KNOPF

75

YEARS·OF·PUBLISHING

Also by Forrest G. Wood

BLACK SCARE
The Racist Response to Emancipation and Reconstruction

(1968)

THE ERA OF RECONSTRUCTION
1863–1877

(1975)

THE ARROGANCE OF FAITH

Forrest G. Wood

THE ARROGANCE OF FAITH

Christianity and Race in America from the Colonial Era to the Twentieth Century

ALFRED A. KNOPF NEW YORK 1990

THIS IS A BORZOI BOOK PUBLISHED BY ALFRED A. KNOPF, INC.

Grateful acknowledgment is made to the following for permission to reprint previously published material:

Edinburgh University Press: *Excerpt from* African Ideas of God: A Symposium, *edited by Edwin W. Smith. Published in 1950 by Edinburgh House Press, Edinburgh, Scotland.*

Ludlow Music, Inc.: *Excerpt from "This Land Is Your Land," words and music by Woody Guthrie. TRO – © Copyright 1956 (renewed), 1958 (renewed) and 1970 by Ludlow Music, Inc., New York, NY. Used by permission.*

Library of Congress Cataloging-in-Publication Data

Wood, Forrest G.

The arrogance of faith: Christianity and race in America from the colonial era to the twentieth century / by Forrest G. Wood.—1st ed.

p. cm.

Includes bibliographical references.

ISBN *0-394-57993-3*

1. United States—Race relations. 2. Race relations—Religious aspects—Christianity—History of doctrines. I. Title.

E184.A1W7 *1990*

261.8'348'00973—dc20 *89-37858* CIP

Manufactured in the United States of America

First Edition

For Teresa

In West Africa, where the population was especially dense and from which the great bulk of slaves was secured, Christianity was practically unknown until the Portuguese began to plant missions in the area in the sixteenth century. It was a strange religion, this Christianity, which taught equality and brotherhood and at the same time introduced on a large scale the practice of tearing people from their homes and transporting them to a distant land to become slaves.

JOHN HOPE FRANKLIN
From Slavery to Freedom

Contents

Acknowledgments

It would be very ego-gratifying to think that this book was the product of one person sitting at the keyboard of an Apple Macintosh and sifting through a mountain of notes extracted from a mountain of sources. Fortunately, the tasks of research and writing—which can often be lonely endeavors—are rarely done alone. Like every writer who has tried to create a serious work, I depended extensively on the wisdom and insights of many others, some of whom are no longer here to accept my thanks. People like John D. Motlow, Edward H. Howes, Sam Ross, A. Hunter Dupree, Lawrence A. Harper, and Charles G. Sellers, Jr., would be surprised—and, I hope, pleased—to know how far their influence has reached over the years. My debt to Kenneth M. Stampp cannot be measured. In the larger sense, he more than anyone else convinced me that it did not matter how great the answers I came up with were if I failed to ask the right questions. In the smaller sense, he forced me to reexamine the words I placed on paper to determine if indeed they meant what I thought they meant. Harold W. Pfautz and Orlando Patterson were under the impression that I had endured those humid summers in Providence and Cambridge because I wanted to use the wonderful libraries at Brown and Harvard when, in fact, I had joined their National Endowment for the Humanities seminars to pick their brains. I am grateful to my editor at Knopf, Jane N. Garrett, who made numerous suggestions for improving the work.

I also owe more than I can ever repay to colleagues and associates who would be easy to overlook because they are just down the hallway or across the quad. Although he never complained, I am sure Charles A. Litzinger—whose intimate knowledge of Chinese culture and language (not to mention his Trappist background) made him an inexhaustible source of ideas, information, and humor—grew weary from my pestering for what must have seemed to him the most trivial of details. Bruce W. Jones, a Congregational minister who converted his clerical training and experience into a commitment to teaching and scholarship in religious studies, saved me from several embarrassing mistakes of fact and interpretation pertaining to race and slavery in biblical times. It occurred to me very early in the progress of this book that I would be foolish not to take advantage of the insights of Solomon O. Iyasere, a writer and native of Benin, whose criticisms enlarged dramatically my understanding of West African religion and philosophy. Richard E. Stockton's impressive Eastern Orthodox background and, especially, his mastery of classical languages enabled him to contribute significantly to my appreciation of the ancient texts that formed the basis of Christian arguments on both sides of the slavery question. A former colleague, Jon Butler of Yale University, provided me with a prepublication copy of his own manuscript on the southern colonial Anglican church and then was gracious enough to set aside whatever he was doing long enough to review a portion of my chapter 7 even though I did not send it to him until two months before the publisher's deadline.

Many people were helpful in ways that probably seemed small to them but, taken together, were critical in enabling me to develop ideas and clarify facts. Dave Brock, Monsignor Ronald J. Swett, and Rabbi Steven J. Peskind responded quickly and generously to my requests for assistance. Emilie Deutsch of Capital Cities/ABC, Inc., directed me to Hugh A. Dempsey, of Calgary's Glenbow Museum, who provided information about the Blackfoot Indians of southern Alberta. Needless to say, whatever flaws remain in this book are there in spite of these people.

I am also indebted to the American taxpayer. A research fellowship from the National Endowment for the Humanities provided me with the scholar's dream: a full year away from the distractions of lectures, examinations, and seminar papers—not to mention committee meetings. I am grateful to Oliver A. Rink, William McKee Evans, and Orlando Patterson for supporting my fellowship application. I also wish to thank the University Research Council of California State University, Bakersfield, for subsidizing a reduction of my teaching load at a crucial time. No researcher can ever repay his obligation to librarians, and every library should have a Leonard Thorp. James E. Segesta, Christy Gavin, Eugenia B. Winter, David Kosakowski, and Gary Hyslop already know how much I appreciate their help. Although she would insist she was just doing her job, Lorna Frost went above and beyond in making available to me the vast resources of the Online Computer Library Catalogue (OCLC) system. Because of the diligence of her staff in the Inter-Library Loan Department of the Walter W. Stiern Memorial Library, I was able to acquire—often within days—books, pamphlets, articles, and micro-documents from all over the United States and Canada. The willingness of participating libraries to send materials—some of them very old, rare, and fragile—has given me a tremendous appreciation of and respect for those who share in the search for truth.

Finally, this book belongs to my wife, Teresa. She did not write, type, or edit a single page. She did not participate in brainstorming discussions, run down sources, or become involved in any of the tedium that spouses are often called upon to do. What she did was listen to me, humor me, chastise me, and, perhaps most important of all, pull me away from the work when I could not recognize the need for a change of environment.

And she did all this while facing the much more formidable task of confronting daily a room full of second-graders, not to mention helping to raise two daughters. The ordeal endured by a writer's family never shows in the finished product. Only Teresa, Jennifer, and Magen know what it is like to live with a person who can spend an entire evening agonizing over one footnote.

Preface

This book took a long time to write. When I first discussed it with Knopf managing editor Ashbel Green, most of what appears on the following pages was still in the thinking stage. At the time, I was rushing to meet a publication deadline for another book, so I even stopped thinking about this one—for a while. But there are some ideas that simply refuse to leave a person alone. For years I wondered if Americans could ever overcome the problems that a racially and ethnically heterogeneous society creates for itself. No nation anywhere can claim a population whose people come from such divergent backgrounds. In fact, many societies strive to prevent such diversity. The Japanese take great pride in their racial and cultural homogeneity and pass laws to ensure its purity. Trying to keep its language free of intercultural pollution, the French government proposed a ban on the official use of certain non-Gallic words for which there were no ready French equivalents, like "weekend" and "hot dog." In the United States, such an idea would be silly, although efforts to have English declared an "official" language suggest that some people do not think so.

At the opposite extreme are the fifteen constituent republics of the Soviet Union, which are organized around a principle of geographic delineation, whereby Ukrainians, Armenians, Georgians, and others occupy politically defined enclaves and, accordingly, retain most of their distinctive ethnic characteristics. Such an arrangement could never work in the United States simply because racial and ethnic minorities are distributed throughout the nation and do not have such geographic prerogatives—assuming they would even want them. But there have been some who thought this would work. Because they insisted on drawing an analogy between Russian nationalities and American racial minorities, the Socialist and Communist parties failed to make significant impressions on black Americans in the early decades of the twentieth century. Similarly, several all-black towns in Oklahoma, for example, Langston and Boley, seemed, for a short time, to offer opportunities for some kind of geographic separation on a small scale.

I have always been convinced that the most destructive and enduring racial discrimination is the kind that is not obvious. Highly visible and vocal white-supremacist organizations like the Ku Klux Klan have always thrived on notoriety. The bigot's inflated ego, limited intellect, and proclivity for recklessness made him incapable of subtlety or resourcefulness. Overt racism was predictable. Also, during the era of legal segregation, laws calling for separate schools, railroad cars, and drinking fountains were there for everyone to see. There was no secret about who was responsible and what needed to be done. While it took a long time to change the rules—fifty-eight years from *Plessy v. Ferguson* to *Brown v. Board of Education*—at least the rules were there to be changed. What was far more difficult to detect was the *covert* racism that lurked within the structures and operations of the nation's most fundamental political and social institutions: government, industry, finance, professions, services, trade unions, schools, and churches. "The way such an institution operates may not have been established with any reference to race," social psychologist Thomas F. Pettigrew wrote; "it may not have been conceived, set up, or maintained by bigoted individuals: nevertheless, the resulting product narrows the opportunities of Negroes just as effectively as if it had been specifically designed to do so."[1]

As I pursued this line of inquiry, the institution of religion—not just churches and communicants but, more fundamentally, Christianity as a belief system—increasingly dominated my notes. I am not suggesting that I was the first person to notice that Sunday morning had become the most segregated time of the week. Rather, what really surprised me was how far Christianity's influence had reached beyond the sanctuary. Biblical maxims, the Puritan work ethic, Pauline moral preachments, Old Testament conceptions of The Elect, and scriptural admonitions like the Ten Commandments—what true believers like to think of as eternal verities—permeate every fiber of secular life. The exalted American commitments to individualism, free enterprise, and the diffusion of democratic principles are, I came to believe, nothing more than secular extensions of the Christian precepts of a personal relationship with Christ, man's dominion over the earth, and the bringing of the Good News to all peoples.

The central thesis of this book is that Christianity, in the five centuries since its message was first carried to the peoples of the New World—and, in particular, to the natives and the transplanted Africans of English North America and the United States—has been fundamentally racist in its ideology, organization, and practice. While popes, bishops, preachers, evangelists, and missionaries proclaimed Christianity to be the ultimate solution to all of the world's problems, their celebration of that belief created and maintained one of the worst of those problems, a problem so pervasive but insidious that for a very long time many observers thought the cause of the disease was its cure. In his *Yankee Saints and Southern Sinners* (1985), Bertram Wyatt-Brown described abolitionism as an evangelical movement "aimed at the creation of a new Republic based on universal rather than local and variant principles," and stated that "antebellum reformers were determined to make the country as homogeneous and puritanical as possible, to eliminate the evil of folk racism but to strengthen the heritage of Christian idealism."[2]

One obvious problem, of course, was that, beyond an irreducible core of general principles, there has always been intense disagreement among Christians as to what principles were universal. More critical was the reformers' attempt to harmonize two purposes that were inherently antithetical. Contrary to the perception of Wyatt-Brown's abolitionists, "Christian idealism" was a major component of the "evil of folk racism." *Weakening* its influence would have been, in the long run, a more effective way of eliminating racism. Underlying this contradiction was Christianity's unshakable premise that everybody should be a Christian, a belief that even infiltrated the halls of secular academe. One historian in the early twentieth century insisted it was very unfair of black writers to lay "the whole burden of the Negro's present sins on the back of the white man because of the Negro's experiences during slavery." Both races share the responsibility, Joseph B. Earnest, Jr., wrote in *The Religious Development of the Negro in Virginia* (1914). "We grant that slavery had its vices, but it also had its virtues, and prominent among its virtues in Virginia, was the care exercized in training the Negro religiously."[3] Only a person who believed that conversion to Christianity justified any means could claim that slavery had "virtues."

Needless to say, recognizing Christianity itself as a source of immorality was unthinkable for the faithful because such recognition would have impugned their most profound beliefs. By and large, Christians had difficulty separating biblical myths from biblical reality. Fundamentalism—the belief that every verse in the Bible is literally true—was pervasive until the later decades of the nineteenth century. Accordingly, it was a lot easier to accept on faith Christianity's basic doctrines and either ignore its errors or blame them on human weakness, a reaction made imperative by the fact that, for a monotheist, the belief in an omnipotent being required a belief in a virtuous being. When Abraham Lincoln, noting in his Second Inaugural Address that Southerners and Northerners prayed to the same God, said, "It may seem strange that any men should ask a just God's assistance in wringing their bread from the sweat of other men's faces," he assumed that his listeners believed in a just God. To such people God could be nothing else and, Lincoln suggested, it was a perversion of the faith to ask for divine protection for something as unjust and invidious as human bondage. Just two years earlier, a visiting European clergyman had wondered about the same thing. "One asks how it is possible," wrote Georges Fisch, pastor of the French Evangelical Church in Paris, "that a country so imbued with Christianity could have maintained slavery; and how it is that a third of its population defends it at all hazards."[4]

But defending slavery did not seem so strange to people whose conception of humanity was far different from Lincoln's or Fisch's. To the white

Southerner, it was perfectly logical to ask for divine help because God had already mandated the slave's subservient level of humanity. "The master who did these things was highly educated, and styled a perfect gentleman," Harriet A. Jacobs wrote in 1857, describing her owner's cruelty. "He also boasted the name and standing of a Christian though Satan never had a truer follower."[5] Thus while condemning her master's hypocrisy, Jacobs, like many abolitionist clergymen, apparently accepted the idea that Christianity embodied an ideal of justice fundamentally opposed to slavery.

But to attribute the sin of racism to the Christian's immoral conduct is to miss more than half the point. In the first place, distinguishing human actions from what the devout believed to be divinely ordained works called for an assumption that a historian is unable to justify. The faithful may find it easy to believe that Moses parted the Red Sea, but the secular scholar needs more evidence than Exodus 14:21. Similarly, more than a few of the authors of histories of the Middle East during biblical times have, regrettably, let their faith lead their judgment. In many of these works, scriptural references to what God said and did were routinely seen as facts. Since I was obliged to observe the canons of scholarship I did not have the luxury of accepting on faith an inerrant Bible and thus was left only with the premise that Christianity itself, the Way and the Word, was man-created—that man created God in his image, or, as Voltaire put it, *Si Dieu n'existait pas, il faudrait l'inventer*—and, accordingly, was the source of many of the evils that Christians insisted were human corruptions.

Needless to say, this idea is universally repudiated by the conservative faithful. While I was writing this book, one of my graduate students submitted a research paper in which he referred to something God had done. I tried to explain that if he were a seminarian studying for a degree in theology, God's existence would be a given, but that in a secular institution he could not present as fact something that existed only as an article of faith. People believe that God exists and their *belief* is a fact. The historian must confine himself to dealing with the significance of that belief; its validity is beyond his analytical powers. But despite my best efforts to persuade the student to rethink his perception, he refused.

It is also necessary for the reader to make certain concessions as to just what constitutes *religion*. To begin with, one must resist the tendency to think of non-Christian religions as simply faiths in which people worship other deities or apotheosize different messengers. The theologies and eschatologies of Native American, African, and Eastern religions are so fundamentally different from the Judeo-Christian belief system that the word "religion" often seems inadequate to identify them, a lesson that I learned early in life. When I was about ten years old I saw in a book of facts a list of the world's major religions, arranged in order of size. I recall that, having been raised in a conservative Protestant family, I was disappointed that Christianity was not the largest religion in the world. That distinction belonged to something called "Confucianism-Taoism." To a child, size is important; but since I knew that China was the largest nation on earth, I understood why a Chinese religion could claim the most adherents.

What I have learned since is how poorly the word "religion" describes the beliefs of other peoples when we try to understand them according to the monotheistic model and that measuring a faith is far less important then defining it, something that every scholar who deals with the subject must do. Very early in *The Ghost Festival in Medieval China* (1988), Stephen F. Teiser pointed out that Chinese religion functioned "*within* such institutions as the family, the community, and the state, and only secondarily as an institution distinct from all other social groupings." In China, "religion" meant "the family of activities in which myth and ritual, symbol and cosmology figure prominently."[6] It is a definition that would be understood by Africans and American Indians but neither understood nor tolerated by Christians.

From its inception this study was based on the premise that the greatest victims of racial injustice were the African men and women who were brought in chains to the New World and their descendants. Asians, American Indians, Hispanic Americans, and other racial and ethnic minorities have also suffered, but their numbers are far smaller and the conditions of their suffering much less severe. Moreover, the Indian confronted Europeans on his home turf, while Asians and most others migrated voluntarily (which did not, of course, make their ordeal any more acceptable). Only Africans were stripped of their humanity through a systematic obliteration of their ancestral heritage, culture, language, and traditions. Only the black person was perceived in stark color terms. And only the African was dehumanized by Christian entrepreneurs and masters through a form of bondage that was, in some respects, the cruelest ever known. Indeed, anti-black racism was so pervasive that it even influenced perceptions of discrimination against other groups. In a section entitled "The Minority Situation" in *America as a Civilization* (1957), Max Lerner vividly described the prejudice faced by Jews, Chinese, Filipinos, Mexicans, recent European immigrants, and other non-black peoples:

> [E]xcept in the South, no local prejudices have been translated into law. . . . [E]xcepting the South, no political candidate or party since the Know-Nothings has run successfully on a platform of racism. . . . [Anti-Semitism is a] case study a little sharper than the other minority groups, although less sharp than the case of the

> Negroes. . . . [A]nti-Semitism took its place, after anti-Negro racism, as the most serious movement of ethnic hatreds in America. . . . Except in the attitudes toward Negroes, the majority of Americans hold . . . enlightened views.[7]

For Lerner, the racism suffered by blacks was the standard against which all other discrimination was measured.

A word on languages and biblical texts is in order. The Authorized (King James) Version of the Bible, which has been the primary American text since the days of the colonial Anglicans and Puritans, has been quoted or referred to whenever it seemed important to know exactly which Bible the people of the time were reading and because it has been, over the years, the most familiar and enduring edition in the United States. But modern versions, especially the New York International Bible Society's *The New International Version of the Holy Bible* (1978), have been quoted whenever differences in wording amplified the narrative or clarified a point. Since it is one of the more conservative modern translations, the *NIV* edition has the virtue of reading in the vernacular while retaining much of the tone and rhythm of the Authorized Version. Colonial North Americans also had access to William Tyndale's translations (1494–1536), Myles Cloverdale's "Great Bible" (1550), and the Geneva Bible (1560), the latter being the common Bible among the early English Puritans. Anyone who needs to be reminded of the problem of relying on one version should know that, as Margaret T. Hillis pointed out, there were over 2,500 different English-language editions published in the United States prior to 1957.[8]

Deciding which Bible to quote was simple compared to untangling the problem of languages. When referring to Chinese materials I followed the 1979 Romanization, but, since many publications were written in the old transliteration, I decided to avoid confusion by showing both—that is, "Xun Zi (Hsün Tzu)" and "*Li Ji— (Li Chi*)." On the other hand, traditional African and American Indian languages, unlike Chinese, evolved from rich oral traditions and in modern written forms have been spelled phonetically in whatever ways suited those who were transcribing them.[9] For the sake of consistency, I have adopted the simplest forms throughout this work, for example, the West African high god Oloroun for Obba Oloroun or Olou-oroun. Finally, while I modernized colonial English writing ("s" for "f"), I did *not* standardize the spelling of plantation argot because there were variations in dialect and pronunciation—as "patterollers" and "paddy rollers" for slave patrols—even within one region.

Part One

CHRISTIANITY

ONE ❦ THE WAY

Whether you turn to the right or to the left, your ears will hear a voice behind you, saying, "This is the way; walk in it."

ISAIAH 30:21

Salvation comes by Christ alone,
The only Son of God;
Redemption now to every one,
That love his holy Word.

Dear Jesus we would fly to Thee,
And leave off every Sin,
Thy tender mercy well agree;
Salvation from our King;

Salvation comes now from the Lord
Our victorious King,
His holy Name be well ador'd,
Salvation surely bring.

JUPITER HAMMON
"An Evening Thought: Salvation by Christ, with Penitential Cries" (1761)

Christian Nurture and Cultural Myopia

In 1944, 20th Century–Fox released a long and somewhat tedious motion picture (based on a best-selling novel by A. J. Cronin) titled *Keys of the Kingdom*, about a Catholic missionary in China. While studying in Scotland, the future priest, played by Gregory Peck, had been summoned before the college rector for asking a question one of his teachers considered an example of "a general mental disobedience." Prompted by a description of Catholicism as the "one true and apostolic faith," the curious student had asked if, since a person's religious orientation was determined largely by the accident of his birth, God had "set an exclusive value on creed." Without explanation the rector replied, "Yes," which seemed to satisfy the student. Most moviegoers probably found the answer lacking, overlooking the fact that the significance of the exchange was in the question.

Religious influence has always been far-reaching because the individual is subjected to it earlier in life than he is to political or economic pressures.

It is second only to the family as a socializing force, and, like racist ideology, it is more *of the mind* than just about any other human activity. It has not been unusual for children to stray from the religion of their parents, especially in a pluralistic society where the national government never placed its official imprimatur on one denomination. Conformity was not easily achieved even during the colonial period. Defections from the faith were major factors in the Puritan adoption of the "Half-Way Convenant" in 1662, whereby two of the three tests required for church membership were dropped, and in the outbreak of hysteria over witches in Salem in 1692—both in oppressively theocratic Massachusetts—and in the spontaneous emergence of the Great Awakening in the 1730s. All of these were, among other things, fearful responses of the clergy to the general decline of the religious zeal that had motivated the early immigrant generations. Nonetheless, in an age when transportation and communication facilities were virtually nonexistent and most people lived in widely separated cultural enclaves, religion played a large role in daily life, and children could be expected to grow up and follow the same spiritual paths as the rest of the family. They were rarely in a position to do otherwise.

To the devout Christian, it was something that careful parents should not leave to chance. Taking to heart the advice in Proverbs 22:6, "Train a child in the way he should go, and when he is old he will not turn from it," Congregationalist minister Horace Bushnell wrote what amounted to a manual for the Christian indoctrination of children. Published in 1846 and revised in 1861 as a book of over four hundred pages, *Christian Nurture* called for the total immersion of the child in a Christian environment, beginning with infant baptism. "Early childhood resists nothing," Bushnell insisted. "What is given it receives, making no selection." Citing Genesis 18:19, in which Abraham "will command his children and his household after him, and they shall keep the way of the Lord, to do justice and judgment," Bushnell contended that the transmission of Christian values to children was not simply a matter of training, but a product of the bond created by the "absolute force" that flowed from the family as a religious unit. The "power exerted by parents" was not only the deliberate power to teach and govern but power "without any purposed control whatever."[1] Bushnell's purpose, one historian pointed out, "was to show how early conditioning, accomplished before the development of independent judgment, could effectively preempt the need for revivals."[2]

To the doctrinaire thinker, the one thing that matters of faith could not tolerate was independent judgment. Bushnell's Christian nurture did not, however, entirely rule out evolution or adaptation. In fact, its "prime feature," religion historian William R. Hutchison pointed out, "was the latitude it allowed within the area of orthodox religious expression." The committed Bushnellian family "conspired to prepare the child to accept neologies that the parental generation, and certainly Bushnell himself, had not accepted." Apparently Bushnell did not consider conditioning as possible for everyone. Though he accepted evolution and adaptation, he did not include Africans as likely candidates for change. Since "intellectual culture, domestic virtue, industry, order, law, [and] good faith" were characteristics that Bushnell believed "could be transferred biologically from one generation to the next," George M. Fredrickson wrote, and since black people presumably did not possess these qualities, they were "condemned to extinction."[3] Slavery is clearly wrong, Bushnell argued, but black people are still inferior. Maybe, he concluded, it was "God's plan to finish this race last, and set them on the summit, when their day shall come."[4]

Bushnell probably should not have worried about inculcating religious conformity. Although modern studies of church membership in the eighteenth century are contradictory,[5] adherence to Christianity in general—especially Protestantism—was widespread. Church *attendance*, on the other hand, left something to be desired. It needs to be remembered that the colonists of English North America were still living in an age when people believed that faith in God was all one needed to understand the universe. The Enlightenment was underway in Europe and scholars were just beginning to explore the scientific and technological fields that produced, among other things, the industrial revolution. But religion was still the "organizing principle of life," historian Gary B. Nash wrote. "Thus people attributed to supernatural forces what could not be understood or governed."[6] It is difficult for a person who receives his weather reports from television satellites to comprehend the importance of religion to people who perceived it as the source of everything. The worst feature of Christian nurture was, of course, the stultification of original and creative thinking. "I know of no country in which, speaking generally, there is less independence of mind and true freedom of discussion than in America," Alexis de Tocqueville wrote in *Democracy in America* (1835). "In America the majority has enclosed thought within a formidable fence. A writer is free inside that area, but woe to the man who goes beyond it. Not that he stands in fear of an *auto-da-fé*, but he must face all kinds of unpleasantness and everyday persecution. . . . One finds unbelievers in America, but unbelief has, so to say, no organ."[7] It may have been true, as John Locke argued in the late seventeenth century, that religious belief was entirely voluntary and could not be forced on an unwilling person,[8] but a society that offered no choices had, in fact, forced conformity.

There were many reasons for this condition, not the least of which was the simple fact that Christian conviction, by definition, was based on faith in an infallible authority; to challenge canons or dogmas with rational arguments could be construed by true believers as heresy. Of course, some religions have been more indulgent of disagreement and divergence than others. For example, the Baha'is of Iran, evolving from the nineteenth-century Babites of Persia, have always stressed principles of universal brotherhood and have acknowledged the validity of almost all faiths. Similarly, many Buddhists see no fundamental conflict between their teachings and those of most other religions. It is the adherents of the other religions that see a conflict. In the United States, the Unitarian-Universalists have long boasted of their absence of creed and their willingness to entertain diverse religious views. But these are exceptions. In most of the Western world, Christianity has been the dominant religion; and while there have been mutual toleration and even occasional cooperation among, say, different Protestant denominations, Christians by and large have not acceded to any way to salvation except through Jesus Christ. There simply was no room in the dogmatic mind for contrary notions, however based in facts they might have been.

It is not possible to discuss the history of religion and race without also raising some fundamental questions about Western culture. If it is true, as intellectual historians have long proclaimed, that the mainstream of Western thought is a product of the confluence of Judeo-Christianity and Hellenism, can a culture that is totally outside of that mainstream ever be compatible with it? Are the political, philosophical, and economic systems of Western civilization eclectic enough to embrace or absorb the values, traditions, and customs of African, Asian, or pre-Columbian New World cultures? How should the Christian "nurture" heathens, especially those with offending skin colors and barbaric customs? There may always have been universal human habits and institutions, but at what point did cultural compatibility become cultural conflict? Can non-Western ideas and patterns of behavior be assimilated intact into Western culture, or must they be modified and eventually undermined and destroyed? How can one enjoy the best of two worlds if one world perceives the other's best as its worst?

Scholars who have offered answers to these questions have created a controversy that has itself become virtually institutionalized. In *The Myth of the Negro Past* (1941), anthropologist Melville J. Herskovits, basing his findings on primarily empirical evidence, concluded that black Americans retained many significant aspects—"persistent Africanisms"—of their ancient cultures.[9] For example, the African tradition of sitting up all night and singing over the dead was practiced on many American plantations. Similarly, an African burial custom that was common in the New World was digging graves in an east-west direction because one should not sleep or be buried "crossways uv de world," a practice that had a Chinese equivalent in which a belief in benevolent and hostile spiritual forces called for burying relatives in a north-south direction. Adapting the directional tradition to a Christian theme, the American slave buried his kinfolk with their heads at the west end of the grave so they would not have to turn around to see Gabriel blow his horn in the eastern sunrise.[10] Denied the use of drums and other loud instruments by masters who feared slaves communicating, the irrepressible bondsman substituted hand-clapping and foot-stomping in plantation dances that ultimately worked their way into the popular dances of the early twentieth century.

Of course, all this simply meant that if the researcher looked long enough in the right places he would eventually find elements of thought and conduct among black Americans that appeared to have ancestral origins—which could be said of almost any ethnic group. Persistent Africanisms were, understandably, more observable in the South, where the much larger black population provided a social milieu that enabled many traditional habits to survive and where a slave was more likely to come into contact with recently imported Africans.[11] Conversely, by focusing on the *lost* qualities of African life, others have called attention to the obliteration of the old social systems.[12] It has made for a provocative debate, but in the last analysis comparing the two views may be little more than a discussion over whether the canteen is half empty or half full.[13]

As it happened, the differences between northern and southern persistent Africanisms in the United States were simply scaled-down versions of the more conspicuous differences between American slavery and slavery in the rest of the New World, where conditions encouraged cultural continuity. Common in the West Indies, for example, but rarely known in the American South were the African magical practices of obeah, voodoo, and myalism. While African influences were becoming obfuscated in America, slaves in Dutch Guiana, Brazil, and the West Indies—especially Haiti—retained customs and traditions that could be traced to specific locations like Nigeria or Dahomey.[14] Yoruba gods with names similar or identical to the African originals—Obakala, Ogun, Oxissi, Xango, Oxalais, and even a counterpart for Satan, Exú—were elements in some black Christian ceremonies in Brazil. Slaves and former slaves in Brazil also acknowledged the spiritisms of Candomblé, Makumba, and Umbanda (or Mbanda), the last of these readily infiltrating the religious rituals of the black Roman Catholic descendants of those who had carried the "pagan" practices in the slave ships—to the dismay of the church hierarchy.

Several scholars have noted that it was the similarity between the pantheon of gods and spirits in African traditional religions[15] and the saints of the Catholic church that facilitated syncretism among slaves in the Spanish and Portuguese New World. Many of the saints of the church were seen to possess powers very much like those of the lesser spirits in Africa. Herskovits pointed out that Arthur Ramos, in his *O Negro Brasileiro*—(1935), "provided full documentation, naming the saints that correspond to African gods, and depicting and analyzing the ritual altars on which crucifix and chromolithographs of the saints jostle African offerings and wood carvings in the African manner."[16] An obvious example was the Virgin Mary, to whom Catholics made supplications for intercession rather than praying directly to God or Jesus, a practice that made sense to people who had never been so presumptuous as to address the high god in their native religions. Moreover, the Catholic's observance of holy days, feasts, fasts, and abstinence and his use of sacraments, candles, holy water, rosaries, vestments, and relics was "more akin to the spirit of African piety than the sparseness of Puritan America, which held such objects to be idolatrous."[17] In reality, the hybridization of the church was, despite the apprehensions of some Catholic officials, fully in accord with Pope Gregory XV's injunction, on founding the Sacred Congregation for the Propagation of the Faith, that the missionary fathers should "do their utmost to adapt themselves to the native customs" and avoid imposing European culture on converts.[18]

The differences between English America and the rest of the hemisphere was also a matter of timing and numbers. For instance, by the early nineteenth century four-fifths of the slave population in the United States was American-born, while, at the same time, the majority of slaves in Jamaica and Santo Domingo had been born free in Africa and subsequently enslaved. For essentially the same reason, the African influence remained strong in Brazil and Cuba, where the transatlantic slave trade flourished until the mid-nineteenth century.[19] Nowhere was this influence more apparent than in so-called Afro-Cuban songs and dances, as the *beguine* in Martinique, the *rhumba* and *conga* in Cuba, and the *samba* in Brazil. There were no North American equivalents.

But even here the compelling force of Anglo-American culture can be discerned. While others have focused on the differences between impalpable Africanisms in the United States and conspicuous Africanisms in much of the rest of the New World, they inadvertently called attention to a disturbing aspect of the American condition: Southern slaves lost most of the vestiges of their African heritage *because* the oppressive institutional forces of Protestant Anglo-American society easily smothered them. Conduct was one thing; belief quite another. Burying the dead in an east-west direction was a mechanical ritual that could be observed and repeated; it was a physical action, not a manifestation of a profound line of thought. On the other hand (and far more important), how much of the African's—

psychological processes—his conceptions of time and space, his philosophical attachment to the natural landscape, his definition of kinship responsibilities, his relationship with his gods and ancestral spirits—survived generations of bondage? In short, how many of these Africanisms, all of which were crucial to his religious world view, persisted?

Whether or not the African's adaptation to his status was an act of submission or of expediency, it certainly was not the kind of "nurture" that Bushnell had in mind. While white Christians condemned the slave's "pagan" practices, there is little doubt that most Americans—including many whose claim to "liberalism" was presumably based on an open mind—had virtually no perception of the narrowness of their own vision. For example, chapter 19 of Ralph Barton Perry's magisterial *Puritanism and Democracy* (1944) is entitled "Equality and Fraternity," but the only equality that he considered worth discussing was Western European and American. Perry frequently used terms like "mankind," "all men," "organized society," "all social classes," "nature," and "race" (meaning the human race), but he rarely included non-Westerners in his democratic ideal.[20] This was typical cultural myopia, and its taproot was Christianity.

Preaching at the ordination of six missionaries at Newburyport, Massachusetts, in 1815, the Reverend Samuel Worcester, pastor of the Tabernacle Church in Salem, perceived the entire non-Christian world as lost in darkness.

> Is the religion, or the morality better in Burma,—in China—in Japan—in Thibet—in Tartary—in any part of pagan Asia? Is it better in the benighted regions of Africa—of Northern or Southern America—or in the islands of the Southern Ocean? Are not those nations and tribes wholly given to idolatry? Are they not all in darkness, in the shadow of death? Have they not all changed the glory of the incorruptible God into images made like to corruptible man, and to bird, and four-footed beasts, and creeping things?[21]

In Worcester's day, "Protestant humanitarians believed that Christianity and especially the liberating spirit of the Reformation had been responsible for all the liberal achievements of their era," according to historian Lois W. Banner, and the "primary effect of the Reformation had been 'the emancipation of the mind from subjection to every restraint but that which common sense and truth imposes.' " Before the end of the century, Walter Rauschenbusch, who, as the leading prolocutor for the Social Gospel movement, could be expected to be sympathetic to the plight of oppressed peoples, echoed that theme when he described the Reformation as a freeing of the mind and "humanity gaining in elasticity and capacity for change."[22]

One is compelled to wonder if Rauschenbusch's "humanity" included

Africans, Eskimos, New World Indians, Australian aborigines, and the teeming millions of the Middle East and Asia. Many of the wonders of Egypt and China were well known even in his day, but there were others lesser known or not known at all. Would he have made such a presumptuous statement had he been aware of the dazzling accomplishments of some of the very people that Worcester had called "pagan" and "benighted"? Twenty centuries before Christ, the citizens of Mohenjo-Daro on the Indus River in what is today Pakistan had developed an effective sewerage system. Similarly, at the same time that the Visigoths and other barbarians were overrunning Europe, the ancestors of the modern Sudanese had devised artificial street-lighting facilities. Two thousand years ago, the forefathers of the Haya people of modern Tanzania produced medium-carbon steel in preheated, forced-draft furnaces, a technique not developed in the West until the nineteenth century. The Moche people of ancient Peru, whose society flourished from A.D. 100 to 700, were wonderful architects and craftsmen who developed sophisticated metal-plating techniques fourteen centuries before the Europeans were to perfect similar skills. Even more remarkable was their construction of an intricate canal network utilizing hydraulic engineering techniques for moving water—techniques that would not be seen in the Christian world for a thousand years—resulting in a sixty-mile intervalley canal that can only be observed clearly from the air.

No less amazing was the eastward migration of a small group of Micronesians in the western Pacific. Setting out over three thousand years ago in hand-carved wooden canoes that the residents of modern Satawal still produce from memory, these early mariners, without charts or instruments, navigated by stars, wind, and ocean swells. By the first century A.D. they had settled the Marquesas Islands and were moving toward both New Zealand and the Hawaiian chain. When Europeans sighted the Pacific Ocean for the first time some fifteen centuries later, almost all of its ten thousand islands had already been explored by these intrepid sailors, who had never heard of a sextant or compass.[23]

How could the Protestant Reformation "emancipate the minds" of such remarkable people, enabling them to gain in "elasticity and capacity for change"? Perhaps more to the point, *why* should it? And Rauschenbusch was a well-educated liberal Christian. One can only shudder at the cultural myopia of the conservative Protestant whose posture was closer to the norm. In fairness to Rauschenbusch, it should be acknowledged that many of the achievements of non-Western societies had not yet been discovered, even as recently as 1907. Nevertheless, on the eve of the twenty-first century, many Christians continue to believe that Christ's mandate in Matthew 28:19 to "teach all nations" still means that only Christianity can solve the world's problems.

This is not to disparage the intellectual significance of the Reformation—which was enormous—but simply to call attention to the Westerner's ethnocentric shackles, a point that should not be minimized because it was the foundation of his assertion that he had the right to dominate everyone else. In looking back on Classical Antiquity, the Dark Ages, the Medieval period, the Renaissance, the Reformation, and the modern era—all moments in the history of the West—Americans and Europeans have been largely unaware of their cultural shortsightedness. To be sure, no one would deny that the technological success of the West has been the source of its economic and political (that is, military) power. Machines make plows *and* guns. But, while it might be true that, as the saying goes, one "can get more with a gun and a smile than with just a smile,"[24] this does not mean that matters of ethics—right or wrong, good or bad, truth or error—should necessarily be defined in Western terms. Yet this is precisely what the Christian mind has always done. For better or worse, power has always been the handmaiden of morality; and there is simply no getting away from the fact that religion is, among other things, a moral system. That is one of its enduring virtues. And one of its abiding curses.

All of this makes it easy to agree with Tocqueville's observation that Christianity was a cornerstone of modern slavery and, *ergo*, modern racism:

> Christianity had destroyed servitude; the Christians of the sixteenth century reestablished it, but they never admitted it as anything more than an exception in their social system, and they were careful to restrict it to one of the races of man. In this way they inflicted a smaller wound on humanity but one much harder to cure.[25]

"What social virtues are possible in a society of which injustice is the primary characteristic," another European visitor asked, "in a society which is divided into two classes, the servile and the imperious?" Christianity proclaims "the fact of the natural equality of men," Harriet Martineau asserted. "How does the existing state of religion accord with the promise of its birth?"[26] Therein lies one of Christianity's greatest enigmas: its supreme usefulness to people of contrary viewpoints. Philosophers and theologians have long called attention to the importance of religion in influencing human thought and conduct. Be it Judaism, Islam, Hinduism, Buddhism, Christianity, or whatever, a society's religion has always been defined as a vital and irrepressible force in its life. But it was Christianity's disjunctions that made it possible for the northern Freewill Baptists and the southern Baptists, both of whom read the same Bible, to be so far apart on the issue of slavery. The Christian justification for exterminating American Indians, the biblical defense of human bondage, the antebellum schisms of the mainline denominations, and the religious rationale for conquest have made it all too easy to conclude that—at least for some people in some places—religious principles have easily given way to economic forces and social customs; and, accordingly, that Christianity, the faith of the first nations to bring the weapons of technology to war and commerce, has been the most corruptible of all the faiths. One can never know if Hinduism, confronted by the irresistible lure of capital and power, would have compromised its fundamental integrity, because it was never in a position to do so. But one can say that, good works notwithstanding, there has been no greater religious force in the dehumanization of humans than Christianity, the self-proclaimed religion of peace, brotherly love, and fellowship.

The Christian Diaspora

Any consideration of religion and race must also deal with the nature of Christianity in general, and Christianity in America in particular; but such an effort immediately collides with a wall of confusion. To begin with, there is no more factious religion anywhere. The term *Christian* has always applied to a wide range of groups, from, on the one hand, the ubiquitous and hierarchical Roman Catholic Church with its vast property holdings and its centuries-old traditions and rituals to, on the other, independent storefront congregations with uneducated preachers who live on the brink of poverty. The Pope claims to be a messenger of Christ, but so, with equal conviction, does the itinerant faith healer who travels through America's rural backwaters or the child evangelist who has "a calling." Among Americans who call themselves Protestants are militant fundamentalists who believe everything in the Bible is literally true and liberal Unitarian-Universalists who eschew dogma, encourage diversity, and even count agnostics and atheists among their members.

Americans tend to think of a colonial period with Puritan oligarchies in New England and state-supported Anglicans in the South, but by the late seventeenth century religious pluralism was the rule rather than the exception in most settlements. To some observers, "Pennsylvania in 1750 was simply a chaos of religious sects," and in North Carolina an Anglican missionary complained about the "great number of dissenters of all denominations . . . particularly Anabaptists, Methodists, Quakers, and Presbyterians." Religious proliferation was so extensive on Long Island, New York, that attempts to count denominations were meaningless because the number changed almost daily. At one time in the nineteenth century there were 150 independent Lutheran sects in the United States. The number dropped to 66 by 1900, but as late as the mid-twentieth century still numbered over a dozen. One of the original aims of the Disciples of Christ—a revivalist group that had emerged in the early 1800s from the movements of Barton W. Stone in Cane Ridge, Kentucky, and Thomas Campbell in western Pennsylvania and whose members sometimes called themselves simply "Christians"—was a unification of all Protestant denominations, an effort that led, not surprisingly, to more divisions and "succeeded only in adding one more separate institution, under that ironically all-embracing name, to the list of competition."[27]

The Disciples of Christ had been only part of a larger unification effort that failed. One of the driving forces behind the revivalism of the early nineteenth century was a desire to bring the churches together around a common understanding of Christ. But the result was more often the opposite. Even worshippers as undoctrinaire as the Quakers splintered into Orthodox, Hicksite, and Wilburite factions. In short, from the late seventeenth century, Christianity in America embodied countless denominations, congregations, sects, cults, synods, episcopates, and splinter groups; and these "churches" were just as diverse in their theologies as in their physical and organizational structures. The only obvious thing they had in common was a professed allegiance to a Christian God; but it was here that they often disagreed vehemently on the nature and message of that God, as a perceptive Seneca chief observed. "If there is but one religion, why do you white people differ so much about it?" Red Jacket asked a young Moravian missionary named Cram in 1805. "These black coats talk to the Great Spirit, and ask for light that we may see as they do, when they are blind themselves and quarrel about the light that guides them."[28] To someone from a culture where there was virtually no disagreement about religion (which described almost every African and American Indian kinship group), the often rancorous diversity among Christians must have seemed strange indeed.

On the other hand, Christianity in the United States may not have been as diversified as a simple count of denominations would suggest. "There is an unnumerable multitude of sects in the United States," Tocqueville wrote, but all "belong to the great unity of Christendom, and Christian morality is everywhere the same." Americans have found "many ways of professing Christianity," Martineau observed just two years later, "but there are very few, very few men, whether speculative or thoughtless, whether studious or ignorant, whether reverent or indifferent, whether sober or profligate, whether disinterested or worldly, who do not carefully profess Christianity, in some form or another." It was the ideological foundation of the most significant and influential American settlements, noted Francis Grund, yet another of the many foreign travelers who visited the United States in the decades after the War of 1812. "The Americans look upon religion as a promoter of civil and political liberty," he added, "and have, therefore, transferred to it a large portion of the affection which they cherish for the institutions of their country."[29]

Both Grund and Martineau were especially impressed by the universality of Christianity in the United States. As a reviewer for the *Methodist Quarterly Review* put it in a critique of Robert Baird's major study of American religion, the United States was "founded on Christian principles, recognizing Christianity as the religion of the country."[30] No one can doubt that the richness of religious diversity created an American society composed of the best elements of dozens of cultures, a favorite theme of historians for years. But also no one should doubt that that same diversity forced each denomination to accept the existence of the others. The cheerful observations of people like Martineau should not obscure the fact that religious toleration was as much a consequence of necessity as of choice, or even more. And while no one can doubt the importance of religion in the American past, the essence of that importance must never be misunderstood.

While these observers—most of whom were citizens of countries with state churches—were impressed by the magnitude of the American religious presence, they also expressed reservations about its benefits. Both Martineau and Tocqueville wondered if the pervasiveness of Christianity was sufficient to make one question the extent of religious pluralism. Moreover, what seemed to be most important for American society, Tocqueville went on, "is not that all citizens should profess the true religion but that they should profess religion." Americans practice a wide variety of creeds, Grund agreed, "yet it is absolutely necessary that a man should belong to some persuasion or other" in order not to be treated as an outcast. Jews are tolerated like any denomination of Christianity, he wrote, "but if a person were to call himself a Deist or an Atheist, it would excite universal execration." The fear of appearing not to be a Christian is compelling, according to Tocqueville. "In the United States it is not only mores that are controlled by religion, but its sway extends even over reason." While most Americans "profess Christian dogmas because they believe them," he concluded, "[there are others] who do so because they are afraid to look as though they did not believe in them."[31] In view of these conditions, it is not unreasonable to wonder just how voluntary religious preferences were—especially in communities where there was only one church—and if the various denominations were as different from one another as they appeared. It may not have been so important that Christianity in America was split into many sects as it was that there were so many sects of Christianity.

It is also important to keep in mind that virtually all of the Christian churches of America have changed dramatically over the past three and a half centuries, despite frequent declarations from the pulpit that Christ is universal and constant and that virtue and sin are always the same. There was perhaps no more vivid example of this institutional metamorphosis than the emergence, in the early 1800s, of the Unitarian church. Unitarianism was an intellectual offshoot of New England Congregationalism, which, in turn, had had its origins in the colonial Puritan church. It is doubtful that there has ever been in America a religious body more dogmatic in theology, straitlaced in conventions, or hostile to outside influences than the Puritan establishment of Massachusetts Bay in the seventeenth century. But the Puritan stalwarts were eventually undone by their emphasis on individual responsibility and their commitment to freedom of intellectual inquiry.[32] As more and more of the outside world revealed itself to the Puritan mind, the only answers to the puzzles of reality that made any sense were those that challenged long-cherished "eternal verities." It was impossible to enforce conformity, which Puritanism demanded, among people who exalted individualism; and this dilemma eventually brought the strict Puritan harshness down to what historian Carl Degler called "the balmy breath of Unitarianism," a movement that in the eyes of many old-line Protestants wandered so far from The Truth that it did not even deserve to be called Christian.[33]

The historical significance of the emergence of the Unitarians should not be exaggerated. To begin with, the Unitarianism of the antebellum era was very different from the twentieth-century church. While the early Unitarians were criticized by mainstream Protestants for rejecting the *deity* of Christ, they did acknowledge the *divinity* of Christ; and their belief that the Bible was divine revelation and that God performed miracles placed them closer to their sectarian critics than one might initially suppose.[34] Although the Unitarians were celebrated in intellectual circles, they represented only a fragment of the old Puritan orthodoxy and, in fact, were far removed from it by over a century of Congregationalism. Confined primarily to a narrow corner of the nation for most of the nineteenth century, they emerged long after Protestant fundamentalism had been well established.[35] With private lives and virtues that had "little room either for moral or religious criticism," many Unitarians, Francis Grund observed in 1837, were convinced that their sect would appeal to a broad spectrum of the population. "Massachusetts liberals of 1825 . . . had expected Unitarianism to spread 'like a prairie fire' across America," historian William R. Hutchison wrote; "but the fire had sputtered out west of Worcester and south of the Connecticut line, and had only with difficulty been re-lighted in more distant places." The Unitarians form a "highly respectable and intellectual class of society," Grund concluded, but the "great majority" of the American people simply considers their doctrines to be "incompatible with pure Christianity."[36] For American Protestantism, the rise of the Unitarians constituted barely a flicker of intellectualism on the religious horizon. To the vast majority of Protestants, liberal Christianity was apostasy, but the example does illustrate the diversity and complexity of this vague but all-inclusive essence called "Christianity."

Go Ye into All the World

Since there were only a handful of dominant religions in early America, it is possible to draw some generalizations about the role that Christians played in shaping racism in the United States. To begin with, Christianity, like most religions, was *dogmatic*; that is, its advocates were convinced that their faith was the one *true* religion and that there was no path to immortality except through Christ. In his study on "the Protestant hope for a Christian America," Robert T. Handy of New York's Union Theological Seminary acknowledged the contradiction inherent in the belief in one true faith in a pluralistic and democratic society. "Committed to the principle of religious freedom and to the voluntary method, the leaders of the thrust to make America Christian failed to sense how coercive their efforts appeared to those who did not share their premises," he wrote in *A Christian America* (1971). "It was hard for them not to view their opponents as agents of evil, for they were convinced that they were unequivocally on the side of good." After listening to a Swedish missionary relate the Genesis account of Adam and Eve, a group of Susquehanna Indians concluded, according to a story told by Benjamin Franklin, that "It is indeed bad to eat apples." When the Indians then related their own legend about a beautiful woman who had descended from the clouds and helped them find maize, kidney beans, and tobacco, the missionary ridiculed their story as "mere fable, fiction, and falsehood." Offended because they believed the "rules of common civility" obliged him to believe their story as they had his, they criticized him for his insolence and bad manners. Condemning the Indian's myths as "nonsense and rank superstition," the Christian saw no similarity between the supernatural events of the Indian's religion and his own biblical "miracles."[37]

In fairness to Christians it should be pointed out that their dogmatism was no more unrelenting than that of many other believers. An exclusive claim to The Truth has been a fundamental characteristic of many faiths, modern and prehistoric (although many non-Western societies believed that each culture can, even must, have its own legitimate religion). Everything else was *superstition*, which, historian James Axtell wrote in his study of the contest of cultures, had "no objective reality" but was "merely an aspersion used by one group to denigrate the religion of another." Discussing the religions of primitive societies, British anthropologist A. R. Radcliffe-Brown pointed out that it was usually customary—he might even have said *necessary*—to consider other religions as "bodies of erroneous beliefs and illusory practices." Debunking someone else's faith legitimizes one's own. The history of religions, he concluded, has been "in great part the history of error and illusion." Unfortunately, Christianity rested on a principle—monotheism—that clearly set it apart from most other religions and actually worked against effective evangelization. As the Swedish missionary's reactions made clear, monotheists began from the premise that no other gods existed. On the other hand, Africans, Asians, New World Indians, and most of the rest of the world's polytheistic peoples, like the missionary's Susquehanna audience, simply saw the Christian's God as one of many. Polytheistic societies often had little difficulty trading gods or acknowledging someone else's spiritual hosts because, while doing so, they could keep the ones they already had. The Christian, on the other hand, demanded that the heathen disavow entirely every vestige of his "false" religion.[38]

By itself, dogmatism was of no consequence. But Christianity was also a missionary faith and the peripatetic adventurers who launched the Age of Exploration carried the colors of Christian nations. To the Jews and Christians of biblical times, the "world" was the lands of the eastern Mediterranean; there is no evidence that Christ or his disciples had any knowledge of peoples or cultures outside of one small corner of the Middle East. Fifteen centuries later the Christian's world encompassed the oceans. From the time of his first voyage, Columbus saw himself as a pilgrim whom God had chosen to bring Christianity to the New World, a view suggested by his frequent use of the signature "Christoferens" ("Christbearer"), and the name that one Juan de la Cosa inscribed on what historians consider the first map of the New World. "God made me the messenger of the new heaven and the new earth of which he spoke in the Apocalypse of St. John after having spoken of it through the mouth of Isaiah," Columbus wrote to the Spanish royal court in 1500, "and he showed me the spot where to find it."[39]

While there were other religions whose advocates extended their doctrines beyond their original territories—Islam being the most conspicuous example—none was pursued as relentlessly or carried as far as Christianity.[40] The missionary purpose was also a major component of

English exploration, first in the 1570s with the voyages of Martin Frobisher, and later with the adventures of George Best, Humphrey Gilbert, Samuel Purchas, and, especially, Richard Hakluyt.[41] In 1583 Gilbert set out across the North Atlantic with orders to convert to the faith any "poor infidels, it seeming probable that God hath reserved the Gentiles to be introduced to Christian civility by the English nation." The following year, Hakluyt, who was also an Anglican minister, proclaimed in his "Discourse" that the crown's title of "Defender of the Faith" assigned to the sovereign the primary responsibility for bringing the gospel of Christ to heathens.[42]

It should come as no surprise, then, that when King James in 1606 granted special charters establishing the Virginia companies of London and Plymouth, he specifically called for "propagating the Christian Religion to such people, as yet live in darkness and miserable ignorance of the true knowledge and worship of God." Special instructions issued the same year required the governing authorities to "provide that the true Word, and Service of God be preached, planted, and used, not only in the said colonies, but also, as much as might be, among the savages bordering among them, according to the rites and doctrine of the Church of England." In 1609 the second charter of Virginia made the missionary objective "the climax of the document."[43] Nor did it end there. "The principal and main ends are *first* to preach and baptize into the Christian Religion," the Virginia Company declared in 1610, and "recover out of the arms of the Devil a number of poor and miserable souls."[44] Contrary to the common historical perception of Virginia as a commercial colony interested only in the accumulation of wealth for stockholders, the early literature of the colony suggests, Perry Miller wrote in *Errand into the Wilderness*, that "the cosmos expounded in the Virginia pamphlets is one where the principal human concern is neither the rate of interest nor the discovery of gold, but the will of God. . . . [I]n thoughts and in reported actions, religion *seems* the compelling, or at least the pervading force."[45]

Virginia was only the first English colony to appear to take to heart Christ's command to "Go ye therefore, and teach all nations, baptizing them in the name of the Father, and of the Son, and of the Holy Ghost."[46] Reviewing the charter of the Massachusetts Bay Company, King Charles considered the conversion of heathen natives to Christianity to be "the principall Ende of this plantacion." The charter itself, dated 1628, called for an effort to "Wynn and incite the natives of that country to the knowledge and obedience of the onlie true God and Saviour of Mankinde and the Christian faith," and charged the governor to "doe your best endeavor to draw on the natives of this country . . . to the true God."[47] In remarks prepared in 1720 for the Commissioners for the Propagation of the Gospel among American Indians, Cotton Mather argued that missionary work was still as important as it had been "when the *Seal* of the Colony was, a Poor *Indian* having as a label from his Lips, expressing this Cry, COME OVER AND HELP US!" The effort should be a fulfillment of Proverbs 25:25: "*As cold waters to a Thirsty soul, so is Good News from a Far Country.*"[48]

Similar missionary intentions were set forth in the charters for Maryland, Maine, Carolina, Rhode Island, Pennsylvania, and in the Articles of Confederation for New England. Of the early charters granted by the English government, only those for Connecticut (1662) and New York (1664 and 1674) were silent on the question of missions to the heathens. But Connecticut did not need a royal mandate to become, with Massachusetts, the first colony to establish Indian missions; beginning in 1641 and continuing through the late nineteenth century, church and state formed a partnership to bring Christianity to Native Americans. Thus many of the earliest settlers of English North America considered themselves only secondarily merchants, exploiters, or Englishmen. "[I]n their own conception of themselves," Miller concluded, describing the planters and promoters of Virginia, "they are first and foremost Christians, and above all militant Protestants."[49] At least those were the public declarations.

In fact, the conception was more militant than Christian or Protestant. Prior to the Great Massacre of Good Friday in 1622, which took the lives of one-quarter of Virginia's white population, there was some missionary sentiment, as several company preachers believed that the Indian was a heathen only because he had never had the opportunity to hear the gospel and that his salvation was simply a matter of reaching out to him with the Word. It was not his fault that he had been an ocean away from the influences of Christianity. Unfortunately, the spirit of the charter and the good intentions of the ministers remained only that. From the first days of Jamestown, most settlers showed little interest in the mission cause. After the massacre, public opinion turned overwhelmingly against the Indians, with many whites calling for "a war of attrition and extermination." Some colonists saw the Indian's extreme hostility as nothing less than a "willful refusal to accept the free gift of God's grace through the gospel" and concluded that whatever catastrophic fate befell him was well deserved.[50] In other words, the Indian was despised because he did not have the good sense to appreciate the true faith that was being offered to him. That conclusion was an ideal religious rationalization because it not only relieved the settler of the responsibility of continuing his missionary efforts, but also justified his use of violence and subjugation. The founders had made a good-faith effort to uplift the savage, the colonists reasoned; if the effort failed, it was the savage's fault.

To Perry Miller's assertion that "religion *seems* the compelling, or at least the pervading force,"one could easily point out that conditions were often not what they seemed. By the beginning of the eighteenth century, memories of the massacre of 1622 had faded sufficiently to allow a renewed attempt to bring Virginia's natives into the body of Christ. Shortly after 1700, James Blair, founder and for fifty years president of the Royal College of William and Mary, tried to establish a program in which young Indian males who had already converted would be trained as missionaries to work among their own people, but the effort did not succeed in training even one Indian. Later, when Governor Alexander Spotswood brought some Indians together to form praying communities (as John Eliot had done in Massachusetts in the seventeenth century), the results were similarly disappointing.[51]

Many Puritans in Massachusetts were not excessively impressed by their charter commitment to convert Indians but, rather, displayed a "garrison mentality" that was anything but Christian-spirited. As part of the colony's security policy, the directors of the Massachusetts Bay Company instructed the first governor, John Winthrop, to train all the men in the use of firearms, keep Indians out of the towns, and deport to England any colonist who sold firearms to Indians. Almost from the first day, in fact, the charter mandate to "Wynn and incite" heathens "to the knowledge and obedience of the onlie true God" was a casualty of what was perceived as a more urgent need to ensure the safety of white Christians. Writing to Winthrop in 1647, Samuel Symonds placed the conversion of Indians in seventh place on a list of why God chose the Puritans to settle New England. Moreover, the idea of reaching out to Indians was complicated by the Puritans' belief that conversion did not mean a simple declaration for Christ, but, rather, required the savage first to give up his pagan ways and adopt the white man's habits—in short, to repudiate his culture. Since that seemed out of the question for any more than a small fraction of the Indian population, the only realistic option was domination. "Missionization," as one historian put it, "officially began only after" the Puritans had exterminated the Pequots in 1637 and "had begun a war of attrition against . . . the Narragansetts."[52]

Anyone who considered that a bit drastic needed only to recall that the idea of a "just war" had long been a part of Christian tradition, going back to the Bible itself and validated in Augustine's *City of God* (c. 423), in which "the only righteous wars were those commended by God, who sometimes withheld victory from His armies in punishment for their own sins."[53] Since many colonists saw the hand of God in the smallpox epidemic that had decimated the Indian villages three years before the arrival of the Plymouth settlers—followed fifteen years later by another outbreak in

1633–34—the suggestion of extermination did not seem so outrageous. Taking up arms against a heathen enemy was tantamount to taking up arms against Satan. "And I saw heaven opened, and behold a white horse," the Puritan read in Revelation 19:11; "and he that sat upon him *was* called Faithful and True, and in righteousness he doth judge and make war." With this ringing principle before him, the Puritan emphatically proclaimed that "every man undertakes to fight manfully under Christ's banner against sin, the world, the devil, and to continue his faithful soldier and servant to his life's end."[54] Accordingly, he found it easy to conclude that prisoners captured in a "just war" must be punished by "either death or slavery," historian Edmund S. Morgan wrote. Following both the Pequot War and King Philip's War four decades later, the victorious Puritans sold their Indian captives "in the West Indies and in return brought back Negroes (captured, presumably, in equally just wars), for Negroes were more docile then Pequots or Mohawks or Narragansetts." In their "Body of Liberties," the Puritan fathers clearly prohibited "bond-slavery, villenage or captivitie amongst us," but excepted, among others, "lawfull captives, taken in just warrs."[55]

As it happened, the missionary impulse was as compelling among those who expressed it through love as it was among those who expressed it through destruction and enslavement. Writing to Abbé Raynal in July 1781, Anthony Benezet, a leading Quaker critic of slavery, insisted that Christianity was the only hope for oppressed black people everywhere. Calling attention to the presumed needs of blacks in both Africa and the Caribbean, Benezet argued that the Christian must help heathens overcome "the corruption of the human heart, and invite them to seek for the influence of that grace, proposed by the gospel, by which they may obtain salvation."[56] No one, not even the benevolent Quakers, ever suggested that the infidel should simply be left alone.

After 1800 the evangelical spirit intensified dramatically. In 1810, the Congregational Church, with some assistance from other denominations, organized the American Board of Commissioners for Foreign Missions. Five years later, speaking at an ordination service for six missionaries, Samuel Worcester, pastor of Tabernacle Church in Salem, Massachusetts, and a founder of the board, exclaimed, "My brethren, *the heathen do need the gospel. There is no other remedy for them.*" Without exception, he pontificated, all other world religions were utterly worthless and their adherents were without hope, salvation, or eternal light.[57] If there was a universal component in evangelical Christianity, it was the unshakable belief that everyone else was wrong and that infidels had to be "rescued." The missionary was not discouraged by resistance because that was simply Satan talking; and besides, the ignorant heathen did not know what was good for him anyway. In fact, Christian missionaries often seemed to imply that the object of their attention not only had the wrong religion but, in fact, had no religion at all. Ugandan scholar Okot p'Biket criticized early European travelers in Africa who had claimed that the natives, "in common with other so-called 'savages,' had *no* religion, but only superstition."[58]

The American missionary spirit kept pace with territorial expansion and reached its peak in the late nineteenth century, when men like Josiah Strong, a Congregationalist minister who has often been exalted as the quintessential Protestant imperialist, asserted that "Christian individuals and nations had a primary obligation to fulfill the missionary charge of world evangelization and that . . . Americans as Christians had a special obligation and opportunity to fulfill this charge."[59] Herein lay the fundamental component of the Christian's racism: his inherent inability to leave other people alone. There has probably never been a time in the history of the nation when the missionary spirit was more contumelious than it was during the three decades before World War I. And it was never more arrogantly expressed than in the words of Robert E. Speer, secretary of the Board of Foreign Missions of the Presbyterian Church in the United States of America:

> But Christianity must continue, and all the more as this transformation advances, to seek to win individual men away from their religions to Christianity. If by proselytizing is meant winning men from all that is false and evil in the world's religions and relating them to the one universal religion, which is all truth and good, in other words, the effort to make Hindus and Mohammedans Christians, then that is just what we are trying to do. We are proselytizing. And we do not see what else in all the world is worth doing. The business of every man is to find truth, to live it, and to get it found and lived by all the world. This is what we are Christians for. And this change in individuals must be a radical and living change.[60]

Speer later differentiated between "false imperialism which is abhorrent to Christianity" and "true imperialism which is inherent in it."[61] Moreover, this attitude reached far beyond the pulpit and moved into the public consciousness and the highest circles of government. Among the justifications for seizing the Philippines during the war with Spain in 1898 was the contention that the United States had a *manifest* right to civilize and Christianize "our little brown brothers," who had suffered so long at the hands of the corrupt Spanish papists. The fact that the Filipinos were overwhelmingly Roman Catholic meant little to white Americans, who were in the midst of an orgiastic outburst of nativistic pride and Protestant chauvinism. Whatever the age and place, the missionary impulse was ubiquitous and the infidels were not always grateful. The tunnel of piety was long and narrow. Religion is man's search for God, Christians liked to say, but Christianity is God's search for man, a reminder that the arrogance of faith is not easily set aside.

A Haughty Spirit Before a Fall

As for the "heathens" themselves, most had no understanding of evangelism and therefore were more than a little bewildered by the Christian's single-mindedness. After listening to John Eliot preach in 1646, several Indians wondered why it was that only the English knew God. Why, "if we are all the children of one father," one of them asked Eliot on another occasion, do "white men know about the ten commandments and Indians do not?" Since most Indians, like most Africans, believed that each culture was served by its own beliefs, many of them were perplexed by the white man's insistence that Christianity was the only true religion. Cultural differences were simply too great to allow for that. It was obvious, one group told Presbyterian missionary David Brainerd, that the red, white, and black races had been created by different gods; and since the Indian's life was "vastly preferable" to the others, his god must have been watching the other gods so as not to make the same mistakes.[62]

The insistence that religion was relative was also the point of Red Jacket's complaint to the missionary Cram. "Brother! You say there is but one way to worship and serve the Great Spirit," the Seneca chief asserted, "yet you Christians constantly disagree among yourselves," an argument that impressed Francis Grund. Red Jacket, Grund wrote in his travel study, was "an Indian chief of great eloquence" who "observed that it was very probable God had intended the white and red races for different purposes," suggesting a belief in cultural pluralism. "To you," Red Jacket said to Cram, "[God] has given the arts; to these He has forever closed our eyes. Why should He have not given you another religion also?" My faith serves me and yours serves you, the Indian seemed to be saying. Why should anyone want to interfere with that? Besides, if Christianity is for everyone, why was it not from the beginning revealed to everyone?

> You say that you are sent to instruct us how to worship the Great Spirit agreeably to his mind; and, if we do not take hold of the religion which you white people teach us, we shall be unhappy hereafter. You say you are right and we are lost. How do we know

> this to be true? We understand that your religion is written in a book. If it was intended for us as well as you, why has not the Great Spirit given to us, and not only to us, but why did he not give to our forefathers the knowledge of that book, with the means of understanding it rightly? We only know what you tell us about it. How shall we know when to believe, being so often deceived by the white people?

After the meeting, Cram refused to shake hands with Red Jacket because "[t]here was no fellowship between the religion of God and the Devil."[63] Several Wyandot leaders took the simple position that if God had intended for them to be Christians he would have written the Bible in their language. Moreover, they added, the fact that the Bible speaks mainly in agricultural terms was proof that it was not written for people who were primarily hunters.[64]

The Indian's resistance to Christianity was also influenced by his inability to understand some of the most fundamental elements of Christian belief, especially the story of the crucifixion and resurrection. The problem was not the miracle aspect of the story. Like the Susquehanna Indians who told the Swedish missionary about the beautiful woman who had descended from the clouds and taught them how to cultivate maize and kidney beans, virtually every society professed a religion based on supernatural origins. Rather, the Indian was dumbfounded by a faith whose omnipotent being allowed his own son to be killed. What kind of omnipotence was that? It just did not make sense. But if there were Indians like Red Jacket who could not reconcile Christian teaching with their world and who questioned the authenticity of a document that had been revealed only to a small fraction of the earth's population, there were others who were impressed by these very qualities. Writing in his *Key into the Language of America* (1643), Roger Williams recounted a conversation he had overheard between two Indians on the subject of the white man's heaven.

> A *Quinnínticut* Indian (who had heard our discourse) told the *Sachim Miantunnômu*, that soules went up to Heaven, or downe to Hell; For, saith he, Our fathers have told us, that our soules goe to the *Southwest*.
>
> The *Sachim* answered, But how doe you know your selfe, that your soules goe to the *Southwest*; did you ever see a soule goe to Heaven or Hell?
>
> The *Sachim* againe replied: He hath books and writings, and one which God himselfe made, concerning men's soules, and therefore may well know more than wee that have none, but take upon trust from our forefathers.[65]

Thus the absence of a written language among at least some Indians was sufficient to raise doubts about the truth of their own religious heritage. The fact that the words of biblical writers and the teaching of missionaries also had to be taken "upon trust" was not enough to discredit the influence of the written word.

Like most North American Indians, the African believed that religion was not a matter of individual conscience or a personal relationship with a supreme being, but a matter of devotion to family and community customs and traditions. There was nothing voluntary about it. Also like the Indian, the African, with no comprehension of evangelism, could not understand why any people should want to impose their religious beliefs on others. While one tribal group might influence the belief system of another through political consolidation or military conquest, such syncretism was coincidental—the by-product of occupation, not of motivation.

Faith was not simply an outer garment that one could shed in favor of another; it was a fundamental component of culture. When Portuguese Catholic missionaries in rural northern China in the nineteenth century ordered converts not to participate in village temple activities or contribute to the temple's support because of the church's opposition to what the missionaries considered pagan rites, the villagers reacted angrily because temple activities were an essential aspect of village life and everyone was supposed to participate. By challenging the missionaries, they were simply trying to preserve a centuries-old tradition.[66] Similarly, since the African's religion was profoundly interwoven into his everyday life, Christian evangelism did far more than merely challenge his belief in his gods. "Each society had its own religious system," a West African scholar wrote, "and the propagation of such a religious system would involve propagating the entire life of the people concerned."[67]

Simply put, the effort to convert the infidel was far more than a matter of asking him to switch churches. In trying to change the African's religion, the missionaries were attacking the foundations of his culture. To be sure, whether or not the Christian realized he was disrupting traditional life was probably irrelevant because he almost certainly would not have cared anyway. The dogmatic mind claimed exclusive access to the truth and thus was inherently incapable of compromising because it saw no reason to.

Given this situation, it is not difficult to see how the true believer could justify any action if it appeared—to him—to serve the faith; and it mattered little if such action required the use of intimidation or force. While Islam has often been associated with the sword, Christianity was no less militant in enforcing its doctrines and safeguarding its territories. Clovis I, the founder of the Frankish monarchy in the fifth century, and his eighth-century successor Charlemagne, who became emperor of the Holy Roman Empire, were among the first and most ruthless advocates of conversion by conquest. Under Charlemagne, refusal to be baptized incurred a death sentence. "It was a temporal sword that made Christianity a world religion," wrote waterfront philosopher Eric Hoffer in *The True Believer.*[68]

Nowhere has the devastating irony of this theme been more exquisitely dissected than in a work of fiction—book 5, chapter 5 of Fyodor Dostoyevsky's masterpiece *The Brothers Karamazov.* "Why hast thou come to hinder us?" the Grand Inquisitor asks the imprisoned Christ, whose return to earth during the "most terrible time" of the Spanish Inquisition threatens to undercut the magisterium. " 'All has been given by Thee to the Pope,' they say, 'and all, therefore, is still in the Pope's hands and there is no need for Thee to come now at all. Thou must not meddle for the time, at least.' "[69] To Dostoyevsky, the institutional church was by its nature incapable of tolerating any challenge to its authority; deviation was ecclesiastical suicide. The whole idea of papal infallibility was based on the premise that, even if the Pope was wrong, he could not be portrayed to the laity as wrong or else some people would begin wondering how often he had been wrong. It was more important to be believed right then to *be* right.[70] Thus for the true believer it was perfectly logical that Christ himself must not interfere with the irrepressible progress of Christianity; and if Christ could not deflect the evangelical impulse, surely heathens should not be permitted to do so.

There are contradictions in every religion; but the missionary quality of Christianity magnifies the consequences of its contradictions. The history of Christianity may be the serene and saintly story of Jesus of Nazareth and the Virgin Mary, St. Francis of Assisi and Mother Teresa, and Martin Luther King, Jr., leading nuns and clergymen in nonviolent resistance. But it is also the cruel and bloody story of crusaders and conquistadores, Pope Innocent II and Torquemada, the Salem witch trials and cross-burning Klansmen. "Kill a Commie for Christ!" bumper stickers shouted during the 1950s. When British philosopher and mathematician Bertrand Russell, well known for his agnosticism, was asked by a reporter which religion he would prefer if he were forced to choose one, he selected Buddhism because, he said, it was the only major faith that had never tried forcibly to impose its doctrines on unwilling alien peoples. "Christianity has been distinguished from other religions by its greater readiness for persecution," Russell wrote in 1954. "The whole contention that Christianity has had an elevating moral influence can only be maintained by wholesale ignoring or falsification of the historical evidence."[71] One can only wonder if Russell had read Thomas Jefferson's *Notes on the State of Virginia* (1785):

> Millions of innocent men, women, and children, since the introduction of Christianity, have been burnt, tortured, fined, imprisoned; yet we have not advanced one inch towards uniformity. What has been the effect of coercion? To make one half the world fools, and the other half hypocrites. To support error and roguery all over the earth.[72]

Jefferson needed to look no further than his own slave quarters to see an "effect" of his own "coercion." Christianity—from Richard the Lion-Hearted to Billy Graham—has almost certainly been responsible for more worldwide proselytizing and obtrusion than any religion in history. One can only wonder how many "infidels" have been killed or enslaved in the name of Christ.

Dogmatism and militancy do not shine in any garments, least of all in a faith whose essence is a loving and merciful Jesus. Protestant efforts to convert dark-skinned infidels may have seemed altruistic, but it was in the nature of evangelical Christianity that the spiritual belief of the heathen was "of the Devil" and must be purged before salvation could be realized. In the 1720s, Gilbert Tennent, a leader of the revivalist faction in the Presbytery of New Brunswick and a major figure in the Great Awakening, argued that no person could ever become a Christian without first becoming aware of the horrors of *not* being a Christian. As religion historian Winthrop S. Hudson described the process, the convert "must first know himself as a sinful creature, estranged from God, and rightly subject to condemnation, before he can apprehend and receive God's forgiveness and acceptance."[73] What this meant, of course, was a public confession and acknowledgment of past transgressions; membership in The Elect was not possible without the catharsis of humiliation.[74] There simply was no other way. Of course, for Africans and Indians this meant a repudiation of beliefs and practices that they and generations of their ancestors had always considered imperative paths to prosperous and righteous lives in this world as well as the next. That so many of them refused to take that step should surprise no one.

Needless to say, the tenacity with which the missionary-minded Christian pursued his evangelical goals also rendered him purblind to the racist constrictions inherent in his faith. In his introduction to the 1965 edition of Samuel Stanhope Smith's *Essay on the Causes of the Variety of Complexion and Figure in the Human Species* (1787), historian Winthrop D. Jordan explains how the work "serves to demonstrate in quietly dramatic terms the way in which a sense of inequality among races infiltrated traditional Christian doctrine in America."[75] That a modern scholar with a background in the history of race relations could so easily set down these words is an example of the insidiousness of institutional racism. To begin with, describing the white Christian's perception of nonwhite races as a "*sense* of inequality" is a gross understatement. In fact, his assumption of superiority was emphatic and profound. And to say that such a "sense" *infiltrated* Christian doctrine is to imply that it did so covertly and that Christianity in America had been, at least up to the point of "infiltration," relatively free of white-supremacist ideology. Actually, the belief in an "inequality among races" was blatant from the beginning. What Jordan called "traditional Christian doctrine" was itself racist.

It was an easy trap to fall into. In discussing the religious defense of slavery in the Anglo-American colonial world, Leland J. Bellot pointed out that, although evangelicals could be found on both sides of the controversy, the English church did not "avoid the moral tension between Christian principles and the institution of slavery which had plagued Christian social thought and practice from its very origins."[76] Like most writers on the subject, Bellot, by juxtaposing "Christian principles" and "slavery," drew the traditional polarity of good and evil. What he did not acknowledge was the racism inherent in the evangelical's advocacy of those very principles and, most important of all, in the principles themselves. Slavery in the New World was a product of the arrogance of Christianity, not its opponent in the creation of "moral tension." The proof of this is best seen in the fact that antislavery Christians exalted love, compassion, forgiveness, and charity only in the context of *conversion*. In other words, the missionary could not invoke "Christian principles" without making their application contingent upon the slave's adoption of the faith.[77]

To rephrase the point as a question: Could Christians welcome a non-Christian into their midst, accord him social and political equality, and, at the same time, not only not try to impose Christianity on him but fully respect his right to practice any faith he chose? Or no faith at all? A Christian who did not try to convert the nonbelievers around him would not have been true to Christ's command to spread the good news to all the world. Since evangelicalism mandated that all peoples should be taught to know Christ, how much love and charity could an infidel expect from his Christian benefactors if he persisted in practicing his "false" religion?

When the Apostle Paul told the Galatians that "You are all sons of God through faith in Christ Jesus, for all of you who were baptized into Christ have clothed yourselves with Christ," he was, in fact, saying that becoming a Christian obliterates all distinctions. "There is neither Jew nor Greek, slave nor free, male nor female, for you are all one in Jesus Christ. If you belong to Christ, then you are Abraham's seed, and heirs according to the promise."[78] Did this mean that the slave who accepted the white man's offer of freedom but spurned his offer of Christianity would forever remain outside of white society? Shunned, ignored, oppressed? Religious agencies like "home and foreign missions, Bible societies, temperance societies, societies for the reclamation of fallen women [but not fallen men], and societies for the accomplishment of every kind of good work" flourished in antebellum America.[79] But all of them did their "good work" only within a Christian context. Presbyterian missionaries, according to one scholar, praised Indians only "*in so far* as they could emulate white Christians."[80] Like the hungry derelict who must sit through a sermon to get a plate of beans at a skid row mission, the heathen was a beneficiary of Christian benevolence only if he joined the community.

The need to equate Christianity with righteousness can be seen even in the work of modern religious scholars. Church historian Franklin H. Littell described as "superior" a definition (not his own) of religious liberty that recognized "the natural and inalienable right of every soul to worship God according to the dictates of his own conscience" without interference and without infringing on the rights of others.[81] The problem with this "superior" definition—and others like it—is its assumption that everyone believes not only in the existence of a god but, as the capitalization of "God" and the absence of an indefinite article would suggest, a Judeo-Christian God. Did Littell's definition apply to someone who believed in more than one god? Or no gods? Modern churches have done as much as any philanthropic institution in the world to ameliorate hunger, poverty, disease, and ignorance, but the fact remains that most Christians have perceived the African, Indian, or any other nonbeliever as an equal—if they have done so at all—only *after* he has been converted. It was impossible for a missionary to accept the heathen for what he was *and* consider him an equal. That would have been real charity.

If the missionary impulse was the driving force behind Christianity's subjugation of its heathen subjects, it should be instructive to review the human price exacted by other missionary faiths. After all, it is unfair to condemn the sins of Christianity without at least acknowledging the sins of all societies whose oppressed classes have owed their condition to the power of religion. Unfortunately for the Christian, it does not help his defense to point out that only one other major religion, Islam, exported its teachings on a grand scale and for reasons and with consequences that had little in common with those of Christianity. Most important was the source and nature of the mission mandate. While Muslims believed that Allah was the one true God, they did not nurture a compelling obligation to force others to believe likewise. For example, the Umayyed dynasty that ruled the Arab world for a century before A.D. 750—the only time in Islamic history that all Muslims were united in a single state—eschewed forced conversions and the persecution of religious dissent. Christians and Jews, considered "people of the book" whose faiths were partially true, only had to pay higher taxes.

As Arab traders established caravan routes across North Africa, the spread of Islam probably depended more on trade and commerce than on the sword. Moving south in the tenth century, Islam was rejected by the rulers of Ghana, who nevertheless welcomed Muslim merchants. Not surprisingly, the Soninke merchant class became, by the eleventh century, one of the first West African social groups to accept the Islamic faith. In fact, Islam was not hostile toward West African traditional religions, and it became a state religion mainly in areas where certain chiefs exploited religion to consolidate their power. Since their adoption of the faith was more an act of political expediency than a spiritual commitment, Islam did not necessarily filter down to the masses or significantly alter popular views of the universe. In most of sub-Saharan Africa the "state" was a kinship group, and the incorporation of Islamic beliefs into the group's code of conduct was not unusual; but tribal leaders never attempted to impose their faith on others. One could voluntarily become a Muslim, but conversion by proselytizing or force was unthinkable.[82]

While the economic and political control of a territory in the name of Allah was more important then the salvation of its infidels, the introduction of the gospel of Christ was the overriding purpose of the Christian mission. If it could be said that faith followed conquest in Islam, it could be said that conquest followed faith in Christianity. The geographic range of Islam, which spread primarily across regions bordering the Mediterranean Sea and penetrated central Asia as far as southern Russia and northern India, did not approach the reach of Christianity. In fact, except for a few places like Indonesia, Islam was largely confined to a single landmass. On the other hand, the biblical mandate to "teach all nations" led to the Christian domination of Europe and virtually the entire New World, from whence it reached back across oceans to every continent. By the beginning of the twentieth century there were few corners of the planet that had not been tapped by the emissaries of Jesus Christ. If anyone needs a vivid lesson on the expansive power of Christianity, he has only to reflect on the fact that on the eve of the twenty-first century the largest Roman Catholic edifice in the world is in Yamoussoukro, Ivory Coast, and the largest Protestant congregation anywhere is in Seoul, Korea.

More to the point than the geographic range of the Muslim's religion was the nature of his relationship to the people he subjugated. To begin with, Islamic law prohibited the enslavement of anyone born a Muslim or converted before being captured. In practice, this injunction was frequently set aside by emirs, sultans, and other state leaders whose political and economic interests took precedence over matters of faith. Even so, the very existence of such a law stood in stark contrast to the Christian's willingness to enslave anyone with a dark skin. The law also prohibited penal slavery, a not uncommon practice in Europe, especially in Russia, where it was a major source of labor. And most Islamic slaves had rights; for example, a slave who was unhappy with his situation could demand a different owner, a demand "which the master was duty bound to honor." Not surprisingly, the manumission rate of slaves was much higher in Muslim countries than anywhere in the Christian world. "Mahomet proclaimed Liberty to all Slaves," Benjamin Rush wrote in 1773. "He not only emancipated his own Slave, but made him his Friend."[83]

Another unusual distinction was the Muslim slaveholder's preference for women. "Among the great majority of Islamic peoples after the ninth century," sociologist Orlando Patterson pointed out in *Slavery and Social Death*, "female captives and kidnapped persons fetched a higher price than males, even where slavery was economically important."[84] This was also the case among Ugandan Muslims in black Africa, where "[c]attle and slaves, especially women, were the major spoils of war."[85] The situation does not seem so unusual in male-dominated societies where a man wealthy enough to own slaves might have a stable of concubines, or where slaves served primarily as domestic servants or where a woman's reproductive capability inflated her value. Furthermore, in most Islamic slave societies, a slave woman and her children became free as soon as she bore a son for her master. On the other hand, a child born to a free woman and a male slave would be free but the father would remain in bondage. In the thirteenth century, the policy that "the child follows the better half" was in effect only in Sweden and Spain.[86] All of this was in sharp contrast to the American situation, first established by law in the southern colonies, where children always assumed the status of their mother.

In the Sudanic belt the condition of the members of a slave family, J. Spencer Trimingham wrote, "ameliorated itself with each successive generation." Even though Islamic law decreed that the children of slave parents remained slaves, in practice it was not uncommon for bondsmen to pass from "slaves" to "serfs" in one generation, and in the case of Africans like the Hausa to redeem themselves completely.[87] But of all the distinctive qualities of Islamic slavery, probably none was more remarkable than the use of slaves as soldiers. In fact, in Islam's unique vertical slave hierarchy a bondsman could distinguish himself in military or political service, eventually rising to a rank just under royalty, or, in the case of the *ghilmān*, actually taking control of the government. As impressive as was the rise of the *ghilmān*, the most startling aspect of the deployment of slave military forces was the simple fact that large numbers of bondsmen could be trusted as soldiers. In the twelfth century, the great Saladin, Sultan of Egypt and

Syria, raised an army of 12,000 *mamluks,* slaves recruited from Asia and Turkey. Five centuries later Mulay Ismail of Morocco purchased black slaves for use in the *abid*, an army that eventually numbered 150,000.[88] The very idea of a slave army would have defied the comprehension of a Christian slaveholder, who, always wary of the possibility of an uprising, could only shudder at the thought of putting weapons in the hands of his bondsmen. That armed Muslim slaves could be trusted not to turn on their masters said a great deal about the differences between Islamic and Christian slave systems.

As preferable as the life of a Muslim slave might seem when compared to that of a slave in the Christian world, there were several areas in which the two were almost indistinguishable. Foremost was the matter of color and race. While slaves of every complexion could be found in Islamic societies, darker-skinned people were almost always treated far worse than Turkish or European captives. In Malaysia, for example, "the Arab rulers viewed the conquered native population with utter contempt"; and in parts of the Sudan a black skin, Patterson noted, "was and still is associated with slavery." But it should also be pointed out that, unlike in Western slave societies, the captive's status as an infidel, not his race or color, was the primary basis of his enslavement. Of course, it is not likely that very many black slaves took much comfort in knowing, if indeed they knew, that people of other races and colors suffered in bondage. Slaves in Islamic and Christian societies also shared similar places in their owners' value systems. It was a matter of honor and respect, for instance, that a Muslim master should have a large retinue of "dependent followers."[89]

Similarly, the American slaveholder measured his social status according to the number of slaves he owned. Just as a Muslim master would be unreasonably offended if any of his slaves were killed (even more so than if one of his sons had been killed) because of the insult to his honor, so also the Christian master in the American South would often keep, or add to, his labor force during periods of low cotton prices when it would have been good business to scale back the number of slaves he had to maintain. It should be made clear that the Muslim, in this situation, never cared about the welfare of his slave but, rather, about the affront to his own personal prestige, again making him little different from the American plantation owner, who dressed his house servants in the finest clothes just to impress visitors. In either case, "the master's existence is enhanced by the slave's," rather than the other way around.[90]

It is also worth noting that slavery in Christian societies did not reach substantial numbers until the advent of capitalism and the opening of the New World. On the other hand, slaves had been a major commodity of Islamic trade long before they were economically essential, a situation that continued well into the nineteenth century.[91] But the Muslim dominance would not last forever. With the markets of Europe and Africa beckoning, the Christian countries raised slavery to levels of quantity and inhumanity exceeding anything seen in the Islamic world—or almost anywhere else, for that matter.

"Sullen Peoples" and the Devil

Of course, it did not require a quantum leap in reasoning to conclude that anyone who believed in an erroneous religion must also be a product of an inferior culture. "If one's own model was superior," Martin E. Marty wrote, "that meant that all others were inferior." With the earliest Christian missions to Asia and Africa sending back reports of idolatry, wickedness, and depravity, Marty concluded, "[t]he picture of others' cultural inferiority was thus deeply impressed." It was "natural," another religion scholar asserted, for European missionaries to regard their own culture "as superior to that of the countries in which they carried on their missionary work." Displaying a "patronizing" and "contemptuous" attitude "towards men whom he could never quite persuade himself to regard as grown up," Stephen Neill wrote, the evangelical Christian believed he could better judge "the real interests of his people than they could themselves." Some Europeans questioned the Indian's claim to the land on the grounds that the absence of Christianity meant there was no legitimate recognition of his jurisdiction. In other words, the Indian was not entitled to live by his own standards or to have others judge him by those standards. Likewise, two students of New England history pointed out that the Puritan, like the later pioneers who crossed the continent in the nineteenth century, "could not reasonably imagine the existence of native societies that were physically distinct from his own without being morally inferior."[92]

In his efforts to establish Indian "praying villages," John Eliot, probably the most aggressive Puritan missionary, was not concerned simply with converting heathens to Christianity but with bringing about a "massive cultural change by the introduction of European social and cultural values and institutions into Indian life." Urging the Indians to "detach themselves from their 'savage' culture," Eliot insisted that they adopt "the ways of 'civilization' " *before* being introduced to Christianity.[93] As a leading historian of the Methodist Church in America pointed out, supporters of the American Colonization Society, who in the early nineteenth century advocated the resettlement in West Africa of former American slaves, "continually emphasized the value of their colonies . . . as posts for the 'Christianization' and civilization of Africa." By preaching the gospel of

Christ, Donald G. Mathews wrote, the missions were supposed to "make civilized people of 'barbarians.' "[94]

Barbarians? If there was one thing that exposed the raw racism of Christianity, it was the name-calling that characterized virtually every missionary account. Wherever the Christian went, his language accompanied him. In his supercilious invocation to "take up the white man's burden" by sending forth "the best ye breed," Rudyard Kipling urged Americans who were debating the decision to occupy the Philippines,

> *To wait in heavy harness,*
> *On fluttered folk and wild—*
> *Your new-caught, sullen peoples,*
> *Half devil and half child.*[95]

Like their English cousins, Americans had no trouble perceiving "sullen peoples" as *barbarian*, *primitive*, *pagan*, *savage*, *idolatrous*, *heathen*, and *superstitious*, all terms with long histories and unequivocal pejorative connotations. In the approximately two hundred letters sent in the eighteenth century by the Anglican "Associates of Dr. Bray" to their superiors in London, all of these terms, and others like them, appeared frequently.[96] During the Creek War of 1813–14, Andrew Jackson referred to his Indian adversaries as "savage bloodhounds," "savage dogs," "cannibals," and "bloodthirsty barbarians." For sixty years after the founding in 1837 of the Board of Missions of the Presbyterian Church in the United States of America, missionaries dispatched to various Indian tribes used many of these same words to describe the natives.[97] By the time John Fiske wrote his *History of the United States* (1894), he simply divided the Indians into three groups: "savage, barbarous, and half-civilized."[98]

In truth, some of these words did not originate as terms of contempt but acquired that meaning through common usage. "Both *infidel* and *heathen* were based upon religious criteria," Robert F. Berkhofer wrote, "and derive from ancient Jewish and early Christian distinctions between themselves and other people."[99] It made little difference to the colonists, Roger Williams noted in 1645, that "heathen" originally included "Babylonians, Caldeans, Medes, and Persians, Greekes and Romanes." The term came to have its present meaning only in recent times as contacts between the English and the Indians became more frequent—and violent.

> I Shall first be humbly bold to inquire into the name *Heathen*, which the English give them, & the Dutch approve and practise in their name HEYDENEN, signifying Heathen or Nations. How oft have I heard both the English and Dutch (not onely the civill,

> but the most debauched and profane) say, These *Heathen* Dogges, better kill a thousand of them then that we *Christians* should be indangered or troubled with them; Better they were all cut off, & then we shall have no more trouble with them: They have spilt our *Christian* bloud, the best way to make riddance of them, cut them all off, and so make way for Christians.[100]

Thus the notion of them-and-us was delineated early. For some people both terms implied nonbelief in any religion. Centuries before Columbus, European Christians had identified Norsemen and Irish Celts by many of the same terms that white Americans later used to describe Africans and Indians. Nor was such labeling simply a bad habit that could be attributed to the widespread ignorance of an earlier age. Western scholars, African writer Okot p'Bitek complained, have always divided the world into two parts: "their own, *civilized*, and the rest, *primitive*."[101] It was not just the *use* of the words; it was the words themselves. However the non-Christian was described, he was oppressed by the Christian's language.

Barbarian, savage, heathen, pagan. Whatever term was used, it designated an incarnation of the source of all evil—Satan. Christianity was the religion that gave evil a human form with human functions. To the artist he was a persona that lurked in dangerous places, waiting to ensnare the innocent. Portrayed in the male gender, Satan spoke in the sinner's language and influenced mortals through intellectual processes and as an extraneous entity that took possession of a victim's body. To emphasize the magnitude of his influence—and, concomitantly, the importance of God's countervailing power—Christianity raised the devil to a level almost equal with God's. Other religions recognized demons and evil spirits that influenced human behavior and created chaos for mortals, but only the major monotheistic faiths—Judaism, Christianity, Islam—acknowledged an evil being who worked against the interests of God. And early American Protestants saw him connected to Africans and Indians.

From the beginning, "sullen peoples" were considered less civilized, backward human beings whose strange beliefs and practices were nothing less than manifestations of Satan. Two years after the founding of Jamestown, Virginia Company officials notified Governor Thomas Gates that the colony's missionaries must make every effort to convert Indian children, who, because they were "chayned under the bond of Deathe unto the Divell," could be forcibly taken from their parents, a sentiment repeated three years later when Captain John Smith wrote of the same Indians that "their chiefe God they worship is the Divell."[102] Thus the Christian not only believed that he was right and everybody else was wrong, but that he had the right to use physical force to impose his religion on others and that the beliefs of infidels were intrinsically evil and must be eradicated from the world.

Similarly, the Puritan defined the natural environment as "Satan's domain" and all aboriginal creatures as enemies of God. "Wherever the Indian opposed the Puritan," Roy Harvey Pearce observed, "there Satan opposed God." To the faithful, he concluded, devil worship "was at the core of savage life." The Puritans, unlike the early Virginia missionaries, did not even give the Indian the benefit of his ignorance. More than other colonists, historian George Fredrickson noted, they "were animated by the belief that Indian religion was not simply an unfortunate error of the unenlightened but quite literally worship of the Devil." The Puritan interpreted the presence of heathens as a crucible of his faith. Convinced that God had "allowed" the Indians to inhabit North America in order to challenge the strength of his religious commitment, he saw them both as "enemies of God's People" and as "pawns in God's plan" to test the true believer and remind him of his superiority and obligation. Hence he believed it was his "God-given duty to stamp [Indian religion] out wherever possible." In 1637, on the eve of the attack on Fort Mystic during the Pequot War in Connecticut, a minister named Edward Johnson urged the Massachusetts militiamen, each of whom he called a "faithful soldier of Jesus Christ," to "execute vengeance upon the heathen" who were "not only men, but Devils." Forty years later, during the war against a Wampanoag chief named Metacom (who subsequently became better known as King Philip), William Hubbard, in *The History of the Indian Wars in New England* (1677), reminded his readers of Cotton Mather's contention that "the Devil decoyed those miserable savages" to New England so that the Gospel would never reach them.[103] To such people, the universe was a stage for the engagement of good and evil in the forms of God and Satan, and primitive religions were allies of the Devil. Since Africans and Indians stood in such stark cultural contrast and their presence loomed as a potential threat to the Christian's well-being, it was no great feat to associate them with the evil force.[104]

Despite the humanitarian efforts of some Christians on behalf of the millions held in bondage, Christian thought and conduct in the first three centuries of American life came down overwhelmingly on the side of human oppression. The "teachings and practice of the church," theologian Ernst Troeltsch believed, "constituted one of the main sanctions for [slavery's] perpetuation."[105] Beginning in 1441, when Antonio Gonsalves returned to Portugal with ten Africans as gifts for his sovereign, Europeans justified enslaving blacks on the grounds that it gave the infidels "the opportunity to cast off their heathenism and embrace the Christian religion," a rationalization that extended well into the modern era. There simply is no way of reconciling the contradiction of the existence of human bondage in a nation founded on principles of independence and self-determination, whose citizens professed a religion that exalted peace on earth and good will toward men, other than to conclude that those principles and that good will were reserved for white Christians only. Racism subverted the best of principles, and racism existed only in the minds of human beings.

Individuals who exalted Christianity as the greatest enemy of human bondage either ignored the facts or were simply naïve. An example of the former was Joseph H. Oldham, an official of the International Missionary Council and editor of the *International Review of Missions*, who, in his *Christianity and the Race Problem* (1924), claimed that Christianity could solve virtually all racial problems. Disregarding entirely the religious racism of the past, Oldham offered the cause of the conflict as its cure. The naïve attitude was exemplified by Jacob Stroyer's exclamation at the beginning of the Civil War that "where Christianity exists slavery cannot exist." The pastor of a northern black church, Stroyer could be forgiven his exuberance. Less forgivable was a recent study by Conrad James Engelder, who drew the absurd conclusion that Christianity was the greatest enemy of human bondage because among the first nations to abolish slavery were those that bordered the Mediterranean Sea where Christianity had been first established, a conclusion that totally ignored the fact that nations that bordered the Mediterranean were also among the first to establish slavery.[106]

The racism of Christianity has been so pervasive that it has always escaped the full force of criticism, a situation encouraged by the fact that the true believer is not likely to acknowledge—or even recognize—the errors of his faith. And if he did he saw it as a failure in human conduct, not an inherent flaw of the Christian faith. The result was a society in which the seductive powers of religion were—and are—formidable, beguiling even the astute. Turning Africa into "a hunting ground for slaves rather than a field for philanthropic and missionary endeavor is one of the world's great tragedies," Sydney E. Ahlstrom wrote in his massive *A Religious History of the American People* (1972). Supporting "one of the largest and cruelest of slave systems" in a nation that claimed to be "the great model of modern democracy" is, he added, "one of the world's greatest ironies."[107]

That a scholar of Ahlstrom's stature failed to see the inherent contradiction of his own words is a measure of racism's insidious tenacity. The enslavement of ten million free men and women was indeed a tragedy of incalculable proportions. But by including the failure to mount a missionary program as an essential feature of that tragedy, Ahlstrom, in assuming that Christianity would elevate the African's quality of life, spoke from the same premise as Oldham. It was Christianity, a cornerstone of those "large" and "cruel" slave systems, that perverted the African's quality of life. Since Europeans justified enslavement on religious grounds, the most "philanthropic" thing the Christian could have done for Africans would have been to leave them alone. Not leaving them alone was the *real* tragedy. Since Christianity had always provided an ideal rationale for enslavement, why should it have been so "ironic" that a predominantly Christian nation nurtured slavery? The contradiction so often seen in the presence of slavery in a democratic society may not have been much of a contradiction after all. English North Americans embraced slavery *because* they were Christians, not in spite of it.[108]

TWO THE WORD

Every word of God is flawless; he is a shield to those who take refuge in him. Do not add to his words, or he will rebuke you and prove you a liar.

PROVERBS 30:5–6

Come, divine interpeter,
Bring my eyes thy book to read,
Ears thy mystic words to hear,
Words which did from thee proceed,
Words that endless bliss impart,
Kept in an obedient heart.

All who read, or hear, are blessed,
If thy plain commands we do;
Of thy kingdom here possessed,
Thee we shall in glory view
When thou comest on earth to abide,
Reign triumphant at thy side.

CHARLES WESLEY, 1762

Not to Err Is Divine

If Christianity was exalted as the one true faith, it followed that its authority must be without error; and if one could find in this authority a justification for differentiation of the races, such a revelation would surely support the contention that some people were meant to be masters and others were meant to be servants. Accordingly, if a person subscribed to the doctrine of inerrancy, there should be no basis for controversy.[1] "In the pre–Civil War era, except for rare circles of freethinkers who were regarded as outside the pale of Christianity," one scholar of religion wrote, "the divine inspiration and infallibility of the Bible were taken for granted."[2] There was no serious challenge to the doctrine of biblical inerrancy until the late nineteenth century, when the liberal theology of people like Presbyterian-cum-Episcopalian Charles A. Briggs raised the issue of the scriptures' reflecting the fallibilities of their human authors. What was important, William Newton Clarke argued, was the Bible's principles, not its words. The result was a controversy over the Bible as, on the one hand, the revealed word of God and, on the other, "the human literary product of an ancient sociopolitical and religious community." The latter was subject to criticism, interpretation, and revision because it was simply the writing of men, much of it allegorical, about their own time. This new liberalism so alarmed conservative Protestants that, to reaffirm their belief in the Bible's inerrant primacy, they began establishing "Bible" colleges, the first one founded in New York City in 1882 by a former Presbyterian minister named A. B. Simpson, followed by the Moody Bible Institute in Chicago in 1889 and the Bible Institute of Los Angeles in 1907. By 1961 there were 194 such schools in the United States, most of them affiliated with fundamentalist denominations and fully committed to the belief that the Bible is without error.[3] Considering the indestructibility of the doctrine of biblical inerrancy, it is more than a little curious that the Holy Bible, the documentary authority on which almost all Christians have based their beliefs and conduct, has been used over the centuries to support virtually every conceivable political, economic, and social position, often being quoted by disputants on opposing sides.

Curious, perhaps, but in the context of the American social and political environment hardly surprising. After 1800 the "hermeneutical awakening" of many Protestant leaders resulted in the appearance of a number of denominations—for example, the Disciples of Christ—based on independent biblical interpretation rather than on the acceptance of authority.[4] The Bible was indeed the foundation of Christian beliefs and conduct; but, unlike the leaders of the Protestant Reformation, American churchmen were inclined to interpret it "less according to the norms of classical Christianity than through the presumed competence of private reason and individual experience."[5] And *reason* and *experience* told both the slaveholder and the abolitionist what each wanted to believe.

To be sure, since Northerners and Southerners had for years quarreled over a document as concise and unequivocal as the United States Constitution, why should their interpretations of something as ambiguous and allegorical as the Bible have been less controversial? Perhaps more to the point, if clergymen had long disagreed vigorously over theological questions, how could they have been expected to be less contentious over secular matters—especially those as economically crucial and emotionally charged as slavery and race relations? The result of this ferment was a host of antislavery preachers waving their Bibles in the air condemning human bondage and just as many southern ministers calling attention to the numerous biblical passages that seemed at least to give tacit—if not specific—approval of slavery.[6] When David Brion Davis outlined the "network of beliefs and associations regarding slavery" shared by the nations of Western Europe, he listed the Bible first, followed by "classical antiquity" and "experience with various kinds of servitude."[7]

If the scriptural association with race had been confined to debates among theologians and clergymen, its influence probably would not have been very far-reaching; intellectual controversies have seldom engaged the interests of large numbers of Americans. But slavery was a reality, the black presence was ubiquitous, and the extreme cultural contrasts between the Christian and non-Christian worlds summoned forth all sorts of dreadful images of superstition and savagery. It was not just a matter of language, or skin color, or religion, or personal habits, but all of these and more; thus the fundamental connection between Christianity and racism could not have been kept out of the public arena for very long. The differences were simply too many and too great.

Presidents Washington, Jefferson, Madison, and Monroe were all Virginia slaveholders who had little trouble reconciling bondage with their religious convictions. And there probably has never been a better example of Christian miasma at the highest levels of public service than the career of Andrew Jackson, hero of the War of 1812, conqueror of the Indian, slaveholder, and President of the United States from 1829 to 1837. Jackson was convinced that one of the reasons slavery was widely accepted throughout the Western world was the biblical endorsement of master-servant relationships. The political and economic circumstances of his time, and his personal experiences, as he understood them, clearly reinforced that view. Reversing in his mind cause and consequence, he saw the profitability of the slave-labor system as evidence of its moral integrity.

As a Tennessean, Jackson was a product both of the South, where racial and caste lines were sharply defined by custom and law, and of the West, where survival and success often depended on quick decisions and bold actions. His was a background that called for direct and simple solutions, not introspection and philosophical meandering. There was simply no place in his narrow spectrum of contemplation for finding merit in divergent moral viewpoints. "It was easy to see that he was not a man to accept difference of opinion with equanimity," Josiah Quincy wrote after traveling with Jackson through Massachusetts; "but that was clearly because, he being honest and earnest, Heaven would not suffer his opinions to be other than *right*."[8]

While every American President has found it politically expedient to show his biblical colors from time to time, none did it so forcefully as the charismatic Jackson, who claimed to have read three chapters of the Bible every day for the thirty-five years prior to his election in 1828.[9] Even if he exaggerated, the statement clearly reflected the great importance he placed on biblical teachings; and it was the claim as well of an astute politician, based on the assumption that such a statement would be popular. To be sure, nowhere did the public see more vivid evidence of God's intervention than in Jackson's stunning victory over the British at New Orleans in 1815, which Francis Hopkinson, in "Lines of an American Poet," described effusively:

But let the few whom reason make more wise,
With glowing gratitude uplift their eyes,
Oh! let their breasts dilate with sober joy,
Let pious praise their tongues and hearts employ
To bless our God, with me, let all unite,
He guides the conq'ring sword, he sways the fight.

The almost total destruction of the forces of the most powerful nation on earth, with practically no losses on the American side, convinced many people that the outcome had to be providential. There simply was no other plausible explanation. As an unknown poet wrote in the *National Intelligencer* barely a month after the battle:

To shew the vanity of human trust,
To shew then that a hand unseen
Directs and guides the whole machine.

The proposition that he was "God's Right-hand Man" was one that Jackson welcomed eagerly.[10]

Jackson's view on the Bible and slavery may have been somewhat circumstantial, but, whether engaging in military operations or defying the United States Supreme Court, he considered his campaigns against Indians as nothing less than holy wars. Concerned about government interference in his attack against the Creeks in 1813, he made it clear that his civilian superiors in Washington should leave him alone so that he could "give peace in Israel." Even a bad situation could be rationalized on biblical grounds. At the battle of Horseshoe Bend, for example, Jackson lamented the heavy loss of lives by explaining that "it is in the dispensation of that providence, which inflicts partial evil to produce general good." When, in the final battle, he came upon an Indian leader who had been struck in the mouth by grapeshot, he surmised that it was "as if Heaven designed to chastise him by an appropriate punishment."[11] Historians have severely criticized Jackson for his mistreatment of Indians (although they have sometimes passed it off as merely a normal consequence of his western background), but they have usually done so to show that he was simply speaking for a generation of Americans who believed they had the right to dispossess Indians in the name of territorial conquest, as in his refusal to enforce the Supreme Court's decision in favor of the Indians in the case of *The Cherokee Nation v. Georgia* (1831). And at least one historian has even called Jackson a protector of Indian rights.[12] What has been missing from both the critical and sympathetic portraits of the seventh President is an examination of the profound religious conviction that was a cornerstone of his public life.[13] Andrew Jackson served in a variety of state and federal positions during his long political career, and to all of them he brought the ardor of a soldier in God's army. And in none of his offices was the biblical imprint more vividly exposed then when he dealt with matters involving race.

While it seems that the Bible has always been a source of controversy—and the religious foundations of the proslavery argument had been laid in discussions, letters, and sermons far back in the colonial period—it was not until the second quarter of the nineteenth century that southern whites, largely in response to the attacks by abolitionists, began to invoke the scriptures in a *systematic* defense of slavery.[14] As the cotton monoculture moved across the South, its primary beneficiaries found it increasingly necessary to justify its labor system. To some observers, southern clergymen seemed unable to talk about anything else. Harriet Martineau complained in 1837 that, with one exception, "I never heard any available reference made to grand truths of religion, or principles of morals." Instead of preaching about virtues like "striving after perfection, mutual justice and charity, and christian liberty," the ministers spent all of their time "pretending to find express sanctions of slavery in the Bible; and putting words to this purpose into the mouths of public men, who do not profess to remember the existence of the Bible in any other connexion." Shortly before the Civil War the Reverend B. M. Palmer claimed that God had entrusted the black race to the care of the white—a "trust providentially committed to us"—which meant that the South was obliged to "*conserve and to perpetuate the institution of slavery as now existing*."[15]

Thus, what emerged in the decades before the war was a philosophical argument—waged in the press, the pulpit, and the halls of Congress—exalting a way of life based on a literal interpretation of selected passages of the Bible. The revivalism of the early nineteenth century had "helped recast the Southern world view by increasingly grounding it in the Bible." The upshot, especially in the South, was a surge of fundamentalism and a reemphasis on the revelations of the Bible.[16]

Word Power

To articulate that defense, it was necessary for Christian defenders of slavery to resolve ambiguities over the definitions of certain English terms. For example, the word denoting servitude that appeared most frequently in the Authorized Version of the Bible was the relatively benign "servant,"[17] but because of the contexts in which it was often used and the conditions that presumably existed in biblical times, many Christians simply assumed that "servant" almost always meant "slave." Of course, such an assumption conveniently served the purposes of the American slaveholder. Accordingly, the use of "servant" to mean "slave" in translating the Greek *doulos*, as lexicographer Walter Bauer pointed out, "is largely confined to Biblical translations and early American times."[18] In both earlier and later translations, on the other hand, the *doulos* was clearly under some kind of bonded obligation. Calling the biblical servant a slave may have been self-serving for Christian masters, but it was closer to the original meaning of the term, as modern English and American translators of the Bible have agreed. At the same time, the Puritans apparently found a middle ground between the Jewish "servant" and the gentile "slave." A slave in New England often lived close to his master's family, "in keeping with the custom of the Hebraic family," and was usually called "servant," a term that, in fact, applied to anyone who worked for someone else, slave or otherwise.[19] Of course, the vast majority of the black population was in the South, where differences over definitions had the most meaning. Almost as though anticipating the southern rationale, English scholars who prepared the Authorized Version translated Paul's terms as "bond" and "servant," which, to one who was looking for a moral justification of slavery, could not, of course, have meant anything other than "slave." As Paul wrote in his letter to the Ephesians:

> Servants, be obedient to them that are *your* masters according to the flesh, with fear and trembling, in singleness of your heart, as unto Christ; Not with eyeservice, as men-pleasers; but as the servants of Christ, doing the will of God from the heart; With good will doing service, as to the Lord, and not to men: Knowing that whatsoever good thing any man doeth, the same shall he receive of the Lord,whether *he be* bond or free.[20]

Needless to say, once this premise was established, it was not hard for the American slaveholder to find numerous biblical examples of slavery and to conclude that God had indeed given the institution his blessing.

Disregarding the fact that they were using a Bible that was an English translation of ancient manuscripts, written in a style common to the highest literary forms of the early seventeenth century and composed primarily for readers who were educated and privileged, defenders of slavery cited three Old Testament categories of servitude that they believed applied to the American situation. The first was based on the Greek *doulos*, which southern clergymen like Thornton Stringfellow and Albert Taylor Bledsoe interpreted to mean "servant" in the sense they were using it: alien peoples purchased or captured.[21] Nor was it an interpretation that was confined to the South. There was no doubt, George Junkin, a Presbyterian minister and president of Miami University in Ohio, maintained in 1843, that *doulos* was a Greek translation of the Hebrew *èbed*, which, since it was often paired with the word *olam*—meaning "forever" or "everlasting"—could only mean "slave." Another Ohio Presbyterian, John Robinson of Ashland, agreed, insisting that the Apostle Paul had used the word *doulos* to signify "a man in a servile state, a male slave or servant, one who servilely yields to another, a servant of God." The fact that Paul also had used specific terms to identify masters—for example, *kurios* and *despotes*—was, Robinson concluded, a clear indication of God's approval of slavery. Oddly, the proslavery argument over the definition of the word *doulos* long outlived the institution of slavery itself, as southern apologists of the post–Civil War years continued to look for explanations and excuses. "It is absolutely certain that a *bondman*, one bound to a master, bought with his money, or transferred to him as being *property*," a Nashville Methodist named William Pope Harrison declared in 1893, "is the meaning of the original word."[22] As the translators of the King James Version saw it, Mosaic law clearly identified who could be enslaved and the terms of their bondage: "strangers" who lived among the Jews and who, in a specific provision for ownership, could be passed on to descendants. As Moses presumably wrote in setting forth God's rules to the Levites:

> Both thy bondmen, and thy bondmaids, which thou shalt have, *shall be* of the heathen that are round about you; of them shall ye buy bondmen and bondmaids. Moreover of the children of the strangers that do sojourn among you, of them shall ye buy, and of their families that *are* with you, which they begat in your land: and they shall be your possession. And ye shall take them as an inheritance for your children after you, to inherit *them for* a possession; they shall be your bondmen for ever: but over your brethren the children of Israel ye shall not rule one over another with rigour.[23]

For many American slaveholders, the rationale was so made to order, it must have seemed providential. The transatlantic slave trade appeared to be a reenactment and fulfillment of ancient law; it was the Africans' status as "strangers," that is, *outsiders*, that made them ideal candidates for bondage. That was what slavery was all about, what set the slave apart "from all other forms of involuntary servitude," Moses I. Finley pointed out. "He is brought into a new society violently and traumatically," and denied "all traditional human ties of kin and nation and even his own religion." Such a condition was admirably compatible with the white Southerner's view of slavery. In America the slave was forced by circumstances, both contrived and coincidental, to surrender a good measure of his cultural heritage—losing his bases of solidarity, a sociologist would put it. But, at the same time, he was not permitted to embrace his new culture in a way that would ensure access to all of its rights and privileges. The enslaved person, Finley went on, was prevented from creating new ties, "except to his masters," and his descendants were "as much outsiders, as uprooted, as he was," which accorded closely with the assertion in Leviticus that slaves passed on from the master to his children shall be "bondmen for ever." With one foot in Africa and the other in the West, the slave was not allowed to remain an African and it was impossible for him to become a Westerner. That meant that, in an era of enlightenment and mercantilism, he was nothing, or, as sociologist Orlando Patterson put it, he was "socially dead."[24] It would seem only natural that an outsider, after being systematically stripped of his extrinsic social bearings, would at least cling to that most fundamental element of his ancestry—his spiritual heritage. One can only wonder why the bondsman at least appeared to adopt so easily his tormentor's religion.

The second category of servitude, defined in Leviticus 25:39–43, 47–53, was similar to the first except that it pertained only to Hebrew servants rather than outsiders and therefore, by isolating the enslaved alien caste, emphasized the inferior status of the "strangers." For example, a Hebrew could pay a debt by selling his labor in much the same fashion as an indentured servant in colonial America. Accordingly, he retained certain rights and was not considered property. He could be redeemed by anyone, including himself, and if not so redeemed he automatically became free after six years or at the time of "jubilee."[25] Significantly, if a poor Hebrew sold himself to a wealthy "stranger," the law ordained that the Hebrew must be considered no worse than a "yearly hired servant." An outsider could not possess a Hebrew slave; thus the special privileges enjoyed by the Chosen People extended to the nature of their servitude. As it happened, the ancient Jewish jubilee—a year-long celebration held every fifty years in which mortgaged land was restored to the original owners, land was left fallow, and all bondsmen were freed—became a liberation theme for both abolitionists and slaves, who saw it as a promise of freedom:[26]

Dear Lord, dear Lord, when slavery'll cease,
Then we poor souls will have our peace;—
There's a better day a coming,
Will you go along with me?
There's a better day a coming,
Go sound the jubilee![27]

The third type of servant was simply an ordinary hired hand who worked for wages. With these categories in mind, the American defenders of slavery concluded that the words "servant," "bondman," "bondmaid," and "bondservant" in the English Bible meant the same as *doulos*, the slave possessed as property. Only when "hired servant" or "hireling" appeared did they consider it to mean a hired hand.

Needless to say, the critics of slavery also played the word game.[28] Recognizing that the English Bible was a translation of older works in other languages, they turned to early Greek texts to substantiate their opposition. To appreciate fully the meanings of scriptural terms and references, one would need to go back beyond the fourth-century Latin Vulgate edition of the Bible prepared by St. Jerome, or the twenty-seven books on the list that Bishop Athanasius of Alexandria compiled in the year 367, which were to become the New Testament, and study not only ancient Greek and Hebrew texts but northwestern Semitic writings, especially Aramaic, and even some of the lesser-known languages of biblical times such as Akkadian and Ugaritic. Except for a handful of biblical scholars like Albert Barnes and George B. Cheever, there were not many people on either side of the slavery controversy who were knowledgeable in even one or two of these tongues.

Cheever pointed out that there was no actual Hebrew equivalent to the English "slave," a word that was common to most modern European languages and had derived from the Old Bulgarian *Slovene*, the name of a Slavic people which had been first used to identify captives from southeastern Europe and, later, the Baltic states. The Greek word *doulos*, Barnes contended in *An Inquiry into the Scriptural Views of Slavery* (1846) and Cheever reiterated in *God Against Slavery* (1857) and *The Guilt of Slavery and the Crime of Slaveholding* (1860), referred simply to servitude in general and, because of its association with the nonpejorative Hebrew *èbed* (or *obed*), did not signify any kind of forced servitude. Quoting an unidentified minister, abolitionist Sarah M. Grimké argued in 1836 that *èbed* "applied to both servants and hired, to kings and prophets, and even to the Saviour of the world." Similarly, antislavery Baptists, meeting in Worcester, Massachusetts, in July 1841, insisted that the English translation of "bondman" meant one who was apprenticed. "Both the Hebrew, Ebed, and the Greek, *Doulos*, simply signify an actor—one who acts or serves."[29] Besides, some critics pointed out, conditions in biblical times were so different from those of the modern world that any search for identical meanings was fruitless. For example, if a society based its laws on what was legal in Abraham's day, then concubinage would be acceptable. The truth is, Horace Bushnell told the Yale alumni in 1843, the laws of Moses were never perceived as permanent and were subject to revision and interpretation by the prophets, Christ, and Paul.[30]

Most antislavery Christian scholars also knew that there were precise Greek words for the various forms of servitude and that a "strict usage" for *doulos* and its derivatives, as biblical lexicographer Gerhard Kittel agreed, "is for the most part found only in the epistles." More important was the status of the *doulos* within Hebrew society. "The judgment on the slave is always material, and it remains so even when it is severe," Kittel noted. "The *doulos* is never despised or rejected simply because he is a slave." In other words, the stigma of inferiority was not significant among the early Jews, a situation that apparently prevailed in colonial America only in New England, where the term "servant" did not necessarily carry a negative connotation.[31] Accordingly, the nature of biblical slavery was such, abolitionists argued, that *doulos* was more properly compared to a "servant" in modern times. Indeed, "had it not been for the arbitrary translation of the word servant into *bondman*," Cheever claimed, "no semblance of an argument could have been found for the existence of any kind or degree of involuntary servitude for them." In a detailed analysis of the "meaning of the words denoting servitude in the Scriptures," Barnes explained that the term closest to the American perception of the slave as chattel personal—that is, the slave who was part of the lowly "mudsill of society," which many Southerners insisted was essential in a civilized culture—was *andrapodon* and it could not be found anywhere in the early Greek manuscripts. The other terms, some of which appeared frequently, were *oiketes*, a household servant; *hypekoos*, a waiter or attendant, especially one who served at a door; *misthios*, a hired man (or *mercenarius* in the Latin Vulgate), meaning anyone who worked for wages; and *latris*, a person who received pay as a soldier or one who served the gods.[32]

The Israelites made none of these finer distinctions in their ancient writings, Barnes noted, using only the perfectly respectable Hebrew *èbed* to identify all kinds of service. "Their language was less cultivated [than that of the Greeks], and much less adapted to express nice discriminations of thought."[33] If some biblical scholars were easily confused, it was understandable. For example, the ancient Greek word δουλεία signified "servitude," "slavery," or "bondage." Moving the accent mark one character resulted in the modern δουλειά, which meant "work" or "business." Since the latter had come into use by the seventeenth century, self-serving, but honest, differences of opinion over the meaning of *doulos* were probably inevitable. Some critics of slavery argued that the word "servant" as used in the Authorized Version meant "hired servant," not "slave"; that is, *doulos* meant *misthios*, not *andrapodon*.

But the supporters of slavery were not dissuaded. John Robinson noted that both Peter (1 Peter 2:18) and Paul (The Acts 10:7) used *oiketes* to identify slaves because the word signified "one living in the same house with another; and by implication, a domestic servant, a household slave." Similarly, George Junkin insisted that the Israelites used *saukeer* to identify a "hired hand," which did not translate as *misthios*. If *saukeer* meant "hired hand," he concluded, "*èbed* must mean slave."[34] However the words were interpreted, the most significant point in the scramble for definitions, Barnes concluded, at the risk of being accused of splitting hairs, was that, while different kinds of servitude were mentioned in the early Greek accounts, the one word—*andrapodon*—that signified the kind of slavery Southerners were defending did not appear anywhere in the scriptures.[35] Anyone who used the Bible to support human bondage, they argued, was simply making the whole thing up.

Hebrew, Greek, Latin. These were the obvious languages that contending forces argued over, an argument aggravated by the fact that it was never possible to know if a translation was exact. The modern critic, of course, would not be bothered by such hair-splitting. Slavery was wrong whether the Bible approved it or not; and in a religiously pluralistic society, especially one that clearly delineated the separation of church and state, there simply was no valid reason why any religious doctrine should be part of secular life.

What was far less obvious, and therefore far more insidious, was the covert, indirect terminology that perverted the Christian's attitude toward dark-skinned peoples. Many European languages are corrupted by their connection to the symbolisms of "black" and "white," which, in the English Bible, are most often written as "dark" and "light" and variations like "night" and "day." From the first chapter of Genesis (1:4)—"And God saw the light, that *it was* good: and God divided the light from the darkness"—to the last chapter of Revelation (22:5)—"And there shall be no night there; and they need no candle, neither light of the sun; for the Lord God giveth them light: and they shall reign for ever and ever"—there are dozens of verses in which darkness signifies evil, sin, death, failure, ignorance, and damnation; while light always means pure, virtuous, good, happy, clean, and salvation. "I am the light of the world," Christ said in John 8:12: "he that followeth me shall not walk in darkness, but shall have the light of life." False teachers who try to lead Christians astray are "wild waves of the sea, foaming up their shame," Jude, the brother of Jesus and James, warned, "wandering stars, to whom is reserved the blackness of darkness for ever."[36] Sometimes the pejorative connotation is intentional. "I *am* black, but comely," said the lover in a confession of deformity, as black "as the tents of Kedar, as the curtains of Solomon." But it is a blackness that was caused by working in the vineyards under the sun, not by inheritance, he explained, therefore it is only temporary.[37] When Jeremiah asked, "Can the Ethiopian change his skin, or the leopard his spots?" he was conceding that one who is accustomed to living an evil life can never do good.[38] However this reference has been used, the assumption that dark skin was undesirable was clear. Why else should the Ethiopian be the example?

Despite the extensive biblical uses of light and dark as metaphors for good and evil and a similar Roman tradition, the negative quality of blackness was not widely associated with skin color—at least in the Western world—until after biblical times. In the *Epistle of Barnabas* (ca. A.D. 70–100) the devil was referred to as the "Black One" and, according to one researcher, "in the visions of saints and monks, demons at times assumed the shape of 'Ethiopians.' " Similarly, in the writing of the early church fathers, the Ethiopian was often identified as the "blackest" of all persons, a symbolism begun by Origen in the second and third centuries and carried on through the fifth century by others, including Jerome and Augustine, both of whom "linked blackness directly with sin." And yet, despite the association of darkness with all that was evil and demonic, early Christians did not, in fact, exhibit a negative attitude toward black people generally. "In classical thought the blackness of the Ethiopian was only skin-deep," Frank M. Snowden, Jr., wrote. "Blacks could have a soul as pure as the whitest of the whites." Consequently, there is no evidence that dark-skinned peoples in early Christian times suffered for their color; there were "no fixed concepts of blacks as evil or unworthy of conversion." The Ethiopians, in fact, "became an important symbol of Christianity's ecumenical mission," Snowden concluded. "Building on classical color usages, the Christian writers developed an exegesis and a black-white imagery in which Ethiopians illustrated the meaning of the Scriptures for *all* men."[39]

But the same could not be said of later generations of Christians and Muslims, who saw the dark skin of the "heathen" as a mark of inferiority. By the tenth century, black Africans were increasingly being used as slaves throughout much of the eastern Mediterranean region.[40] Nor was the disdain for dark skin an exclusively Western attitude. The Han Chinese considered the dark-skinned Lolos who lived along the border to be fit only for servitude. Retaliating against this treatment, the Lolos of Taliang Shan, in a contemptuous reversal of the color code, kidnapped and enslaved many of their tormentors. "White skin, so highly prized by the Han Chinese," Patterson observed, "was despised by the swarthy black Lolos and became a mark of servility and a way of identifying the Han slaves."[41] Whatever the causes, the imprint of color could be devastating. There may have been no specific biblical connection between blackness and bondage, but when European explorers began penetrating the non-European world, they had little trouble fashioning the scriptural color code into a touchstone of modern slavery.

In fact, French sociologist Roger Bastide argued, it was Christianity that first introduced the black/white color code into Western thought. "White is used to express the pure, while black expresses the diabolical," Bastide wrote. "The conflict between Christ and Satan, the spiritual and the carnal, good and evil come finally to be expressed by the conflict between the white and black." In other words, monotheism was inherently dichotomous. Polytheism, on the other hand, perceived the powers on a continuum, with good gods, bad gods, and in-between gods, a universe filled with shades of gray. In the Middle Ages the Black Madonna, or Black Virgin, was a sorceress to be feared rather than a Loving Mother to be adored. Pictorial representations of the Three Wise Men usually showed the black king, Balthazar, behind the other two. Of course, graphic portrayals of Christ had to be "as far removed as possible from anything that could suggest darkness or blackness." The result was a Renaissance image of Christ that recorded his transmogrification from Semitic to Aryan, his dark hair and beard evolving into "the color of sunshine" and his dark eyes magically taking on the "color of the sky from which he descended and to which he returned." In his fanatical condemnation of abolitionism, *Slavery, As It Relates to the Negro, or African Race* (1843), Josiah Priest insisted, amazingly, that God preferred a white complexion or else he would not have given Jesus light hair and blue eyes. By the time the Enlightenment had replaced the "old Christian code of ethics," Bastide concluded, the association was so universal that its "symbolism had become secularized."[42]

Nowhere was this color symbolism more thoroughly institutionalized than in the New World. Before the sixteenth century was over, Portuguese and Spanish explorers had introduced African slavery to most of the Caribbean and parts of eastern South America, where, for some time, slave women were the only females accessible in large numbers. With a large population of mixed extraction, colonial authorities found it prudent, if not necessary, to establish certain rules of color. In Jamaica one's social status at birth and one's color defined a complex arrangement in which the percentage of black blood ranged from the darkest "negro" and "sambo" to the lightest "mustee," "mustifino," and "quintroon." It did not take long to discover that extending limited privileges to "in-between" classes was one way of reducing security problems. Eventually, any person lighter than mustee was considered white. Similarly, Brazilians defined social status by a combination of skin color and wealth. This resulted in as many as twelve classes between "negro" and "white" and reflected a pragmatism best expressed in the saying "Money whitens."[43]

The closest to privilege-by-shade in North America was a mixed-blood class first defined under the French as *les gens de couleur libres*—"free people of color"—who subsequently became part of the American population with the acquisition in 1803 of the Louisiana Territory. Elsewhere in English North America and the United States, color differentiation was mainly a private matter. "Some slaveholders preferred to use 'bright mulattoes' as domestics," Kenneth M. Stampp noted; "a few paid premium prices for light-skinned females to be used as concubines or prostitutes."[44] The preference of the white male for slaves in both kitchen and bedroom followed the same color code.[45] And it was a code adopted by the slaves themselves. A "yellow" Negro was higher in the hierarchy of slavery than a dark-skinned one, a former slave told Scottish traveler David Macrae, and the greatest insult among black people was to be called a "charcoal nigger." It was often said of a slave who had converted to Christianity that his skin might be black but his soul was white. "[W]e slabes is black only in dis prezzen worle," one bondsman allegedly told Negrophobe Hinton Rowan Helper; "in de nex worle, we is gwine to be white fikes too! You see den dat we's not niggers." It was a recognition that appeared even as one denied it. "The souls is all white or black," a former slave told a WPA interviewer, " 'pending on the man's life and not on his skin."[46]

While southern slaveholders may not have been aware of the biblical color symbolism, the Puritans of New England defined almost everything within a religious context. Responding to accusations that she had bewitched some of the young girls of Salem Farms, Tituba, the mixed-blood servant of the Reverend Samuel Parris, claimed to have had hallucinations involving a black dog and two rats, one red and one black—the two biblical colors signifying evil.[47] The fact that Tituba, one of the first to be accused, was part black and part Indian may have been only coincidental. Other witnesses testified that some of the "afflicted" girls claimed to have seen a black man whispering in the ear of the wife of Giles Cory, one of the men accused of witchcraft.[48] When it came to the color symbolism of the Bible, there was an unbroken line from Job 34:22, "There is no dark place, no deep shadow, where evildoers can hide," through Proverbs 4:18–19, "The path of the righteous is like the first gleam of dawn, shining ever brighter till the full light of day. But the way of the wicked is like deep darkness; they do not know what makes them stumble," and Hebrews 12:18, "You have not come to a mountain that can be touched and that is burning with fire; to darkness, gloom and storm," to the Puritans of Massachusetts Bay. Nathaniel Hawthorne and Arthur Miller saw it clearly.[49]

The authors of the books of the Old and New Testaments, of course, were not responsible for creating the symbolic values of black and white. To begin with, the languages of their time probably had some words that were not fully translatable into English or other European tongues. Modern biblical scholars are still questioning the meanings of certain scriptural words and terms; for example, what early translators called "leprosy," many researchers have argued, was probably not the dreaded Hansen's disease but a minor skin ailment, similar to eczema, that was common in the eastern Mediterranean part of the world.[50] More important, the good-bad significations of light and dark seem to be universal; only people who were born blind could be unaware of the benefits of light and the limitations of darkness. The bride in a Christian wedding wears white, the color of purity; the widow at a funeral wears black, the color of death. Even in those cultures where white is a color of mourning—as in Korea, rural China, and other parts of Asia—the purpose is to memorialize the cleansing of a soul as well as to express grief or sadness. Thus the meanings are still the same.

The point, of course, is not to find blame or place responsibility but, first, to acknowledge the extent of the pejorative connotations inherent in biblical references to colors and shades and, second, to identify those aspects of skin color that became critical elements in perpetuating slavery and racism. In his classic *Notes on the State of Virginia* (1785), Jefferson remarked how "unfortunate" it was that it had pleased God to make Africans black, to which the black abolitionist David Walker angrily replied: "As though we are not as thankful to our God, for having made us as it pleased Himself, as they [whites] are for having made them white."[51] Biblical color symbols, by themselves, were no worse than any others; but it was to the Bible that Christians looked for the meaning of life, thus the symbolism was pervasive.

Mosaic Law, Christ, and the Golden Rule

It is possible to distinguish a half dozen or more biblical arguments defending human bondage, but, in the last analysis, they can be grouped under three general headings. The first argument is found in the Old Testament, where various forms of servitude are described and where major figures like Abraham, Isaac, Jacob, and Job all apparently possess slaves—or, at least, people whom some Bible translators have identified as "slaves."[52] "Hagar, from whom millions sprang, was an African slave, brought out of Egypt by Abraham, the father of the faithful and the beloved servant of the Most High," Representative Charles Pinckney, one of the framers of the Constitution, declared in 1820; "and he had, besides, three-hundred-and-eighteen male slaves."[53] Most important, bondage was part of Mosaic Law, especially as set forth in the twenty-fifth chapter of Leviticus, which sanctioned "buying, selling, holding and bequeathing slaves as property" (although a careful reading of these verses could lead to conflicting conclusions). Prior to this time, the master-servant relationship had "rested on the custom of the Patriarchs," but Leviticus gave it the authority of law.[54]

The prophet Isaiah acknowledged slavery when he described to the people of Jerusalem and Judah how God's destruction of the world would be the same "for master as for servant, for mistress as for maid."[55] The belief among some whites that Africans were inherently lazy and would not work unless enslaved may have been based on Proverbs 12:24: "The hand of the diligent shall rule: but the slothful shall be under tribute." Other defenders of slavery claimed that when God banished Cain to the Land of Nod, the "mark" that Cain bore was really a black skin. This may have been the basis of the popular southern opinion that God had imposed slavery on man as "just punishment for his sins."[56] Indeed, this interpretation seemed to be confirmed in the twenty-eighth chapter of Deuteronomy, where the Jews were warned of the many curses that would descend upon them if they disobeyed God, including returning to Egypt as slaves.[57]

It was in passages like these that slaveholders found many of their favorite arguments. A stern and vengeful Jehovah who punished wrongdoing by bringing down his wrath upon sinners was, presumably, a much more effective medium of control than a loving and merciful Jesus who preached brotherly love, forgave sinners, and turned the other cheek. While slavery was defended from virtually everywhere in the Bible, many slaveholders considered the books of the Patriarchal Age[58] from Noah to Moses, to be the foundation of the religious justification.[59]

In fact, slavery existed long before there were people called Jews. The first record of human bondage in the Near East dates to the early Bronze Age, about 3000 to 2000 B.C., when increases and shifts in population led to hierarchies of occupation and leadership. "The family commune was replaced by a governing assembly of adult freemen," Harry M. Orlinsky wrote, "this assembly usually headed by a council of elders." All others were excluded from positions of responsibility, and a class of slaves, usually foreigners captured in war, performed much of the common labor. Beginning around the end of this period, a group of primarily Semitic nomads called the 'Apiru (or Habiru)—described by Old Testament scholar John Bright as "a class of people without citizenship, who lived on the fringes of the existing social structure" and included Joseph—wandered about the region, many of them hiring themselves out "as mercenaries and as private or government slaves." While some 'Apiru achieved positions of wealth and influence, others "became prisoners of war and state slaves doing forced labor (*corvée*)." Some of the ancient texts from Nuzi indicated that the 'Apiru could be found in virtually every occupation, including serving the court and the rich as soldiers and workers. Whatever its origins, a servile class appeared very early in the history of Israel:[60]

> When Israel became strong, they pressed the Canaanites into forced labor but never drove them out completely. . . . Neither did Zebulun drive out the Canaanites living in Kitron or Nahalol, who remained among them; but they did subject them to forced labor. . . . And the Amorites were determined also to hold out in Mount Heres, Aijalon and Shaalbim, but when the power of the house of Joseph increased, they too were pressed into forced labor.[61]

Following their flight from Egyptian captivity, the Israelites subjected both Gentiles and other Israelites to bondage which was often occasioned by an incurrence of debt that could be paid no other way. In fact, debt was the second most important cause of enslavement of Israelites by Israelites, especially among males, although, according to sociologist Orlando Patterson, it was against "strict religious law."[62] In this instance, the law, obviously, had little effect on economic conditions. By the later Old Testament period, it seemed to be almost a law of nations that the enrichment of one class should be sustained by the impoverishment of another. As upper-class Judeans grew prosperous in the last centuries before Christ, it became increasingly common for the poor to sell themselves and their children into bondage. "Although we are of the same flesh and blood as our countrymen and though our sons are as good as theirs, yet we have to subject our sons and daughters to slavery," the people complained to Nehemiah in the fifth century B.C. "Some of our daughters have already been enslaved, but we are powerless, because our fields and vineyards belong to others."[63]

Needless to say, American slaveholders who defended their "peculiar institution" on biblical grounds could only do so by ignoring certain important features of Old Testament slavery that were in direct opposition to the most fundamental principles of bondage in the modern American world. To begin with, slaves in ancient Israel enjoyed many rights and privileges, some of them guaranteed by law. According to the first eleven verses of Exodus 21, God instructed Moses to set forth a policy governing Israelite servants that was intended mainly for their protection.[64] For example, a slave was to be freed automatically after six years (a condition that was similar to the indentured servitude of the American colonial period) unless he chose to remain his master's servant for life, which was the only way he could keep a wife his master had provided. Considering the circumstances, of course, such a choice could hardly be called one that was freely made; and the slave who made it carried a permanent badge of bondage in the form of one ear pierced by an awl. If, on the other hand, the slave had brought his wife into bondage with him, she left with him. Another rule provided that a woman who was sold into slavery by her father could not then be sold to another person. If the master selected her for his son, she must be treated as a daughter. "If he marries another woman, he must not deprive the first one of her food, clothing and marital rights." Any violation of these terms required her immediate redemption with no compensation to the former master.[65]

Included in other laws and practices were provisions that an injured slave should be set free; a slave could inherit his master's estate if there were no heirs. A strict observance of the Sabbath was imposed "so that your manservant and maidservant may rest, as you do"; and a slave who died on the same day he had been beaten by his master was considered a murder victim and the master prosecuted accordingly.[66] What the law obviously tried to do was make the slave as close to being a member of the master's family as possible. For example, all male members of the household over eight days of age must be circumcised, including those "bought with money from a foreigner."[67]

In fact, some slaves actually became family. Convinced that she would never bear a child, Sarah persuaded Abraham (who, at eighty-six, was still named Abram) to have a child with Hagar; this was Ishmael. Thus the family precedent had been well established by the time Rachel, the wife of Abraham's and Sarah's grandson Jacob, prevailed upon her husband to have a child with her maidservant, Bilhah, whom Rachel then claimed as her own and named Dan.[68] There were many American Hagars and Bilhahs, but there were no American Sarahs or Rachels.

Underlying all of these laws and customs extending favorable conditions to slaves was a fundamental and long-standing aversion toward bondage that was tied to the legacy of the Israelites' Egyptian captivity. "Know for certain that your descendants will be strangers in a country not their own," God said to Abram in Genesis 15:13, "and they will be enslaved and mistreated for four hundred years." Twice again in Genesis (17:8 and 28:4) and in Exodus 6:4, the Israelites were reminded that they were aliens in the land of Canaan. Moreover, in at least four different places in the Old Testament where bondservants were the issue, the Israelites were admonished to remember their own suffering as alien slaves in Egypt.[69]

The two references to aliens, which are only sixteen verses apart in Exodus, were especially important because "the heathen that are round about you" and "the strangers that do sojourn among you," who were identified in Leviticus 25:44–45 as the most suitable candidates for bondage, were seen by American defenders of slavery as the biblical equivalents of modern Africans. If it could be shown that these ancient outsiders were entitled to some measures of justice and equality, the Americans' biblical defense of slavery would be substantially discredited. For this reason it served the slaveholder's purpose to ignore any scriptural lesson calling for sympathy for foreigners, for example, Genesis 23:4, in which Abraham asked the Canaanites to overlook his status as an alien and stranger and sell him a plot of land so he might bury Sarah, or Matthew 25:35, in which Christ related to his disciples on the Mount of Olives the story of the stranger who was clothed, fed, and cared for.

It did not require a particularly scrupulous reading of Exodus 21 to see that it was the intention of the law to minimize the control of the master, not codify the obligations of the servant.[70] This meant that, although the Israelites had been urged in Leviticus to purchase their bondsmen "from the nations around you," if they found it necessary to enslave fellow Israelites they had to observe certain limitations not otherwise imposed. In other words, ancient law defined slavery as a necessary evil, not a condition to be preferred. While it is impossible to know the actual number of slaves of all nationalities in Israel, historian Abraham Leon Sachar estimated that at least 20 percent of the population was in bondage at its height during the years after the exodus. As for Israelite slaves, Salo Wittmayer Baron, possibly the preeminent student of Jewish history and author of the twenty-volume *The Social and Religious History of the Jews*, insisted that their numbers began to decline toward the end of the "Second Commonwealth."[71] Enslavement for debt had been the major reason for bondage, but by the time of the Ptolemaic dynasty, 305 to 30 B.C., the institution had all but disappeared almost everywhere in the Near East.[72]

If the Old Testament of Moses and the prophets carried the message of bondage, it also carried the message of emancipation. Critics of slavery pointed out that for every passage that appeared to sanction forced servitude, there was one that repudiated it. For example, both Exodus and Deuteronomy prescribed the death penalty for selling a kidnap victim into slavery, especially if he was a fellow Israelite. According to Old Testament scholar Dale Patrick, the verb "steal" in the Eighth Commandment referred to "the arbitrary seizure of persons or property." To seize someone and sell him into slavery, as Joseph's brothers did, was punishable by death. It did not matter how a slave was originally acquired; if he ran away it was a violation of Mosaic Law to chase after him and return him to his master. Anyone who "stealeth a man, and selleth him," then "that thief shall die."[73] Indeed, the law went even further. Should a runaway slave fall into the hands of an Israelite, that Israelite must protect him, provide him with shelter, and allow him to live wherever he chose.

By the time of the prophet Isaiah, this protection was extended to virtually all fugitive slaves: "Take counsel, execute judgment; make thy shadow as the night in the midst of the noonday; hide the outcasts; bewray not him that wandereth."[74] This would mean, abolitionist George B. Cheever deduced, that the law requiring anyone who found a lost animal to return it to its owner was indirect proof that a slave "was never regarded as property, and could not be treated as such."[75] Warning the people of Judah that they would suffer dire consequences for their wickedness, Jeremiah told the Israelites that any master who had broken God's covenant by reenslaving a fellow Israelite would fall "to the sword, to the pestilence, and to the famine." The punishment of the guilty would be so terrible that God would "even give them into the hands of their enemies, and into the hand of them that seek their life: and their dead bodies shall be for meat unto the fowls of the heaven, and to the beasts of the earth."[76] Similarly, Obadiah warned the people of Edom that anyone who killed or captured fugitives would surely be punished by the Lord: "Neither shouldest thou have stood in the crossway, to cut off those of his that did escape; neither shouldest thou have delivered up those of his that did remain in the day of distress. For the day of the Lord *is* near upon all the heathen; as thou has done, it shall be done unto thee: thy reward shall return upon thine own head."[77] No equivocation here.

Though it seems that the Bible has been used to justify virtually everything, that use was only significant insofar as people considered the scriptures the inerrant word of God. In America before the twentieth century, that was almost everybody.

That *everybody* included slaves, as ironically it was in the same Old Testament that they—and even a few Indians—found many of their favorite stories. The most popular biblical episode was, naturally, the exodus of the Jews from Egypt, which was reflected in plantation spirituals like "Let My People Go" and "Go Down Moses."[78] The escape themes of "Swing Low, Sweet Chariot" and "Follow the Drinking Gourd" specifically referred to the underground railroad through which slaves crossed the "River Jordan" and escaped to the "Land of Canaan." Other Old Testament figures whose success in overcoming adversity made them popular subjects of slave songs included Daniel—"O My Lord Delivered Daniel"—and Job:

> *Job was a man whom God did love;*
> *God gave Job a home above,*
> *The time came he had to die.*
> *Then Job was taken up in the sky.*[79]

Whatever the specific situation, the general theme was that of an oppressed minority calling upon God for deliverance. Samson, Moses, Joshua, Elijah, and David were also heroes to many converted Algonquin Indians, Puritan missionary John Eliot discovered, some of whom honored their favorite characters by taking their names.[80] It is plausible—though unprovable—that people who had not been raised in a Judeo-Christian culture found the highly charged dramatic quality of the Old Testament more appealing—and certainly more entertaining—then the relatively sedate tone of the New Testament. Whatever the reason, there is no doubt that Old Testament characters dominated the slaves' religious music and folklore.

While the defenders of slavery found their first biblical argument in what the Old Testament said emphatically (if equivocally), they found their second in what the New Testament did not say at all. The fact that bondage was not specifically condemned by Christ, or anyone else, was not lost on its defenders, northern as well as southern. To be sure, it could be argued that while Old Testament passages supporting slavery were balanced by others that condemned it, there was virtually no analogous criticism of New Testament arguments defending bondage. As the Reverend Richard Fuller, an influential Baptist preacher from Beaufort, South Carolina, declared in 1845 in a published exchange of letters with Francis Wayland, one of the North's most distinguished Baptists, "What God sanctioned in the Old Testament, and permitted in the New, cannot be sin."[81]

By the time abolitionism had become a major force in American life, dozens of advocates of defense-by-omission had taken public positions, and none was better known or more widely respected than James Henley Thornwell—president of South Carolina College, editor of *Southern Presbyterian Review*, and professor of theology at Columbia Theological Seminary. "[H]as the Bible, anywhere, either directly or indirectly, condemned the relation of master and servant as incompatible with the will of God?" Thornwell asked in his 1851 report to the Synod of South Carolina. "Where the Scriptures are silent [the Church] must be silent too. What the Scriptures have not made essential to a Christian profession, she does not undertake to make so. What the Scriptures have sanctioned, she does not condemn." The Word of God is its own interpreter, Thornwell concluded; the critics of slavery cannot therefore claim to interpret it one way or another.[82]

But what of the Savior himself? Certainly, the Prince of Peace would never approve something as terrible as human bondage! In 1773, long before the antislavery crisis of the nineteenth century, a preacher named Richard Nisbet considered it quite logical that Christ, if he had disapproved of slavery, would have prohibited it "in direct terms." But he did not. In his debate with Wayland seventy-two years later, Fuller noted that Christ certainly had numerous opportunities to criticize bondage—for example, in Luke 7:2–10, when he healed the sick slave of the centurion—but he said nothing.[83] Even more to the point were Christ's comments to the disciples in Luke 17:7–10, where he made a parabolical reference to the master-servant relationship.

> Suppose one of you had a servant plowing or looking after the sheep. Would he say to the servant when he comes in from the field, "Come along now and sit down to eat"? Would he not rather say, "Prepare my supper, get yourself ready and wait on me while I eat and drink; after that you may eat and drink"? Would he thank the servant because he did what he was told to do? So you also, when you have done everything you were told to do, should say, "We are unworthy servants; we have only done our duty."

To the defenders of slavery, only one conclusion could be drawn from these seemingly missed opportunities. Addressing the Presbyterian General Assembly in 1845, John Robinson, pastor of the church in Ashland, Ohio, contended that since Christ and the apostles had not opposed slavery, modern Christians "have no authority to do so."[84] Similarly, George Armstrong, in *The Christian Doctrine of Slavery* (1857), pointed out that "Christ and his apostles saw fit to present detailed lists of sins but in these make no mention of slavery."[85] Surely if they had been so specific about everything else they would not have omitted slavery unless they had meant to. Nor did the Civil War and emancipation end the matter. In 1867, Robert L. Dabney, in *A Defence of Virginia*, repeated the by-now-moot argument that Christ's silence was simply one more example of his approval of slavery.[86] The logical conclusion was nothing if not obvious: If slavery was evil, Christ would have spoken out against it. Since he did not, it was presumptuous for man to do so.[87]

Of course, the problem with an argument based on what was *not* said was that, by switching the burden of proof, the reverse was equally true. In 1857, Albert Barnes, pastor of the First Presbyterian Church of Philadelphia and a prominent member of the New School division of his denomination, carried the defense-by-omission reasoning to its logical but obviously absurd conclusion when he contended that the New Testament *disapproved* of slavery because nowhere did Christ or any of the apostles specifically *approve* of human bondage. In turning the argument on its head, Barnes was really calling attention to the fact that such tortured logic was nothing more than the refuge of one who simply did not have much solid evidence on his side.

As early as 1816, George Bourne, an English-born Presbyterian minister in Virginia, condemned as "baseless" the argument that the New Testament's silence was tantamount to approval. Christ may not have spoken directly against bondage, Bourne wrote in *The Book and Slavery Irreconcil-*

able, but all of his teachings on love, mercy, and fellowship were antithetical to everything slavery represented, a theme echoed later by abolitionists who were convinced that "the general spirit of Christianity" would ultimately prevail. If Christ's silence meant anything, this argument proposed, it was opposition to bondage. Likewise, the Apostle Paul did not condemn slavery, Goldwin Smith wrote in 1864, but he proclaimed those principles that would eventually call for its abolition. More than a few antislavery spokesmen—such as James Dana, Jonathan Edwards, Jr., and David Barrow—also contended that the existence of slavery in biblical times did not necessarily mean that it had God's blessing. The Bible was silent on many things, George Williams of Harrison County, Virginia, pointed out, but one should not draw erroneous conclusions from that. When Joshua asked the sun to stand still, he asked, did that mean that the Bible was an authority on astronomy?[88]

In explaining the relative silence of Christ, Smith and others also called attention to some of the practical considerations of life in the first century. Christians believed they had a mandate to spread the faith through all the world; but the world, at least in the beginning, was mainly the Roman world. If advocates of Christianity were to enjoy access to nonbelievers, they had to avoid "interference with civil institutions." To have spoken out against slavery during the reign of Caesar, Smith argued, "would have arrayed the two parties in deadly hostility throughout the civilized world; its announcement would have been the signal of servile war; and the very name of the Christian religion would have been forgotten amidst the agitations of universal bloodshed." Like missionaries who justified enslaving the heathen African in order to convert him to Christianity, abolitionists like Smith rationalized Christ's silence as a necessary expedient for evangelizing the world. Not to be ignored, on the other hand, was the matter of whether Christ had really been silent on the subject. Speaking before the Methodist General Conference in Baltimore in 1842, South Carolina's Alexander McCaine claimed slavery had been "sanctioned by Almighty God" in the Old Testament and "renewed and confirmed by the Saviour in the New."[89]

McCaine did not explain what he meant by "renewed and confirmed" but may have had in mind Christ's words in Luke 12:42–47, where, in response to a question from Peter, he said that the servant who knows his master's will and carries it out will be rewarded, but the servant who does not "shall be beaten with many *stripes*." Since the passage described a servant who supervised others, it would have been easy for McCaine to see the similarity between this parable and the southern cotton plantation managed by an overseer or slave boss. Whatever conclusions one might draw, here at last, defenders of bondage could say, was a scripture in which Christ himself specifically alluded to the duties of a slave and prescribed the punishment for one who was disobedient. Did that sound like someone who was opposed to servitude?

That the defenders of slavery interpreted Christ's presumed silence as an endorsement of bondage should surprise no one. But that they also claimed the support of the Golden Rule from Christ's Sermon on the Mount gave new meaning to the word "rationalization." "Therefore all things whatsoever ye would that men should do to you," Christ told his disciples in Matthew 7:12, "do ye even so to them." Abolitionists, of course, saw nothing equivocal about the message: any man who was not himself willing to be enslaved should not impose bondage on another. Beginning with the publication of John Hepburn's *The American Defense of the Christian Golden Rule* (London, 1713) and carried on in the writings of Ralph Sandiford, Elihu Coleman, and Benjamin Lay, the Quakers—the only Christians to speak out consistently against slavery in the colonial era—made the Golden Rule the centerpiece of their condemnation.[90] In *A Caution and Warning to Great Britain and Her Colonies* (1766), Anthony Benezet recalled Quaker founder George Fox's message to the slaveholders of Barbados almost a century earlier:

> Consider with yourselves if you were in the same condition as the blacks are, who came strangers to you and were sold to you as slaves; I say, if this should be the condition of you or yours, you would think it hard measure, yea, and very great bondage and cruelty. And therefore consider seriously this, and do you for and to them as you would willingly have them or any other do unto you were you in the like slavish condition, and bring them to know the Lord Christ.[91]

When mainline Protestant churches began their official assault on slavery, they followed the Quaker precedent; the Presbyterian General Assembly concluded its famous declaration of 1818 by quoting the New Testament passage.[92] So obvious was the application of the rule that the enslaved Olaudah Equiano, recalling the kidnapping of his sister and himself in his native Eboe, instantly recognized its significance:

> O, ye nominal Christians! might not an African ask you, learned you this from your God? who says unto you, Do unto all men as you would men should do unto you. Is it not enough that we are torn from our country and friends to toil for your luxury and lust of gain? Must every tender feeling be likewise sacrificed to your avarice?[93]

Actually, the do-unto-others principle had been implied as early as 1641, when the Massachusetts Bay government, in the first colonial statute on slavery, prohibited bondage except for captives of war and "strangers" who submitted voluntarily or were purchased from others, a position endorsed three years later by the founder of Connecticut, Thomas Hooker, who argued that, unless a master-servant relationship had been entered into freely, no person should have authority over another.[94] Hooker considered as "truth" the necessity of servility in relationships between masters and servants and husbands and wives, provided the subservient party, by "a mutuall ingagement, each of the other," had submitted willingly. There was no natural justification for forced servitude, he declared, but two individuals, "by their free consent," could establish such a relationship.[95] Hooker did not explain how an association that two individuals consented to could be called "forced." Similarly, he saw no contradiction between the assumption of human equality in nature and the legitimacy of a relationship in which one person exercised power over another.

Since the abolitionists' attraction to the Golden Rule was so obvious, it must come as a surprise to some that the defenders of slavery, in what was certainly one of the most tortured rationalizations of the southern argument, not only found it compatible with bondage but actually considered it one of Christ's most important statements on the subject. It was, of course, an issue that slavery interests could not ignore. Since no one doubted that critics would leap at the opportunity to invoke Christ's words, the defenders of slavery would have to come up with something. And they did. Resorting to what can only be described as rhetorical acrobatics, proslavery apologists so perverted the Golden Rule's logic that it was possible to conclude that—since humans were so manifestly unequal in physical and mental qualities—Christ had never suggested that people were equal.

Such a position not only would have been contrary to reality, they argued, but it would have destroyed the sanctity of the marriage relationship, in which men, according to the Apostle Paul, were patently superior to women and where the husband was explicitly given dominion over the wife.[96] Since the husband's superiority was self-evident, they concluded that Christ had not advocated equality but that each man—master and slave—had certain duties to perform in accordance with the political and social position that God had placed him in and in the relationships with others that this position called for. In short, the master needed only to treat his slaves as his duty as a master required of him.[97] In one of his published letters to Francis Wayland, Richard Fuller insisted that Paul's exhortation to slaveholding Colossians to "give unto *your* servants that which is just and equal" was obviously a "special application" of the Golden Rule, which only obliged the master to give his slave "whatever was equitable, and due to one intelligent, social, immortal being, standing in such a relation to another."[98]

Perhaps the most revealing—and most disturbing—aspect of the slaveholder's perversion of the Golden Rule was his total inability (or unwillingness) to put himself in the shoes of an oppressed slave, which, after all, was what the rule called for. Writing for the South Carolina Baptist State Convention in 1822, Richard Furman brushed aside the Golden Rule's emancipationist implications by declaring that "surely this rule is never to be urged against that order of things, which the Divine government has established; nor do our desires become a standard to us, under this rule, unless they have a due regard to justice, propriety and the general good." In other words, Christ never intended to establish a principle contrary to the nature of relationships that he himself had prescribed, just as a free person cannot do whatever he wants if it is wrong. In fact, the Golden Rule required no more of a master, Furman added, "than what he, if a slave, could, consistently, wish to be done to himself, while the relationship between master and servant should be still continued." The concluding clause, of course, rendered the preceding proposition meaningless. Writing for the *Southern Presbyterian Review* in July 1850, James Henley Thornwell echoed Furman's theme when he maintained that the Golden Rule only required that "we should treat our slaves as we feel that we ought to be treated if we were slaves ourselves."[99] Eleven years later, with the Civil War already underway, he included an identical argument in his address for the newly created Presbyterian Church in the Confederate States of America. Apparently it never occurred to Thornwell—or he never publicly acknowledged it—that the *first* thing he would "feel that he ought" to receive if he were enslaved would be his freedom. Knowing what it meant to be free, he could not, had he been pressed to explain, admit to anything else and sustain his thesis.

But that did not mean that no one tried. "The rule of our conduct to our neighbor is not any desire which we might have, were we to change places," another leading Presbyterian, Robert L. Dabney, argued after the Civil War; "but it is *that desire which we should, in that case, be morally entitled to have.*" In short, under the Golden Rule, the master was obliged to give slaves only what slaves, *as slaves,* deserved. Of course, the master defined the obligation. Even in the North, where the plight of the black person was less severe, there were whites who seemed to be incapable of comprehending the nature of his situation. On a trip through New England in the 1830s, Harriet Martineau told of a "Boston gentleman" who contended that the "people of colour" he saw "were perfectly well-treated." But this same gentleman would think it "anything but good treatment," Martineau concluded, were he to endure the same offenses. "If he felt himself excluded from every department of society, but its humiliations and drudgery," she scoffed, "would he declare himself to be 'perfectly well-treated in Boston'?"[100]

In fairness to the slaveholding Christians of the South, it needs to be noted that their convoluted interpretation of the Golden Rule found support among more than a few northern denominations, including some whose national leaders had condemned slavery. When, in 1835, four abolitionists in the Methodist church published an "Appeal" for support from members of the New England and New Hampshire conferences, eight "prominent churchmen, including the President of Wesleyan," responded by arguing that emancipation could not be justified unless there were reasons to believe that it would "add to the sum of happiness." To "do unto others," they suggested, meant to do whatever was best for those "others." Since the learned clergymen believed freedom would have a deleterious effect on the bondsman's welfare because he would be unable to compete with the white man, they were certain that, practically speaking, emancipation was contrary to the spirit of the Golden Rule. In other words, the best possible situation for the African was in bondage to the white man. Keeping him there was fulfilling the rule. Surely the slave must realize what fate awaited him, Presbyterian George Junkin surmised. "No man but a fool would wish to be thus set free."[101]

Speaking at the Oneida Conference in 1837, Bishop Elijah Hedding, one of the highest-ranking officials of the Methodist church and a vociferous critic of abolitionism, defended "our brethren in the southern states" and unabashedly proclaimed that "the right to hold a slave is founded on this rule."[102] He ignored the invocation of the Golden Rule by his own church at the famous Christmas Conference of 1784, where Methodist leaders declared that slavery was "contrary to the Golden Law of God on which hang all the Law and the Prophets."[103] Hedding may have had in mind Paul's letter to the Christians of Ephesus in which the Apostle urged slaves to serve their masters as they would serve Christ, admonishing them not to shirk their duties but to work hard and with cheerfulness because God would eventually "reward everyone for whatever good he does, whether he is slave or free." At the same time, Paul reminded masters that they themselves are "slaves" to Christ and that they should treat their servants kindly because God had no favorites.[104] By thus making Christ's words fit Paul's meaning, the Christian slaveholder managed to convince himself that the rule merely directed him to treat his slave in the manner that his position as a firm but benevolent master required of him, just as a husband must treat his wife as his position of strong and protective husband required him to.

Invoking Christ's Sermon on the Mount to justify bondage was preposterous enough, but no biblical defense was more bizarre than that of clergymen like William Andrew Smith, the president of Randolph-Macon College, who in 1844 conceded that slavery was "a great evil," but was "not necessarily a sin," a contention that was especially popular among northern churchmen who sympathized with their beleaguered southern brethren. Addressing the Triennial Baptist Convention in Philadelphia in the same year, Francis Wayland declared: "I believe slavery to be a sin, but consider many of the Southern slaveholders to be as free from the guilt of slavery as I am." Up to that time most northern Baptists, both preachers and laymen, "held that slavery was an evil, a misfortune, to be deplored," retired Baptist clergyman Jeremiah Bell Jeter reminisced, "but that slaveholders of the South, under their circumstances, might or might not sin in holding slaves." In 1855, Samuel Blanchard How, pastor of the First Dutch Reformed Church in New Brunswick, New Jersey, expressed an almost identical opinion when, addressing a gathering of his colleagues, he argued that God did not necessarily oppose something just because it was wrong, a view maintained by the Dutch Reformed leadership on both sides of the Atlantic since the days of New Netherland. Slavery "is an evil much to be lamented," he conceded, "but we deny that it is a sin against God and a crime against man." In both cases, the contradiction inherent in the differentiations of *evil*, *sin*, and *crime* was exceeded in its sophistry only by the equivocation that slavery was not *necessarily* a sin. Did this mean that slavery was always an evil, but only occasionally a sin or crime? If so, how was anyone to determine which was the case? An only slightly less tortured opinion was expressed in 1852 by Ohio Presbyterian John Robinson, who contended that the relationship between master and slave was not "necessarily and under all circumstances sinful," but described no circumstances under which it might be so. It may seem like a strange theology, but at about the same time that How made his pronouncement, Norwegian Lutherans in the Midwest were arguing over this very point.[105]

Of course, the obvious question was: If slavery was an evil, then who—if not the slaveholder—was guilty of committing it? An "evil" could not materialize by itself, independently of a cause; the very word denotes wrongdoing, which in turn means the commission of a sin. Did Smith, Wayland, and How believe in a Satan who created evil institutions with no mortal involvement? To Wayland the matter was not that simple. Certain conditions, both good and evil, existed in biblical times, he explained, that can be dismissed as "merely history." Although slavery was one of those conditions, in reality nothing in the Bible was "morally binding" unless it was clearly set forth as God's will. For example, if God had commanded that everyone should own slaves, not to own them would have been a sin.

Conversely, if he had ordered that no one should own slaves, to own them would have been a sin. He did neither. As "merely history," human bondage had been extraneous to divine concerns. Some things in the Bible were obligatory, he concluded, while others were not. A decision not to own slaves would be one of the latter. Moreover, if God commanded an individual to do something, that did not necessarily mean everyone should do it. The idea that slavery could be evil but not sinful was an essential feature of the conservative Christian's theology because, in answering the charge that an all-good, all-powerful God would never permit evil, suffering, and injustice to exist, it enabled him to fit wrongdoing into God's greater plan of the ultimate good. That is, in order to root out evil, it must first be there. The lesson was that man "should not meddle with affairs," as Edward H. Madden put it; "he should not try to reform the world until God's time comes."[106] Which meant that slavery was one of those evils that should be left alone. It was the ultimate rationalization.

The Pauline Manifesto

The problem for those who invoked Mosaic Law to justify modern slavery was one of *post hoc, ergo propter hoc*. After all, Old Testament mandates like those in Leviticus applied only to a small segment of humanity living three thousand years ago in an isolated corner of the planet. By what stretch of the imagination could they be projected to people everywhere in modern times? Moreover, the contradictions between some Old Testament laws that approved slavery and others that condemned it could not be resolved in anybody's favor. As for the New Testament, the fact that Christ said virtually nothing about bondage was cited by advocates for both sides. While Christian teaching seemed to favor the oppressed slave, the absence of a specific reference to slavery left the whole matter in dispute. In short, the two arguments simply could not stand on their own.

But there was a third proslavery biblical argument that was neither equivocal nor noncommittal. The letters of the Apostle Paul, together with selected passages from some of the other epistles, constituted the most important—and extensively quoted—biblical weapon in the arsenal of the Christian slaveholder. The message was consistent and undeniable: servants were to obey their masters in all things; defiance toward civil authority was also defiance toward spiritual authority; the road to salvation was disciplined and orderly; and freedom in the next life did not require freedom in this one. For example, in Romans 13:2, Paul warns that any person who rebels against legitimate authority would be rebelling against what God had instituted and would therefore suffer the consequences. In

Galatians 4:30, Paul, invoking Old Testament law on inheritance (Genesis 21:10), wrote: "Get rid of the slave woman and her son, for the slave woman's son will never share in the inheritance with the free woman's son." Similarly, calling attention to the mutual responsibilities of masters and servants, he admonished in Colossians 4:1: "Masters, provide your slaves with what is right and fair, because you know that you also have a Master in heaven." Although this passage was sometimes cited as an admonition to slaveholders to be kind to their bondsmen, its real significance lay in the fact that it never even occurred to Paul that the only thing the master could provide his slave that was "right and fair" was freedom. But there was no way to misinterpret Titus 2:9–10: "Teach slaves to be subject to their masters in everything, to try to please them, not to talk back to them, and not to steal from them, but to show that they can be fully trusted, so that in every way they will make the teaching about God our Savior attractive." What more appropriate code of conduct could the slaveholder find? Especially popular among defenders of slavery was Ephesians 6:5–8:

> Slaves, obey your earthly masters with respect and fear, and with sincerity of heart, just as you would obey Christ. Obey them not only to win their favor when their eye is on you, but like slaves of Christ, doing the will of God from your heart. Serve wholeheartedly, as if you were serving the Lord, not men, because you know that the Lord will reward everyone for whatever good he does, whether he is slave or free.

In other words, the slave should not only obey his master, but he should enjoy doing it, suggesting that Paul could very well have been thinking about Christ's relating of the Parable of the Talents on the Mount of Olives. "Well done, good and faithful servant!" Christ told his disciples. "You have been faithful with a few things; I will put you in charge of many things. Come and share your master's happiness!"[107]

All of these lessons quickly found their way into the litany of the slaveholder. In 1835, Episcopal Bishop Nathanial Bowen circulated a pastoral letter in South Carolina that listed ten biblical references "relating especially to servants" with instructions to include them in any service for slaves.[108] A favorite was Peter's admonition to the persecuted Christians in the northern provinces of Asia Minor:

> Slaves, submit yourselves to your masters with all respect, not only to those who are good and considerate, but also to those who are harsh. For it is commendable if a man bears up under the pain

> of unjust suffering because he is conscious of God. But how is it to your credit if you receive a beating for doing wrong and endure it? But if you suffer for doing good and you endure it, this is commendable before God.[109]

Nor were such passages pointed out only by slave-owning Southerners. In the same year that Bishop Bowen sent out his letter, nine prominent Methodist ministers in the New England and New Hampshire conferences, growing anxious over the controversy created by some of their antislavery colleagues, cited I Timothy 6:1—"Let as many servants as are under the yoke count their own masters worthy of all honour"—as "an impregnable demonstration that *slaveholding is not in all cases and invariably, sinful.*"[110] They did not specify in which cases it was not sinful. And if the endorsement of northern clergymen was not convincing, one could even find a slave who would invoke God to justify his own bondage. To avoid joining a new master in Georgia, a slave named William Grimes actually believed that God wanted him to remain a slave when, after praying for help to break his own leg with an axe so that he would be left behind, the leg would not break. "I then prayed to God," Grimes wrote in 1855, "that if it was his will that I should go, that I might willingly."[111] Nor was this an isolated example. "I have met many religious colored people, at the South," Frederick Douglass wrote, "who are under the delusion that God requires them to submit to slavery and to wear chains with meekness and humility."[112] One such person was so convinced that he set it down in print.

In 1861 the Franklin Printing House of Atlanta published a tract purportedly written by a slave named Harrison Berry—the property of one S. W. Price of Butts County, Georgia—who justified his own enslavement by citing various biblical incidents. During Old Testament days, he wrote, Abraham, "being a righteous man," had "some three hundred [slaves] born in his own house." Berry's most far-fetched rationalization involved Christ's pronouncement to the Pharisees when he recognized Caesar's image on a Roman penny. Since slavery was legal under Roman law, Christ's acknowledgment of Caesar's temporal authority was tantamount to an approval of bondage.[113] Berry might have been stretching to make the same point as that of Southern Methodist leaders who proclaimed that the church must yield to any civil statute that was not a direct violation of biblical law.[114]

The epistles were clear on this. Everyone should submit to the established government, Paul wrote to the Romans, because it was an instrument of God. "Obey your leaders and submit to their authority," the anonymous author of Hebrews told the vacillating Christian Jews. "They keep watch over you as men who must give an account." Similarly, Peter instructed the Christians in Asia Minor: "Submit yourselves for the Lord's sake to every authority instituted among men: whether to the king, as the supreme authority, or to governors, who are sent by him to punish those who do wrong and to commend those who do right."[115] But the centerpiece of Berry's servile declaration was Paul's short epistle to Philemon which included the passage that, among Southerners, was probably the most frequently cited Pauline justification for slavery. And for Protestants like the Disciples of Christ, who were dedicated to a "literal restoration of primitive Christianity," it was "an almost insurmountable obstacle to mass conversion to abolitionism."[116] After converting the runaway servant, Onesimus, to Christianity, Paul instructed him to return to his master, Philemon.[117] For the Bible-quoting slaveholder, it was the perfect example.

As it happened, Onesimus was not the first biblical fugitive to serve the proslavery purpose. In Genesis 16:9, the angel of the Lord ordered the runaway servant, Hagar, to return to her mistress and "submit to her." When Secretary of State John Forsyth, who served under both Andrew Jackson and Martin Van Buren, intimated that Pope Gregory XVI opposed slavery, Bishop John England of the Charleston diocese, in one of several letters to Forsyth, cited both the Onesimus and Hagar stories as part of an elaborate biblical defense of slavery.[118] But the Onesimus episode was far more than a story of a prodigal servant returning to his master. If Berry, England, and other defenders of slavery had read past verse 15 they would have discovered that Paul asked Philemon not only to welcome the fugitive back into the household but to forgive him for running away and for whatever other misdeeds he may have committed. Paul even offered to compensate Philemon for any damages or losses he may have incurred. What really undermined the slaveholder's use of this episode was verses 16 and 17, in which Paul urged Philemon to receive Onesimus no longer as a slave but as a "brother beloved." Moreover, Paul added, Philemon should welcome Onesimus just as though he were welcoming Paul himself. In other words, the fugitive was not returning as a slave but as an *equal*, which, needless to say, was a proposition slaveholders must have found incomprehensible. In contrast to Bishop England, Father Edward Purcell, editor of the *Catholic Telegraph* in Cincinnati, saw the Philemon story as a clear argument against slavery, an opinion shared by most abolitionists.[119] Yet even this passage was used by proslavery advocates, among them Presbyterian cleric George Junkin of Miami, Ohio. In a convoluted argument, Junkin contended that Paul's use of the words "brother beloved" and "in the flesh" carried the same meaning as his earlier admonition to Ephesian servants to "be obedient to them that are *your* masters according to the flesh."[120] In other words, the master and servant were "brothers" only in the body of Christ.[121] It was characteristic of the slavery controversy that both critics and defenders generated thousands of words to explain a scriptural passage that, in the Authorized Version, ran to only twenty-nine lines.[122] Like many biblical arguments, the story of Philemon and Onesimus could be reconstructed to fit virtually any purpose.

Of course, if Christian slaveholders found it easy to ignore Old Testament lessons that did not support their position, they would certainly disregard New Testament messages that did the same. Interpreting the Bible has seemed almost to be an exercise in evading the application of Newtonian law: one eschews the suggestion that for every lesson there is an equal and contrary lesson. Although the defenders of bondage considered the Apostle Paul to be one of their most important biblical authorities, they carefully avoided any of his pronouncements that appeared to argue against slavery. Paul agreed, for example, that certain laws of Moses were meant to punish "menstealers," a clear indictment of the slave trade. Even more remarkable, he wrote to the Christians in Corinth that slaves should take advantage of every opportunity to gain their freedom, a passage that masters feared bondsmen would see as a license to run away.[123] Finally, John, in Revelation 13:10, warned that anyone who led another into captivity would himself go into captivity. But these were passages that, like the verses in Philemon calling upon the master to receive the runaway servant as a "brother beloved," the Christian slaveholder never felt obliged to accommodate; and he had no trouble finding a "good" slave—like Berry—who recognized what whites perceived as God's will. In 1863 a northern sympathizer of the Confederate war effort named J. F. Feeks published a long poem entitled "Da Yaller Ringlets," in which an old slave woman said to her white ward:

De dear Lord Jesus soon will call
Old mammy home to him,
And he can wash my guilty soul
From ebery spot of sin.

And at his feet I shall lie down.
Who died and rose for me;
And den, and not till den, my chile,
Your mammy will be free.[124]

Harrison Berry may have been just as fictitious as Feeks's black mammy, but, either way, both examples reflected the arrogance with which whites could put into the mouth of a slave a Christian theme to justify his own bondage.

It should surprise no one that Pauline doctrine on obedience became a leitmotif in the gospel of the Christian slaveholder, and the place where that doctrine could most often be found was in something called the "slave catechism."[125] As early as 1704, when Elias Neau, a French Huguenot who had converted to Anglicanism, was appointed "catechist" for New York, the church's missionary arm, the Society for the Propagation of the Gospel in Foreign Parts, established a program for "instructing" slaves in the ways of the Bible.[126] Two years later, none other than the great Puritan divine Cotton Mather, in *The Negro Christianized*, formalized the doctrine with the publication of two catechisms, one of which included this exchange:

Question: If you serve Jesus Christ, what must you do?

Answer: I must Love God, and Pray to Him, and Keep the Lords-Day. I must Love all Men, and never Quarrel, nor be Drunk, nor be Unchaste, nor Steal, nor tell a Ly, nor be Discontent with my Condition.

Mather exhorted the slave to honor everyone, especially, in an obvious reference to the Fifth Commandment, "the master and mistress, as father and mother." And in an "answer" based on the Tenth Commandment's warning against covetousness, the slave was admonished to be "Patient and Content with such a Condition as God has ordered for Me."[127] Another early author was Henry Patillo, a pioneer missionary in North Carolina, who published his slave catechism in 1787; and in the decades before the Civil War, several more were written by Baptist, Methodist, Presbyterian, and Episcopal clergymen.[128] To many religious leaders, the catechisms seemed the only means of spreading the word among people who were overwhelmingly illiterate. Since, in response to the Nat Turner rebellion in 1831, the southern states called for stricter enforcement of laws prohibiting the teaching of slaves to read and write, one historian noted, "religious instruction had to be exclusively oral."[129] In the last analysis, it hardly mattered who wrote a catechism or when it was written; the one thing all of these question-and-answer training manuals had in common was an emphasis on obedience:

Who gave you a master and a mistress?
God gave them to me.
Who says that you must obey them?
God says that I must.
What book tells you these things?
The Bible.[130]

Simply put, the obedience to God that Moses called for also meant obedience to one's master; and for Paul, who stood squarely in the Mosaic tradition, this Old Testament idea was a cornerstone of his teaching.[131] When Paul told his friend Titus, who was leading the church on Crete, to "*Exhort* servants to be obedient unto their own masters," he meant *teach* them.[132]

Of course, it is virtually impossible to assess the actual influence of the catechisms. Talking to a government interviewer in 1938, ninety-year-old Sarah Fitzpatrick had no illusions about their purpose.

> White preacher he preach to de white fo'ks an' when git thu' wid dem he preach some to de "Niggers." Tell 'em to mind deir Marster an' b'have deyself an' dey'll go to Hebben when dey die. Dey come 'round an' tell us to pray, git 'ligion, dat wuz on Sun'dy, but dey'ed beat de life out'cha de next day ef ya didn't walk de chalk line. Our white fo'ks made us go to church an' Sun'dy School too. Dey made us read de Catechism. G'ess de re'son fo' dat wuz, dey tho't it made us min' dem beder.[133]

Forty-nine-year-old Joseph Smith of Maryland and his wife both claimed that they never heard a white preacher say anything except "obey your masters."[134] In 1910 a former slave from Alabama named Bill Pickens told the same story.

> I 'member in de ole days how one er my marster's slaves wanted to go to dat church. "You min' your business an' hear de preacher what I sen' you," marster says. Once a month his preacher 'ud come an' talk ter de colored folk. He'd tell 'em how dey must obey deir marster an' missus an' not steal any chickens. He wouldn't say much more dan dat. No real preachin'.[135]

"Black Christians were given to understand that slavery was God's will and his enactment," C. Eric Lincoln wrote. "It was a consequence of black people's peculiar sinfulness and depravity that they should suffer, and that white men should be agents of providential justice set over them."[136] But knowing the intentions of whites who endorsed the catechisms does not reveal much about the sincerity of the slaves' response. Some blacks rejected the teaching of the catechisms outright, while others, like Sarah Fitzpatrick, were determined to make life as easy for themselves as possible and went along mainly to mollify their masters.

On the other hand, there were bondsmen who genuinely embraced Christianity but considered the catechisms, in the words of three former slaves, a "hypocritical perversion of holy scripture."[137] They did not accept Pauline teaching on obedience, but they clung to a belief in the fundamental truth of Christianity. To call what they were told a "perversion of holy scripture" was to affirm the validity of scripture but to condemn the white man's misuse of it. Solomon Northup, a free black who had been wrongfully enslaved for twelve years, was incredulous that one of his owners, Peter Tanner, could piously serve as a church deacon and, at the same time, repeatedly warn his slaves, in a reference to Luke 12:42–48, that Christ prescribed many whiplashes for the disobedient slave.[138] The slave was rarely in a position to question overtly the truth of Christianity itself, thus whatever racist elements were inherent in the faith were not challenged by his criticism of the catechisms. It is not uncharacteristic in the study of race relations that the catechisms, as instruments of control, revealed more about the thinking of the slaveholding society and its clerical leaders than they did about the slaves.[139]

To the Christian slaveholder, the beauty of the Pauline doctrine on obedience was its unique separation of the world of the body from the world of the spirit, a condition made imperative by Paul's insistence that respect for God's laws went hand in hand with respect for man's laws. Like the white preacher in Virginia who warned slaves that offenses against their masters and mistresses were "faults done against God himself," Paul warned that rebellion, overt or otherwise, toward legitimate civil authority was rebellion against God. Of course, once one separated the world of the body from the world of the soul, it then became necessary to rank them. Unfortunately for the oppressed, Paul insisted that "spiritual freedom surpassed and transcended in importance civil status."[140] In a proposition that stated that all souls were equal in the spiritual world but not all mortals were equal in the temporal world, freedom under man's law was less important than "freedom" in the eyes of God, which the slave could achieve by faith and good works—and it was not necessary for one to enjoy the former in order to realize the blessings of the latter.[141] "Spirit stands for the divine life and power as manifested to men," W. David Stacey wrote in *The Pauline View of Man*. "The flesh stands for the weakness and frailty of man which entertains evil and so separates from God and leads to death."[142] Of the three major monotheistic faiths, only Christianity applied this principle to the structure of society. In "medieval Christendom under the conservative spell of Saint Augustine," sociologist Orlando Patterson observed, Christians rationalized their "exclusion of the slave on the secular level" by including him "in the sacred community." Thus he was an insider in the city of God but an outsider in the city of man.[143] The idea quickly found its advocates in America. In its famous Declaration of 1818, the Presbyterian General Assembly condemned slavery only to find its position undermined by the insistence of subsequent assemblies that the church should be concerned only with the "moral" aspects of bondage, not its "civil" aspects. The legality of the institution of slavery was a civil matter for which, conservative "Old School" Presbyterians declared, the church had no responsibility.[144]

Of course, the absurdity of this doctrine could be exposed by merely suggesting that the slaveholder exchange places with one of his bondsmen. If freedom in the spiritual world was more important than freedom in the temporal world, the master should not make so much of the latter. But the critical issue here was not so much Paul's vision of man's relationship to God, but how men—especially nineteenth-century Americans—perceived that vision. The Pauline dualism of body and soul made it easy for them to reconcile the fundamental contradiction between the call for salvation and the acceptance of bondage. Separating the body from the soul made it easy to separate the world of the body from the world of the soul. A plea for subservience to earthly masters that also held that all races will be equal in heaven could not be sustained any other way.[145] Perhaps the most amazing expression of this principle was that of the Reverend Jacobus Elisa Joannes Capitein of the Dutch Reformed Church, who, in his *Dissertatio Politico-Theologica de Servitute, Libertati Christianae non Contraria* (1742), flatly declared that "slavery was not contrary to Christian freedom," a declaration that was widely embraced by the Dutch Reformed clergy on both sides of the Atlantic. The fact that Capitein's parents were native-born Africans meant nothing.[146]

Of course, if freedom meant only freedom from sin, then it was fair to raise questions about the definition and use of the word. When Paul told the Galatians that "[t]here is neither Jew nor Greek, slave nor free, male nor female, for you are all one in Christ Jesus," more than a few slave-holding ministers concluded that he was simply pointing out that the only freedom that mattered was freedom in salvation in Christ. Life on this earth was brief and temporary; the hereafter was forever. "[T]he freedom of the Soul for Eternity is infinitely preferable to the greatest Freedom of the Body in its outward Condition upon Earth," Anglican minister Benjamin Fawcett told a group of slaves in 1755. When Christ told the Jews in the temple square, "[Y]e shall know the truth, and the truth shall make you free," they said they could not be set free because they were no one's slaves. But every sinner, Christ replied, is a slave to sin. "If the Son therefore shall make you free, ye shall be free indeed."[147]

In other words, true freedom came from "the emancipation of the will from the power of sin," southern Presbyterian James Henley Thornwell argued. Salvation grants freedom from the grip of Satan, not freedom from the secular chains of slavery. Nor was it a lesson used only by southern clergy. Both George Junkin, a prominent Ohio Presbyterian, and C. F. W.

Walther, head of the conservative Missouri Synod of the Lutheran church, argued publicly that biblical freedom meant only freedom from damnation and that it "could be preserved within the framework of a servant-master relationship."[148] It was a universal Christian blind spot; when salvation was at issue, it mattered not if one was slaveholder or abolitionist. Although he was an outspoken critic of slavery, Congregationalist Jedidiah Morse insisted that "belief in Christ, which freed man from sin, the worst kind of slavery, was the supreme good, far greater than all temporal blessings."[149] Since it was the Christian master who kept the bondsman in chains and the Christian minister who defended that bondage, it is difficult to avoid the conclusion that the problem was Christianity.

Coinciding neatly with Protestant teachings about the dualism of body and soul, this definition of *free* clearly allowed for the "liberation" of the latter without interfering with the enslavement of the former. The upshot, as David Brion Davis put it, was "bondage as a reciprocal relationship between loving master and loyal servant, instituted by God for the better ordering of a sinful world, but limited by the rational terms of the social covenant." Among English and American Protestants in the seventeenth century, "servitude appeared to balance natural freedom and worldly fate, human authority and the equality of men under the supreme rule of God." Simply put: it mattered not what a person's status was according to man's law; and for that matter, for some people the best guarantee of freedom in the next world, if Paul was to be believed, was to surrender it in this one. "God did not expect His children, black or white, to wrangle with each other over right or wrong, justice or mercy," Donald Mathews wrote. "Rather, He desired His people to wrestle with the demons within themselves."[150] And if the idea of dualism was unclear to some people, they were further confused by the fact that the words "freedom" and "slavery" could, paradoxically, mean the same thing. To be free and a sinner is to be a slave to sin; but to be free from sin is to be a slave to Christ. In the words of a plantation hymn published in 1854 by a Boston minister named Nehemiah "South-Side" Adams, whose sympathy for slaveholders was criticized by other northern ministers:

How sad our state by nature is!
Our sin how deep it stains!
And Satan binds our captive minds
Fast in his slavish chains.[151]

A few biblical lexicologists have agreed that some scriptural references to slavery, especially in the New Testament, did not signify physical bondage at all but merely meant absolute submission to Christ, a principle that could be traced back to the servant poems of the book of Isaiah and the concept of the "Servant of Yahweh."[152] There were others, including members of the same church, who disagreed over the significance of the principle of dualism. For example, while Quaker founder George Fox accepted slavery as "an institution that could be rationalized by the ancient dualisms of body and soul," his American contemporary, William Edmundson, took the position that "physical slavery and Christian liberty were incompatible," a belief that gained a measure of currency during the Great Awakening of the 1740s, when Christian equalitarianism meant "physical as well as spiritual freedom."[153]

Whatever disagreements churchmen may have had, the principle of dualism was ideally applicable to slavery. Masters realized that persuading the slave to accept his lot was much easier if he could expect "eventual deliverance," and there was plenty of biblical testimony to back them up.[154] In his letters to the Christians of Corinth, Colosse, and, especially, Ephesus, Paul urged servants to be content with their condition, however intolerable it might be, because God ultimately would reward their suffering, a promise that the disciple Peter also endorsed in his first letter to the Christians in Asia Minor.[155] Apparently it worked—at least for some bondsmen. In 1783, Jupiter Hammon, the first published slave poet in America, repeated this theme in fifteen of the thirty stanzas of "A Dialogue Entitled the Kind Master and the Dutiful Servant."

Come my servant, follow me,
According to thy place;
And surely God will be with thee.
And send thee heave'nly grace.

Dear Master, I will follow thee,
According to thy word.
And pray that God may be with me.
And save thee in the Lord.[156]

When, in 1822, the court in Charleston, South Carolina, sentenced Denmark Vesey for conspiring to lead a slave insurrection, the judge chastised him for trying to undermine the "divine influence of the Gospel" which was "to reconcile us to our destinies on earth." Seven years later, in a speech before the South Carolina Agricultural Society, Charles Cotesworth Pinckney, nephew and namesake of the former Federalist presidential candidate, proclaimed that the slave can endure severe hardships if he believes they are only temporary, and if he is convinced that his good behavior, "founded on Christian principles," will guarantee "superior rewards in that which is future and eternal."[157]

Give me Jesus
Give me Jesus
You may have all the world,
Just give me Jesus.[158]

Eighty-seven-year-old Anderson Bates of South Carolina remembered a song his mistress sang to the slaves:

Dere is a happy land, far, far, 'way,
Where bright angels stand, far, far, 'way,
Oh! How them angels sing!
Oh! How them bells ring!
In dat happy land, far, far, 'way![159]

How could anyone resist a promise of paradise? A guarantee of happiness in eternity was hard to beat.

The Slave's Bible

If anyone needed an object lesson on the effectiveness of Paul's be-a-good-slave-go-to-heaven theme, he needed only to review the slave's religious music. There is a strong case to be made for the argument that the easy adaptation of many slaves to Christianity, fortified by their belief in the promise of a heavenly reward, was the primary reason for the absence of major slave uprisings in the United States. Nowhere was this adaptation more vivid than in the literally countless plantation songs and spirituals that were heard throughout the South in the antebellum era.[160] Returning home after a long day in the fields, the sea island slaves sang of the Jordan River and moved their oars to words that were more than just a balm to ease the strain on aching muscles:

Jordan stream is wide and deep
Jesus stand on t'oder side.[161]

But the slave also portrayed the passage to heaven in a way that Christian defenders of slavery certainly never intended. Crossing the Jordan River may have meant going to heaven to some, but to many others it was a metaphor for running away to freedom and was the major theme in many spirituals, as in "Oh, Give Way, Jordan," "Oh, Wasn't Dat a Wide Riber," "I'm Crossing Jordan River," "My Army Cross Over," "Deep River," "Way Over Jordan," "I'm Just a-Goin' Over Jordan," and "Roll, Jordan,

Roll" (which was the title of at least two completely different songs and was an expression that appeared in the lyrics of many songs). The words varied, but the meaning—saving the soul or the body—was always the same:

I look over Jordan, and what did I see,
Coming for to carry me home.
A band of angels coming after me,
Coming for to carry me home.[162]

Oh, Jordan's riber am chilly an' cold
One more riber to cross,
But I got de glory in my soul.
One more riber to cross.[163]

Deep River, my home is over Jordan.
Deep River, I want to cross over into campground.[164]

Jordan River
Deep and wide,
None can cross
But the sanctified.[165]

And there was no shortage of biblical transportation. According to musicologist Harold Courlander, it was from 2 Kings 2:11, in which a "chariot of fire" appeared and carried Elijah "up by a whirlwind into heaven," that "the inspiration for the constantly recurring image of Elijah's chariot" came.

I wonder what chariot comin' after me?
Judgement goin' to find me!
Rock, chariot, I told you to rock!
Judgement goin' to find me!
Elijah's chariot comin' after me!
Judgement goin' to find me![166]

It mattered not whether one crossed the Jordan River, rode in Elijah's chariot, climbed Jacob's ladder, or boarded the Gospel Train, the journey to Heaven—or freedom—was an omnipresent theme in slave spirituals.[167]

While many slaves sang of fleeing by crossing over Jordan, the vast majority knew they were not going anywhere. The reality was that the slave would remain in bondage for the rest of his life; and it was in this realization that he made his most meaningful adaptation to the Pauline doctrine of freedom after death.[168] The machinery was biblical, but the product was a blend of Judeo-Christian symbolism and the traditional West African belief in a well-defined universe filled with ancestral spirits. In the colonial era many slaves believed that when they died their souls would return to their original African homes, "there to live free in their former condition."[169] By the nineteenth century, the Christian slave, his native beliefs in an afterlife diminished, nonetheless welcomed death as a journey to "Beulah Land," where he would see all those who had gone before him:

Sister Rosy, you get to heaven before I do,
Sister, you look out for me,
I'm on de way.[170]

I got a mother over yonder,
On the other shore.
By and by I'll go and see her,
On the other shore.[171]

I'll meet my mother over there,
I'll meet my mother over there,
We goin'a have a good time,
Way bye and bye.[172]

A spiritual popular in black churches in Virginia could refer specifically to any recently deceased friend or relative:

Oh, Peter go ring dem bells
Oh, Peter go ring dem bells
Oh, Peter go ring dem bells
I heard from heaven to-day.

I wonder where my mother is gone
I wonder where my mother is gone
I wonder where my mother is gone
I heard from heaven to-day.[173]

Repeat verses replaced "my mother" with "Sister Mary," "Sister Martha," "brudder Moses," "brudder David," and so on. Reflecting on his early days in the South, Jacob Stroyer, pastor of a black church in Salem, Massachusetts, described a song that was often heard from slaves as they were being separated and sent to different homes.

When we all meet in Heaven,
There is no parting there,
When we all meet in Heaven,
There is no parting more.[174]

Sometimes a slave who believed his death was imminent would sing sadly of leaving his friends but would also promise to wait for them on the other side.

When dat ole chariot comes,
I'm gwine to lebe you,
I'm boun' for de promised land,
Frien's, I'm gwine to lebe you.

I'm sorry, frien's, to lebe you,
Farewell! oh farewell!
But I'll meet you in de mornin',
Farewell! oh farewell!

I'll meet you in de mornin'
When you reach de promised land;
On de oder side of Jordan
For I'm boun' for de promised land.[175]

Surely no God-fearing slave would want to jeopardize his passage through the pearly gates to meet Sweet Jesus and to see his loved ones again. For many true believers, happiness would not begin until one's earthly life ended. If, as historians have so often declared, plantation music is a "window" into the world of the slave, then the biblical promise of "everlasting life" was an imperative part of that world.

Whether or not the slave's ancestral perception of life after death had any influence on his understanding of Christian theology is problematical, but apparently there were more than a few bondsmen who did not see anything especially wonderful about entering the white man's heaven. There certainly was nothing equalitarian about the heaven described by a white preacher to slaves, where the races would be separated by a wall, but where "there will be holes in it that will permit you to look out and see your mistress when she passes by," a description of heaven repeated in a sermon by a local black preacher who "was afraid to say anything different." Or the one described by the white preacher who told Molly Finley of Honey Creek, Arkansas, "[Y]ou may get to the kitchen of heaven if you obey your master, if you don't steal, if you tell no stories." If this was what the white man's heaven was like, it was easy to understand why most slaves did not want to share their eternity with their oppressors. While many bondsmen earned places in paradise "on account of their present sufferings," wrote Charles Ball, an American-born slave who had grown up listening to stories about Africa from his grandfather and other slave immigrants, they would not be willing to "admit the master and mistress to an equal participation in their enjoyments." White Christians can tell the slave that heaven is a place where all races live harmoniously, but it "is impossible to reconcile the mind of the native slave to the idea of living in a state of perfect equality and boundless affection with the white people," Ball added. "Heaven will be no heaven to him if he is not to be avenged of his enemies. I know from experience that these are the fundamental rules of his religious creed, because I learned them in the religious meetings of the slaves themselves." Whether or not revenge was a factor, there were many slaves who did not enjoy the prospect of sharing heaven with whites. Far more gratifying was the belief, especially popular among African-born male slaves, that "after death they shall return to their own country and rejoin their former companions and friends in some happy region, in which they will be provided with plenty of food and beautiful women from the lovely daughters of their native land."[176] In the African's afterlife, there was no place for a white master.

If the slave had had only his master to contend with, there might have been reason to anticipate some kind of improvement in his condition. It was simply a matter of numbers. At no time in the antebellum era were the slaveholders ever more than a fraction of the southern white population. On the other hand, a growing number of northern and foreign critics were challenging the moral premises of bondage. With a few more people calling for emancipation, the weight of public opinion and economic coercion should eventually, at least in theory, produce pressures that would bring about the slave's eventual freedom.

Unfortunately, the idea that the slave should accept this condition because it assured him a place in paradise also found support among people who professed to be his friends. None other than Dr. Benjamin Rush of Philadelphia, signer of the Declaration of Independence and founder of the first American Antislavery Society, believed, according to one researcher, that slavery "was a special means of salvation granted to Negroes by God." It was a view not excessively different from George Whitefield's suggestion that bondage actually enhanced the possibility of the slaves' conversion because the heightened "Sense of their natural Misery" would better prepare them for "faith in Christ."[177] Because of the enormity of their suffering, the argument went, God would make it easier for them to get into heaven. Rush and Whitefield may have gotten the idea from the Apostle Paul, who, writing from prison in Rome, told the people of Philippi that by knowing the fellowship of sharing in Christ's sufferings, he will become "like him in his death."[178] No purgatory for the bondsman; by simply *being* a slave, he had *earned* a place in paradise. "Better a poor man whose walk is blameless than a rich man whose ways are perverse."[179]

In 1840 a white preacher named John Mason told a group of slaves that they should not complain if they were wrongly punished because God "will reward you for it in heaven, and the punishment you suffer unjustly here, shall turn to your exceeding great glory, hereafter."[180] Did not sweet Jesus himself say, "Blessed *are* they which are persecuted for righteousness' sake: for theirs is the kingdom of heaven"?[181] On the other hand, according to this logic, God would require a free person to suffer through a long waiting period before admitting him to heaven. It was almost enough to make a free man wish he were a slave. While people like Rush may have intended to call attention to the bondsman's plight, they inadvertently made clear their belief that the relatively short earthly misery suffered by slaves was preferable to the affliction that would be endured by the souls of white sinners. It was a thin distinction from the Pauline manifesto.

While the Old Testament clearly earmarked *strangers* and *heathens* for servitude and the Apostle Paul's admonitions to masters and servants were emphatic (if debatable), in none of the biblical passages directly or obliquely sanctioning slavery could one find a specific reference to race or color. But that did not present a formidable problem for the Christian slaveholder. Indeed, it would be foolish to assume that anyone who could see in the Golden Rule an argument supporting slavery, or who suggested that God did not necessarily oppose something just because it was evil, should have had trouble finding a scriptural endorsement of racial or color differentiation.

THREE THE CURSE

God gave it [religion] to Adam and took it away from Adam and gave it to Noah, and you know, Miss, Noah had three sons, and when Noah got drunk on wine, one of his sons laughed at him, and the other two took a sheet and walked backwards and threw it over Noah. Noah told the one who laughed, "Your children will be hewers of wood and drawers of water for the other two children, and they will be known by their hair and their skin being dark." So, Miss, there we are, and that is the way God meant us to be. We have always had to follow the white folks and do what we saw them do, and that's all there is to it. You just can't get away from what the Lord said.

GUS "JABBO" ROGERS,
to a WPA interviewer

What God Hath Put Asunder, Let No Man Join Together

It is revealing that the most popular biblical story in the slaveholder's arsenal was also the most preposterous: the Old Testament episode, found in Genesis 9:21–27, in which Noah, after sleeping off a drunken stupor, placed a "curse" on his grandson Canaan.[1] It seems that one of Noah's younger sons,[2] Ham, had watched his father sleeping naked and had shown disrespect by telling his brothers Shem and Japheth about it. Not sharing Ham's taste in humor, the brothers covered their father with a robe, all the while respecting his privacy by looking the other way. When Noah awakened and learned what had happened, he punished Ham by placing a curse on Canaan, the youngest of Ham's four sons, making him a "servant of servants"—that is, a slave—to Shem and Japheth. That is all there is in those seven verses. But by the time the American antislavery movement launched its campaign against human bondage in the nineteenth century, the Curse of Canaan had acquired a life that was to become as real for a slave like "Jabbo" Rogers as it had been for any Bible-thumping slaveholder.[3]

There was no biblical explanation as to why Canaan was singled out, why such a seemingly innocuous offense called for such terrible punishment, and, more to the point, why a son should be punished for a father's sin. But that did not stop some defenders of slavery from creating one. Presbyterian minister Robert L. Dabney of Virginia wrote in 1862 that Noah, on God's orders, acted as "patriarchal head of church and state, which were then confined to his one family." Canaan was punished, he concluded, because he "probably concurred in the indecent and unnatural sin of Ham."[4] In other words, Canaan was guilty of being a partner in his father's offense simply because, as far as Dabney was concerned, it was convenient to believe so.

Dabney's reasoning was typical proslavery thinking. To the Christian slaveholder who was convinced there must be a good reason for something he wanted to believe but could not explain, the Genesis story was exceedingly plausible. Accordingly, his easy acceptance of Noah's curse and his certainty that Ham was black, as William A. Clebsch wrote in his foreword to Thomas V. Peterson's *Ham and Japheth*, "referred cultural dissonance to the divine will."[5] In other words, to attack slavery was to attack God's judgment. "So scrupulous is the reverence of the slave-owners for Scripture, so great is their zeal for God's honor," abolitionist Goldwin Smith sarcastically observed, "that upon a merely conjectural interpretation of a passage in the most obscure and difficult part of the Bible, they feel bound to condemn to hopeless slavery on their plantations a whole race of mankind who, in common with other races, have been redeemed by Christ."[6]

Even if it could be argued that God had cursed Ham for gazing on a naked Noah and afterward showing disrespect, there was still the matter of explaining why he would punish an entire race of people, not to mention all of their descendants, for the sin of one person, especially when there was not even a suggestion of such an eventuality in the Bible. The twenty-fifth verse of Genesis 9 simply determined that Canaan shall be a servant "unto his brethren," and the two following verses called for Canaan specifically to serve Shem and Japheth. No one else serving, no one else being served. Although he would never have disputed the Genesis account, even Cotton Mather suggested in 1706 that it was possible that Ham was not the common ancestor of *all* Africans. In 1864 a Boston minister named Increase N. Tarbox, pointing to the significant accomplishments of the Egyptians, Assyrians, Phoenicians, and Carthaginians—all Hamitic peoples—repudiated entirely the Curse of Canaan defense of slavery with the argument that God would never be so unfair. "If any one here asks on what moral grounds we can justify this setting apart of a fourth part of the race of Ham, and putting them under a curse because of the misconduct of their father," Tarbox argued, "we reply by asking on what moral grounds you can justify this setting apart the *whole* of the descendants of Ham, and putting them under a curse, in consequence of the misconduct of their father?"[7] Certainly a just God would never condemn people who had not yet been born. "To suppose it right" that an innocent person today should be enslaved because of a sin presumably committed by an ancestor who lived four thousand years ago, Quaker John Woolman argued in the late eighteenth century, "is a Supposition too gross to be admitted into the Mind of any Person, who sincerely desires to be governed by solid Principles."[8]

It is not possible to determine just when the idea that all of Canaan's descendants should be enslaved in perpetuity as a result of Noah's curse became widely accepted. The 1839 edition (1955 printing) of the King James Bible supports Genesis 9:25 with a footnote reference to Joshua 9:23, in which the Gibeonites, a Canaanite nation, were cursed to be "wood cutters and water carriers" to the Israelites. But the first twenty-two verses of Joshua 9 make clear that that curse was for the Canaanites' deception in leading the Israelites to negotiate a treaty under false pretenses. There is no allusion to Noah's curse. The same edition of the Bible also associates Genesis 9:25 with 1 Kings 9:20–21, in which Solomon enslaved the remnants of several Canaanite tribes; but as with the reference in Joshua, these passages make no connection, direct or indirect, to Noah's curse.[9]

The clearest mandate for natal slavery was Leviticus 25:45–46, in which the Israelites were told they could will their human property to their children. "What is remarkable too it was negro slavery, or the bondage of the Canaanitish descendants of Ham," Baptist preacher Iveson L. Brookes of South Carolina wrote in 1851, "whom God authorized to be held in hereditary bondage, under the laws of the Jewish polity."[10] Of course, such a conclusion required a leap that the Bible itself never made. As was so often the case with people looking for biblical justifications to subjugate others—for example, the Spanish Inquisition's persecution of Jews under the principle of *Limpieza de Sangre*[11]—Christian defenders of slavery pieced together fragments of Old Testament references to bondage into an elaborate rationale for the enslavement of Africans. Moreover, if the children of Canaan had been condemned to serve in perpetuity, Baptist critic David Barrow pointed out in 1808, their descendants would still be enslaved and in the possession of the descendants of the original masters. But those masters had been Jews, and their descendants, he concluded, "have long since been scattered among, and are now tributaries to other nations."[12]

Actually, all of this is moot, an abolitionist preacher wrote in 1864, because New Testament revelations superseded the Old Testament laws and precedents. Noah's words were only a curse, not a prophecy, and "all curses have been taken away by Christ." In fact, Goldwin Smith insisted, God himself removed the curse long before Christ "when Abraham was told that 'in his seed all the nations of the earth should be blessed.' "[13] Ironically, even the critics of slavery, unable to set their arguments outside of an orthodox interpretation of the Bible, were victims of the same constraints inherent in the Christian theology that served the defenders of slavery. Tarbox, Woolman, and Smith did not deny the literal truth of the book of Genesis; they only denied that Noah's curse had anything to do with modern slavery.

That white Christians were able to concoct an elaborate defense of human bondage out of three Old Testament verses (a total of fifty-one words in the Authorized Version), and that most of the Christian world failed to challenge that defense, is difficult for the modern mind to comprehend. In reality, the myth of Noah's curse had become a rationale for a theory of human relationships before the first African set foot in an English colony. As early as 1521, a German scholar named Johan Boemus speculated that all of the primitive and barbaric peoples of the earth were descendants of Ham while everyone else had descended from Shem and Japheth.[14] Of the later accounts by "learned" Americans, none was more widely circulated than the published letters of Dr. Samuel A. Cartwright of Natchez, Mississippi. Cartwright, a physician, wrote a series of letters to the Reverend William Winans in which he purported to prove the "Truths of the Bible and the Justice and Benevolence of the Decree Dooming Canaan." In a transparent attempt to claim a measure of credibility by calling attention to his scientific background, Cartwright wrote in 1843 that he had "no pretension to theological knowledge, and if I had, my subject does not permit me to leave the natural sciences," but his published *Essays* was in fact nothing but a proslavery theological argument.[15]

Nor were Southerners the only spokesmen for the book of Genesis. Canaan's descendants were condemned to slavery because, in the words of Vermont Episcopal Bishop John H. Hopkins, Noah "*judged it to be their fittest condition.*"[16] Some defenders of slavery were even more specific. "Shem was blessed to rule over Ham," the Reverend Frederick Ross, a prominent northern Presbyterian minister, declared in 1859, "[and] Japheth was blessed to rule over both."[17] From here it was only a short step to the belief that the three men were the founders, respectively, of the yellow, black, and white races, a belief based almost certainly on Old Testament passages like "of them was the whole earth overspread" and "by these were the nations divided in the earth after the flood."[18] The connection between the three brothers and what were perceived as the world's three races was so simple and logical it understandably appeared, to the fundamentalist Christian, to be divinely ordained. And, since Ham was by universal agreement the designated progenitor of the African peoples, *ergo*, black servitude.

Of course, anyone with even the most rudimentary knowledge of biology would be quick to point out that Ham himself could not have been black or his parents would have been also, not to mention his sons and brothers and their children—although Presbyterian minister Thomas

Smyth of Charleston devoted some fifteen pages of *The Unity of the Human Races* (1850) trying to explain how it would be possible for some of Ham's descendants to be black but not others. Cartwright argued that the secret to the connection between Ham and Africans might be found in the Hebrew language. "The Hebrew verb, from which the noun Ham is derived," he wrote to Reverend Winans, "signifies generator or parent, also *hot*, and in the Coptic and other dialects, *hot* and *black*, or *burnt black*."[19] Obviously, it was necessary to search for a nonscientific explanation because if one based his conclusions on scientific principles—even only those that were recognized in the mid-nineteenth century—the entire biblical defense of slavery would have come crashing down. Bondage-by-curse could be sustained only on the assumption that God either changed the color of Ham's skin instantly or that of his descendants in a relatively brief period. This was orthodox Christian thinking. Cartwright apparently had no problem with the fact that calling attention to the antecedents of the word *ham* was putting the conclusion before the fact. Unless Noah had some way of anticipating the curse and named Ham accordingly, there was no reason for trying to show that Ham's name had had anything to do with his presumed black descendants.

Christian explanations of the origins both of Africans and of their skin color ranged from the implausible to the ridiculous. In his two-volume *Narrative* published in 1789, Nigerian Olaudah Equiano, who had apparently converted to Christianity during a residence in Virginia, claimed that his people had descended from the ancient Jews through Abraham's children Afer and Afra, born of Abraham's wife and a concubine named Keturah. In other words, racial mixing began early and ultimately produced all of the peoples of sub-Saharan Africa. Apparently, this idea had been suggested by an English minister, one Dr. Gill, in his *Commentary on Genesis*, and supported by the works of fellow Britons, especially Dr. John Clarke's *Truth of the Christian Religion* and Reverend Arthur Bedford's *Scripture Chronology*. In 1663 an English traveler to Massachusetts suggested that the mystery of Ham's skin color might simply be explained by the possibility that Africans were actually white people who over time had acquired an additional outer skin. When John Josselyn took under his care a "*Barbarie-Moor*," he discovered that the man "had one more skin than *Englishmen*," the underlying skin being "bloudy and the same Azure colour with the veins" as whites and the outer skin "a tawny colour" which, together, "makes them appear black." A version of this idea appeared as recently as 1903, when a conservative Protestant named W. S. Armistead, replying to a theory that Africans were not humans, wrote that black people had, in a very short period, developed a dark epidermis over a white dermis in accordance with the same God's "law of *accommodation*" that was responsible for other physical differences, such as hair color and texture. To any person, Christian or otherwise, who had trouble believing the argument that a white person could become black instantly or in a very short period, the two-skin thesis seemed like a plausible rationalization. Even a self-proclaimed friend of the slave, Dr. Benjamin Rush, believed that color differences were only skin-deep. The African's darker skin was the result of a leprous disease, Rush theorized. Once a cure was found, the black person's skin would begin to lighten.[20] In other words, it was a medical problem.

Then there were those who were not at all bothered by empirical contradictions or impossibilities. One exponent of the Old Testament account, a New York harness-maker named Josiah Priest, whose several works on contemporary America were for a short time widely read, simply ignored genetic principles altogether and argued that God had turned Ham black in his mother's womb, although there is absolutely no biblical basis for such an allegation. "Japheth He caused to be *born* white, differing from the color of his parents," Priest wrote in *Slavery, as It Relates to the Negro, or African Race* (1843), "while He caused Ham to be born *black*. . . . It was, therefore, by the miraculous intervention of the Divine power that the *black* and *white* man have been produced, equally as much as was the creation of the color of the first man, the Creator giving him a complexion, arbitrarily, that pleased the Divine will."[21] There was, Priest contended, a widely accepted scientific explanation for this: "Into these two [white and black] *new* bloods God infused, or created, two *secreting* principles; *one* depositing between the *outer* and secondary skin of the body of one of these men a *white mucus*, causing the skin of the man to be *white*, and between the outer and inner skin of the other a *black mucus*, causing that man to be *black*."[22] In other words, it was all *in* the skin.

Needless to say, Priest did not identify a single scientist who supposedly held this opinion. Perhaps more important, if Ham had acquired his darkness before Noah's curse, this would have meant that slavery had had nothing to do with skin color, a proposition that most Christians would not accept. For them it was simply an article of faith that Ham's—more specifically, Canaan's—descendants defied all of the laws of genetics and became black in a very short time as a result of both Noah's curse and their geographical distribution. Canaan had not been born black, the argument went, but had been *blackened* by God. Taking comfort in the thought that with God anything was possible, the true believer did not trouble himself with scientific contradictions.

To conservative American Protestants, these were trifling objections. Considering themselves moderates on the slavery issue, most members of the fundamentalist Disciples of Christ, a sect which grew out of the evangelistic fervor of the early nineteenth century, nonetheless held strongly to the conviction that Africans had inherited the Curse of Canaan, although no one ever bothered to explain how—or why—it was possible for an entire race of people to inherit a curse. Biblical defenders of slavery assumed that God, acting through Noah, had reasons that one could discern by making certain inferences. Working backward from what he saw, the white man perceived Africans as so clearly inferior and their habits so obviously contrary to biblical teaching that subjugating them was merely a matter of fulfilling God's condemnation. The *result* was self-evident; all that remained was to find the *cause*.

Among European Protestants the concept of *original sin* "was being virtually discarded as a theological foundation, and human nature and conduct were increasingly used as a basis for faith."[23] But some Americans worked to keep the idea alive. In 1856, the Reverend Howell Cobb of Georgia insisted that bondage was simply God's way of punishing Africans "for their wickedness." Barely one month before the Civil War, in the first of three articles in the New York *Journal of Commerce*, Thomas Smyth insisted that "slavery is a part of the original curse pronounced on earth, on man, on woman, and is therefore to be classed among the evils incident to a sinful nature in a sin-polluted world and a providential remedial agency for accomplishing wise and beneficent results." This view was echoed in 1862 by Smyth's Presbyterian colleague Robert L. Dabney, who saw slavery as God's "punishment of, and remedy for . . . the peculiar moral degradation of a part of the race."[24]

Such assertions were, in fact, incompatible with the story of the curse. If God had cursed Canaan to punish Ham, how did that translate into punishing people not yet born for being wicked or degraded? Yet, reprehensible though it may have been, it was an idea that died hard. As recently as the 1940s, a Methodist congregation in Mississippi approved a resolution that declared that God, in his eternal wisdom, "lifts and casts down races that he blesses and curses," and that it behooves all races not to question his reasons.[25]

Nor did the true believer ever feel obliged to explain why something as irrelevant as the African's black skin should have become a badge of bondage. In fact, it is difficult to determine precisely just when slavery became a matter of color. The Romans had enslaved black Africans as early as Virgil's time (70–19 B.C.), and in the first two centuries A.D. black slaves could be found throughout many of the Roman territories. By the sixth century, Ethiopian slave traders were importing blacks from central Africa.[26] But, although dark-skinned slaves were not uncommon in Roman times, their color may have been coincidental. In fact, there is no evidence that the Ethiopians who came into contact with whites in the first centuries after Christ suffered discrimination. "The early Christians did not alter the classical color symbolism or the teachings of the church to fit a preconceived notion of blacks as inferior, to rationalize the enslavement of blacks, or to sanction segregated worship," Frank M. Snowden, Jr., wrote. Indeed, black members of the early church "found equality in both theory and practice." Scholars disagree as to just when black skin became associated with subservience, but they are virtually unanimous in their contention that the idea "cannot be placed upon the shoulders of the ancients." Ten centuries elapsed between the first appearance of the story of Noah's curse and the rabbinic literature explaining it. "During these centuries," historian William McKee Evans argued, "the face of servitude had darkened in the Near East" with successive accounts by rabbis, but by the sixth century A.D. the "racial stereotyping of slaves by Jews" appears to have diminished. There also is evidence that the Muslims played a major role in making slavery a racial institution. Most Egyptian slaves were black as early as the middle of the tenth century, and it may have been the beginning of the eleventh century before slaves in the rest of the Islamic world were predominantly black.[27] Adding to the uncertainty was the fact that the word *Moor*, used by Europeans as a synonym for "Negro" as far back as the year 1390, also often referred to lighter-skinned peoples of the Mediterranean region.[28] It should not be forgotten that the Medieval European still drew many of his impressions of slavery from the bondage imposed on the Slavic peoples of the western steppes of southeastern Europe and the Balkan peninsula. No color symbolism here. In almost every European language the word *slave* was originally *slav*, and as late as the fifteenth century the Western interpretation of Noah's curse "remained innocent of racial overtones."[29] The Christian's exploration of Africa and the New World changed all that.

Enlarging the Curse

The absence of an early association between color and bondage notwithstanding, the Christian's definition of slavery invariably worked its way back to Ham, although it was Canaan who had been cursed. The reason was obvious: Since Canaan was only one of four brothers—the others were Cush, Mizraim, and Phut—making Ham the source of black servitude fit in with the popular belief that Noah's three sons were the progenitors of the white, black, and yellow races. It was all very neat—not to mention convenient. Besides, Ham had committed the original offense. It only seemed fair and logical to carry the indictment back to him. On the other hand, focusing on Canaan would diminish the credibility of the Genesis story because it would raise questions about the status of his brothers, especially Cush. "Cush was the father of the thick-lipped and crisp-haired races, to which we give the common name of negroes," the Reverend Hollis Read wrote in 1864, and "no curse was recorded against Cush or his descendants." Mizraim "was the founder of the Egyptians," he added, and the Canaanites, "whose country stretched along the eastern shore of the Mediterranean Sea," included such peoples as "Hittites, Jebusites, Amorites, Girgasites, Hivites, Arkites, etc.," none of whom were black. In fact, "[t]he Canaanites were Asiatics, and not Africans at all."[30] To deflect arguments like this, supporters of the Genesis account believed it was crucial to the three-race theory that Ham be designated as the father of the African race. Accordingly, the "blackness of Ham was," Olli Alho concluded, "always accepted uncritically in the development of the 'theology of slavery.' "[31]

It probably does not even need to be pointed out that in a matter with so many bizarre convolutions nothing would be too strange. In 1867 an obscure publisher in Nashville, Tennessee, named Buckner H. Payne—who was trying to prove that Africans were not humans because they were the soulless descendants of lower animals—suggested that Christians concluded that Ham had been "blackened" because biblical scholars like Samuel A. Cartwright had erroneously translated the ancient Hebrew word *ham* to mean "black."[32] Africans are inferior and deserve to be enslaved because they are subhuman, Payne reasoned, not because they are a condemned race of humans. The obsession with finding a biblical justification for bondage, he concluded, had led whites to look for it where it did not exist. It is true that *ham* at one time meant both "dark" and "hot"; but Payne, naturally, presented no evidence for his thesis and, in fact, there did not appear to be any connection between these definitions and the later belief in Ham's blackness, a belief that had spread to Europe by the Middle Ages. At about the same time that Payne's publication appeared, a small booklet, *The Color Line*—sometimes attributed to a Reverend Thompson writing under the pseudonym of Sister Sallie—agreed that it would have been impossible for Ham, a white man, to beget a black race.[33] Sister Sallie only implied what Payne had stated explicitly: black people must have come from some other, presumably lower, place in the animal world.

The presumed geographic distribution of biblical peoples also influenced the theorists' association of slavery with race. "God sent Ham to Africa, Shem to Asia, [and] Japheth to Europe," the Reverend Frederick A. Ross stated in 1859.[34] Accordingly, the people known as the Canaanites had occupied approximately the area of modern Israel; and the Cushites, the presumed descendants of one of Ham's other sons, were scattered around parts of eastern Africa, including most of present-day Ethiopia. The proximity of these peoples to the black populations of sub-Saharan Africa must have been a factor in the Christian's assumption that all blacks were descendants of Ham. But such an assumption also called for a complete suspension of disbelief. Since the dispersion of the Bantu-speaking peoples throughout the lower two-thirds of the African continent was well underway by the time of Christ, the one hundred or so generations that had come and gone since Noah's day would hardly have been enough to account for the number and distribution of people whose skin colors ranged from brown to true black and included the tallest and shortest humans in the world.

To nineteenth-century Christians who believed that human life began with Adam and Eve, a thousand years seemed like a very long time, but there was already a growing body of empirical evidence that easily deflated the Curse of Canaan myth. Some of the most significant scientific research in the antebellum period emphatically contradicted the traditional Protestant view. Excavations into newly discovered Egyptian tombs and other artifacts demonstrated beyond any doubt that for at least the previous five thousand years there had been no noticeable change in human types.[35] This meant that even before Noah's time (2000 B.C.?), people with Negroid facial and physical features existed essentially in the same color and form as they did in the modern era. "The Caucasian, Mongol, Negro, &c., are found distinct on the monuments of Egypt nearly three thousand years before Christ," Dr. Josiah C. Nott declared in 1849 in the first of his two "lectures" on the biblical and physical history of man. "Query, how much time did it take to produce this diversity?"[36] In other words, if there had been virtually no change in the past five thousand years, how many more thousands of years would have been required to produce from a common ancestor the great variety that presently existed? Moreover, in placing the entire population of the world under the sons of Noah, the defenders of slavery never bothered to explain where the sons' sons[37] found wives to start their new nations. If the only women who survived the Flood were the wives of the four men, where did these new women come from?

Of course, such questions never troubled conservative Protestants, most of whom trusted without question their long-held religious proclivities and, concomitantly, had little respect for scientific opinion. Nevertheless, as antibiblical scientific findings accumulated, Christian defenders of slavery increasingly tried to find a systematic way to squeeze the appearance of an entire race of people into a handful of centuries. In *The Unity of the Human Races* (1850), Thomas Smyth, calculating events down to an exact number of years, argued that "[t]he Negro race is known to have existed 3,345 years ago," or "68 years later than the earliest of the white race." Accordingly, Africans did not appear until "842 years *after* The Flood," he concluded, allowing "ample time" for the "multiplication and diffusion" of "all the various races of men." Trying to demonstrate that time was not a problem, a contemporary of Smyth's, Lutheran preacher John Bachman, published *The Doctrine of the Unity of the Human Race* (1850), in which he set out a mathematical model that he claimed proved that the entire population of the earth could have reached its current number in just six thousand years. Because of divine intervention, he surmised, humans in ancient times evolved much more rapidly than they do in the modern age.[38] Theoretically, a single pair of humans could produce over 2.3 quadrillion people in just fifty generations.[39] Apparently Bachman assumed that every female on earth would produce one child per year from the onset of her menses until her menopause, that is, about thirty children—or fifteen more females—per woman. In the light of these figures, how, he wondered, could anyone "doubt the possibility of the derivation of all the individuals in the races of animals, and men from single pairs."[40]

Like most other Christian apologists for slavery, Bachman exemplified the fact that someone motivated by religion to find an answer will find it wherever he wants to. At least it could be said of Smyth and Bachman that they tried to devise statistical explanations, farfetched though they were, for a matter that had heretofore been understood primarily as an article of faith. Of course, the problem with their arguments was not that they only made sense theoretically. Rather, both clerics completely ignored the fact that it was not accounting for numbers in a brief period that was the issue but accounting for *change*.

The problem with a curse is that true believers consign to it a mystique that gives it a life of its own despite the best evidence against it. One fiction that survived the centuries was the belief that, although it was Noah who had spoken, it was God who had actually cursed Canaan. Noah himself, of course, made no such claim, a fact that Protestant abolitionists lost no time in pointing out. In 1857 George B. Cheever of New York City, a leading spokesman for the "New School" Presbyterians, argued that the curse was exclusively Noah's and, since it fell upon Canaan, "who was as white as the Hebrews or ourselves," the action had nothing to do with race or color. The essential point was not that there had been no curse; Cheever was, in effect, saying that it was irrelevant. Seven years later, Hollis Read, emphasizing that there was no explicit biblical indication that Noah's action was divinely inspired, repeated Cheever's contention.[41] In other words, Noah's outburst was clearly—and solely—the result of a father's anger over the disrespect shown by a son, hardly the kind of thing that would justify the enslavement of an entire race of people.

Nevertheless, the widespread conviction that everything in the Bible was divinely inspired was enough to convince believers that the curse was

God's, and the contention that Noah had spoken only for himself was not a popular one. The assumption that it was God who cursed Canaan has appeared even where least expected. David Brion Davis, in his highly acclaimed *The Problem of Slavery in Western Culture* (1966), summarized Quaker William Edmundson's antislavery views and concluded by declaring that "perpetual bondage was an 'oppression on the mind' which could not be justified by *God's* curse on the children of Canaan."[42] Edmundson believed that God's curse of Canaan had no historic significance, but apparently accepted the existence of such a curse. It is not clear if Davis was simply paraphrasing Edmundson's beliefs or if he was assuming that the Old Testament account actually identified God as the source of the curse. Whichever the case and whatever the reason, the idea that the curse was attributable to God survived long after the belief in its validity. Edmundson—like Cheever and Read—was simply one more ardent Christian critic of slavery who was a captive of the same biblical myths that drove the most zealous defenders of slavery.

A claim that God had placed a curse on a group has always been a convenient device for subjugating alien peoples. Colonial depredations against Indians were often based on the assumption that the natives, with their red skin color, were agents of a Satan whose red coloring and association with fire had been one of the popular mythologies of medieval Europe. Thus it was easy for John Winthrop, the first great Puritan leader of Massachusetts Bay, to believe that the smallpox epidemic that had decimated Indian villages in 1616–18 was simply God's way of "thinning out" the heathen aboriginal population in order to facilitate the later English migration. With no acquired immunity to the Europeans' diseases, more than three-quarters of the Indian population living along the New England coast—from the Penobscot River to Narragansett Bay—numbering in the tens of thousands, succumbed in an incredibly brief period.

The actual number of victims can never be known, but even conservative estimates are staggering. Only a few years before the first permanent English settlement in North America, the Indian population from southern Maine to western Connecticut may have been as high as 144,000. One researcher estimated that the epidemic took the lives of between 70 and 90 percent of the Massachusetts Indian tribes, including the entire Patuxet tribe of Plymouth. By 1631 the Massachusetts tribes were down to 750 from an original 24,000—a decline of over 97 percent![43] English visitor John Josselyn, after trips to New England in 1638 and 1663, claimed that the population of the "three Kingdoms of the Sagamorships" had been reduced from 3,000 to 300; while Cotton Mather gave the casualties as more than nine-tenths—"yea, 'tis said, *nineteen* of *twenty*"—of their original number. The "sweeping *mortality*" killed the Indians "in such vast multitudes," Mather wrote, "that our first planters found the land almost covered with their unburied carcasses."[44] The fact that the Indians had originally contracted the disease from visiting English fishermen was not acknowledged. In the end, the actual number of Indians who died may have been less important than the way their deaths changed both their relationship with the conquering Puritans and the Puritans' understanding of their own destiny.

The belief that God had cursed the Indian population in order to prepare New England for his children was preached from every pulpit and quickly became an enduring part of Puritan folklore. Shortly after the end of the Great Migration, the anonymous author of *New England's First Fruits* (1643) reminded believers that "the good hand of God" had swept "away great multitudes of natives by small pox, a little before we went thither, that he might make room for us there." When a second outbreak of the disease struck in 1633–34, Winthrop was prompted to write to Nathaniel Rich that "the natives are neare all dead of the small Poxe, so as the Lord hathe cleared out title to what we possess."[45] This new "virgin soil epidemic" killed thousands more from Maine to the Connecticut Valley, historian Gary Nash wrote, "proof that God had intervened in the Puritans' behalf at a time when the expansionist impulses of the settlers were beginning to cause friction over rights to land." In his *Magnalia Christi Americana* (1702), Cotton Mather recalled how the lessons of the "prodigious pestilence" had been passed down through the generations: "We have heard with our ears, O God, our fathers have told us, what work thou didst in their days, in the times of old; how thou dravest out the heathen with thy hand, and plantedst them; how thou did'st afflict the people, and cast them out!" As late as 1760, Nathaniel Appleton preached a sermon giving thanks to God for sending "a mortal Sickness among the Indians who inhabit near the Sea-Shore, in this part of the Country, which destroyed multitudes of them, and made room for our Fathers."[46] Already believing they were The Elect of God, it was no great stretch of the imagination for the Puritans to see the removal of the Indians by disease as simply part of a divine plan to establish the Kingdom of Christ in the New World.

The early Puritans were not, of course, the last Christians to perceive themselves as the beneficiaries of a curse. A more recent example of racist damnation by deity was the teaching of the Church of Jesus Christ of Latter-Day Saints (Mormons) that certain people who at one time had been white—Indians and Africans—had had their skins darkened because of past sins against God, and, accordingly, were not eligible for full membership in the church. "And he had caused the cursing to come upon them, yea, even a sore cursing, because of their iniquity," it was written in *The*

Book of Mormon (1981 ed.); "wherefore, as they were white, and exceedingly fair and delightsome, that they might not be enticing unto my people the Lord God did cause a skin of blackness to come upon them." Mormon doctrine also condemned interracial sexual contacts—"cursed shall be the seed of him that mixeth with their seed"—and countenanced racist stereotypes—"because of their cursing which was upon them they did become an idle people, full of mischief and subtlety, and did seek in the wilderness for beasts of prey."[47]

Well into the twentieth century, most Americans considered Mormonism a cult whose general influence on American life was virtually nonexistent. Since they were confined to an isolated section of the country, the Mormons' ennobling of their "exceedingly fair and delightsome" fellow saints and, conversely, their condemnation of dark-skinned peoples had little effect on blacks or Indians. But the doctrine's existence served as a reminder of how so-called curses that had been conceived in less enlightened times could survive as long as enough people believed in them. In 1978, President Spencer W. Kimball of the Church of Jesus Christ of Latter-Day Saints, after claiming to have received a "revelation" from God, announced that otherwise qualified black men henceforth would be admitted to the Mormon priesthood. All women continued to be excluded from the church's leadership. As it did when it outlawed polygamy, the Mormon church—when it became politically expedient to do so—responded to the social pressures of the times.[48]

Polygenesis: If Not Ham, Who?

One explanation for the diversity of humankind that most conservative Christians were not inclined to accept was that the several races had been created independently and that Adam and Eve (not to mention Noah and Ham) had never been exclusive progenitors in the development of humankind—a view that Thomas Jefferson in his *Notes on the State of Virginia* considered plausible.[49] Pondering the differences between the kind and number of languages in Asia and those of North American Indians, Jefferson wondered if "not less than many people give to the age of the earth."[50]

The doctrine of *polygenesis* could be traced back to the Renaissance, when many orthodox beliefs, including the idea of the Great Chain of Being, were being challenged. But as George M. Fredrickson pointed out, the first systematic classification of the savage as a "permanently distinct and inferior species of humanity" did not appear until 1676–77, when an unpublished paper of Dr. William Petty of the English Royal Society appeared.[51]

Coinciding with what is usually considered the beginning of the Age of Reason, Petty's essay could be considered the first shot of a scientific assault on the Christian explanation for the origins of man. However it began, the notion that the races had come into existence independently of each other at least had the virtue of accommodating the Christian's belief that the earth was only a few thousand years old. More to the point, any argument that relegated Africans to a lower level of humanity made it easier to justify slavery.

Ironically, one of the first American advocates of this thesis was not a defender of slavery but a Philadelphia physician named Samuel George Morton whose research had convinced him that the various races had evolved from separate origins. Beginning in 1820, Morton started collecting human and animal skulls, eventually accumulating what was believed to be the largest collection of crania in the world. Basing his conclusions on a lifetime of study in paleontology, anatomy, medicine, and anthropology, Morton concluded that the secret of polygenesis could be found in the evolution of the mulatto. Equating humans of different races with horses and donkeys, he argued that a person of mixed extraction did not have the same reproductive capacity as a person of pure blood and, accordingly, the hybrid strain would eventually die out. The word "mulatto" derived from the Spanish and Portuguese *mulato*, which, originally referring to a young mule, could be traced back to the Latin *mulus*. Here was empirical proof. The mule was a product of the union of two different species but was itself sterile. Since fecundity was universal within each species of animal life, Morton, apparently assuming that an object always displays the characteristics of its name, theorized that whites and blacks must have had completely different origins.[52] Of course, humans were not mules, but it was such an easy association that anyone who wanted to believe it had no trouble doing so. Although no one ever found even the slightest trace of evidence that mixed-breed sterility existed in humans, the belief remained popular well beyond Morton's time, even among a few Christian leaders.[53] During the "miscegenation" debate prior to the presidential election of 1864, the editor of the New York *Daily News*, a staunchly Democratic newspaper, invoked the Curse of Canaan myth and filled three full columns with "scientific" testimony on sterility among hybrids.[54]

Even Morton, despite his antithetical views on human origins, placed his argument within the context of the story of Genesis. "It is difficult to imagine that an all-wise Providence, after having by the Deluge destroyed all mankind except the family of Noah," he wrote in 1839, "should leave them to combat . . . the various external causes that tended to oppose the greater object of their dispersion." If one is to accept the biblical account, the only conclusion that could be drawn, he went on, was that each race "was adapted from the beginning to its peculiar destination." In short, the characteristics that distinguished the races were "independent of external causes."[55]

At least partially inspired by the growing debate between abolitionists and defenders of slavery, the idea of multiple origins was, in time, expounded by some of the leading scientific figures in the United States. In two lectures published in February 1844, Josiah Nott, whom H. Shelton Smith called the "South's most vigilant exponent of the new ethnology," angered conservative Protestants because he proposed that, since Canaan's descendants were white, Africans must have had different ancestors. There was no other plausible explanation. Agreeing with Morton's hypothesis on the sterility of "hybrids," Nott identified many species of animals and races of humans that had existed far longer than the four thousand years since the Flood. But the conflict could be easily resolved, he concluded, by simply acknowledging that the nonwhite peoples of the world had separate origins and that the Bible, therefore, applied only to Caucasians.[56]

Speaking in 1847 before the Literary Society of Charleston, South Carolina, Harvard's Louis Agassiz surprised—and dismayed—his listeners with the assertion that he "believed in an *indefinite* number of original and distinctly created races of men." There are superior and inferior races whose distribution could only have come about by multiple origins, Agassiz declared. The idea that people as different as Chinese, Africans, and Europeans had developed from a common pair in just a few thousand years, he concluded, was preposterous. Even the rational mind of a scientist as eminent as Agassiz was trapped in a Christian universe. "Before Darwin," Edward J. Larson noted, "American scientists typically accepted the biblically orthodox view that God directly created every type of species, with each thereafter reproducing true to form." Accordingly, in an effort to reconcile the doctrine of polygenesis with the biblical account of creation, Agassiz, following Nott's lead, suggested in an article in Unitarianism's *The Christian Examiner* (1850) that Adam and Eve were the progenitors only of the white race.[57] Unable (or unwilling) to challenge the chronology of Genesis, he could not (or would not) see human history reaching back beyond the few thousand years accounted for in the Old Testament.

Despite the incredulity of Nott's and Agassiz's audiences, what William Sumner Jenkins called the "pluralist" account of human origins found considerable southern support. For the defenders of slavery, the polygenetic argument could not have come along at a better time. The editors of two of the most influential southern periodicals, the *Southern Quarterly Review* and *De Bow's Review*, "recognizing that the theory of polygenesis would provide a sound, scientific basis for enslaving the black race," gave the idea extensive coverage in the years prior to the Civil War. Although Nott had challenged the Christian belief that all humans had descended from the sons of Noah, he never suggested that black people were not inferior. Speaking to the Southern Rights Association in December 1850, he said that he had advocated polygenesis to persuade abolitionists that God had permitted slavery to exist because black people had never been part of the Judeo-Christian world. If Northerners could be convinced that Africans had not descended from Adam and Eve, he contended, they might find black slavery less reprehensible. Although Nott took positions contrary to popular biblical defenses of slavery, and his repudiation of the Christian tradition on the unity of man directly challenged the Curse of Canaan myth, he was, in fact, a staunch advocate of white supremacy, holding that the only ultimate solution to the race problem was colonization.[58] Like Morton and Agassiz, Nott set his unorthodox theory of human origins within the chronology of orthodox Christianity. "The religion of Christ, too, is advancing as the world becomes more enlightened," he noted in 1844, describing the progress made in the fields of geology and astronomy, "and they can and will march on together, receiving light from each other, and upholding the wisdom, goodness and glory of God."[59] Even men of science would only go so far.

Although the theory of polygenesis found support among a few influential people—including James Hunt, the leader of the British anti-abolitionist movement—it was contrary to the dominant school of thought that prevailed in both Europe and the United States and it faded rapidly after the emancipation of American slaves.[60] William Petty's unpublished essay for the English Royal Society in 1677 did not open a floodgate of works challenging the belief in the unity of humankind. When, almost a hundred years later, Lord Henry Homer Kames published his "Discourse on the Original Diversity of Mankind" in *Six Sketches on the History of Man* (1774), the idea was considered bizarre if not heretical.[61] Still struggling to wrench loose from an era when the church dominated serious thinking, most scholars held that, while there were certainly varieties of color, form, and behavior among races, the human species in the Great Chain of Being sprang from a common origin.[62]

In an effort to accommodate orthodox Protestant thinking, one popular scientific explanation for the diversity of human types that did not directly challenge the "Christian's conception of monogenesis" was that all of the world's societies had degenerated from their original state of purity during the time of Eden and that inferior peoples were simply the most conspicuous products of such decay. According to Robert F. Berkhofer, American colonists saw the Indians as "corrupt copies of the Jewish or other high civilizations of the past or, at worst, the very agents of Satan's own degeneracy." Even a person as compassionate and sympathetic as Roger Williams could not help seeing the Indians as "wandering Generations of *Adams* [*sic*] lost posteritie." Under conditions in which heathenism and idolatry flourished, the argument went, rapid change was possible. So as all these ideas came along, a division developed among Southerners—between, in William Sumner Jenkins's words, "scripturalism and rationalism"—who had been allies in the defense of slavery. Among the rationalists were scientists like Nott and Egyptologist George R. Gliddon, both of whom took particular pleasure in tweaking the noses of clergymen over the fundamentalist insistence on the unity of the races.[63] Nott, especially, so enjoyed "parson skinning" that he could not resist mocking the assertion of Columbia Seminary's George Howe that Adam and Eve could have produced 200,000 descendants in just 130 years.[64] Though not as mind-boggling as John Bachman's 2.3 quadrillion offspring in fifty generations, Howe's claim did nothing for the credibility of "scripturalism."

Unfortunately for Christians, the belief in *monogenesis* could not be easily reconciled with the scientific insistence that far more time was necessary for creatures to evolve into their present forms than the handful of years allowed by the Bible. The Christian's dilemma was obvious: the more he insisted that all of humankind began with Adam and Eve, the more untenable was the belief that the earth was only a few thousand years old. "In rejecting the doctrine of polygenesis as an attack on religious orthodoxy," one historian wrote, "Southern Christians spurned the only scientific defense of slavery that could have justified enslaving the black race."[65] If the slaveholder had been inclined to evaluate his tenets objectively, he would have had no choice but to concede either that the black man was his equal or that the Bible was not literally true. Polygenesis held that the entire Judeo-Christian line of "begats"—from Abraham to Jesus—was just a small fraction of humanity. This would mean that, from a global perspective, Christianity was insignificant, an absolutely unthinkable proposition. "If Agassiz is correct," Robert Graves, the editor of *The Baptist* (Tennessee), wrote in February 1868, "we are hopelessly lost—we are without a *Bible*, without a *Savior* and without *heaven*."[66]

Although he rejected a literal interpretation of the Bible, Jefferson did try to find an explanation for the origins of life that could at least partially accommodate Christianity. Because he believed in the primacy of reason and inquiry, he could not accept on faith something as contrary to common sense and logic as the unscientific—and unarguable—contention that all things are possible with God. The observable world was simply too full of facts that contradicted everything the Christian believed in about the human origins. To resolve this contradiction without repudiating the biblical chronology, Jefferson postulated a view of nature in which every creature still existed in its original physical form. "Every race of animals," he wrote in *Notes on the State of Virginia*, "seems to have received from their Maker certain laws of extension at the time of their formation."

> Their elaborative organs were formed to produce this, while proper obstacles were opposed to its further progress. Below these limits they cannot fall, nor rise above them. What intermediate station they shall take may depend on soil, on climate, on food, on a careful choice of breeders. But all the manna of heaven would never raise the Mouse to the bulk of the Mammoth.[67]

This meant that the different human races first appeared exactly as they now were. In a static universe, creatures did not become extinct or change significantly into other forms.[68] Jefferson was, of course, both right and wrong. He was right in his belief that the great variety of human and animal species could not have developed into their present forms in just a few thousand years. But he was wrong in assuming that the universe was static and that living creatures did not change. As a resolution for what seemed to be an unsolvable problem, the pluralist explanation was clean and simple; but its fatal flaw was that it also required Christians to renounce one of their most sacred beliefs. To the true believer it was not much of a trade-off. Moreover, it opened a Pandora's box of questions that no one wanted to try to answer. For example, if Africans were not really the descendants of Ham and Canaan, then who were?

Most Americans were not troubled by the question because the overwhelming majority accepted the biblical story of Noah and his sons as it was set forth in the Old Testament and interpreted by the Protestant clergy. Any other explanation of the origins of humankind was apostasy; had this been an earlier time and a different place, Morton, Agassiz, and Nott might have found themselves sharing the fate of Galileo.[69] Americans—especially Southerners—were conservative when it came to science and religion. Thus they were not inclined to question a biblical lesson that they had learned as children, such as that in Paul's declaration to the Athenians: "And [God] hath made of one blood all nations of men for to dwell on all the face of the earth."[70] Paul had drawn his authority from Genesis, where "Adam named his wife Eve, because she would become the mother of all the living" and where "the whole world had one language and a common speech."[71]

While the belief in a common origin of humankind was held by almost everyone in the Christian world, the rationalism and skepticism of the European Enlightenment was bound to raise doubts about ideas that could not be substantiated by scientific inquiry. Sixty-three years before

Thomas Smyth published his explanation of how the races had diverged since the time of Noah in *The Unity of the Human Races* (1850), Samuel Stanhope Smith's *An Essay on the Causes of the Variety of Complexion and Figure in the Human Species* (1787, revised 1810) devoted twenty-six pages to a refutation of Lord Henry Holmer Kames's earlier work on polygenesis. It never occurred to Smith to address the slavery issue because he did not think it was relevant. By the middle of the nineteenth century it was an entirely different matter. George Howe, a professor of biblical literature at Columbia Seminary in Georgia, was so upset by Nott's two lectures in 1848 on the biblical and physical history of man that his critique in the *Southern Presbyterian Review* (1850) ran to sixty-three pages. Similarly, Smyth, recalling Christ's admonition to the multitudes in Matthew 23:8 that "all ye are brethren," devoted an entire chapter of his ponderous work—which was more a biblical defense of slavery than a criticism of multiple origins—to a condemnation of Agassiz's use of the Bible to support polygenesis.[72]

One of the more intriguing arguments against the principle of multiple origins, first advocated by Smyth and enlarged two years later by Presbyterian William T. Hamilton, pastor of the Government Street Church in Mobile, held that if Africans were not descendants of Adam and Eve, then there would have been no reason to try to convert them "since doctrinally Christ was the 'second Adam' who offered salvation to all members of the fallen race." The Bible, Smyth had noted, taught that all races are of "Adamic origin, seed, or blood" and that Christ was the savior of all humankind, but the doctrine of polygenesis embodied the contention that Christ "lived, and suffered, and died" only for the white race. Since thousands of slaves and Africans had renounced their heathen beliefs and happily embraced Christianity, both men argued, the supposition that they were not eligible for redemption because they were not members of the Adamic race seemed absurd. In other words, if Africans had not been among those whom God, through Christ, had given the opportunity for salvation, they would not—indeed, could not—choose to become Christians. The fact of their conversion was *prima facie* proof of their common origin with the white race.[73]

More persuasive than either Hamilton or Smyth was Lutheran minister John Bachman, who, as professor of natural science at the College of Charleston, enjoyed a measure of credibility denied most clergymen. Drawing upon his years of research in crossbreeding plants, birds, and mammals, Bachman contended that since different species of animals cannot be crossbred, the fact that the races can produce mixed offspring and that those "hybrids" can, in turn, reproduce—in direct contradiction of Morton's theory on the progressive sterility of mulattoes—is proof that they are of a single species, *ergo*, they have a common ancestor. This was incontrovertible evidence that the Bible was in complete harmony with the laws of nature and that, indeed, every "Biblical student" could better understand scriptural teaching by studying astronomy, geology, and physiology. Bachman also chastised southern supporters of polygenesis for aggravating the sectional controversy. "The advocates of plurality should especially be on their guard," he wrote in 1850, "lest the enemies of our domestic institutions should have room to accuse them of prejudice and selfishness, in desiring to degrade their servants below the level of those creatures of God to whom a revelation has been given, and for whose salvation a Saviour died, as an excuse for retaining them in servitude." In other words, the Southerner who believed in multiple origins was only giving the abolitionists one more argument with which to attack slavery. In another work published five years later, Bachman accused Agassiz of inconsistency for saying that all humans spring from a single origin and then, later, suggesting that different types of humans developed independently of one another.[74] Such a contradiction, he was convinced, was a proof of the weakness of the plurality argument.[75]

The mathematical calculations and scientific arguments of Smyth and Bachman were typical of the thinker who lived in the Age of Reason but whose mind was still a captive of the Age of Faith. Bachman, in particular, brought respectable scientific credentials to the debate over multiple origins. But, though he proudly identified himself as both a minister of the Gospel and a professor of science, he always made his scientific findings conform to his religious beliefs, never vice versa. He was, in short, a personification of the inherent incompatibility of rationalism with faith.

Bachman the scientist looked for answers by formulating a hypothesis that could be verified, modified, or even discredited. Accordingly, he tested his hypothesis to eliminate false assumptions because only by filtering out errors could he get closer to the truth. Objectivity meant accounting for the variables and accepting the validity of what remained. But Bachman the man of faith *began* with the answer. By selecting only the evidence that served his religious purpose and disregarding the rest, he claimed to prove what he already believed was true. When it came to explaining the origin and condition of the human species and the place of black people in that explanation, Bachman the scientist gave way to Bachman the minister of the Gospel. The only thing he really proved was that he could not be both a man of science and a man of faith. If the classic definition of "faith" was then (as it is now) "belief in the unknown," then the overwhelming majority of Protestant Americans were indeed, at least in matters of religion and race, people of faith.

The advocates of unity were right about humankind's springing from a common ancestor, but wrong about the identity of that ancestor. Of course, the critics of unity were also correct in their assertion that it was simply impossible for the great variety of races to have developed in the six thousand years since Adam and Eve. The former argued from a position of faith and rejected anything that was not compatible with their religious beliefs. The latter trusted their observations and reasoning ability but still came to an incorrect conclusion because they were unable to contemplate the existence of humanity outside the biblical model. The Christian's justification for black slavery was based on—and reinforced by—a monumental ignorance over the length of time it would take to change an entire population's skin color. But the idea took hold because, in the first place, the Christian never doubted God's power to do anything and, perhaps more to the point, it fit in nicely with the status quo and with what the defenders of slavery wanted to believe.[76]

The doctrine of polygenesis not only conflicted with the belief that all of humankind had descended from Noah's sons, a belief that at least a few Christians had already discarded as archaic myth, but it threatened to undermine the foundations of Christianity itself by implicitly questioning the universal assumption that the Bible was the divine word of God. Since Christian slaveholders would certainly never agree with such a blasphemous implication, they "turned to the story of Ham to legitimize their peculiar institution in a way that was consistent with their biblical constitution."[77]

Like almost every biblical story pertaining to slavery and race, the Curse of Canaan myth had its aberrations. Buckner Payne, that imaginative Nashville publisher who came up with the idea that Christians associated Ham with Africa because they erroneously defined the ancient Hebrew word *ham* to mean "black," devised what he considered to be a simple solution to the disagreement over multiple origins. Writing under the *nom de plume* of "Ariel," Payne argued that the controversy arose because whites had long ago mistakenly assumed that Africans were human beings. The truth is, he went on, black people are nothing more than the highest form of lower animals, occupying a place in the order of primates between the ape and the white man. In other words, they are *beasts!* The beauty of this thesis was its inescapable conclusion. If Africans are not humans, Payne reasoned, they do not have immortal souls and, more to the point, they did not descend from any of Ham's sons. The alternative was obvious: Negroes must have been among the pairs of animals that Noah had carried on the Ark.[78]

While it was certainly a unique explanation and it coincided perfectly with the white belief in black inferiority (not to mention its conformity to the biblical account of the Flood), the idea attracted few supporters because, like the doctrine of polygenesis, it dismissed Noah's curse as irrelevant, a conclusion that conservative Protestants simply could not accept. One of the first to criticize Payne was another Nashville resident, Robert A. Young of the Shelby Female Institute, whose lengthy book title reflected his orthodox Protestantism: *The Negro: A Reply to Ariel. The Negro Belongs to the Genus Homo—He Is a Descendant of Adam and Eve—He Is the Offspring of Ham—He Is Not a Beast, but a Human Being—He Has an Immortal Soul—He May Be Civilized, Enlightened, and Converted to Christianity* (1867).[79] Yet, as different as Payne and Young might have been in their interpretations of Old Testament myths, they shared two fundamental beliefs: that the Genesis account of the Flood was literally true and that black people were inherently inferior.

Although even by nineteenth-century standards, Payne's whole idea seemed too ridiculous to be taken seriously, ridiculous ideas can take on lives of their own. In the turn-of-the-century aftermath to Payne's diatribe, William G. Schell replied to Charles Carroll's sequel to "Ariel" by actually quoting Charles Darwin's *Descent of Man* to refute Carroll's contention that black people are inhuman. "Evolutionists acknowledge the zoological distinctions between man and the apes," Schell wrote in *Is the Negro a Beast?* (1901). "They also acknowledge that the various races, the blacks, the browns, reds, and whites, are all men and proceeded from one common origin."[80] While Darwin's views became the most effective argument against orthodox Christianity's perceptions of the origins of humankind, their support for both biological and social hierarchies did not augur well for dark-skinned peoples. Nevertheless, it had to be the ultimate irony that Schell, in a book produced by the Gospel Trumpet Publishing Company of Moundsville, West Virginia, invoked Darwin, the *bête noire* of Christian fundamentalists, to defend a biblical explanation of human origins.

The Perils of Fundamentalism

Needless to repeat, the widespread acceptance of the Curse of Canaan story rested on an unwavering belief in the literal truth of the Old Testament. Christian fundamentalism was a cornerstone of institutional racism in the United States. Long before the debate over slavery reached the abolitionist level, 266 residents of Brunswick County, Virginia, signed a petition that justified slavery on the basis of Noah's Curse.[81] Except for "rare circles of freethinkers who were regarded as outside the pale of Christianity," as Ralph L. Moellering described them, the vast majority of Americans in the antebellum period took for granted the divine inspiration and literal infallibility of the Bible. "The idea that the races of men were descendants of the three sons of Noah and that their destiny had been prophetically determined by God," the author of a history of the Disciples of Christ wrote, was held by a "large majority" of the Disciples in the early nineteenth century.[82] And they were typical. The various Protestant denominations of America, at least up to 1900, were overwhelmingly fundamentalist in their interpretations of the scriptures. While Old Testament stories like Creation, the Flood, the parting of the Red Sea, Jonah and the whale, Daniel in the lions' den, the feats of Samson, the age of Methuselah, and New Testament events such as the virgin birth of Jesus, feeding the multitudes, raising Lazarus from the dead, and even the Resurrection have been recognized by many modern biblical scholars as allegories, fables, and parables designed to influence the common folk of an ancient and more simple time, they were held to be literally true by most Christians who lived before the twentieth century.[83]

The story of Noah's Curse was so ingrained into the orthodox Protestant mind that it was sometimes invoked far from the pulpit. Speaking before the Mississippi Democratic State Convention in 1859, none other than Jefferson Davis defended chattel slavery and the foreign slave trade by alluding to the "importation of the race of Ham" as a fulfillment of its destiny to be "servant of servants."[84] The story also long outlived the institution it had been called forth to justify. Speaking before the Mississippi Synod of the Presbyterian Church shortly after the United States Supreme Court's landmark desegregation decision in the case of *Brown* v. *Board of Education* (1954), the Reverend G. T. Gillespie reaffirmed his belief in the Genesis account. The white-supremacist Citizens' Council of Greenwood subsequently distributed copies of the address under the title "A Christian View on Segregation."[85] In 1958 Judge Leon M. Bazile of Virginia ordered an interracial couple, Richard and Mildred Loving, to leave the state for twenty-five years as punishment for violating Virginia's anti-miscegenation law, a sentence subsequently upheld by the Virginia State Supreme Court. "Almighty God created the races white, black, yellow, Malay and red, and He placed them on separate continents," Judge Bazile later explained, "and but for the interference with His arrangement there would be no cause for such marriages."[86] In June 1967, the United States Supreme Court, in the case of *Loving* v. *Virginia*, invalidated the anti-miscegenation laws of seventeen southern and border states. But the spirit of Buckner Payne and Charles Carroll has endured in the ravings of people like minister C. E. McLain, whose 1965 vanity book *The Place of Race*—fifty-six pages of incoherent rambling supported by numerous biblical references—is a vivid reminder that the Curse of Canaan idea is alive and well among poorly educated, politically right-wing, and fanatical Christian fundamentalists.[87]

It should also be remembered that the Christian slaveholder assumed that all forms of servitude, whether ancient or modern, were essentially the same and that the societies in which they flourished were not significantly different from one another. If comparisons to biblical times were to have any meaning, conditions in all eras would have had to be comparable. But when the periods in question were forty centuries apart, such an assumption seemed absurd to the critics of slavery. Some antislavery clergymen noted, for example, that it was not unusual in Old Testament days for poor men to sell themselves into service, a practice more akin to the indentured servitude of seventeenth-century England and America than to the involuntary enslavement of Africans. Even more important to these critics when considering biblical slavery was the special status of the people of Israel. The Jews "were the select people of God in a unique situation," one religious writer noted. "They were God's chosen instruments in meting out punishment against the 'seven nations' whose abominable transgressions evoked God's wrath." But such a limited and exclusive "permission for slavery" in Old Testament times did not necessarily mean human bondage could be justified in other times and places. The Christian defenders of slavery also assumed that scriptural translations were historically accurate and, probably most important of all, that the Holy Bible was a divinely inspired work whose authority and authenticity no one questioned. This created a dilemma for the abolitionists. Most of them were no less enthusiastic in their belief in the divine origins of the Bible than the staunchest defenders of slavery. Gilbert Haven, whom Timothy L. Smith identified as "the best-known Methodist abolitionist," called for complete racial equality, including the right to intermarry. There was probably no more militant spokesman for antislavery before the Civil War, or outspoken champion of complete racial equality afterward, than Haven; but even he clung to the "absolute oneness of the race of man, in Adam, Noah, and Christ."[88] In other words, the disputants could be poles apart in their interpretations of scriptures and how they applied to slavery, but there was no disagreement that all of humanity descended from a common ancestor and that the Bible was the Word of God.

Herein lay a crucial factor in understanding the history of religion and racism in America. Since most people professed to believe in a Judeo-Christian God—and there is no evidence that they did not—they were constrained by their acceptance of the Bible as the only source of truth. In order for scriptural defenses of slavery to have any validity, everyone had to share this assumption. The upshot was that the critics of slavery were handicapped by their inability, or unwillingness, to challenge the Bible itself. It was easy to accuse a Presbyterian minister from South Carolina of distorting scriptures to suit his purposes; but it was very difficult to take the position that Noah and the Apostle Paul, or, for that matter, even Jesus, were simply wrong. Any suggestion that the Bible's teachings were false would be considered blasphemous—and both critics and defenders of slavery knew that. It was not by accident that most abolitionists chose not to challenge head-on the widespread and long-held belief in the Curse of Canaan myth but rather eluded the issue by simply shaping their arguments to conform to the Old Testament calendar, contending that the Canaanites had never settled in Africa and that black people were, in fact, the descendants of Cush, one of Canaan's brothers. This meant, of course, that many people opposed to bondage believed, like most proslavery Christian conservatives, that an entire race of people could materialize in less than two thousand years. And it did not matter anyway, as Goldwin Smith had suggested, because the curse had expired when Abraham's descendants lost their inheritance to the land of Canaan.[89] The First Amendment to the United States Constitution may have guaranteed each person the right to be free from the suasions of any religion; but in reality there was little respect in America, at least prior to the twentieth century, for any person who wanted to take a public stand based on a refutation of the Holy Bible.

To the researcher, one of the greatest problems in using the Bible as a historical document has always been separating mythology from fact. Generally, historians recognize that major portions of the scriptures cannot pass the tests of credibility that modern scholarship demands. Thus the controversy between the religious conviction that the Bible is the revealed word of God and the academic proposition that it is "the human literary product of an ancient sociopolitical and religious community" cannot be resolved because there is no common ground for reconciliation.[90] The one is an article of faith not subject to criticism or modification. The other is an intellectual hypothesis subject to criticism, interpretation, and revision—and even rejection—because it views scriptures as simply the writing of men about their own time.

Yet, while it is not an exaggeration to point out that the overwhelming majority of the American people living before the twentieth century believed in a perfect Bible, there were critics of slavery who insisted that the scriptures contained serious errors and distortions and who were not afraid to speak out publicly. Henry Clarke Wright, a follower of abolitionist William Lloyd Garrison, characterized any biblical passage that could be interpreted to support slavery as a "Self-Evident Falsehood," and Charles Stearns concluded that the Old Testament was no more divinely inspired than the Koran or the Book of Mormon. Shortly before the beginning of the Civil War, English traveler Isabella Lucy Bishop reported that Wendell Phillips had told a New England antislavery convention that both George

Washington and Jesus Christ were "traitors to humanity; the one as author of the Constitution, the other of the New Testament, both of which encourage slavery."[91]

Needless to say, this kind of militant abolitionism was not supported by the churches, and most Christians, clerical and lay, repudiated any argument that called into question the Bible itself.[92] The error, they would say, was not in the word but in the mind of the reader. Nevertheless, the fact that there were men like Wright and Stearns illustrates clearly that nothing in Christianity was above criticism, including Christ himself.

Since a literal reading of the Bible left no doubt that some kind of bond servitude was widespread in biblical times and that it was not specifically condemned anywhere in the scriptures, the burden of proof was on the shoulders of the critics of slavery. "The slaveholder's case based on the Bible stood until refuted," William Sumner Jenkins pointed out. "In order to rebut its conclusiveness and make out a contrary case, the anti-slavery moralist had to depart from a strict construction of the literal text." Fortunately for the antislavery cause, the abolitionist preacher was not usually placed in the uncomfortable position of contradicting scriptures because proslavery religious arguments tended to emphasize Old Testament precedents while he depended mainly on the New Testament lessons of a loving Jesus.[93] Unfortunately for the slave, most Protestant Americans on both sides of the debate believed the Bible to be literally true. To challenge traditional interpretations of the scripture by pointing to implicit lessons was to undermine everything that fundamentalist Christians held dear. To them, the Bible was explicit; it implied nothing.

In the twentieth century, Protestant fundamentalism may no longer be a major factor in the cultivation of racist attitudes (except for a few militant white-supremacists who claim a Christian authority), but an examination of its character does nonetheless reveal a rigidity of thought that in earlier times did not bode well for racial minorities. To be so inflexible about the meaning of the written word—a written word that has passed through many translations since its origins and that continues to be subject to a wide range of interpretations—suggests a mind set that was relatively unaffected by rational arguments and scientific evidence.[94] Beliefs and habits, like just about everything else, evolved over the centuries, but there always seemed to be some things that hardly ever changed. It is not unreasonable to assume that the person who refused to be influenced by the facts was the one least likely to acknowledge changes.

This obduracy was not always immediately evident, but its consequences were certainly far-reaching. It is not unfair to ask if those Southern Baptists who believed that women should not be ordained because of scriptural sanctions on sex roles could be expected to embrace an equalitarian view on race. More generally, could the members of any Christian denomination in which women were consigned to a position subordinate to men—such as Roman Catholics, Seventh-Day Adventists, and Mormons—overcome earlier views on black people without continuing to nurture some reservations? Was the world supposed to believe that Mormon president Spencer W. Kimball's claim to a divine revelation, in which he alleged that God told him to declare black men eligible to enter the priesthood, instantly eradicated racist thinking and habits among church members? Even the Catholic Church, which has made sweeping changes and which on some issues—at least in the United States—has occupied the most liberal positions, still clutches tenaciously to the tradition of a celibate, all-male priesthood. The common underlying question in all of these examples is: If the insidious blade of discrimination could, for whatever reason, cut sharply in one direction, could it not swing back quietly in another? Such a question assumes that an institution—especially one as comprehensive and influential as a church—that so easily relegated one segment of the human race to a subservient status might not fully escape the inclination to do the same to others. Discrimination easily became a habit. Laws changed and human behavior evolved; but once a long-established notion became tucked away in some corner of the mind, it was not easily dislodged. Not even by a revelation.

Part Two

RACE

FOUR WHOLE CHRISTIAN OR NONE

I want to be ready, I want to be ready,
I want to be ready to walk in Jerusalem
Just like John.

O John, O John, what do you say? . . .
That I'll be there at the coming day.
John said the city was just four square,
And he declared he'd meet me there,
Walk in Jerusalem just like John.

A SLAVE SPIRITUAL
Author unknown

Baptism and the Common Law

To cite the Bible in defense of human bondage was one thing. To impose upon the bondsman the religion of that Bible was quite another. Asking the slave to embrace the "inerrant" teaching of the same scriptures that had been used to justify his enslavement was the crowning affront of evangelical Christianity. When he sought to convert his slaves, the slaveholder was, in effect, asking them to tighten their own shackles. The result was the fragmented adaptation of a faith that its most zealous adherents had insisted was founded on eternal "truths." To the slaveholder, Christianity was a divine blueprint for class delineation and social order. To his antislavery critic, it was a foundation for the liberation of oppressed peoples. But to the enslaved it could be a sanctuary from the burdens of bondage, a political rationalization intended to appease the master, or absolutely nothing at all.

As religion and race became increasingly entangled, the debate over baptism and bondage provided an all-too-vivid look at the corruptibility of Christianity. In the seventeenth century many Europeans defended the enslavement of heathens because they considered it a convenient and expeditious method of bringing pagans into the Christian "sphere of influence." The importance of winning souls to Christ overrode all other considerations. Indeed, to some people the only valid reason for enslaving heathens was to facilitate their conversion. Bondage was an unpleasant but necessary expedient because entering the "democracy of grace" would quite properly be followed by "enfranchisement." Obviously, the principle itself was unjust because, despite its ostensibly good intent, it rested on the premise that there was nothing wrong with enslaving certain people, at least temporarily, so long as the ultimate objective was morally valid.

Of course, the logic of this argument cut both ways. If the purpose of enslavement was to convert the heathen, the moment he embraced the faith he should have been given his freedom. It was an idea that, as William Sumner Jenkins put it, "grew out of the old patristic theory that slavery was based on man's original sin rather than upon nature," and it presumably had the strong support of James I, King of England from 1603 to 1625.[1] If that sin was washed away, according to the theory, the basis for enslavement ceased to exist. (But that also meant that in a perfect world there would be no slaves and therefore no one to do the slaves' work.) Accordingly, early efforts by colonial missionaries to baptize bondsmen stumbled over the English common-law principle, which dated at least from the Protestant Reformation, that one cannot enslave a Christian.[2] Needless to say, if the common law had been strictly observed, the big loser would have been the slaveholder. Unfortunately for the slave, the slaveholders, with their social prestige and economic and political power, pinioned the rule by simply denying missionaries access to their bondsmen.

It was at this point that, as has often been the case, expedience overcame principle. Clergymen learned quickly that they would continue to enjoy access to the slave population only if they stopped insisting on compliance with the common law, and some, to ingratiate themselves further with the masters, became staunch defenders of slavery. As outrageous as it may seem to a liberal Christian of the twentieth century, the fact is that more than a few of the Protestant clergy in colonial America believed that the African's salvation was dependent on his remaining a slave, a tribute to the realization that the power of the purse was mightier than the power of the pulpit.

If there were very many Protestant ministers who were troubled by this practical abrogation of the common law—not to mention the moral contradiction of upholding human bondage in order to win souls to a loving and merciful Jesus—their relief was not long in coming. Perhaps most compelling was the pronouncement of James's grandson, Charles II, who condemned as "impiety" the practice of denying baptism to slaves "out of a mistaken opinion" that it made them "*ipso facto* free."[3] The problem of insincere conversions made it easy for some clergymen to rationalize their dilemma. "If freedom was a reward of baptism, could any slave resist it, no matter how rudimentary his theology," Helen Tunnicliff Catterall asked in her monumental work on slavery and the law, "or could any masters welcome it?" Worried about just such a situation, the lower house of the Maryland legislature in 1663–64—barely ten years after the colony was founded—proposed "to draw up an Act obligeing negros to serve *durante vita* . . . for the prevencion of the dammage Masters of such Slaves may susteyne by such Slaves pretending to be Christned And soe pleade the lawe of England." Three years later, so that masters "may more carefully endeavour the propagation of christianity," the Virginia General Assembly, without alluding to the matter of insincere confessions of faith, adopted an act declaring that "the conferring of baptisme doth not alter the condition of the person as to his bondage or freedome."[4]

Despite the unequivocal wording of both laws, officials in these two colonies seemed to have trouble convincing themselves. In 1692 and again in 1715 Maryland lawmakers enacted measures affirming the original act, while the Virginia law of 1667 was reenacted or enlarged at least three times—in 1682 (with a proviso also applying the exclusion from the common law specifically to Indians, Muslims, and other "pagans"), 1705, and 1748. As English settlers in the plantation colonies moved south and west, the law went with them. In 1670, only seven years after the Crown had granted eight investors and friends of the Court a charter for the colony of Carolina, the "Fundamental Constitutions" of that province extended to the slave the privilege of church membership but would not exempt him "from the Civil Dominion his master has over him." Lest anyone for a moment doubt the meaning of that exclusion, legislators in South Carolina, like their brethren in Maryland and Virginia, passed confirming laws in 1690 and 1712.[5] And this was just the beginning.

The relative scarcity of slaves in the northern colonies should have meant less concern over the connection between baptism and emancipation, but that was not necessarily the case. Because of the close interlocking of church membership and political participation in New England, some Puritans were quite anxious about the civil liberties a baptized slave might claim. To deflect potential problems over the situation, the Puritans granted slaves some rights, including the right to marry. Between 1631 and 1664, all church members in Massachusetts claimed the right to vote, although black converts apparently were excluded from ecclesiastical functions.

But, if Rhode Island was the first New England colony to have a law denying freedom after conversion, it was not because the leaders of the other colonies had not tried. In May 1694, a group of ministers in Massachusetts petitioned the governor and the legislature for the passage of a law declaring that baptism did not change the slave's status. The petition was denied, but that did not diminish the worries of at least some church leaders over what they considered to be the unpleasant side effects of slave conversion. On the other hand, the eminent Cotton Mather argued that all of the fuss was unnecessary because, he said, no law specifically calling for the emancipation of converted bondsmen had ever existed and, like King

Charles, he criticized slaveowners who used that as an excuse to deny baptism to slaves.[6] In *The Negro Christianized* (1706), Mather asked "What *Law* is it, that Sets the *Baptized Slave* at *Liberty*?" The "*Law of Christianity*" does no such thing. There was, in fact, a longstanding de facto recognition of slavery because, he reasoned, English laws acknowledging slavery had been passed after many slaves had already become Christians, and those laws had not been repealed.[7] There simply was no basis for the apprehension over emancipation, he concluded, and therefore no reason to call for legal sanctions against baptism.

Nineteenth-century legal scholar John Codman Hurd argued in his massive *The Law of Freedom and Bondage in the United States* (1858–62), that the fact that English common law recognized slavery in one part of the empire "is a proof that the state did not at that time regard such slavery as contrary to Christianity, or being *for that reason* forbidden by the common law." In time almost everyone denied that the common-law principle had ever existed. A 1671 amendment of the original Maryland law had called the fear of emancipation an "ungrounded apprehension." Similarly, in 1704 the New Jersey colonial legislature described the idea as a "groundless Opinion," the exact term used two years later by New York lawmakers in "An Act to incourage the Baptizing of Negro, Indian and Mulatto Slaves."[8]

That there continued to be a great deal of confusion over what so many people referred to as only an "opinion" should have surprised no one. After all, if Mather and the others denied that a conversion-emancipation law had ever existed, just what law was it that the Maryland legislators had referred to when they insisted that baptized slaves could not "soe pleade the lawe of England"? Even more to the point, why pass laws repudiating something that did not exist? It was these very contradictions, of course, that fed the continuing uncertainty. Despite the Carolina law of 1670 calling for the continued endorsement of converted bondsmen and the South Carolina confirmation of 1690, Francis Le Jau, a missionary for the Anglican Church's Society for the Propagation of the Gospel in Foreign Parts (SPG), thought it necessary in 1709 to reinforce those mandates by requiring every slave preparing for baptism to take the following oath: "You declare in the presence of God and before this congregation that you do not ask for the Holy Baptism out of any desire to free yourself from the duty and obedience you owe to your master while you live; but merely for the good of your soul and to partake of the grace and blessings promised to the members of the Church of Christ." Since the law did not appear to allow for exceptions, one can only wonder why Le Jau thought such an oath was necessary. As it happened, South Carolina's slaveholders were similarly apprehensive. In 1712 the colonial legislature, still obviously nervous about a possible misunderstanding of the earlier rules, proclaimed that "Negro or Indian slaves" who were baptized "shall not thereby be manumitted or set free," and that they "shall remain and continue in the same state and condition."[9]

With clerics like Le Jau showing the way, it was only a matter of time before legal principle became canon law. When Bishop of London Edmund Gibson proclaimed in 1727 that "Christianity does not make the least alteration in civil property," the Anglican Church became the first Protestant denomination to adopt a formal no-emancipation policy. Invoking the Pauline dualism of body and soul, Gibson, in one of his two famous letters on the subject, declared: "The Freedom which Christianity gives, is a Freedom from the Bondage of Sin and Satan, and from the Dominion of Men's Lusts and Passions and inordinate Desires; but as to their outward Condition, whatever that was before, whether bond or free, their being baptised, and becoming Christians, makes no manner of Change in it."[10] All that really mattered, he asserted, was to escape the eternal "enslavement" of damnation. It followed that the African should cheerfully accept physical enslavement in this world because it was transitory and of little consequence. Baptism guaranteed freedom in the next world; everything else was trifling.

Although historians have usually viewed the problem as a conflict between English common law and colonial profit, the English were not the only Protestants in colonial North America to grapple with the dilemma—or the only ones guilty of duplicity in resolving it. Dutch-owned slaves began arriving in New Amsterdam about 1626.[11] Since the first African immigrants to settle in Virginia seven years earlier appear to have been indentured servants, there is a probability that the first real slaves in what later became the United States were Dutch-owned, not English-owned. Within twelve years, the Dutch Reformed Church had taken a position on slavery and emancipation, albeit an ambivalent one. "As early as 1638," one church leader argued, the primary reason for enslaving Africans was "to bring them to the knowledge of God and salvation."[12]

But while the Dutch did not have to deal with the dictates of English common law, they did have to respond to the dictates of common sense and decency. If the slaves "want to submit themselves to the lovely yoke of our Lord Jesus Christ," church official Dominie Udemans wrote in the same year in his *'t Geesttelyk Roer van 't Coopmansschip*, "Christian love requires that they be discharged from the yoke of human slavery." This, however, was only an opinion, and the Dutch in fact were no more conscientious about emancipating baptized slaves than anyone else. Within two years of the English conquest of New Netherland in 1664 (without either side firing a shot), the new government declared that the "Duke's

Laws" for the colony of New York "shall not extend to sett at Liberty Any Negroe or Indian Servant who shall turne Christian after he shall have been bought by Any Person." Similarly, the Dutch Lutheran church in New Netherland had launched a mission program for imported Africans, but its effort did not usually include any suggestion of emancipation. Arriving in New York in 1725 to serve a Dutch congregation in the Hudson Valley, the German pastor William Christopher Berkenmeyer, after acquiring slaves for himself, "inserted in the church constitution of 1735 a provision that baptism does not 'dissolve the tie of obedience.' "[13] Apparently, the "Duke's Laws" of 1666 and the New York law of 1706 were not enough for Berkenmeyer.

To the Christian missionary, then, ensuring the salvation of heathens took precedence over every other consideration. For example, SPG leaders insisted that making a Christian of the slave was far more important than making a free man of him. It seemed never to occur to most missionaries that giving the slave his freedom *first* might have made Christianity more attractive, thereby facilitating his conversion. Of course, the power of profits made the former impossible, the latter only difficult. Even the pious Moravians, who were among the most active Christians working to convert slaves during the colonial period, agreed that where "their salvation was regarded, it was under the circumstances, proper to own and employ them."[14]

And the law, not to be left behind where the prosperity of the realm was concerned, kept pace with the ecclesiastical position. Two years after Bishop Gibson's pronouncement, Attorney-General Sir Philip Yorke in London, responding to British and colonial merchants who were asking "for his opinion on the matter" and to a request from Bishop George Berkeley for a ruling, declared that "baptism doth not bestow freedom . . . nor make any alteration in [the slave's] temporal condition."[15] And yet the common-law principle persisted, a consequence, perhaps, of the fact that some of the English court cases that addressed the issue between 1667 and 1772 were ambiguous.[16] It is not unreasonable to assume that revoking the common-law provision for emancipating a converted heathen could be troubling to those who believed that conversion was the only reason for his enslavement. "If conversion to Christianity did not change slaves' civil status, then heathenism was not the basis of slavery," one historian pointed out, "and if it were not, then what was?" As late as 1781 the legislature of Prince Edward Island in Canada, still unsure of the law, considered it necessary to reconfirm the rule that baptism had no effect on a slave's status.[17] It should surprise no one that the lingering doubts over the converted slave's status were always resolved in the slaveholder's favor. In the last analysis, what really mattered was not the validity of some nebulous quasi-religious principle with uncertain origins but the interests of the political and economic élite.

If the Christian missionary's primary objective was to save souls at all costs, then the controversy over baptism revealed just how high that cost would be, a cost, since he was not paying it, he willingly accepted. In a later variation of this theme, some northern missionaries who had been sent by the American Board of Commissioners for Foreign Missions to work among the Cherokees and Choctaws, opposed the demands of their superiors to take a stand against Indian ownership of slaves because, they argued, any interference with the Indians' social institutions would reduce the number of Indians converted to Christianity. Like the seventeenth-century missionaries to slaves, these nineteenth-century missionaries to Indians were perfectly willing to "sacrifice" the black person's freedom for the sake of winning souls to Christ—and in this case it was not even the slave's soul that was the object of the missionary's attention. As it happened, there were also some practical reasons for not antagonizing the Indians. Most of them lived in sparsely populated areas and the mission workers were convinced, for numerous reasons, that slave labor was essential to the economic and spiritual welfare of the tribes. If the Indians were forced to give up their slaves, the missionaries feared, the entire mission program would almost certainly collapse. It was virtually the same argument that could be made for all slaveholders, and critics condemned it for the same reasons. The American Board of Commissioners had been founded and was controlled by northern churchmen—mostly Congregationalists and Presbyterians—who were among the leaders in the emerging assault on slavery. As the Protestant church's circle of influence widened, antislavery clergy and laymen "questioned whether it could maintain an institutional Christianity without forthrightly pronouncing slavery a sin," Robert T. Lewit wrote. "To evade this question, in their eyes, was to evade Christian morality."[18]

The problem for the missionaries to the Indians was compounded by the fact that many of them had gone south early in the century before abolitionism had become a dominant issue among northern Protestants, and they therefore had remained isolated from the rapidly growing Christian antislavery movement. The result was an impasse. "The missionaries failed to realize that their northern brethren saw freedom, or rather, the absence of slavery, as a prerequisite for the existence of a Christian society," Lewit concluded. "On the other hand, the missionaries did not see in their acceptance of slavery any compromise in their Christianity." Since "acceptance" was tantamount to endorsement, these representatives of northern churches had, in the eyes of their brethren, adopted the conventional southern religious view justifying slavery, which, besides being antithetical to their own churches' teachings, was an example of how a person with ostensibly altruistic intentions could easily accommodate the forces of his social environment, however anathematic they might have been. With both sides unyielding, the outcome was not difficult to foresee. At its annual meeting in 1860, the American Board of Commissioners ratified a proposal to discontinue support of the remaining Cherokee mission stations. The old missionaries quit the scene never understanding why.[19]

It needs to be remembered that the ease with which white Americans reconciled the contradiction between human bondage and Christian love was just one part of the larger question of justifying slavery in general. "True, it had come to be the general conviction in England and upon the Continent, that Christians ought not to be reduced to slavery," the Reverend Jesse T. Peck of Albany, New York, wrote in 1868; "but captives in war and accredited pagans were not included in this exemption." Enslavement was exactly what "the *law of nations* for Christian powers" mandated for "prisoners in war with heathen and infidel nations," one of Peck's contemporaries, legal scholar John Codman Hurd, declared. From the very first, Peck insisted, Africans had not been brought to the New World to be Christianized and emancipated. Of course, feelings of guilt could be easily assuaged by the belief that the black person was culturally degenerate and that enslavement in a Christian society was therefore an improvement in his condition. None other than George Whitefield, the leading Anglican of the Great Awakening in the 1740s, openly defended his purchase of a plantation and slaves in South Carolina on the grounds that the enslavement of blacks made their conversions possible. Horrified by the terrible conditions on the slave-trading ships, educator Emma Willard nonetheless insisted in 1845 that the Africans' welfare in the colonies was "better than it was elsewhere; incomparably better than it had been in their own country, where scarce a gleam of moral light illuminated the darkness of their minds."[20] After the Revolution, the opposition to the slave trade—as much a consequence of political and economic fears over large concentrations of blacks as of moral indignation—generated enough heat among the delegates to the Constitutional Convention in 1787 to make the issue one of only three constitutional references to slavery.[21] But the belief that the African was better off as a slave in America than as a free man in Africa lingered, and the abolition of the trade in 1807 did little to change that belief. On the eve of the Civil War, for example, the Augusta (Georgia) *Despatch* defended slave smuggling by describing one shipment as a "cargo of sturdy laborers, delivered from the darkness and barbarism of Africa, to be elevated and Christianized on our shores."[22]

The rationale—or, more accurately, rationalization—that slaves benefited from the Christianizing influence of bondage was even endorsed by some blacks. After moving to Liberia to study theology, a Caribbean-born convert named Edward Wilmot Blyden argued that enslavement was God's way of elevating heathen Africans to a higher level of civilization and preparing them for conversion and mission work in their native land. No less surprising was the action of black Christians at the 1856 General Convention of the African Methodist Episcopal Church, founded earlier in the century by northern black Methodists protesting the racist attitudes of their white brethren. The delegates rejected a proposal to bar slaveholding members from the denomination because they feared that masters would retaliate by denying the clergy access to slaves—a justification virtually identical to that of the early colonial missionaries who had acquiesced in the slaveowners' opposition to baptism.[23] Since it was unlikely that any slaveholder would seek membership in a black church, one can only wonder why the matter ever came up. In any event, the widespread belief that the African benefited from slavery endured long after the institution itself ceased to exist. There is more than a little irony in the fact that an idea that had been conceived as a rationalization for a morally reprehensible practice acquired a life all of its own—the lie told so often that the liar believed it.

In contrast to the Protestants in the English colonies, the Catholic missionaries in the New World territories of Spain, France, and Portugal were unencumbered by the sanctions of English common law and thus were not faced with an emancipation dilemma. Under the Code Noir of 1685, French slaveholders were required to baptize and provide Christian instruction for all slaves. When Ferdinand and Isabella approved the introduction of slavery into Hispaniola (modern Haiti and the Dominican Republic), they advised Governor Nicolás de Ovando to admit only "Negro slaves or other slaves who were born in the power of Christians, our subjects and natives." In other words, slaves who had been born free in non-Spanish territories could not be brought to the island. Later in the century, Africans shipped directly to all Spanish colonies in the transatlantic slave trade had to be baptized before they were allowed to disembark. Of course, mass baptisms for the purpose of qualifying for migration could hardly be called genuine. When the Jesuits arrived in 1572, they "manifested an active interest in the spiritual lives of the slaves," and "some of the larger plantations and haciendas employed resident priests to minister to the needs of all the people, including the slaves."[24] Having had frequent contacts with the African world long before the time of Columbus, the Spanish and Portuguese enjoyed a familiarity with slavery that could be traced back to the old Roman slave code. "Large numbers of Negroes mixed freely in slavery" in both Muslim and Christian Spain, according to Herbert S. Klein, and "the Iberian peoples had long accepted the individuality, personality, and coequality of the Negro."[25] Accordingly, the closest thing to a crisis of conscience was resolved when, in 1516, Bishop Bartolomé de Las Casas proposed the importation of "Negroes or other slaves" in order to deflect pressure to enslave the Indians, an action that, an American clergyman wrote in 1868, "sought to mitigate the horrors of Indian servitude by simply changing the victims." In fairness to Las Casas, it should be noted that he subsequently renounced the proposal.[26]

Otherwise, throughout colonial Latin America, Dominicans, Jesuits, and others worked to reduce the harshness of slavery and to provide religious education and counsel. The upshot was that the English churches could win souls among slaves but could not proclaim the equality of all Christians; while the Latin American churches could declare all people equal in the eyes of God without threatening the legality of slavery. This is not a qualitative comparison, and there were certainly few slaves who stopped to ponder the relative merits of the two systems; but at least it can be said that in the Catholic colonies religious leaders were not persuaded to abandon a fundamental principle in the name of convenience.

But the Catholic slaveholder deserved little praise. Recent research has shown that the differences between the slave systems of the Protestant and Catholic New Worlds were not as great as had been commonly believed. In the urban centers of Latin America where church authority was strong, "the treatment of slaves was indeed more humane than in areas of the American South," but in the outlying regions, where slavery was more extensive and the church had less influence, there was little to distinguish the Catholic sugar grower in Brazil from the Methodist cotton planter in Georgia. In her study of the Roman Catholic church in Louisiana under French jurisdiction, Mary Veronica Miceli contended that black religious life there "was far less harsh than that to the east, and also than later in Louisiana's history," because baptism for slaves "was the key not only to spiritual freedom from sin, but also opened to the slave access to all the Church had to offer."[27] Such a comparison implies that slaves in Protestant America benefited little, if at all, from their association with the church. But the same could be said of the Catholic slaves in Louisiana; "spiritual freedom" was not freedom and "access" to the church was not citizenship. Miceli, undoubtedly influenced by her devotion to her faith, ignored altogether the fact that the Catholic slaveholder was under no pressure to emancipate his slaves—even in theory—and thus was never reluctant to convert as many slaves as possible and keep them in bondage. Unlike many of their Protestant counterparts in the English New World, Catholic missionaries saw no sin in enslaving Africans.[28] It is a hair-splitting distinction, but it needs to be made. There may have been few black Protestants whose faith saved them from enslavement, but there were certainly *no* black Catholics who were so fortunate.

By the nineteenth century, the American slaveholder's view on baptism had turned the original common-law position on its head. While many English Protestants in the early colonial period had viewed the slave's conversion to Christianity as at least a theoretical justification for emancipation, defenders of bondage in the decades prior to the Civil War, extending Whitefield's logic to its inevitable conclusion, considered enslavement an essential condition that benefited the black man because, as the editor of the *Despatch* noted, it exposed the heathen to Christianity and other civilizing influences. In other words, while some people in the seventeenth century considered slavery an unfortunate means to a worthwhile end, the nineteenth-century Protestant defenders of slavery were convinced that bondage was what made the slave's salvation possible. It was the ultimate rationalization.

From the 1830s onward, the southern "proslavery" argument was filled with paeans to the importance of slavery as the best way of getting Africans to heaven. In 1852, Dr. Samuel A. Cartwright of New Orleans and the University of Louisiana, one of the South's most fanatical critics of abolitionism, insisted that it was impossible to "Christianize the negro without the intervention of slavery." Reminiscing about his plantation days in Missouri, former slave William Wells Brown recalled that his master, who became obsessed with converting his slaves after he had "got religion," believed that bondage was God's way of reaching the heathen Africans. "I regard our negroes as given to us by an All Wise Providence for their especial benefit," Brown's owner declared, "and we should impart to them Christian civilization." Even critics of slavery supported the cause. Episcopal Bishop Chase of Illinois, in a letter to a group of English bishops, agreed that the clergy could "tolerate the evil because of the good they could do for the souls of the slaves."[29] It was an argument that, in fact, had been articulated two centuries earlier by the first Christian missionary to the slaves who found it expedient to brush aside the old common-law principle. The systematic defense of slavery may not have emerged until the second quarter of the nineteenth century, but long before that the master had convinced himself that he was doing the slave a favor.

Christian slaveholders, of course, had no monopoly on greed. As Orlando Patterson pointed out, "all of the monotheistic religions revealed striking similarities in their teachings, practices, and hypocrisies." While all of them repudiated the idea that conversion mandated emancipation, all of them also insisted that the slave should be converted before he would be eligible for emancipation. "Except in isolated cases none of these religions seem to have had any influence on the rate of conversion," Patterson concluded. "Only when economic and political expediency coincided with piety did religion seem to count."[30] Which meant, of course, that it did not really count then either. The ultimate rationalization made it unmistakably clear that when the spiritual interests of God conflicted with the material interests of men, God did not have a prayer.

Compliance or Defiance

It needs to be remembered that the slaveowner's interest in Christianizing his slaves was profoundly influenced by the fact that the taproot of the slave system was *power.* This meant that a slave's religion had to be compatible with that power or he would ultimately challenge the master's authority. Accordingly, in the last two decades of the seventeenth century, authorities in London instructed the governors of New York, Virginia, and Maryland to do everything possible to facilitate the conversion of the bondsmen, although the slave population's growth surge was still to come. One of the Established Church's earliest advocates of conversion was Morgan Godwyn, "the angry clergyman," who had served in both the British West Indies and Virginia and whose *The Negro's and Indians* [sic] *Advocate* (1680), Herbert S. Klein wrote, "created a good deal of sentiment."[31] As it happened, Godwyn was to become a harbinger for the church's missionary arm, the Society for the Propagation of the Gospel in Foreign Parts.

Beginning in 1702 and continuing even beyond the American War for Independence, the SPG sent clergymen and teachers to North America to work for the conversion of slaves and, through thousands of copies of its *Annual Sermons*, urged slaveholders "to encourage and promote the instruction of their Negroes in the Christian faith."[32] It was an objective that, at least in theory, made sense. Once masters were convinced that conversion did not mean emancipation, it was understandable that at least some of them would want their bondsmen to become Christians if for no other reason than to induce passivity. But even more fundamental was the fear that any religion other than the master's was potentially a platform for resistance. In order for a slave society to flourish without the constant threat of rebellion, logic seemed to dictate that the only religion that could be permitted to exist was the master's. From this it followed that the ideal condition, at least for slaveholders, was for all slaves to become Christians.

While the fear of slave rebellions may have been foremost in the minds of many masters, most missionaries also saw nothing wrong with trying to make a passive Christian out of what they perceived as a potentially dangerous heathen. In *The Negro Christianized* (1706), Cotton Mather told slaveholders in New England that a "dutiful," "patient," and "faithful" Christian servant would do nothing "that may justly displease you."[33] It was an argument that, in a rather perverse way, even appealed to Quaker

William Edmundson, one of the most militant critics of slavery in the colonial era, who warned that masters could not afford *not* to encourage their bondsmen to become Christians. Threatened with arrest on the grounds that his views might inspire a rebellion, Edmundson defended his proposal with the novel but pragmatic contention that "the only way to keep blacks *from* cutting white throats was to make them loving Christians." During the Great Awakening in the mid-eighteenth century, Anglican George Whitefield and Presbyterian Samuel Davies were among those who argued that Christian slaves made better servants, and that the masters' interests would be advanced if all slaves were converted.[34] It was an idea that found a home in the hearts of some of the most influential Protestant leaders of the colonial era.

It was also an idea that would not go away. Following the aborted Denmark Vesey revolt of 1822, Charleston Baptist leader Richard Furman, addressing the governor of South Carolina on behalf of the state Baptist convention, argued that religious instruction and biblical lessons could prevent slave uprisings.[35] Seven years later, in a widely publicized speech before the Agricultural Society of South Carolina, Charles Cotesworth Pinckney, nephew and namesake of the one-time Federalist presidential candidate, argued that if all slaves were converted to Christianity "a greater proportion of domestic happiness would prevail, and render them more contented with their situation, and more anxious to promote their owner's welfare."[36] Describing the intolerable conditions that he had fled thirteen years earlier, William Wells Brown in 1847 recalled that while he was owned by Dr. John Young, religious teaching consisted of "teaching the slave that he must never strike a white man, that God made him for a slave; and that, when whipped, he must not find fault—for the Bible says, 'He that knoweth his master's will and doeth it not, shall be beaten with many stripes!' and slaveholders find such religion very profitable to them."[37] As a former slave named West Turner told a Federal Writers' Project interviewer in the 1930s, the only thing he was taught in Sunday school was to be "nice to massa and missus; don't be mean; be obedient and work hard."[38]

As it happened, masters who urged or even merely permitted their slaves to convert—for whatever reason—remained a small minority of the slaveholding population. Despite the pleas of churchmen like Godwyn, Mather, Whitefield, and Davies, the overwhelming majority of slaveholders during the colonial period, Dutch as well as English, tenaciously resisted attempts to bring Christianity to their bondsmen, and for a far more compelling reason than an unwillingness to comply with a common law that everyone ignored anyway. Similarly, later arguments from prominent Southerners like Pinckney persuaded few masters. Historian Lawrence W.

Levine's observation that "whites debated the wisdom" of converting their slaves was more than an understatement.[39] Indeed, the slaveowner's hostility to religious instruction for his bondsmen was no less furious than if slavery itself had been attacked. When Morgan Godwyn "urged Virginia masters to do their religious duty by their slaves," he was answered by angry retorts demanding, "*What I had to do with their servants?*"[40]

Almost from the first day, the letters and reports of SPG missionaries in America to their superiors in London complained of the virtually universal refusal of masters to permit their slaves to hear the gospel. "The conversion of slaves . . . seldom happens," missionaries in South Carolina wrote in 1713. "[A]s the opportunities are neither great nor frequent for carrying on so good a work so the success must be little and inconsiderable in comparison of what might be expected because there are so many rules and impediments that lie in the way." Since devotions interfere with work and plantations are scattered and remote, they added, most masters "are generally of the opinion that a slave grows worse by being a Christian" and they quickly "malign" anyone who tries to give him religious instruction.[41]

In his 1724 report on "the state of the church and clergy" in Virginia, the Reverend Hugh Jones conceded that most whites opposed the conversion of blacks and Indians because, first, it made the slaves proud and not good servants and, second, to Christianize someone who still practiced "barbarous Ways" would be a "Prostitution of a Thing so sacred." Only the young children of Indians and slaves, he concluded, would be promising candidates for conversion. But even in this instance efforts were disappointing because the Anglican clergy required masters to "stand as sponsors" for slave children to be baptized and few were inclined to do so. Two years later, Lieutenant-Governor Hugh Drysdale, in his report on the present state of Virginia, regretted that when it came to the church's mission effort, the "majority of slaveowners paid no attention to it." Since the Established Church was not properly organized for missions to slaves, he added, it was up to individual clergymen to take it upon themselves, and many—perhaps most—were not interested.[42]

Similarly, the clerical authors of the *Annual Sermons* repeatedly cited owner resistance as the cause of the low conversion figures. A missionary in South Carolina blamed slaveowners for the fact that, from 1703 to 1706, he had converted only four slaves and baptized just one out of a total slave population of one thousand! In 1710, Anglican Bishop William Fleetwood expressed doubt that there were any masters "who cause their slaves to be Baptized." Another bishop accused slaveholders of harboring "an irrational contempt of the blacks, as creatures of another species, who had no right to be instructed or admitted to the sacraments"—a complaint that also appeared frequently in the collection of approximately two hundred letters known as the American Correspondence of the Associates of Dr. Bray, a missionary organization founded by Thomas Bray for the purpose of establishing schools for blacks. Some SPG missionaries noted that many slaveholders cared so little about their own spiritual well-being—"unconverted masters," church historian Robert Baird called them in the nineteenth century—that it should not be surprising that they cared not at all about their bondsmen's religious welfare.[43] What it amounted to, in the end, was a much weaker sentiment for Christianizing slaves on the New World side of the Atlantic, where the bondsmen lived, than on the other, where English church leaders perceived the missionary needs of the colonies from a distance.[44] Not until the Great Awakening of the 1740s, another historian pointed out, "did incidents of slave conversion occur in any sizable numbers."[45]

Yet even this revivalistic phenomenon of the mid-eighteenth century may have had little import. While the Great Awakening has often been portrayed by historians as a harbinger of a more democratic America, it did not significantly change the common pattern of race relations, especially in places where the size and distribution of the slave population was intimidating. In fact, whatever increase there may have been in the number of converts after the 1740s should be attributed not so much to the effectiveness of the missionaries as to the increase in the size of the slave population. Since the fear of large numbers of slaves worked against efforts to convert them, it is not unreasonable to surmise that as the black population increased, the percentage that became Christians actually declined, a conclusion sustained by the obvious adaptation of evangelicals "to the exigencies of southern society." In South Carolina, SPG missionaries like Gideon Johnston—who complained of "rubbs and impediments that lye in the way" of his efforts—reported that the early support they had enjoyed among local whites dropped precipitously after 1708, when blacks surpassed whites in numbers. The complaint was repeated in Virginia when, in the years from 1680 to 1740, the black portion of the colony's population rose from less than 10 percent to about one-third. Traveling through the southern colonies in 1740, George Whitefield claimed to have found "only a few" slaves who were Christians. Two years later the Bishop of London noted that only eleven out of twenty-nine blacks in one parish in Virginia attended church and that the situation was far worse in some of the more densely black-populated parishes in South Carolina. It was not until after the Revolution that significant numbers of black Virginians looked to Christianity. When a Quaker missionary observed in 1765 that "the life of religion is almost lost where slaves are very numerous," he was only affirming what had long since become the rule. Conversely, the fact that Maryland remained at a relatively low 12 to 18 percent black during the first three decades of the eighteenth century apparently accounted "for the greater willingness of white masters there to allow slaves to be baptized and catechized.'[46] Writing from St. Mary's County in 1734, the Reverend Arthur Holt reported that he had much more success in converting slaves in Maryland than he had had in Barbados, where their population was more concentrated.[47]

Nor did independence and nationhood change things much. In the decades following the American Revolution, it could readily be said of a state or county that the higher the percentage of blacks, the more fearful whites were about allowing them to participate in religious activities. One of the first things Frederick Law Olmsted noticed was that it was usually the wealthier masters—that is, those who owned the most slaves—who were most obdurate in denying Christian instruction for their bondsmen, a condition, he added, that was most common in areas "where the enslaved portion of the population outnumbers the whites."[48] A bondsman on a large plantation in Louisiana claimed that of the 150 slaves owned by his master, perhaps 10 could be considered Christians.[49]

By the late antebellum decades, the emerging political conflict between sections had begun to displace every other consideration. As antislavery attacks became increasingly acerbic and southern reactions stiffened, the slaveholder's determination to protect his privileged position became the critical factor, not the number of slaves he owned. When a white preacher told slaves in North Carolina that "God judges men by their hearts, not by the color of their skin," Harriet A. Jacobs noted that that was "strange doctrine from a southern pulpit" and it "was very offensive to slaveholders . . . [who] said he and his wife had made fools of their slaves, and that he preached like a fool to the negroes."[50]

Reflecting on his slavery days, William Wells Brown wrote in 1880 that in Missouri, the slave state with the smallest percentage of blacks, most planters "cared but little about the religious training of their slaves, regarding them as they did their cattle,—an investment, the return of which was only to be considered in dollars and cents."[51] For Missouri slaveowners, at least, it seemed to be principal over principle. Another former slave, eighty-two-year-old Sarah Douglas of Alabama and Arkansas, told a WPA interviewer that her master's church required family members to vouch for the honesty and worthiness of prospective slave members. "Then they let us join," she added sardonically. "We served our mistress and master in slavery time and not God."[52]

If anyone doubted the seriousness of the master's prohibition against religious instruction, he needed only to measure the risk. "[M]any masters and overseers will whip and torture the poor creatures for going to meeting," John Leland wrote in *The Virginia Chronicle* (1790), "even at night, when the labor of the day is done."[53] By the middle of the nineteenth century, the slaveholder's use of violence to control and intimidate slaves was commonplace. When Henry Bibb learned he was to receive five hundred lashes for attending a prayer meeting that he had been ordered to stay away from, he and his wife and daughter ran away. "[T]he regulations [of Louisiana], as well as public opinion, generally," he later wrote, "were against slaves meeting for religious worship."[54]

In the 1930s, several former slaves told Federal Writers' Project interviewers that the punishment for worshiping Jesus was whipping, but if they prayed with their faces down they could usually avoid detection because the sound of their voices would not carry. Singing and praying could only be done in secret, they added, and various tricks—such as speaking over a container of water to muffle the voice, tying grapevines across the road to trip the slave patrol's horses, and placing pots over doors as alarms—were used to escape apprehension. "[S]ome dey would for git to put ol' pot dar an' the paddy rollers would come an' horse whip every las' one of 'em," seventy-seven-year-old Minnie Fulkes testified. "You haven't time to serve God," the "paddy rollers" proclaimed. "We bought you to serve us." Fulkes later told the interviewer, "I jes kno' if I knowed how to write, an' had a little learning, I could put off a book on dis here situation."[55] If these conditions had been common across the South, it would be easy to conclude that more slaves probably became Christians in spite of the master than because of him.

In the last analysis, the fear of the defiant slave easily overwhelmed the quest for a submissive one. Despite the pleas of prominent Protestant leaders, the overwhelming majority of masters were unwilling to take the risk, a conviction that the preachers, as their acquiescence in the baptism dilemma forewarned, were quick to acknowledge. Writing to the Reverend John Waring in London in the fall of 1753, missionary Joseph Ottolenghe conceded that slaveholders refused to permit their bondsmen to receive religious instruction because "a Slave is ten times worse when a Christian, than in his State of Paganism."[56] He did not specify what he meant by "worse," but such a description almost always meant, at the very least, disobedient. "Even the evangelical churches themselves," Herbert S. Klein wrote in his comparative study of Virginia and Cuba, "after a brief period of strong support for Negro conversion and religious instruction, by the early decades of the nineteenth century had conformed to planter opinion and had kept slave conversions and participation to a minimum." In 1710, after an especially impressionable convert in South Carolina provoked fear among fellow slaves by making dreadful predictions about an impending apocalypse that had been forecast in the book of Revelation, Anglican missionary Francis Le Jau, trying to squelch rumors about the end of the world, leaped at the opportunity to criticize the practice of teaching slaves to read.[57] In fact, Le Jau was doing no more than calling attention to the popular slaveholder's complaint that for every biblical reference supporting the master-servant relationship there was one calling for escape from bondage, a message that any literate slave could easily find:

He delivered Daniel from the Lion's den,
Jonah from the belly of the whale,
The Hebrew children from the fiery furnace,
Then why not every man?[58]

Slave literacy—which many Protestant leaders believed was essential to understanding the Bible—was almost universally condemned in colonial and state laws, laws that grew more restrictive after the Nat Turner uprising of 1831, in which sixty whites were killed, sent shock waves of fear across the South. Henry Bibb described how, just two years after the revolt, "a poor white girl," whom he only identified as "a Miss Davis," tried "to teach a Sabbath School for the slaves, notwithstanding public opinion and the law was opposed to it." The school actually began operating, but when word got out that "Miss Davis" was also teaching her students to read, local whites forced her to close. "There are thousands, who . . . are thirsting for the water of life; but the law forbids it, and the churches withhold it," Harriet A. Jacobs wrote in 1857. "They send the Bible to heathen abroad, and neglect the heathen at home." When he told his master that he saw no harm in reading the Bible to other slaves, thirty-five-year-old Sella Martin of Alabama was ordered to "[r]ead nothing to the slaves." If biblical stories could really inspire running away or insurrections, Martin was a perfect example of why a literate slave was dangerous. After a southern Episcopal minister suggested to Olmsted that the slaves' distrust of white preachers could be overcome if the bondsmen were taught how to read the Bible, a slaveowning member of the congregation warned the pastor to keep his "dangerous views" to himself. "The laws of the country forbade the education of negroes," the dissident worshiper added, "and the church was, and he trusted always would remain, the bulwark of the laws." Similarly, Solomon Northup, a free black who had been kidnapped and forced into slavery for twelve years, described how, after his master had converted another bondsman, several local whites complained that anyone who allowed his slaves to have Bibles was "not fit to own a nigger." The common view among virtually all southern whites was that an informed slave was a dangerous slave. From the time of the earliest colonial settlements to the Civil War, Christianity and education were virtually synonymous; but when the master denied religion to his slaves he was far less worried about their knowing Christ than he was about their knowing too much.[59]

There is no evidence that conversions to Christianity actually led to slave rebellions. In fact, the only colonial uprisings that appeared to have any direct religious connections were the New York City insurrection of 1712 and the Virginia revolt of 1730, and there were even doubts about the former. Initially, New York City authorities believed the uprising had been led by slaves from an Anglican school run by a French Protestant named Elias Neau. But, after about two dozen blacks had been killed, they learned that the rebels were mainly dissident slaves owned by masters opposed to religious instruction for bondsmen. "However a great jealousy was now raised," abolitionist Joshua Coffin wrote in 1860, "and the common cry very loud against instructing the negroes." Fear was a compelling force and the Protestant slaveholder, perhaps subconsciously recognizing the humanity of the slave, certainly knew what he would do if he were in the slave's predicament. He would not be so foolish as to think the slave would do any less. The lessons of the exploits of Moses, Daniel, Elijah, Jonah, David, Jesus, and other biblical heroes who struggled against oppression and overwhelming odds were well known to those slaves whose masters had permitted religious instruction, and, accordingly, were conspicuous themes in many slave songs and sermons.[60]

You may talk about yo' king ob Gideon,
You may talk about yo' man of Saul,
Dere's none like good ole Joshua,
At de battle ob Jericho.[61]

One song portrayed Samson—who was almost as popular in plantation spirituals as Joshua—prophesying his ultimate triumph:

If I had my way,
If I had my way,
If I had my way,
I'd tear this building down.[62]

It should not have taken a particularly astute observer to notice that the double meanings of many songs were betrayed by their titles, for example, "Let My People Go," "The Walls Came A-tumbling Down," and "Steal Away to Jesus."[63] And, of course, no destination was as longed for as the Land of Canaan:

O Canaan, sweet Canaan
I am bound for the land of Canaan.[64]

There were often "tag lines" to those verses in which freedom was equated with going to heaven, but they were for the benefit of unsuspecting whites. Hidden within almost every spiritual that exalted a heavenly salvation was the hope of being free in *this* world.[65] Describing the misery of a slave woman he identified only as Patsey, Solomon Northup wrote: "Her idea of joy of heaven was simply *rest*, and is fully expressed in these lines of a melancholy bard":

I ask no paradise on high,
With caves on earth oppressed,
The only heaven for which I sigh,
Is rest, eternal rest.[66]

Although slave insurrections in colonial North America and the United States never reached the scale or frequency of those in Brazil and some of the Caribbean islands, there were enough to feed the fears of white Southerners. And the biblical connection was obvious in all of them. Gabriel Prosser—who, in his abortive revolt of 1800, saw himself following in the tradition of Moses and Samson—believed he was doing no more than fulfilling the seventeenth-century English Puritan dictum that "rebellion to tyrants is obedience to God." To Prosser, the Old Testament analogy was a mandate. "I had heard in the days of old when the Israelites were in service to King Pharaoh," he declared, "they were taken away from him by the power of God and carried away by Moses," a theme echoed by his brother Martin, himself a preacher, who told his fellow conspirators that "five of you shall conquer an hundred and a hundred a thousand of your enemies." Two decades later, Denmark Vesey, who understood well the story of Moses, launched his uprising with the support of the African Methodist Episcopal Church of Charleston, South Carolina. "Behold the day of the Lord Cometh, and thy spoil shall be divided in the midst of thee," he read from the scriptures to his followers. "For I shall gather all nations against Jerusalem to battle, and the city shall be taken." In fact, some slaves believed, according to Vincent Harding, that the "black song of faith and struggle, 'Go Down Moses,' " had been inspired by the Vesey rebellion. In his famous seventy-six-page pamphlet *Appeal to the Colored Citizens of the World*, published in Boston in 1829, David Walker, who had been born free in 1785, included several references to Moses and concluded by asking, "Have we any other master than Jesus Christ?" Black peoples everywhere should not fear to take up the struggle for that "glorious and heavenly cause" because, Walker assured them, "Jesus Christ the king of heaven and of earth who is the God of Justice and of armies, will surely go before you." The best-known religious slave insurrectionist—and the only one whose uprising resulted in a heavy loss of white lives—was, of course,

Nat Turner. A slave preacher and the leader of a rebellion that terrorized Southampton County, Virginia, for weeks, Turner, on May 12, 1828, proclaimed:

> I heard a loud noise in the heavens, and the spirit appeared to me and said the Serpent was loosened, and Christ had laid down the yoke he had borne for the sins of men, and that I should take it on and fight the Serpent, for the time was fast approaching when the first should be last and the last should be first.

To achieve this, "all the whites we meet should die, until we have an army strong enough to carry out the war on a Christian basis."[67] Did anyone, the slaveholder readily asked, need a more convincing example?

It should be reiterated that slavery in English North America, compared to slavery elsewhere in the New World, was relatively free of violent eruptions, which is all the more remarkable considering that students of institutionalized bondage have described slavery in the American South as among the most oppressive in human history. In an area the size of Western Europe and with a slave population of almost four million in 1860, the most surprising aspect of slave insurrections in the United States is that there were so few. Estimates as to the actual number vary because Herbert Aptheker and others who researched the subject disagreed on what constituted an uprising. Some of the so-called revolts, historian Carl N. Degler wrote, were little more than "temporary work stoppages," but even the most inflated estimate meant an average of only about one per year.[68]

One reason for the docility of the American bondsmen was the widespread rural distribution of the slave population in the United States, a distribution that made organization and communication difficult compared with, say, Brazil, where as many as a thousand slaves lived on one plantation and where an independent state like the Republic of Palmares, organized by runaway slaves, flourished for sixty-seven years. In the United States, only a few thousand planters owned more than a hundred slaves each and agricultural units were relatively small. To diminish further the opportunities for expressing discontent—and, perhaps more to the point, unwittingly to reveal their own insecurity—state lawmakers prohibited slaves from owning drums and other loud instruments because they believed that Africans had an innate primitive ability to beat out secret messages. Also, slave uprisings may have been discouraged by the fact that, as the utter dependence of the bondsman on his master sometimes made him a willing collaborator in his own enslavement, the insurrectionist was never sure whom he could trust. Denmark Vesey was betrayed by a slave informer who wanted to protect his master.

It also should be pointed out that there were less controversial reasons for the slaveholder's opposition to religious instruction for his slaves than his fear of their reactions to provocative biblical lessons. A frequent criticism, for example, was that time taken for religious activities was time taken from essential duties. The slave "has work enough from the White Folk on his hands," Gideon Johnston wrote, to take up whatever Sunday time he was allowed. Except during the winter months, slaves in the cotton regions worked seven days a week. Accordingly, a Sunday holiday was "entirely a gift of the master," which the exhausted bondsman more than likely used for rest and entertainment. "Why, Sundays they sleep mostly," a slaveholder told Olmsted; "they've been at work hard all week, you know, and Sundays they stay in their cabins, and sleep and talk to each other." Then there were those whites who simply believed that a society dependent on slave labor must, to ensure the quality and perpetuation of its way of life, keep its slaves in the deepest ignorance. Olmsted reported that in South Carolina 350 "leading planters and citizens" signed a remonstrance against a Methodist clergyman, one Reverend T. Tupper, a "cautious and discreet person" who, because he could be trusted to "confine himself to verbal [i.e., oral] instruction in religious truth," had been earlier chosen by his superiors "to preach especially to the slaves." But even this the "leading planters and citizens" did not want. Such "verbal instruction," they charged, would "increase the desire of the black population to learn. . . . We thus expect *a progressive system of improvement* will be introduced . . . which, if not checked . . . *will ultimately revolutionize our civil institutions.*" The Reverend Tupper certainly knew what that meant. With no illusions about the prudent course, he "retired from the field" because, in the words of the Greenville *Mountaineer*, "the great body of the people were manifestly opposed to the religious instruction of their slaves, even if it were only given orally."[69] To the slaveholder, "a progressive system of improvement" for black people was a threat to everything he believed in and simply could not be tolerated.

Nor was this disapproval of the "leading planters and citizens," Olmsted went on, the expression of "a merely local or occasional state of mind." Rather, such an attitude appeared to be widespread throughout the South, and "even where the economy, safety, and duty of some sort of religious education of the slaves is conceded, so much caution, reservation, and restriction is felt to be necessary in their instruction, that the result in the majority of cases has been merely to furnish a delusive clothing of Christian forms and phrases to the original vague superstition of the African savage." Typical was the Louisiana planter who told Swedish traveler Fredrika Bremer in 1850 that "no religious instruction has been allowed to the slave on the plantations, nor is it even to this hour." Instances of

Christian education for slaves were thought by some to be so unusual that their existence surprised even the most experienced travelers. Learning of a Presbyterian minister in Liberty County, Georgia, who for thirteen years had been paid by slaveowners to minister to their slaves, Olmsted described the situation as "almost unparalleled" and said that in "no other district has there been displayed as general and long-continued an interest in the spiritual well-being of the negroes." But even here, in "a district in which more is done for the elevation of the slaves than in any other of the South," this same minister complained that the property interests of the masters often presented insurmountable obstacles to the slaves' spiritual well-being.[70] If this was the case in an area that a northern visitor perceived as having a liberal slave code, one can only wonder what conditions obtained elsewhere.

The Missionary Failure

Despite the slaveholders' unrelenting opposition to slave conversion and the fundamental contradiction between Christianity and bondage, many northern whites continued to believe that most slaves eagerly embraced Christianity—a belief reinforced by the symbolism and the most obvious of the double meanings in popular plantation songs and stories. Almost certainly the best-known example was the association between "Swing Low, Sweet Chariot" and the underground railroad. But many others were less conspicuous. For example, the Jubilee spiritual "Steal Away to Jesus," which included the line "I hain't got long to stay here," was to most whites a simple longing for relief from the burden of slavery. But, as Fisk University folklorist Thomas W. Talley pointed out, since slaves had sometimes met "in the dead of the night in some secluded lonely spot for a religious meeting even when they had been forbidden to do so by their masters," the song was sung in the late afternoon as field hands from neighboring plantations passed each other on the roads, giving notice "that a secret religious meeting was to be held that night at the place formerly agreed upon for meetings." Most Northerners, Olmsted argued, would be surprised that such stealth was necessary. "The prevailing impression among us, with regard to the important influence of slavery in promoting the spread of religion among the blacks," he confessed, "is an erroneous one in my opinion"; and the realization that Christianity had little influence on the masses of slaves "was unexpected and painful to me." The northern clergy had always assumed that slaves received "regular daily instruction" in "the truths of Christianity," Olmsted went on, but, although family prayers were regular features in many of the planters' houses he visited in Mississippi and Alabama, he did not observe a single instance in which field hands were involved in such devotions.[71] The simple fact was, the great majority of slaveholders were convinced that the disadvantages of slave conversion—ominously exemplified by Nat Turner—far outweighed the advantages.

The available statistical data suggest that the number of slaves who became Christians was far smaller than anyone imagined—then or since. There had never been a strong effort to convert slaves during the colonial period, and conversions actually declined after the Revolution. In the seventeenth century the Moravians made a sincere effort to convert blacks, but such a small sect could never make a significant impact, and there were no serious missionary programs for slaves among the larger denominations. Puritan clergymen John Eliot and Cotton Mather called for missions for blacks, but the former was more interested in working among Indians and the latter advocated Christianizing slaves mainly as a means of control. The percentage of slaves converted was probably slightly higher in the northern colonies, especially in New England, where their numbers were fewer and where most of them lived in white households, a situation that facilitated the African's adoption of his master's faith. But even here there was little reason to celebrate.

One writer noted that the first recorded conversion in New England had occurred in 1641, barely three years after the African's arrival, but that over a century later the overwhelming majority of the region's black people were still unsaved. The situation was not much different among the other sects. "[B]y the mid-eighteenth century many black children were attending schools opened by Anglicans and Quakers," Gary Nash observed. "In the Northern towns Protestant ministers performed slave marriages and baptized their children." But, again, Christian leaders still counted far more failures than successes. The low conversion rate was also influenced by denominational rivalries. Anglican missionaries dispatched by the London-based Society for the Propagation of the Gospel in Foreign Parts ran into a wall of opposition from Puritans, who did everything they could to keep blacks away from the Established Church. Official SPG records for New England reported one slave converted in 1729 by a pastor who, twenty-one years later, boasted of baptizing five black children, only one of whom was a slave. In 1739 the society's agent in New London, Connecticut, reported converting "one mulatto servant and one Negro child." It also appears that many Anglican missionaries sent to work among the Indians had little stomach for the hardships of life in the wilderness; thus most left the frontier areas after only brief sojourns for the "more pleasant life in the settlements."[72]

In the plantation colonies mission efforts were even less successful. In

1720 an Anglican minister in South Carolina admitted sadly that during the previous eleven years he had baptized only eight or nine slaves out of an estimated 800 in his parish. Eight years later another minister resigned after five years of service because, he complained, he had failed to convert any of the 1,500 slaves in his charge. Nor were such efforts helped by the fact that many missionaries simply found it less troublesome to worry about the souls of whites. For example, Samuel Davies, "the evangelist who laid the foundations of Presbyterianism in Virginia," had little success in introducing slaves to the Gospel because his efforts were nothing more than extensions of his program for establishing a white church. Halfhearted attempts produced less than halfhearted results. In 1762 a minister in South Carolina estimated that there were only 500 Christians in a black population of 46,000—a little over 1 percent, a figure that was not contradicted by official surveys. The First Census (1790) counted 306,193 slaves in Virginia, but only 13,000—barely 4 percent—were actually considered to be church members.[73] The fact that there was an increase in conversions is far less revealing than the fact that it was so small. Although Davies apparently was unaware of his own shortcomings when he complained in 1756 of "the almost universal neglect of many thousand poor slaves," his assessment was hard to disagree with.[74]

While most efforts to make Christians out of heathen Africans were, by almost any yardstick, complete failures, some denominations were more successful—or, perhaps more accurately, less *un*successful—than others. By the early nineteenth century, the Baptists and the Methodists were clearly the most effective Protestant churches in winning black people to the faith.[75] Their success probably had something to do with their demonstrative style of worship, a feature that was characteristic of traditional African religions and in America was most conspicuous in the southern camp meeting. It should not be forgotten that the slave had brought from his ancestral homeland a religious tradition that was rich in color, symbols, rituals, and appeals to nature, and that embodied an exuberant physical expression through art, music, dance, and even work. He was sometimes criticized by Christians who considered "emotional wildness and extravagance" to be "strong survivals of superstition and paganism," but he could not be anything else.[76]

At times, Christianity, especially its more puritanical and intellectual varieties, must have seemed to him to be cold, rigid, unnatural, and boring. With its boisterous promise of quick redemption and its inherent propensity for emotional rather than intellectual persuasion, revivalism, certainly America's most distinctive contribution to Christianity, had its strongest appeal among the rural poor, a group in which blacks always loomed large. "Revival conversions came in the immediacy of the moment, usually suddenly," one historian observed, "and with little relation to the traditional nurturing of the church." Having emerged from their inception in the Great Awakening and nourished by the movement that had centered in Kentucky in the late eighteenth century, the camp meetings, although originally Presbyterian, eventually came to be identified mainly with the Methodists.[77]

The Presbyterians, in turn, criticized the emotionalism of the Methodists and, perhaps not surprisingly, had only modest success in converting bondsmen.[78] One study has calculated the number of black Presbyterians in Florida in 1858 as probably less than 100, which was so small—especially when compared to Florida's total black population two years later of almost 63,000—as to be statistically nonexistent. Quoting an article in the Charleston *Observer* in 1834, abolitionist Sarah M. Grimké complained that few slaves in South Carolina had joined the church and that at least 100,000 slaves living in the South Carolina Synod had "never heard of the plan of salvation by a Redeemer." Since there were at the time about 330,000 blacks in the state, Grimké's estimate was probably on the low side. A report of all southern Presbyterian churches in 1850 claimed 5,389 black worshipers, which was only about 10 percent of the slaves owned by white members. Apparently Presbyterian masters cared little about the spiritual well-being of their bondsmen. And the Episcopalians, whose condescending manner and stiff formality certainly had little attraction for slaves, were the least effective of all Protestants—despite the fact that their church was "dominant in the states where Blacks were most populous." In 1860 less than 1 percent of South Carolina's black population were members of the Episcopal church.[79]

Ironically, the singular success of the Methodists serves best to illustrate just how few slaves were actually converted to Christianity. At the beginning of the nineteenth century there were 15,688 slave and free black Methodists in the United States, or less than 2 percent of the total black American population. Sixty years later they numbered 215,000, which was 4.8 percent of the black population—hardly a spectacular increase in view of the relatively small size of the church in 1800.[80] As unimpressive as these figures are, they become even less impressive when it is seen that in the same six decades the overall Methodist membership nationwide increased at almost exactly twice the rate of the black membership—2,455 percent to 1,270 percent. The deception of numbers could also be seen in Florida, where, in the fifteen years before the Civil War, black Methodists never constituted less than one-third of all the Methodists in the state and reached 43 percent by the end of that period. But when compared to Florida's total black population rather than to the total Methodist membership, that percentage drops to just 10.6.

Elsewhere in the South, Methodist numbers were similarly unimpressive. In 1829—the same year that Pinckney extolled the virtues of Christianized slaves to the South Carolina Agricultural Society—church members in that state could boast only two plantation missions with a total of 417 members. By the time of the schism in 1844, the mission movement had spread to several other southern states, with sixty-eight stations served by seventy-one missionaries and claiming 21,063 members, an average of 310 per station.[81] Increasing at an average annual rate of 2.6 percent during the two decades before the Civil War—compared to an increase in the state's slave population of 1.1 percent—black Methodists in South Carolina numbered 42,000 by 1860; but that was still only 10.2 percent of the state's black population—essentially the same as Florida's—compared to 8.2 percent in 1840, not an especially impressive increase for a twenty-year period.[82]

Nor do the figures for the entire South change the situation significantly. In 1849, a former slave named James W. C. Pennington, who subsequently became a Presbyterian minister in New York, recalled enjoying the "rare privileges in attending Sabbath school" at a time (1829) when 700,000 slave children "had no means of Christian instruction." By 1830, Donald G. Mathews wrote, "there were at most 140,000 blacks in the South who were members of an evangelical church," but that was still just 6.5 percent of the southern black population. Ten years later, the Sixth Census counted 2.5 million slaves in the United States, of whom only 200,000—barely 8 percent—were officially listed as members of Protestant churches. In 1860 the *Christian Observer* counted 468,000 black members of all Protestant denominations—about 12 percent of the total slave population and less than 11 percent of the black population, North and South.[83]

In view of these growing but still meager figures, it was easy to be impressed by the boast of Southern Methodists on the eve of the Civil War that there were 171,857 free and slave black members in their church, so long as one overlooked the fact that that seemingly large number was, in reality, just 4 percent of the black population in the fifteen slave states and the District of Columbia.[84] On the other hand, northern black Methodists accounted for almost 18 percent of the black population in the free states. Since the Methodist church had what has been universally acclaimed as by far the best conversion record of all American Protestant denominations, one is only left to doubt the success of other missionary efforts, especially in the South.

Efforts to Christianize the other large nonwhite American minority, the Indians, were even less successful. Perceived by many early colonists as, at best, savages who were beyond salvation or, at worst, personifications of the devil, Native Americans have been victims of four centuries of Christian racism. "White clergymen who tried to convert natives may have been prompted by altruistic ideals," one historian wrote, "but their daily activities helped to destroy the cultures of the people they wanted to aid." For example, John Eliot's insistence that the Indian must first become "civilized" before he could be baptized meant, in effect, that before the Indian could become a Christian he had to stop being an Indian. The rush to convert Native Americans came in the decades following the War of 1812, when the surge in revivalistic enthusiasm that accompanied the Second Great Awakening led to the organization of various missionary societies, which claimed spectacular successes. Founded in 1810, the American Board of Commissioners of Foreign Missions worked extensively among the Cherokees and Choctaws, proclaiming a primary objective of making Christians out of Indians and a secondary objective of helping the Indian to practice "Christian living." While Congregationalists and, to some extent, Presbyterians, worked through the Board of Commissioners, Methodists and Baptists "spread over the whole godless frontier and strove indiscriminately to evangelize both white men and red," Roy Harvey Pearce wrote in his classic *The Savages of America* (1965), while Quakers and Moravians continued their work on a smaller but no less enthusiastic scale. But Indians proved to be unreceptive and missions began closing. For all the expense and effort, the Indian missions, in the words of their historian, Oliver W. Elsbree, were a "virtual failure." When the missionary effort declined in the 1840s and afterward, the federal government enlisted clergymen as agents and thus "continued to attempt to reconcile the Indian to his fate by religion."[85] Since the government was interested in Indian removal and control, not in Indian religious practices, such a policy was nothing more than an obvious effort to subdue a troublesome racial minority under the pretense of Christian paternalism.

The Conspicuous Convert

If the number of slaves and other southern blacks who could be officially counted as members of Protestant churches remained small throughout the antebellum era, how can one explain the almost unanimous historical opinion that most slaves eagerly embraced their masters' religion? "From the moment they arrived in America and began to toil as slaves," Eugene D. Genovese wrote, "they could not help absorbing the religion of the master class." In fact, there is even a consensus as to just when the missionary appeal was most effective. By the late eighteenth century, Genovese went on, "black conversion to Christianity started to assume noticeable proportions," reaching a peak in the early nineteenth century, when, Lawrence

W. Levine agreed, there was among the bondsmen a "wholesale conversion to Christianity." Reflecting on the refusal of West Indian planters to allow their slaves to hear the gospel, sociologist Orlando Patterson wondered how one could "account for the Protestant slave South where, during the late eighteenth and the nineteenth centuries, both masters and slaves were highly religious." To E. Franklin Frazier, Christianity, providing "a new basis for social cohesion," played a major role in helping the slave adapt to his condition. Historian Timothy L. Smith saw "evangelical Protestantism" as the "folk religion of Black people in the United States while they were yet slaves," and John B. Boles claimed that within a century after 1750 "the majority of slaves were worshipping in one fashion or another as Christians." While the conversion rate reportedly leveled off after 1830, the number of blacks who adopted Christianity presumably remained high right up to the Civil War. For example, Joel Williamson tabulated the South Carolina slave membership in 1860 of the four mainline denominations—Methodists, Baptists, Presbyterians, and Episcopalians—at 72,000, a number he found "impressively large."[86]

The assumption has become so universal that all kinds of claims have been based on it. "An obvious fact of American religious life," Winthrop S. Hudson wrote in *Church History*, "is that the vast majority of the descendants of Africans who had been brought to North America became Baptists and Methodists."[87] Not just Christians or even Protestants, but Baptists and Methodists! Similarly, Yale historian John W. Blassingame asserted that "An overwhelming majority of the slaves throughout the antebellum period attended church with their masters."[88] Notice that Blassingame did not limit himself to a modest majority, a specific time period, or merely slaves who worshiped just anyplace.

But such conclusions raised more questions than they answered. For example, since Williamson's figure for South Carolina was only slightly over 17 percent of the state's black population (and the uncounted slave members of the lesser denominations was insignificant), one must ask: "impressively large" compared to what? A count of 72,000 black Christians did indeed look "impressive"—until it was held up to the state's black population of 412,000. No one is questioning the fact that many black men and women embraced Christianity. Despite the resistance of their owners, more than a few slaves became devout Christians by "praying with their faces down"; and in the northern states the church was one of the most important institutions in black life and a major force in challenging the status quo. But that still does not say a great deal about the amplitude of Christian influence and its overall impact, for good or bad, on the black population at large. Frazier's and Smith's assessments were hard to question because neither made a quantitative judgment and both looked only at those slaves who had converted; but they were not applicable to those—the large majority of the black population—who remained outside of the church's influence.

What was the basis of Genovese's assumption that the transplanted Africans "could not help" adopting their oppressors' religion? Such an assertion implied that the heathen was "helpless" in the face of an irrepressible Christianity. If the slave's ancestral religious faith could not be sustained under the conditions of bondage in the New World—and that is far from having been established with any degree of certainty—did that mean he was compelled to snatch up the only religion available? And what was an inexact term like "noticeable proportions" supposed to mean? In an area where there were few converts, one convert would be noticeable. The same question could be asked of Levine's "wholesale conversion" and Patterson's "highly religious."[89] Such vague quantitative terms will always be necessary and useful parts of the scholar's vocabulary; unfortunately, scholars will continue to use them even when their vagueness leads to inaccurate conclusions. For example, students of American slavery have always looked at the vast body of plantation spirituals as a reliable indicator of the slave's attraction to Christianity. But is it possible that all the time they were counting songs they should have been counting singers instead?[90]

Part of the answer to these questions may be discerned by a close look at the nature and extent of the white Christian's perception of his religion. If the members of a society were predominantly of one religion, there was a tendency for most of them—like those Northerners whose "prevailing impression" Olmsted found to be erroneous—to *assume* that everyone subscribed to the common faith, especially since that was what they *wanted* to believe. Since white Americans defined their society as "Christian," it did not even occur to them that a substantial number of the population did not qualify, a perception that made it easy for British visitor Isabella Bishop, who lived in the United States for a year just before the Civil War, to identify all four million southern slaves as "nominally Christians." Likewise, editor and clergyman William Aikman, writing in the *Presbyterian Quarterly Review* in 1862, referred to the entire population of four million slaves as "a Christian race" and, indeed, "a *Protestant* people." That Bishop was cautious enough to include the modifier "nominally" did not significantly attenuate the exaggeration because the evidence suggests that most slaves were not even nominally Christians. Robert Baird, a Presbyterian minister who "travelled extensively in England and Europe as an agent of the American Sunday School Union" and one of the most eminent church historians of the antebellum period, admitted that the incidence of slave conversion was adversely influenced by unsympathetic masters, but he added that he knew of no state where the slave was not permitted to hear the gospel, a naïve conclusion that was wholly contrary to both Olmsted's observations and the testimony of the slaves themselves.[91]

Even one who has been critical of Christianity's treatment of racial minorities can have a blind spot. In his *Righteous Empire: The Protestant Experience in America* (1970), Lutheran historian Martin E. Marty of the University of Chicago called his chapter on black Americans "The Overlooked Protestants," a dubious choice of words in view of the reality that the vast majority of blacks were not Protestant. In fairness to Marty, it should be noted that he acknowledged that "most blacks who were religious were Protestant," and that not all blacks were religious.[92] What is missing is an acknowledgment that most blacks were not Christians.

Erroneous generalizations about the popularity of Christianity among slaves may also have been a result of the seductive appeal of very large numbers. Baird was understandably impressed by a report that there were 300,000 black Christians in the South in 1850. In his mind's eye he may have visualized a vast sea of upturned black faces. Like Williamson's estimate for South Carolina, all those zeros gave the impression that hordes of people were participating. Such a figure would indeed seem imposing if at the same time someone happened to note that four slave states—Arkansas, Delaware, Florida, and Texas—each had smaller *total* populations. Imposing but, of course, irrelevant. Large numbers could be especially delusive because the missionary spirit always tended to prefer optimism to reality. Puritan clergyman Daniel Gookin's estimate that there were at least 1,100 "praying Indians" in the Boston area in 1674 was based more on wishful thinking than on factual evidence.[93] Bishop, Aikman, Baird, and others like them were evangelical Protestants who wanted to believe that certain things were true. But the significance of that six-digit number diminished considerably when recognized as barely 9 percent of the slave population—even less if southern free blacks had been included. When the heart was filled with hope, the head was not prepared for the worst.

Then there is the matter of all those plantation spirituals. From the moment slaves started singing, they exalted Moses, Joshua, Jesus, and a host of other biblical figures and themes. No one really knows how many religious songs the slaves composed and sang; but the number is mind-boggling and is certainly far larger than any other category of Afro-American musical literature. To contemporary observers, the songs were unequivocal evidence of the importance of Christianity in the typical slave's life, a conclusion that remained unchallenged until recent times. How could it be otherwise for people whose lives were so profoundly laid bare in their sacred music?

Well, it was possible, John Lovell, Jr., wrote, because the slave was not as *religiously* influenced by his music as it appeared he was, at least not in the sense in which most whites perceived that influence. In his comprehensive *Black Song: The Forge and the Flame: The Story of How the Afro-American Spiritual Was Hammered Out* (1972), Lovell compellingly challenged the contention that black people attended camp meetings in large numbers or embraced Christianity early *and* in equally large numbers. It was a myth perpetrated by the white Christian's wishful thinking and his inability, or unwillingness, to understand the black personality. Many researchers, Lovell wrote, "failed to consider the natural tendency of the African to sing wherever he was and his further tendency to utilize whatever was in the air around him." The production of thousands of plantation spirituals was not so much a result of widespread Christianity among slaves as it was a result of the enslaved African's using Christian metaphors to express his feelings about his condition. "The ante-bellum Negro was not converted to God," anthropologist Paul Radin declared. "He converted God to himself." As a "fixed point" from which the slave could measure everything else, God was an anchor in a world of "endless shifting." In other words, Christianity was *convenient*, not *necessary*. "The religious quality of the poems is often there for reasons other than expression of Christian doctrine," Lovell explained. "[T]he principle of religion being followed is African. The songs merely recall the totality of religion as a unifying and organizing force." The real significance of the spiritual, historian Sterling Stuckey agreed, was its relationship to the circle dancing that accompanied it, which, in turn, "generated the continuing focus on the ancestors and elders as the Christian faith answered to African religious imperatives."[94] As it happened, the spiritual suited perfectly both the cathartic needs of the slave and the restrictive expectations of the slave-master. Slaves could vent their defiance and rage in verses with double meanings and the master was content in the thought that they were singing about going to heaven.

The slaveowner's resistance notwithstanding, there is still the matter of accounting for the facility with which many transplanted Africans embraced Christianity. It is essential, of course, to distinguish between, on the one hand, an infant born into slavery who was several generations removed from his immigrant ancestors and, on the other, a free adult from Africa who had endured the *process* of enslavement. The former, who knew no life but bondage, may, at least for comparative purposes, be considered a *tabula rasa* who was shaped largely by his experiences. But for the latter, enslavement demanded the obliteration of the fundamental institutions and practices by which human beings were socialized—that is, the bases of solidarity: family, community, nationality, and religion—producing a form of adaptation that fell within what some modern psychologists have called "operant conditioning."[95] To be sure, many slaves had been brought into the white church, in Vincent Harding's words, "as part of the continuing assault on African history and traditions, as part of the attempt to root out all living connections with the homeland, as a program of pacification."[96]

No longer part of his mother country, the slave was "left in suspense between two societies and isolated between two peoples, sold by one and repudiated by the other," Alexis de Tocqueville observed in *Democracy in America* (1835); "in the whole world there is nothing but his master's hearth to provide him with some semblance of his homeland." Transplanted Africans began to lose many of their cultural habits within one generation, historian Kenneth M. Stampp asserted, "not only because of the general decay of Negro culture but also because new problems and experiences created an urgent need for a new kind of religious expression and a new set of beliefs." Frightened and bewildered by an alien and hostile environment, the slave needed a religion that did not threaten the interests of the master, would relieve the boredom of routine labor, and promised a better life ahead. While he might cling to certain familiar adjuncts, the focus of his new faith was determined largely by his status and therefore he "embraced evangelical Christianity eagerly." It is not an exaggeration to suggest that Christianity, with its promise of a heavenly reward for Jobian behavior, probably served the slave's spiritual needs better than could his traditional African religion, where the focus was on the *here* rather than the *after*. In short, the Christianized slave was the product of a social class's response to the painful realities of slavery.[97]

How else can the conversion of Phillis Wheatley—brought as a slave from Africa to Boston when she was only about seven years old and within six years writing verses glorifying her new faith—be explained?

> *'Twas not long since I left my native shore*
> *The land of errors, and* Egyptian *gloom:*
> *Father of mercy, 'twas thy gracious hand*
> *Brought me in safety from those dark abodes.*[98]

It would have been perfectly understandable if an average child of this age, thrown into an alien and threatening world, had been easily persuaded to adopt the faith of her captors. But Wheatley was anything but average. Almost immediately she showed herself to be a person of remarkable intellect. In just a little over a year after her arrival in Massachusetts she was, according to one of her principal chroniclers, reading "fluently the most difficult parts of the Bible." With an appetite for learning that can only be described as voracious and omnivorous, Wheatley studied history, geography, astronomy, and the ancients, "especially the works of Virgil and Ovid." Alexander Pope's translation of Homer was "her favorite English classic."[99] She was certainly not much more than sixteen when she published her first poem; and three years later her first book of verses—*Poems on Various Subjects, Religious and Moral*—appeared in London.[100] If any slave, especially one not born into bondage, had the intellectual strength to resist the master's religious blandishments, it should have been Phillis Wheatley.

But she did not merely accept her newfound Christianity—she reveled in it! Many of Wheatley's verses were euphoric paeans to her faith, and the words themselves left no doubt about her gratitude to her captors for snatching her from the heathen abyss of her native land. In the lines above notice her joy at the "gracious hand" that brought her in "safety" from Africa, that "land of errors" filled with "dark abodes" and "gloom." As the opening stanza of "On Being Brought from Africa to America" show, it was a theme she repeated frequently.

> *'Twas mercy brought me from my* Pagan *land,*
> *Taught my benighted soul to understand*
> *That there's a God, that there's a* Saviour *too;*
> *Once I redemption neither sought nor knew.*[101]

The antithetical italicized juxtaposition of *Pagan* and *Saviour* is almost too obvious. Moreover, an insight into Wheatley's self-image may be seen in the last verse of this poem, where she inadvertently revealed a negative feeling toward the color of her own skin:

> *Some view our sable race with scornful eye.*
> *"Their colour is a diabolic die."*
> *Remember*, Christians, Negroes *black as* Cain,
> *May be refin'd, and join th' angelic train.*[102]

The racist implications were clear. Africans—who could realize salvation despite their "diabolic" color—were "refin'd" by conversion to Christianity. Owned by a respected tailor whose family recognized her talents and encouraged her to cultivate them, Wheatley could certainly never have been accused of embracing Christianity in order to ease the burden of bondage. She was a slave, to be sure, but her condition was comparatively easy and, indeed, was probably more comfortable than that of many white young women anywhere.[103] There were not many slaves in the rice fields of South Carolina who were familiar with Pope's translation of Homer.

Phillis Wheatley as conspicuous convert could also be a product of what French sociologist Roger Bastide called the "worst" thing that could happen when slaves assimilated "North American values" and, becoming predominantly Christians, saw "no other way to demonstrate their identification with America than by adopting a kind of Puritanism." Unfortunately, embracing the white man's religion so fervidly also meant introducing "a factor historically linked to the condemnation of the Indian and the Negro as inveterate savages," which then led to one's "own condemnation."[104] But the analysis can also be overdrawn. For example, Max Lerner, in his classic study of contemporary American life, *America as a Civilization* (1957), argued that the "religion of the Negro came close to the primitivism of the early Christian church, when religion was the creed of the slave and the persecuted." Places like heaven and Canaan promised eventual freedom, and the slave's religion "took its place, along with New England Calvinism and frontier revivalism, as one of the crucial influences on the American religious consciousness—not in the sense of influencing Christian ritual or theology but in investing again with a naive wonder the early strivings of Christian faith."[105]

The comparison seems neat, but while Lerner described a parallel between Africans oppressed because of their blackness and early Christians persecuted for their religious beliefs, he apparently attached little significance to the fact that the latter were persecuted, in part, *because* they were Christians, while the slaves—or, at least, some of them—turned to Christianity because they were persecuted. The difference is fundamental; and to what extent the slave's conversion was a consequence of his bondage, as a convenient escape mechanism or a genuine spiritual commitment, is a question that has never been—and probably can never be—fully answered.

Alien though his master's theology may have been, there is more than a little evidence that many slaves, whose culture and folklore had been steeped in religious meaning, embraced it eagerly for reasons known and unknown. Orlando Patterson argued persuasively that "fundamentalist Christianity became at one and the same time a spiritual and social salvation for the slaves and an institutional support for the order of slavery." Perhaps the most important practical aspect of Christianity was that it served, in varying degrees, both the slaveholder and the enslaved. The theological dualism of Pauline Christianity paradoxically "allowed for the spiritual support of both groups and of the system as a whole." In this way masters found "spiritual and personal dignity and salvation in the ethic of the justified and redeemed sinner," Patterson wrote in *Slavery and Social Death*, and the slaves found "salvation and dignity in this same interpretation of the crucified Lord." The idea of "Jesus as Messiah King and Jesus as comforting savior" was harmonious with both the world of the slave-holder and the world of the slave.[106]

But there is an abiding problem with all of this that intrudes upon the complacent satisfaction of such a conclusion. The ease with which some slaves became Christians should not obscure the fact that many, perhaps most, bondsmen did not convert at all or did so for other than religious reasons. There seems to be little doubt that the slave's use of Christianity to assuage the devastation of bondage was much less far-reaching than the master's use of Christianity to justify it. The facility of slave conversions loses much of its significance when viewed against the much larger number of bondsmen who remained outside the faith.

The ease with which many slaves adopted Christianity may also have been the result of an apparently unique West African susceptibility to external religious influences. The most obvious consequence of this has been the success of the two missionary religions—Christianity and Islam—in virtually every tribal area of West Africa.[107] Contrary to the implications of scholars like Stampp and Genovese, it was not necessary to enslave the African in order to give him a reason for becoming a Christian. In trying to explain the West African's unusual proclivity for syncretism, Patterson called attention to a peculiar sense of inferiority that was reflected in "the strong belief that the magical practices of neighbouring or distant tribes are always more powerful than one's own." Since many students of African religion have agreed that there is "a remarkable uniformity in the supernatural beliefs of all West African Negroes," it would not be hard to assume that groups that lived close together had been easily influenced by each other's doctrines until their beliefs became similar or even identical. And, since the African perceived his gods as functional and utilitarian rather than recondite and ethereal, he concluded that the European's technological and military superiority was proof that Christian "magic" was more powerful than his own. The concept of *power*, as Geoffrey Parrinder noted, was an omnipresent element in African religions and, considering "the dynamic nature of the universe and human life," Africans believed that the powers of various spiritual forces were often in contention with one another.[108] Accordingly, as the African's resistance to his captors crumbled, he found it increasingly difficult to maintain faith in a god who would allow his people to be so easily conquered.[109] In addition, since he had always believed that there were many gods, he never denied the existence of a Christian God; thus his inability to resist the white man's power left him only to conclude that his High God had failed him and that he had no choice but to embrace the "victorious" Christian God.

A belief in competing gods also made American Indians vulnerable to

Christian proselytizing. In 1644 a Sagamore chief and four of his aides agreed to worship the Puritans' God because "we see He doth better to the English, than other gods to others."[110] Over two centuries later another Indian leader called Chief Sealth said essentially the same thing, albeit more forebodingly, when he told a white negotiating party.

> Your God is not our God! Your God loves your people and hates mine. He folds his strong and protecting arms lovingly about the pale-face and leads him by the hand as a father leads his infant son—but He has forsaken His red children—if they are really his. Our God, the Great Spirit, seems also to have forsaken us. Your God makes your people wax strong every day. Soon they will fill the land. Our people are ebbing away like a rapidly receding tide that will never return.[111]

A variation of this theme was expressed by a Cherokee chief named Attakullaculla, called Little Carpenter by whites, who conceded in a speech that the Indians' defeat at the hands of whites must mean that God had intended for whites to prevail. In this case, the Indian believed that both races were served by one God, who had, for his own reasons, made white people superior.

> As to what happened, I believe it has been ordered by our Father above. We are of a different color from the white people. They are superior to us. But one God is father of us all, and we hope that what is passed will be forgotten.[112]

One God or two, the fundamental principle was the same. Whites clearly had been favored by the deity and the Indian had little choice but to accept the consequences.

Conversion was also served by the fact that there were some rather remarkable similarities between African religious notions and certain European ideas about spirits and devils. For decades, one of the most popular arguments against emancipation and racial equality had been the charge that the heathen slaves had come from a primitive culture—they were almost always perceived as having come from one culture—where religious traditions embodied all sorts of superstitions and occult practices, an argument that could be heard among both northern and southern whites up to the Civil War. For example, the West African practice of voodooism, with its belief in the power of sorcery and charms, had been transplanted virtually intact to the Americas, especially to the Caribbean islands. As late as the middle of the twentieth century voodooism was still to be found in some parts of the West Indies and, reportedly, even on Edisto Island, South Carolina.

In the eighteenth century, an Anglican missionary—obviously familiar with biblical condemnations of occult practices like divination (using various clues such as the positions of the stars and planets to predict God's will), necromancy (communicating with the dead), witchcraft, sorcery, casting spells, interpreting omens, black magic, enchantments, and astrology as "an abomination unto the Lord"—complained that "the native religious beliefs [Africans] brought with them were so at odds with Christianity as to preclude their conversion." Another described those born in Guinea as "strangely prepossessed in favour of superstition and idolatry."[113] To him it was clear that the chants, the dances, the music, and the physical gyrations all bespoke the influence of supposed Satan-inspired magical forces.

Yet the irony of it all was that a belief in mystical powers was one of the things that Africans most had in common with their Christian oppressors. The latter may have believed that all such powers were inherently evil, but they never doubted their existence. When it came to "popular religion and folk beliefs," Lawrence W. Levine noted, "the African and West European systems, long assumed to be totally diverse, had enough in common to facilitate syncretism."[114] The idea of a witch whose pact with the devil had given her supernatural powers did not develop in Europe until the late Middle Ages, but then it erupted in an outburst of hysteria far beyond anything witnessed in colonial America.[115] "Between 1560 and 1680 in England's Essex County," David E. Stannard wrote, "it is estimated that at least 400 individuals were accused of over 1,500 witchcraft-related crimes." This was trifling compared to the situation that obtained on the continent. "Thousands of people were tried for witchcraft during the craze that swept over Europe in the sixteenth and seventeenth centuries and crossed the Atlantic with the first white settlers," another historian observed. In some villages up to one-third of the population was accused of witchcraft, with almost 10 percent put to death. "In one small canton in Switzerland between 1611 and 1660 alone, 2,500 people were accused of having made pacts with the Devil," Stannard noted. "All were executed."[116]

There were "aspects of witchcraft in the complex societies of Western Europe," another student of the subject wrote, "that no amount of theoretical refinement can reconcile with witchcraft in simple societies." The European variety, "with its New England derivative, was somehow more convulsive, less stabilizing, and bloodier than its African counterpart."[117] This may have had something to do with the fact that the Christian always considered witchcraft to be an aberration—something to be destroyed;

while the African saw it as an inherent constituent of nature—something to be appeased.

While Christians sanctimoniously condemned African and Indian religious beliefs as delusions, the traditions and fables of these "strangers who do sojourn among you" were certainly no more fantastic than some of their own. When it came to the bizarre and incredible, Judeo-Christianity marched with the best—or worst—of them. What true believers unquestioningly accepted as acts of God, infidels could have seen as nothing more than fairy tales. Old Testament stories of Noah gathering pairs of all the animals, Moses parting the Red Sea, Daniel in the lion's den, Samson pulling a building down with his hands, Jonah in the stomach of a "big fish," and Joshua making the sun stand still were among the biblical myths that severely tested a potential convert's credulity. Similarly, New Testament parables about feeding five thousand people with five loaves of bread and two fishes, Lazarus rising from the dead, and the Resurrection and Ascension were supposed to show the divine power. Skeptics called them fables and allegories conceived to impress the uneducated common people of a simpler time. Believers called them miracles.

One can only wonder what the heathen was supposed to think when he was told he must disavow his false magic and embrace the Christian's equally extravagant mythology. Pagan or Christian, such supernatural phenomena were essential to the promulgation of the faith. If God could not perform miracles, he was not God. It was no different with people whom Christians perceived as heathens. What the European called superstition, witchcraft, and sorcery among Africans were really essential aspects of their traditional religion, in which a belief in magic was associated with natural events such as earthquakes, volcanoes, and floods.[118]

One scholar argued that the most convenient distinction between magic and religion rested on whether or not a person believed that, on the one hand, he benefited from some special power "inherent in the object," or, on the other, if the "object was devoid of any inherent power, but derived its efficacy from God."[119] Conveniently ignoring the fact that God himself could be construed as an object with "inherent" power, he concluded that Christians considered African religions as examples of the former. The best that can be said about separating superstition from faith is that it was, and always will be, difficult to determine where magic starts and religion ends. Some scholars maintain the determination can never be made because there is no real difference.

The European's proclivity for the occult came to the New World right along with his religion and, indeed, was often used to promulgate it. There were few Christians in English North America who did not believe in the power of satanic rites, astrology, witchcraft, and other religious eccentricities. Potions, charms, omens, and various mystical practices, Kenneth M. Stampp pointed out, were commonplace among "Puritans, Baptists, Methodists, and other religious sects who first obtained possession of their ancestors." More than a few English Christians, including John Wesley himself, believed that the Bible recognized witchcraft, albeit as an "abomination."[120] From the earliest days of Christianity, the devout perceived a dichotomous world of good and evil. A belief in the existence of God required a countervailing belief in the existence of Satan, otherwise there would be nothing for God to do and no way of defining the limits beyond which the faithful must not go. The Devil, playwright Arthur Miller observed in his notes to *The Crucible*, was "a necessary part of a respectable view of cosmology," in which the world is "gripped between two diametrically opposed absolutes."[121]

Rare indeed was the Puritan preacher who did not have on his desk a copy of *A Discourse of the Damned Art of Witchcraft*—as did Samuel Parris, the minister of Salem Farms, whose nine-year-old daughter was one of the young girls who claimed in 1692 to have been bewitched by local women. Asked by Sir William Phipps, Governor of Massachusetts Bay, to find "moral and theological support" for the outbreak of hysteria in Salem, Cotton Mather wrote *On Witchcraft: Being the Wonders of the Invisible World* (1692) "to countermine the whole PLOT of the Devil, against *New-England*, in every branch of it, as far as one of my *darkness* can comprehend such a *Work of Darkness*." Trying to justify the trials, Mather claimed there is a Devil who "possesses" people and this could have been the case in Salem.[122] Still defending the prosecutions a decade later in *Magnalia Christi Americana*, Mather pointed out that the judges and justices "consulted the precedents of former times, and precepts laid down by learn'd writers about witchcraft" when arriving at their decisions.[123] Mather may have been alluding to the ninety-five witchcraft incidents recorded in English North America, almost all of them in New England, *before* the Salem outburst. He did not mention that only the Puritans actually executed witches.[124]

When it came to the chimerical world of demons and sorcerers, the transplanted African had plenty of company; American colonists who condemned the slaves' traditional religion as idolatrous and superstitious were simply ignoring their own powerful traditions of magic and witchcraft. Moreover, that condemnation may have been a subconscious acknowledgment of the unique role black-skinned people played in those traditions. In one account of apparitions claimed by allegedly bewitched persons, "scores of Miserable People were troubled by horrible appearances of a Black-Man, accompanied with Spectres," while another described the presence of the Devil, "appearing to me like a black."[125] In every such reference, the equation with evil was clear. One may wonder if it was only a coincidence that Tituba, one of the first persons charged in Salem, was part black.[126]

The Reluctant Convert

A fundamental question remains to nag at the inclination to acquiesce in the obvious. It is difficult to disagree with the conclusion that Africans easily embraced Christianity if—like Patterson, Genovese, Levine, and Stampp, among others—one spends most of the time wondering how and why many slaves adopted the faith. Focusing on a particular segment of the population should reveal a great deal about *that* segment; but it can also obfuscate, or at least distort, the truth about everyone else. One must wonder if the common assumption about the slaves' proclivity for Christianity is based on the fact that, like the person who searches for a lost object under a lamp post because that is where the light is, historians were interested mainly in why—not, how many—slaves became Christians and therefore focused their attention on those who had converted.

Seventeenth-century Puritans who saw the Indian "praying villages" as effective missionary arrangements only saw the Indians who were there. A historian who surveyed the congregations of antebellum southern Baptist churches concluded that "over much of the South biracial churches seems to have been the norm."[127] Did he mean that most Baptist churches were biracial, or that most black Baptists attended biracial churches—or what? Whatever the purpose of his generalization, he was still talking only about blacks who were in church. The researcher sees what he looks at. What many did not, apparently, look at—besides the complaints of both missionaries and slaves—was the membership reports of the various denominations. If even only remotely accurate, these lead to the inescapable conclusion that the great majority of slaves did not become Christians. And, as those scholars who have focused on black religion have pointed out, Christianity among slaves was, in both thought and practice, far different from that of their white counterparts.

Such a conclusion therefore makes it hard to disagree with Frederick Law Olmsted's observation that slave religion was a convenient anodyne, serving useful purposes as recreation and an escape from the tedium of work, but little else. "On many plantations," he wrote, "religious exercises are almost the only habitual recreation not purely sensual, from steady dull labor, in which the negroes are permitted to indulge, and generally all other forms of mental enjoyment are discouraged." Converting to Christianity could also ease the burden of work. By the time of the Great

Awakening, one writer pointed out, bondsmen were well aware that church attendance where allowed meant resting on Sunday. And Christianity created opportunities for recreation and entertainment not otherwise available. In those places where religious exercises were permitted, slaves enjoyed more freedom of expression, Olmsted observed, "than is ever tolerated in conducting mere amusements or educational exercises." In other words, a master was more inclined to allow his bondsmen to "let off steam" if their actions seemed to have a religious purpose. This, in turn, suggests that plantation music was usually spiritual because the slave was not allowed any other kind and that its preponderance, therefore, has exaggerated the importance of religion in the slave's life. If Olmsted's impression that the slaves who were given religious instruction received nothing more than a "delusive clothing of Christian forms and phrases" was the rule throughout the South, the quality of the slave's new faith certainly must be questioned.[128] This means that the researcher is obliged to examine the forces that worked against the conversion of many transplanted Africans, whose religious heritage was so radically different from the dominant faith and, perhaps, from the faith of the researcher himself. There is nothing wrong with asking why many slaves became Christians. There is also nothing wrong with asking why many more did not.

Whatever successes the various denominations claimed, it is impossible to determine with any accuracy the conversion rate of slaves; and the numbers that are available are misleading. As with virtually everything else in his life, the slave could never be sure of his religious options. One researcher who studied black and white Protestants in antebellum Florida, for example, concluded that many slaves who accompanied their masters to church had no choice. If converting to Christianity was supposed to be a voluntary act of contrition, how sincere was the conversion of the slave who was compelled to attend services? "Faithful service was preached to them as a Christian duty, and they pretended to acknowledge it," Olmsted wrote, "but the fact was that they were obedient just so far as they saw they must be to avoid punishment." The Episcopal planter in South Carolina who ordered his overseer to take away the "weekly allowance of bacon, sugar, molasses, or tobacco" of any slave who failed to attend weekly chapel services was not unique. It can never be known how many bondsmen were simply poseurs who wanted only to please their owners. But there is abundant evidence that in many of their contacts with the master the slaves tried to outwit him by "outdumbing" him—"puttin' on ole Massa," some of them called it—the wily practice of feigning stupidity in order to accommodate the white man in one direction while thinking in another. Needless to say, conversions based on fear, expediency, or deception could hardly be called genuine. One slaveowner who had urged his slaves to become Christians later complained that they were all "called to prayers, but none came." On the other hand, how many slaves became sincere Christians, or at least wanted to, but never identified with a particular denomination and therefore were not listed in any official report? Was one who *believed* any less important because he was not counted? The Protestant churches may have failed the black person, Levine argued, but "it does not follow that the spiritual message of Protestantism failed as well."[129] Of course, while the absence of a slave's name on a church roster did not necessarily mean he was not among the faithful, the reverse was equally true. The writer who described the "genuine religious response" of some slaves to the entreaties of an Episcopal minister did not explain how anyone could be sure.[130] A roomful of happy, singing slaves was not necessarily an indication of "genuine religious response."

While many of the historians who claimed to see wholesale conversions looked for reasons why a slave would want to become a Christian, few have asked why he would *not*. Those who did would find it virtually impossible to avoid the conclusion that the hypocrisy inherent in a faith that claims to free the soul at the same time that it imprisons the body was certainly a major reason for repudiating Christianity. Also common was a well-justified unwillingness to trust white churchmen. Convinced that the most pious masters were also the cruelest, forty-nine-year-old Joseph Smith of Maryland declared that he would "rather live with a cardplayer and a drunkard than with a Christian."[131] Only her enormous faith enabled Harriet A. Jacobs to continue believing in the basic goodness of Christianity and at the same time recognize the obvious hypocrisy of her devout but brutal master.

> *Ole Satan's church is here below;*
> *Up to God's free church I hope to go.*[132]

Replying to a question from Olmsted about the slaves' "habitual lack of trust of the white race," an Episcopal cleric conceded that the slaves were skeptical enough to wonder why, if the Bible was addressed to all peoples, he was afraid to put it in their hands and let them read it for themselves. In 1849, Henry Bibb recalled that his fellow slaves had no confidence in white ministers "because they preach a pro-slavery doctrine." The only preachers the slaves trusted were black, he added, and masters often kept them away from the plantations.[133]

Underlying all of this was the slave's understandable reluctance to worship the God of his oppressor. What would have been the attraction in that? In 1729, Elihu Coleman, a Quaker "minister" in Nantucket, Massachusetts, asked why any bondsman would want to belong to a religion whose members "tell the Negroes they must believe in Christ, . . . receive the Sacrament, and be baptized, and so they do, but still they keep them slaves." The point was repeated in 1776 by another antislavery clergyman, the Reverend Samuel Hopkins of Newport, Rhode Island, when he accused "Christian masters" of mistreating their slaves, thus creating among them "the deepest prejudices against the Christian religion." Others were outwardly bitter. After he and his mother were caught trying to run away by "slave-catchers" hired for the purpose, William Wells Brown described their journey back to what he sarcastically called "the land of whips, chains, and Bibles." Among some former slaves the operative word was *hatred.* "It is impossible to reconcile the mind of the native slave to the idea of living in a state of perfect equality, and boundless affection, with white people," Charles Ball wrote in 1858. "Heaven will be no heaven to him, if he is not avenged of his enemies."[134] To Ball, loving a god whose teachings had been used to subjugate him and his people made no sense whatsoever.

If the slave had good reason to spurn Christianity, the Indian had a better mechanism for doing so. In the early colonial period, English missionaries had used the "image of the bad Indian" to prove that he needed Christianity and his good qualities to show that he deserved it.[135] But, while the transplanted African was understandably bewildered and overwhelmed by the forces of an oppressive and alien environment, the Indian, a member of a unified and continuous culture, occupying much of the same land that his ancestors had roamed for thousands of years, was better able, for the most part, to resist the blandishments of white missionaries. The African had been wrenched from his traditional homeland; the Indian was in the middle of his. In the early nineteenth century, a Seneca chief named Red Jacket, calling attention to the common Indian belief in religious pluralism, vigorously opposed Christian proselytizing among his people. To the Indian, religion was, above all, a utilitarian belief system that explained a person's origins and destiny and defined his relationship to the universe, a belief system that was typical of most polytheistic cultures. When there are many gods, every group can claim a share. Each society has its own way of understanding the origins and meaning of life, Red Jacket pointed out, and none is more valid than or superior to the others. In short, people use what works. If the members of a society are satisfied with their faith, the Indian asked, why should an outsider want to force his religion on them?[136] "Then saith the native, let the fault lie upon me, and if I may be saved in the religion of my own country, I shall need no further instructor, nor shall I desire any change."[137]

To the Indian—as to the African—religious influences reached into every corner of life. Accordingly, conversion to Christianity, since it meant abandoning ancient beliefs, was nothing less than cultural treason. When some missionaries began urging Indian converts to get control of their tribal government, Indian leaders, realizing that large-scale conversion would undermine tribal unity, decided they had no choice but to resist the "black coats," even if it meant violence. "The massacre of the Reverend Marcus Whitman and a few other Americans in Oregon during 1847," Robert F. Berkhofer suggested, looked very much like a reaction to religious proselytizing.[138] Two years later, Father Eugene Casimir Chirouse expressed his fear that the same fate might befall him at the hands of the Yakima Indians in the Washington Territory.

> At this moment savages from nearly all the neighboring nations are assembled at Holy Cross. I count sixty cabins in my village, around one hundred families. There I have *Yellow-Serpent* with his following as an opponent. He himself presides at all the abominations which are spoken or committed in his infernal den. An old trickster does his best to help him embarrass me: irritated because my instructions are contrary to his maxims and diabolical acts, he invented this strange calumny in order that I might be put to death: "The Blackrobe," he says, "catches rattlesnakes, and makes them vomit a black poison with which he poisons the tobacco with the intention of killing everyone."[139]

Unfortunately, but understandably, since the Indians perceived religious forces as pervasive rather than selective, they did not distinguish between missionaries and farmers. In matters of faith, every white man was an enemy.

If it is difficult to determine how many slaves who were encouraged or permitted to become Christians actually did so, it is impossible to know how many did so in spite of the master. Cut off from the physical underpinnings of their traditional religions, many recent African arrivals certainly would have developed new spiritual anchors. The question was not whether transplanted Africans fell back on Christianity but how many of them actually did so, and in what form. The result would have been, as Genovese surmised, a hybrid faith that combined the slave's "African inheritance with the dominant power," producing a distinctive faith all his own. It is not unreasonable to suggest that if this sort of syncretism could happen to Africans who remained fully under the influences of their traditional religious beliefs, it certainly could happen to those who had been torn away from their ancestral homelands and dragged across thousands of miles of ocean. In the seventeenth and eighteenth centuries, Christian missionaries in the Kongo reported that the natives had no difficulty superimposing Christianity on their tribal religions. "Christianity was thoroughly Africanized," John Kelly Thornton wrote, "in that there was a more or less direct translation of Kongo cosmology and religious categories onto Christianity," a translation facilitated by the fact that various Christian titles, rituals, and adjuncts were easily associated with similar African counterparts, for example, Catholic saints perceived as the equivalents of the African's pantheon of lesser gods. It could be argued, of course, that true conversion required the converts to make radical changes in their behavior—which Kongo Africans did not do—but the missionaries also realized that few natives would have even listened to them if there had not been some kind of accommodation with traditional beliefs and practices. Accordingly, "some truly remarkable combinations of Christianity and local religions were considered to be orthodox, at least for a time, as in China and some parts of India."[140]

Then, also, there were those slaves who were not exposed to Christianity simply because of indifference on the part of their masters. These faceless thousands are impossible to acknowledge because they were an unknown part of that vast majority whose names did not appear in any official church records. Even those who could be accounted for revealed little about the nature of their involvement. That the missionary outreach to slaves quickened dramatically during the Second Great Awakening in the early nineteenth century, especially among Methodists and Baptists, there seems to be little doubt. But that was only a measure of the *white* interest in converting blacks; it revealed little about the number of blacks who actually converted or the circumstances of their conversion. It also revealed little about the nature of the slave's Christianity. For example, what kind of Christian was the slave whose only religious instruction was monotonous lessons on obedience?

When all of the factors that influenced religious participation are considered, attempts to estimate the actual number of Christian slaves are little more than educated guesses; but it is hard to disagree with the proposition that the number of believing, practicing communicants was considerably less than has long been supposed. And overriding all of this was the fact that it was almost always the interests of the master—who, as one observer put it in 1680, had "no other God but money, nor Religion but profit"[141]—and not the efforts of missionaries or the spiritual predilections of the transplanted African, that determined a slave's real religious status.

For many years it was—and, in some ways, still is—common wisdom in the Anglo-American world that the Judeo-Christian world-view imposed certain attributes on all peoples under its influence: independence, perseverance, probity, and moral rectitude, to name a few. Moreover, if all humans were the descendants of an Original Pair, as the biblical view would seem to insist, the fundamental oneness of humankind could not be denied, and it was only a matter of time before adherence to the faith produced a unified culture. In other words, all races and societies were essentially the same; national and regional differences, it was assumed, were the consequences of environmental influences and cultural nurturing. "The repetition of identical impressions from a common environment," Oscar Handlin wrote, summarizing this idea, "in time produced the national characteristics of a people." Accordingly, it was easy for white Americans to conclude that social forces would ultimately mold all immigrants into "the common cultural pattern being shaped by conditions in the United States." When applied to most of the newcomers to the English-speaking New World, the expectation seemed logical. Although English culture had always been dominant, it was obvious almost from the very beginning that many northern and western Europeans—especially white Protestants like the Scotch-Irish, Dutch, Swedes, and Germans—could easily homogenize into the great Melting Pot.[142] All that was needed for the evolution of the Christian Everyman was sufficient exposure to a Christian culture.

For a time, there were those who believed this logic should apply to non-Europeans as well. In New England, John Eliot worked to bring about a "massive cultural change by the introduction of European social and cultural values and institutions" before introducing the Indians to Christianity.[143] "They must 'come up into civil Cohabitation, Government and Labor,' " Eliot's biographer wrote, "and have a fixed condition of life before they would be entrusted with the sacred ordinances of church communion." But other seventeenth-century missionaries sanguinely assumed that it was only necessary to convert the native and he would spontaneously and happily abandon his "savage" culture. The great civilizing factor was conversion to the faith: as soon as the heathen became a Christian—Protestant, of course—he would think and act like one. After all, "the importance of conversion was one of the standards under which the Reformation marched," one historian wrote, and its fundamental axiom was the reorientation of one's life.[144]

A basic premise of the SPG mission to the slaves was, according to Frank J. Klingberg, "that the Negro would, when civilized, work for his own economic survival and security for exactly the same reasons that actuated the white man." By the time of the American Revolution, however, it had become clear that such a radical metamorphosis was simply out of the question for both Indians and slaves. There were "enormous cultural differences" separating blacks from whites, Handlin concluded, and slavery "had shaped those differences into an unbridgeable gulf." Recording his impressions after living in the United States for ten years, Austrian-born Francis J. Grund wrote in 1837 that "[i]t is in vain to talk of civilizing

[Indians]"; and even if it were possible they would eventually become outlaws because whites would never accept them as equals.[145] For Christian reformers who believed in the spiritual oneness of humankind, the desire to make outsiders into cultural clones of themselves was far more than just an example of religious arrogance. It was a denial of reality.

FIVE SQUARE PEGS IN ROUND HOLES

Say, Righteous Sire, shall Afric ever mourn
Her weeping children from her bosom torn?
Chained, sold, and scattered far in Christian lands;
Scourged, beaten, murdered, too, by Christian hands!

DANIEL A. PAYNE
Untitled (1841)

O great Jehovah! God of love,
Thou monarch of the earth and sky,
Canst thou from thy great throne above
Look down with an unpitying eye?—

See Afric's sons and daughters toil,
Day after day, year after year,
Upon this blood-bemoistened soil,
And to their cries turn a deaf ear?

JAMES M. WHITFIELD
"Prayer of the Oppressed" (1853)

The Ancestral Gods

In August 1986, approximately seventeen hundred people and more than three thousand cattle died by suffocation when a cloud of carbon dioxide erupted from Lake Nyos in Cameroon, West Africa, cutting off oxygen over the lower valley.[1] Survivors described the odor of rotten eggs and complained of burning eyes and difficulty breathing before losing consciousness for up to forty-eight hours. Eventually, as many as seven thousand refugees had to be evacuated from the region.

As to what natural forces caused the disaster, Western scientists offered a number of theories. Some suggested that carbon dioxide and other gases had collected in a pocket on the lake bottom and were suddenly released by an unknown geological action, although there was no evidence of any seismic activity. Another theory, based mainly on the fact that Lake Nyos was one of more than thirty volcanic crater lakes in Cameroon, posited that gas from deep within the earth's crust had escaped through a fissure. Only a few centuries old, Nyos had formed when molten rock deep within the earth rose to heat groundwater into steam, a development reflected in local legends of exploding lakes. Others simply argued that the pressure of hundreds of feet of water became too heavy for the one billion cubic meters of carbon dioxide that had been accumulating over the years. Adding to the mystery were the ominous changes in the lake itself: for almost two months the water was the color of dark cocoa, stained by a rusting iron compound called ferric hydroxide that had been pushed up by the escaping gas, and it was over 11 degrees Celsius warmer than the water of the other lakes in the region.

Nor was this the first time such an event had struck the area. Almost exactly two years earlier, Lake Monoun, ninety-five kilometers south of Nyos, had spit up a cloud of gas that smothered thirty-seven people. Meeting in Yaoundé, Cameroon's capital, in March 1987, American, French, and Italian scientists could not agree on the causes of the disasters. But the Bantu people of the region did not need outsiders to tell them what had happened. To local villagers who had long believed that the spirits of their ancestors lived in the lakes the explanation was obvious: *The Gods were angry!*

In Africa it was to the gods and spirits of the physical landscape that one prayed for health and prosperity—or blamed for natural disasters; and, since no one would ever be so foolish as to curse the High God, the lesser gods were convenient targets of criticism. The reactions of the local villagers to the Lake Nyos catastrophe was a reminder of how easy it is to underestimate the persistence and durability of traditional religious beliefs. Accordingly, it is hard to agree with the common assumption that the American slave could have put aside his ancestral religion as easily as some scholars have suggested.[2] There were simply too many critical differences to account for. For example, how did the African's belief in many gods—not to mention his obeisance to the spirits of the dead—accommodate Christianity's insistence on one God and its condemnation of what it considered idolatrous and pagan rites?

Moreover, the slave must have had difficulty understanding a religion that called for a two-hour meeting in a church building on Sunday morning and was then forgotten for the rest of the week. "Africans who traditionally do not know religious vacuum, feel that they don't get enough religion from this type of Christianity," Kenyan John S. Mbiti observed, "since it does not fill up their whole life and their understanding of the universe." In the stateless societies of West Africa, another writer pointed out, religion was "first and foremost a theoretical interpretation of the world, and an attempt to apply this interpretation to the prediction and control of worldly events." The African's religion was not a hat he put on just for special days and observances, but was, rather, a way of thinking and behaving that was a fundamental aspect of his everyday life, what

Galbraith Welch called "an almost indistinguishable mingling of the social with the religious."[3] Many American slaves embraced Christianity, and their sincerity need not be doubted; but researchers who have cited these conversions as evidence of the mass appeal of Christianity simply have not addressed the basic problem of accounting for beliefs and practices that had been nurtured by centuries of tradition and habit.

Generalizing about these beliefs and practices called for the ability to find the usual among the unique. What has been commonly called African traditional religion—sometimes shortened to "ATR," or even the acronym "ATIAR"—was, in fact, a collection of many different religious practices.[4] But there was no tribal group that did not recognize a High God who was responsible for the creation of the universe. To many Bantu-speaking peoples he was "the 'great Muntu,' a person and a force, from which all other beings and creatures come."[5] A young Ijebu man named Osifekunde, who had been sold into slavery in Brazil, identified the god of his people as Obba Oloroun, "king of heaven," also known as Olou-oroun, which means, similarly, "master of the sky," or Olodumare, "owner of the heavens." There were no statues or temples for Obba Oloroun, Osifekunde wrote, because "he is an immaterial being, invisible, eternal, the supreme will which created and governs all things."[6]

This description is almost identical to that of another New World convert, Olaudah Equiano—who had spent part of his captivity in Virginia and was best known to Americans by his Christian name of Gustavus Vassa. In *Interesting Narrative* (1789), Equiano described the supreme god of the Ika people in his native province of Benin as the "Creator of all things, [who] lives in the sun, and is girded around with a belt, that he may never eat or drink; but according to some, he smokes a pipe, which is our own favorite luxury."[7] Variations of Oloroun were common throughout West Africa, and the High God was known by a seemingly infinite variety of names, one "Index of God-Names" running to over three double-column pages.[8] The names may have been different, but in virtually every case the High God was far too important to be considered a personal god who had the time to notice, or even care about, the trivial and mundane problems of common mortals.[9] Unlike the Christian God, to whom one prayed for blessings and forgiveness and who presumably filled the believer with his spirit, the African supreme deity was a remote entity whose essence was beyond the reach and comprehension of ordinary human beings.[10]

This meant, of course, that the typical African's relationship with the supreme deity was far different from the Christian's. As early as 1705, long before European missionaries established permanent stations in West Africa, William Bosman noted that the people of the region believed in the existence of a supreme god but they did not *worship* him. "They have a faint idea of the true God, and ascribe to Him the attributes of Almighty and Omnipresent," Bosman wrote, "but they do not pray to Him, or offer any sacrifices to Him."[11] It was a perception that carried over into the songs and verses of the plantation. "Much of the oral religious literature of the African layman consisted less of 'prayers' (as we think of them)," one musicologist noted, "than of dramatic statements, in the form of songs, relating to the deities."[12]

Not surprisingly, there were few temples or organized cults in sub-Saharan Africa, where formal prayer and worship were practiced. In West Africa only among the Akan peoples of the Ashanti kingdom did one find temples and priests of God. Most of the others were like the Yorubas, who had "no temples of *Oloroun*, no priests dedicated to his service, no cult-houses or convents for the training of devotees," Geoffrey Parrinder observed. "No offerings are made to *Oloroun*, for there are no shrines, and hence no communal prayers or sacrifices, not even the simplest libations of wine, such as are made in honour of the ancestors." It was somewhat paradoxical, at least in the minds of Christians, that although virtually all Africans believed they faced the High God after they died, most of their religious ceremonies and practices had little to do with him.[13] Herein lay the fundamental difference between the Christian and African perceptions of God: There was no African equivalent to the Christian idea of a personal commitment to God based on faith, thus the Christian abstraction of an omnipotent and omniscient being who sits in judgment and punishes a person for his sins simply was not part of the African's eschatology.[14]

As in most polytheistic cultures, the Africans acknowledged a hierarchy of gods and spirits who occupied natural places such as the sky, rivers, and mountains, and lesser heavenly beings like the spirits of the rocks and the huts, plus ancestral spirits who were everywhere. Fetishism, the belief that spirits and gods manifested themselves in material objects, was a critical element in virtually every West African religion. Polytheism was so universal in sub-Saharan Africa that when reports appeared that monotheism might have existed among some of the ancient societies of the upper Nile Valley, Christian missionaries denied the possibility; they refused to believe the idea could have originated before any biblical influence had touched the continent. "It was abhorrent to think that God would have placed in the minds of these savages the instinctive realization of Himself as Creator and Supreme Being," Galbraith Welch remarked, "which had required explanation, revelation and argument to convey to our own ancestors." Reinforcing the Christians' incredulity was the fact that African polytheism was everywhere and multifarious. The Yoruba counted as many as 601 divinities "on every hill, and under every green tree." Many of these intermediate and lesser gods were not actually revered as deities, but, since they had the power to intervene for good or ill in everyday affairs, it was always considered necessary to conciliate them with gestures and words of deference and sometimes with material offerings like chickens, sheep, or an ox.[15] Along the West Coast, where tornadoes are common, rain and thunder gods, not surprisingly, were among the most important deities. The complex belief system of the Yoruba people included homage to Shango, one of the most important of the lesser gods, who blew fire (lightning) and smoke (thunder) from his mouth. In modern times it is still a custom among the Yoruba to say, following a clap of thunder, "Welcome to your Majesty!"[16]

Among the most feared of these *pneumas* were spirits who were to be avoided or appeased because they could bring upon a family, or an entire community, anything from laziness and impotence to epidemics and natural disasters.[17] It was these "swarms of tribally assorted little gods and spirits and demons," Welch wrote, "who came into the life of the bookless Africans and were to them so real that they seemed to be constantly underfoot, constantly giving them shudders and shivers, and less often comfort."[18] To Christians, of course, a belief in spirits and spells, like any occult practice, was one of the most terrible aspects of heathen religions. "When you enter the land the Lord your God is giving you, do not learn to imitate the detestable ways of the nations there," Moses presumably told the Israelites as they were about to go into the Promised Land.

> Let no one be found among you who sacrifices his son or daughter in the fire, who practices divination or sorcery, interprets omens, engages in witchcraft, or casts spells, or who is a medium or spiritist or who consults the dead. Anyone who does these things is detestable to the Lord, and because of these detestable practices the Lord your God will drive out those nations before you.[19]

But to the American slave "detestable practices" were part of Christianity itself, as ninety-three-year-old William Adams of Fort Worth, Texas, recounted to a WPA interviewer.

> There is some born under the power of the devil and have the power to put injury and misery on people, and some born under the power of the Lord for to do good and overcome the evil power. . . . Don't forgit—the agents of the devil have the power of evil. They can put misery of every kind on people. They can make trouble with the work and with the business, and with the family and with the health. So folks must be on the watch all the time.[20]

On the plantation, Gilbert Osofsky noted, Satan was "Old Sam," a familiar figure combining both the traditional Christian devil and African spirits, "like Anansi the spider, or the Afro-Brazilian Exú, or the Haitian Legba, [who] regularly toy with man's fate and have a comic as well as tragic aspect to their characters."[21] The icon of the troublesome demon even appeared in a Civil War slave song in which the bedevilment of the Confederate President was taken for granted:

If de Debble do not ketch
Jeff. Davis, dat infernal wretch,
An roast and frigazee dat rebble,
Wat is de use of any Debble?[22]

The idea of the Devil is one that appears to be almost exclusively a concept of the monotheistic traditions of Judaism, Christianity, and Islam. A culture in which there is one god who is the source of all that is good in the world must also acknowledge a countervailing evil to account for all that is bad.

The embodiment of good *and* evil in one god-figure was not uncommon in some non-Western religions; but this was not possible in Christian eschatology, thus the Devil became a necessary device to absolve God of responsibility for the evil in the world. Conversely, African traditional religions had no equivalent to the biblical Satan, no projections of a "fallen angel" whose purpose was to tempt souls away from God. Since polytheistic religions recognized both good and bad gods and spirits—and some that could go either way depending on the circumstances—their adherents did not need a Satan as a focal point of all wrongdoing. In other words, Africans did not blame their sins on an inscrutable external influence. Rather, the source of evil was close to home, located "in the human world among the ambitions and jealousies of men."[23] But in the Christian universe of good and evil, the latter was incarnated in a Satan figure, which the transplanted African reconstructed in the only way that made sense to him.

Old Satan is one busy ole man;
He rolls dem blocks all in my way;
But Jesus is my bosom friend;
He rolls dem blocks away.[24]

Instead of a transcendent Lucifer, who tormented condemned souls in a place called hell—a place rarely mentioned in plantation spirituals—or an undefinable force who could be everywhere at the same time, the slave's

"Prince of Darkness" was a popular personage who could materialize any time and under the most mundane conditions.

> When my first wife died 'bout thirty years ago, I was going up to Gaston to see Sara Drayden, old Scot Drayden's wife, and I took out through Kennedy Bottom 'bout sundown right after a rain. I seed something a-coming down the road 'bout that high, 'bout size a little black shaggy dog, and I says, "What's that I sees coming down the road? Ain't nobody round here got no black shaggy dog." It kept a-coming and kept a-gitting bigger and bigger and closer and closer, and time it got right to me 'twas as big as a half-growed yearling, black as a crow. It had four feet and drop ears, just like a dog, but 'twa'nt no dog. I knows that. Then he shy out in the bushes, and he come right back on the road, and it went on the way I was coming from, so I went on the way it was coming from. I ain't never seed that thing no more. But I's got a pretty good notion 'bout who it 'twas.[25]

Reminiscing about his slavery days, William Wells Brown recalled that "[t]he early traditions, brought down through the imported Africans, have done much to keep alive the belief that the devil is a personal being, with hoofs, horns, and having powers equal with God." Even some poor whites perceived Satan as a real person, "sporting a club-foot, horns, tail, and a hump on his back," whose influence "was far greater than that of the Lord." He was "a snake in the grass" luring the unsuspecting soul toward damnation.[26] As one plantation song proclaimed:

Shout! Shout! Satan's about.
Just shut your door, and keep him out.

and warned:

Old Satan's just like a snake in the grass,
He's a-watching for to bite you as you pass.

But the slave also knew that there was a sure way of escaping the impending destruction:

But now I'se come a Christun,
I kneels right down an' prays,
An' den de Devil runs from me—
I'se tried dem other ways.[27]

To the transplanted African, a product of a culture in which wrongdoing began in the hearts of individuals and where virtually every material object possessed a spirit, the purveyor of evil took the visible form of an ordinary creature that a person could see and touch and even talk to. The African's High God was remote and unconcerned, but his devil was down to earth and everywhere.

Soul, Sin, Salvation

There were, of course, many more differences between Christianity and African traditional religions than the number of gods and spirits. For example, African conceptions of what Christians call the "soul" were unlike anything in Judeo-Christian theology. While the African understanding of the human spirit was complex and varied from one society to the next, most scholars agree that it had many "spiritual components." In the beliefs of some peoples the "personality-soul" appeared before God to account for the decedent's earthly deeds, approximating the Christian's Judgment Day. A number of West African peoples identified the soul with the voice since "the voice has a personal note of its own which distinguishes it from others." Other spiritual components included a guardian spirit and a moral guide.[28] Sometimes the concepts of god and soul merged. The Ewe people recognized a High God, Mawu, but they also alternated that name with *se*, which was their term for the soul. When someone said "my *Mawu*," he meant "my *se*." Thus to the Ewe, all living things were imbued with the spirit of god:

> *Man has a soul* (se), *the wild animal has a soul,*
> *The bird has a soul, the tree has a soul,*
> *All these souls, who knows them?*
> *God-life* (Mawu-gbe) *is their soul.*[29]

Some societies, such as the Dogon, believed an infant was born only with twin male-female souls but gradually acquired others through maturation and the various rites of passage. To others the soul emerged during dreams. The Gã people, for example, believed a dream was simply a wandering soul, a belief that was similar to one held by the Huron Indians of the northeastern United States.[30] Even more profound was the belief of the Pawnee Indian of the central plains that his dream was a preview of his soul's ultimate destination, where he would dwell forever with his supreme god, Ti-ra'-wa.[31]

While virtually all Africans recognized a human spirit that survived the body, they had no counterpart for, and little understanding of, what Christians called "sin," especially the notion of "original sin," a doctrine of depravity that saw "heredity as transmitting moral disease."[32] The Apostle Paul's confession that, despite his best intentions, his "sinful nature" prevented him from doing good, was beyond the comprehension of people who could never understand how—or, more important, why—a newborn infant inherited a sinful condition that only the grace of a "savior" could expiate.[33] This did not mean that Africans had no recognition of wrongdoing. As in virtually every culture, certain behavior was defined as immoral and conduct that harmed others was universally condemned. One could expect punishment for actions that inflicted suffering on another; but that punishment was conceived as a deterrent to future offenses, retribution for violation of group rules, and compensation to the victim. It was wrong and unjust to steal another man's cow, and a thief would be dealt with by the elders of the society; but such acts were merely the consequences of ordinary human vices like greed and envy. Moreover, a person may have been influenced by others, whom he perceived as witches and sorcerers; but those people, in turn, were only part of a "demonic humanity," whose presence constituted a form of hell-on-earth. In other words, the commission of a sin, for which one should feel guilt, ask for forgiveness, do penance, and seek redemption, was simply not part of the African's spiritual understanding. The Bushmen of the Kalahari Desert did not even have a word in their language for "guilt." And the "dualism of good and evil" that was inherent in Christian eschatology was, Parrinder noted, "unknown to the people of West Africa."[34]

Similarly, before an American Indian could be admitted into the Puritan family, he had to *learn* to be contrite, as missionary John Eliot discovered when he was asked by some New England Indians to explain "humiliation," a word they had often heard in Christian sermons but that was not translatable into their tongue. The ideas of sin and salvation, historian Henry Warner Bowden wrote in his study of Indian missions, were "areas where missionaries found no common ground with native thought." Like people everywhere, Indians understood good and evil, but they could not "fathom the concept of universal guilt." Wrongdoing called for compensation, not repentance. Why, they asked, did Christ have to die for their sins? The spilling of blood was demanded only from enemies.[35]

If the slave was bewildered by the Christian notions of *soul* and *sin*, it is not unreasonable to wonder if he was able to comprehend the idea of *salvation*, which for most Protestants "demanded renouncing the old self and reconstructing a new one under the Spirit." Concomitantly, in a universe defined by the opposing forces of good and evil, salvation, after which paradise awaited true believers, could not exist without *damnation*, which condemned sinners to eternal punishment in the clutches of Satan. It was perhaps this promise of a heavenly reward for good behavior (and, conversely, the threat of condemnation to hell for disobedience) that most distinguished Christianity from the slave's ancestral religion. In the traditional beliefs, one African writer pointed out, there was no paradise to be sought, hell to be feared, or "messianic hope or apocalyptic vision with God stepping in at some future moment to bring about a reversal of man's normal life." God did not exist in an "ethical-spiritual relationship with man" and worship and prayer were "pragmatic and utilitarian rather than spiritual or mystical."[36] For the deceased, happiness in the next life was largely dependent on the tributes of the living.

For example, an English traveler described a village where it was customary, following the death of the governor, "for two of his favorite wives to quit the world on the same day, in order that he may have a little pleasant social company in a future state."[37] The spirits of the departed would, in turn, intercede with the gods on behalf of the living. It was a mutually beneficial arrangement. In traditional African cultures, appeals were made to the spirits mainly to ensure the attainment of earthly objectives like success, health, and prosperity. Africans acknowledged a world occupied by ancestral spirits who had an ethereal *presence*; the hereafter was *here*, and communication with the ghosts of deceased relatives was part of everyday life. Some believed in a sort of filial regeneration. For example, the Edos of Nigeria believed in reincarnation involving the rebirth of a dead person's soul back into the same family, thus strengthening the continuity of family life.[38]

As it happened, the African's acknowledgment of the importance of ancestral spirits was one of the most enduring aspects of the American slave's preparation for death. While some Christian slaves sang of rejoining loved ones in "Beulah Land,"[39] others were heard to say on their deathbeds that they would soon be returning to Africa to join the spirits of their ancestors; and it was not unusual to be asked to carry messages to specific individuals who had already passed over. "Those born in Guinea are strangely prepossessed in favour of superstition and idolatry," the Reverend Philip Reading wrote to an Anglican colleague in England in 1748. "They have a notion, that when they die, they are translated to their own country, there to live in their former free condition."[40]

An important consequence of this belief—which has no Christian counterpart—was "the relation between the living and the dead." Whether or not the deceased was in some place called "heaven" was not a major concern. "Unlike Western religious thought," Benjamin C. Ray pointed out, "speculation about the meaning of human existence does not project forward to a distant and transcendent future; it projects back upon itself to the present, in cyclical fashion, to the all important *now.*" While there were some West African societies—such as the Dogon, Yoruba, and LoDagaa—that were exceptions to the rule, in most of the sub-Saharan region the existence of an afterlife and the notion of personal immortality were only important when associated with the affairs of the living.[41] While the Christian prayed to God in preparation for a future life, the African called upon the spirits of dead relatives to help him in the present one. Thus the southern preacher's lesson that the bondsman should happily endure the temporary hardships of this world in order to realize the permanent blessings of the next was contrary to everything the black African understood about life before and after death.

The black African's puzzlement with understanding how departed Christian souls got to paradise was anchored in a perception of time unlike anything that existed in the West. The Christian's belief that one's earthly life should be spent preparing for an ultimate place called heaven was based on a concept—the future, or perhaps more to the point, eternity—that the African found difficult to understand.[42] Olaudah Equiano, who described his own conversion to Christianity in his *Interesting Narrative*, agreed that the people of his native Benin believed in a supreme being who controlled events, "but, as for the doctrine of eternity, I do not remember to have heard of it." What Africans did not conceive of was an indefinite future, Ray noted, "stretching beyond the *immediate* future of the next two or three years."[43] Understanding the Christian idea of an endless future was one of the most difficult adaptations the converted slave had to make.

Consequently, while white Christians envisioned spending eternity in heaven, black converts were inclined to anticipate a more worldly "Day of Judgment." With spirituals including lines like "You'll see de world on fire," "the stars a fallin'," "the moon a bleedin'," "the righteous marching," and "My Jesus coming," the slave focused on a definite point in the future when he would be relieved of his burdens, not on a vague infinity in which everyone would simply be happy. It was a logical, even imperative, consequence of his cultural foundations. In African thought there was no understanding of history moving forward through stages to a climax, and thus no expectation of redemption in a "world to come," as one finds in Islam, Judaism, and Christianity.[44] The biblical Armageddon, in which the forces of goodwill finally triumph over the forces of evil, was simply not comprehensible to a people whose conception of time projected only to the end of the growing season.[45]

In the African's thinking, rewards for good deeds and punishment for wrongdoing were received in the present world. Is it any wonder, then, that to the American slave almost every Christian figure and idea—not just the Devil—were here and near, not abstract and remote. "Heaven and Hell were not concepts but places which could be experienced in one's lifetime," Lawrence W. Levine wrote. "God and Christ and Satan were not symbols but personages with whom meetings or confrontations were quite possible." The Jesus of the slave songs was not a distant and untouchable High God whom one would meet only in the next life, but a close personal friend who could pop up any time.[46]

When Jesus met the woman at the well,
Oh, she went running to tell.
She said come and see a man at the well,
He told me ev'ry thing that I done.[47]

"It is not at all uncommon to hear [the slaves] refer to conversations which they allege, and apparently believe themselves to have had with Christ, the apostles, or the prophets of old," Frederick Law Olmsted observed in his extensive travels through the South before the Civil War, "or to account for some of their actions by attributing them to the direct influence of the Holy Spirit, or the devil." A later traveler, Scotsman David Macrae, recalled the numerous stories told by former slaves in whose dreams and songs God, Jesus, and Satan appeared and talked.[48]

> I came to a building where I saw God. He sat writing, and without stopping he said to me, "I shod you with the gospel of peace at the greedy jaws of hell. Your name is written on the lamb book of life. Go back in yonder world and stay until I come, for when I come again it is without sin unto salvation." When he spoke those words, the whole place seemed to sound in a moan, "Amen."[49]

Similarly, a twelve-year-old child described a vision he had had after going to bed:

> I saw God sitting in a large armchair, his head up and looking into space. He neither moved nor spoke. He wore a full armor, and across his chest was a breast-protector that shone as if it was made of bars of gold. My mother was standing there, and showed me my two brothers who had died. I looked around and saw hosts of angels around two long tables, and they were shouting and clapping their hands.[50]

One slave convert, struggling to overcome his belief in traditional healing practices, described a God who "came to me in person while I was in a trance and said, 'There ain't no such thing as conjurers.' " But old habits died hard. "I believe in root doctors," he added, "because, after all, we must depend on some form of root weed to cure the sick."[51] However the slave adapted Christianity to his needs, God was not so much an omnipotent creator of the universe to be reckoned with on Judgment Day as a "Great Comforter" who helped folks get through, not just life in general, but the tribulations of each day. "O when I talk I talk wid God" and "Mass Jesus is my bosom friend," like the common appellations of various biblical characters, such as "Sister Mary" and "Brudder Moses," were expressions that reflected a close personal association.[52]

By casting divine beings in human forms, the slave was trying to make comprehensible and comfortable a world in which he was powerless. The dying bondsman—who feared being buried near his white master, who he believed was going to hell—pleaded with his family to be buried elsewhere because he was afraid the devil might mistakenly take the wrong body. "Few Negro songs project mystical or abstract philosophical concepts," musicologist Harold Courlander conceded. "They tend to concentrate on particular events, episodes, stories, and revelations." In a plantation folktale entitled "The Devil's Doing," God and the Angel Gabriel were out for a walk after dinner "along back down the Big Road, picking their teeth," when they came upon a man who was scraping scales off several catfish. Angry at a human trying to undo his work, the Lord ordered the man to toss the fish back into the river. The fish tried to ease the pain of having their scales removed by rolling in the mud on the river bottom, but although the pain eventually subsided, "the scales never grew back, and from that time on the catfish haven't had scales."[53] In the African world, one called upon familiar ancestral spirits to intercede with the gods. Since the Christian world would not tolerate this, it made more sense—and was more compatible with his traditional religion—for the converted slave to equate God and Jesus not with an African High God like Oloroun but with the everyday gods.

One Christian institution that must have appeared strange to the slave was the *church*. Unlike most of the world's polytheistic religions, which have little formal organization, Christianity (like Islam and Judaism) has almost always been characterized by some kind of consecrated place of worship—a magnificent cathedral or simply an open space on a field—where the faithful gather on the day of the week set aside for fellowship. In contrast, some Eastern religions, such as Buddhism and Hinduism, even with traditional priesthoods and monastic orders (for men only, of course), did not mandate systematic obligations for worshipers, as members of a formal group, to visit a pagoda or temple on a weekly or other calendar basis. Pagodas and temples had always existed throughout the

Asian world, but they were primarily places where individuals prayed and meditated.

Similarly, Muslims in North Africa congregated in mosques for prayer and observed certain holy days, but no such organized rituals could be found in the traditional religious practices of most of sub-Saharan Africa.[54] Tribal African religion was centered in the home and village and focused on family sacraments like the naming of babies and the rites of passage through the experiences of adolescence, marriage, and burial. Prayer and veneration were common, but they were usually invocations to the lesser gods and ancestral spirits, asking them to be generous in bestowing health and prosperity. There were numerous "holy" days during the year commemorating important religious events, but the organized church service at which worshipers gathered on the same day each week was not familiar to the black African. "In all cases," Geoffrey Parrinder wrote, "African temples are small constructions, and are not meant for large gatherings of people."[55] In short, there simply was nothing in African traditional religion comparable to the Christian congregation.

The Unsaved Universe

The Christian's certainty that his God was the one true god and that accepting Christ was the only way to salvation, and the smugness that went with that certainty, would have been shaken had he been inclined to look at the way much of the non-Christian world—which was most of the world—perceived its relationship with the supernatural. Like the West Africans, the Chinese practiced an olla-podrida of cosmology, mythology, shamanism, and the cult of ancestors and, more to the point, did not believe in a single god who had laid down a path to eternal life based on an exclusive belief. Five centuries before Christ, Confucius, probably the most influential thinker in Chinese history, questioned the usefulness of speculating about a hereafter. "Till you know about the living," Confucius said as recorded in the *Analects*, "how are you to know about death?"[56] Westerners have often called Confucianism a "religion" because they tended to think of Confucius in the same way they thought of Christ and Mohammed: one who purports to speak for a supreme being. In fact, Confucius—who passed on a *code of conduct*, not a religion—made no divine claims.

A comparison of Chinese and African belief systems can go a long way to show how much polytheistic cultures have in common and, by contrast, to illuminate the enormous gulf between Christianity and the traditional religions of slaves and American Indians. The Chinese feeling for hierarchy, a cornerstone of Confucianism, could be equated with the West African pyramid or triangle, where the High God reigned over the natural gods, the ancestral spirits, and the magical powers. The ancestors and the nature gods occupy two sides of the triangle, Geoffrey Parrinder observed, while "the base is composed of lower magical powers, and in the centre is man subject to influences from every side."[57] In Africa, as in China, appeasing the spirits was simply a way of influencing one's destiny. It was the *here*—not the *after*—that counted, and one appealed to many gods and spirits who, if properly entreated with prayers and offerings, would bestow health, happiness, and prosperity.[58] The striking similarities between African and Chinese religious beliefs should surprise no one. Virtually all polytheistic cultures recognize a hierarchy of deities and spirits. Even the gods of the Hindu trinity—Brahma, Vishnu, and Shiva—were ranked (in that order) with corresponding powers, followed by lesser heavenly beings, including Krishna, the most important human incarnation of Vishnu, and Ganesh, the god of wisdom. By worldwide standards, it was Christianity that was strange.

One African religious practice condemned by Christians but shared by Chinese—as well as by ancient Greeks and Romans and countless non-Western societies—was what often has been inaccurately called "ancestor worship." While the spirits of ancestors were not actually considered deities, they were acknowledged as living pneumas who were frequently beseeched for both protection and prosperity. Filial piety and the reverence paid to the spirits of deceased relatives also reflected the importance of stability and continuity in family life. It could almost be said that age and death elevated one in the social hierarchy. Although the Chinese did not agree on just what it was that survived the death of the body, and their conceptions of the afterlife changed over time, among the earliest terms used to describe the spirits that occupied the world beyond the grave were *gui* (禨), the malevolent pneuma, and *shen* (神), the souls of glorified ancestors. On a darker side were *hun* (魂), the vengeance seeker, and *po* (魄), by which one could literally be frightened to death. "Later, these souls are even further subdivided," one scholar wrote, "in stark contrast to the Western conception of a unitary, immaterial soul."[59] The duality of the monotheistic world forced souls into heaven or hell. In the Chinese world, they branched off in all directions.

The spirits of ancestors were no less significant in the beliefs of the almost ten million people carried to the New World in slave ships. Africans invoked the good spirits of dead friends and relatives, Olaudah Equiano wrote, to protect them from the bad spirits of their enemies. Even more important, among many West Africans—for example, the Ibos, Edos, and Yorubas—ancestral spirits were viewed as family messengers to the higher gods. "The connecting link between the gods and the ancestors," historian Olli Alho noted, "is in some cases . . . a sort of cultural hero who is believed to have created the clans." Thus the kinsmen's homage to the spirits of their forebears was not so much a religion as a "social obligation" that embodied an "intense loyalty to the health of the family tree . . . which was their philosophy of life," as Galbraith Welch pointed out. "To fail to show ancestor reverence would have been a civic crime." At a London symposium in 1950, the Anglican Archdeacon to the Ashanti noted that "older people never drink without pouring out a few drops of palm-wine on the ground for the spirits of the departed, and *okra aduane*, 'food for the soul,' is often provided for them." The ancestral spirits can "influence their living descendants for good or evil," H. St. George T. Evans wrote, "and in many districts it is customary to thank them for such benefits as a good harvest or recovery from sickness."[60]

For the Christian, the heathen's recognition of ancestral spirits who resided in some invisible dimension of the real world was one of the first evils that had to be eradicated. Admonishing the Jews not to adopt the "abominations" of other nations, Moses had warned that God would not tolerate anyone who consults with the dead.[61] In Ecclesiastes the "Teacher" wrote:

> For the living know that they will die, but the dead know nothing; they have no further reward, and even the memory of them is forgotten. Their love, their hate and their jealousy have long since vanished; never again will they have a part in anything that happens under the sun.[62]

As it happened, a belief in ancestral spirits was far more universal than any Christian could imagine. Among the earliest peoples, according to anthropologist A. R. Radcliffe-Brown, the individual's primary duties "are those of his lineage," a notion that the Chinese articulated over twenty-one centuries ago. Since one received his children, land, and cattle from his forebears, paying homage to them was also a declaration of dependence. Accordingly, "by giving solemn and collective expression to them the rites reaffirm, renew and strengthen those sentiments on which the social solidarity depends."[63] In his study of the Tallensi people of West Africa, British social anthropologist Meyer Fortes pointed out that, even in the absence of a belief in the immortality of the human spirit, paying tribute to ancestors was part of the need "to define a person's place in society and his rights, duties, capacities and privileges."

> The Tallensi have an ancestor cult not because they fear the dead—for they do not, in fact, do so—nor because they believe in

> the immortality of the soul—for they have no such notion—but because their social structure demands it. To put it in other words, they have a complex and elaborate body of ritual beliefs and practices for perpetuating and regulating the significance of the dead in the lives of their descendants.[64]

It could be argued that the Tallensi practice might be compared to the study of history in the West. By such "perpetuating and regulating," the members of the kinship group recognized their obligations to their forebears, their status in society, and their duties to each other. But a belief in the actual existence of ancestral spirits may have been only coincidental. Like all peoples who exalted their ancestors, the Tallensi could take comfort in the thought that they would one day be included among the significant dead. The man who paid tribute to the memory of his forefathers could expect his descendants to pay tribute to his memory. Recognizing the importance of ancestors was crucial to cultural stability and it was a reflection of the devotion to families and kinship groups that has always been a fundamental condition of life among Africans, Chinese, and American Indians. Unlike the Tallensi, most of these peoples did believe—and continue to believe—in the immortality of the human soul. "It is the general belief of the Indians that after a man dies his spirit is somewhere on the earth or in the sky," Mato-Kuwapi ("Chased by Bears"), a member of the Santee-Yanktonai Sioux tribe, said just before his death in 1915. "[W]e do not know exactly where but we are sure that his spirit still lives."[65] It is not an exaggeration to suggest that for the enslaved African who was torn from his traditional homeland, cast among hostile strangers, and dragged in chains to the New World, the term *uprooted* seems woefully inadequate.[66]

A look at the belief systems of non-Christian peoples who came under the influence of Christians thus reveals one of the most fundamental elements of racism in the history of American religion: In order to become the same kind of Christian as his white oppressor, the slave had to renounce not only his traditional religion but his traditional culture as well. The essence of Christianity was the voluntary personal commitment that the individual made through his belief in Jesus Christ.[67] In theory, at least, such a commitment was not inherently dependent on familial obligations and there were no legal or cultural imperatives that had to be observed. Practically speaking, of course, family and ecclesiastical pressures could be extremely difficult to resist, especially among some of the more dogmatic and homogeneous Christian groups, such as the Puritans and the German sects in the colonial period and Mormons and immigrant Catholics in the nineteenth century. Yet, while conformity was an essential condition of the Puritan faith, Puritanism, paradoxically, was also "one of the principal sources" of the American veneration of individualism. As Anne Hutchinson vividly demonstrated, even "in the seventeenth century it was possible for individuals to find the form of religion that best suited their inclinations"; and the revival movement of the eighteenth century clearly reflected the growing emphasis on personal experience and the concomitant decline of church discipline.[68]

To the Protestant leaders of the early republic, Christianity was the foundation of two cherished American ideals: "Religion made men republicans," a writer for the *Christian Examiner* declared in 1833; "it also made them individualists."[69] By 1850, religion, operating with "a new emphasis on the individual and the voluntary association," Robert N. Bellah and his associates wrote, no longer "fit into the stable harmony of an organic community." Also, as waves of both citizens and immigrants spread across the continent during the nineteenth century, the commitment to individualism reshaped the Puritan tradition of migration into a westward movement in which Americans became Americans by leaving home.[70] It was only in Western society—and especially in pluralistic Anglo-America—that one found the cult of the individual and a dominant religion supremely compatible with it.

On the other hand, among Africans, American Indians, Asians, and, for that matter, most of the non-Western world, Bellah's "stable harmony of an organic community" was obligatory, while the impulse toward personal independence was eschewed and in some places was virtually nonexistent. In a critique of the treatment of Indians in history textbooks, Frederick E. Hoxie pointed out that Anglo-Americans have often had difficulty understanding aboriginal cultures because those cultures "are rooted in obligations of kinships rather than the appeal of political ideology." The Indian's social relations are "not individualistic, Christian, or monotheistic [and his] traditional values and ceremonies have both civic and religious ramifications." After burying several individual skeletons together in a single pit, for example, the Hurons "used poles to mix all the bones together in final community," symbolizing that they "belonged to one another in death as in life." More than any other tribal ritual, the "Feast of the Dead" reminded them that "they were a people defined by the group and from it drew their sense of being."[71]

In the West one sought his identity as an individual. In an African, Chinese, or Indian society one found his identity as a member of a group—a family, a village, a clan. The Chinese *guanxi* (关系)—for which the closest English equivalent is "relationships" or "connections" to family, friends, and community—meant far more than loyalty to a national leader or political *Weltanschauung*.[72] Similarly, the written Chinese characters for "individualism" — 個人主義 (*geren zhuyi*)—and "freedom"— 自由

(*zi yu*)—usually implied selfishness and lack of concern for others. The connotation was clearly pejorative. In classical Chinese, in fact, there was no word that meant "freedom" in the Western sense. Moreover, the *tao* (道), the "way" or "state of affairs," similar to the "paths of righteousness and ways of the Lord" in the Bible, embraced, in Benjamin I. Schwartz's words, "the 'outer' sociopolitical order and the 'inner' moral life of the individual." In Christianity the "way" usually "refers to the course of individual moral life," but in the *Analects* "it refers to nothing less than the total sociopolitical order."[73] For Christians, "the vision projected in the Hebrew Bible of a divine code of laws wholly within the range of the people's understanding," Schwartz concluded, "suggests a community life not wholly dependent on the wisdom of a ruling elite."[74]

The same could be said of African and New World Indian societies, where the security of belonging to an established social order is crucial. African thought acknowledged the "transcendence of individuals over their own sociocultural conditions," Benjamin C. Ray pointed out, but it never embraced the Western notion of individualism. "Freedom and individuality are always balanced by destiny and community, and these in turn are balanced by nature and supernatural powers," an attitude perhaps best seen in the Dinka idea of *cieng*, which means both "morality" and "living together."[75] In the religious and ethical systems of the Kongo nation in the seventeenth and eighteenth centuries, one student of African history wrote, "individual advancement would be seen as occurring at the expense of the community at large,"[76] a belief virtually identical to the Chinese views concerning *geren zhuyi*. Similarly, Ashanti law held that any offense against "the sacred or supernatural powers on which the well-being of the whole community depends [must] be expiated by the punishment of the guilty persons [or] the whole tribe will suffer."[77] In other words, a crime against the faith was a crime against everyone. When the Christian missionary urged the heathen to give up his traditional religion he was, in fact, calling for the commission of an offense against the well-being of the whole community.

There is perhaps no better example of the Western myopia than John Stuart Mill's classic work on individualism, *On Liberty* (1859), in which he repeatedly used terms like "mankind" and "humans" but made few references to non-Christian societies—"Mohammedans, Hindoos, and Chinese"—except to castigate them. When Mill described "Civil, or Social Liberty [as] the nature and limits of the power which can be legitimately exercised by society over the individual," he described a condition that most Africans, Asians, and American Indians would never have understood.[78] In their worlds, religion was not so much a philosophy of life for the individual as it was a code of behavior for the community or kinship group, a collectivist organism in which shared cultural values ensured that beliefs and traditions would be passed on to succeeding generations. Continuity. The enslaved African had been part of a culture in which the group—especially the family—was the linchpin of the social order.[79]

The individual who detached himself from his religion, Kenyan John S. Mbiti explained, was "severed from his roots, his foundation, his context of security, his kinships and the entire group of those who make him aware of his own existence."[80] The excommunication or "shunning" of a Christian who disavowed his faith in no way approached the frightful isolation that awaited an African who was foolish enough to do the same. In a society of masters and slaves, the slave, in the words of sociologist Orlando Patterson, was "socially dead," but no less could be said of the African who fell from grace in his native society. Outside of his kinship group, he was a nonperson. When the slave traders uprooted the African from his family, tribe, and religion, they destroyed his cultural anchor. "Separated from African society, its production, division of labour, kinship organization and indeed its whole structure," Olli Alho wrote, "the African tradition could survive only to the extent that the new structure it was planted in provided it with new functions and meanings."[81] And that new structure was bondage.

There was yet another aspect of African religions that made the slave especially vulnerable to the assault of evangelical Christianity. Unlike people in European and American societies, where religion (especially since the Protestant Reformation) came to be considered primarily a matter of *belief* rather than *rites*, Africans, Indians, Chinese, and many other non-Christians shared the idea that religion was primarily an expression of correct behavior, not a body of beliefs about right and wrong, truth and error, salvation and damnation. What mattered was not so much what one thought about a situation as how one reacted to it. In other words, conduct was more important than creed. For most West Africans, Benjamin C. Ray pointed out, "ritual behavior is a way of communicating with the divine for the purpose of changing the human situation." In central Africa, according to another writer, ritual "is spiritually more profound than any theology."

Similarly, the teachings of the Chinese philosopher Xun Zi (Hsün Tzü), which were collected in the *Li Ji* (*Li Chi*), *Book of Rites*, set forth the argument that "religious rites have important social functions which are independent of any beliefs that may be held as to the efficacy of the rites." There is no word in classical Chinese, A. R. Radcliffe-Brown pointed out, that means "just what we understand by the word religion." The closest term might be *li*, which, depending on the context, means the rites, rituals, ceremony, propriety, or rules of good manners that, Schwartz concluded, "bind human beings and the spirits together in networks of interacting roles within the family, within human society, and with the numinous realm beyond." Accordingly, the *Yue Ji* section of the *Li Ji* held that religious music was meant to "unite hearts and establish order." Such rituals "are the bond that holds the multitudes together, and if the bond is removed, those multitudes fall into confusion."[82]

The rituals that bound human beings and the spirits together constituted the most critical feature of the African's religious expression. Songs were more than merely words. The "totality of religion as a unifying and organizing force," according to a leading scholar on plantation spirituals, was recalled in music and dance. Culminating the first stage of initiation and puberty rites of the Akamba people, "dancing and rejoicing strengthen community solidarity, and emphasize the corporateness of the whole group," Mbiti noted. African music was "the nucleus of creed and religious history," Geoffrey Parrinder wrote, while the "words, music and movement of the dance express the character and actions of the deity that is being praised, and the nature of human petitions to him." From the earliest colonial days in America, slave converts had included the "shoutin' " or the "ring-shout" in their religious ceremonies. Such loud and ecstatic behavior during revival meetings was similar to the expressions of "spirit possession" that was part of numerous African religious practices. Rhythmic clapping, ring dancing, and singing were West African religious responses that moved virtually intact to the New World. But while music and dance expressed for Africans "the life of the family and society and the meaning of the world," American slaveholders discouraged rituals that their Christian consciences told them were pagan and provocative. Many whites simply assumed that dancing invoked only the false gods of Africa. By the early nineteenth century, Methodist, Presbyterian, and Baptist leaders condemned dancing as sinful and told slave converts they could not continue the practice.[83] As Virginian Moncure Conway observed in 1864,

> The impression has gone around the world with ubiquitous sable minstrels that the slaves are a merry, singing, dancing population, far removed from the cares that gnaw the hearts of more civilized classes. In all the twenty-three years of my life in the land of Slavery, I never saw a Negro-dance, though in those years I have heard of a few in our neighbourhood. The slaves of the Border States are almost invariably members of Baptist and Methodist societies, which are particularly rigid in denying them such amusements. On the large plantations of the far South, dances are encouraged, and formerly were frequent; but of late years they have become infrequent, through the all-absorbing tendencies of the Negroes toward religious meetings.[84]

"In most of Africa, dance, like singing and drumming, is an integral part of supplication," folklorist Harold Courlander noted, but in the Christian world "dancing in church is generally regarded as a profane act."[85]

Whether plantation dances were manifestations of African spirituality, spontaneous emotional outbursts, expressions of religious exuberance, or just jokes played on white folks, their full significance will probably never be known. The slave may have danced just for the sheer enjoyment of feeling his body move, a reasonable assumption in view of the fact that he had few physical pleasures and little opportunity to express his feelings overtly when whites were present. Indeed, slave dances, with their seemingly uncontrolled arm and leg movements—"for their bodies rocked, their heads nodded, their feet stamped, their knees shook, their elbows and hands beat time to the tune and the words which they sang with evident delight"—were often condemned by whites, who believed that only a person under the control of the Devil would make such outrageous body gyrations. Convinced that dancing was not inherently "evil," but aware that he could not openly defy the white man's orders, the slave looked for plausible explanations. "[H]it ain't railly dancin' 'less de feets is crossed," a participant explained after a white observer complained; "dancin' ain't sinful iffen de foots ain't crossed." One student of slave religion contended that, as similar as African spirit possession and the slave shouting tradition might seem, they were fundamentally different on "the level of theological interpretation and meaning." Actually, the slave's boisterous behavior probably owed more to the influence of Protestant revivalism than to his African religious tradition. "The African gods with their myriad characteristics, personalities, and myths do not 'mount' their enthusiasts amid the dances, songs, and drum rhythms of worship in the United States," Albert J. Raboteau wrote. "Instead it is the Holy Spirit who fills the converted sinner with a happiness and power that drives him to shout, sing, and sometimes dance."[86]

While Raboteau could be accused of hair-splitting, in the end it may not have mattered if plantation singing and dancing could be traced to Africa or found in the revivalist tradition of evangelical Christianity. To the slave, they were fundamental elements of his religious expression. By denying him these traditional rites, the slave master removed the "bond that holds the multitudes together," and the slave was thus cut off from the most critical aspect of his spirituality—his religious *practices*.

It would be easy to conclude that the body of slave religious music is large because slavery was a lamentable condition and the slave had little else to sing about. In fact, there was nothing coincidental about it. Protestant leaders who railed against "sinful" singing and dancing left the slaves with only religious music "to articulate many of their deepest and most enduring feelings and certainties."[87] In addition to the presumed evil inherent in such behavior, some masters worried that slaves would wear themselves out. "They would be singing and dancing every night in their cabins, till the dawn of day," one planter complained, "and utterly unfit themselves for work."[88] As always, the master's economic interests came first.

Even more disquieting for the slaveholder was his suspicion that plantation music was a conduit for conspiracies. Most slaves were illiterate, and contact among those belonging to different owners was not always easy. Slave song lyrics often had hidden meanings, thus singing by bondsmen working in adjacent fields was sometimes perceived by whites as a form of secret communication. Even the songs heard in one's own slave quarters were suspect; religious music was only the least suspect. Despite the slaveholder's insistence that his blacks were contented and trustworthy, neither he nor anyone else could be completely sure. When fear was mixed with ignorance, there was no limit to what the imagination might concoct.

But the slaves were not without their own resources. If Christian music was the only kind they were permitted to have, they would adapt it to their purposes. Finding white music "too cold and static to allow for the full expression of [their] religious sentiments,"[89] they created songs that were expressions of sorrow and hope and, through the messages of certain biblical stories, disguised calls for escape and resistance. The ostensible theme of most plantation spirituals was a joyful anticipation of eternal happiness in the next world, but hidden in the words of many of them were pleas for freedom in this world. One can only wonder how long it took masters to discover that the "chariot" in "Swing Low, Sweet Chariot" was the slave's euphemism for the underground railroad. Overwhelmingly illiterate, the transplanted Africans and their descendants did not leave behind an extensive written record documenting their impressions of bondage; thus the publications of their music and folklore are priceless windows into the world of slavery.

Denied the opportunity to observe the rituals of his traditional religion, the slave was bewildered by a faith in which belief was more important than behavior. A student of Puritanism wrote that to a Westerner "turning to God involved leaving one's old religious culture and accepting a new ethic." This meant "asking more of the person than lip-service to ceremony or willingness to perform moral obligations." But "ceremony" and "moral obligations" were the warp and weft of the African's ancestral beliefs. To ignore or minimize the significance of his rituals was to diminish his religious existence. Could the slave casually set aside his spiritual practices simply because their physical adjuncts were no longer accessible? Perhaps more to the point, could he easily shed, like an unwanted garment, a religious heritage in which the concept of a conversion or repentance—the Christian rebirth in Christ or Hebrew *shûbh*, "to go back again" or "to return"—was incomprehensible? The common Christian approach to civilizing Indians served as a vivid example of what was expected of a new convert. A white missionary recorded in his diary in 1828 that he hoped to change the Indian into a typical Yankee: industrious, honest, punctual, and sober. Similarly, in 1854 an evangelist wrote to a colleague that Christians should teach the natives "Yankee enterprise." Reflecting on the efforts of Protestant missionaries to mold Indians into Christian farmers, Roy Harvey Pearce criticized the white man's naïve assumption that "throwing off one way of life for another would be relatively simple." Of course, the basis of such naïveté was the unwavering belief that the cause of Christ was irrepressible. What evangelical advocates seemed not to understand, Pearce wrote in his classic *The Savages of America*, was that culture is a "delicately balanced system of attitudes, beliefs, valuations, conditions, and modes of behavior; the system does not change and reintegrate itself overnight, or in a generation or two."[90] Being thus for the Indian, should it have been any easier for the African?

Missionary frustration over the heathen's apparent inability to "reintegrate" was evident almost from the beginning. John Eliot's efforts, beginning in the 1630s, to bring the Indians of New England into the Puritan fold were frequently frustrated by his inability to understand why the Indians could not simply adopt the white man's customs and habits. Writing in 1748, to an associate in London, the Reverend Philip Reading of Apoquiniminck, Delaware, complained that the slaves in his parish "have no abstracted ideas, cannot comprehend the meaning of faith in Christ, the nature of the fall of man, [or] the necessity of a redeemer."[91] In colonial Virginia the Anglican church's "cherished Elizabethan formularies of worship spoke with a cadence wholly foreign to black African experience," one historian wrote. "Insistence upon memorization of the catechism and acceptance of its alien moral admonition proved to be an almost insurmountable barrier to meaningful membership." No one would deny that, in time, many slaves (and a few Indians) adapted to Western culture and became devout Christians, but such an admission only generates more questions. Because African traditional religion did not include a "God-man" who directly connected the High God to man—no Jesus or Mohammed—were Africans, as one English traveler asked, inordinately susceptible to the blandishments of Christianity and Islam?[92]

Was the bondsman's will to survive so compelling that he eventually created an entirely new world that his descendants still live in, or was he simply a pragmatist who was resigned to accepting a religion that was nothing more than treacle for the needs of the moment? Whichever was the case, the facility with which the enslaved African converted an already splintered Christianity to his purposes was a reflection of his remarkable adaptability.[93]

But one is then compelled to wonder what kind of Christian such a convert would be. For any American to change his faith from, say, Jew to Christian, Catholic to Protestant, or even one Protestant denomination to another, would demand more than a little psychological and social adaptation. Indeed, as the popular play *Abie's Irish Rose* demonstrated, the adaptation could be the source of considerable humor. But such a change, even in a less enlightened age, was simply not comparable to the cultural upheaval that thousands of Indians and descendants of enslaved West Africans were expected to endure.[94]

The question still nags: Was the converted African able to shake off centuries of cultural conditioning and appreciate his new faith, with its strange and unyielding theological baggage, in much the same way as a person for whom Christianity was a familiar religion? There will probably never be a definitive answer, but it is reasonable to assume that the transplanted African (and his children)—*as long as he clung to traces of his traditional religion*—was never able to harmonize completely his religious ideals with orthodox Christianity. After all, if slaves embraced Christianity as readily as so many researchers have suggested, why did census counts and official church records always list such small percentages of slave converts? And if these calculations were even reasonably accurate, was the slaveowner's resistance really the main reason for such sparse numbers? Could an observer as astute as Frederick Law Olmsted, raising the additional question of the quality of the slave's Christianity, have been so far off the mark in generalizing about the gross deficiencies in the slave's religious education? The opportunity to convert to Christianity, where it existed, may have satisfied the slave's spiritual needs, enabling him to adapt more readily to the conditions of bondage—and that was no small matter. But the evidence also indicates emphatically that he was never granted full membership in the Christian family, a family already so fractured that it should not, it would seem, have been bothered by yet another stepchild. In other words, the slave may have embraced Christianity, but Christianity almost certainly did not fully embrace the slave. The upshot was a church that was divided not only by color but, perhaps more important, by psyche.

The Wages of Sex

The African may have left his gods behind, but not his libido. In no area of human behavior has Christian teaching been applied with a heavier hand than in matters dealing with sexual morality. "For Christianity alone, among world religions," Nigel Davies wrote in his study on the world's sexual customs, "sex was little but a necessary evil."[95] From the early Puritans of the seventeenth century who took to heart biblical admonitions against lust,[96] to modern Victorians who campaign against "prurient" entertainment, conduct involving sex and nudity has been tenaciously circumscribed in America by laws and customs that had their roots in the Judeo-Christian tradition. There are numerous biblical references—especially in the New Testament—to the sinfulness of adultery, sexual promiscuity, prostitution, and homosexuality. "For out of the heart come evil thoughts," Christ told his disciples, "murder, adultery, sexual immorality, theft, false testimony, slander."[97]

In some of the Epistles the Apostle Paul seemed almost obsessed with the importance of sexual restraint.[98] "Flee from sexual immorality," he warned the Corinthians. "All other sins a man commits are outside his body, but he who sins sexually sins against his own body."[99] Writing to the Christians of Thessalonica he reminded them that "It is God's will that you should be holy; that you should avoid sexual immorality." Later he told the Hebrews that "Marriage should be honored by all, and the marriage bed kept pure, for God will judge the adulterer and all the sexually immoral,"[100] an admonition that carried over into the teachings of early church fathers like Tertullian, a Latin theologian born in the second century A.D., who identified original sin with sexuality. "Christianity portrayed the body, and particularly its sexuality," one historian noted, "as an obstacle to salvation."[101] During the four centuries after Christ, church leaders produced a sexual revolution involving suppression and abstinence every bit as radical as the twentieth-century revolution for women's rights and sexual liberation.[102]

In explaining Paul's views on sexuality, modern Christian writers have, for the most part, remained fettered by their own evangelical blinders. "As with the Old Testament and Jesus," Stephen Sapp wrote in *Sexuality, the Bible, and Science* (1977), "Paul's concern is with the *misuse* of sexuality, not sexuality *per se*." Sexual sins "are only a few among many," he went on, "and it is always the *improper* use of sex that is condemned." There are two obvious problems with this explanation. First, by insisting that Paul saw sexual sins as "only a few among many" and that he "was not preoccupied with sex as the 'root of all sins,' " Sapp implied that sex was simply not as important to the Apostle as many people assumed. A few pages later, however, he wrote: "Sexuality is one of God's most powerful and therefore most important gifts to humanity." More serious than this contradiction was Sapp's imperative perception of sexuality solely within a Christian context. In assuming that what was "improper" to Paul should be improper to everybody, he defined sexuality according to Christian standards—standards that were contrary to the beliefs and practices of virtually every non-Christian society.

Sapp's evangelical moorings became even more evident when he argued that "one cannot engage in sexual activity for pleasure *alone*, solely for the gratification of the body, because the 'body alone' does not exist." Any activity that is physical, he concluded, "necessarily involves the psyche, the 'spirit,' as well." Such a conclusion, of course, is a metaphysical assumption with no empirical or scientific validity. Nor was Sapp the first modern Christian writer to criticize the physical exuberance of sexual gratification. "The trouble is that when sex becomes fun and nothing else," Joseph Blenkinsopp wrote in *Sexuality and the Christian Tradition* (1969), "it generally ceases to be fun." Obviously unaware of the sexual practices of hundreds of millions of non-Christian peoples, Sapp and Blenkinsopp conveniently ignored the fact that for thousands of years people everywhere engaged in sexual activities for the sheer fun of it and there is no evidence that very many of them suffered dire consequences.[103]

Herein lay the fundamental error in an evangelical Christian analysis of what was essentially a nonreligious issue: it always began with a narrow *assumption of faith* for which there was no historical proof. Quoting Oswald Schwartz's *The Psychology of Sex* (1949), Sapp declared that human nature is "permeated with spirit," and that human "sexuality is not mere happening, it is a deed for which we are responsible, and if we meekly submit to the physical impulse, we incur guilt." By aligning "human nature," "spirit," and "guilt," Schwartz—and Sapp—argued, in essence, that all peoples share a common moral attitude toward sexual matters. Not only is there no evidence for such an assertion, but the implication that guilt is a natural human feeling is similarly fallacious. For example, in the seventeenth century, Catholic missionaries working among the Indians of the western Andes, especially in the region that later became Ecuador, noted that the natives had no word for "guilt" in their language and therefore had to be taught to feel guilty. Similarly, Puritan missionaries in New England had to teach the Indians the meaning of "humiliation." In both examples, the Indian response was a reaction that went to the heart of the differences in moral principles between Christian and non-Christian cultures.

Like most people with Christian worldviews, Sapp and Blenkinsopp defined sexuality in Christian terms, then condemned everyone who did not conform. And such pontification was not confined to evangelicals. Reinhold Niebuhr, who considered the sexual drive, like hunger and survival, to be "at the foundation of human vitality," may have put it more eloquently, but his reasoning was no less flawed. Warning against sexual excesses, he claimed that "sex can also become the perverse obsession of man because he has the freedom to center his life inordinately in one impulse, while the economy of nature preserves a pre-established harmony of the various vitalities."[104] Words like "perverse," "inordinately," and "obsession"—like Sapp's "misuse"—were significant only to the extent that they related to one's own standards; and the Christian's "nature" had no imperative association with *human* nature. And "pre-established harmony" could only mean that some greater being had already laid down the rules of sexual behavior. Obscure evangelical writer or renowned theologian, the blinders of dogmatism were the same.

In the almost two thousand years from the Apostle Paul to modern evangelicals, Christianity's obsession with sexuality has been unrelenting. One of the first prominent advocates of sexual repression and, by almost universal acclaim, the greatest of the early fathers was Augustine (354–430), Bishop of Hippo, who, aware of "the tension between the mystical ideal and his own sensual nature," as theologian Paul Tillich put it, "denied sex and praised asceticism," an antagonism that has persisted "through the whole history of the church."[105] Confessing to God "my past wickedness and the carnal corruptions of my soul," which almost always afflict adolescent males, Augustine was unsurpassed when it came to graphic lyricism:

> [T]he mists of passion steamed up out of the puddly concupiscence of the flesh, and the hot imagination of puberty, and they so obscured and overcast my heart that I was unable to distinguish pure affection from unholy desire. Both boiled confusedly within me, and dragged my unstable youth down over the cliffs of unchaste desires and plunged me into a gulf of infamy. . . . Where was I, and how far was I exiled from the delights of thy house, in that sixteenth year of the age of my flesh, when the madness of lust held full sway in me—that madness which grants indulgence to human shamelessness, even though it is forbidden by thy laws—and I gave myself entirely to it.[106]

The words explode from the page. Wickedness, carnal, hot, infamy, flesh, madness, lust, indulgence, shamelessness. For this ascetic, the passion *against* sex was more powerful than the passion *of* sex, and the march was on. When the Bishop of London, in a 1727 pastoral letter, urged American slaveholders to support efforts to convert slaves because the "Freedom which Christianity gives" is freedom from "the Dominion of Men's Lusts and Passions and inordinate Desires," he was working a field that seventeen centuries of Christian morality had cultivated.[107] The word "morality" generally refers to the rightness or wrongness of an action, but to many Christians it began—and sometimes ended—with sexuality. The libido—or, more properly, the sublimation of the libido—was the yardstick by which faith and virtue were measured.

What was to become the most characteristic aspect of Augustine's mandate was his contention that "natural, sexual desire" was always "accompanied by shame." A member of a sexually liberated generation would be repelled by the suggestion that one should be ashamed of a natural condition. But to an Augustinian, salvation, the ultimate spiritual objective, demanded that man rise above the natural world—a world of physical urges in which affection was "pure" but desire was "unholy." Ralph Barton Perry wrote that in Puritan North America, Christianity's "practical teaching is against nature," that is, man must overcome his own depraved nature in order to realize salvation. It was Augustine's view that "sexual pleasure could be justified only by a married couple's attempt at procreation; and some medieval and early modern Catholic authorities thought sex sinful even for reproductive purposes." For Augustine, Nigel Davies put it bluntly, "all coitus was repellent." In fact, Augustine's association of pleasure with sin was so far-reaching that some of his successors, such as Pope Gregory, took the position that "any consent of the soul to the pleasure of sex was sinful" and that "even married couples fell into sin while making love, at the moment when passion overcame their reason."[108] Which was simply another way of saying that sexual activity was all right so long as no one enjoyed it. The real sin was pleasure.

Then strike your lyre! your voices raise
Let gratitude inspire your song!
Pursue religion's holy ways.
Shun sinful Pleasure's giddy throng![109]

The sanctification of asceticism was nothing if not durable. Over a thousand years after Augustine, the leaders of the Protestant Reformation, though holding a somewhat more positive view, nonetheless "were suspicious of everything sexual," Tillich concluded, a suspicion that has endured to the present in "countries under Protestant influence."[110]

Things were dramatically different almost everywhere in the non-Christian world. Sex and sensuality were omnipresent in the life of ancient Greece, where male homosexuality—especially pederasty (the love of boys)—and paeans to the gods Priapus and Dionysus were essential features of orgies. And the Romans, who have often been accused of imitating the best of the Greeks, were not far behind. In Asia, the celebration of sex was virtually universal. "From time immemorial," Nigel Davies pointed out, "Chinese sages had taught that sexual abstinence was wicked and that for the good of the soul a man needed constant copulation with as many women as he could afford and preferably with several at a time." If sexual intercourse was exalted by the Chinese, it was almost worshipped by the ancient Indians, who left behind a veritable treasure of erotic art and literature. Indeed, some of the finest Indian and Japanese artworks—the kinds of things for which artists in the Christian world would have been imprisoned and even executed—depicted various sexual activities. Long before the emergence of the Indian cult of Shiva, the god of reproduction, whose symbol was an erect penis, there were unmistakable signs of sexual obsession. Among the indigenous peoples of the New World—except the Aztecs and Incas—premarital sexual activity was "not only tolerated but even encouraged," and the variety of activities ranged from oral and anal intercourse to transvestitism and group cohabitation.[111]

Some of these early societies have had their sexual habits thoroughly scrutinized. Beginning in the 1930s, George Devereaux published a series of articles on incest and homosexuality among the Mohave Indians of North America; while Bronislaw Malinowski, in his classic study of the sex lives of the natives of the Trobriand Islands, described in lavish detail the "bachelors' houses" where young unmarried lovers engaged in various feasts and sex games.[112]

In short, sexual indulgence—primarily for men, of course—was a common ingredient of life in almost every part of the world that had never heard of the Apostle Paul or St. Augustine; and it never occurred to any of the participants that there was anything evil, shameful, or degrading about it.[113]

There was nothing like this anywhere in the Christian world. "From Catholic moralists to Victorian doctors, and from American Methodist women to St. Bernadette of Lourdes," Peter Gardella wrote in *Innocent Ecstasy* (1985), "the protagonists of this narrative all believed that human beings came into the world already tainted by sin, and that this disordered condition involved the corruption of human sexuality."[114] The rules of social conduct changed over the centuries, but the Christian moral code continued to influence sexual behavior—and women paid a much higher price than men for transgressing. In English literature, female virtue was a dominant theme—as novelist Samuel Richardson unabashedly proclaimed—and the Victorian code decreed that a woman who had fallen from grace must either somehow die by the end of the story, like Thomas Hardy's Tess, or be banished to some place like Australia.[115] A maiden was pure, but a harlot was wicked. Men were only randy. Well into the twentieth century, the Puritan consciousness influenced behavior at almost all levels: Female clothing could not reveal so much as an ankle without raising eyebrows; bathing suits covered most of the body. Words and expressions for genitalia and sexual acts were never used in mixed company. Various groups, both secular and sectarian, reviewed books, magazines, and theatrical performances for prurient content. Some states passed laws against prostitution, incest, sodomy, bestiality, necrophilia, and even "unusual" sexual practices between a husband and wife (oral sex was illegal in many places; and a city ordinance in Compton, California, prohibited cheek-to-cheek dancing). Fundamentalist preachers railed against dancing and other forms of suggestive behavior. Sexually transmitted diseases were considered God's way of punishing the wicked; homosexuals were persecuted; parents severely admonished a child who touched his "private parts"; and restraints were placed on other activities in which sex and sin were synonymous and guilt and frustration were frequent consequences. To some it was the taboo of sex—the fascination of "forbidden fruit"—that made it appealing, adding the quality of hypocrisy to an already heavily proscribed area of human conduct.

The Augustinian model thus found a natural home in orthodox Puritanism. Since one measure of a believer's spiritual commitment was his or her ability to resist worldly temptations, self-denial was not simply a virtue; it was a barometer of piety.[116] Needless to say, the more powerful the temptation, the more significant the test of faith; and since the degree of temptation was in direct proportion to the degree of physical pleasure, there was no greater vice than sexual indulgence—and no greater test, even in the marriage bed. Abner Hale, the recently married Congregational missionary in James Michener's novel *Hawaii* (1959), was troubled by "his deep and growing appetite for his wife's consoling body." Convinced, like Augustine, that "such surrender on his part must be evil," he spent each night wrestling "with his sweet perplexing temptation."[117] The essence of immorality was the assumption that sexual pleasure would control a man's feelings and hence detach him from God. Affection for a spouse, historian Edmund S. Morgan pointed out, was seen by many Puritans as "a rival to the affection for God." When a man and woman "exceedingly delight" themselves, John Cotton wrote in *A Practical Commentary* (1656), it "much benumbs and dims the light of the Spirit." They will forget God when they are "so transported with affection." Single people, Morgan noted, were advised to "substitute love of God for forbidden lusts of the flesh."[118] "Art thou troubled with lust after women?" Cotton asked;

> and God calls thee not to Marriage, why turn the strength of thy affection to another Spouse, *that is white and ruddy, the fairest of ten thousand.* The more you set your heart to consider, how amiable, and beautiful, and excellent he is, you shall finde he will satisfie your heart, that you will finde little content in any other thing besides.[119]

Sexual gratification itself was not necessarily sinful, the Puritans maintained, but "human depravity" led to excessive sexual ardor, which so easily came between man and God that all physical communication had to be severely circumscribed.[120] While large families were quite common in pre-industrial America, not surprisingly there were also more than a few parents who, though considering children as both blessings from God and more hands to work in the fields, saw each child as a vivid reminder of a moral lapse. Groping for an acceptable way to explain his children's origins, Cotton Mather, convinced that sexual intercourse was an act of "Vileness," prayed that his participation would not prejudice God against the children who were products of that act.[121] There was an abiding Puritan ambivalence about something that was an essential element in God's plan to replenish the species and populate the earth and yet was to be enjoyed only at the risk of offending God.

Such a posture was Augustinian through and through, and the myths it concocted could only be described as bizarre. One notion held that if married partners copulated for pleasure alone their passion would corrupt the seed with its heat and conception would not occur. According to one historian, Jonathan Edwards, without specifically referring to the penis, called the foreskin, a "constant reminder of the 'peculiar need' of bridling and restraint." A New Hampshire preacher named Nicholas Gilman kept a notebook that included "Rules for Suppressing Voluptuousness" and listed an admonition to "Suppress your sensual Desires at the first approach." Recalling the Apostle Paul's Epistle to the Corinthians, Gilman, citing rules against defiling one's body, urged all Christians to "Give no entertainment to the beginnings of Lust."[122]

Nor were Protestant spokesmen of a later era any more enlightened. Arguing that giving children the wrong food "teaches them to value bodily sensations, makes them sensual in every way, and sets them lusting in every kind of excess," Congregationalist minister Horace Bushnell, in his acclaimed *Christian Nurture* (1847 and 1861), cautioned parents to restrict their children's diets to foods that do not arouse such passions, a view shared by many prominent religious leaders, including Charles G. Finney, Lyman Abbott, Mary Baker Eddy, and Alexander Campbell, and one that ultimately led to food products that still grace American tables. Both Dr. John Harvey Kellogg, the inventor of cornflakes and a devout Seventh-Day Adventist, and Sylvester Graham, a Presbyterian minister who created the whole-wheat cracker that bears his name, vigorously championed the view that "eating cereals instead of meat and eggs would weaken the passions and reverse the effects of original sin." The failure to restrain sexual appetites, such people believed, would have disastrous consequences. The Reverend William T. Duryea, speaking in 1895 on "Social

Vice and National Decay" before the National Purity Conference, insisted that sexual passion was the principal cause of epilepsy, tuberculosis, and possibly even leprosy.[123]

It would be unfair, of course, to lay Protestant America's excessively restrictive moral codes at the feet of the Puritans alone. In fact, prudish attitudes toward sex were common throughout all of the English colonies. As Carl Degler noted, "strict moral surveillance by the public authorities was a seventeenth-century rather than a Puritan attitude," and the Puritans themselves were guilty of frequent lapses in moral rectitude.[124] In his seminal article "The Puritans and Sex," Edmund S. Morgan pointed out that there were abundant public testimonies and court records indicating that formal rules against sexual "crimes" were often violated and that punishment was rarely as severe as it could have been. "They passed laws to punish adultery with death, and fornication with whipping," Morgan wrote. "Yet they had no misconceptions as to the capacity of human beings to obey such laws."[125]

In a more recent and comprehensive work focusing on a single community, another historian echoed this view. The choices made for romantic liaisons among the young people "were dictated not by economic factors but by physical attraction and love," Roger Thompson wrote in his book on sex in Middlesex, Massachusetts. "The unmarried, far from being erotically repressed, were fascinated by sexuality." Moreover, they did not just think about it but, apparently, "relieved sexual tensions by various means short of, or including, sexual intercourse." According to two researchers studying blacks in Massachusetts during the seventeenth century, the records indicate that "fornication" among both races (though not between them), for which the usual punishment was whipping or fines, "was a considerable problem." It should surprise no one, then, that the Indian converts of Puritan missionary John Eliot who took up residence in the "praying village" of Noonatomen, trying to break themselves of their former "sinful" habits, drew up a moral code that included a fine of twenty shillings for "any unmarried man who shall live with a young woman unmarried." The same code imposed a fine of two shillings and sixpence for any woman who walked around "with naked breasts" and required unmarried men to establish separate wigwams "and not be shifting up and down to other wigwams."[126]

None of this, however, diminishes the validity of the common perception of Puritan sexual morality. The *existence* of laws calling for death and whipping for sex offenses, even though rarely fully enforced, speaks for itself. More important, Puritan practice was probably less than the faithful would have preferred, but the Puritan *ideal* was a reality and its influence was far-reaching.[127] The young people of Middlesex may have violated the law in relieving their "sexual tensions," but the very existence of those tensions was more than likely a partial consequence of repressive moral proscriptions. It would be easy to conclude that, since fornication was the kind of offense that often would not be reported, the number of documented cases suggested a virtual epidemic of illicit behavior. But, on the other hand, that number would also have to be viewed against the total population. Popular wisdom has portrayed an obsessively puritanical New England in the seventeenth century. Against such a portrait one case a month in a community of one thousand people might appear excessive. But that number would also show that the vast majority of the population did not engage in such activity. James Michener's Abner Hale may have been a caricature of the orthodox Puritan sexual model, but he personified the classic Augustinian attitude about sexuality. While the Puritan church in New England evolved into the less formidable Congregational church, the Puritan consciousness survived in the moral posturings of Protestant denominations, especially in the South and Midwest, that did not always maintain a clear distinction between love, which Christianity exalted, and lust, which it condemned.

Without Awareness That Sex Is "Sin"

This, then, was the moral code that the transplanted African was supposed to understand, although he was not allowed to become a member of the society that promulgated it. Speaking at a convention in Danville, Kentucky, in 1792, the Reverend David Rice complained that the bondsman was "accountable to his Creator" and told how to get to heaven, but then was denied the right to make moral choices. Legally prohibited from marrying in Christian ceremonies and unable to arrange relationships in accordance with their ancient religions, slave men and women formed ad hoc unions and carried on as best they could under laws that defined them as property rather than people.[128] In the meantime, the slave had to contend with contradictory pressures from whites who were themselves ambivalent about what to expect from their bondsmen. On one side, the master told his slaves to eschew their ancestral heathen "superstitions" and learn to conduct themselves in accordance with Christian principles—monogamy rather than indiscrimination; love rather than lust; spirituality rather than animalism. But on the other, he conceded, since it served his purpose to do so, that his slaves were still Africans who, because of their supposed primordial instincts, would quite naturally cultivate carnal habits that a white man would never lower himself to—a reflection of the Apostle Paul's warning to the Thessalonians to control their bodies "in a way that is holy and honorable, not in passionate lust like the heathen, who do not know God." In the social lexicon of the Bible, Paul's "heathen" were nothing more than New Testament descendants of the "strangers" whom the author (or authors) of the Book of Leviticus had proclaimed were fit to be enslaved.[129] Besides, money was to be made from slaves who reproduced frequently. With the master's desire for profit overriding all other considerations, whatever moral compunction he may have had about restraints on his slaves' sexual habits became a casualty of his greed. Profit, as usual, was more powerful than piety. What could be more un-Christian than the systematic slave breeding practiced by many planters?[130]

Thus did the white man's aversion to the nefarious images of blackness and the Christian's perception of sexual morality come together in the person of the slave. In his rebuke to Samuel Sewall's *The Selling of Joseph* (1701), one of the first antislavery tracts in America, John Saffin described the African's character as

> *Libidinous, Deceitful, False and Rude,*
> *The Spume Issue of Ingratitude.*[131]

From the earliest times, Europeans and Americans, equating sexuality with aboriginal cultures, had imputed libidinous excesses to dark-skinned people. Sex was thought to be a consuming interest of the lower animals, and people with black and brown skins were more animal-like than people with fair skins. No one pushed the sexual buttons better than Shakespeare, who, in his cast of characters for *The Tempest*, identified Caliban as a "savage and deformed slave." In *Titus Andronicus*, Tamora, Queen of the Goths, was condemned for falling in love with the dark-skinned Aaron. "Believe me, queen," Bassianus fumed, "your swarth Cimmerian doth make your honour of his body's hue, spotted, detested, and abominable." Why did you descend from your "snow-white goodly steed" to wander with "a barbarous moor?"[132] When Aaron was brought in with his bastard child, Lucius condemned to death the "incarnate devil" and "the base fruit of his burning lust."[133] And, of course, no one embodied dark-skinned debauchery more than the hapless Othello. "O thou foul thief," Brabantio raged, "where hast thou stowed my daughter?" Accusing the Moor of practicing magic and trickery, the distraught father was convinced that his Desdemona, "so tender, fair, and happy," would never run from him "to the sooty bosom of such a thing as thou," unless she had been seduced by "foul charms" or drugs.[134] It is not an exaggeration to say that almost everywhere in the English-speaking world it was commonly believed that any white woman who consorted with a black male had been "seduced."[135]

For white Americans it was a theme with endless possibilities. Thomas

Jefferson believed that black men and women possessed sexual appetites that had nothing to do with love or tenderness but, rather, were simply manifestations of their primitive animal natures. Male slaves were "more ardent after their female," he wrote in *Notes on the State of Virginia* (1787), "but love seems with them to be more an eager desire, than a tender delicate mixture of sentiment and sensation."[136] Jefferson, who would certainly have to be considered one of the most enlightened men of his time, also assumed that black men preferred white women for much the same reason that, as he put it, the "Oran-ootan" in Africa pursued black women, although he never stipulated just what that reason was.[137] Consequently, he was convinced that freeing the slaves would unleash hordes of sex-crazed black men who would lust after the helpless white female population.[138]

Jefferson's concern with the sexual appetite of the black male, long an ingredient in the white man's fears of slave rebellion, was echoed in succeeding years by more than a few Protestant spokesmen. In 1843, Josiah Priest published his biblical defense of slavery, *Slavery, As It Relates to the Negro, or African Race, Examined in the Light of Circumstances, History and the Holy Scriptures*, in which he tried to prove that the descendants of Ham, that is, black men, had excessively large penises and had been natives of the city of Sodom, which God had destroyed (along with Gomorrah) as punishment for their terrible sins of the flesh.[139] "The baleful fire of unchaste amour rages through the negro's blood," Priest declared, "inflaming their imaginations with corresponding images and ideas." In 1858, Bishop of Natchez William Henry Elder, writing to the Catholic Church's missionary arm, despaired of ever converting slaves who were "so entirely animal in their inclinations, so engrossed with the senses, that they have no regard for any thing above the gratifications of the body."[140]

By the end of the nineteenth century—a time of virulent racist attitudes throughout the United States—sex-centered Negrophobia erupted in a frenzy with the publications of Charles Carroll's "*The Negro a Beast*" (1900) and *The Tempter of Eve* (1902), both printed by fundamentalist Christian publishing houses in St. Louis.[141] Because of the African's apelike behavior, Carroll wrote, it was almost a certainty that it had been a black man, and not a serpent, who had tempted Eve in the Garden of Eden. At about the same time, racist theories of African carnality received "scientific" support when Dr. William Lee Howard, in an article in *Medicine* (1903), claimed that the black man's "sexual madness" could be attributed to the large size of his penis and the fact that he lacked "the sensitiveness of the terminal fibers which exist in the Caucasian."[142]

Although it was the black-skinned African who dominated the white man's fantasies about interracial sex, the Indian did not escape an association. Colonial Anglicans, according to one historian, saw in Shakespeare's Caliban the "gabbling, ridiculous monster . . . dark-skinned [and] heathen," a prototype of the American Indian. "Not yet truly human," John Woolverton wrote, Caliban "is possessed of savage uncontrolled sexuality."[143] In a study focusing primarily on the Indians of New England and New Netherland, Francis Jennings described natives whom Europeans saw as violating "supposedly natural laws without compunction," showing "small concern about their nakedness, [and] happily loose about premarital sex." Moreover, "[t]here was no crime of fornication or 'unnatural vice' " among Indians; women "were mistresses of their own bodies" and all sexual relations "were personal matters outside the jurisdiction of sachem and council."[144] Although white Americans rarely lived in the kind of intimate proximity with the Indian population that they did with slaves, by the 1830s many of them nevertheless claimed to see in the native the same "sexual aggression and lust" that was so evident in Africans.[145]

It was a subject that easily lent itself to fictional exploitation. Among the most popular works in the early twentieth century were two novels by Thomas Dixon, a well-known Baptist preacher who found the mythology of race far more to his liking than the mythology of Christianity. In *The Leopard's Spots* (1902), Dixon gave full expression to the view that the black male was a sexual madman. His second book, *The Clansman* (1905), became the inspiration for D. W. Griffith's classic silent film *The Birth of a Nation* (1915), which built up "to its sustained climax from two attempted rapes of white women by black men"—a dramatic fulfillment of Jefferson's worst fear. Casting the role of the ingénue, Griffith replaced the "mature figure" of Blanche Sweet with the more virginal and fragile Lillian Gish because he wanted to shift "sexuality from the white woman to the black man," Michael Rogin wrote in his study of political demonology. "The regression to the presexual virgin and the invention of the black demon went hand in hand."[146]

Some modern psychologists argue that the white phobia over black male sexual prowess is the product of a dominant group's refusal to acknowledge in itself sins that it sees in a minority group. Describing the emptiness of their lives, psychoanalyst Helen V. McLean claimed that whites in a small southern town believed "the Negro has what they lack." Their contacts with local blacks, however, were "fraught with the terror of the forbidden," she added. "Their inflexible consciences, in seeking a victim to punish for all manner of forbidden impulses, must keep in subservience those who represent the temptation." White Americans have always seemed to be obsessed with sexual matters, but because of the Christian influence, sex, according to the theory, was perceived as "dirty," so they imputed "abnormal" sexuality to other peoples.[147] By projecting "immorality" onto Africans, the white man, believing that every black man considered the seduction of a white woman to be the ultimate achievement, justified his subjugation of them.[148]

Paradoxically, the modern white phobia over interracial sexual relations was not a problem for the early Christians, and the Latin writers who referred to interracial marriages reflected no abiding concern or fear about racial mixing. "Neither the biblical account of Moses' marriage to a Kushite nor that of Josephus condemns the union," Frank Snowden wrote. "Josephus in his version does not suggest that there was anything unusual about the overture of the Ethiopian princess or about Moses' acceptance of her proposal." But in more recent centuries, Christianity played a major role in producing a society where sexual conduct often did not coincide with moral preachments and where Africans and Indians must have wondered about the efficacy of the white man's religion and the strength of his faith. In 1630 a Virginian named Hugh Davis was whipped for "defiling his body in lying with a negro," behavior the authorities considered an "abuse to the dishonor of God and shame of Christians."[149] But less than two centuries later a much more celebrated Virginian, perhaps emulating the conduct of his father-in-law, apparently established an intimate relationship with a slave woman that lasted thirty-eight years and produced as many as seven children. Some of Thomas Jefferson's biographers—most notably, Merrill O. Peterson and Dumas Malone—have taken strong exception to the suggestion that he maintained a romantic association with Sally Hemings, but the evidence is abundant enough to make it highly likely. These critics have usually based their dissent chiefly on the argument that such behavior would be totally out of character for a man of Jefferson's stature and temperament. But too often their complaint has seemed motivated by the fact that they simply could not believe someone whom they had admired and exalted their entire lifetimes could possibly engage in conduct that they personally considered reprehensible. To place Jefferson above such behavior is to place him outside of an era in which sexual relations between slaveowners and female slaves were commonplace, even among the presumably genteel élite of plantation society. Why should Jefferson, whose beloved Martha died when he was only forty-one, have been any different?[150]

It would not be inappropriate to wonder why the members of a society that not only tolerated but actually exalted an institution as barbaric as human bondage should be squeamish about anyone's private sexual behavior. By the middle of the nineteenth century sexual liaisons between masters and slave women were so widespread that they could no longer be called aberrations. "Any lady is ready to tell you who is the father of all the mulatto children in everybody's household but her own," Mary Boykin

Chesnut wrote in her diary in 1861. "Those, she seems to think, drop from the clouds."[151] Thus, in a nation in which the relationships between religion and sexuality ranged from the celibacy and complete abstinence of the Shakers to the complex marriages of John Humphrey Noyes's Oneida community, where sexual intercourse with multiple partners was encouraged and even given religious ratification, physical contacts between dominant white men and submissive black women were so mundane that they were almost always publicly ignored.[152]

One question that must have occurred to more than a few slaves was how the white man was able to reconcile biblical admonitions against lust with his practice of concubinage—a practice that, as Lillian Smith wrote in her classic *Killers of the Dream* (revised, 1961), made the footpath from the Big House to the slave cabins one of the most heavily traveled in the South. Similarly, what could the slave have thought about the conflict between scriptural teachings on sexual behavior and the slave-breeding operations of many Bible-quoting planters in the upper South during the decades just before the Civil War? What a strange religion was this Christianity that condemned adultery as a mortal sin, but saw nothing wrong with unmarried slaves cohabiting. Nor did the end of bondage bring anything other than a nominal change in the situation.

One of the most hypocritical conditions faced by former slaves was state laws that made interracial marriage a crime while casual relationships (between white men and black women, of course) were usually considered less than minor indiscretions and, among some white men, were smirkingly envied. Shortly after the war a black delegate to the Mississippi State Constitutional Convention agreed to support a proposal against intermarriage only if it was coupled with one against white men keeping black mistresses. In an inverse application of the same idea, delegates to an 1883 convention of black men in Texas pleaded for a law against concubinage with punishment at least equal to the law against intermarriage. Three years later, a black man and a white woman in Maryland, who had lived together for a number of years and had several children, were each sentenced to eighteen months in jail because they had married. Clergymen pleaded, unsuccessfully, with authorities to pardon the couple because, they said, the law against intermarriage was simply "a cloak for immoral living." In other words, marriage was a crime but promiscuity was not.[153]

As nervous as the white man was about the alleged sexual powers of black men and their concomitant attraction for white women, it was the black woman who became the central character of the white man's hypocritical posturing between his public professions of piety and his private sexual behavior.[154] To maintain the appearance of a traditional Christian community, slaveholders imposed upon their wives and daughters a veil of innocence and purity. Exalted and protected, the white female was placed on the pedestal of "Sacred Womanhood"; but, as Smith noted, "the higher the pedestal, the less he enjoyed her whom he had put there, for statues after all are only nice things to look at." It was to the arms of the slave woman, who, the Reverend David Rice observed as early as 1792, dared "neither resist nor complain," that the white man turned for his own sexual liberation. If early Christian leaders had had access to such a convenience just outside their back doors, they certainly did not publicly take advantage of it. Rather than acknowledge "the madness of lust," as Augustine had called it, church fathers exorcised their own smoldering sins by projecting them onto the objects of lust—women. In order to "sublimate his passions and be rid of the tormenting visions of dancing girls," Jerome—sometimes known as the "patron saint of misogyny"—buried himself in Hebrew studies and biblical translations; and Tertullian, the same person who had equated original sin with sexuality, called women the "devil's gateway." Well beyond the Middle Ages, church fathers perceived females as the "more lascivious of the sexes," the sirens who lured holy but helpless men into sin and away from "ascetic spirituality." Accordingly, Oscar Handlin argued, the master, "drawn to the slave by her availability and repelled by consciousness of her inferiority, could purge himself of self-hatred only by locating the responsibility for the low passion in her, and in her not as an individual but as one of a degraded race of beings."[155]

Thus the American slaveholder was able to create for himself what must have sometimes seemed like the best of heaven and hell. By elevating his own women above the carnal world, he maintained an illusion of Christian spirituality; and by succumbing to the allegedly irresistible allure of the black female, he found full expression for his sexual appetite. As long as he indulged this "weakness" with a woman whose inferiority had been divinely ordained, it did not seem so sinful.[156]

A shadow victim of all this, Lillian Smith wrote, was the white woman for whom "sex was pushed out through the back door as a shameful thing never to be mentioned," and who unleashed her wrath not upon her philandering husband but upon the female slave. In her *Incidents in the Life of a Slave Girl* (1861), Harriet A. Jacobs described in painful detail the anguish of a jealous mistress who tried to trick an innocent slave woman into confessing. It was not the man who was at fault, one southern white woman complained, but his slave paramour, "of strong sex instincts and devoid of sexual conscience, at the white man's door, in the white man's dwelling." In other words, the vulnerable white male, simply too weak to resist the allure of forbidden sex, was the victim. After the Civil War, a white missionary named Marcia Cotton blamed her inability to persuade black prostitutes to give up the business on the "African heathenism" to which these "poor degraded women clung." The black woman's sexual impulses, she maintained, must be culturally ingrained. "How else can I get any excuse for this predominance of Animal habits which show themselves all the while with most of them."[157]

Of course, the most obvious consequences of these associations were everywhere. In 1860 the United States Census Bureau counted almost 600,000 Americans of mixed blood, which was over 13.2 percent of the total black population—and this was unquestionably a conservative figure.[158] The bureau had instructed its canvassers to classify as mulatto any black person who had a "perceptible" trace of white blood. Since this left a great deal to the visual discretion of the individual enumerator, there must have been many uncounted blacks with an imperceptible trace of white blood—not to mention many whites with an imperceptible trace of black blood. If the discernible percentage of people who were of mixed blood was 13.2, one can only guess what the true figure was. In any event, by this time their presence had become, as John Hope Franklin put it in his presidential address to the Southern Historical Association in 1971, "an integral part of the perfect society to which the white southerner had become so attached and committed."[159]

Unfettered by the white man's religious shackles, the slaves at least had each other, and physical intimacy was one of the few areas of fulfillment left to them. Christianity, with its endless litany of "thou-shalt-nots," could not take that away from them. "Down by the quarters in the still night, the blacks in their darkness gave themselves over to heedless abandon," Oscar Handlin wrote. "No constricting reason held back the flow of their passion." In contrast to the puritanical slaveholder's deflection of "the instinctual drives of the body," the unchurched slave was, in Smith's words, "without awareness that sex is 'sin,' " and was full of "a marvelous love of life and play, a physical grace and rhythm and a psychosexual vigor that must have made the white race by contrast seem washed-out and drained of much that is good and life-giving." While white children in the front yard were taught lessons on "sin, sex, and segregation," black children in the back yard were "naked and unashamed [and] did all the naughty things little white children were punished for."[160] No hypocrisy, no frustration, no guilt; and no Augustinian association of shame with a natural act.

Needless to say, the white male was never aware of the obvious contradiction in his juxtaposition of sexuality and animalism. In denigrating Africans for their allegedly excessive sexual appetites, whites implied that civilized humans engaged in sex solely for procreation and that sexual indulgence for any other reason was simply an expression of one's lower animal proclivities. In other words, sexual behavior should not be sensual behavior. The first was a natural function, the other was lust. Of course, anything that would make the black person appear to be subhuman coincided with the Christian's dichotomous universe and, accordingly, reinforced the white person's claim to superiority.[161] What whites did not realize, or simply chose to ignore, was that the very quality they criticized was a uniquely human characteristic. The fact that a man and a woman could enjoy a sexual relationship without being driven by a biological purpose was one of the things that elevated them above lower animals. Since many mammals breed only during certain seasons when the female is receptive and conception is likely to occur, the person who engaged in sexual relations only to have children was the one who was really behaving "like an animal." And, of course, it was the black woman's so-called animal appeal that some white men apparently found so compelling, an attraction which suggested that their ignorance of animal behavior was matched only by their hypocrisy.

This does not mean that slaves did not have sexual taboos and codes of sexual morality. In some African societies, bridal virginity was very important, while in others premarital (though not usually extramarital) sexual relations were acceptable and even encouraged. In his *Interesting Narrative* (1789), Olaudah Equiano compared the reserved sexual behavior of the women in his native Benin, one of the largest kingdoms along the African Guinea coast, with those in other parts of West Africa, where they "were not so modest as ours, for they eat, and drank, and slept with their men." To a Christian, African sexual customs ranged from bizarre to shocking. Among the Nyakyusa, a nursing mother avoided her husband because it was believed that semen was dangerous to infants. Ibo women, who attached great significance to cleanliness, went into seclusion during their menstrual periods, after which they underwent a purification process involving washing and offerings. In many societies, the buttocks and genitals were recognized as the "gates of life" and had to be well covered at all times. Within some kinship groups physical contacts between certain relatives—such as a man and his mother-in-law or a woman and her father-in-law—were scrupulously avoided. There were tribes that practiced sexual hospitality, a host making his wife (or daughter or sister) available as a sleeping partner for a visiting male; and among the Masai, people within certain age groups shared sexual favors. In a few places, tribal ceremonies required a woman to have actual or symbolic intercourse with her husband or with officials. Sex could also be simply a matter of practicality. For example, in some societies, especially those where military campaigns kept a husband away for long periods of time, another male—usually his brother—had intercourse with the wife both to satisfy her physical urges and to impregnate her so she could get on with the business of raising a family.[162]

One should not confuse the African's rules of sexual conduct with his rules of marriage. However outrageous his morality seemed to a Christian, it was always a fundamental component of his social system. In the Kongo nation an adulterer faced the death penalty, a punishment that Equiano claimed was widespread across much of the continent, "so sacred among [the men] is the honour of the marriage-bed, and so jealous are they of the fidelity of their wives." Anything that undermined a family's stability threatened the community's stability. In a society in which kinship was the foundation of almost everything, relationships were what really counted. Sexual behavior was governed by rules of relationships, not rules of good and evil. In 1638 a Massachusetts planter named Samuel Maverick, looking to increase his retinue of slaves, tried to breed his "Negro woman" with a young black man. But the woman, who it seemed had been a "Queen in her own Countrey," rejected her unwelcome bed partner because "this she took in high disdain beyond her slavery." When the master "commanded him will'd she nill'd she to go to bed to her, which was no sooner done but she kickt him out again."[163] It was not so much that she objected to having sex as it was to having it with one who, to her, was a common person. Social status, not morality, was the critical factor.

The important point in comparing the sexual behavior of Christian slaveholders and that of their bondsmen is not that the African's sexual customs were sinful, as the Christian perceived them, but that they were very different and that they generally were part of a long-established code of behavior. As Mbiti pointed out, the "religious and social uses of sex are held sacred and respectable."[164] Moreover, the African, unlike the white Christian, did not pay lip service to a religious moral standard, all the while practicing just the opposite. As strange as his sexual customs were to a Westerner, they were consistent with, and sometimes integral parts of, his religious traditions. Every culture has had its share of hypocrites, but among most sub-Saharan African societies sexual practices were scrupulously intertwined throughout the kinship structure and were not characterized by the contradiction and deception that the New World slave found so common among white Christians.

SIX THY KINGDOM COME, THY WILL BE DONE

Blessed is the nation whose God is the Lord; and the people whom he hath chosen for his own inheritance.

PSALMS 33:12

This land is your land, this land is my land,
From California to the New York Island.
From the redwood forest to the Gulf Stream waters,
This land was made for you and me.

WOODY GUTHRIE
"This Land Is Your Land"

A People Not Chosen

There is in the Judeo-Christian tradition an implied form of racism that has sometimes consciously—and often unconsciously—influenced the thinking of many Jews and Christians. The Old Testament is, among other things, a history of the early Jews, an epic tale of trial and tribulation in which the children of ancient Israel, selected by God to illuminate his divine presence by both word and action, are portrayed as a unique and favored people.

> The Lord had said to Abram, "Leave your country, your people and your father's household and go to the land I will show you. I will make you into a great nation and I will bless you; I will make your name great, and you will be a blessing. I will bless those who bless you, and whoever curses you I will curse; and all peoples on earth will be blessed through you."[1]

"Now if you obey me fully and keep my covenant," God purportedly told Moses on Mount Sinai, "then out of all nations you will be my treasured possession." It had been just three months since the flight from Egypt. "Although the whole earth is mine, you will be for me a kingdom of priests and a holy nation."[2] Forty years later, Moses, repeating almost these exact words, admonished the Jews to defeat and destroy "totally" the seven larger and stronger nations that God had driven out of the land before them.[3] "Make no treaty with them, and show them no mercy," he commanded. To avoid the risk of losing your sons to their gods, he added, shun them socially and destroy their pagan altars. "For you are a people holy to the Lord your God," who has "chosen you out of all the peoples on the face of the earth to be his people, his treasured possession."

As it happened, the minority status of the Israelites probably magnified the importance of their selection. "The Lord did not set his affection on you and choose you because you were more numerous than other peoples, for you were the fewest of all peoples," Moses reminded them. "But it was because the Lord loved you and you kept the oath he swore to your forefathers that he brought you out with a mighty hand and redeemed you from the land of slavery, from the power of Pharaoh king of Egypt."[4] There was nothing equivocal about that.

But while being God's "treasured possession" carried certain privileges, it also imposed some terrible burdens. In ancient times, abolitionist Goldwin Smith wrote in 1864, almost every society considered itself the "chosen people" of its own gods. For these nations, the belief that they were chosen was a foundation of national pride, which, in turn, inspired military aggression, justified territorial conquest, and obfuscated cultural shortcomings. On the other hand, Smith explained, the Israelites were the chosen people of the "true God," whose objective was to teach them "national humility."[5] Because they often lived amidst or near unfriendly nationalities, they were destined to suffer for their exclusive claim to The Truth: "Then the Lord said to [Abram], 'Know for certain that your descendants will be strangers in a country not their own, and they will be enslaved and mistreated four hundred years.' "[6]

It was their blessing *and* their curse. After all, when the members of a minority insist that everyone else's gods are false, they should not be surprised by hostile reactions. In the age of Abraham, when beliefs were shaped by faith rather than science, the suppression of heresy was routine. Of course, it also could be argued that God had not actually favored the Israelites at all, but rather had chosen them to suffer as a demonstration of his will to all of humankind. "The chosen people can rightly be punished," Conor Cruise O'Brien declared in his William E. Massey, Sr., Lectures at Harvard, "and God can use other people as instruments of their punishment."[7] It had all been a cruel trick. But since overcoming adversity was also a yardstick of strength and achievement, that thesis could conveniently be turned around. It mattered not if God exalted the Israelites or condemned them; the fact that they had been persecuted was in itself sufficient reason for feeling chosen. If something special was worth having, it was worth suffering for. For some that conviction carried with it a form of penance that bordered on psychological self-flagellation, an attitude perhaps best expressed in the Yiddish saying *Schwer zu sein a Yid!* ("It's hard being a Jew!") But also obvious was the implication that only the Jews, thanks to God, were strong enough to survive such an ordeal. Indeed, not merely to survive but to flourish in the face of persecution was a measure of one's true holiness. No others were worthy of such a test; to pass it one had to be superior. Accordingly, it is not difficult to understand why British historian Arnold Toynbee, in an interview with *Life* magazine, called the Jews one of the most "race-conscious" people in the world.[8] There is nobility in martyrdom.

Whatever believers presumed his reason to have been, when God selected a small segment of humanity and placed it apart from all others, did he not, in effect, discriminate against everyone else?[9] While there may have been no explicit scriptural basis for the belief that God made nonwhite people inferior, it should not be difficult to understand how a religion that had in its origins a necessary element of ethnic selection could continue to convey and even encourage a posture of cultural arrogance toward outsiders.

For example, what did the Old Testament say about the many nations that had *not* been chosen? Did God's selection of the Israelites mean that all other societies in existence at the time had been abandoned by him and, accordingly, were condemned to eternal damnation? When Abram passed through Sechem and the plain of Moreh to the "promised land," the Canaanites were already there, "but the Lord appeared to Abram and said, 'To your offspring I will give this land.' " What had the Canaanites ever done to deserve this? When God later made a covenant with Abram for the land between the Nile and the Euphrates, he specified ten nations that would be displaced.[10] In at least six other places in Genesis, God reaffirmed his land grant to the Israelites, first to Abraham (13:14–15; 15:7, and 17:8), then to Isaac (26:3–4), and finally to Jacob (28:4 and 35:12). In Exodus 6:4, God made the same promise to all the Israelites. Later, in Leviticus 20:23, he reminded Moses that the Israelites must lead righteous lives and not "according to the customs of the nations I am going to drive out before you."[11] And in Psalms 2:8–9, God is both specific and relentless. "Ask of me, and I shall give *thee* the heathen *for* thine inheritance, and the uttermost parts of the earth *for* thy possession. Thou shalt break them with a rod of iron; thou shalt dash them in pieces like a potter's vessel."

What was never explained was why God thought it necessary to dispossess so brutally these condemned nations just to create a homeland for one small group. One American clergyman believed that God simply wanted to demonstrate to the Israelites his willingness to discriminate against others. In 1819, in a sermon commemorating the ordination of two missionaries to the Sandwich Islands, the Reverend Heman Humphrey of Pittsfield, Massachusetts, commenting on the problems faced by Moses and Joshua during the Israelites' occupation of the plain of Jordan, pointed out that the several nations that remained in the promised land had been condemned by God to "utter destruction."[12] To Humphrey it was a lesson in power that the Israelites were expected to remember.

It was also, ultimately, a lesson in discrimination by omission for everyone subject to the influences of Judaism and Christianity. If Jews and early Christians suffered persecution because they had to face the test of having been selected by God, were the many millions who had not been selected totally out of God's favor? Did Christians in the modern era ever raise the point that the scriptures never took into account the Jews' geographic isolation? These are questions that cannot be answered without calling attention to the provincialism of biblical writers. The "nations" written about in the Old Testament occupied a tiny corner of the planet; and Christ, in his lifetime, traveled only a short distance from his birthplace. When Moses said that in Abram "all the peoples on earth will be blessed," did he believe that all there was to the "earth" was the Near East that he knew? Specifically, since biblical writers made no mention of nations not known to them, how did the societies of China and India—old and flourishing civilizations even in Moses' day—fit into Old Testament teachings and prophecies? When explorers from the Christian world encountered strange peoples for the first time, did any of them think to wonder about the "eternal truths" that had been passed down over the centuries? Of course, none of these questions have been answered by historians because scholarly research calls for objective analyses of factual data, and the chosen-people concept, like most religious myths, is an article of faith; but it should not be difficult to see how a religion based on a favored-people notion encouraged believers to *disfavor* others. The significance of a myth rests solely on the influence of the people who believe it is true, or, at least, useful. When one has been weaned on an assumption of cultural and spiritual exclusiveness, it is not always easy to be magnanimous about things like equality and justice among all peoples.

Although only the Israelites were singled out in the Old Testament for special treatment, most Christians, pointing to the coming of Christ as a fulfillment of ancient prophecies, claimed favored status as an inheritance from God. "The Old Testament is the New Testament concealed," Bible readers like to say, "and the New Testament is the Old Testament revealed." As Peter told the Christians living in the northern provinces of Asia: "But you are a chosen people, a royal priesthood, a holy nation, a people belonging to God, that you may declare the praises of him who called you out of darkness into his wonderful light."[13]

The children of Israel may have been the original Chosen People, but God favored all who believed in Christ; and to be a Christian *and* an

American was to be in the best of all possible worlds. Accordingly, the early Puritans believed that "England was a new Israel, a holy people favored of God," as one historian put it. But the church had fallen into error, making England's sin "all the greater because [she was] held so high in the esteem of the Maker." The Puritan migration of 1630–42 was nothing more than an extension of the divine mandate. New England was also called New *Canaan*; and every hardship that the Puritans encountered was overcome because of God's favor. The story of the "epidemicall sickness" that had been inflicted on the region's Indian population just before the arrival of the English became legendary among the faithful. Similarly, many Puritans were convinced that their military successes against the Indians, such as the virtual annihilation of the Pequots in 1637 and the defeat of King Philip in 1676, were God's way of keeping the land safe for his chosen people. Just as God had driven out the various tribes of Canaan before the ancient Israelites, he was now driving out the Indian tribes of New England before the Puritans. The Chosen People mandate was ultimately enlarged by the principles of the Revolution, in which it was made clear that the destiny of the American people was not duty to a single monarch but, in William R. Brock's words, "to God and mankind."[14] Thomas Jefferson probably said it better than anyone else in the closing sentence of his Second Inaugural Address.

> I shall need, too, the favor of that Being in whose hands we are, who led our forefathers, as Israel of old, from their native land, and planted them in a country flowing with all the necessaries and comforts of life; who has covered our infancy with his providence, and our riper years with his wisdom and power; and to whose goodness I ask you to join with me in supplication, that he will so enlighten the minds of your servants, guide their councils, and prosper their measures, that whatsoever they do, shall result in their good, and shall secure you the peace, friendship, and approbation of all nations.[15]

But while God's selection had brought trial and suffering to the Jews, it meant power and conquest for Anglo-Americans. In 1874, Samuel Harris, Dwight Professor of Systematic Theology at Yale College, argued in his *Kingdom of Christ on Earth* that God has always acted by chosen peoples, and to the Anglo-Saxon "more than to any other the world is now indebted for the propagation of Christian ideas and Christian civilization." Thirteen years later, James M. King, a prominent Methodist clergyman in New York, declared that God had chosen the Anglo-Saxon "to conquer the world for Christ by dispossessing feeble races, and assimilating and molding others."[16] Nowhere did Harris or King say anything about the Catholic and Protestant countries of continental Europe. Did they mean that only Great Britain and the United States could claim to be chosen?

Whomever they may have excluded, thus did an idea enunciated millennia earlier to exalt victims of oppression ultimately come to justify an imperialistic crusade against "weaker" people. "We will not renounce our part in the mission of our race," Senator Albert J. Beveridge of Indiana proclaimed in a speech defending the American acquisition of the Philippines following the Spanish-American War, but "will move forward to our work, not howling out regrets like slaves whipped to their burdens, but with gratitude for a task worthy of our strength, and thanksgiving to Almighty God that He has marked us as His chosen people, henceforth to lead in the regeneration of the world." Later in the same speech, he added: "And of all our race He has marked the American people as His chosen nation to finally lead in the regeneration of the world. This is the divine mission of America, and it holds for us all the profit, all the glory, all the happiness possible to man. We are trustees of the world's progress, guardians of its righteous peace."[17]

The proof of this divine mandate was so self-evident as to be almost redundant. How else could one account for America's natural abundance, economic progress, and political success? From the Puritans' New Canaan in the seventeenth century to Woodrow Wilson's messianic resolve to "save the world for democracy" in the twentieth, Americans perceived themselves as The Elect in the fullest religious sense. It was an idea that had come a long way from what Goldwin Smith had called ancient Israel's "national humility."

It was also a perception that almost all Americans shared. There were few Jewish or Christian sects whose members did not believe that they had "responded to a divine call and made a covenant to walk with God," religion historian Timothy L. Smith noted. "Covenant theology, which Perry Miller has demonstrated was central to the Puritan 'errand into the wilderness,' turns up at least occasionally in the faith of almost every American ethnic group." If the various denominations understood the "covenant" in its theological sense—the promises made by God to man, as recorded in the Bible—then it was inescapable that they would consider themselves chosen. The fact was, both Protestant and Catholic immigrants easily embraced the notion that they had been favored by "divine sanction and direction to their long pilgrimage toward a more just, happy, and humane tomorrow."[18]

It should, thus, surprise no one that the northern independent black churches that had organized in the early nineteenth century as groups feeling persecution identified with the "exodus" theme. So powerful was the idea of selection that even the slaves embraced it. "The single most persistent image that slave songs contain," Lawrence W. Levine wrote, "is that of the chosen people." Titles like "De People Dat Is Born of God," "We Are the People of God," and "We Are de People of de Lord," reflected clearly the exclusive status claimed by all Christians.[19] Paradoxically, the slave's affinity for the chosen-people thesis more closely paralleled the original Old Testament situation of an oppressed people fleeing enslavement than did the white Christian's invocation of dominion. Whether or not his perception had been part of an Islamic or African tradition was irrelevant, the principle of the chosen people was inherent in Christianity. Of course, there was a critical difference between the European immigrant's recognition of a "divine sanction and direction" and the transplanted African's sense of religious fulfillment. The former came to it by choice, the latter by necessity.

It should be pointed out that being preferred by God could have beneficial results for others because the sense of obligation that accompanied the privilege of being chosen sometimes cultivated humility, generosity, humanitarianism, compassion, and an open mind. But on its dark side the favored-people doctrine bred arrogance, conceit, indifference, contempt, and closed minds—all components of institutional racism. And, like Frankenstein's monster, it could also return to destroy its creator.

In 1837, an English preacher named John Wilson founded the Anglo-Israelites, an ultra-fundamentalist group organized around the belief that the modern Anglo-Saxon, not the Jew, was the true descendant of Joseph and the ten lost tribes of Israel. As "proof," Wilson invoked Genesis 49:24, in which he somehow saw Jacob's tribute to Joseph's bow as a "prophecy of the English yeoman with his long bow." Thirty-three years later, the missionary Edward Hine brought the movement to the United States, where he eventually converted Charles A. L. Totten, a professor of military science at Yale.[20] By the 1980s, several right-wing "Christian" groups—some of them organized in heavily armed paramilitary encampments—were making the same kind of claim. In a letter to *Time* magazine, a member of something called the Christian Identity Movement argued that for centuries the "Jewish leadership" had tried to "usurp our birthright from true Israel, which is Anglo-Saxon, Germanic, Scandinavian and other white peoples."[21] Thus the doctrine of the chosen people cut in both directions.

Modern Christian advocates of the doctrine are nothing if not arrogant. Being chosen by God carried with it, as religion scholar William A. Clebsch put it, "a sense of deserving to have been chosen." Accordingly, few Americans considered it necessary to explain how an idea that was inherently antidemocratic could be consistent with democracy. If this contradiction could be expected to give thoughtful people reason to pause, there was little evidence that it did. It was also a recipe for demagoguery. A democratic society depended on the will of the people; but when these same people accepted a leader who they believed was "marked by God, as Andrew Jackson was at New Orleans," they risked being subjected to a leader who claimed he knew God's intentions better than they did. In Europe it was called "divine right" of kings; but in a democratic United States, all citizens were supposed to be equal under law. In fact, adherence to the chosen-people doctrine inevitably had led to the conclusion that, as some of the old Republicans who tried to reconcile their privileged status with the equalitarian ideals of Jefferson had noted, some people simply were "more equal" than others. Well into the twentieth century, most Americans proudly and unabashedly claimed to be citizens of the freest and most democratic society on earth *and* to be chosen by God to lead humankind to a higher level of civilization. Few saw the contradiction. "Americans as Christ's special messengers were," in William R. Hutchison's words, "a people sent as well as chosen."[22] They even had a special name for it: *Manifest Destiny*.

The Obligations of Destiny

In most traditional histories of the United States, Manifest Destiny is presented as a political and economic theme—the grand story of pioneers who overcame suffering and adversities to bring civilization to an untamed wilderness. It was a heroic and ennobling drama of epic proportions, and, as the subject of countless films, novels, and television programs, it is probably better known to American schoolchildren than any other single aspect of the nation's past. Concomitantly, white Americans have always believed that their political system is so demonstrably superior to any other, and their economic institutions so irrepressibly expansive, it should be obvious to anyone of intelligence that territorial conquest was as inevitable as the tides. Was it not reasonable to believe, Congregationalist Josiah Strong asked in 1893, "that this race is destined to dispossess many weaker ones, assimilate others, and mould the remainder, until in a very true and important sense, it has Anglo-Saxonized mankind?"[23] Convinced of their invincibility, the agents of conquest—traders, soldiers, missionaries, miners, farmers, stockmen, merchants, politicians, railroad builders, and adventurers—swept across the continent. It mattered little what was in their way, human or otherwise; if it did not move, it would be pushed aside.

Once the white American had convinced himself that he was culturally and intellectually superior to the nonwhite peoples he encountered, it was not hard for him to justify his aggression against them. The Indians were heathen and uncivilized; and the Mexicans, who were also mostly Indian, were corrupt and decadent—qualities inherited from the effete Spanish. "The annexations of the Mexican War," wrote Albert K. Weinberg, the godfather of modern research on Manifest Destiny, "represented a conscious change to a toleration of amalgamation with other races."[24] Similarly, the Filipinos, who also had been victimized by Spanish occupation, deserved to be liberated from the Catholic yoke.

Some Americans believed that once the indigenous populations realized how much they would gain from American conquest, they would welcome their Anglo-Saxon benefactors and join them in the march into the future. The moral and social theory of *cultural regeneration* claimed the power both to transform lives into a new Christian perfection and to uplift backward peoples to the American ideal. Needless to say, the effort might have been better appreciated if the conquerors had embraced rather than ghettoized their dark-skinned victims.

In all of this the hand of the government was omnipresent. As territory was purchased or conquered, federal authorities established land policies, encouraged migration and settlement, subsidized transportation developments, authorized territorial and local governments, and set up programs of Indian removal. The American appetite for expansion was insatiable, and the government and the citizen were partners in a venture that did not end even at the water's edge.

At almost exactly the same time that "Manifest Destiny" became a popular expression among ambitious politicians and peripatetic settlers, a new school of "naturalists" began publishing findings that appeared to establish a scientific foundation for a racial hierarchy. For the expansionist, they could not have come at a better time. Probably the most influential American scientific work—and, published in ten editions in sixteen years, almost certainly the most popular—was *Types of Mankind* (1855), written by physician Josiah C. Nott and Egyptologist George R. Gliddon. Nott also assisted in the English translation of Comte Joseph Arthur de Gobineau's *Essai sur l'inégalité des races humaines* (1853–55), considered by many European and American scholars to be the most authoritative statement on "Aryan superiority and racial determinism"; and in 1857 he added another volume, *Indigenous Races of the Earth*, to the growing list of scientific publications supporting white supremacy.[25] Even Swiss-born Louis Agassiz of Harvard, probably the most respected zoologist in the United States, was, despite his close association with a number of New England abolitionists, convinced that people of African origin were inferior to Caucasians; and at the 1850 meeting of the American Association for the Advancement of Science in Charleston, South Carolina, he and Nott appeared on the same program.[26]

While the ideas of people like Nott and Gliddon probably did not have an immediate effect on the average person's perception of race, the scientific authentication of white supremacy nonetheless coincided neatly with slavery and territorial expansion. Manifest Destiny and racism fed on each other. The more exalted Manifest Destiny became, the more blacks and Indians were degraded; and the more blacks and Indians were degraded, the more exalted Manifest Destiny became.[27]

Although the racial theories of Gobineau, Nott, and the others were debated primarily in scientific circles and quoted extensively in the white-supremacist writings of fanatics like John H. Van Evrie,[28] the idea that propelled Manifest Destiny into the twentieth century was a variation of Charles Darwin's theory of natural selection. Developed by English philosopher Herbert Spencer and popularized in the United States by Yale's William Graham Sumner, Social Darwinism—the application of the principle of biological evolution to social institutions—became the leitmotif of, first, expansionists calling for the dispossession of American Indians, then, entrepreneurs justifying their predatory business practices, and, finally, imperialists defending the acquisition of overseas possessions. Just as the strongest members of each animal species survived by dominating the reproductive processes, monopolizing limited food supplies, and adapting to environmental conditions, the argument went, so would "superior" nations assert their political and economic hegemony over weaker states. "Orientals" and "Malays" are incapable of self-government, Senator Beveridge exclaimed in his speech calling for permanent American acquisition of the Philippines. No nation was better qualified to subdue "savage and senile peoples" than the United States; thus we must exercise our natural superiority or the world will "relapse into barbarism and night." If we do not seize the opportunity, he concluded in what sounded more like a concession to the compelling influence of finance capitalism than a desire to civilize backward people, we will lose the China trade and, ultimately, control of the Far East to England, Germany, and Russia. Colonel—and later Brigadier General—Frederick Funston, commander of the 20th Kansas Volunteers, was apparently one of more than a few Americans, including Presidents William McKinley and Theodore Roosevelt, who saw clear parallels between the need for subduing the rebellious Filipinos led by Emilio Aguinaldo and the earlier justification for the subjugation of the Indians. After setting fire to village huts in Caloocan, Funston vowed to "rawhide these bullet-headed Asians until they yell for mercy" in order to teach them not "to get in the way of the bandwagon of Anglo-Saxon progress and decency."[29] The beauty of Social Darwinism was its devastating simplicity: The strong competed for domination of the weak. And the "weak," in almost every case, were people with dark skins.

While the Anti-Imperialists called the acquisition of the Philippines a violation of the traditional American principles of liberty and independence, one opponent condemned American possession for essentially the same racist reasons that some imperialists favored it. Even before Beveridge raved about the importance of subduing "savage and senile peoples," Senator John W. Daniel called for the rejection of the Treaty of Paris, in which Spain had ceded the islands to the United States, because Americans would be asked to embrace a "witch's caldron" of "mixed races" consisting of Chinese, Japanese, and "Malay Negritos." Travelers returning from this part of the world, he went on, have described people of all "concatenations and colors," including some with spots and stripes! "This mess of Asiatic pottage, 7,000 miles from the United States, in a land that we can not colonize and can not inhabit," he charged, "we are told . . . we must take up and annex and combine with our own blood and with our own people, and consecrate them with the oil of American citizenship." Rather than raise the quality of civilization of these "alien races," Daniel concluded, the American people will be dragged down to their level of degradation. Everything will be reduced to the lowest common denominator. If the treaty is ratified, future historians, if there are any, "will say at that moment commenced the decline of American institutions and of the great career which America had set forth to herself to lead upon this earth."[30] Thus the most incriminating spectacle of the debate over the acquisition of the Philippines was the revelation that the American political ethos—divinely mandated or self-imposed, imperialistic or democratic—was irreversibly grounded in a belief in white supremacy.

Christian Imperialism

This, then, has for a long time been the textbook version. But this version is incomplete. It does not require a particularly careful examination to discover that, underneath all of the political shibboleths and economic realizations, Manifest Destiny was, in the final analysis, a *religious* concept that was exalted by Americans of all social levels and had been an essential element in the adventures of every European colonial power. In fact, it is difficult to imagine Manifest Destiny without its Christian credo. When the Nicene Creed was adopted in 325 during the reign of Constantine and later codified by Theodosius (379–395), Christianity became, in Conor Cruise O'Brien's words, "the official cult" of the Roman Empire. "Christ had said that his kingdom was not of this world, but the cult of Christ now becomes that of a worldly empire and is about to become the cult of many kings and princes."

By the sixteenth century, the Reformation itself had become "the grand means employed by God in preparing a people who should lay the foundation of a Christian empire in the New World." During the reign of Queen Elizabeth I, according to religion historian Winthrop S. Hudson, "returning exiles devoted their energies to making clear England's identity and mission as a chosen people." Even more important than the new "national self-consciousness" that had sprung from the glory of Drake, Raleigh, Shakespeare, and the defeat of the Spanish armada "was the strong conviction that England had a God-given vocation to fulfill."

The European theory of the right of discovery, another historian observed, "derived from the ancient claim that Christians were everywhere entitled to dispossess non-Christians of their land," a theory reinforced by the tradition of *vacuum domicilium*, which held that land not "occupied" or "settled" was available to any "civilized" person—that is, Christian—who, of course, had the exclusive right to determine whether or not a land was "settled." In the fifteenth century this theory was codified in a papal declaration authorizing the enslavement of "all saracens and pagans whatsoever, and all other enemies of Christ wheresoever placed," and the seizure of their land. There was never even a suggestion of equality. Applied to Indians of the New World, the theory led to "violence rather than assimilation or coexistence." In fact, it mattered not if the land was vacant, as Europeans questioned whether people who lived without knowing Christianity and "without the customs deemed necessary for equality in international relations at the time" could claim title under "natural law."[31] In other words, only Christians had a *natural* right to the land.

The right of discovery and occupation was also a guiding principle of the Puritan migration of the seventeenth century, during which John Winthrop and his company launched an "Errand into the Wilderness" to establish a "New Canaan," where God's latter-day chosen people could worship free from the danger of error.[32] In his "Attestation" to Cotton Mather's *Magnalia Christi Americana* (1702), John Higginson described how God had intentionally opened the land for the Puritans so they could subdue the wilderness, plant colonies, erect towns, and settle churches.[33] By the time the spiritual fervor called the Great Awakening had swept across the colonies three decades later, reinforcing "the conviction that God had a special destiny in store for America," Manifest Destiny was an old idea.[34] Benjamin Rush, one of the signers of the Declaration of Independence and the founder of the first American Antislavery Society, was convinced that the American Revolution had been divinely inspired and that the United States had been chosen by God to reform the world. Referring to the expulsion of monarchy and the establishment of the American republic, Rush, apparently unaware of the cruel irony of his words, said that God had selected America for man's "ultimate deliverance from slavery."[35]

In the early nineteenth century, John Holt Rice, founder of the

Presbyterian Union Seminary in Virginia and co-founder of the American Bible Society, tried to stem the increasing divisiveness both within and among evangelical denominations—especially Presbyterians and Congregationalists—because, he believed, it was undermining America's divinely ordained role of Christian world leadership. Rice's sentiments were identical to those of Alexander Campbell, founder of the Disciples of Christ, whose efforts to unify all Protestant denominations was based on a conviction that God had charged "Protestant England and Protestant America" with the fortunes, "not of Christendom only, but of all the world."[36] Perhaps no one articulated that belief better than the Reverend Heman Humphrey, pastor of the Congregational Church of Pittsfield, Massachusetts. In September 1819, while delivering a missionary ordination sermon based on God's declaration to the elderly Joshua that "there remaineth yet very much land to be possessed," Humphrey proclaimed:

> As the land of Canaan belonged to Israel, in virtue of a divine grant, so does the world belong to the church; and as God's chosen people still had much to do, before they could come into full and quiet possession of the land, so has the church a great work to accomplish, in subduing the world "to the obedience of Christ."

There are vast areas of the earth belonging to the church that "are still unsubdued," Humphrey concluded, including the region from "our western frontier to the Pacific Ocean."[37] Humphrey seemed unconcerned by the fact that the United States had just negotiated a treaty with Great Britain calling for joint jurisdiction of the Oregon country and that the rest of the land from America's "western frontier" was under Mexican and Spanish control. Thus the United States possessed *no* territory "to the Pacific Ocean." Apparently, God did not recognize political boundaries.

Needless to say, an idea as racist-oriented as Manifest Destiny was certain to be popular among Christian defenders of slavery. When a fanatical commitment to expansion joined a fanatical commitment to bondage, there was no limit to the Christian's imagination, and none was more ludicrous than that of physician and Louisiana University professor Samuel A. Cartwright. In a series of nine letters written to Reverend William Winans and published as a sixty-eight-page booklet that rambled in repetitious detail through all of the biblical arguments based on Noah's curse of Canaan, Cartwright insisted that God had always intended for white men to enslave Africans and carry them to the New World. From the moment that Canaan was condemned to servitude, he and his descendants were marked for enslavement at the hands of the Christian American slaveholder. God's promise in Genesis 9:27 to "enlarge" Japheth, the presumed progenitor of the Caucasian race, was a prophecy of the European discovery and settlement of the New World, and the designation in the same verse of Canaan as Japheth's slave was a ringing endorsement of the slave trade. "No sooner did Japheth begin to enlarge himself, and to dwell in the tents of Shem," Cartwright wrote, "than Canaan left his fastness in the wilds of Africa where the white man's foot had never trod, and appeared on the beach to get passage to America, as if drawn thither by an impulse of his nature to fulfill his destiny of becoming Japheth's servant."[38] In other words, not only was the African inexorably drawn by the power of God to submit to bondage in order to fulfill the promise of Manifest Destiny, but he knew exactly where to go to make himself available.

It would be easy to point out that the absurdity of the argument was exceeded only by the naïve credulity of those who believed it, but that would only obfuscate the more fundamental revelation of how far Christian defenders of slavery were willing to go. Any inclination to deride such preposterous ramblings is quickly overcome by the recognition that Cartwright was one of the antebellum South's most respected and admired intellectuals.

In the North, the growing threat of sectional division in the decades leading up to the Civil War generated ambivalent reactions among clergymen who were trying to balance their commitment to America's role to carry out its divine mission with their opposition to human bondage. As the debate over slavery intensified, one Baptist spokesman expressed his concern that the conflict would impede not only the Christian's duty to evangelize America, but also "the master work of evangelizing Foreign Nations." Disunion would "jeopardize what to the nineteenth century were religious values," Timothy L. Smith argued. "Most evangelical clergymen believed that the nation's chief mission was to cradle a faith which should conquer the world." Twelve years before the Civil War, missionary Hollis Read voiced much the same spirit in *The Hand of God in History*. When the mission of Manifest Destiny collided with the cause of human freedom, there were more than a few critics of slavery who knew where they had to compromise. Lyman Beecher, president of Lane Theological Seminary in Cincinnati, was one of many leading abolitionists who saw themselves as major figures in the nation's millennial role to evangelize the world and tempered their antislavery enthusiasm to avoid doing anything to jeopardize that role. Of course, the good news was that with the end of the war and the emancipation of the slaves, Christian America was free to fulfill its divine mission without distractions, a mission that was endorsed by as avid a spokesman for the rights of the former slaves as Methodist Bishop Gilbert Haven, who saw America as "God's empire."[39] When, shortly before the Spanish-American War, Monsignor John Ireland, Roman Catholic Archbishop of St. Paul, Minnesota, described the United States as a "providential nation" that had a "divine mission to prepare the world, by example and moral influence, for the universal reign of human liberty and human rights," he obviously had no idea how cruelly duplicitous his words might sound.[40]

Duplicity was not a problem for Senator Beveridge. In his highly charged speech in the Senate in January 1900, and in his subsequent "March of the Flag" address, which he delivered several times, he made frequent allusions to God, whose "great purpose made manifest in the instincts of our race . . . is the redemption of the world and the Christianization of mankind," a message not lost on religious leaders. The smell of gunpowder still hung in the Cuban air and the Filipino rebel resistance would last another two years, but every mainstream Protestant denomination, and some of the minor sects, had already formulated plans to take advantage of the new missionary opportunity.[41] Calling Anglo-Saxons "the great missionary race," Josiah Strong, in his immensely popular *Our Country: Its Possible Future and Its Present Crisis* (1885, revised 1891), proudly declared his conviction that the American was the "exponent" of a "pure *spiritual* Christianity,"[42] although the subsequent American venture into the western Pacific was far more physical than spiritual.

The publication of Strong's book had been anxiously anticipated by the Protestant clergy. By the time of the First World War, 175,000 copies had been sold and individual chapters had been reprinted in pamphlet form and in dozens of newspapers and magazines, a public response that the chief librarian of Congress compared to that for Harriet Beecher Stowe's controversial and enormously popular antislavery novel, *Uncle Tom's Cabin* (1852).[43] Strong's was only the most acclaimed declaration of Christian imperialism.[44] Less known but equally sanctimonious were James S. Dennis's *Christian Missions and Social Progress* (1897–1906) and Robert E. Speer's *Christianity and the Nations* (1910). Seventeenth century or twentieth, it seemed not to matter. Manifest Destiny in its most fundamental and compelling form was the idea that by some kind of divine fiat the American people had been elected—indeed, had an obligation—to elevate, by precept and example, all of humankind.

The New Chosen People

However one chose to perceive Manifest Destiny, it was not a spontaneous phenomenon and could not be understood outside of a religious context, for one very obvious reason. If Americans were destined to occupy the continent, some *One* had to make that determination. The term "destiny" assumed—no, proclaimed—the presence of a supreme force, an original mover. Inherent in the belief of being chosen was a belief in the existence of a Chooser, be it God, providence, nature, fate, or some other mystical entity. Once that belief was recognized, the rest was just a matter of carrying out the divine mandate so that its consequences coincided with the national interest.

For example, displacing Mexican authority from California and the Southwest in the 1840s simply meant replacing a weak and corrupt government with a strong and democratic one, whose citizens had been endowed by their Creator with unalienable rights. Similarly, Indians were conveniently perceived not so much as ordinary human beings but as part of the fauna, along with buffaloes and coyotes, to be driven off or killed. Does the Indian have "the right to prevent others from developing the resources of the soil," a Methodist editor asked, "and hold as his own ten thousand acres per capita, when multitudes of honest, hard-working men have not a yard of earth that they can call their own?" Because the Indian "delights in hunting buffalo and deer," he went on, the soil will "be doomed to perpetual barrenness."[45] Surely this was not what God had intended. The American farmer had the right to dispossess the Indians because, Senator Thomas Hart Benton of Missouri insisted, they were not using the land "according to the intentions of the CREATOR."[46]

As it happened, God's favor was one of the more durable political themes in American history. While most presidents did not invoke a divine mandate as unabashedly as did William McKinley, there were few who were unwilling to call on the deity, including the leaders on both sides of the Civil War. At his inauguration as President of the Confederate States of America in February 1862, Jefferson Davis called upon "the favor of Divine Providence" to project and perpetuate the Confederacy, and concluded his speech with a prayerful hope "reverently fixed on Him whose favor is ever vouchsafed to the cause which is just." Even when the "cause" was all but lost, his resolve did not waver. Three years later, with Richmond captured by Union forces and the end of the war only days away, Davis, stubbornly refusing to admit defeat, urged his fellow Southerners to rely "on the never-failing mercies and protecting care of our God" and to "meet the foe with fresh defiance, with unconquered and unconquerable hearts."[47]

In fairness to Davis, it should be noted that calling for God's support in time of war was as old as war. "I saw heaven standing open and there before me was a white horse, whose rider is called Faithful and True," John wrote in Revelation 19:11. "With justice he judges and makes war." From time immemorial, soldiers have marched off to fight what Saint Augustine called a "righteous war,"[48] calling attention to a contradiction that was more than obvious to Abraham Lincoln. "Both [sides] read the same Bible and pray to the same God, and each invokes His aid against the other," he said at his second inaugural in March 1865. But Lincoln also thought it was presumptuous to expect divine favor just because he believed his cause was worthy; and, in fact, he recognized in the Civil War a greater paradox than that of opponents asking for the support of the same God. "It may seem strange that any men should dare to ask a just God's assistance in wringing their bread from the sweat of other men's faces," he went on, "but let us judge not, that we be not judged." Thus did Davis and Lincoln exemplify the extreme uses of God in war. While the one, incorrigible to the end, prayed for a divine miracle to save a society that fed on human bondage, the other, calling attention to the fundamental contradiction in that position, charitably refused to agree that any person can know what God intends.

The period of the Spanish-American War may have been the high-water mark of Christian imperialism, but William McKinley was not the last American president to raise the banner of Manifest Destiny. Just as Andrew Jackson believed he was fulfilling God's mandate in defining the national character, Woodrow Wilson saw himself doing the same for the nation's international role. With his strict Calvinist background and acclaimed as the leader of the world's leading nation, he could almost be forgiven for his self-indulgence. Certainly no president was more committed to the idea that the United States had a duty—or, perhaps more to the point, *right*—to lead the world out of darkness than Wilson, the most messianic of all American chief executives. And nowhere was this commitment more evident than when he chose as Secretary of State William Jennings Bryan, the Bible-thumping populist from Nebraska, who saw America as "the supreme moral factor in the world's progress." Similarly, when Calvin Coolidge justified American intervention in Nicaragua in 1927 by claiming that the United States had a "moral obligation" to enforce the Washington Treaty of 1923—to which the Managua government was not a party—"in order to encourage the Central American States in their efforts to prevent revolution and disorder," his view was less than Wilson's only in scale.[49]

And changing the name of the idea did not change its intent. Lyndon Johnson's campaign to "Vietnamize" the Vietnam War by calling for a greater use of South Vietnamese troops appeared to be a scaling back of the American presence, but the objective was unchanged. The effort may have been less obtrusive in its self-righteousness than McKinley's and Theodore Roosevelt's determination to "Americanize" the Filipinos sixty-five years earlier, but it was based on the common belief that Americans know what is best for the rest of the world—especially the nonwhite, non-Christian part of it—because God had bestowed a special responsibility on them. From the moment the United States emerged as a leading world power in the late nineteenth century, this belief has been a fundamental principle of American foreign policy. "I have always believed that this anointed land was set apart in an uncommon way," Ronald Reagan said in 1982, "that a divine plan placed this great continent here between the oceans to be found by people from every corner of the earth who had a special love of faith and freedom."[50] The fact that the public adored Reagan for this kind of claptrap suggests that the idea that God had chosen Americans to lead the world out of darkness was as popular as ever.

In claiming a divine mandate, Americans did not consign responsibility to some vague universal *élan vital* like "Providence" or "Nature," or, for that matter, even something so general as a biblical God. The Christian imperialist was nothing if not specific. From the first colonial settlement to the late twentieth century, Christian America meant *Protestant* America. Of course, by the nineteenth century the proliferation of sects, not to mention constitutional proscriptions of established churches, had made it impossible for one denomination to prevail. But Protestantism itself remained the dominant religious force in America. In the 1850s, the geography books, spellers, and readers used by the majority of American schoolchildren almost always designated the United States as a Protestant nation; and, as Timothy L. Smith observed, "leading citizens assumed that Americanism and Protestantism were synonyms and that education and Protestantism were allies."[51]

Ultimately, Protestant fanaticism became the taproot of the nativistic upsurge that produced secret patriotic organizations like the Order of the Star-Spangled Banner and its political offspring, the American Party, which added a new shibboleth—though not a new character—to the American political vocabulary: the Know-Nothing. In fact, many Roman Catholics, Jews, and other non-Protestants had immigrated to the United States in the two decades before the Civil War, and by 1860 there were more Catholics in the nation than any single Protestant denomination. But that made little difference to traditional America; as Martin E. Marty pointed out, "by observation and instinct Americans had come to call their territory Protestant."[52]

After the Civil War this assumption took on a missionary fervor. From his platform as general secretary of the Evangelical Alliance, Strong expressed his "enormous confidence in America's destiny under Protestant leadership."[53] Echoing the virtually unanimous refusal of Protestant spokesmen to acknowledge that most Filipinos—members of a Roman Catholic Church that had been established three centuries earlier—were already Christians, McKinley told an audience of visiting Methodists that only after "I went down on my knees and prayed [to] Almighty God for light and guidance more than one night" did it "come to me this way" that the impropriety of a democratic nation possessing colonies was outweighed by the need to "civilize and Christianize" people, who were, after all, "our fellow-men for whom Christ also died."[54] If the United States acquiesced in their claim to independence, he added almost as an afterthought, the Filipinos, who "were unfit for self-government," would be easily exploited by foreign powers like France and Germany.[55] Later, on a speaking tour through the Midwest during the congressional campaign of 1898, McKinley, defending his decision to occupy the Philippines, was reassured by the ovations he received whenever he used code words and phrases like "destiny," "duty," "humanity," and "the hand of the almighty God."[56]

Meanwhile, keeping an eye on the home front was the American Protective Association, a conservative Protestant group opposed to the heavy influx of Catholic, Jewish, and Eastern Orthodox immigrants in the three decades before the World War.[57] The Protestant claim to divine sanction subsided after the war, but it did not die out entirely, and its popularity among fundamentalists remained strong. By the 1980s, evangelical Protestants, led mostly by an ever-changing number of television preachers, fostered a resurgence of the belief that only the United States, directed by a Christian God, could save the world from the destruction guaranteed by self-inflicted moral degradation.

Whatever it was about clergymen like Josiah Strong and politicians like Albert J. Beveridge, who could so easily blend Christian piety with the racist ideals of Anglo-Saxon supremacy, it was part of the Protestant ethos that nineteenth-century students of American religious history had grown up with. Writing in 1844, Presbyterian Robert Baird, whom Marty called "the first major American church historian," declared that the "Germanic" and "Teutonic" peoples have been charged with the "theoretical and practical mission of Protestantism for the world." This theme may have been what impressed visiting German scholar Philip Schaff, who, returning home in 1854 after a ten-year sojourn among his Reformed brethren in Pennsylvania, proclaimed that the American Protestant was "best fitted for universal dominion."[58]

Strong echoed the "Germanic" emphasis; and when he published the first edition of *Our Country* in 1885—with a chapter on "The Anglo-Saxon and the World's Future"—he had in fact borrowed a title that had been used for over forty years for articles published by the American Home Missionary Society. Perhaps most contumelious of all was Leonard Bacon, who audaciously claimed that God had deliberately delayed the exploration of the New World until after the Protestant Reformation had begun in order to reserve North America for Protestant discovery. "By a prodigy of divine providence," he wrote in 1898, "the secret of the ages had been kept from premature disclosure." As religion historian William R. Hutchison put it, "God had wondrously kept the New World hidden from human knowledge until the Protestant movement . . . could assure settlement under the auspices of true religion."[59]

In fact, the belief that God had saved North America for Protestant discovery and settlement could be traced back at least to the sixteenth century, when the first English explorers claimed a share of the New World. During the reign of Queen Elizabeth, Sir Humphrey Gilbert sailed across the North Atlantic with instructions to work for the conversion of the "poor infidels, it seeming probable that God hath reserved these Gentiles to be introduced into Christian civility by the English nation."[60] In a variation of this theme, Samuel Purchas, a contemporary of Gilbert's, argued that God had intended for Englishmen to possess the New World, otherwise he would not have led them to it. As recently as 1964, British religious writer Stephen Neill, in an assertion that was painfully close to the African belief that a people can only be defeated if the enemy's god is stronger than theirs, held that the ease with which Europeans overran the natives was evidence that it had been God's purpose for the white man to prevail. Cotton Mather and Jonathan Edwards were just two of the colonial religious leaders who believed that "God had hidden America until such time as the Reformation could guarantee that the religion planted on these shores would be pure and evangelical." Mather, in his *Magnalia Christi Americana*, put a reverse spin on this argument when he speculated that God had directed the Puritans *away* from the Hudson River area where the Indians were numerous because the "little feeble number of Christians" might have "been massacred by these bloody salvages . . . whereas the good hand of God now brought them to a country wonderfully prepared for their entertainment."[61]

Divine geographical design was a proposition that even found an advocate in the scientific world. In his "Lectures on Coal," published in the Smithsonian Institution *Annual Report*, 1857, geologist Joseph LeConte of Georgia, who had trained as a physician and later joined the faculty of the new University of California, held that God had created coal to facilitate the Anglo-American's industrial supremacy through the use of the steam engine, and that, as a corollary, America's abundant coal reserves were part of God's preparation for the "glorious destiny" of the United States. In 1851, Baird had speculated that Hernando de Soto's decision to sail from Cuba to the west of the Florida peninsula instead of east led him away from the Atlantic coast of the North American continent, thereby denying the region to Catholic Spain. "It is said that a very trifling circumstance decided him!" Baird theorized. "But all was ordered by the Being who knows how to make the most significant as well as the greatest occurrence subserve His glorious purpose."[62] To Baird, it was obvious that God was a Protestant.

As Yale University's Sydney E. Ahlstrom pointed out in his comprehensive history of religion in the United States, there was an "almost universal American conviction that the United States had a mission to extend its influence throughout the world. To mainstream Protestants a denial of manifest destiny bordered on treason." The typical American of the nineteenth century was convinced that "the kingdom of God would be realized in history, almost surely in American history."[63] It has always been a popular theme among Protestant evangelists that Armageddon would come in the lifetimes of people already born, and that God had singled out the United States to lead the world to salvation.[64] Of course, the prediction that the end of the world was imminent had been heard for centuries, but that meant little to a generation hearing it for the first time.

Dominion Over All *the Earth*

While being chosen by God was inherently unjust to those who were unchosen, there was an even more fundamentally racist consequence of the white American's romance with Manifest Destiny, namely, his belief that God had created the natural universe and all of the creatures in it for his exclusive use. As a Kentucky preacher told English traveler Ebenezer Davies in the 1840s, "the 'world' belongs to God's people." The preacher, of course, was only repeating an old theme—and one with political applications. In the eighteenth century, a Boston minister named John Lathrop condemned British restrictions on colonial trade because, he insisted, God had designed the American landscape for "extensive business," and Americans were "entitled to all the natural and improvable advantages of our situation." Another New Englander, James Knowles, a Congregational minister and Professor of Pastoral Duties at Newton Theological Institution, acknowledged that the early Puritans had no other choice when they advocated the extermination of all Indians because the savages had refused to obey "the great law of God," which "obliged them to become civilized, and to adopt those modes of life which would enable their territory to support the greatest possible number of inhabitants."[65] In December 1830, in a speech that would infuriate a modern conservationist, Andrew Jackson called for the removal of Indians by saying almost the same thing.

> What good man would prefer a country covered with forests and ranged by a few thousand savages to our extensive Republic, stud-

ded with cities, towns, and prosperous farms, embellished with all of the improvements which art can devise or industry execute, occupied by more than 12,000,000 happy people and filled with the blessings of liberty, civilization, and religion[?][66]

Since the Fifth Census reported a total population of 12,866,020, Jackson was apparently including the 2,328,642 black Americans—86 percent of whom were slaves—among his "happy people."

It should be obvious to everyone, future Democratic presidential candidate Lewis Cass wrote in the *North American Review* in the same year, "that the Creator intended the earth should be reclaimed from a state of nature and cultivated; that the human race should spread over it, procuring from it the means of comfortable subsistence, and of increase and improvement." That not only meant turning over the sod, hunting down mountain lions, dispossessing Indians, and extending the slave-labor system; but, eventually, digging for coal, drilling for oil, clear-cutting timberlands, and damming up rivers. "[M]an, when he is strong, conquers nature," declared William Lawrence, a Massachusetts Episcopal bishop. Anything that gets in the way will be brushed aside. "Dominion over the earth is the condition of man's residence upon the globe," William Pope Harrison, an editor for the Methodist Church, South, reflected in 1893, "and wherever any tribe or race shall cease to exercise that dominion in the measure possible to the opportunities of the age, that tribe or race will fade away and be no longer a cumberer of the ground."[67] Thus were two hallowed American precepts—Manifest Destiny and agricultural fundamentalism—joined. The divine right to exploit nature's resources was nicely complemented by the universal belief that tilling the soil was closer to God than any other vocation.

In fact, the belief that God had invested in man the ultimate use of the landscape had been widespread in the Christian world long before western farmers looked for an excuse to chase Indians off the prairie. A seminal idea of the European Renaissance was that scientific inquiry would be a critical tool in overcoming natural barriers. "Only let Mankind regain their rights over Nature, assigned to them by the gift of God," Francis Bacon wrote in *Novum Organum* (1620), "and obtain that power, whose exercise will be governed by right reason and true religion," a sentiment not dissimilar to René Descartes's "practical philosophy," which, as set forth in *Discours de la Méthode* (1637), defined humans as "the lords and possessors of Nature." In his commentary on *Hakluytus Posthumus, or Purchas His Pilgrimes* (1625), the Reverend Samuel Purchas made clear his conviction that God had "enriched the Savage Countries, that those riches might be attractive for Christian suters, which there may sowe spirituals and reape temporals." However, unlike Professor Knowles two centuries later, Purchas absolved the Indians for "not working their land according to God's revealed will" because they could not have known better. At the same time, though, "the English, knowing God's will, have an obligation to work that land; for it is almost bare of inhabitants and it is rich in all those things which make for 'merchandise.' " Twelve years later English Puritan Richard Sibbes, convinced that "worldly things are good in themselves, and given to sweeten our passage to Heaven," declared that "this world and the things thereof" were made by God "for the benefit of his creature."[68] Before the century was over, Cotton Mather made the same claim for his own Puritans:

> The *New-Englanders* are a People of God settled in those, which were once the *Devil's* Territories; and it may easily be supposed that the Devil was exceedingly disturbed, when he perceived such a People here accomplishing the Promise of old made unto our Blessed Jesus, *That He should have the Utmost parts of the Earth for his Possession*.[69]

Needless to say, these declarations of divine indulgence also looked very much like after-the-fact rationalizations of the greed of the "Christian suters."

Of course, there was no shortage of biblical support for all of this. People like Cass and Harrison could cite Genesis 1:26, where God gave man the right to "rule over the fish of the sea and the birds of the air, over the livestock, over all the earth, and over all the creatures that move along the ground," a mandate repeated almost verbatim in verse 28. By the time of King David, God had ranked man only "a little lower than the angels, and . . . crowned him with glory and honour." Having given him dominion over all of nature, God had everything placed under his feet: "[A]ll flocks and herds, and the beasts of the field, the birds of the air, and the fish of the sea, all that swim the paths of the seas."[70]

Nor was the situation changed much in the New Testament. While many Mosaic principles and Old Testament prophecies were revised by Christ, the order that man "should replenish the earth, and subdue it" was not one of them. In the Sermon on the Mount, Christ told his disciples not to worry about things like food, drink, and clothing because God would provide as he had for the birds, who were, after all, far less important than humans: "Look at the birds of the air; they do not sow or reap or store away in barns, and yet your heavenly Father feeds them. Are you not much more valuable than they?" Later, addressing the multitudes, he repeated the sentiment: "Don't be afraid; you are worth more than many sparrows."[71] In a lesson on the sins of boasting, cursing, and speaking evil, James, the brother of Jesus and one of the leaders of the church in Jerusalem, urged Christians to tame their tongues just as the many "animals, birds, reptiles and creatures of the sea are being tamed and have been tamed by man."[72]

It was the Israelites of Yahweh, more than any other ancient peoples of the eastern Mediterranean, who elevated humans above the rest of the living world. In a comparison of Israelite and Mesopotamian law, Jacob J. Finkelstein noted that the former placed humans over nature while the latter—like Africans, Asians, American Indians, and most of the people of the non-monotheistic world—viewed human society as just one constituent of nature and subject to all of its forces.[73]

It should come as no surprise, then, that Americans perceived a dichotomous world, with God, man, and the angels on one side and everything else on the other. To the Puritan, nature was the revelation of God's will. "[A]t the moment of creation Adam did not possess 'experimental knowledge,' " Edward Reynolds wrote in 1658, "but he did have already in his mind . . . so much of *Natural Knowledge* as should dispose him for the Admiring of God's Glory, and for the Governing of other Creatures over which hee had received Dominion."

> Looke upon bruit beasts, we see no actions but may arise from the temper of the matter; according to which their fancies and appetite are fashioned. . . . It is true indeed, in a man there are fancy and appetite, and these arise from the temper of the body; therefore as the body hath a different temper so there are severall appetites, dispositions & affections . . . but come to the higher part of the soule, the actions of the will and the understanding of man, and they are of an higher nature; the acts which they doe have no dependence upon the body at all.[74]

In the eighteenth century, Jonathan Edwards had envisioned a three-tiered universe consisting of God and the heavenly hosts; humans, who were in the divine image; and the natural world, which displayed none of the "qualities of mind which distinguish angels, saints, and men." In fact, when it came to determining positions in the hierarchy of living creatures, Christian mythology portrayed man not as the highest form of animal life but as the lowest form of heavenly life. "The beasts are so made that they commonly go with their heads down to the earth seeking their food with their mouths in the dust or down to the ground," Edwards exclaimed. "But how very different is man from them, with his head towards heaven, which shews that the highest good of the beasts is earthly, but that man's proper happiness is heavenly." It is certainly beautiful, he added later, "that in the various ranks of beings those that are nearest to the first being should most evidently and variously partake of his influence."[75] Accordingly, man, since he had been molded in God's image and was the only creature with an immortal soul, had a divine right to exploit the natural landscape for his own profit and for the glory of God.

The biblical mandate even worked its way into the antislavery argument when, in 1836, Quaker abolitionist Sarah Grimké, who fifteen years earlier had moved out of her family's Charleston home because she could no longer tolerate the slave system, published a letter to the "Clergy of the Southern States" in which she insisted that the eighth Psalm gave man dominion only over lower animals, not over his fellow man. "Man may shed the blood of the inferior animals, he may use them as *mere means*—he may convert them into food to sustain existence," but the African, like the European, was created in God's image.[76] In the same year, Sarah's younger sister, Angelina, published her own antislavery treatise, *Appeal to the Christian Women of the South*, in which she invoked the same Mosaic principle:

> It has been justly remarked that "*God never made a slave*," he made man upright; his back was *not* made to carry burdens, nor his neck to wear a yoke, and the *man* must be crushed within him, before *his* back can be *fitted* to the burden of perpetual slavery; and that his back is *not* fitted to it, is manifest by the insurrections that so often disturb the peace and security of slaveholding countries. Who ever heard of a rebellion of the beasts of the field; and why not? simply because *they* were all placed *under the feet of man*, into whose hand they were delivered; it was originally designed that they should serve him, therefore their necks have been formed for the yoke, and their backs for the burden; but *not so with man*, intellectual, immortal, man![77]

While rejecting the argument that man was vested with dominion over other men, Angelina agreed that God had given man dominion over "*all things*."[78] Unfortunately, it was the widely held latter principle that made Christianity a partner in the enslavement of millions of Africans and their descendants. Like all abolitionists, the sisters defended the slave's right to be free; but like all Christians, they also inadvertently exalted a principle that helped whites justify bondage for blacks. When God gave man dominion over all creatures, he made it easier for defenders of slavery to perceive the heathen African as something less than human.

Nor did civil war and emancipation change much. The institution of slavery may have been abolished, but the idea that black people were innately inferior survived and even flourished. As the traditional belief in biblical causes of racial differences began to decline, an emerging belief in "scientific" explanations led to, among other things, Social Darwinism, where "weaker" peoples were consigned to a subservient status. "Competition is a law of nature," William Graham Sumner wrote. "Nature is entirely neutral; she submits to him who most energetically and resolutely assails her. She grants rewards to the fittest, therefore, without regard to other considerations of any kind."[79] Faith in an unforgiving nature was as dogmatic for people like Sumner as faith in the Bible was for others.

Actually, the belief that the man who energetically and resolutely assails nature will prosper is, in its consequences for the natural landscape, painfully similar to the belief that God gave man dominion over all the earth. The popularity in the nineteenth century of pre- and post-millennial sects—which held that Christ will return one day, believers will ascend to heaven in the "rapture," and the world will end—easily led to a diminished regard for the physical environment. Not only is human existence on earth temporary, millennialists believed, but the earth itself is temporary. Accordingly, the impulse is to exploit the landscape while it is still here. If God can be invoked as the authority for depleting natural resources, how much respect for those resources can one expect from someone who believes that Judgment Day might occur at any moment? If the end of the world is imminent, one can afford to be extravagant.[80]

All of this is very different in most of the polytheistic world, where man is considered to be merely one of many beings who survived and, indeed, prospered not because he subdued the forces of his natural environment, but because he harmonized with them. To the Chinese, for example, a prosperous and healthy man lived in accordance with the principle of *feng shui* (風水)—seeking harmony with nature. While Christianity bestowed upon man dominion over the natural landscape, Buddhism taught that all of the creatures of the earth, including humans, were on paths of enlightenment and that, indeed, any living being could become a Buddha—one who embodied divine wisdom and virtue. "A heron flew over bamboo wood," Swiss novelist Hermann Hesse wrote of his spiritual explorer, "and Siddartha took the heron into his soul, flew over forest and mountain, became a heron, ate fishes, suffered heron hunger, used heron language, died a heron's death." Shintoism, the state religion of Japan, emphasized the worship of nature and, like Buddhism, perceived man as only one creature among many in a vast natural landscape. In the teachings of Lao zi, according to historian Benjamin Schwartz, the "processes of nature are not guided by teleological consciousness and . . . the *tao* [道] is not consciously providential. . . . To the extent that human beings as creatures 'abide' in the *tao*, they are part of that world of nature which [Lao zi] affirms."[81] To the Hindu, whose veneration of living things was the foundation of his faith, the universe was an eternal closed system in which nothing was created or lost, only rearranged.

Probably no one respected the physical environment more than the Gagudjus, an aboriginal people who have lived in the Kakadu region of northern Australia for forty thousand years—by far, the longest unbroken culture in existence. Believing that all living things (including humans) were manifestations of a single "life force," the Gagudjus have always considered it their sacred duty, since the land and its creatures provided them with everything they needed, to protect the natural environment.[82] From Buddhist to Gagudju, as diverse as these societies were they shared the belief that man is one with nature and must care for it or perish.

Similarly, American Indians from every era and every part of the continent spoke reverently of the relationship between nature and a divine being. "Holy Mother Earth," a Winnebago wise saying proclaimed, "the trees and all nature, are witnesses of your thoughts and deeds." Arguing in 1855 against a federal reservation plan in the Northwest, Young Chief of the Cayuses maintained that the Great Spirit created the earth and told it "to take care of the Indians, to feed them aright," and that men should care for the ground and "do each other no harm," a sentiment virtually identical to one expressed forty-five years later by a member of the Wabanaki Nation in the Kennebec River area of New England. "The Great Spirit is our father, but the Earth is our mother," Bedagi, or Big Thunder, proclaimed in describing the relationship between death and nature. "She nourishes us; that which we put in the ground she returns to us, and healing plants she gives to us likewise." A Sioux medicine man named Tatanka-ohitika talked of honoring the "works in nature" of Wakan tanka, the higher being who was the maker of all things. "Kinship with all creatures of the earth, sky and water was a real and active principle," declared Chief Luther Standing Bear of the Lakota tribe. "For the animal and bird world there existed a brotherly feeling that kept the Lakota safe among them and so close did some of the Lakotas come to their feathered and furred friends that in true brotherhood they spoke a common tongue."[83] Criticizing the white man's attempts to convert Indians, eighty-seven-year-old Tatangi Mani, a Stoney Indian from Alberta, Canada, told a London audience in 1958 that Christian missionaries condemned his people as idol worshippers because "they didn't understand our prayers."

> You didn't try to understand. When we sang our praises to the sun or moon, you said we were worshipping idols. Without understanding, you condemned us as lost souls because our form of worship was different from yours.
>
> We saw the Great Spirit's work in almost everything: sun, moon, trees, wind, and mountains. Sometimes we approached him through these things. Was that so bad? I think we have a true belief in the supreme being, a stronger faith than that of most whites who

> have called us pagans. . . . Indians living close to nature and nature's ruler are not living in darkness.[84]

How different all of this was from the Puritan's conception of nature, in which "All the creatures . . . have an end; the end of the Sunne, Moone and Starres is, to serve the earth; and the end of the Earth is, to bring forth Plants, and the end of Plants is, to feed the beasts."[85] And, of course, the end of the beasts was to serve man, who, in turn, served God.

While the Indian venerated the natural world, he did not miss a chance to denounce the white man's abuse of it. An elderly Wintu woman in California noted that Indians shake nuts out of trees, while whites cut the trees down; Indians use downed wood for homes and fires, but whites pull down trees for these purposes; Indians use rocks as they are, while whites blast them into smaller pieces. "The Indians never hurt anything, but the White people destroy all," she lamented. "Everywhere the White man has touched [the earth], it is sore." More recently, five leaders of the Hopi tribe petitioned President Richard M. Nixon to overrule a proposal for strip mining on land leased from the Navajo and Hopi peoples. "The white man, through his insensitivity to the way of Nature," they complained, "has desecrated the face of Mother Earth." The Christian's religion told him to exploit the land; the Indian's told him to respect and replenish it. Not understanding the English conception of property rights, the Indian resisted land sales and cessions or acquiesced in them without fully realizing the consequences. The idea of individual ownership of land appeared in New England as early as 1623, when Governor William Bradford of Plymouth, after a plan for communal property ownership had failed, divided the land among individual households. In the years since, Max Lerner wrote, property ownership became an essential constituent of the American drive for freedom, individuality, and self-reliance. The Anglo-American intoxication with property ownership was so compelling that even Thomas Jefferson, according to Henry Adams, saw nothing "improper or immoral" about ordering "Indian agents to tempt the tribal chiefs into debt in order to oblige them to sell the tribal lands which did not belong to them, but to their tribes."[86]

In fact, the idea of private ownership of land was often incomprehensible to the Indian. A person might grow crops on the land and claim the fruits of his labor, but he could not claim ownership of the land itself because, like the sky and the sea, it was created by God and thus belonged to everyone. Offered trinkets in exchange for territory, the Nez Percé leaders of the Pacific Northwest refused because they did not believe they could sell something they were part of but did not own. "The plains are large and wide," Crowfoot, chief of the Blackfeet of southern Alberta said a few days before joining other chiefs to sign a land-cession treaty. "We are the children of the plains, it is our home, and the buffalo has been our food always."[87] At the signing ceremony Crowfoot pleaded with government officials that they would not cheat his people.

> Great Father! Take pity on me with regard to my country, with regard to the mountains, the hills and valleys; with regard to the prairies, the forests and the waters; with regard to all animals that inhabit them, and do not take them from myself and my children for ever.[88]

"Strangely enough [white men] have a mind to till the soil and the love of possession is a disease with them," Sitting Bull told the Powder River Council in 1877. "They claim this mother of ours, the earth, for their own and fence their neighbors away; they deface her with their buildings and their refuse."[89]

To no one was the natural landscape more important than the African, whose reverence for the earth was a major element of his religion, and one that he carried into slavery and Christianity.

Ol' trouble it come like a gloomy cloud
I know de udder worl' is not like dis
Gadder thick an' thunder loud.

Thund'ring and lightning and it looks like rain,
Hol' the win', don't let it blow.

My Lord calls me, He calls me by the thunder; . . .
My Lord calls me, He calls me by the lightning,
The trumpet sounds within-a my soul.

Wind blows hard, wind blows cold,
What you goin' to do when your lamp burns down?
Lord have mercy on my soul.

Mountains—dominant features of the landscape, conveying a sense of power that slaves could only dream about—held a special fascination.

Way up on de mountain, Lord!
Mountain top, Lord!
I heard God talkin', Lord!

I 'ntend to shout an' never stop, . . .
Until I reach the mountain top,

Lord, I'm climbin' high mountains.
Tryin' to get home.

And rocks or stones, as powerful obstacles to be cast aside or as part of the Christian perception of Christ (or Peter) as The Rock, provided the slave with another familiar metaphor.

Daniel saw de stone, Rollin', rollin'
Daniel saw de stone.

I got a home in-a dat Rock, Don't you see?
Between de earth an' de sky,
Thought I heard my Savior cry,
You got a home in dat rock, Don't you see.[90]

Of course, the fauna, those very creatures that "creepeth upon the earth" and "passeth through the paths of the sea"—creatures that Christians believed God gave man dominion over—were everywhere in the African's universe.

Oh, I thought I heard them say,
There were lions on the way.[91]

Deeply embedded in the consciousness of the New World slave, the African's affinity with the animals around him was, ironically, first brought to the attention of the American public by a white journalist named Joel Chandler Harris. Traveling through the sharecropping back country of his native Georgia, Harris collected legends, folk tales, and sayings that ultimately led to the publication of the "Uncle Remus" tales. Using familial appellations like Br'er Fox, Br'er Bear, Sis Nanny Goat, and Br'er Rabbit—the latter a direct counterpart of the African Shulo the Hare—Harris demonstrated the blacks' belief that even among animals who were natural enemies there was a common brotherhood, that all living creatures were integral parts of a single universe.[92] To the African and his New World descendants, animals were metaphors for almost every human condition:

I went down to de Fair.
Dem varmints all wus dere.
Dat young Baboon
Wunk at Miss Coon;
Dat curled de Elephan's hair.

De Camel den walk 'bout,
An' tromped on de Elephan's snout.
De Elephan' sneeze
An' fall on his knees;
Dat please all dem monkeys.[93]

The equality of "lower" animals with humans was further suggested in the fact that conversations often took place between the two:

Snail! Snail! Come out'n yō' shell
Or I'll beat on yō back till you rings lak a bell.

"I do ve'y well," sayed the snail in de shell.
"I'll jes take my chances in here whar I dwell."[94]

"One day I heard a turkey hen say, 'We are poor, we are poor,' " seventy-year-old Will Dill, of Spartanburg, South Carolina, told a Federal Writers' Project Interviewer. "The old turkey gobbler said, 'Well, who in the hell can help it.' Yes sir, they talk just like we do, but 'tain't everybody can understand 'em."[95] Further exemplifying the equality of all living creatures was the fact that animals occasionally got the best of their encounters with humans:

I went up on de mountain,
To git a bag of co'n.
Dat coon, he sicked 'is dog on me,
Dat possum blowed 'is ho'n.

Dat gobbler up an' laugh at me.
Dat pattridge giggled out.
Dat peacock squall to bust 'is sides,
To see me runnin' 'bout.[96]

Though the relationship between the animals and humans was sometimes antagonistic, the fundamental condition underlying that relationship was the African's harmony with nature and his perception of animals as creatures with whom he shared the environment, not as obstacles to be overcome. It was a perception that was diametrical to the Christian's view of the physical universe.

The idea that man was not part of the natural world was also a fundamental element in some Christians' hostility toward scientific explanations of nature. One of the reasons why conservative Protestants vigorously rejected the Darwinian principle of natural selection was that it held that man had evolved from lower forms of life, making him only the most recent and highly developed link in the natural order of beings, not someone divinely set apart from it. To be sure, the explosion in scientific knowledge that began around the middle of the nineteenth century must have been so overwhelming that the traditional Christian simply found it easier to deny all of it. Throughout this period, most Protestant clerics continued to proclaim that the earth was less than ten thousand years old and that it would not have been physically possible for human evolution to occur over such a brief period—although they apparently had no trouble with the notion that God had turned one of Noah's grandsons black in an instant. In 1836, Moses Stuart of Andover Theological Seminary, who has been called "the leading American biblical scholar of the era," challenged the entire science of geology, insisting, in a debate with Edward Hitchcock, Professor of Chemistry and Natural Science at Amherst College, that the earth was less than six thousand years old and scoffing at the idea that each of the "days" in Genesis represented thousands or millions of years.[97]

But the march of reason was relentless. As the study of plant and animal fossils became a major scientific discipline in the twentieth century, conservative Christians continued to cling to the belief that the age of the earth was measured in thousands of years. Most of them understood—and, perhaps, feared—that if man was merely a creature *of* the earth, they could claim no divine favor, an idea that was contrary to everything they believed about the origin and nature of the human species. When compared with the life forms that spanned the 600 million years of the Paleozoic, Mesozoic, and Cenozoic eras, hominids—here for perhaps a few million years—would appear to be little more than experiments of nature, destined to survive for a far shorter time than dinosaurs, sharks, or even the lowly cockroach. That is not a proposition that modern Christian fundamentalists have found easy to deal with.[98]

The Human as Creature

It is possible to discern any number of racist incentives lurking within the Christian's dichotomous universe. For example, if man claimed a divine right to exploit the natural landscape, he could also claim a right to define its parts and dimensions. If Africans and Indians were perceived as subhuman, what place did they occupy in that landscape? In early Virginia, English settlers considered slaves to be so physically and culturally inferior that "before the end of the seventeenth century many of the white colonists came to regard them as not of the human kind." The attitude easily found its way to New England, where, in 1731, Puritan minister Dean Berkeley of Rhode Island exhorted his parishioners to "consider Blacks as creatures of another species, who [had] no right to be admitted to the sacraments."[99] The Puritans envisioned a Christian commonwealth that would "shine like a beacon." But to accomplish this, "[l]and, beast, and man must be brought under control," historian Gary B. Nash wrote. "To do less was to allow chaos to continue when God's will was that Christian order be imposed." Bringing man "under control," however, meant subjugating Africans and Indians, which could only be justified by dehumanizing them. Herein lay the racist catalyst of the Christian's claim to dominion over all creatures. Once the heathens were defined as something less than complete human beings, it was much easier to slide them over to the other side of his dichotomous universe, where they could be treated like beasts of the field or seen as obstacles to be overcome. For many New England Puritans the environment was not a world of nature where humans interacted with all of its forces—as Africans, Asians, and American Indians perceived it—but a realm of God where moral imperatives tested the believer's faith. "Wherever the Indian opposed the Puritan, there Satan opposed God," Roy Harvey Pearce wrote in 1953; "Satan had possessed the Indian until he had become virtually a beast."[100]

In fact, it is possible to trace the reduction of some humans to the level of beasts as far back as Aristotle, whose doctrine of "natural slaves" had been included in the Spanish justification of slavery. Debating the issue in 1550–51 with Bartolomé de Las Casas, the jurist Juan Ginés de Sepúlveda insisted that "barbarous" persons who refused to submit to the European's "overlordship" may be "warred against as justly as one would hunt down wild beasts."[101] Thus defined as savage and vicious animals, Indians and Africans ultimately became, in the minds of many whites, among those creatures that "creepeth upon the earth." And if one began with that assumption and worked backward to its biblical antecedents, it was possible, as Pearce observed, to find the dark-skinned-man-as-beast in Satan himself: "Now the serpent was more crafty than any of the wild animals the Lord God had made."[102] With the juxtaposition of animals and evil the dichotomy was complete.

"But these [false prophets] blaspheme in matters they do not understand," Peter wrote to the Christians living in the northern provinces of Asia Minor. "They are like brute beasts, creatures of instinct, born only to be caught and destroyed, and like beasts they too will perish."[103] To both the English and the Dutch, Roger Williams lamented, Indians were nothing but "*Heathen* Dogges," who, like Peter's false prophets, should all be killed.[104] It is inherent in every monotheistic faith that there are only truth and error, good and evil. When God gave man dominion over the earth and its creatures, he put humans in opposition to nature. Since the dark-skinned heathen obviously did not belong on the side of truth and good, the Christian assigned him, along with the rest of nature, to error and evil.

It was not necessary, of course, to cast Africans and Indians in biblical terms to dehumanize them. Recounting the explorations of one Bartholomew Gosnold, who in 1602 had been the first European to set foot on Cape

Cod, Cotton Mather described how Gosnold had "found such comfortable entertainment from the *summer-fruits* of the earth, as well as from the *wild creatures* then ranging the woods, and from the *wilder people* now surprised into courtesie." Responding to an attempt in 1716 to change the Massachusetts law defining "Indian, Negro, and Mulato servants" as personal property, Judge Samuel Sewall complained in his diary that he was unable to prevent them from "being rated with Horses and Hogs." Nor was the law liberalized any time during the colonial period. "And thus they continued to be rated," George H. Moore wrote in *Notes on the History of Slavery in Massachusetts* (1866), "with horses, oxen, cows, goats, sheep, and swine, until after the commencement of the War of the Revolution." Gideon Johnston added his voice to those of other Anglican missionaries in South Carolina who reported to their superiors in London that the Cherokees were "Savages" who "seem to have nothing but the shape of Men to distinguish them from Wolves & Tygers." By the time of the Creek War in 1814, Andrew Jackson found it easy to refer to the Indians as savage "bloodhounds" and "dogs." By the time of the Civil War, American defenders of racial subjugation were quoting the writings of European travelers to Africa—such as British naturalist Richard F. Burton—who had described the "animal-like" behavior of the natives, including reports of women allegedly copulating with gorillas.[105] In such a climate it should have surprised no one when the state of California conducted a census at the end of 1867 and included among the numbers seven thousand "domestic and wild Indians."[106] Similarly, no one was surprised when Theodore Roosevelt, often hailed as the first conservationist president, apparently saw the Indian as just another part of the fauna, along with bears, bobcats, and bison. "I don't go so far as to think that the only good Indians are the dead Indians," he was quoted as saying just before the end of the nineteenth century, "but I believe nine out of ten are, and I shouldn't inquire too closely into the case of the tenth."[107]

Long before Theodore Roosevelt, of course, invoking God to denigrate Indians and slaves had become a popular rationale for anyone who stood to profit from it. In 1830 Governor George R. Gilmer of Georgia, perhaps taking a page from Jefferson's order to the Indian agents, freely admitted that the land-cession treaties negotiated with the Indians in his state were nothing more than expedients designed to secure for civilized people the God-given right to subdue the earth. One did not need to justify stealing land from a person who should not have had it in the first place, an idea that had its counterpart among slaveholders who believed that the slave, because of his innate inferiority, was not entitled to the kind of treatment that whites presumably accorded each other. Commenting on his impressions of the privileged classes of the South in the decade before the Civil

War, Frederick Law Olmsted noted that there was a "broad assertion that the negro is not of the nature of mankind, therefore cannot be a subject of inhumanity." It was not hard to subjugate a person if he had first been reduced to something less than human. For anyone who thought that this was inevitably a result of a black person's status as a slave, he needed only to observe its continuation after the institution of slavery ceased to exist. As one of a legion of northern writers and journalists who toured the South in the months after the Civil War, Sidney Andrews found this feeling endemic. "All the talk of men about the hotel indicates that it is held to be an evidence of smartness, rather than otherwise, to kill a freedman," he wrote from Orangeburg, South Carolina; "and I have not found a man here who seems to believe that it is a sin against Divine law."[108] Obviously, it was not bondage that had made the slave a victim of the white man's religion; it was racism.

Certainly one of the most outrageous expressions of the African as beast was Buckner Payne's booklet *The Negro: What Is His Ethnological Status?* (1867), which held that Africans had no souls because they were really nothing more than beasts that Noah had included among the primates and other animals carried on the Ark. The year after Payne's work appeared, Scottish traveler David Macrae constructed an imaginary conversation—which he suggested was a composite of many conversations he had heard—between a moderate Virginian and a radical white supremacist from Mobile, Alabama, in which the latter concluded that the black man "hangs on to a different part of creation altogether."[109] Although a few anonymous writers agreed with Payne,[110] Macrae concluded that only the most poorly educated and narrow-minded whites held such a view; and most of the Protestant clergy who thought the argument deserved attention at all scoffed at the idea. This moved Payne—still writing under the pseudonym of "Ariel"—to reply to his critics in an extended revision of the book and a new pamphlet.[111]

While the proposition that black people were soulless animals faded rapidly under the heat of vociferous fundamentalist opposition, it was resurrected early in the twentieth century, when conservative Christian publishing houses in St. Louis came out with two books by Charles Carroll—"*The Negro a Beast*" (1900) from the American Book and Bible House, and *The Tempter of Eve* (1902) from the Adamic Publishing Company. In the first work, a 382-page tome with ten illustrations, Carroll paid tribute to Payne and essentially repeated the soulless-Negro argument. In the second book, Carroll, discussing biblical chronology in great detail, theorized that the serpent that had persuaded Eve to eat the forbidden fruit in the Garden of Eden had, in fact, been a black man who had descended from an "ape-like man" who, in turn, had evolved from the "man-like ape" of the tertiary period.[112] After all, the serpent in Genesis 3:1–4 was more clever than any animal and could speak. Thus the image of Satan as serpent became the image of the black man as serpent, an idea that had been implied at least as early as 1841, when the Reverend Thornton Stringfellow theorized that "the ancestors of the negroes now in the United States were the *slaves of serpent*."[113] Carroll certainly spoke for only a small minority of the conservative Christian population, but two of his contemporaries—William H. Campbell, author of *Anthropology for the People: A Refutation of the Theory of the Adamic Race Origin of All Races, by a Caucasian* (1891), and Alexander Harvey Shannon, who wrote *Racial Integrity and Other Features of the Negro Population* (1907)—set forth similar arguments, although neither specifically declared Africans to be without souls.

It should be reiterated that the ideas of men like Payne and Carroll were popular only among the most fanatical religious racists and that the overwhelming majority of Christians considered the suggestion that black people had no souls as too ridiculous to be taken seriously. Among the few who did take it seriously were five Protestant preachers—one a former slave—whose books condemning Carroll, published by Christian publishing companies between 1901 and 1906, were primarily statements of their belief in the biblical unity of humankind.[114] One writer, W. S. Armistead, expressed amazement that a reputable publishing firm like the American Book and Bible House would stoop so low as to publish and endorse what he considered a blasphemous work. Another, H. P. Eastman, claimed the proof that Africans belonged to the family of man was that "Ham really had a negress for a wife." As willing, even anxious, as some Protestant fundamentalists were to acknowledge African inferiority, believing that the black person was a beast would force them out of their cozy and long-held assumption that all of the human race had descended from the sons of Noah. It was no surprise when, in 1902, the delegates to a Baptist convention in Texas called upon all ministers and members "to expose and denounce the insulting and outrageous book."[115]

While most Christians did not go to the extremes that Payne and Carroll did, their belief in a biblical universe in which God and man were set against everything else did make it a little easier for them to think of black people as something less than human. Undoubtedly, many slaveholders recognized the slave's innate humanity. After all, the master's children often grew up with the children of the house servants. Slave nannies usually cared for their owners' small children with the same love and affection that they cared for their own. Serious romantic relationships, especially between white men and slave women, were not rare. All of these situations must have created feelings that could not be easily dismissed.

But most whites were also well aware of the social mores of a slave society in which they could not treat the black person as completely human without at least tacitly admitting that he was completely equal. If all humans are equal in the eyes of God, should they not also be equal in each other's eyes? By consciously—or subconsciously—placing blacks on the other side of the natural universe, whites were able to obfuscate this fundamental contradiction.

This meant, of course, that masters were sometimes faced with a dilemma of conscience. There is considerable evidence that more than a few slaveholders agonized over their legal status as owners of human property and their recognition that the slave possessed the full range of human feelings. "It is difficult to handle simply as property, a creature possessing human passions and human feelings," Frederick Law Olmsted observed in his travels through the South, "while on the other hand, the absolute necessity of dealing with property as a thing greatly embarrasses a man in any attempt to treat it as a person."[116]

And conversion to Christianity, if anything, compounded the dilemma. "Allowing the slave the privilege of salvation implied a recognition of him as a Christian person," Arnold A. Sio wrote. "The definition of the slave as a physical object overlaps that of the slave as a social object, since only social objects can perform and have intentions." Nor did there seem to be any way to untangle the two roles. "The value of a slave as property resides in his being a person, but his value as a person rests in his status being defined as property."[117] Whatever the reason, the slaveholder's recognition of his slave's basic humanity did not change the central point that, in a Protestant world of masters and slaves, there did not need to be a conscious attempt to classify black people as subhuman. The fact that so many white Americans believed in a divinely ordained dichotomous universe simply made it easier to perceive nonwhites as being fundamentally inferior. It was inherent in the faith.

Part Three

CHURCHES

SEVEN THE PURE AND PROFANE: COLONIAL CHURCHES

She say, Celie, tell the truth, have you ever found God in church? I never did. I just found a bunch of folks hoping for him to show. Any God I ever felt I brought with me. And I think all the other folks did too. They come to church to share *God, not to find God.*

Here's the thing, say Shug. The thing I believe. God is inside you and inside everybody else. You come into the world with God. But only them that search for it inside find it. And sometimes it just manifest itself even if you not looking, or don't know what you looking for. Trouble do it for most folks, I think. Sorrow, lord.

ALICE WALKER
The Color Purple

The Institutional Church

It is difficult to exaggerate the importance of the church as a cultural form in the American past, especially in the pre-industrial era, when it served not merely as a place of worship but, in fact, as a nexus of an agrarian neighborhood's social and political activities.[1] Indeed, in early America, when the continent was populated by immigrants with compelling—and competing—religious interests, the church was a psychological breakwater against both the threatening forces of a hostile natural environment and the encroachments of other denominations. Nor did the establishment of a constitutional government publicly committed to the separation of church and state significantly diminish the sectarian influence. Alexis de Tocqueville, Harriet Martineau, and Francis Grund were just three of the many foreign visitors during the antebellum period who were impressed by the proliferation of churches in both urban east and rural west. After living and traveling in the United States for ten years, Grund, in *The Americans in Their Moral, Social, and Political Relations* (1837), described a nation dominated by churches. There was "no village in the United States without its church," the Austrian-born journalist observed, "no denomination of Christians in any city without its house or prayer, no congregation in any of the new settlements without the spiritual consolation of a pastor." The American "eagerness for religious instruction and the means of social worship are so great," Martineau wrote in *Society in America* (1837), "that funds and buildings are provided wherever society exists."[2]

English travelers, Max Berger noted, "pointed to the fact that America, though still largely a primitive country, had as many churches as the British Isles, that religious assemblages were being held at one place or another practically all the time [and that] . . . [C]hurch services were always crowded on Sunday."[3] One Briton, Archibald Prentice of Manchester, was impressed that New York City in 1848 had 215 places of worship while his hometown "with a comparable population supported only 114."[4] Within a community, the common faith held everything together and the church, one historian insisted, became one of "the most powerful cohesive factors in American civilization."[5]

This meant that whatever else a church was, it was a *socializing* institution, a communal arrangement where codes of conduct were clearly drawn, virtues like loving and sharing were exalted—though not always practiced—and, above all, the quality of *belonging* was reinforced. Whether large or small, the fellowship of a church often described itself as a family, a condition symbolized by the popular appellations, especially among traditional Protestants, of "brother" and "sister." "The Christian God is conceived after the analogy of the familial relationships because these relationships typify an interest that is personal, comprehensive, and undiscriminating," Ralph Barton Perry wrote in *Puritanism and Democracy* (1944): "It is in the family that each can be most certainly assured of the solicitude of others, no matter what may be his place in the world, and his level of talent or attainment."[6] With the members of a congregation seeing themselves as "brethren," the familial nomenclature extended throughout the Christian community.

To be sure, nowhere has the filial hierarchy been more carefully formalized than in the Roman Catholic Church, where a priest is a *father* to whom sinners confess their sins, *brothers* are teachers, and a nun is a *sister* or even a *mother* superior. And all, to use the slave's vernacular, are God's "chillun." It was also in the family where the line of authority was standardized and extended to the church. The hierarchy of bishops, priests, pastors, elders, and deacons was analogous to paternal, maternal, and avuncular relationships, where age and birthright defined one's position. Thus the church, like the family, constituted a community of shared feelings and mutual responsibilities, but also imposed structure and order for the common good.

Yet one should not assume that the presence of churches everywhere meant that everyone was present in church. Scottish traveler Peter Neilson observed in 1830 that, despite the ubiquity of places of worship, Americans did not appear to be very conscientious about worshiping. "Speaking generally we may say that all [of the people of Mississippi] profess to be Christians," Bishop William Henry Elder of Natchez wrote in 1858 to the Catholic church's missionary office, but many of them "do not belong to any particular Denomination, & even among those who do, a considerable number have never been baptized." In fact, it appears that the generation to which the founding fathers belonged was far less enthusiastic about organized worship than modern political and religious orators would like everyone to believe. "Presumably it was well before 1800, the earliest date for which a general estimate can be made," social historian Rowland Berthoff wrote, "that church membership fell below 10 percent of the adult population." Projecting backward from the more comprehensive data of the early nineteenth century, Franklin H. Littell of the Chicago Theological Seminary estimated that on the eve of independence only 5 percent of the American population claimed membership in established Protestant churches.[7]

Of course, the numbers varied widely from place to place and time to time, but even the most optimistic appraisal for a single-minded Christian community like Massachusetts in the seventeenth century was far lower than one might suppose. Just ten years after the great Puritan migration of the 1630s, according to Yale University's Jon Butler, official church rolls in New England—a region that was always perceived as dominated by an oppressive theocratic oligarchy—probably included no more than one-third of the population; and in 1776 perhaps 15 percent of all colonists were regular churchgoers, a number three times Littell's figure for the same year and over twice his estimate of 6.9 percent for 1800—but still surprisingly low. In fact, Littell wrote, church membership nationwide, despite the evangelizing influence of the Second Great Awakening (1825–40), did not reach 15 percent until 1850 and during the Civil War was still under 20 percent.[8]

Needless to say, historical opinion on the paucity of practicing Christians has never been unanimous. In her study of religion, politics, and society in colonial America, Patricia U. Bonomi challenged these figures with her own calculation that "no less than some 60 percent of the adult white population attended church regularly between 1700 and 1776."[9] Of course, such disagreements may be strictly academic. Membership and attendance figures did not necessarily equate with the numbers of believers, and the influence of clergymen often reached far beyond their pulpits. Then, as now, there were many people who, when challenged, professed their belief in a biblical God but who did not subscribe to any formal doctrine or denomination. But, even allowing for all of this, the conclusion that Americans never clung to their churches as tenaciously as patriotic mythology would have it is still inescapable.[10]

On the other hand, it would be misleading to go too far with this. Although the Protestant churches could never be characterized as a cohesive and monolithic entity, it is nonetheless true that Protestantism generally has been the dominant religious movement in America from the earliest colonial times. By the middle of the nineteenth century, as church historian Winthrop S. Hudson observed, Protestantism "had established undisputed sway over almost all aspects of national life." And the influence of the churches reached far beyond the "somewhat narrowly defined membership." The Puritan-inspired "blue laws" of colonial New England spread across the country and came to rest mainly in the so-called Bible Belt states of the South and Midwest, where legislatures and local authorities, intimidated by Protestant fundamentalists, set down codes of behavior that appeared to have no other purpose than to keep people from enjoying themselves. One should also not make too much of the fact, as one English visitor did, that a small community may not have had a church at all. "A stranger taking up his residence in any city in America must think the natives the most religious people on earth," Frances Trollope wrote while traveling through the United States during Andrew Jackson's first term; "but if chance lead him among the western villages, he will rarely find either churches or chapels, prayer or preacher; except, indeed, at that most terrific saturnalia, 'a camp meeting.' " While it is true that in the eighteenth and nineteenth centuries many Americans—probably most—were not actively affiliated with churches, they nevertheless were inclined to consider themselves "adherents" of one denomination or another. Even the man who did not think of himself specifically as a Baptist or Methodist still professed a belief in God and subscribed to the truths of the Good Book. Thus, throughout the nation, including the frontier areas where organized congregations were relatively scarce, the "patterns of belief and conduct" had been established by the Protestant churches.[11]

It is indicative of the importance of the church that its power, in some ways, was more compelling than that of the government. Within a denomination, there was a line of authority that might have been as well-defined and autocratic as the episcopal hierarchies of the Anglican, Roman Catholic, and Eastern Orthodox churches, or as decentralized and democratic as independent neighborhood congregations that hired and fired pastors for the most trivial of reasons.[12] And where there was a line of authority, however diffuse it might be, there was an uneven distribution of power—power that could be benevolent and just or arbitrary and capricious. Such power was especially far-reaching because if it was abused a victim had little recourse.

An authority based primarily on secular law was, at least in theory, less autocratic because an offended party could appeal through the courts or, in a democratic society, change the law by changing the lawmakers. In an establishmentarian society, however, the church and government were partners in defining and enforcing ecclesiastical policies. Sectarian and secular law were virtually interchangeable. In a monarchy the church and state were fused; since kings claimed to rule by divine right, they considered resistance to their authority as nothing less than defiance toward God, *ergo*, a political crime was also a sin. Similarly, many of the early colonial laws were either created by the clergy, as in New England, or shaped by the influence of church leaders. But in all these instances, the church's power could be, again at least in theory, diminished or even eliminated simply by overthrowing the existing political leadership.

While an independent church did not enjoy the benefits of association with the government as was the case in much of Europe and Latin America before the twentieth century, it also was not at great risk if that government was displaced. Whenever a church was perceived as an agent of government persecution, that risk was indeed great. Having assembled in 1640, the revolutionary Long Parliament impeached Archbishop of Canterbury William Laud, imprisoned King Charles, chased many Anglican clergymen from their parishes, prohibited the use of the common prayer book, and even persecuted Independents, Baptists, and some of the lesser sects. In November 1789, the French Assembly, in its zeal to bring down an Old Regime that had grown arrogant and profligate partly because of the influence of the seventeenth-century Cardinals Armand Jean du Plessis de Richelieu and Jules Mazarin, nationalized virtually all of the property of the Catholic church. The Mexican Constitution of 1917 not only confirmed the Reform laws of the 1850s, which had stripped the Catholic Church of its landed wealth, but even declared buildings of worship to be state property. In February 1918, the Soviet Supreme Council of National Economy severed relationships between the Russian Orthodox Church and the state and confiscated all church property, which subsequently could be used for religious purposes only by private groups upon application to the government. In the last three examples the state also abolished sectarian education and declared family matters such as licensing of marriages and recording of births to be exclusively civil affairs.

All of this was very different for the American churches, which, without the protection of the government, exercised their authority because their subscribers had come by choice, not by rule. It could be argued that an unencumbered church was more influential than a state sect since its authority was enlarged by the fact that one who wanted to believe more readily submitted than one who was told to believe. In a situation where the church did *not* enjoy the official support of political leaders, those who disputed an ecclesiastical position had few avenues of appeal because the church's authority rested solely on the universal acceptance of a supreme being whose infallibility was a given.

In a sense, the church was a military organization and the ministers were its field commanders. A denomination organized on an episcopal or presbyterian system had a chain of command that, at least in principle, demanded respect and obedience. Open challenges to church authority could result in the excommunication of individuals, the defrocking of clergymen, and even the expulsion of congregations. From the perspective of the leadership, it could be no other way. For example, until 1978, when Spencer Kimball, president of the Church of Jesus Christ of Latter-Day Saints, claimed he had received a "revelation" from God calling for a change in racial doctrine, black Mormons were not eligible for full membership. God had cursed dark-skinned people, church doctrine held, and only God could remove the curse. Accordingly, to question the authority of the church and its leaders was to question, at least by implication, the authority of God.

It is essential to a proper understanding of the Christian churches in America to recognize that the mantle of moral infallibility claimed *ex cathedra* by the Pope was something that all Christian clergy, by virtue of their positions, to some extent slipped under. An institution that was not upheld by either the laws of man or the laws of science was entirely dependent on the faith of its supporters. This meant that strict adherence to doctrines and unquestioning obedience to leaders were crucial. The enforcement of ecclesiastical rules may have been effective only among the faithful, but that was enough. While a person's body was out of the reach of the church, his soul was not. For believers, canon law was more compelling than secular law because the punishment for violating the latter was only in this lifetime but the punishment for violating the former was forever. Or so one was taught to believe.

Complicating the situation was the fact that the Protestant churches of America have always been an ever-changing mixture of diversity and uniformity. After 1800, the "hermeneutical awakening," a movement by congregations calling for independent interpretations of the Bible instead of unquestioning obedience to authority, produced a sharp increase in the number of denominations, thereby fragmenting even more what had never been a very unified arrangement to begin with. Calls for Protestant unification were fruitless because direct appeals to a single Bible produced an increase rather than a decrease in the number of sects. Since there were small Catholic and Jewish populations in the United States prior to the 1850s, only the Episcopal Church stood as an authoritarian body. A society that had begun with mostly Anglicans, Congregationalists, Quakers, Baptists, Presbyterians, and Dutch Reformed became heavily populated with Methodists, Disciples of Christ, Lutherans, and members of many independent churches. Yet, at the same time, there was an underlying unity that cut across most Protestant denominations. Europeans who traveled in the United States during the nineteenth century noted that American churches, despite "institutional differences," were remarkably similar and that this conformity could be traced back to the early churches of the colonial period. The apparent variations in both doctrinal and methodological matters did not alter the fact that the Protestant churches were, in many respects, more alike than they were different.[13] The critical question here is whether or not there was a common attitude toward race.

At the time of the drafting of the federal Constitution in 1787, virtually every Protestant church in the nation had adopted an official position against slavery, a stance that began to erode almost immediately.[14] Moreover, opposition to slavery did not necessarily mean support for racial equality. In fact, only the most radical emancipationists—of whom there were few—publicly advocated complete equality among all races. By this time slavery had become so institutionalized in the plantation states that the official positions announced by national church leaders had virtually no effect on slaveholders, who were far more interested in profits than piety. The shallowness of Protestant opposition to slavery could also be seen in the clergy's "hearty endorsement" of the American Colonization Society, a group organized in 1816 to encourage former slaves to emigrate to territories outside the United States. Supporters argued that the program would provide an incentive for masters to free their slaves because it would give the freedmen a place to go. But since it applied only to free blacks, colonization, like earlier protests against the slave trade, would actually have served to strengthen slavery by eliminating a potentially disruptive element, a consideration not lost on slaveholders. Notwithstanding the fact that free black men and women had been permanent residents of North America for two centuries and had as much right to the country as anyone else, colonization was, in the last analysis, not so much an attempt to get rid of slavery as it was an attempt to get rid of people who happened to have been slaves. As the population of the cotton-producing states moved westward, American Protestantism, not surprisingly, adapted to the realities of economic power. By the time of the Civil War, every major denomination that had condemned slavery by 1787 had a southern division that was a staunch champion of bondage.[15]

Even northern Protestant leaders who had, despite opposition from within their own hierarchies and congregations, maintained an unwavering opposition to slavery had to deal with the incriminating question of motivation. For example, how much of the Christian condemnation of bondage was based not on a sincere belief that the African was entitled to all of the rights and privileges of human existence but on a desire to exorcise a terrible evil from one's midst? No religious body was more equalitarian in spirit than the Society of Friends. Yet at the time of the reform movement within the organization in the 1750s, many Quakers disapproved of bondage because, in the words of Richard Bauman, slavery had become "a symbol of an avaricious attachment to the cumbers of the world, as well as an embodiment of the weak-spirited willingness to compromise with principle." Similarly, early Baptist emancipation sentiment was primarily concerned with "maintaining a godly distance from an ungodly world."[16] In short, it appeared that many "emancipationists" were not so much calling for the abolition of the institution of slavery as for the removal of its corrupting influence. In all fairness, it should be noted that there was nothing inherently wrong with this reaction as long as it was not accompanied by sanctimonious claims of moral superiority, which, of course, was not always the case.

The Chosen of the Chosen

In a pluralistic society like the United States, where religious proliferation and ethnic diversity have reached levels far beyond those found anywhere else in the world, it is difficult—if not impossible—to consign to a single religious group or doctrine a preponderant influence on anything. But if there is one theological impulse whose impact on American life has been more far-reaching than that of any others, it would almost certainly be Calvinism, especially as practiced by the Covenant Puritans of Massachusetts Bay and later embraced by Protestant Americans almost everywhere. From the founding of Massachusetts to the early national period, the Puritans—and their Congregational descendants—constituted the largest Calvinist sect in North America.

On the eve of the Revolution, according to Ralph Barton Perry, almost half of America's estimated 2.5 million people were "adherents of Calvinistic or closely allied sects," and over half of those were Congregationalists.[17] In time, the Puritan influence was omnipresent. As the fertile plains and valleys of the western territories beckoned, the New England farmer turned away from the rock-bound soil of Massachusetts, Maine, and Connecticut and followed the setting sun. The custodian of the Puritan tradition was nothing if not peripatetic. Familiar place names—Portland, Concord, Springfield, Lexington, Salem—reappeared everywhere. In time, Ohio, Illinois, Kansas, and Oregon were only a few of the places that could claim to be *new* New Englands.

But while the spirit moved, it also evolved. One of those inexact general terms that even the colonists defined in several ways, "Puritanism" could mean, depending on time and place, almost everything or anything. As the Puritan ideal began to drift away from its New England birthplace, "it became evangelistic and fundamentalist," Max Lerner wrote in *America as a Civilization*, "and the mentality of Calvinism gave way to the mentality of what Mencken joyously called the 'Bible Belt.' "[18] Ironically, as this mentality moved southward and westward, it began to diminish in its northeastern birthplace. By the early nineteenth century, the liberalism of Congregationalism and Unitarianism had flushed out most of the old habits, and the inclusiveness of secularization had replaced the exclusiveness of the church as the moving force of public life. Eventually, the Puritan tradition came to rest in Protestant bosoms everywhere, but particularly among the rural folk of the midwestern and southern regions of the United States. Political conservatism, blue laws, and other trappings of the traditional seventeenth-century conscience—all of which had long characterized the religious ethos of New England—permeated the social fabric of the nation. In their moral suasions the Puritan and the Victorian became as one. Be it Congregational, Reformed, Presbyterian, Baptist, Methodist, Disciples of Christ, or whatever, Puritanism was a *way of thinking* that reached far beyond the realm of faith and worship. Ultimately shaping the development of government, education, and the workplace, it became a cornerstone of American culture.

Yet it was this very pervasiveness of the Puritan tradition that also made it the religious ideal most difficult to associate with the emergence of a racist culture. Some reasons are obvious. Although heavily involved in the colonial and early national slave trade, New England was not a region that easily accommodated large numbers of transplanted Africans. Ships in Boston and Providence were outfitted as slavers, but they picked up and deposited their cargoes everywhere. As late as 1680 there were only about two hundred slaves in all of New England, with perhaps 60 percent of that number in Massachusetts. By 1700 the count had increased to approximately one thousand blacks in the region, a few free but mostly slaves; and fifteen years later Massachusetts claimed two thousand, a figure that looks substantial until seen as barely 2 percent of the colony's population. And it may even be a little high. In 1754, according to figures compiled by the "Assessors of the several towns and Districts within the Province," there were 4,489 slaves in Massachusetts. Subsequent tabulations recorded a high in 1764–65 of 5,779; followed by a gradual decline to 5,249 in 1776, 4,377 in 1784, and 4,371 in 1786.[19]

These numbers were for slaves only; and the decline was probably the result of increased emancipation. Reporting no slaves at all, the First Census (1790) counted 5,369 black people in Massachusetts, but this figure still looks unimposing when it is seen as just 1.4 percent of the state's population and less than 1 percent (.71 percent, to be exact) of the total black American population. Just under 32 percent of the blacks in the six New England states resided in Massachusetts; but Connecticut and Rhode Island, both with smaller white populations, actually had higher concentrations.[20]

Since the Puritan of the seventeenth and eighteenth centuries simply did not have very many opportunities—or reasons—for making personal decisions about race, church leaders did not bother to adopt a formal position concerning slaves or black people. "Except for military policy, no laws were passed applying only to Negroes until the 1680's," Robert C. Twombly and Robert H. Moore wrote. "Old and New England had fitted the black man into the social system without legally recognizing slavery as a slave caste." In most of colonial New England, Edmund S. Morgan noted in his study of Puritan families, any person who worked for someone else, "in whatever capacity," was called a *servant*, including slaves and Indians. The result was an obfuscation of class lines. "Within the broad guidelines of the Common Law and Puritan religious views," Twombley and Moore concluded, "Massachusetts had extended century-old rights of Englishmen to Negroes."[21]

This absence of involvement has been reflected in the writing of some of the most influential students of early New England history. For example, in almost seven hundred pages of *Puritanism and Democracy* (1944), Ralph Barton Perry barely mentioned slavery.[22] Similarly, in two of his most important books on Puritan thought, *Errand into the Wilderness* (1956) and *Nature's Nation* (1967), Perry Miller, the quintessential student of Puritanism in America—and certainly its most eloquent—made only the sketchiest references to Indians and, in his one comment on slavery, innocuously speculated that Willie Mays's baseball skills might have been a consequence of the fact that only the fittest Africans, the New World's only involuntary immigrants, were selected for bondage and survived the ordeal of the slave trade.[23]

Despite the dearth of Africans in New England and their conspicuous absence from some of the most important studies of the early Puritan world, they were part of that world almost from the beginning and were not entirely unnoticed. Because Africans arrived in the New World in a state of subservience, the Puritan saw them as "strange and exotic creatures," who were "uncivilized without much tradition behind them," in contrast to the Indians, who were "descendants of once proud tribes with a distinct cultural heritage." The first record of blacks in New England appeared in Governor John Winthrop's journal in 1638, just eight years after the founding of Massachusetts Bay.[24] Three years later, the ninety-first article of the famous Massachusetts "Code of Fundamentals," also known as the "Body of Liberties," acknowledged, under the heading of "Liberties of Forreiners and Strangers," that "there shall never be any bond-slaverie, villinage or captivitie amongst us; unles it be lawfull captives, taken in just warres, and such strangers as willingly selle themselves or are solde to us," a passage that implied bondage had existed there for some time.[25] It is not possible to know if the word "strangers," which was deleted from the 1660 and 1672 editions of the code, referred specifically to Africans; but its use in the 25th chapter of Leviticus (Authorized Version) to identify outsiders who were subject to forced servitude under Mosaic law, defenders of slavery later claimed, made Africans the most logical candidates for enslavement.

A few miles to the south, authorities in relatively equalitarian Rhode Island passed two seemingly contrary laws within months of each other. On May 19, 1652, the Commissioners of the General Court of Providence and Warwick, "being lawfully mett and sett," called for the conditional emancipation of a slave after serving ten years or reaching the age of twenty-four:

> Whereas, there is a common course practiced among Englishmen to buy negers, to that end they may have them for service or slaves for ever; for the preventing of such practices among us, let it be ordered, that no blacke mankind or white being forced by covenant bond, or otherwise, to serve any man or his assighnes longer than ten yeares, or until they come to bee twentiefour yeares of age, if they bee taken in under fourteen, from the time of their cominge within the liberties of this Collonie.

It was the first—and for a long time, only—such law anywhere in the colonies, but, despite the Commissioners' ostensibly good intentions, the law was never enforced, "even in the towns over which the authority of the Commissioners extended."[26] Closer to reality, the preamble to a Rhode Island statute acknowledged that it "is a common course practised amongst Englishmen to buy Negers, to that end they may have them for service or slaves forever," a statement that, like the 1641 Massachusetts statute, intimated that human bondage was already well established.[27]

Despite the paucity of the black population, the articulation of legal measures so early belied a perfunctory concern for the status of black people. And the common practice went far beyond the law. For example, a slave in Massachusetts may have had some theoretical rights prior to 1664, but they were almost universally ignored. "It is doubtful whether the General Court ever considered the Negro a member of the Company of Massachusetts Bay, even though he were a communicant," one writer noted. "To have done so would have been the equivalent to a writ of emancipation."[28] In a theocracy, membership in the church meant membership in everything, and the Puritan had a moral obligation to ensure the salvation of the souls in his charge. "All the Members in a Family are therein equal, in that they have Souls equally capable of being saved or lost," Samuel Willard wrote in *A Compleat Body of Divinity* (1736): "and the Soul of a Slave is, in its nature, of as much worth, as the Soul of his Master."[29] Yet, when it came to according rights and privileges to black or Indian members, the Puritan was just as duplicitous as any other Protestant. Despite the fact that church membership in most of New England was supposed to include political rights and full participation in church matters, that was rarely the case. "Although nearly every church made some provision for Negroes," Lorenzo Johnston Greene wrote, "they were generally set apart from white members." Before 1730, only a few white Puritans seemed interested in converting slaves to the faith, fewer slaves joined the church, and even fewer slaves showed much interest.[30] Considering the contradiction between the Puritan's professed commitment to saving souls and his repulsion toward black converts, no one should have been surprised.

No one epitomized the early Puritan apprehension over slavery better than Cotton Mather, pastor of one of Boston's largest churches. Certain that slavery was divinely ordained, Mather, like most Protestant clergymen, matched closely William Sumner Jenkins's description of Puritan missionaries whose concern for the slave was "humanitarian, for the care of his soul and for the amelioration of his physical hardships, rather than equalitarian, for the absolving of his status." Although a civil libertarian of the twentieth century might have trouble understanding a political vocabulary that recognized no inherent connection between *humanity* and *equality*, it was a distinction that the Puritan had little difficulty making. In 1693, convinced that bondage was both an ideal foundation for conversion and a legitimate system of control, Mather organized a prayer and study group for slaves and published *Rules for the Society of Negroes*, in which he told them they were the "miserable children of Adam and Noah" and that they should be submissive and faithful to their masters.[31] Thirteen years later, in *The Negro Christianized*—his major publication on the subject—Mather reminded the bondsman to be "Patient and Content with such a Condition as God has ordered for [you]." At the same time, he told masters that a slave who is a Christian will be "dutiful," "patient," and "faithful," and will do nothing "that may justly displease you." Accordingly, since the condition of slaves in this life must be "low, and mean, and abject," let something therefore be done "towards their welfare in the *World to Come*."[32]

It mattered not if the master was cruel or benevolent or whether the servant was a slave or an employee, Puritan ministers were quick to argue, the master's interests always came first.[33] Was it not Christ himself, some of them argued, who said that the path to salvation was through subservience? "[W]hoever wants to become great among you must be your servant, and whoever wants to be first must be your slave—just as the Son of Man did not come to be served, but to serve, and to give his life as a ransom for many."[34] Submission to an earthly master may not have been what Christ had in mind, but the meaning of a scripture was often what one put into it. Mather certainly did not speak for all Puritans, but his views on slavery and subservience were close to those of Protestants everywhere.

If the slave could not find much comfort in the views of Puritans who believed he belonged in a state of servitude, neither did he find much in the arguments of those who claimed to be his friends. The Congregational church eventually did more than any other Protestant denomination to nurture the nineteenth-century antislavery movement, but the effort did not spring from some ancient fountainhead of Puritan equalitarianism. For example, Samuel Sewall's pamphlet *The Selling of Joseph, a Memorial* (Boston, 1700) has for many years enjoyed the distinction of being one of the first genuine antislavery tracts in colonial North America.[35] But was it, really? In a section entitled "Caveat Emptor!" Sewall suggested that former slaves "seldom use their freedom well" and that "there is such a disparity in their Conditions, Colour & Hair, that they can never embody with us, and grow up into orderly Families, to the Peopling of the Land."[36] It was one thing to oppose slavery in theory; it was quite another to accept black people in reality. As Louis Ruchames wrote in his introduction to a reprint of the pamphlet, Sewall "shares the contemporary prejudice which regarded Negroes as inferior, foreign beings who could never be integrated into New England Society."[37] Was this the view of a person who opposed slavery, or of one who could not accept the presence of free blacks? If the latter was the case, then Sewall had more in common with the nineteenth-century founders of the American Colonization Society and the members of the later Free Soil Party—who disliked black people more than they disliked slavery—than he had with the abolitionists.

Historians have paid relatively little attention to a reply to Sewall by John Saffin, a Boston merchant and jurist, who, in *A Brief and Candid Answer to a Late Printed Sheet, Entitled, the Selling of Joseph* ([Boston], 1701), "defended slavery on the ground that it was specifically sanctioned in both the Old and New Testament."[38] While "all Mankind are the Sons and Daughters of *Adam*, and the Creatures of God," Saffin wrote in what may have been the first published defense of slavery in the colonies, "it doth not therefore follow that we are bound to love and respect all men alike."[39] Later Christian supporters of bondage needed to look no further than Saffin's writing for the classical biblical articulation of their position.

Somehow, it is painfully easy to agree with the proslavery speculation that had New England had a large black population the cause of slavery would have found some of its most vociferous champions among the bluebloods of Boston, Hartford, and Providence. In fact, the economic growth of the region owed not a little to the institution. For one and a half centuries Yankee merchants realized enormous profits from the slave trade, a practice about which only Quakers and Mennonites complained. Puritan entrepreneurs were also involved in capturing slaves from Spanish colonies in the Caribbean for sale on New Providence Island.[40] Church leaders may have had little to say about human bondage, but when a commercial opportunity beckoned there were more than a few of the faithful who had no difficulty brushing aside all thoughts of slavery's brutality in order to realize a profit, thereby making what most Americans have always considered a virtue—the Puritan work ethic—a partner in the subjugation of an entire race of people (and later fueling the Marxist accusation that capitalism is inherently racist).

Whatever can be said of the Yankee's involvement in human suffering, his lack of daily contact with large numbers of black people made him an easy target of southern scorn, a condition that has persisted to recent times. During the antislavery crusade of the decades before the Civil War, the reconstruction period after the war, and the civil rights movement of the twentieth century, a common complaint from Southerners was that if black people had been as numerous in the North as they were in the South, the Northerner would be far less sympathetic toward advancing their cause. Although the allegation always produced angry denials from northern political and religious leaders, a lingering public uneasiness suggested that the charge was probably more than half right.

As a vital commodity in the European's struggle for commercial supremacy, the African was swept up in the maelstrom created by the convergence of Puritanism and capitalism. "Both an intense individualism and a rigorous Christian Socialism could be deduced from Calvin's doctrine," R. H. Tawney wrote in his classic *Religion and the Rise of Capitalism* (1926). "Which of them predominated depended on differences of political environment and of social class."[41] It is not possible to understand the Puritan's willingness to exploit the suffering of slaves without considering the fundamental link between economic growth and what Max Weber called the Protestant ethic.[42] "To the Puritan, a Christian's work was a part of his offering to God," historian Carl Degler wrote. Being chosen by God also meant being chosen to be successful. "To work hard is to please God."[43] Work was part of the glorification of God and God glorified work. "Piety and strict moral standards came first," another historian noted, "but material success was a social necessity and earned its own rewards."[44]

The Protestant ethic is not, of course, confined to New England or even the New World. Like American missionaries working among slaves and

Indians, the later Calvinists of South Africa tried to teach the Bantus the importance of "saving money and the use of capital, standards of ethics for labor, morals, and divine vocation." But the natives, wasting their meager earnings on feasts and what whites perceived as "licentious or erotic" activities, made little provision for the future and seemed interested only in satisfying their immediate needs.[45] Ultimately, the Puritan work ethic ravaged the slave in ways that carried far beyond his political liberation. Africans worked as hard as people anywhere. Moreover, the African's labor, like almost everything else in his life, was profoundly intertwined with his spiritual perception of the universe. But enslavement obliterated that connection and removed all incentives: As a tool in the Christian's enlargement of a capitalistic system, but sharing none of its wealth, the slave had every reason to resist the requirements of his master and to withhold efficiency. Of course, the slaveholder then complained that his bondsmen were natural malingerers because they would only work when threatened with pain and punishment. The image of the lazy black person thus became indelibly imprinted in the mind of white America.

The "Veriest Ruines *of* Mankind"

It is in the Puritan's posture toward the Indian that one can find the clearest and most abundant evidence of his racial thought, but even there it is not always easy to define the significance of that thought. Like their counterparts in Virginia and elsewhere, colonists in New England had initially expressed a strong desire to convert the native population to the faith, a desire cultivated by early Puritan writers, who had expressed optimism about the Indian's future in a Christian society, for example, Edward Winslow, *Good Newes from New England* (1624), Francis Higginson, *New-England Plantation* (1630), and William Wood, *New England Prospect* (1634). More than a few Puritans believed that the native was just as eligible as anyone for salvation or damnation—"equal in sin on the lowest level and in divine grace on the highest." The most celebrated of the missionaries to the Indians, and certainly the most effective, were Thomas Mayhew—whom Alden T. Vaughan called the "most impressive of the early missionaries"—and John Eliot, pastor of First Church of Roxbury.

Yet, as Perry Miller warned, it would be a mistake to compare the seventeenth-century Puritan's efforts to a modern missionary enterprise. The Puritan did not try to bring Christ to the Indians by living among them, sharing their lives, and otherwise trying to appreciate their culture and understand their needs. Rather, he brought the Indians to Christ by moving the most compliant of them into nearby "praying villages" like Natick, Nonantum, or Noonatomen, where they would be shielded from the corrupting influence of their heathen brethren, exposed to regular sermonizing, and taught "English mores." In other words, the full burden of adaptation fell on the Indian, not on the missionary. Coincidentally, relocating the Indians also helped ensure the security of neighborhood whites who, ironically, did not appreciate having the Indians close at hand. Foremost among the relocation advocates was Eliot, who, speaking the local native dialect, could by 1646 "preach with some effectiveness to Indian audiences." In time, his mission to the Indians dominated his life. Over a twenty-two-year period, beginning in 1651, Eliot "modeled the fourteen praying towns of Massachusetts Bay on his utopian vision of a 'Christian Commonwealth,' " each governed according to a legal code based on the Bible but drafted by him.[46]

Bringing the Indians together into a Christian community was just the beginning. To ensure that every one of them had a chance to read the Bible for himself, Eliot embarked on the prodigious task of translating the scriptures into Algonquin, the most widely spoken tongue of the New England tribes, a task that seemed to be impossible since there was no written Algonquin language. Undaunted, he decided to invent one by simply using the English alphabet to transcribe the phonetics of the Indian's spoken language, a task so formidable that it would be easy to conclude that Eliot was a man possessed. For example, the Algonquin language included many long compound words, each with a combination of meanings and without verb substantives; thus "forgive us our sins as wicked-doers" came out as *ahquontamaiiunnean nunmatch eseongash neane matchenekuk queagigu.*

Of course, finding Indian equivalents for English words was probably the least of Eliot's problems. What he appeared to disregard altogether was the fact that most Indians did not understand the English alphabet; learning to read the Algonquin Bible meant, in effect, learning to speak and read a foreign language. It would have been more practical simply to teach the Indians to speak English, then teach them to read the English Bible (a method that would have been applicable to all Indians). But Eliot, seeing his efforts finally appear in print in 1663, clearly wanted to create an Indian-language Bible for posterity, one that could be recopied and disseminated among the tribes in perpetuity. What the Authorized Version was to the English-speaking world, Eliot hoped his translation would be to the Algonquin world. As a child of a culture with a rich written literature, he could not imagine a Christian society without the printed Bible. "The whole Bible Translated into the *Indian*-Tongue, by Mr. *John Eliot* Senior," John Josselyn rejoiced in the same year, "was now printed at *Cambridge* in

New England."[47] Unfortunately, Eliot's zeal got in the way of his common sense. What he seemed not to take into account was that every generation of Indians would have to learn the new written language or the Algonquin Bible would be useless. What was the point of translating something into another tongue if no one could read it?

As it happened, getting the Indians into a Christian community was a lot easier than turning them into Christians. The ultimate objective was, in fact, to obliterate completely every vestige of the Indian's traditional culture so that, as Eliot put it, he could "rightly enjoy visible sanctities in ecclesiastical communion." For example, by laying out the fort and praying house at Natick along "several broad, straight streets," Neal Salisbury wrote in his study of the "Red Puritans," the missionaries disrupted the "vital communal pattern" of the multifamily roundhouses and longhouses that had formed the Indian's traditional village. Even his normal clothing was taken away from him in favor of European garb. To discourage the wearing of animal skins, he was cut off from his customary source of furs, which also reduced his access to the bear grease he smeared over his hair and body. Concomitantly, Indian women were to keep their hair long—but not hanging loose—while men had to cut theirs short. "Whether English or Indian, the principal sin of long hair was pride," James Axtell wrote. "And seventeenth-century Englishmen did not need reminding that pride was the original sin of their spiritual parents." In addition, many forms of "unChristian" behavior were proscribed, ranging from philandering and idleness to the killing of lice between the teeth—an Algonquin habit that Eliot found especially disgusting.[48]

At least one visitor was impressed by all of this. After recounting the torture and deaths of two Mohawks by fire and slow dismemberment at the hands of some "Barbarous" Eastern Indians, John Josselyn praised Eliot's converts. "These go clothed like the *English*, live in framed houses, have stocks of Corn and Cattle about them, which when they are fat they bring to the *English* Markets," Josselyn wrote in the second of his *Account of Two Voyages*; "the Hogs that they rear are counted the best in *New England.*" At least the apparent successes, Perry Miller said, were enough to induce other Protestant colonies, all of whom "advertised that they intended to convert Indians," to imitate the New England example. To reach the heathens, the Dutch Reformed and Scottish Presbyterian churches, like that of the Puritans, tried "to hew a civilization out of the wilderness, to put a church into the center of the new community, and then to pray that the grace of God would flow through these channels as already it had flowed through the societies of Europe and Britain."[49] All the Indian had to do was give Christianity a chance. God's love would do the rest.

In the end, the Puritan's determination to inseminate the natives with "English mores" undermined whatever chances for conversion might have existed. It would be easy to assume, in looking back from the vantage point of the twentieth century, that Eliot had been embarrassingly naïve in expecting the Indian to effect what anthropologists have called "transculturation."[50] But such an assessment would probably be unfair. When one is driven by the passion of faith, nothing else matters. As the decades passed, the Puritan enthusiasm—if that is the right word—toward converting Indians hardened, and even missionaries as sympathetic as Daniel Gookin despaired of ever being able to Christianize a significant number of them.

Accordingly, by the end of the seventeenth century, more than a few Puritans agreed with Cotton Mather's description of the Indians as "doleful creatures [who were] the veriest *ruines* of *mankind*, which [were] to be found any where upon the face of the earth," and whose religion was "the most explicit form of *devil-worship*."[51] When God brought down his "speedy vengeance" upon them during King Philip's War in 1675, Mather wrote in *Magnalia Christi Americana*, he was punishing them for rejecting the Gospel:

> Their city was laid in ashes. Above twenty of their chief captains were killed; a proportionable desolation cut off the inferiour salvages; mortal sickness, and horrid famine pursu'd the remainders of 'em, so we can hardly tell where any of 'em are left alive upon the face of the earth.[52]

In fact, Mather piously speculated, God probably had originally populated America with the Indians in order to keep them from the gospel. "But, as probably, the devil seducing the first inhabitants of America into it, therein aimed at having them and their posterity out of the sound of the *silver trumpets* of the *Gospel*." There were times, he added, when "*the most unexceptionable piece of justice in the world*" would have been to exterminate the Indians.[53]

The Puritan's failure to establish a constructive relationship with the Indian was a consequence of Puritan devotion to a faith that allowed only absolutes and employed methods dependent on force and grounded in Old Testament exhortations. The missionaries, making little effort to compromise with or understand the natives, would not be satisfied with a "good" or "peaceful" Indian but, rather, insisted on creating converts who were "copies of themselves." Of course, this was impossible and the praying villages, monuments to the naïveté of the Puritan mind, were dismal failures. The actual number of Indians converted under these arrangements cannot be known. At one time, there were 263 and 242 native residents of Natick and Nonantum, respectively, but that did not necessarily translate into converts. Apparently trying to make the situation look as good as possible, Gookin reported in 1674 there were at least 1,100 "praying Indians" in all 14 villages, a number that is difficult to corroborate. By that date there were only 145 residents remaining in Natick, of whom none were baptized and no more than 50 were taking communion. Using Gookin's calculations, Francis Jennings produced figures that show barely 4 percent of all village Indians baptized and between 6 and 7 percent taking communion. And historian Alden T. Vaughan, first crediting Thomas Mayhew with being responsible for a "rapid conversion of the natives," later conceded that the missionary, after seven years of full-time work among the Indians of Martha's Vineyard, could count only twenty-two converts to Christianity.[54]

Eliot himself only claimed responsibility for the conversion of "a few hundred of the several thousand Indians of Massachusetts Bay." Whatever success he might have had was doomed by the "rigorous social and theological demands made of converts to Puritanism." By bringing the heathens to Christ rather than bringing Christ to the heathens, Eliot had hoped to transform the Indian into nothing less than an English Puritan with red skin. Although they sincerely believed that what they were doing was in the Indians' best interests, missionaries as dedicated as Mayhew, Eliot, Gookin, and John Sergeant, describing Indian tradition as "backward," "uncivilized," and "immoral," were convinced that there was no other way to bring them to Christianity.[55] The Indian's only access to heaven, they held, was through his adoption of the white Christian's culture. To remain an Indian was to ensure damnation. "The frightening paradox was that," in Roy Harvey Pearce's devastating words, "the savage heathen was lowered, not raised, by his contact with the civilized Christian."[56]

Pearce looked at the effect that the coming of the English colonist had on the native American. His judgment on that effect was understandably cynical. There have been others, however, who focused on what they perceived as positive efforts of the white man to "improve" the quality of life of the Indians and, accordingly, believed they saw something less ominous. One of the most sympathetic examinations of the Puritan's effort to bring Christianity to the Indian—or, more accurately, to bring the Indian to Christianity—is Alden T. Vaughan's study of the early New England frontier. Despite the Puritan's failure to introduce a significant number of Indians to the Christian way of life, he did "make a brief noble effort," Vaughan maintained, to avoid the traditional European way of dealing with "savages," and his policy toward them did not change until after 1675—the year of King Philip's War—when "it became clear . . . that the Indians would never fulfill Puritan hopes."[57]

But it is difficult to sustain this optimistic picture in the face of certain not-so-noble facts, foremost of which was the missionaries' conscious efforts to eliminate all traces of the Indian's native culture. Similarly, how should one interpret the prayers of the early settlers who thanked God for sending the terrible epidemic that decimated the Indian population in 1617, prayers repeated for years afterward in many Puritan pulpits?[58] And it is hard to see the Puritans' annihilation of the Pequot people as anything other than the traditional European way of dealing with savages. All of these occurred before Vaughan's watershed year of 1675. Vaughan also unflinchingly described an incident involving a group of Narragansetts who had promised—under duress—not to assist King Philip. "When it later appeared that the tribe had failed to live up to this treaty," he concluded without critical comment, "a force of soldiers was dispatched to obliterate the covenant-breakers before they could openly move to aid the Wampanoags."[59]

Excusing the Puritans because they did what they believed was in the Indian's best interests was beside the point. Needless to say, it never occurred to them that what would have been in his best interests would have been to leave him and his land alone. It did not really matter how "good" the Puritan's intentions were if the consequences of those intentions were destructive. The essence of Christian racism has always been the harm done by people who thought they had a monopoly on the truth.

When the Indian refused to "give up his natural liberty . . . and bow to the superior law of the Christians as laid down in the Good Book," Puritan divines like Cotton Mather saw this as nothing less than proof of the native's certain condemnation to hell. Thus emerged a fundamental question about the Puritan's perception of race relations that is impossible to ignore: What influence, if any, did the Calvinist doctrine of predestination have on the Puritan attitude toward Africans and Indians? "We call predestination the eternal decree of God by which he has determined in himself what he could have every individual of mankind become," John Calvin argued in *Institutes of the Christian Religion* (1559 edition); "but eternal life is foreordained for some and eternal damnation for others."[60] It would have been more accurate had he said eternal life for a *few* and damnation for *many*, that is, "few grains of wheat are covered by a pile of chaff."[61] While Calvin agreed that the logic of this principle is "incomprehensible," he also proclaimed that, since God is not capable of error, it stands as "just and irreprehensible."[62] The trick, of course, was for each person to determine if he had been chosen by God—to search for the marks of election—or others would likely determine that he was not.

With dismal chains, and strongest reins,
like Prisoners of Hell,
They're held in place before Christ's face,
till He their doom shall tell.
These void of tears, but fill'd with fears,
and dreadful expectation
Of endless pains, and scalding flames,
stand waiting for Damnation.[63]

When the critics assailed Calvin for advocating a principle that excluded so many, he comforted them with the argument that the immediate cause of predestination was not some extraneous force but man's *free will* "through which God acts when he makes his decree."[64] In other words, a person made an independent choice to live a Christian life, and it was through his conduct that everyone realized his preferred status. Somehow, this made it sound all right.

But it also excluded the overwhelming majority of the human race. Needless to say, the ramifications of a strict application of the principle of predestination were staggering. Except among the favored few, there is no suggestion anywhere in the doctrine of The Elect that all men are equal. If there were such things as "marks of election," how many Africans and Indians displayed them? The only way they could be admitted to the exclusive circle was to live exactly like those who were teaching them and, as Eliot unwittingly made clear, that was impossible. "[A]ll of these who teach predestination have observed something empirically," theologian Paul Tillich observed, "namely, that there is a selective and not an equalitarian principle effective in life." Thus, if a basic doctrine of a person's faith was the belief that God had already ordained his destiny, could anyone properly argue against the Indian's and African's suitability for rejection? Perhaps more to the point, did the principle of election, by which God had already chosen those who would receive eternal life, reduce all others to degradation? If the Puritan believed that it did, then he must have considered the *un*elected—the condemned majority of the human race—as people whose earthly conduct must be closely controlled.[65] The Christian should love everyone, Calvin added, but he should reserve the greatest concern for those "whom God hath joined to us more closely and with a more holy tie."[66]

If everything that happened was God's will, then there must have been a divine purpose in placing the white Christian and the heathen Indian together in this small corner of the world. Since life was a drama featuring a struggle between the forces of God and the forces of Satan, and since the Puritan perceived himself as one of The Elect, then the Indian was obviously an "unregenerate" agent of evil.[67] There was no place left to put him. To the Puritans—not to mention the Presbyterian, Dutch Reformed, Huguenot, and other Protestant sects that drew their theological impulse from the teachings of Calvin—the logical conclusion was inescapable.[68] If a belief in predestination was even no more than a subconscious premise of the Puritan's world view, would he be able to do anything other than consign Africans and Indians, whose cultural habits were so clearly alien to everything he understood about civilization and Christianity, to "eternal damnation"?

Calvin admitted that he did not know why God had favored some and not others, but he also insisted it was not necessary to know the reasons. "If, therefore, we can assign no reason why he grants mercy to his people because such is his pleasure, neither shall we find any other cause but his will for the reprobation of others." Though God's choices may be "incomprehensible" to mortals, Calvin added, he nonetheless had in his "just and irreprehensible" judgment "barred the door of life to those whom he has given over to damnation."[69] But dismissing the issue of fairness with the weak palliative that God is always just was simply not enough. In questioning the validity of the doctrine, Tillich pointed out that Calvin overlooked the fact that not everyone had the same historical opportunity to know Jesus, a point the Puritan poet Michael Wigglesworth freely, but uncompromisingly, acknowledged in his description of Judgment Day:

Thy written Word (say they) good Lord,
we never did enjoy:
We nor refuse'd, nor it abus'd;
Oh, do not us destroy.[70]

Others did not have the same opportunity because, Tillich went on, "their condition is such that they cannot even understand the meaning of what is said to them."[71] To Wigglesworth, that was irrelevant.

Their place there find all Heathen blind,
that Nature's light abused,
Although they had no tydings glad,
of Gospel-grace refused.
There stands all Nations and Generations
of Adam's *Progeny,*
Whom Christ redeem'd not, who Christ esteemed not,
through infidelity.[72]

Tillich's reading of Calvin, then, suggested that the subjugation of Africans and the extermination of Indians were little more than coincidental, though unfortunate, consequences of geographic circumstance. On the other hand, the true believer never doubted his own destiny. The marks of election that Calvin recognized were, first, "an inner relationship to God in the act of faith," followed by the "blessing of God" and one's "high moral standing." In other words, it was through commitment to Christ, economic abundance, and purity in conduct that one was assured of election.[73] Hard work (the Protestant ethic) and clean mind (Puritan morality) were the tickets to salvation.

In theory, the doctrine of predestination would seem to be an ideal rationale for defending hostile behavior toward nonwhite peoples. To begin with, the believer was absolved of all responsibility. Who would quarrel with God's decisions? Besides, since God was all-knowing, he surely would know who would be saved; *predestination* was just a word that the faithful used to identify God's ability to know the future. More to the point was the doctrine's obvious application to the American situation. Predestination validated the Puritan's existential world. The Calvinist gained certainty of his salvation by witnessing in himself the empirical conditions of moral rectitude and economic good fortune.

Conversely, it was easy to conclude that those who did not manifest either must have been condemned to "destruction." Could one expect the provincial colonist in the seventeenth century, with a dogmatic passion for his faith and a narrowly focused understanding of the world, to believe any different? To him, the Indian and the African—with dark skins, primitive religious practices, incomprehensible languages, and strange habits—were as unlike himself as one could possibly be. Whether or not the Puritan consciously applied the principles of his theology to his immediate environment is arguable; after all, his first priority was to survive in a new and sometimes dangerous world. But he also was committed to construct a Christian community as he perceived it should be. It was not likely that an "outsider" who exhibited no marks of election would find a very warm welcome there.

In the end it was the polycentric nature of the Puritan's congregationalism, rather than the monolithic nature of his theology, that fostered the denomination's ambivalence toward slavery. With no centralized ecclesiastical policy-making authority and no established forum for entertaining divergent viewpoints, it was possible, on the one hand, for the congregation in Suffield, Connecticut, to appropriate for its pastor "£20 towards the purchase of negroes" while, on the other, Samuel Hopkins's First Congregational Church in Newport, Rhode Island, admitted slaves as members.[74] But the spirit of the Enlightenment was relentless and changing political conditions eventually forced the New England cleric to look beyond his own churchyard. If Puritans could not always agree on whether or not to condemn bondage, the Calvinist impulse eventually touched many other Protestant leaders.

By the time of the Revolution, according to one historian of race relations, the "Puritan heritage" had moved American clergymen to "collectivize the personal sin of slaveholding and thereby threw responsibility for reformation onto the entire community." If slavery was a communal sin, as Puritan thinking had it, the consequence would surely be communal punishment. From his pulpit in Newport, Hopkins, whom William W. Sweet called the "father of the antislavery movement in America," demanded the marshaling of the collective will against bondage and became the "most effective influence in colonial New England against slavery and especially the slave trade." Sweet's major sin was certainly no worse than exaggeration. During the colonial era several Congregational ministers owned a small number of slaves, but by the beginning of the nineteenth century, this particular group of clergymen were probably close to unanimous in their opposition to slavery.[75]

This did not mean that all of them—or even most of them—were abolitionists. One influential Congregational minister in the antebellum period was Horace Bushnell, who criticized slavery but, making clear his belief in white supremacy, also favored colonization as a solution to the racial problem. Returning from a three-month visit to the South in 1854, Nehemiah Adams, who held pulpits in Cambridge and Boston from 1834 until his death in 1878, claimed to be "an ardent friend of the colored race" but thought that slavery had virtues worth preserving. After publishing his impressions, *A South-Side View of Slavery* (1854), Adams became known in antislavery circles as "Southside Adams." Nevertheless, Congregational and Unitarian leaders—unlike the Baptists, Presbyterians, and Methodists—managed to avoid serious internal divisions because neither had significant southern constituencies or slaveholding brethren to mollify. Ultimately, the slave population and the heirs of the "Puritan heritage" were divided by geography no less than principle. As the sectional crisis deepened in the years prior to the Civil War, the "liberal fringes of religious life were snipped off," in Carl Degler's words, and the Unitarian Church "all but disappeared from the South."[76] Puritan *thinking* worked its way into most of the Protestant denominations in America, but the Congregational and Unitarian churches remained confined generally to the northeastern corner of the country.

Rice or Righteousness: The Established Church

It is more than a little ironic that the first Protestant denomination to establish an official missionary program for the New World was also the denomination of the most powerful slaveholders. Like the Puritan Church in New England, the Anglican—or Established—Church in the southern colonies enjoyed a formal association with the colonial governments, but in this instance the clerical leadership was also backed by the highest ecclesiastical authority in London through the Archbishop of Canterbury all the way to the Crown. In June 1701, at the behest of the Reverend Dr. Thomas Bray, whose six-month assignment in Maryland as commissary for the Bishop of London had reinforced his concern for the spiritual welfare of English subjects in the colonies, church officials chartered the Society for the Propagation of the Gospel in Foreign Parts (SPG). Although "foreign parts" signified a service in a foreign land, the society, since its primary purpose was to minister to people who were already Christians, was not so much a missionary organization as it was an Anglican watchdog agency. In 1702 the society sent its first contingent of workers; and for the next eighty-three years a steady stream of missionaries, catechists, and teachers—not to mention countless Bibles, Common Prayer Books, and official church publications (including ten thousand copies of Bishop of London Edmund Gibson's 1727 letter on the importance of converting slaves)—crossed the Atlantic Ocean under its auspices.[77]

Although the society's original purpose was to tend to the pastoral needs of the settlers, the decision to include slaves and Indians did not come as an afterthought. As early as 1673, copies of Richard Baxter's *Christian Director*, calling for slave conversion, had circulated extensively throughout the South. After a two-year missionary apprenticeship in Virginia and ten more years in the West Indies, Morgan Godwyn published his broad plan for Christianizing Indians and blacks in *The Negro's and Indians Advocate* (1680), which, like Baxter's work, subsequently became a blueprint for the SPG. It should be noted that there was absolutely no emancipationist sentiment in either of these efforts, and, indeed, the society's missionaries never openly criticized slavery. Godwyn, George H. Moore wrote in his *Notes on the History of Slavery in Massachusetts* (1866), "hardly intimates a doubt of the lawfulness of slavery, while he pleads for [the slaves'] humanity and right to religion against a very general opinion of that day, which denied them both." By the eighteenth century slavery in the New World had become so institutionalized that any agitation for freedom would, in Frank J. Klingberg's words, "have ended [the missionary's] usefulness at once, both in the West Indies and in the South." No one defended the importance of converting heathens more vigorously than Godwyn, another historian wrote, but even he "insisted on the divine origin of social hierarchy including slavery as the lowest rank." Like the Puritans in New England and the Catholics in Latin America, the English church saw no fundamental contradiction between human bondage and Christianity.[78]

Nowhere was this accommodation more evident than in the society's commitment to make Christian education available to the non-English heathens. Convinced that conversion without education was meaningless, Thomas Bray in 1723 created a new group, whose members, after his death in 1730, became known as The Associates of the Late Dr. Bray and who saw themselves as "Instructing in the Christian Religion the Young Children of Negro Slaves & such of their Parents as shew themselves inclinable & desirous to be so instructed."[79] It seemed like a move in the right direction, a move whose necessity was underlined by the fact that the initiative to establish such a missionary arm came from London rather than the resident colonial clergy. In 1699, two years before church officials approved his organization of the SPG, Bray had founded The Society for Promoting Christian Knowledge, which eventually established almost forty libraries from Boston to Charleston, with the largest, at Annapolis, Maryland, one of the first semi-public lending libraries in the New World. Considering the urban locations of most of the libraries and the obvious literacy requirement, no one could argue that they had been intended for anyone other than English settlers.

As a logical extension of the SPCK, the organization of the Associates was the only serious effort to provide Christian education for slaves. But if the letters written by its field workers—collected under the title The American Correspondence of the Associates of Dr. Bray—was any indication, it, like the missionary effort of the SPG, was not even marginally successful. While almost all of the letters reflected their authors' religious enthusiasm, few of them claimed much in the way of results. In the approximately fifty-year existence of the Associates,[80] perhaps two or three thousand black people were reached, which was less than 1 percent of the estimated colonial black population. And of those who did receive some instruction, there is little evidence of many long-lasting conversions. Nor was the contemptuous attitude of the movement's leaders likely to endear them to many slaves. The Reverend John Bartow of West Chester, New York, told the SPG that he believed it was "very rare that [blacks] can be brought to have any true sense of the Christian religion," a not uncommon view.[81] "Bray's own ideas about blacks were not equivocal," the editor of the correspondence wrote. "He considered them barbarous and heathen, and he accepted the institution of slavery. His concern was for the blacks' immortal souls, not their temporal condition."[82]

The arrogance with which English-speaking Christians like Bray looked down upon the "uncivilized" heathen was typical and continued well into the nineteenth century as part of the proslavery argument that the African had no distinctive history or culture. In fact, the irony of that arrogance was inescapable. Most white Americans were—and are—unaware that as early as the fourth century Christianity had reached the upper Nile as far as the Semitic kingdom of Axum, which was at the height of its power under its greatest conqueror, King Ezana (320–350), the first African monarch to accept Christianity. It was not until the fifth and sixth centuries that fair-haired Nordic invaders—Jutes, Angles, and Saxons—brought their brand of paganism to a Britain already populated by various Celtic tribesmen, blue-painted Picts, and even a few remnants of the now-departed Romans. "The [SPG'S] missionary activities were in some respects a curious turn of history," C. Eric Lincoln wrote, "for the African involvement in Christianity was centuries old long before the English had given up some pagan practices very similar to those from which they now decided the Africans ought to be rescued."[83]

None of that would have mattered anyway. To the modern Briton, the African was a heathen and the evangelical mandate was clear. It was up to the pure of heart to do what he had to do. Bray launched his religious-education program because, like John Eliot, he "held that civilising coloured men was a necessary preliminary to their conversion."[84] Naïvely assuming that by simply *telling* heathens about Christianity he could erase the cumulative influence of thousands of years of cultural conditioning, Thomas Bray was no different from Eliot, Baxter, Godwyn, or any other single-minded Christian envoy. Like Eliot's Indian, the African did not respond to the missionary appeal because he *could* not.

In South Carolina, the pure of heart included Anglican clerics Samuel Thomas, Francis Le Jau, Ebenezer Taylor, Thomas Hasel, John Whitehead, and William Tredwell Bull, none of whom had much success in a region where the number of slaves was growing rapidly and political and economic considerations made the slaveholders' resistance insurmountable. In this colony, at least, Indians were not readily converted because they saw nothing to be gained by adopting the faith of people whose presence they resented. But in the case of the slaves, conversion was difficult, if not impossible, mainly because the masters did not permit it. "There was a consistently patronizing quality to the remarks about Indians and blacks by the South Carolina ministers," John Frederick Woolverton wrote. "Clergy were often prone to caution, even obsequiousness, before slaveholders who held the power of hiring and firing."[85] The situation was little different in Virginia, where the planters' influence was so "all-embracing" that ministers learned very early not to challenge existing social rules. The vestrymen—those lay leaders who managed the church's temporal affairs—who really controlled the parish, were in many cases also the wealthiest slaveholders.[86]

When Quaker reformer Anthony Benezet in 1767 asked the SPG to "condemn the slave trade," a society spokesman refused on the ground that such a declaration would make masters "more suspicious and cruel, and much more unwilling to let their slaves learn Christianity," a specious reply, since few masters were doing so anyway.[87] Anglican churchmen throughout the plantation colonies placed a higher priority on maintaining the good will of the white laity—especially of affluent slaveholders, whose financial contributions kept most of them living in comfort—than they did on the spiritual well-being of the slaves. It should therefore surprise no one that, despite what had begun as an ostensibly sincere effort to win slaves to Christianity, the number of bondsmen actually converted remained embarrassingly small throughout the colonial era.[88]

In fairness to Bray and the Anglican missionary movement, it should be repeated that, as British historian C. P. Groves wrote, the SPG's "main concern" was the "pastoral care of Europeans," not the salvation of Africans, Indians, or any other heathen peoples. Missionaries in South Carolina, working alongside clergymen supported by the colonial government, had, in Frank J. Klingberg's words, "a double duty" of instructing "the Negroes as well as the whites."[89] Obviously, the society was not a missionary organization in the modern sense. Despite the fact that Bray's inspiration came while he was serving the church briefly in Maryland in the 1690s, the mission of the SPG is best understood when set against the larger backdrop of British imperialism in the eighteenth century.

Having begun its colonial ventures during the reign of Elizabeth, England, by the time of William of Orange, was ready to challenge the Spanish, Portuguese, and French domination of the New World. With Englishmen serving his majesty—or, in the case of Queen Anne (1702–14), *her* majesty—across the oceans, the Society for the Propagation of the Gospel in Foreign Parts was a logical, almost necessary, extension of the Anglican faith. But since the society's first priority was the souls of English settlers, thirty-three-year-old John Wesley, working in newly established Georgia in 1736–37 with his younger brother Charles, "found that the claims of the settlers at Savannah left him no time for the plan he had cherished of preaching to the Indians." The society's obligation to English colonists can also be seen in its efforts in places where slaves were relatively scarce. Faced with a Puritan leadership that feared the establishment of an Anglican episcopate in America, SPG missionaries in New England had little success in reaching anyone, black, red, or white.[90] Wesley's dream would have to wait until his Methodist movement emerged to forge the most effective missionary program in the former British colonies.

It also should not be forgotten that many of the Anglican ministers, including the celebrated George Whitefield, were themselves slaveholders and therefore undoubtedly held most of the same racist convictions as the rest of the southern white population. Visiting the South in the late eighteenth century, English evangelicals James Habersham and William Knox were convinced that "their role in the slave system, far from being a moral evil, was in truth part of a divine plan for converting Africans." Settling in Georgia, Habersham became a protégé of Whitefield; while Knox returned to England and, in 1789, published *Three Tracts, Respecting the Conversion and Instruction of the Free Indians, and Negro Slaves in the Colonies.*[91]

Nineteenth-century white Southerners, who, in response to the growing chorus of abolitionist criticism, espoused the infamous "proslavery argument," found plenty of earlier clerical testimony to reinforce their views. Indeed, according to Jon Butler it was the Anglican churchmen of the *later* colonial period, that is, from 1690 to 1790 (which coincided almost exactly with the SPG's sojourn in North America), who were most responsible for creating a race consciousness that other denominations later inherited. In Butler's opinion, the Established Church in the colonial South did far more to ensure the subjugation of black men and women than merely tolerate the institutionalization of slavery. When Anglican clergymen articulated a clearly defined theology of slavery, they in fact cultivated a lay population that was already well attuned to the notion that Christianity was completely compatible with black subservience. The main point here is that while Protestant capitulation to economic reality was not something that necessarily emerged along with slavery itself, as would be so easy to assume, it was nonetheless formulated later by Anglican missionaries who cultivated the racist culture that subsequent southern denominations so eagerly embraced. In short, the southern Baptist and Methodist churches that black men and women in the nineteenth century found so appealing had inherited from their Anglican forebears the foundations of the slave philosophy and "became defenders rather than the critics of the new, revolutionary slave society of the southern colonies."[92]

Nor was the Anglican Church's record with the Indians any better. In 1680 Morgan Godwyn had called for the conversion of Indians and in the early eighteenth century missionaries for the SPG had been instructed to make every effort in this direction, but little was attempted and less was accomplished. Like the Puritans in New England—though not necessarily for the same reasons—Anglican missionaries made little effort to travel among the tribes. Of the more than three hundred SPG agents stationed along the Atlantic coast, William R. Hutchinson noted, not one ever lived among the Indians. If the efforts of the Associates of the Late Dr. Bray to provide Christian education for slaves were unproductive, an earlier Anglican proposal to do the same for Indians was a total disaster. When all of the parishes in Virginia established a fund to build an Indian "college," Virginia Company officials embezzled most of the money or used it for other company expenses, and no college was ever built nor a single Indian converted under such an arrangement. An example of the general white contempt for Indians could be seen in a Revolutionary War incident involving a large number of natives living along the Ohio River. Converted earlier by Moravian missionaries, the Indians were massacred by Virginia militiamen, who had mistaken them for hostile tribes whom Virginians had been fighting bitterly for years. "The Christian Indians came out of their villages to meet the militia as friends," George Maclaren Brydon wrote in his massive *Virginia's Mother Church and the Political Conditions Under Which It Grew* (1947), "and were totally exterminated."[93] It is not hard to conclude that Brydon would have considered the incident less tragic had the Indians not been Christians. Certainly the Virginia militia would have thought so.

Since the Established Church had never called for an equalitarian accommodation for slaves and Indians, its ministers could not technically be accused of surrendering a vital principle to the slaveholding interests. But on another level surrender they did; and if there was one figure who personified the church's adaptation to the reality of slavery, it was George Whitefield, whom religion historian Sydney E. Ahlstrom called the "hero-founder" of the evangelical tradition in America. As one of the ministers in the eighteenth-century Great Awakening and the southern counterpart of Jonathan Edwards in New England and Gilbert Tennent in the middle colonies, Whitefield has often been portrayed as an advocate of the equalitarian spirit that declared that all men are equal in the eyes of God, a spirit whose rejection of convention and authority ultimately found its political expression in the American independence movement. The Great Awakening—"that tumultuous series of outdoor revivals and camp meetings that swept the country around 1740," as historian C. Eric Lincoln described it—was one of the most important social events in the evolution of American democracy, historians have always been quick to point out, and Whitefield was one of its giants. It would seem that the movement's emphasis on the spoken, rather than the written, word should have appealed to blacks and Indians, both of whom had come from cultures with strong oral traditions. One minister "reported in the mid-1760's that his Newport congregation was composed of 500 whites and 70 blacks; with 55 blacks being communicants." Another writer observed that one hundred blacks " 'constantly' attended Anglican services at Newport, Rhode Island, in 1743." At the same time, reports from field agents for the SPG indicated an increase in the number of black converts.[94] It is, of course, impossible to know if any of these numbers had been influenced by the Great Awakening.

For his part, Whitefield, telling slaveholders that there were no differences between white and black souls, staunchly supported programs to convert slaves and advocated more humane treatment for them. Calling some masters "Monsters of Barbarity," he also criticized slaveholders for neglecting the bondsmen's religious needs. An extremely popular figure, who became an itinerant, open-air preacher because the English clergy refused to let him speak in their churches, Whitefield considered slave labor—because it provided the planter with the lavish wealth to engage in "midnight balls and amusements," "drinking and dancing," and other sins of the spoiled—to be the fundamental cause of South Carolina's "degeneracy."[95] It was a familiar theme: criticizing slavery because of its allegedly pernicious effect on the master class.

It needs to be pointed out that no one has ever produced evidence that Whitefield actually favored emancipation, although some historians have implied just that.[96] In fact, if the historical assessment of George Whitefield's accomplishments had been based solely on his racial policies, he would be far less than a leading godfather of democratic principles as so many political historians have portrayed him. Conscious of the interests of the British settlers who were trying to establish "civilization" in the middle of the southern wilderness, his first priority was to minister to their spiritual needs, not to those of the heathens. Salvation for slaves was important, but it would come as a by-product of his primary mission. Unlike his close friend John Wesley, who insisted that no amount of economic benefit could justify "the injustice and cruelty of the slave system" and with whom he later split over doctrinal issues,[97] Whitefield had always perceived Africans to be a degraded, inferior people, whose bondage was their best insurance for salvation.

Whitefield was so convinced that there was no other effective way of reaching African souls—and that, perhaps more important, slave labor was critical to the future of the colony's survival—that "in 1741 he agreed to testify before Parliament in support of [slavery] in Georgia and later lamented that the trustees had deprived the colony of slave labor these many years."[98] Exalting the myth that "hot countries cannot be cultivated without Negroes," he celebrated the reversal of the ban on slavery in the colony.[99] One historian has concluded that Whitefield, trying his best to conceal "a deep-seated fear of blacks," was the probable author of *A Letter to the Negroes Lately Converted to Christ in America* (London, 1743), which, urging "blacks to die rather than disobey . . . propped up the institution of slavery with evangelical braces." By 1747–48 he had become a slaveholding owner of his own plantation and one of the South's most outspoken champions of bondage. The same man who a few years earlier had argued compellingly for a more humane treatment of slaves saw nothing inhumane about the institution of slavery.[100]

The Anglican accommodation continued virtually unchanged to the

Civil War. While every other major Protestant denomination took an early position against slavery—positions that most of them later modified and even divided over—the Episcopal Church remained aloof from the controversy. A traditionally conservative sect, the Episcopalians were mostly élitists who represented the upper classes, among whom there was little disposition for social reform. It drew a disproportionate share of its membership from the slaveholding population. This meant they did nothing, in effect leaving the church's supporters of slavery, as religious historian Winthrop S. Hudson noted, free to speak out "while their opponents were urged to avoid creating dissension by remaining silent." Or by falling back on the traditional rationalization. For example, after he was asked how any sincere man of God could remain silent on the slavery issue, Episcopal Bishop Philander Chase, who had moved into the Ohio-Illinois country after 1815 to organize churches and schools, replied in a letter to a group of English bishops that the southern clergy could "tolerate the evil because of the good they could do for the souls of men."[101] Chase's observation was revealing because, first, he was conceding that slavery was inherently evil, and, second, his use of the verb "tolerate" implied that at least some southern churchmen agreed with him, although none was courageous enough to acknowledge it publicly. What Chase could not—or would not—do was admit that a "necessary" evil was still an evil.

As the cotton plantation system became institutionalized throughout the South in the second quarter of the nineteenth century, economic reality silenced all possible dissent. Cynical though it may sound, it is not an exaggeration to submit that the critical factor in determining who opposed slavery and who supported it was, with every church that claimed a national constituency, a consequence entirely of political and economic factors. All of the Christian conviction in the world could not dent the purse of one slaveholder.

As the sectional conflict polarized opinions in the decades before the Civil War, Episcopal clergymen took aggressive positions on both sides of the issue. Opponents of slavery, who, at least publicly, were clearly in the minority, included E. M. P. Wells, Evan M. Johnson, John McNamara, and William and John Jay. A southern critic was Joseph Dodderidge of western Virginia (where slavery was not as extensive as in the eastern portion of the state), who in 1824 published a book that condemned both slavery and its popular defense. "We debase [the slaves] to the condition of brutes," he wrote in a variation on a popular abolitionist theme, "and then we use that debasement as an argument for perpetuating their slavery."[102] On the other side were Bishop George W. Freeman of the southern church and, most notorious of all, Bishop John Henry Hopkins of Vermont. As a highly visible official in the northern church, Hopkins was controversial because his views were as extreme as any Southerner's, and he laid them out in widely circulated wartime publications like the pamphlet *Bible View of Slavery* (1863)—which became part of the radical Democratic political series *Papers from the Society for the Diffusion of Political Knowledge*—and the 376-page book *Scriptural, Ecclesiastical, and Historical View of Slavery* (1864).[103]

At about the same time, the General Council of the Protestant Episcopal Church in the Confederate States of America met in Georgia and issued a pastoral letter that, while urging religious instruction for all black people, insisted on the moral rightness of the slave system, "upon which we are about to plant our national life." This view was repeated in even angrier terms in the anonymous *Negroes and Religion* (1863?), which was purportedly written by a member of the southern church to his northern brethren.[104] The southern Episcopal accommodation of slavery was perhaps best represented by Bishop Leonidas Polk of Louisiana, owner of four hundred slaves, who, as a Confederate general, made the supreme sacrifice in defense of the "lost cause."[105] Despite the southern Episcopal clergy's almost unanimous support for the South, the national leadership, through its Freedmen's Commission, had become involved in several aid programs, including the founding of what later became St. Augustine College in Raleigh, North Carolina. But the Old South died hard. Well into the twentieth century, Episcopal leaders like Quincy Ewing were still struggling against the racist myths that had started over two centuries earlier with the likes of Morgan Godwyn and Thomas Bray.[106]

Quakers and the Arrogance of Humility

It has long been acknowledged by students of early American history that only certain Moravians, Mennonites, and Quakers were openly critical of slavery, and that, since the first two denominations were too small and isolated to be noticed, only the Quakers were numerous enough to have much influence. In 1657, long before any Puritan or Anglican had taken a stand, George Fox, the founder of the Society of Friends, wrote from England to Quaker missionaries in the New World cautioning them against the temptation to possess "Blacks and Indian slaves." Fox did not criticize slavery directly, but the letter did reflect his belief that all people were equal in the eyes of God.[107] It was not much of an antislavery declaration, but it was a beginning. The first colonial Friend to speak out against bondage was probably William Edmundson, a "traveling Irish Quaker," who in 1675 wrote to Friends in several colonies—including the plantation colonies of Virginia and Maryland—condemning the ownership of slaves.

Indeed, Stephen B. Weeks wrote, "slavery was the subject which differentiated Friends in the South from other religious bodies."[108]

Writing from Newport, Rhode Island, the following year, Edmundson asked, in a general letter to Quakers in America, how, since it is "unlawful to make slaves of Indians," anyone can justify enslaving black people. Newport was a major slave-trading center and Edmundson was first in what Thomas E. Drake called "the great succession of antislavery apostles." What is now probably the best-known Quaker antislavery statement was the Germantown Protest of 1688, drafted by Dutch-speaking Friends, who, because of the suffering endured by their European ancestors in the sixteenth century, traditionally opposed institutional persecution.[109]

From the Germantown Protest (which did not actually appear in print until 1844) to the early nineteenth century, the Society of Friends was virtually the only American religious body that circulated published arguments against bondage. The first of these appeared in 1693, when William Bradford of Philadelphia, a follower of the Scottish-born Quaker George Keith, published Keith's *An Exhortation & Caution to Friends Concerning Buying or Keeping Negroes.* Defining four antislavery arguments based on various biblical passages, Keith articulated themes that were to reach a peak of popularity a century and a half later in the flood of religious abolitionist literature that was virtually everywhere in the North before the Civil War. Subsequent Quaker publications condemning slavery included John Hepburn's *The American Defense of the Christian Golden Rule* (1715), Ralph Sandiford's *A Brief Examination of the Practice of the Times* (1729), Elihu Coleman's *A Testimony against that Antichristian Practice of Making Slaves of Men* (1733), and Benjamin Lay's *All Slave-Keepers that Keep the Innocent in Bondage, Apostates* (1737), which, taken together, historian William Sumner Jenkins called "the seeds of the antislavery movement in America."[110] In 1790, an anonymous poet, assuming the character of a Pennsylvania slave who had been recently liberated, memorialized two of these antislavery writers:

> *Long, long remember'd, from my earliest years,*
> *Prophetic sounds still tingle in my ears,*
> *Still gentle* Sandiford *methinks I see,*
> *Proclaiming Blacks by God and nature free.*
> *To wasting zeal and sympathy a prey,*
> *Methinks I hear the venerable* Lay,
> *Now, at distress and wrong for pity sigh,*
> *And now, "All Slave-Keepers, Apostates," cry.*[111]

Certainly the most acclaimed of all Quaker critics of slavery were John Woolman and his close friend Anthony Benezet. In 1754, Woolman, who has been described by more than one scholar as the greatest of all American Quakers, published *Some Considerations on the Keeping of Negroes: Recommended to the Professors of Christianity of Every Denomination*, which, according to the leading historian of the Quakers and slavery, received the widest circulation of any antislavery document in any language.[112] In the same year, Woolman drafted the Philadelphia Yearly Meeting's *An Epistle of Caution and Advice*, in which he wrote: "To live in ease and plenty by the toil of those whom violence and cruelty have put in our power is neither consistent with Christianity or common justice."[113] It is interesting to speculate as to whether or not Abraham Lincoln might have been thinking of this passage when, in his eloquent Second Inaugural Address, he wondered, with a tone of understanding and forgiveness that even Woolman did not display, how Confederate leaders could morally justify asking God to help sustain a society built on the backs of slaves.

Benezet—born in St. Quentin, France, in 1713—was easily the most prolific of all Quaker antislavery writers, with *Observations on the Inslaving, Importing and Purchasing of Negroes* (1759); *A Short Account of that Part of Africa Inhabited by the Negroes* (1762 and 1763); *A Caution and Warning to Great Britain and Her Colonies, in a Short Representation of the Calamitous State of the Enslaved Negroes in the British Dominions* (1766), and *Some Historical Account of Guinea; Its Situation, Produce and the General Disposition of Its Inhabitants* (1771). This last Alice Felt Tyler claimed John Wesley had plagiarized extensively for his *Thoughts on Slavery*.[114] The same poet who eulogized Sandiford and Lay had this to say about Woolman and Benezet:

> *Columbia use had sear'd to Negro-groans,*
> *And distant Europe heard not Afric's moans,*
> *Until thy meeker spirit,* Woolman, *rose,*
> *Aiming to soften rather than to oppose;*
> *And thou, lov'd* Benezet, *of kindred mind,*
> *The World thy country, and thy Friends mankind.*[115]

Nor did Benezet confine himself only to seeking justice for slaves. In 1750 he opened in his home an evening school for black children which he operated for twenty years. Any people who suffered at the hands of the English had a friend in Benezet. In a letter to John Smith in June 1758, he expressed his anger over the treatment of the Minisink Indians by both Quaker and other "back-settlers, . . . especially in the settlement of their lands, for which, I doubt, they have received little or no consideration." Five years later, in a long letter to Jeffrey Amherst, the Governor-General of British possessions in America, Benezet condemned the cruel treatment of Indians by government forces who were frustrated over their inability to defeat Pontiac. Just before Benezet died in 1784, he published anonymously *Some Observations on the Situation, Disposition, and Character of the Indian Natives of this Continent.*[116] To this Quaker, every human was a child of God.

The Quaker sense of freedom from bondage can be better understood if considered within the context of the sect's theology. Contrary to the Puritan idea of God as a separate being whom one addressed or confronted, Quakers perceived a spirit of God that lived within each human. To the Puritan, the spirit of God was imposed on the convert from without; to the Quaker it had always been there, needing only to be illuminated. The purpose of organized religion was to help each individual become aware of that spirit, to enlarge and share experiences through fellowship as the spirit moves one, and thus to lead a more godly and loving life. Since this spirit dwelt within every human, to place a person in bondage was to enslave the spirit of God. "The idea of property in man entailed the control of the slave as a moral being," Jenkins wrote, "and this was the basis of the evil to the Quaker who believed in the doctrine of the inner light whereby the individual and the deity came into direct moral contact." Moreover, because of this perception of God-in-man, Quakers saw no significance in skin color. The dominant European fought wars and enslaved heathens, they believed, because he was driven by greed and a lust for power, not because of deeply held prejudices against nonwhite races.[117] "The Colour of a Man avails nothing," Woolman wrote, "in Matters of Right and Equity." One of the pitfalls of the Quakers' simplicity of thought was an unshakable naïveté. That people who so persistently condemned the enslavement of Africans could at the same time be oblivious of the importance of color or race in that enslavement was indeed a strange paradox.

But, if the advanced position occupied by the Society of Friends made it the most equalitarian of all early American Christian churches, it also provided the most compelling example of the insidiousness and pervasiveness of institutional racism. George Keith may have been a pioneer in the early antislavery movement, but his views reflected the opinion of only a tiny minority of the Quaker population, and he paid dearly for them. Disowned in 1692 by Philadelphia Quakers who considered him an apostate, he and like-minded members founded the Keithian Friends' Monthly Meeting.[118] While the new group provided him with a platform for his views, it also served to alienate him even more from the main body of Quakers. Seven years after the publication of the first antislavery tract in American history, its author quit the only major denomination in the colonies to speak against slavery and joined the Anglican Church.[119]

Nor did some of the later advocates fare much better. While Hepburn's essay was merely ignored by most Quakers, Sandiford's brought down the wrath of wealthy Philadelphia Friends and led to his eventual exclusion from the church. Lay, whose personal eccentricities and four-foot-seven-inch hunchbacked figure made him easy to reject, was, like Sandiford, ostracized by the Quaker establishment; but, true to his inner light, he continued to consider himself a member. As for the general Quaker population, it was not until 1758 that the Philadelphia Yearly Meeting became the first to outlaw slavery within the church, a precedent followed over the next three decades by numerous regional yearly meetings. Finally, in 1775—eighty-seven years after the four Germantown Friends had drafted their protest—a group of Philadelphia Quakers formed the first secular antislavery organization in America, the Society for the Relief of Free Negroes Held in Bondage. With Pennsylvanians Woolman, Benezet, and John Churchman leading the way, Quaker officials began their antislavery drive by moving to erase all traces of bondage from within the Society of Friends.[120]

That a religious denomination so far ahead of its contemporaries could for well over a hundred years be racked with internal controversy over human bondage was as much a commentary on the nature of Anglo-American culture in the seventeenth and eighteenth centuries as it was on the Friends. For example, the issue of *gradual* emancipation that was to torment politicians and abolitionists from the Revolution to the Civil War was first proposed by the early Quakers. Despite his admonition to the New World missionaries, Fox "accepted Negro slavery as an institution that could be rationalized by the ancient dualisms of body and soul, matter and spirit," and in 1671, in a letter to the Governor of Barbados, he even suggested thirty years "as an appropriate term of service for Negroes." In his best Pauline posture, Fox went on to say that he and his associates, in "several meetings with [the slaves] in divers plantations," had "exhorted them to justice, sobriety, temperance, chastity, and piety, and to be subject to their masters and governors." The letter was subsequently printed in pamphlet form, with copies circulating throughout English North America. Four years later, William Penn proposed a policy for his planned colony, in which "blacks" who were imported as "servants" would be granted their freedom in fourteen years, "after which they would work their 'own' land in return for two-thirds of the produce for life."[121] He said nothing about the slaves already there.

Although Penn's proposal was never implemented, it is worth noting, as religion historian Lester B. Scherer pointed out, that it "did not provide for freedom in any sense that Anglo-Americans would have recognized." Fourteen years was twice the length of service required of most white indentured servants, making the plan a "system of serfdom that no one would have thought of offering to white people." By 1691, when a wealthy New

Yorker named Lewis Morris, who had made his fortune in Barbados, bequeathed one of his slaves to Penn, the colonizer of Pennsylvania was himself already a slaveowner. Thus did the founder of the Society of Friends and its most celebrated American advocate yield to the common purpose. Taking his cue from Fox and Penn, Keith recommended freeing slaves "after some reasonable time of moderate Service." By the beginning of the eighteenth century involuntary servitude had become, in Thomas E. Drake's words, "deeply woven into the pattern of American Quaker life." Indeed, the principle of gradualism was more "deeply woven" than anyone realized, as even Anthony Benezet suggested that all slaves should be freed "after a definite term of servitude." And none other than John Woolman—who one historian suggested "did not blame a person who retained [slaves] for good reason"—concluded his discussion with a slaveholding Quaker couple "in a good degree of satisfaction" because he ostensibly had persuaded them to free their slaves "after their decease."[122] To this paragon of Quaker virtue, gradual emancipation meant enslavement during the lifetime of the *owner*.

It was in the plantation colonies that Friends met their real challenge and, of course, where they were least effective. Southern Quakers began raising questions about slavery as early as the Virginia Yearly Meeting of 1722, but—aside from angering slaveholders—little was accomplished, and many who could no longer reconcile the existence of human bondage with their faith resolved the dilemma by simply leaving.[123] By the time of the independence movement, slavery in the plantation colonies was completely institutionalized. In 1773, Virginia Quakers, making what for the South was certainly a radical proposal, called for all slaves born after a certain date to be emancipated at the ages of eighteen and twenty-one, females and males, respectively. Nothing came of the suggestion, of course, but its terms revealed the pervasiveness of the belief in gradualism and that, whatever peaceful method was devised, the pace of emancipation would be agonizingly slow. It had been a century since Fox and Penn had offered their respective thirty- and fourteen-year proposals, but the idea of a "grace period" remained popular even among people as committed to equality before God as the Quakers. In North Carolina, the substantial Quaker population continued to devise ways of freeing slaves—for example, purchasing and manumitting them—well into the nineteenth century, but the hardening southern attitude toward emancipation made these efforts increasingly ineffective, and in any event the number of bondsmen who won their freedom this way was always a very small fraction of the total slave population.[124] There were many Christians—and not all of them Quakers—who recognized human bondage as a horrible sin, but the idea of universal and immediate emancipation was still inconceivable to white Americans of virtually every religious persuasion.

As impressive as were the arguments of men like Edmundson, Keith, Woolman, and Benezet and the strong antislavery policies of some of the yearly meetings, a careful examination of the Quaker position reveals at least three basic contradictions that illuminate the pervasiveness of institutional racism within the society. To begin with, many of the earliest critics condemned the slave *trade* rather than slavery itself. For example, the pious German, Swiss, and Dutch Quakers of Germantown began their protest with a remonstrance "against the traffick of mens-body" and insisted that a good Christian at least should refuse to purchase slaves.[125] The antislavery significance of the document—which had been submitted by Garret Henderich, Derick op de Graeff, Francis Daniel Pastorious, and Abram op de Graeff—was also diminished by the failures of the monthly meeting in nearby Dublin and the subsequent regional quarterly and yearly meetings to endorse it. It was clearly a minority position. In fact, the protest was not printed and was quickly forgotten until it was discovered 156 years later tucked away among the records of the Philadelphia Yearly Meeting (Orthodox) and printed in an 1844 edition of *Friends.* Historians have since cited it for being the *first* document of its kind, not for being the most important. Similarly, in a letter made public in 1754 by the Philadelphia Yearly Meeting, Benezet noted that it had "frequently been the concern of our Yearly Meeting, to testify their uneasiness and disunity with the importation and purchasing of negroes and other slaves."[126] In other words, it was the business of buying and selling slaves—not owning them—that was the greatest evil.

The Quakers were not the only ones who appeared to be more concerned with the slave trade than with slavery itself. The later and more widely publicized political protests over the trade came, for the most part, not from critics of slavery's inhumanity but from critics of its dangers, that is, southern colonists who feared the increasing likelihood of uprisings inherent in large concentrations of black people. Southerners had not forgotten the Stono rebellion of 1739 near Charleston, where thirty whites and forty-four blacks had died, the greatest slave insurrection of the colonial era. This same fear was a major element in the independence movement, when colonial legislatures complained about earlier British rejections of their attempts to limit the importation of Africans. The Whig party had controlled Parliament during most of the time between 1689 and 1760 and, because of its close ties to London's commercial interests, had pressed for laws that promoted the welfare of the merchant class.[127] Yielding to the pressures of the highly profitable British trading companies, the Parliament managed to keep alive an issue that ultimately worked its way into the drafting of the Declaration of Independence in 1776 and the debates at the Constitutional Convention in Philadelphia, where slaveowners and slave-trading interests extracted a guarantee that the trade would not be interfered with for twenty years. The racist significance of this entire matter, of course, was its exclusive concern for the safety of the white population and its utter lack of concern for the welfare of the enslaved, an aspect of the situation that implicated even the benevolent Friends.

Second, for most of the colonial period the Society of Friends, despite its intrinsic antipathy to bondage, did not make a serious effort to win slaves to the faith. There were some aggressive missionaries among the brethren, but it is rather paradoxical that Quaker missionary zeal did not match Quaker antislavery zeal. Church leaders finally made a move in this direction in 1756, but the "exclusiveness of the Society, reinforced by the rigorous obligations of membership," David Brion Davis noted, "made it difficult [for Quakers] to consider bondsmen as spiritual equals." While Davis may have been endorsing the suggestion that Quaker theology was simply incompatible with the African temperament, the fact that more than a few black Jamaicans joined the faith would appear to belie that contention. If Quaker missionaries did not aggressively pursue black converts, that deficiency was magnified by the fact that the few blacks who were members were only grudgingly admitted by the yearly meetings. When abolitionists, in a move designed to force churches to make a commitment, asked black worshippers to refuse to sit in segregated pews, two members of a Quaker congregation stopped attending services because they objected to sitting in the back of the church and, in their words, to being "treated with contempt."

It is easy to understand why blacks were not attracted to Quaker theology or the Quaker style of worship, but the problem was compounded by the Quaker inability to understand what one historian called the anthropological principle of "cultural complexity," a deficiency that affected relations with Indians as well. Appearing to apply the simple solution to everything, Quakers, according to Roy Harvey Pearce, offered the Indians love, not dogma or ritual. Needless to say, it did not take the Indians long to discover that they could enjoy that sort of thing without converting. If that was all there was to salvation, they must have thought, why bother? Like Africans, Asians, and almost all other polytheistic peoples, Indians believed that rites and rituals were the essence of religion. "Indian converts were virtually non-existent," Pearce argued, "since the savage knew that religion meant ceremony and ritual, and since Quakers offered only the law which God had placed in the heart."[128] Quaker theology was, in many ways, unlike that of any other Christian denomination; but like all the others, it was inherently incapable of accommodating the heathen's culture. When one believed that Christianity was the only way to eternal life, then one also believed that the Christian way was the only way of living.

Finally, and perhaps most significant, was what is probably uncharitably called the selfish reason for the Quaker position. It seems that for almost everyone the worst thing about slavery—from George Fox, who in 1671 called upon Friends in Barbados to be kind and generous to their slaves because "an account will be required by him who comes to judge both quick and dead, at the great day of judgment,"[129] to the radical Friends who saw the American Civil War as "God's punishment of a slaveholding nation"[130]—was that slaveholders were committing a *sin*, and any person who did not speak against bondage was no less guilty in the eyes of God. Long before other Christians were to take such a position, William Edmundson stood first "in Britain's empire to proclaim slavery a sin."[131] By the 1730s, many Friends had taken up the call. For example, Benjamin Lay, one of the Quaker writers whom William Sumner Jenkins called pioneers of the antislavery crusade, described bondage as a "Hellish Practice," a "filthy sin," the "Capital Sin," and "the Greatest Sin in the World."[132] Like an assailant who needed to be saved from his anger, the slaveholder was a sinner who must be rescued from his sin. No one gave a great deal of thought to rescuing the slaves from the slaveholder's sin.

It was a condition that afflicted the noblest of them all. Both Benezet and Woolman opposed slavery because they were against "all worldliness and spiritual decline," Richard Bauman wrote.[133] For example, in his letter to the Philadelphia Yearly Meeting in 1754, Benezet argued that tolerating slavery "draws down the displeasure of heaven."[134] Similarly, writing to Samuel Fothergill in October 1774, he pointed out the need to protect the "rising generation" of fellow Quakers from "being defiled with this mighty evil." It seems almost an embarrassment to suggest that Woolman, whom Thomas E. Drake called "the greatest Quaker of the eighteenth century and perhaps the most Christlike individual that Quakerism has ever produced," was bothered by the slave trade "not so much because of the hardships upon the Negroes, but because of the effects upon their masters." This from the person who was to become, in Drake's words, "the channel through which the antislavery impulse flowed into the conscience of the Society of Friends in America." In 1770, two years before his death, Woolman warned that God would unleash his wrath on those Friends who refused to give up their slaves. Although he was largely unsuccessful in actually persuading masters to free their bondsmen, he nonetheless felt redeemed for his efforts. After pleading with several slaveholding Quakers and explaining "the exercise I was under; . . . I found myself discharged from a heavy burden." Later, following a second visit to Quaker slaveowners in which he was accompanied by Churchman, Woolman claimed to have found "inward satisfaction."[135] To feel contentment for having tried with no concomitant remorse for having failed suggested a larger concern for one's own salvation than for the welfare of the enslaved. Similarly, those Friends in Virginia and North Carolina who resolved their inability to accept slavery by simply leaving probably did wonders for their own consciences.

Needless to say, what was glaringly absent from most of these expressions on the sinfulness of owning slaves was a concern for the suffering of the enslaved. If slavery was an abomination for the slaveholder, *what was it for the slave?* Bondage was a horrible violation of the humanity of what would ultimately be an estimated ten million Africans and their descendants, but these pious spokesmen for Christ saw it mainly as a collective sin that white society must exorcise in order to avoid God's wrath. In other words, they saw *themselves* as victims. In letters to John and Henry Gurney, Granville Sharp, and Richard Shackleton, written between January and June of 1772, Benezet made almost identical references to the suffering of the slaves' "oppressors," but expressed no concern for the suffering of the oppressed.[136] Such Christian critics were, as it happened, little different from the later abolitionists who called for the purging of slavery by demanding the expulsion of the southern states from the Union. This might have done wonders for the guilt-ridden. It would have done nothing for the slaves. By the nineteenth century, the Quaker position began moving, ever so slowly, closer to a genuine concern for the welfare of the enslaved. For instance, Samuel Janney of Virginia condemned slavery because "it degrades men by regarding them as property, and not only as property, but *chattels personal.*"[137] Similarly, John Parrish published *Remarks on the Slavery of the Black People* (1806), a surprisingly equalitarian plea for emancipation with no self-serving lament about the sins of slaveholders or of those who tolerated slaveholders.[138]

But old habits die hard. Three years before the Civil War, the Yearly Meeting of the Quakers of the northeast United States, while addressing the condition of the slaves, began its forty-eight-page pamphlet *The Appeal . . . on Behalf of the Coloured Races* with a protracted description of divine retribution and how God punishes nations for their sins. "The annals of those that have preceded us furnish abundant evidence that national sins have incurred national calamities," the delegates warned, and those nations "have sunk into moral and political degradation, and their very existence has been blotted out from the earth." It needs to be remembered that the Quakers, initially decades ahead of all Christian denominations in their antislavery policies, never became major participants in the religious wing of nineteenth-century abolitionism. Indeed, some Indiana Quakers were so conservative that they succeeded in driving Levi Coffin—the celebrated "President of the Underground Railroad"—and Charles Osborn into organizing a separate Yearly Meeting. Even the relatively liberal Hicksite Quakers forced from their ranks abolitionist members who subsequently formed the Congregational or Progressive Friends, a movement that began in Indiana but, like the Coffin-Osborn defection, eventually spread across the Midwest and into Pennsylvania. By the election of 1860, most Quakers supported antislavery candidates and issues but few were politically active.[139]

It may be unfair to single out the Quakers for being more concerned with their own salvation than with the condition of the slave, especially since the save-your-own-skin attitude was an affliction endemic to virtually every religious group that spoke out against slavery. But the Quakers are easy targets because everyone has come to expect more from them. From the very beginning, the Society of Friends held the advanced position in the religious war against bondage, and its spokesmen were at least half a century ahead of all other Christian leaders. When the standard is seen to be less than perfect, everyone who is measured against it is diminished. While it is certainly an unfortunate commentary on the Quakers that they were too often concerned only with themselves and the punishment that God would impose on them for holding slaves or allowing others to do so, it is an even more unfortunate commentary on all of the other Christian groups of colonial America that they were so far behind the Quakers.

It also needs to be reiterated that Quaker efforts against slavery were initially directed against slaveholding members of the church. It was an excruciatingly slow struggle in the North as well as the South; but, having "won the battles within their own Society" by 1783, the Quakers believed that they were also best qualified to "campaign against slavery in the outside world," a belief strewn with racist pitfalls. For example, because it was against the law to liberate a slave without meeting strict conditions, the so-called North Carolina plan did not call for the legal emancipation of slaves but rather established a class of Quaker slaveholders who granted "virtual freedom" to those whom they had purchased. From a strictly pragmatic point of view, the plan made sense. The black person remained technically a slave, but he enjoyed most of the rights and privileges of any free black. Unfortunately, the fear that state authorities might ignore the technicality persuaded some slaves who had been "freed" under this procedure to run away, often leaving behind homes and farms. This, in turn, created a situation in which Quakers elsewhere were something less than sympathetic when it came to emancipation. In 1831 the legislatures of Indiana and Illinois, fearing the immigration of large numbers of recently freed slaves, passed laws against the entry of any black person whose freedom had been won in this manner. Quakers in both states were among the supporters of the laws.[140]

EIGHT PROFIT OVER PIETY: SLAVERY AND SCHISM

I urge you, brothers, to watch out for those who cause divisions and put obstacles in your way that are contrary to the teaching you have learned. Keep away from them. For such people are not serving our Lord Christ, but their own appetites. By smooth talk and flattery they deceive the minds of naïve people. Everyone has heard about your obedience, so I am full of joy over you; but I want you to be wise about what is good, and innocent about what is evil.

ROMANS 16:17–19

I appeal to you, brothers, in the name of our Lord Jesus Christ, that all of you agree with one another so that there may be no divisions among you and that you may be perfectly united in mind and thought.

1 CORINTHIANS 1:10

The Church as Moral Agent

If there was one place in antebellum American religion where the race issue opened wounds that did not heal for decades—and, in some respects, still have not healed—it was in the churches. For the great debate eventually led to the sectional divisions of the three mainline Protestant churches: the Presbyterians (1837), Methodists (1844), and Baptists (1845). From the liberal afterglow of the American Revolution to the thunder of cannons at Fort Sumter—from the Confederation to the Confederacy—the leaders of these denominations agonized over human bondage and its place in a Christian society. Nor did the controversy move exclusively along geographic lines. Denouncing abolitionism's threat to ecclesiastical unity, conservative northern clergymen probably had more in common with their southern counterparts than they had with their liberal northern brethren.[1] Opinion within one denomination could be spread across a wide continuum. Of course, by insisting on denominational unity, conservative Northerners were, in effect, advocating submission to proslavery interests, because unity could not be ensured any other way.

To the white Southerner, slavery simply was not negotiable. Only in the South, where there were few counterbalancing liberal clergymen, was opinion relatively uniform, especially after 1831, when the Nat Turner uprising chilled all discussion of freedom for slaves. Since the Congregational and Unitarian churches did not have significant southern constituencies, their hierarchies remained intact, eventually producing some of the North's leading abolitionists, and sweeping along many otherwise indifferent preachers and lay persons.[2]

For two centuries the enslavement of Africans had been a fundamental constituent of the status quo, and religious leaders were, for the most part, conservatives who did not want to disturb convention. But the antislavery clergy refused to be silenced. Accordingly, the emerging sectional conflict found one of its earliest platforms in the pulpits of America; it was through the mainline denominations that Southerners first acted on their secessionist impulses. The division of the churches was, in fact, a harbinger to the division of the states. "As the crisis grew," one historian wrote, "there was a striking congruency between earlier arguments for splitting the churches and those for breaking the federal Union."[3] As with the nation itself, it was *secession*, not expulsion, that produced the schisms; for both proslavery preacher and slaveholding politician, the solution to the Great Problem was simply to take a walk.[4]

But that did not occur without a great deal of soul-searching acrimony and self-serving rationalization. For centuries Christians had quarreled over everything else. Why should slavery have been any different? In the end, the ability of the Protestant churches to agree over any controversial issue, assuming their leaders and members were so inclined, was seriously diminished by two fundamental conditions. The first was the underlying contradiction between, on the one hand, a church as a collectivist institution, and, on the other, a congregation made up of individuals whose participation was voluntary. Protestantism in the United States never followed the European pattern of monolithic state-supported systems. When the freedom of choice enjoyed by Americans in secular life was applied to already divided religious institutions, the result was simply more division.[5] "Dissenters from the majority opinion, viewing the church as a free agency, which they have every right to leave, in the face of institutional pressure will simply leave," religion historian George Marsden wrote. "Preaching and propaganda may, of course, alter social mores; but the American denominations as institutions lack any power to effect social revolution." In the early nineteenth century, another writer noted, "the correction of social problems had been considered less important than the conversion of individuals," an attitude that accounted for the widespread belief among many Protestants that antislavery was not a religious issue. A logical corollary of this attitude was the prevailing assumption that, since every group consisted of individuals, once enough people made conscious decisions to lead Christian lives, the resolution of social problems would follow naturally. The mission of evangelical Christianity was "to reform individuals, not society, although society would benefit indirectly from the reformation of individual conduct."[6] When conservative preachers argued that the best way to abolish slavery was to instill Christian values into the individual, they assumed that converting *individuals* would transform *groups*.

By the time of the Civil War, however, an increasing number of northern Protestant clergymen began to address directly the idea that, while saving souls was still—and would always be—their primary objective, they also had a duty to work for justice for oppressed peoples. The difficulty did not arise from the Christian's emerging recognition of that duty but from his failure to realize that only individuals can act morally. Terms like "collective morality" may be useful abstractions, but they do not exist in reality; the members of a group do not fuse their minds into a single consciousness. "Though it is very important for man as an individual that his religion should be true, that is not the case for society," Tocqueville observed in 1835. "Society has nothing to fear or hope from another life." Individuals go to heaven or hell, not congregations. Thus, while an individual has a conscience and can make personal ethical judgments, Reinhold Niebuhr argued in *Moral Man and Immoral Society* (1932), a group is a political entity and is inherently incapable of putting someone else's interests above its own. According to Kyle Haselden, Niebuhr believed that it was difficult, if not impossible, "for human societies and social groups to act on the basis of a high and radical morality," and that it was easy for "the individual Christian to exempt himself from all sense of personal responsibility for the actions of his group and from his involvement in its failings and to do so on the basis of what he considers to be the prior claims of his religion and by the substituting of personal piety for social justice." Accordingly, as small groups grew into large ones, "Niebuhr saw human relations becoming increasingly ruthless."[7] Individual ministers and church members could make speeches, sign petitions, and join movements calling for the abolition of slavery; but, as constituents of a collective, they were powerless against the vested interests of the institution.

The second obstacle to effective church opposition to slavery lay in the relatively secular independence of each denomination and the absence of an established church whose leaders did not serve at the sufferance of the parishioners, a condition that Frances Trollope found quite lamentable. "As there is no legal and fixed provision for the clergy," the captious English visitor wrote in 1832, "it is hardly surprising that their services are confined to those who can pay them." Trollope believed that the church—like the schools, the courts, the military, or any public institution—served the general good and therefore should be supported by the government.

Similarly, Harriet Martineau was convinced that the American clergymen's financial dependence on sympathetic congregations made ministers "the most backward and timid class in society." Spending most of his time "in the study of moral relations," who else more than a man of God, she asked in 1837, should not be "blinded by life-long custom and prejudice [or] pecuniary interest"? When a preacher draws his salary from the state, as was the case in most European countries, he can speak honestly against what he perceives as a popular evil because he does not have to worry about alienating parishioners. But as long as "the living of the clergy depends on the opinion of those whom they serve," they will inevitably "undergo a perversion of views about the nature of their pastoral office." Except for a few Presbyterians and "some professors at Oberlin Institute," Martineau added, the vast majority of Protestant clergymen are "as fierce as the slaveholders against abolitionists." Even the Unitarians, who make a lot of noise about freedom and justice, leave it "to the laity to carry out the first pressing moral reform of the age." Following a journey through the eastern and southern states after the Civil War, Scottish visitor David Macrae made the same observation as Trollope and Martineau, though in somewhat more colorful language. The dependence of ministers on the people, he wrote in 1870, "tends to make dumb dogs of many who would like to bark, and who see plenty to bark at," but who do not have the courage to offend the people who pay their wages.[8] All three critics were apparently oblivious of the fact that the European clergyman was no more independent than the American; he just had to avoid offending a different constituency.

This clerical impotence was magnified by the fact that most Protestant denominations, by their very nature, were simply "too democratic for effective social action."[9] The legacy of the Revolution and the spirit of the Declaration of Independence reached into every aspect of life, nurturing the cult of the individual and negating any collective effort that required group discipline. In a nonsectarian society committed to the separation of church and state and to such noble principles as justice and liberty, no church, however dogmatic and well established, could invoke the law to compel adherence to its doctrines. It was Tocqueville's opinion that while Catholicism demanded obedience and Protestantism encouraged independence, neither was especially compatible with equality. Hierarchical sects like the Episcopalians, Methodists, Catholics, and to a lesser extent Presbyterians could, raising the threat of expulsion, impose internal sanctions against recalcitrant members. But apparently that possibility did not discourage many people from following their personal inclinations, and the leaders of these denominations, perhaps fearful of the probable consequences, looked for excuses to avoid enforcing rules against slavery.

Among churches organized under the congregational system—such as Congregationalists, Baptists, Disciples of Christ, Unitarians, and Universalists—there was no central church government whatever to enforce a common discipline. It was here, paradoxically, that some of the most outspoken clerical abolitionists preached, making it easy to conclude that any ecclesiastical hierarchy would have been oppressive.

Finally, most of the several interdenominational groups organized and supported by the churches were similarly ineffective. The American Missionary Association, formed in 1846 by northern Protestants who were unhappy with both the general apathy toward slavery of denominational leaders and the shrill anti-Christian arguments of some abolitionists, made no secret of its commitment to the antislavery cause. But national organizations like the American Bible Society, the American Tract Society, and the American Home Missionary Society scrupulously avoided any actions that might offend the members of any of its constituent denominations. In what was a typical rationalization, spokesmen for the American Bible Society maintained that their primary mission was to "circulate the Bible, not to conduct campaigns to correct evil laws"; while the American Tract Society, in thousands of books and tracts, condemned every sin imaginable—except slaveholding.[10]

The upshot was a Christian church that, ultimately, did not play a major role in the cause of human equality and in which sectional differences among the denominations were not as great as one would suppose. In the eighteenth century, defenders of slavery among men of the cloth were far more numerous than opponents. "For every John Wesley who was critical," David M. Reimers wrote, "there were several George Whitefields who considered slavery a blessing." That church leaders in the slaveholding states were outspoken defenders of bondage should surprise no one. Commenting on the sermons she had heard, Martineau reported that, with only one exception, southern preachers, some of whom were themselves slaveowners, never referred to the "grand truths of religion, or principles of morals." Such things as "striving after perfection, mutual justice and charity, and christian liberty" were scrupulously avoided by ministers who, on the other hand, took advantage of every opportunity to find "express sanctions of slavery in the Bible." Throughout the antebellum era—and afterwards—the racial paranoia of white Southerners was evident everywhere. "Scratch a reformer and you'll find an abolitionist," they liked to say. Traveling through the South in the 1840s, English visitor Ebenezer Davies was incredulous when he learned of the expunging from the catalogue of the American Sunday-School Union of a painting entitled *Jacob and His Sons* because, "in reprehending the sale of Joseph to the merchants, it reflected upon the *internal* slave trade." Southern Protestant clergymen were virtually unanimous in their support of the Confederate war effort.

After the war the southern churches, continuing the legacy of slavery, were among the first institutions to call for the separation of the races; by the twentieth century they had become bastions of segregation. With no desire to intrude into places where they were not welcome, most black Southerners were more comfortable in their own congregations. During the years 1889–1915 virtually every southern Protestant denomination "was active in missionary labors among Negroes," but because of the postwar exclusion of blacks from white churches and the active recruitment by southern black churches, the number of people influenced by this effort was "minuscule."[11]

This was to be expected in a region that for two centuries had exploited human slavery for profit. What was not expected was the dismal record of the Protestant churches in free states. A great deal has been said and written over the years about the role of Christianity in the antislavery movement. In particular, the findings of Gilbert H. Barnes and Dwight L. Dumond in the 1930s went a long way to attempt to rescue the abolitionism story from the William Lloyd Garrison–James G. Birney "libel" that the Protestant churches had been "bulwarks" of slavery.[12] But while the antislavery movement owed much of its impetus to the efforts of individuals like former evangelist Theodore Dwight Weld, Presbyterians Charles Grandison Finney and Henry Ward Beecher (who later assumed the pulpit of a Congregational church), the Quaker sisters Sarah and Angelina Grimké, and the Presbyterian brothers Arthur and Lewis Tappan, the *institutional* involvement of northern denominations and congregations was virtually nonexistent. It is not an exaggeration to assert that the clergyman or church member who marched with the abolitionists did so in spite of his denominational connection, not because of it.[13]

The fact was dramatically underscored by the emergence of antislavery splinter groups that broke away from the mainline churches. The presence in the northern states of *only* the Wesleyan Methodists, the American Free Baptist Mission Society, the Free Presbyterians, the Franckean Evangelical Lutheran Synod, the Indiana Yearly Meeting of Anti-Slavery Friends, and the Progressive Friends—each representing just a tiny fraction of its parent sect—was an embarrassing reminder of how many churches did *not* take an official position against human bondage. The church "does not lead public opinion on such matters as the slavery issue," William Warren Sweet observed, "but rather, tends to follow public opinion." At the adoption of the Federal Constitution in 1787, the three mainline denominations took emphatic stands against bondage. By the Civil War, Sweet wrote in another book, all three had made 180-degree turns and had divided geographically. The inability—or refusal—of the Protestant churches in antebellum America to come to terms with the "racial factor," C. C. Goen lamented in *Broken Churches, Broken Nation* (1985), "has been a single constant in the American experience."[14] It is difficult to avoid the conclusion that Garrison and Birney were more than half right.

Nowhere was this inability more conspicuous than in the churches' support of the movement to colonize free black people somewhere outside of the United States, a movement that began after the War of 1812; received a new breath of life from a President—Abraham Lincoln—who considered it a viable solution to mass emancipation; and on the eve of the twentieth century was still considered by some discouraged black people as the only realistic course of action.[15] While the American Colonization Society was founded in 1817 as a secular organization and included among its members and supporters some of the most visible political figures in the United States—Henry Clay, John Randolph of Roanoke, Andrew Jackson, William Crawford—it quickly drew the endorsements of every mainline Protestant denomination. Jedidiah Morse, an eminent New England Congregationalist, was one of the first clergymen to speak out in behalf of colonization.[16]

Because some people exalted it as a way out of the slavery crisis, colonization even won the early support of Garrison and several other prominent abolitionists. But when the abolitionists subsequently repudiated the ACS as a racist organization, which was primarily interested in making slavery more secure by getting rid of potentially troublesome free black people, the churches continued to campaign vigorously for the idea, not because of any presumed emancipationist or humanitarian purpose but because of the opportunity that colonization ostensibly created for fulfilling Christ's mandate to "teach all nations." What better way was there to introduce the gospel to Africa than with civilized and Christianized free black Americans, who would not only carry the word but would also serve as role models for the natives? The first black Americans to leave would be the vanguard of a mission to millions. If there had been any antislavery sentiment in the Protestant support of colonization, it was quickly displaced by a desire to evangelize the world.

The opportunity was so attractive that one could argue it had been foreordained, that God had planned the European enslavement of Africans to provide a conduit to the heathen masses of Africa. In a speech before the Kentucky Colonization Society, Henry Clay made frequent references to God and to the distribution of the races on different continents.[17] Speaking in 1832 to the Vermont Colonization Society in Montpelier, John Kendrick Converse, pastor of the First Congregational Church of Burlington, claimed that the book of Exodus was a blueprint for colonization. In 1851, traveler Fredrika Bremer, writing to the Queen Dowager of Denmark, insisted that the opportunity to evangelize Africa was the primary reason so many American clergymen supported colonization.[18]

But while missionary-minded Protestants supported the effort with their sermons, they did not support it with their money. To send a significant number of black people to Africa would have required a far greater financial commitment than anyone was willing to make. The Fifth Census (1830) counted 320,000 free black people in the United States. If anyone wanted an object lesson on the ineffectiveness of colonization he needed only to note that in the twenty-five years from the founding of Liberia to conferring of full independence, a mere 12,000 emigrants had moved under the auspices of the society. Considering the time and money spent on the program—not to mention the energy—it had not been a bargain.

"Old" and "New" Presbyterians

As it happened, the Presbyterian division of 1837 into New School and Old School factions was the only one of the mainline schisms that was not *primarily* the result of disagreement over slavery and, therefore, did not produce the usual sectional alignment until some years later. From the very beginning of the debate over slavery in the eighteenth century, the polarization of opinion among Presbyterians was considerably less acute then it was among Methodists and Baptists. Like most mainline Protestants, individual Presbyterians initially took enthusiastic but sometimes ambivalent stands against both slavery and the mistreatment of Indians. Inspired by the example of John Eliot in Massachusetts and swept up by the spiritual fervor of the Great Awakening, David Brainerd, after being expelled from Yale because of his excessive religious enthusiasm as the leader of the New Light students, began in 1743 what he hoped would be a long and productive mission as pastor to the Mahican Indians in Kaunameek, New York, and the Delaware Indians in Pennsylvania and New Jersey. Unfortunately, the Indians did not appear to be very interested. Perplexed by the Judeo-Christian concept of monotheism, they saw no reason to adopt a new god when theirs served them very well. Brainerd, a typical Protestant missionary, thought that all he had to do was *tell* the infidels what to believe, but his only significant accomplishment was the baptism of thirty-eight converts at Crossweeksung, New Jersey. Whereas Eliot's mission to the Indians a century earlier had lasted for four decades, Brainerd's ended after only four years. He died in 1747 at age twenty-nine, convinced that he had failed.[19] But, as sometimes happens with individuals who live short but deeply committed lives, Brainerd's influence reached far beyond his own lifetime. For years afterward, readers of Jonathan Edwards's "The Life of David Brainerd" were inspired to mission work by the example of this young Presbyterian.[20]

While Brainerd labored to bring the gospel to Indians, one of the first prominent Presbyterians to advocate the conversion of African slaves was Samuel Davies, whom Andrew E. Murray, the leading chronicler of the denomination's racial history, called "the evangelist who laid the foundations of Presbyterianism in Virginia." But Davies's time in the mission field was even briefer than Brainerd's. Since he worked among blacks for only a year and a half, in 1756–57, his effort was little more than a momentary outreach from his primary ministry to white settlers. Referring to Africans as "stupid despised black Creatures," Davies never advocated emancipation or, for that matter, any other program to improve their quality of life. When, in 1787, Samuel Stanhope Smith, minister and president of Princeton, calmly explained in the first edition of his *An Essay on the Causes of the Variety of Complexion and Figure in the Human Species* how the differences among races should be perceived as part of God's great plan, he expressed an opinion shared by many of his clerical and lay brethren.[21] Unlike the later angry replies to abolitionists, Smith's statement was not a polemical argument but a simple, straightforward statement that barely mentioned slavery. Nevertheless, Presbyterian ambivalence began to emerge almost immediately. In the same year, spokesmen for the Synod of New York and Philadelphia supported "the general principles in favour of universal liberty that prevail in America, and the interest which many of the states have taken in promoting the abolition of slavery." The synod did not, however, call for immediate emancipation, and it agreed that whatever was done must be "consistent with the interests of the state of civil society," that is, emancipation must be gradual and not disruptive.[22] Subsequent sessions of the Presbyterian General Assembly—the church's national governing body, which had grown out of the New York and Philadelphia Synod—repeated the call, climaxing with its ringing declaration of 1818:

> We consider the voluntary enslaving of one part of the human race by another, as a gross violation of the most precious and sacred rights of human nature; as utterly inconsistent with the law of God, which requires us to love our neighbor as ourselves; and as totally irreconcilable with the spirit and principles of the Gospel of Christ, which enjoins that "All things whatsoever ye would that men should do to you, do ye even so to them."[23]

As the *ne plus ultra* of the Presbyterian church's stand against bondage, it sounded unequivocal, but, as in 1787, its sponsors hedged right from the beginning. Though the General Assembly published its "Expression of

Views" condemning slavery, it did not specifically call for slaveholding members to emancipate their bondsmen. And church officials continued to take refuge behind the *gradualism* argument when they cautioned that emancipation should not proceed without regard "to the public welfare." Of course, the bondsman's welfare was never discussed and the General Assembly did not again mention slavery for seventeen years.[24]

Nowhere was Presbyterian equivocation more dramatically revealed than in its reactions to the activities of George Bourne, almost certainly the church's most virulent critic of slavery. After studying at Homerton Academy in London, Bourne emigrated to the United States in 1805 and became co-publisher of the Baltimore *Evening Post,* where, through his editorials, he frequently criticized the Governor of Maryland. Since he had thus cultivated an appetite for controversy, it should not have been surprising that, following his ordination in 1812 as pastor of the South River Church in the Lexington Presbytery, Virginia, he lost no time in angering many people by calling for the *immediate* emancipation of the slaves, an argument that he circulated four years later with the publication of his strident *The Book and Slavery Irreconcilable, with Animadversions Upon Dr. Smith's Philosophy.* "Moderation against sin is an absurdity," Bourne reasoned. "Can any man cojoin stealing and honesty, or dare he admonish a headstrong transgressor partially to desist from his ungodly practices." There is no such thing as a half-sin. If it is not possible to break into a house or rob a person with moderation, he asked, "with what moderation can you break up a whole country, can you pillage and destroy a whole nation?"

Not even the most outspoken Quakers of the seventeenth and eighteenth centuries had taken such a resolute position. Though he was widely known and highly regarded as a preacher, Bourne's vocal and uncompromising opposition to slavery quickly incurred the wrath of his Virginia brethren and eventually led to his deposal from the pulpit, an ejection that, paradoxically, was ratified by the same General Assembly of 1818 whose statement condemning slavery was the high-water mark of the Presbyterian church's institutional stance against bondage. There has never been an adequate explanation of this contradiction and, as Murray suggested in his study for the Presbyterian Historical Society, it would be safe to conclude that the General Assembly of 1818 probably was not the equalitarian body that it has sometimes been made out to be. In any case, Bourne, no longer subject to institutional restraints, devoted all of his energies to the emerging antislavery cause, becoming "a powerful force in the northern abolitionist crusade of the 1830's" and advocating immediate emancipation long before William Lloyd Garrison and other militant abolitionists took up the banner.[25]

But few Presbyterians followed Bourne. The "rise of immediatism" was, as one historian noted, "a religious crusade, [but] it was not a church movement." Ministers who criticized slavery were a small minority and few of their congregations supported them. There were several Presbyterian centers of strong antislavery sentiment—especially in upstate New York—but for the most part abolitionism did not enlist a large number of church members and, in time, the leadership withdrew into the safety of evasion and neutrality. Despite the General Assembly's condemnation of bondage in 1818, southern ministers gradually acquired control of the national leadership, and one of their most eminent clerics, James Henley Thornwell, president of South Carolina College and editor of the *Southern Presbyterian Review*, became, in Alice Felt Tyler's words, "the real leader of American Presbyterianism." By 1845, spokesmen for the Old School were proclaiming that slavery "under the circumstances which it is found in the Southern portion of this country is no bar to Christian communion." The domination of the national leadership by Southerners may have been the reason one northern Old School critic of slavery chose to hide behind a pseudonym. In 1856, "Smectymnuus" published a forty-four-page pamphlet, *Slavery and the Church*, that consisted of three letters refuting the biblical proslavery arguments of two of his Old School colleagues.[26] The emergence of the "Old" and "New" schools had been, in part, a response to the Presbyterian-Congregational Plan of Union of 1801, a call for interdenominational cooperation that conservative Presbyterians considered a serious breach of faith. Smectymnuus would not have found much agreement here.

But anyone who expected the supposedly more liberal New School to take a strong stand against slavery was in for a surprise. It was the liberals who in 1826 organized the joint American Home Mission Society, and its members, like the colonial missionaries who had argued against emancipating baptized slaves, avoided saying anything that would offend the master for fear of losing access to his bondsmen. Because of the inclusion of some southern presbyteries that had joined for doctrinal reasons, the New School General Assembly voted in 1843 to table all discussion on slavery: any vote, no matter which way it went, would be so close that a large minority of the membership would be alienated. It was not until 1850, thirteen years after the Old School–New School division, that the northern New School finally resolved that slavery was "intrinsically an . . . oppressive system opposed to the proscriptions of the law of God." But it was still a minority position among all northern Presbyterians. Two years later professors at Princeton joined ranks with southern ministers to declare, through the columns of the *New York Observer*, that the doctrine of *predestination*, in which "certain men were elected to be saved and others to be damned," also determined who would be masters and servants.[27] Considering the importance of the Calvinist tradition in Protestant theology, it is surprising that someone had not thought of that argument sooner.

While George Bourne personified the extreme antislavery faction in the Presbyterian Church, Charles Colcock Jones exemplified the southern Presbyterian compromise with the emerging power of the cotton kingdom. In an 1829 letter to his fiancée written while he was in the North studying for the ministry, Jones had condemned slavery as a "violation of all the Laws of God and man," a "complete annihilation of justice," and an "inhuman abuse of power" that was "fearful in the extreme." But, returning to the South, he soon realized that he could never maintain such a view publicly. The only realistic option for a Christian minister, he concluded, was to bring the faith to as many blacks as possible. Originally, "the problem had been slavery and the solution, emancipation," Donald G. Mathews wrote, "but prudence and piety altered his goal," and now his objective was "not to challenge social systems but to transform individuals."[28]

It was a fast change of heart. In 1832, Jones, while still in his twenties, resigned the comfortable pastorate of the First Presbyterian Church in Savannah to devote himself to religious education for slaves in Liberty County, where he had been raised and where, except for three years as a professor at Columbia Theological Seminary, he spent most of the next thirty years, earning the title "missionary to slaves." Reporting two years later to the Synod of South Carolina and Georgia, Jones bravely repeated the familiar antislavery stricture that the white race first reduced the slave to ignorance and then condemned him for being ignorant. The solution, he added, was education *and* conversion, a course of action that accommodated the bondsmen's status because it enabled the missionary to "separate entirely their *moral* and their *civil* condition."[29] Thus in only five years he had swung 180 degrees from the view he had first expressed to his fiancée.

Jones also was one of several Protestant ministers who wrote "slave catechisms" that were ostensibly designed to instruct the slaves in the lessons of Christianity but that, in fact, served to indoctrinate them with the virtue of obedience. In two publications (1834 and 1837—the latter published in at least three editions), he called attention to the duty of masters to treat their slaves humanely, but at no time did he publicly criticize slavery. Despite his best intentions, Jones, like virtually every southern clergyman, never doubted the innate inferiority of the black race. It should be remembered that the slave catechisms were, after all, religious guides to help the slave get to heaven by being a good slave, not manuals for challenging the status quo.[30]

In fact, they were part of a larger policy in which virtually every effort that appeared to be in the slave's behalf was really designed to reinforce the security of his bondage. Jones was one of many Presbyterians who had always boasted of their commitment to Christian education, but when southern churchmen defined the advantages of that education, the slave's welfare almost always received short shrift. Agreeing that missionary work among slaves was important, for example, the leaders of the same Synod of South Carolina and Georgia which Jones had addressed in 1834 listed the benefits of conversion but placed the saving of black souls after: (1) understanding mutual duties between masters and slaves, (2) serving the master's economic interests, (3) promoting safety for both races, and (4) benefiting *white* morality. As for freedom for slaves in this world, the subject, to no one's surprise, was not on the list. On the eve of the General Assembly of 1836, spokesmen from the same synod repeated their complaints about the antislavery pressures of northern members; and ministers from the Hopewell (Atlanta) and Charleston Union presbyteries echoed the widely held southern conviction that slavery was "a political institution with which Ecclesiastical Judiciaries have not the smallest right to interfere."[31] The Presbyterian schism was just one year away.

There has been a tendency to associate the slavery issue with the Presbyterian fracture of 1837 into Old School and New School divisions because the schism occurred as the sectional controversy was heating up and at about the same time that the Methodists and Baptists divided into northern and southern denominations. But if the Presbyterian Church was, as John C. Calhoun had asserted, one of the "three great evangelical churches" that had been "torn asunder" by the slavery question, the "tearing" was only in contrast to those denominations, such as the Episcopalian and the Congregationalist, whose geographic distribution or hierarchical organizations precluded the internal agonizing that led to disunion. The Presbyterian split was the result of dissension over several issues; and since the denominational leadership had not taken as strong an early stance against slavery as had those of the Baptist and Methodist churches, its eventual acquiescence in the reality of the slave power did not present so sharp a contrast. Disagreement over slavery was only the final chapter in a half century of dissension that had been simmering at least since the adoption of the Plan of Union of 1801 with the Congregationalists. For the first three decades of the nineteenth century, Old School doctrinal conservatives had angrily opposed the New School liberals, who had called for cooperation with other Protestant churches and with interdenominational groups like the American Home Missionary Society.[32] Disagreements over slavery appeared occasionally, but they were almost always sectional rather than doctrinal; resolutions passed by southern state synods and presbyteries from both Old and New schools were virtually identical in their support of slavery and their assertions that it had God's approval.[33] To many—perhaps most—Presbyterians, there were more important things to quarrel over.

But to leave the matter there is to obfuscate the reality of the Presbyterian posture toward race. While slavery may not have been the most visible issue at the 1837 General Assembly, its underlying influence clearly "tipped the balance toward schism." It was obvious to Seymour Boughton Treadwell of the American Antislavery Society, writing in *American Liberties and American Slavery* the year after the Old School–New School fracture, that "advocates and apologists for slavery" at the convention "applied the keen but cruel excision knife indiscriminately, to all the northern 'rotten branches' of this '*strange vine*,' that they supposed to be in the least infected with the fanatical doctrine."[34]

In his important study *Revivalism and Social Reform* (1957), Timothy L. Smith agreed that the Presbyterian division may indeed have been primarily over theological and organizational issues, but it was also partly the result of "a covert 'deal' between [northern] conservative Scotch-Irish churchmen who opposed the revivalists' doctrinal heresies and Southerners who feared their antislavery principles." Similarly, religion historian Winthrop S. Hudson argued, the "disruptive effect of the slavery issue upon the churches was foreshadowed by its role in the hidden agenda" of the schism of 1837. While national Presbyterian leaders did not openly debate slavery, yet another writer insisted, it was the antislavery propensity of the New School ministers that frightened Southerners and moved them to call for the faction's expulsion.[35] In other words, these scholars suggested, proslavery Presbyterians pursued their cause while hiding behind the skirts of doctrinal dissidents, a conclusion verified by the significant incidence of slave ownership among Presbyterians.

It was an incidence that was deceiving. In his standard textbook on Afro-American history, *From Slavery to Freedom: A History of Negro Americans* (six editions, 1947–86), John Hope Franklin, arguably the preeminent black historian in the United States in the twentieth century, took the position that southern Presbyterians (and Quakers) were the "most liberal in their attitude toward Negroes, but they were not large slaveholders." Rather, he went on, the largest number of Protestant slaveholders could be found in "the Episcopal church on the Atlantic seaboard and in the Baptist and Methodist churches in the cotton kingdom." If one looked at the most volatile issues in the three major schisms and simply counted slaveholders, Franklin's conclusion was correct. It was also misleading. The reason he counted fewer Presbyterian slaveholders was that there were fewer Presbyterians. In the decade before the Civil War, according to Isabella Bishop's calculations, the number of Presbyterians in the United States was less than one-fourth the number of Methodists and less than one-half the number of Baptists. Even the Disciples of Christ, which had not been founded until 1812 and whose members were concentrated in the border states, could claim almost as many members as the Presbyterians.[36]

But counting heads did not say a great deal about the importance of slavery within a denomination. What Franklin should have done was assess the incidence of slavery *among* church members, as others have. In *Presbyterians and the Negro*, Andrew E. Murray cited figures that indicated that as many as 50 percent of all southern Presbyterian families owned slaves, a much higher percentage than that of the southern white population at large or of any other southern denomination.[37] In 1849 the Reverend James Smylie of Mississippi, who himself at one time had owned fifty-three slaves and in 1830 had been the third-largest slaveholder in Amite County, estimated that three-fourths of the members of the southern Presbyterian church owned slaves. That was almost certainly an exaggeration, but it did reflect at least one person's impression. As another student of the denomination noted, Presbyterians clearly "owned a disproportionate number of slaves" and they "were at least as fully involved in slavery as any denomination and had to come to terms with the religious and moral questions that the institution raised."[38] Ironically, it was a Presbyterian slaveholder, Robert J. Breckinridge of Kentucky, who, after emancipating his bondsmen, became a lightning rod of the denomination's antislavery faction.[39]

As abolitionism became increasingly respectable and the sectional controversy intensified, Presbyterians seemed determined to disassociate themselves from the very issue that had disturbed Jefferson like "a firebell in the night." In an 1849 declaration, Old School leaders, clinging tenaciously to the conservative position, repeated the familiar rationalization that slavery was "a civil institution which should be dealt with by legislatures rather than churches," a popular argument at the 1837 General Assembly and one that found its fullest expression in Ashland, Ohio, minister John Robinson's 256-page *The Testimony and Practice of the Presbyterian Church in Reference to Slavery* (1852).[40] It was an expedient contention, but it flew in the face of the fact that the church itself submitted to civil law and thus, in effect, approved slavery. In other words, a declaration of neutrality was tantamount to a declaration in favor of bondage. One must wonder if very many Presbyterians noticed the "personal liberty laws" passed by northern state legislators, who recognized their "moral" responsibility and dealt with the "civil" question by frustrating the enforcement of federal fugitive slave laws, a practice that increased sharply after the passage of the Fugitive Slave Act of 1850.

In 1846 a newly elected Whig congressman from Illinois named Abraham Lincoln had been among those objecting to increasing the range of slavery through war with Mexico. The "conscience" in Conscience Whigs was a proclamation of moral, not political, indignation. In the United States Senate, Henry Clay, Daniel Webster, and John C. Calhoun were closing out brilliant careers in debates over California's admission as a free state, a draconian fugitive slave law, and other slavery-related issues; while younger luminaries, like Stephen A. Douglas and Jefferson Davis, were launching their futures and fortunes from the same platforms.

Out of the turmoil emerged a new political party committed to the territorial containment of slavery. In Kansas the issue was resolved with gunpowder and blood, and in the United States Congress an outspoken antislavery senator was beaten into sensibility by an irate southern representative. While conservative churchmen like Robinson saw no moral issues at stake, politicians like Senator Charles Sumner of Massachusetts invoked moral righteousness to justify legislative behavior. To the abolitionist, the political status quo was inherently immoral. The irony of it all should have been obvious even to the most indifferent: As politicians argued—and Kansans killed each other—over issues that invoked the *morality* of slavery, the Presbyterian clergy, from whom one had a right to expect moral leadership, decreed that human bondage was a *political*, not a moral, issue!

While the Presbyterian schism of 1837 may have been over "doctrinal heresies," by the late 1840s the New School had begun moving closer to a hard-line abolitionist position. Within two decades, slavery was to be the primary cause of the withdrawal of its southern members, who—constituting only one-eighth of the national membership—objected to the strong antislavery position taken by the northern leadership. In 1857, these New School proslavery dissidents, with seven presbyteries and 15,000 members, organized the United Synod of the Presbyterian Church in the United States of America—which was a misnomer because all of its congregations were in the southern and border states. Despite the early rhetorical heat of George Bourne and others—or, perhaps, because of it—the slavery issue was swept along with, and sometimes obscured by, differences over doctrine, procedures, and, finally, political loyalty. Had there been very many southern Presbyterians who disagreed with the proslavery position, all, except for a few like Breckinridge, suffered in silence.

In an earlier era, Bourne had been forced from his Virginia pulpit because the church simply could not tolerate such an outspoken antislavery critic in its ministerial ranks. By the late antebellum period, the slightest suggestion of opposition to slavery could be equally costly. According to Carl N. Degler, in 1861 Eli W. Caruthers, "an obscure Presbyterian minister in Greensboro, North Carolina," lost his pastorate because, while praying for the safe return of Confederate soldiers, he lamented that the southern war effort was for "a bad cause." Aware of the risks, Caruthers withheld from publication a four-hundred-page manuscript entitled "Negroes Not a Degraded Race Suited Only for Slavery" because he believed its antislavery views "would not have been tolerated in any of the Southern States." Tracing African history through the ages, Caruthers pointed out that it took Christianity fifteen hundred years to elevate "Anglo-Saxons and Germans . . . to a civilized position." How, he wondered, could anyone criticize Africans, "who have been for long centuries shut out from this light of heaven and from these benign influences?"[41] Obviously even Caruthers could not escape the racism inherent in the missionary mentality. That Africans were "uncivilized" and could be elevated into the "light of heaven" only by Christianity was an assumption that he shared with white Americans everywhere.

In the spring of 1861—four years after southern New School Presbyterians had established the United Synod and with the Civil War already underway—Old School Southerners, in an action praised by church luminaries Charles Colcock Jones and David H. Porter, walked out of the General Assembly in Philadelphia and, insisting that slavery was clearly sanctioned in both the Old and New Testaments and that Africans could "never be elevated in the scale of being," reconvened on December 4 in Augusta, Georgia, as a *new* Old School denomination—the Presbyterian Church of the Confederate States of America. Representing forty-seven presbyteries from eleven southern states, the commissioners adopted a statement drafted by Thornwell that was directed "to all the Churches of Jesus Christ Throughout the Earth" and which repeated many of the conventional biblical and moral justifications of slavery.[42]

The sectional division was complete. On matters of slavery and race, Presbyterians had finally caught up with their Methodist and Baptist brethren. Moreover, because of the long-standing doctrinal disputes, there were now four churches where two and a half decades earlier there had been only one. And yet the brevity of that condition spoke volumes about the real priorities of the southern factions. Only three years after the southern Old School defection, its leaders invited the New School United Synod into their ranks. Apparently, those irresolvable doctrinal differences that Presbyterians had been agonizing over for more than sixty years were, at least to the southern clergy, far less important than maintaining a united front on the question of slavery. The war would end within a year and the Confederate cause was rapidly becoming the "Lost Cause," but southern Presbyterians once again had a common home. If anything, the prospect of a humiliating military defeat and the certain death of slavery seemed to bring them even closer together. In December 1863, speaking before the

South Carolina state legislature, the Reverend Benjamin Morgan Palmer praised the Confederate war effort because it was essential to protect the slave "from the schemes of a false philosophy which threaten his early and inevitable extermination." God had ordained, Palmer went on, that the African should be enslaved to ensure his survival.[43]

Concomitant with the belief that God had called for the enslavement of Africans was the belief that he would not forsake the Confederate cause. Writing to his son shortly after the beginning of the Civil War, Jones called attention to Jefferson Davis's recent declaration that the South would rely on "a just and superintending Providence" to ensure its victory. The following year, the younger Jones, by now an officer in the Confederate army, wrote his father that "God still favors our cause and inspires our armies and leaders as He has done in such a marked manner for some time past," to which the senior Jones replied by condemning the "execrable proclamation" and reassuring his son that God was still with the Confederacy. "Up to this hour we can say the Lord has been on our side," he wrote eight days after Abraham Lincoln had issued the preliminary Emancipation Proclamation; "to Him let us constantly commit our cause."[44]

This was the same Charles Colcock Jones who, while studying for the ministry thirty-three years earlier, had written to his fiancée that slavery was a "violation of all the Laws of God and Man" and was "fearful in the extreme." Here was one more living example of the power of politics and profits over piety and principle. The argument that bondage was essential for the slave's continuing existence because he would perish in a world dominated by whites had long been a part of the traditional defense of slavery. A few months after Palmer's speech to the legislators, the General Assembly of the Presbyterian Church CSA, meeting at Charlotte, North Carolina, repeated its belief in "the divine appointment of domestic servitude," and "the peculiar mission of the Southern Church to conserve the institution of slavery, and to make it a blessing to both master and slave."[45] For the leaders of a major Protestant denomination to claim that they actually had a *mission* to "conserve" human bondage must boggle the modern mind. It mattered not that the war had taken a disastrous turn for the South and that it was only a matter of time until the Union armies would be in complete control of the slave states. It appeared that no amount of reality could shake the southern Presbyterian's single-minded conviction on the rightness of slavery. The overwhelming sentiment that God had appointed the black man to a lifetime of servitude endured; *ergo,* to oppose slavery was to oppose the will of God.

The thunder of cannons had barely faded when the race question returned to antagonize southern Presbyterians. In December 1865, at a meeting of the General Assembly in Macon, Georgia, the delegates rejected a proposal to reunite with the northern church because of the latter's position allegedly advocating social equality for the freedmen (which, in fact, it had not). The institution of human bondage *may* have been wrong, they conceded (less than two years after insisting on its divine justification), but the respective positions of master and servant were correct. On matters of "social morality and Scriptural truth," the "relationship" was unassailable.[46] With the smell of gunpowder still burning their nostrils and having just lost slave property whose market value was incalculable,[47] the defenders of the "Lost Cause" could hardly be expected to be contrite. In the years following the war, the southern Presbyterian church drifted in and out of efforts to include black worshipers and ministers until, in 1874, the General Assembly, meeting in Columbus, Mississippi, called for the organization of a separate black denomination. The parent body would lend moral and some small—as it turned out, *very* small—financial support; and it was a course that would ensure permanent racial harmony because it was, the delegates argued, preferred by black members themselves.

The unreconstructed view of the postwar era was nowhere better seen than in the words and actions of Robert Lewis Dabney, one of the most respected—and certainly one of the most virulently racist—leaders of the southern Presbyterian church. A professor of theology at the Union Theological Seminary in Virginia and later professor of moral philosophy at the University of Texas, where he also established a Presbyterian seminary, Dabney expounded his fanatical opinion in *A Defence of Virginia, and Through Her, of the South, in Recent and Pending Contests against the Sectional Party*. Written in 1862 but not published until 1867, this work blamed the Civil War entirely on northern abolitionists, who, Dabney claimed, provoked the conflict to "gratify their spite." From George Bourne in 1816 to Robert Lewis Dabney in 1867—that pretty much describes the evolution of the Presbyterian church in Virginia. In 1882 Dabney condemned a proposal by the southern church's General Assembly to establish "fraternal relations" with the northern Presbyterian Church in the United States of America because, he argued, it would involve "ecclesiastical amalgamation with negroes" and would "seal the moral and doctrinal corruption of our church in the South, and be a direct step towards that final perdition of Southern society, domestic amalgamation."

Although he resisted internal pressure to ordain black preachers, Dabney agreed that the only solution to the racial problem was the establishment of a totally separate black Presbyterian church. As late as 1894 (four years before his death at age seventy-eight), he was still defending the "human justice of slavery" and calling for the abolition of the federal union. On the matter of black membership, southern Presbyterians dragged their feet and found excuses. As a result of the continuing southern hard line, northern Presbyterian missions moved into the South during the last decades of the nineteenth century and organized black congregations in which blacks were given full equality in church governance.[48]

Slavery may not have been the decisive factor in the schism of 1837, but the race issue nonetheless cut deeply into the Presbyterian psyche. Following the theme popularized by Dabney and others, the Reverend John W. Stagg, who had served major congregations in Tennessee, North Carolina, and Alabama in the late nineteenth and early twentieth centuries, launched a series of tirades against racial equality in which he called the Fifteenth Amendment to the Constitution "the most egregious wrong ever perpetrated in the history of the Republic." Writing in the *Presbyterian Quarterly* in 1900, Stagg insisted that racial distinctions were ordained by God and that there "will never be a church, in the South, of any denomination, that will allow negroes in its courts or within its walls as equals so long as the race question is involved." Some might say that, at least for his own church, Stagg was prophetic. In 1954, delegates to the Southern Assembly of the Presbyterian Church voted 283 to 169 to invite its presbyteries to consider merging with two northern branches, the Northern Presbyterian Church and the United Presbyterian Church of North America. But the enthusiasm of the leadership did not filter down to the local clergy as the presbyteries decided *against* the proposal, 43 to 42—not even a simple majority on a ballot that required a three-fourths vote.[49]

Coming in the wake of the United States Supreme Court's landmark desegregation decision in *Brown* v. *Board of Education*, the response of the presbyteries carried the undeniable smell of "backlash." Four years later, the United Presbyterian Church of North America merged with another northern group, the Presbyterian Church in the United States of America; but when the southern church—by now called the Presbyterian Church of the United States—considered reunion, its presbyteries rejected the proposal by a margin, one noted historian pointed out, that "correlated markedly with black-and-white population ratios in the respective districts."[50] A century after white Southerners in the New School had gone walking, the unrelenting grip of racism in the southern Presbyterian church was as strong as ever.

Mission Over Mercy: The Methodists

If slavery had been obfuscated by doctrinal differences in the Presbyterian division of 1837, it was virtually the only issue leading to the Methodist schism of 1844. Unlike the Presbyterians and Baptists, whose American origins could be traced back to seventeenth-century Puritan dissenters, the colonial followers of John Wesley had only the Anglican experience to draw upon. Except for various Methodist Societies, the denomination was not organized in America until the later years of the eighteenth century. Thus its leaders and missionaries did not have an opportunity to address the slavery issue outside of the hierarchy of the Established Church until long after bondage was thoroughly institutionalized. Baptists and Presbyterians grew up with slavery; Methodists were introduced to it.

Yet, if there was one American sect that was a microcosm of the Christian ambivalence on race and slavery, it was the Methodist Episcopal Church, which, beginning with about four thousand members in 1775, had by the 1820s surpassed the Baptists as the largest Protestant denomination in antebellum America, eventually claiming some of the nation's most militant defenders of slavery and some of its most passionate abolitionists. According to Donald G. Mathews, the leading chronicler of the antebellum church, "a discussion of slavery and Methodism explains the fate of antislavery thought among Southerners, the significant relationship between the early and later antislavery movements, the character of the abolitionist crusade, and its effect upon the majority of Americans."[51] Quite a role for a denomination that did not even exist for the first century and a half of the nation's past.

Not only did Methodism in America start late and small, but, in the beginning, it was mainly a southern denomination, which, considering the preponderating influence of the Established Church in the plantation colonies, was to be expected. At the time of the famous Christmas Conference of 1784—the event from which the church dates its official origin in the United States—between 80 and 90 percent of all Methodists lived below the Mason-Dixon Line, primarily in Virginia and Maryland.[52] Furthermore, according to C. Eric Lincoln, "fully one-fifth of its membership was black." But the number and distribution of that membership changed dramatically. While there were disparities in the various reports, even the most conservative calculations indicated a growth that was nothing less than phenomenal. When the continental colonies declared their independence from Great Britain, American Methodists declared their independence from the English church. One historian estimated that the number of Methodists went from about one in two hundred Americans at the end of the Revolutionary War to one in twenty by 1845.[53] Another account reported an increase in membership from 10,500 to 76,150 in the ten years prior to 1791, with 20,000 new converts in Virginia alone in just one year.[54] The significance of these increases might be diminished somewhat by the fact that many of these new Methodists—perhaps most—were simply Episcopalians following their leaders into the new denomination. Yet, even allowing for this, the growth was impressive.

But this did not explain the tremendous growth of Methodism in the North, where the Established Church had never enjoyed the preeminence that it had claimed in the South. By 1812 the numbers of members in the free states had surpassed those in the slave states, a trend that obviously corresponded to the more rapid growth of the northern population. At the General Conference of 1816, northern delegates outnumbered southern 42 to 35, with 13 others from the western states. By 1844 the North-South ratio was 118 to 58.[55] Between 1800 and 1840 almost all American churches experienced dramatic increases, and several new evangelical denominations—such as the Disciples of Christ—appeared, but the number of Methodists exploded. While the Baptist membership grew from 170,000 to 560,000 (slightly over 300 percent) during these four decades, the Methodist enrollment for the same period soared from 70,000 to 820,00, an increase of almost twelvefold![56] In 1849, the number of Methodists in the now-divided church was, according to its own calculations, 1.1 million; by the time the armies of Virginia and the Potomac began stoking up their cannons, the combined membership was over 1.6 million.[57] In the seven and a half decades from the Revolution to the Civil War, the Methodist Church went from a handful of dissidents in the Protestant Episcopal Church to the largest Protestant denomination in the United States.

There was a great deal more to the emergence of the Methodist Episcopal Church than the growth of its membership. As a predominantly southern denomination in its early years, the church had, by the time of the division of 1844, a vested interest in bondage, and it was unlikely that very many of the clergy or laity gave much thought to manumission or any other effort to improve the quality of life for the slaves. In the year before the schism, 25,000 communicants owned 208,000 slaves—over 9 percent of the total slave population—and 1,200 Methodist clergymen were themselves slaveholders. If anyone needed a barometer to measure the southern Methodist's official commitment to bondage he had only to consider the fact that every minister elevated to the rank of bishop in the Methodist Episcopal Church, South, between 1846 and the Civil War was a slaveholder. Like supporters of slavery in other denominations, southern Methodists argued that slavery was approved by God and that its status was a government concern, not an ecclesiastical one. The church must be neutral in such matters. Needless to say, neutrality was an evasive concept. By attacking critics of slavery, these same Methodists were, in fact, subjecting themselves to the state and identifying "what was right and Christian with what was southern." The Methodists' inability, or refusal, to compromise on the slavery issue may have hurt more than helped the slaves because after the schism the southern members, though isolated, were free from the pressures of their northern brethren. As for those southern Methodists who might have been inclined to speak against slavery, few, if any, were bold enough to do so. For the first half century of the Methodist Church's existence in North America, its unity depended "on the strict enforcement of silence or neutrality on the slavery question," Sydney Ahlstrom observed.[58] Its only charitable involvement with the slaves was converting as many of them as possible, which may, incidentally, have been the way some Methodists eased their consciences about being unable to influence emancipation. Then again, that may also be a charitable speculation.

Whether or not very many Methodists saw slave conversion as a consolation for emancipation is problematical, but there is no doubt that their efforts to convert slaves were the most successful of all American Protestants. Always aggressive missionaries, the Methodists had established several mission stations in the southern colonies during the 1770s. By the early nineteenth century, they were able to claim more slave members than any other church except possibly the Baptists, whose independent congregations never supported missionary efforts as the Methodist episcopate was able to.[59] There was some Episcopal and Presbyterian missionary activity among the slaves, but none rivaling the Methodists. By the time of the Sixth Census (1840), the Methodist and Baptist churches each had about 80,000 slave members. The total national memberships were 700,000 and 500,000 respectively.[60] At the same time, however, the emancipationist leadership within Methodism, lukewarm though it may have been, had caved in to the slavery interests. In 1816, church leaders had conceded that "the evil of slavery appeared to be 'past remedy,' " H. Shelton Smith wrote, and they "turned their main attention to evangelizing the slaves and to promoting the colonization movement."[61]

But, despite their well-publicized successes, they failed here also; boasts of large-scale conversions were convincing only when compared to the efforts of the other denominations. The Methodist church's missionary zeal, conspicuous though it was, exposed the pathetic weakness of the total Protestant interest in black people's souls. As late as 1830, the number of slaves converted was painfully small, even in South Carolina and Georgia, where missionary work had been most active. Ten years later, church officials reported 94,532 black members nationwide, which was approximately 12 to 13.5 percent of the total membership—depending on whose numbers are used—a figure consistent with accounts from other churches.[62] However, it would be a mistake to match the 10 to 12 percent national black church membership with the slightly larger black percentage of the American population. The Eighth Census (1860) counted the number of slaves and free blacks in the United States at 14.2 percent of the total population. But blacks in the free states constituted only 1.7 percent of the population, while those in the fifteen slave states—where the Methodist missionary effort was concentrated—were almost 35 percent of all Southerners. Since the slave did not have the same access to church as the northern black, it is against the latter figure that the success of missionary efforts should be analyzed. If there had been very many white Methodist missionaries who believed that the road to heaven was lined with the souls of black converts, more than a few must have been nervous about their own salvation.

Like the Baptists and Presbyterians, many Methodists initially had opposed slavery, including the three most important figures in the early American church—John Wesley, Thomas Coke, and Francis Asbury.[63] Wesley's *Thoughts on Slavery* (1774), since it had been heavily plagiarized from Anthony Benezet's *Some Historical Account of Guinea* (1772), was an especially strong denunciation of bondage.[64] Asbury, the first resident Methodist Episcopal bishop in the United States and the only one of Wesley's English preachers who did not return to Britain, declared in the 1770s that the abolition of slavery must be a goal that all church members should work toward.

In 1780, four years before the church was officially organized in the United States, Methodist leaders issued a statement condemning slavery as "contrary to the laws of God, man, and nature, and hurtful to society." At the Christmas Conference of 1784—the high-water mark of the church's attack on slavery—officials, including Asbury and Coke, approved a resolution calling for the expulsion of all slaveowning members. The delegates also included in the "Discipline," the "authoritative rule book on American Methodism," a provision requiring every slaveholding member to draw up a legal document "agreeing to free all of his slaves at a time depending on their age at the time the document was drawn up." Ministers (more than a few of whom were themselves slaveholders) were to keep detailed records and members had one year to comply or leave the church, while converts applying for membership had to agree, as a condition of membership, to accept the ban. There were a couple of soft spots in the rule: Slaveholders living in a state in which manumission was illegal were excepted, and Virginians, because of "special" circumstances, were given an extra two years to comply. Needless to say, most slaveowners ignored the 1784 declaration and the hierarchy made no attempt to enforce it. Despite the growing recalcitrance of what was still a predominantly southern denomination, in 1801 the General Conference repeated its "deepest abhorrence of the practice of slavery."[65]

But that was about the last antislavery expression that would be heard from the Methodist leadership for some time. As southern resistance to emancipation mounted, Asbury made "preaching to slaves the alternate to preaching about slavery."[66] Slavery would continue to exist for many years because "there is not sufficient sense of religion nor of liberty to destroy it," he wrote in his diary on January 9, 1798, in a statement that sounded very much like a lament; "Methodists, Baptists, Presbyterians, in the highest flights of rapturous piety, still maintain and defend it."[67] In fairness to Asbury, it should be noted that his capitulation was the rule, not the exception. But the Methodists also had no one to match Presbyterian George Bourne and Baptists John Leland and David Barrow, all of them Virginia preachers on the cutting edge of southern abolitionism. Later in the nineteenth century, Virginia was to produce Moncure Conway, a young Methodist minister whose father had owned "fifty or sixty slaves" and who until 1850 had never "seen any free society, and was unaware of the existence of any region without the evils to which [he] had become accustomed."[68] But the South had long since slammed the door on all discussion of emancipation, a situation that Conway resolved by moving to England.

It was no accident of circumstance that the Methodist turnaround, like those of other mainline denominations, coincided almost exactly with the emergence of cotton as the South's most important commodity and the nation's leading export crop. By the end of Andrew Jackson's presidency the official church position had become so equivocal that delegates to the General Conference of 1836 spoke against *both* slavery and abolitionism—especially abolitionism. A year earlier four antislavery members had been chastised by church officials, including the president of Wesleyan University, for circulating an "Appeal" to the New England and New Hampshire conferences calling for action against slaveholders. Thus the delegates were primed to approve a resolution criticizing "in the most unqualified sense the conduct of two members [Orange Scott and La Roy Sunderland] who were reported to have lectured . . . in favor of moderate abolitionism." After certain northern members challenged a southern declaration that slavery was a blessing rather than a curse, the delegates, despite a substantial free-state majority, voted 122 to 11 in favor of a gag rule against criticizing slavery.[69]

By an almost identical vote (120 to 14), the delegates in their "Pastoral Address" further disclaimed "any right, wish, or intention, to interfere in the civil and political relation between master and slave," a position endorsed in subsequent years by several state and regional conferences.[70] Except in New England, these conferences "were dominated by preachers who tried to check antislavery militancy within Methodism," and who routinely denied applications for ordination from candidates who were known to be abolitionists. Like their colonial brethren, who had been pressured to renounce emancipation as a consequence of conversion, many

Methodist preachers believed their first duty was to convert heathens to Christianity and thus were perfectly willing to strike any bargain in order to retain access to the slaves. What had been to Asbury in 1798 only a reluctant concession to save bondsmen's souls rather than free their bodies became for Methodist leaders in 1836 the foundation of their slavery policy. "Their purpose was not emancipation," Mathews conceded, "but conversion and pastoral care."[71] It was little more than a modern version of the Pauline rationalization: Life on earth is brief and transitory; the hereafter is forever.[72]

Thus, in its short, fifty-year existence in the United States, the Methodist Episcopal Church had moved 180 degrees from its original position condemning slavery. By 1840, one religion scholar wrote, "Methodism had fallen to a new low in subserviency to its proslavery faction." It was a strange irony that while the number of Methodists in the free states had by the second decade of the nineteenth century surpassed the number in the slave states, the national leadership's official position on slavery had traveled essentially in the opposite direction, backing away from its original call for the expulsion of slaveholders to a declaration that it had no desire to challenge slavery. The consequences were predictable. In 1833–34, Orange Scott managed to coax most of the Methodist ministers in New England into the antislavery camp. By the end of the decade small groups of frustrated dissenters in Ohio, Pennsylvania, New York, and Michigan were organizing independent congregations, a movement that culminated in 1841 with the founding of the "perfectionist" Wesleyan Methodist Church. The great schism was underway. Two years later, Scott, weary from several years of defying the conservative leadership of Bishop Elijah Hedding, led a large contingent of "New York laymen and their pastors" into the Wesleyan Methodist Connection, which by this time claimed six thousand members. Contemptuously called the "Scottite" church by conservative Methodists, the Wesleyans constituted less than 1 percent of the national Methodist membership, but the chorus of antislavery criticism was growing ominously and the likelihood that the number of dissidents would soar was great.[73]

At the national church's General Conference of 1844, the northern majority, trying to avoid alienating any faction, angered both the antislavery delegates by refusing to criticize slavery and the proslavery participants who demanded more than just neutrality. The fact that almost three-fourths of the southern representatives were slaveholders virtually guaranteed rancor and deadlock, thus neither side was feeling conciliatory when the break finally occurred. The incident that triggered the fracture was the leadership's order to Bishop James Osgood Andrew of Georgia and South Carolina not to resume his administrative and clerical duties until he relinquished two recently acquired slaves. To the southern participants, this demand "abolitionized" the hierarchy. When a majority of the delegates, under a threat from the New England representatives to withdraw and join the Wesleyans, refused to endorse a proposal that would have defended the morality of slaveholding, the Southerners announced their intention to secede and the leadership drew up a Plan of Separation to divide church property. Although northern officials later repudiated the plan and continued to court slaveholding members in the border states, the division into northern and southern branches was now a reality. The following year the southern defectors assembled in Louisville, Kentucky, and formally organized the Methodist Episcopal Church, South. There would not be another nationwide general conference of the Methodist Episcopal Church for almost a century.[74]

While the seceding Methodists left behind northern factions that continued to quarrel among themselves, they soon discovered that secession was not all it promised to be. Among the disaffected Southerners were clergymen who remained ambivalent about slavery and who actually spoke in favor of some emancipation plan if it included a provision for removing the black presence altogether. As with the earlier colonizationists, the objective was to get rid of undesirable people rather than an undesirable institution. Actually, a few southern Methodists conceded that bondage was not an ideal situation but that there was, under the circumstances, no other practical way to govern such people.[75] Of course, the overwhelming majority of the clergy and lay membership supported not only slavery and schism but, led by ardent proslavery advocates like Holland Nimmons McTyeire, editor of the church's *Christian Advocate* (Nashville), the southern secession movement and the Confederate war effort as well.[76]

Nor did the departure of the southern members bring instant harmony to northern Methodists, who, in H. Shelton Smith's words, "remained surprisingly conservative on the bondage question for the next twenty years." It could be argued that no one should have been "surprised" by this resistance to antislavery pressures. The longstanding northern Methodist antipathy to abolitionists had been based on more than simple obsequiousness toward slaveowning ministers and bishops. Biblical justifications for bondage notwithstanding, the ultimate issue was not slavery but *race.* And on this matter white Northerners were little different from white Southerners. At the northern General Conferences of 1856 and 1860, motions to expel slaveholding members by rewriting the General Rules were defeated, thereby convincing a number of New York abolitionists that they should organize the Free Methodist Church as a haven for all those who could not associate with anyone who refused to condemn bondage.[77]

There were now two antislavery Methodist factions. Herein lay the seed of the racist malaise that afflicted virtually every Protestant denomination and could even be traced back to the colonial Quakers: Antislavery Methodists, like many abolitionists in every denomination, were more concerned with ensuring the future of their own souls than with the present suffering of four million slaves. Human bondage was a sin that they could not tolerate, thus their solution was to disassociate themselves from all vestiges of it. By the late antebellum period it had become a familiar refrain: Getting rid of slaveholders was more important than getting rid of slavery.

But there is one matter that nags. In view of the denomination's episcopal organization, the Methodist schism raised the question of just how influential a church's leaders were—or could be—when addressing fundamental issues of human rights, and whether or not its ecclesiastical structure was significant or even relevant. The congregational system of the Baptist Church may indeed have been a major reason for that denomination's vulnerability to the forces of disunion. There is probably more than a little truth in the proposition that all religious practices, like all politics, are local. On the other hand, the Methodist Episcopal Church, like the Protestant Episcopal (Anglican) Church, was governed by a hierarchy of bishops working within well-defined and carefully organized regional and national conferences.[78] Unlike the Episcopalians, however, the Methodists were unable to avoid the internal acrimony that eventually forced them into northern and southern branches.

The next question is obvious: Was the power of the slavery interest so formidable that it simply crushed whatever institutional obstacles it confronted, or was the organizational structure of a denomination simply irrelevant? It could also be argued that it was the episcopal system itself that fractured the church. In an ecclesiastical hierarchy in which authority is vested in a select few, the leadership must either enforce its moral doctrines or, faced with the destruction of its credibility, redefine them as insignificant, which, in turn, would almost certainly diminish its own significance. Unwilling, and probably unable, to carry out the former, church officials settled for the latter, a solution that the contending sides repudiated by defection and secession.

Unlike Catholics and Episcopalians, who boasted of strong hierarchies but lacked an emotional ethos, or the Baptists and Presbyterians, whose national organizations were weak or nonexistent and, in the case of the Baptists, whose style of worship leaned heavily toward emotions, the Methodists possessed the two qualities—an established hierarchy and a fervid antislavery element—that "united explosive material and rigid structure," as John Nelson Norwood put it in 1923. "The result was that while other denominations had suffered in slavery struggles, nowhere was the issue so clear-cut or the outcome so destructive to the historic church as among the Methodists." Compounding the dilemma was the fact that the Methodists were less theologically oriented than, say, the Presbyterians, and thus, as Sydney E. Ahlstrom put it, "placed far greater emphasis on visible matters of discipline."[79] The episcopal system inherently emphasized order, form, and ritual rather than ideology—conduct rather than belief. Unfortunately, the more rules an institution sets forth, the more opportunities it creates for dissension—and defeat.

After the Civil War, northern Methodists continued to exhibit a split personality toward the race question. On the one hand were a few radical churchmen like Bishop Gilbert Haven of Massachusetts, who before the war had been one of the first abolitionists to focus on the psychological issue of racism rather than the moral issue of slavery and who advocated complete social equality among the races, including intermarriage:[80] "And the hour is not far off when the white-hued husband shall boast of the dusky beauty of his wife, and the Caucasian wife shall admire the sun-kissed countenance of her husband, as deeply, and as unconscious of the present ruling abhorrence as is his admiration of her lighter tint."[81] In fact, Haven's ideas were so anomalous that he was formally repudiated by his own church just four years after his 1872 election to the episcopate.[82] But Gilbert Haven was in a class by himself. On the other side were those northern Methodists who, more pragmatic about the realities of race relations than Haven, favored the reunification of the church at any cost, a cost that the former slaves would ultimately pay. Some of the Methodists who had gone south to work among the freedmen during the reconstruction years made occasional attempts to integrate religious activities but almost always encountered angry resistance from local whites. When, in 1874, a church official in Atlanta ordered that black members be permitted to use certain facilities that they had never had access to before, white members simply renounced their allegiance to the denomination and set up an independent congregation. Faced with virtually universal white opposition, church leaders, slavishly conceding that segregated congregations were "for the good of all concerned," capitulated the following year.[83]

Thus, what began as an extremely modest move during the reconstruction era to bring some blacks into southern congregations became in the 1880s a hard-line segregationist policy of "racially pure denominationalism." By 1895 all of the Methodist General Conferences in the South were segregated, a condition that black Methodists themselves publicly favored. It was to be the prevailing view of most white Americans for the next seventy-five years, North as well as South. In the late 1880s, the Reverend J. Benson Hamilton, pastor of the Cornell Methodist Church in New York

City, spoke in direct opposition to his northern liberal colleagues who, like Haven, continued to call for the integration of all southern Methodist congregations. Sounding more like an antebellum southern preacher than the pastor of a big-city northern congregation, Hamilton was convinced that the South would never survive without the total separation of the races. In seventy years the black population, if unchecked, would number fifty million, he predicted, and, being "illiterate, licentious, and intemperate," it would easily overwhelm the southern white population. The result would be "a bloody war of races."[84]

If Hamilton sounded like an antebellum southern preacher, Atticus Greene Haygood, who advocated "Liberal" Christianity and called for religious education for the former slaves, was as close as one could expect to get to a white southern clergyman who supported the elevation of the black race. In the context of southern Methodism, Haygood, president of Emory University in Atlanta, was indeed conspicuous, and the high praise he received from both northern reformers and southern blacks was apparently justified. In his Thanksgiving sermon of 1880, he asked whites to be patient, understanding, and compassionate toward the freedmen. He was also one of the first advocates of reunification with the northern church. But Haygood was no Gilbert Haven. Recognizing fundamental racial differences that he believed would always require the separation of the races, Haygood, like other Christians who considered themselves friends of the black race, never wavered from the assumption that the black man was acceptable only when he lived the way white Christians thought he should live. Haygood insisted that blacks, in order to enjoy the opportunities of freedom (*equality* was never mentioned), must give up their "habits of thoughtlessness, drinking, fornication, and 'debasement of worship services.' "[85]

In other words, Haygood was guilty of the same arrogant dogmatism that had always afflicted Christian missionaries everywhere. Offerings of fellowship and opportunity were extended only to those who displayed a willingness to embrace the faith and live according to its tenets. The former slave must become, to paraphrase Kenneth M. Stampp, a white Christian with black skin, nothing more, nothing less.[86] If he remained true to his ancestral heritage he could expect nothing. The black person would always be different; but, if he ever expected to partake of the benefits of freedom, religion could not be one of the differences.

The persistence of controversy in the decades after the Civil War supported the suspicion that the bitter debates over slavery that had produced the schism of 1844 had actually obfuscated the more fundamental issue of *racism*. After all, the ratification of the Thirteenth Amendment to the Constitution in 1865 had, finally and unequivocally, eliminated the problem of association with slaveholders, an action that should have satisfied all those Christians who had insisted that freedom for the slaves was a political, not a moral, issue. With the disputes that had ignited the divergent causes of people like Orange Scott and Elijah Hedding now resolved, there should have been nothing left to argue about.

As it happened, when the Reverend Hamilton insisted that "race preference and prejudice has built a wall between the two races," he was only reflecting a Methodist opinion that could be traced back at least a century. When, in 1787, three black worshipers were pulled from their knees while praying in St. George's Methodist Episcopal Church in Philadelphia and, despite their request to complete the prayer in progress, ordered to the back of the sanctuary, they left and vowed never to return. Slavery had been abolished in Pennsylvania seven years earlier and therefore was not a factor in the incident, but it triggered one of the most significant movements in American social and religious history: the emergence of the independent black church. One of the men who had been jerked to his feet was Richard Allen, an extremely devout former slave, who previously had been permitted to preach at St. George's several times and who had, with one of the other men, Absalom Jones, just established the Free African Society, a private black mutual-aid organization. In 1794, Allen founded the Bethel African Methodist Episcopal Church; and twenty-two years later, after congregations had been established in Maryland, Delaware, Pennsylvania, and New Jersey, he brought them together as the national AME Church. At about the same time and for virtually the same reasons, black Methodists in New York City, led by Peter Williams and James Varick, withdrew from the John Street Methodist Episcopal Church and formed the African Methodist Episcopal Zion Church. Although AMEZ leaders struggled for many years, by the early 1820s the church had stablized and had launched an expansion program. The black Methodist church, created not from a desire to be separate but from a desire to worship without discrimination at the hands of white brethren, was to become the most enduring legacy of Methodism's refusal to accord to the black communicant all of the rights and privileges of membership in the body of Christ.[87]

Independence or Provincialism?: The Baptists

While the events leading to the Methodist schism of 1844 were indeed foreboding and dramatic, they were no more so than those that divided the Baptists one year later. Begun in Rhode Island by Roger Williams and his band of dissident Puritans, the church had its most rapid early growth in New York and Pennsylvania; the first colonial Baptist Association outside of New

England, representing five congregations, convened in Philadelphia in 1707. Although there were relatively few congregations before the Revolution, the denomination, consisting primarily of independent churches, grew steadily, especially in the South.[88] Of the approximately 65,000 Baptists in the United States in 1790, Virginia claimed 20,000, while Kentucky, Georgia, and the Carolinas together counted another 18,000. For a short time it appeared that the Virginia church would take the leadership in condemning slavery when, in 1785, the state's Baptist General Committee proclaimed that hereditary bondage was "contrary to the word of God." Nor was it just a momentary exercise. Four years later, the same body, acting on a resolution introduced by John Leland—who had moved from Massachusetts to take up his Virginia pastorate—declared slavery repugnant and called for its legal abolition; and the following year the committee resolved to use "every legal measure, to extirpate this horrid evil from the land."[89] For slaves in the state with the largest slave population, the Baptist church's official stance seemed too good to be true.

Another Virginia minister who enthusiastically supported his denomination's position was David Barrow, who, after freeing his own slaves, preached for twenty-four years in his home state before moving to Kentucky in 1798. As the leading southern Baptist voice against bondage, Barrow published a fifty-page booklet, *Involuntary, Unmerited, Perpetual, Absolute, Hereditary Slavery, Examined* (1808), which, one historian wrote, "easily ranked as one of the strongest antislavery tracts of its time."[90] When Barrow arrived in Kentucky, he found what were probably the most pugnacious of all southern reformers. Accordingly, in 1807, he and Carter Tarrant formed an independent antislavery organization called Friends of Humanity, whose antislavery creed was soon adopted by twelve churches. With its long-standing doctrinal commitment to "liberty of conscience," the Baptist church appeared to be the ideal Christian platform from which to launch the antislavery movement. But what seemed too good to be true, was too good. Although the Friends of Humanity spread north and east, it was difficult to sustain an intractable position on slavery in a region "where slavery was commonly practiced," and the fellowship eventually died out in Kentucky.[91]

While Baptist officials below the Mason-Dixon Line were the first to confront the slavery issue, their northern brethren soon joined the cause. In 1789, church leaders in Philadelphia urged congregations to form their own antislavery societies—slavery was still legal in much of the North—and by the turn of the century the Baptists had succeeded the Quakers as the leading northern antislavery denomination. As northern bondage gradually disappeared in the next two decades, the emancipationist impulse spread rapidly among the churches, and when Illinois was admitted to the

Union in 1818, it was already a center of Baptist antislavery activity. Afterward, the greatest growth occurred in New England, especially Maine. With over 13,000 members by 1830 (not counting the militantly abolitionist Freewill Baptists, who numbered 9,000), Baptist congregations in Maine united behind the antislavery cause until, by January 1841, one report identified 184 of the state's 214 ministers as "decided abolitionists"—among them influential preachers like Edwin R. Warren, James Gilpatrick, and Samuel Adam.[92]

Nine months earlier, 110 clergymen had convened in New York City to organize the American Baptist Anti-Slavery Convention. Before adjourning, the delegates warned slaveholding members that bondage was "a violation of the instincts of nature,—a perversion of the first principles of justice,—and a positive transgression of the revealed will of God." Those who continued to hold slaves were declared unfit for Christian fellowship.[93] Whether or not the delegates had considered all of the ramifications of such a forceful position is open to question, but their language was sure to fire up the resistance of the proslavery interests in the church, resistance that in just five years resulted in schism.

The Baptist sentiment against slavery also carried over into the mission field as church leaders, in the years immediately after the Revolution, began serious religious work among slaves. In the early national period, the Baptist church was one of the fastest-growing Protestant denominations, and clearly the most successful in winning black converts. By 1800, black Baptists and Methodists numbered in the tens of thousands, with Presbyterians "a distant third."[94] Black Baptist converts, at least in some places, were "accepted for church membership in the same manner as whites."[95] American Baptist churches were unique in granting black converts—slave and free—all of the rights and privileges of membership (although slaves usually had to have their masters' written consent), and it therefore should surprise no one that many black men and women were drawn to the Baptist church. In fact, some congregations were so democratic that they did not think it necessary to minister to the special needs of the slaves, a situation that probably cultivated a measure of white indifference to the black person's spiritual development.

Whatever the consequences, white Baptist "acceptance" of black members reached all the way into the pulpit. One of the first black Baptist pastors was George Leile, who had been licensed to preach in South Carolina before the War for Independence and who also ministered to the Silver Bluff Church near Augusta, probably the first all-black Baptist church in the United States. Other black Baptist clerics of the early national period included Andrew Bryan, who founded the First African Baptist Church in Savannah, Georgia, in 1788 and who by 1812 counted

1,500 members; William Moses and Gowan Pamphlet in Williamsburg, Virginia, in 1776; Colin Teague and Lott Carey in Richmond, who later became missionaries to Africa; and John Jasper, also of Richmond. By the beginning of the nineteenth century, black Baptist preachers "were not uncommon in Virginia," one writer noted, and as late as 1830 many were still being admitted to the Baptist ministry.[96]

The attraction of the Baptist church for transplanted Africans, however, probably had less to do with formal missionary efforts—in which Baptists never enjoyed the success of the Methodists—than with the inherent characteristics of the denomination. A product of a culture that was guided more by feelings than intellectual analysis or philosophical introspection, the slave was understandably attracted to the form of worship in which he was a participant rather than a spectator. The revivalistic style, the untrained preachers who "offered a fervent gospel, both simple and personal in its appeal, that attracted the unlettered regardless of race," the presence of black ministers, and the opportunity to participate in virtually all congregational activities were features of Baptist worship that seemed to suit best the African's religious temperament. Perhaps most important of all was the practice of baptism by immersion. "Are your negroes Baptists or Methodists?" Frederick Law Olmsted asked a slaveholder in northern Mississippi just before the Civil War. "All Baptists; niggers allers want to be ducked, you know," the master replied. "They ain't content to be just titched with water; they must be ducked in all over. There was two niggers jined the Methodists up here last summer, and they made the minister put 'em into the branch; they wouldn't jine 'less he'd duck 'em."[97]

Such a statement, at least in the opinion of one noted scholar, was not a superficial observation. Baptism by immersion, according to anthropologist Melville J. Herskovits, was favored by many slaves because of the lingering influence of African river cults, for "the river spirits are among the most powerful of those inhabiting the supernatural world," and their priests "are among the most powerful members of tribal priestly groups." Herskovits may have been reaching a little, but it is certainly plausible that transplanted Africans in the New World adapted to their environment by, among other things, adhering "to that Christian sect which in its ritualism most resembled the types of worship known to them."[98] The operative word here is *ritualism*. The slave's ancestral religion had been filled with demonstrative physical expressions, and bodily immersion in water was a lot more demonstrative and physical than being sprinkled on the head.

Calculating the syncretic effect of the Baptist style, Herskovits drew what was at least a safe empirical conclusion. As people to whom religious practice was more critical than religious belief, slaves were attracted to the denomination that appealed more to feelings than to the intellect. Of course, all of this was irrelevant as far as the slave's secular status was concerned. Whatever the reasons for the slave's propensity for the Baptist church, they had little to do with easing the burdens of his bondage. Baptist officials may have initially assumed a militant antislavery position, slaves may have been inordinately attracted to the denomination, and black Baptist preachers may have been fairly commonplace in parts of the United States in the early nineteenth century; but the good times were about to end.

To begin with, many lay southern Baptists had never supported the positions of their antislavery clerical leaders. The relatively high biracial composition of the southern Baptist churches should not obscure the fact that the races remained socially separated throughout the antebellum period. In fact, since there were more black worshipers in white Baptist churches than in any other white churches, the pattern of segregation that became standard for all biracial churches was probably first established here. In the face of growing resistance from the lay membership, most churches in Virginia simply tabled debate over the General Committee's 1785 resolution condemning slavery as "contrary to the word of God." Once public opposition emerged, it did not take long for Baptist leaders to change their minds. Eight years after the 1785 declaration, four years after the endorsement of Leland's proposal calling for the legal abolition of bondage, and only three years after denouncing slavery as a "horrid evil," the Virginia General Committee "consented lamely to relegate the slavery question entirely to the civil authorities."[99] For religious leaders to determine that the resolution of a *moral* issue was the government's responsibility was indicative of the power of white racism. Moreover, whatever persuasive power ministers like Leland might have had was undermined by their inability to articulate a well-defined plan for emancipation. Without a coherent, unified program, the opposition to slavery was rudderless and had no purpose.

The debate over slavery at the Constitutional Convention in 1787, the federal government's decision in 1807 to ban the foreign slave trade, and the ominous implications of congressional wrangling over Missouri's statehood application made it clear that time was an enemy of the enslaved. As sectional differences exacerbated personal sensitivities and the free and slave states polarized, it became increasingly difficult for an advocate of what essentially were the interests of one region to be effective in the other. Discouraged by his inability to influence his Virginia congregation, Leland quit his fourteen-year ministry and returned to New England, where he remained active in the antislavery movement until his death in 1841.

Some southern Baptists also rationalized that it would be inhumane to emancipate illiterate and unskilled slaves who, unable to compete with whites for land and jobs, would quickly become destitute. Appointed in 1836 to the pastorate of Richmond's First Baptist Church, Jeremiah Bell Jeter had originally opposed bondage, until he tried to manumit several slaves his wife had inherited. Speculating that the freedmen would face terrible hardships and, as a minister of the gospel, expected to be compassionate, he decided that the only humane thing to do was to keep them enslaved. Similarly influenced was Iveson L. Brookes, a planter and Baptist minister in Jasper and Jones counties, Georgia, who also had criticized slavery but changed his thinking after two marriages into slaveowning families. "The more I have investigated the subject," he wrote, "the more I have become convinced of the true character of African Slavery as an Institution of God and fraught with the highest degree of benevolence to the Negro race." Of course, Jeter and Brookes were simply echoing a common proslavery rationalization and one that conveniently ignored the existence of thousands of free blacks in both North and South—almost a half million by 1860—including many former slaves. While few of them lived in the lap of luxury, most were getting by. Nevertheless, the prediction that the government—and, perhaps more to the point, the churches—would be obligated to provide for the former slaves' well-being remained popular throughout the antebellum era.[100]

Such speculation had been part of every debate over emancipation—what was to be done with the freed slaves?—speculation that was probably based more on the fear of a large and vindictive black population seeking vengeance than on an altruistic concern for the freedmen's welfare. The unspoken realization that the slave had good reason to be vindictive might have persuaded Baptists, like Southerners everywhere, and not a few Northerners, that while bondage was indeed evil the consequences of emancipation would be worse.

The best evidence of the southern Baptist's belief in the morality of bondage could be seen in the fact that, while emancipationist sentiment was growing among members elsewhere in the nation, the Virginia church's submission to the reality of slavery was complete long before the economic pressures of cotton production became the dominant fact of life in most of the antebellum South. Only in retrospect could anyone have noticed that the Virginia General Committee caved in to slavery interests in the same year—1793—that a Yankee inventor named Eli Whitney completed the machine that was to revolutionize the southern economy and ensure the phenomenal growth of plantation slavery. While the nineteenth-century capitulation of the other mainline Protestant denominations could be at least ostensibly associated with the rise of the Cotton Kingdom, the proslavery motive of the Baptists appeared to be firmly entrenched in their belief in white supremacy.[101]

In 1822, Richard Furman, pastor of Charleston's First Baptist Church and organizing president of the South Carolina Baptist State Convention, addressed the governor of the state and, claiming to speak for all South Carolina Baptists, set forth "a biblical defense of slavery as a positive good." Furman was actually protesting against laws passed in the wake of the Denmark Vesey uprising prohibiting religious instruction for slaves. Teaching the slave the way of Christianity, he argued, would prevent rebellions.[102] Whether or not Furman was actually the first person to use the term may be arguable, but the "positive good" theme quickly evolved into a social theory. It became a fundamental element of John C. Calhoun's defense of the southern economic system and the centerpiece of George Fitzhugh's exposition on the perfect hierarchical society.[103] During the decade preceding the southern Baptist tergiversation, many local ministerial associations—such as the Charleston Baptist Association, the Savannah River Association of Baptist Ministers, and the Goslien Association (Free Union, Virginia)—condemned abolitionism and passed resolutions proclaiming the biblical justification of slavery. In time, the influence of the southern churches even reached into the national Baptist organizations—the General Tract Society and the missionary agencies. When the General Missionary Convention (for foreign missions) was established in 1814, its first president was a slaveholder, who retained his post without incident for twenty-one years. The Home Mission Society, which had been organized in 1832, made its position clear in February 1841, when it circulated a statement warning against the introduction of "secular conflicts" into church affairs.[104] Once again, a moral issue was not a religious matter.

Nor should it be assumed that every Baptist preacher who spoke out against slavery did so because of moral convictions. Because of the small percentage of slaveholders among church members—compared to, say, Episcopalians, Presbyterians, and Methodists—Baptist preachers were far less concerned with the interests of masters than were the ministers of other denominations. Indeed, the lower economic level of the Baptist lay population was a fundamental element in the emergence of some of the South's most militant white supremacists. As northern abolitionist pressures mounted and the sectional debate over the issue of slavery in the territories heated up, many southern plain folk saw themselves as the first and worst victims of the catastrophe predicted by slaveholders. The prospect could be terrifying. Former slaves would demand the rights and privileges enjoyed by everyone else, many Southerners warned, ultimately dragging the common white population down to the lowest level. The poor white farmer—the "Swamp Angel," the "Cracker," the dirt eater, and the hillbilly, names that do not suggest a high standard of living—whose economic condition was often little better than the slave's, at least could claim two distinctions that set him above the bondsman—his freedom and his color. Emancipation would leave only one.

The vast majority of the 1.3 million men who fought for The Cause during the Civil War did not own slaves. That so many people were willing to lay down their lives to defend a society whose riches they would never share was a measure of the compelling power of racism. Moreover, if the small independent landowner—that sturdy yeoman whom Jefferson exalted as the American ideal—could no longer aspire to become a great planter, he would lose his incentive to expand and move up in social status. It needs to be remembered that the enormous social prestige that derived from slaveownership drove the nonslaveholder to acquire bondsmen as relentlessly as it drove the slaveholder to hang on to the ones he had and, in fact, to acquire even more. When all of these factors are taken together, it should come as no surprise that, as northern Baptists grew more strident in their condemnations of slavery, southern members found themselves drawn together under what they perceived as a common banner of self-preservation. On May 8, 1845, in Augusta, Georgia, the Southern Baptist Convention was born.[105] A Protestant denomination whose leaders in Virginia a half century earlier had condemned slavery as a "horrid evil" and "contrary to the word of God" was fractured by a cause that its defenders now proclaimed had a divine origin.[106] And yet, if one looks back at the distinctive characteristics of the Baptist church, it may not have been as great a leap as it appeared.

The Baptist schism of 1845 was not so much over slavery as over slave*holding*. Like the Methodists before them, the antislavery Baptists were more concerned with ostracizing masters than with doing anything to alleviate the suffering of the almost three million human beings held in bondage. In 1844 Baptists in Georgia had forced the Home Mission Society, which had been evasive about whether or not a slaveholder could be appointed missionary, to accept or reject James E. Reeve, a slaveholder whom the Georgia Baptist Convention had nominated. When the society voted 7 to 5 to deny the appointment, the southern members resigned and it became, for all intents and purposes, a northern organization. Following the Triennial Convention in Philadelphia in the same year, the Alabama State Baptist Convention adopted a resolution asking the church's Foreign Missionary Board in Boston for a "distinct, explicit avowal" that slave-owners would not be discriminated against when it came to foreign-mission appointments. When the Boston officers refused the request and, in fact, invited members who could not support its antislavery policy to withdraw, the gauntlet had been thrown down. The board's action, according to Jeremiah Jeter, was the spark that ignited the schism. "This decision terminated all hope of union between the Baptists of the two sections in missionary work," he wrote in his *Recollections* (1891), and "filled the brethren of the South with amazement and sorrow." Meeting in Richmond in April 1845, the Virginia Baptist Foreign Mission called for a meeting to be held in Augusta the following month. There 293 delegates convened and formed the Southern Baptist Convention. And at a subsequent meeting in Providence, Rhode Island, led by Francis Wayland and attended by Jeter and one other southern Baptist minister, all parties agreed that a separation was the only viable course of action remaining. Slavery was the fundamental and irreconcilable issue, but nowhere in his four-page review of the affair did Jeter even mention it.[107] The Baptist schism of 1845, it would appear, was exclusively a consequence of the Southerner's anger over being criticized for owning slaves and for defending slavery.

The shift of the Baptists to a hardline proslavery stance was also a consequence of the denomination's emerging status as a recognized church. Beginning in the 1630s as a maverick sect among Rhode Island Puritans, the church by the nineteenth century had grown so large and respectable that it became, in the words of one of its major chroniclers, "more deeply committed to the preservation of the social order" than Roger Williams could ever have foreseen. Like the members of most institutionalized religious bodies, Baptists were conservative when it came to the question of religious intrusion into social issues. This conservatism could be found even among the ranks of the critics of slavery. In 1840, northern Baptists, led by 130 ministers from Massachusetts, had formed the American Baptist Anti-Slavery Convention, an action that Southerners feared would place the mission societies under the leadership of abolitionist zealots. But at the same time the organizers elected as their first president a man, Elon Galusha, who was also a vice-president of the same Board of Foreign Missions that had criticized abolitionists. His appointment did not, of course, mollify Southerners, who threatened to cut off all contributions to Baptist agencies. Galusha was, in fact, an ardent critic of slavery, whose denunciation based on biblical arguments drew a point-by-point rebuttal from none other than Thornton Stringfellow, one of the most ardent southern defenders of bondage.

By this time, the two sides had become so belligerent that neutrality was unacceptable to either. Northern Baptist abolitionists opposed any compromise with a moral evil, while southern Baptists, not content simply to be tolerated, insisted on a positive endorsement of slavery. When the Home Mission Society in 1841 tried to placate its contumacious southern members by taking the position that the controversy was outside of its area of responsibility, these same members demanded an official declaration from the society *supporting* slavery. Responding to the harsh criticisms of the New England ministers, the Charleston Baptist Association described its antislavery critics as "deluded and mischievous fanatics." Interfering with an institution that was sanctioned by the Bible, the report went on, was "incendiary and murderous in its tendency" and not in the interests of the slaves themselves. The Charleston ministerial association was only the first of many southern Baptist groups to proclaim its unrelenting support of slavery.[108]

While Baptists had always taken extreme pride in their congregational independence, the ensuing structural disjunction made the denomination one of the most contentious *pro*slavery religious bodies in the nation. Unlike the Episcopal, Methodist, and Presbyterian churches, all of which organized into regional and national hierarchies, individual Baptist churches recognized no higher ecclesiastical authority than the officers of the local congregation. There were voluntary collective activities in home and foreign missions and in various state general committees, but there was no official chain of command or court of appeals beyond the local pulpit. Even the Baptist General Convention, founded in 1814 mainly to promote the foreign missions and confined to appointing missionaries and raising money, was essentially an *ad hoc* organ of the church. John Leland and David Barrow and their supporters were unable to articulate a unified policy on emancipation because, in part, there was no established congregational network through which to communicate and to provide a forum. And if, somehow, there had been an official policy on slavery or race, there would have been no mechanism to enforce it. When the leaders of the general associations in Virginia and Kentucky announced their resolutions condemning slavery, most of the churches in those states simply ignored the statements and a few threatened to resign from the societies.[109] Paradoxically, the local autonomy that had facilitated the admission of black converts and the ordination of black Baptist preachers was also the source of resistance to emancipation.

The remarkable willingness of southern Baptist congregations to accept slave members and their steadfast unwillingness to endorse freedom for those same members was one of the great enigmas of the Protestant church in antebellum America. Fiercely jealous of their independence, southern Baptists were provincial in ecumenism and suspicious of outsiders (Leland had come from Massachusetts), a posture dictated in large measure by the early history of the denomination. In the seventeenth century, the Baptists had rebelled against authority imposed from above, and the rebellion resulted in their almost fanatical commitment to "liberty of conscience." When organizations like the Virginia General Committee began handing down denunciations of slavery, many church members bristled because, as a specialist in the church's history observed, they "had no intention of relinquishing their consciences to a new episcopacy of Baptist elders."[110]

Congregational independence had come too hard to be so easily set aside. It would not be an exaggeration to suggest that the early Baptist sentiment for emancipation, such as it was, easily became a victim of an abiding Baptist passion for independence.

As openly racist as the southern faction was, it had no monopoly on white supremacy in the Baptist church, even in those places where leaders boasted of their antislavery zeal. There was probably no situation more bizarre than the one in Massachusetts where members of a black family discovered that a pew they had purchased in a previously all-white Baptist church had disappeared. Refusing to be intimidated, they sat on the open floor—only to find the flooring removed the following Sunday. Undaunted, they stood through the services. As late as 1834, a petition calling for the immediate emancipation of all slaves had been signed by only eleven ministers from New York and New England, the region with the largest number of Baptist churches in the nation and claiming the most abolitionist clergymen.[111] The inclusion of *immediate* might have scared a few away. During the antebellum decades, churchmen opposed to abolitionism dominated the Baptist General or Triennial Convention and its Board of Foreign Missions, as well as the Baptist General Tract Society.[112] Like the Home Mission Society, each of these agencies hid behind the specious argument that the specific function for which it had been created did not include taking a position on slavery.

While many northern Baptists made a great deal of noise about opposing human bondage, it is not to their credit that their opposition, like that of the Quakers and many other Christians, was too often a cry for self-purification rather than an effort to lift the burden of enslavement from the backs of millions of black men and women. Their first priority, rather, was to excommunicate slaveholding members lest God punish the church for the sin of tolerating slavery. Describing the posturing of antislavery evangelicals in the years following the Revolution, one historian asserted that they believed the young nation could not "find favor in the eyes of the Lord" until it had been "redeemed from the *sin* of holding Africans in bondage."[113] Even the Freewill Baptists, who were almost as militant as the Franckean Lutherans and the Indiana Yearly Meeting of Anti-Slavery Friends, did not shift their attention to working directly in the slaves' behalf until 1842. As threats of sectional division mounted in the 1840s, there were more than a few northern church leaders who were pleased by the prospect of expelling the slaveholders but who seemed not at all concerned with abolishing the institution of slavery. Accordingly, in April 1845, the editor of the *New York Baptist Registry* called for a peaceful parting of the ways. The following month—almost simultaneously with the birth of the Southern Baptist Convention—Francis Wayland, the president of

Brown University and "one of the most prominent Baptists in the antebellum North," reluctantly acknowledged the departure of his southern brethren, but he continued to oppose efforts to impose sanctions on slaveowners on the ground that such an action would eliminate any possibility of reconciliation.[114] He said nothing about emancipating slaves as a condition of reconciliation.

Such equivocation was vintage Wayland. In *The Elements of Moral Science* (1835), he condemned slavery; but, criticizing abolitionists for putting "the cart before the horse," he was also skeptical about their ability to get rid of it. Cautiously conservative when it came to reform, Wayland was convinced that society would never change until the people in it had changed first. In other words, he clung to the naïve belief that the path to improving the quality of life for oppressed peoples was through the hearts of individuals, not through institutional actions. Three years later, in *The Limitations of Human Responsibility*, Wayland enlarged on this theme when he argued that individuals "have the right to attempt to change southern opinions . . . And to show the master . . . that it is his duty to liberate his slave"; but, at the same time, institutions like the government and the church have no "power whatever either to abolish slavery in the southern States; or to do anything, of which the direct intention is to abolish it." Completely disregarding the fact that it was the institutions of government and the church—through laws sanctioning slavery and the slave trade and religious doctrines of racial superiority—that had created slavery, he concluded that the worst consequence of such efforts would be "to excite the slaves to insubordination and civil war." Indeed, antislavery agitation could easily do more harm than good because, Wayland reasoned, it could so anger slaveholders that they would take it out on their bondsmen.[115]

But reason was not always something he used well. In one of the fifteen letters he exchanged with the Reverend Richard Fuller of Beaufort, South Carolina (beginning in the same year as the Baptist schism), Wayland made it clear that he considered slavery to be a sin and "forbidden in the Scriptures." But he later wrote that "to hold slaves is not of necessity a guilt, and under peculiar circumstances it may not be wrong; it is, therefore, *in itself*, no scripture ground for ecclesiastical excommunication."[116] Condemning and justifying bondage in virtually the same breath, Wayland took the morally indefensible and inherently contradictory position that slavery was evil but, at the same time, possessing slaves was not; and, furthermore, no one—congressman or Christian—had a right to interfere with the institution.

The events of the 1850s moved quickly and emphatically, making it difficult for Wayland to continue splitting hairs over responsibility for emancipation and impossible for him to remain conciliatory toward slaveholders. Despite his longstanding conservatism, he was so angered by the actions of the "border ruffians" and other proslavery forces during the Kansas crisis that he eventually came to believe that the entire South must secede or the free states would be corrupted by their continuing association with the slave power.

By the time the Civil War began, events had driven him to conclude that war was, in fact, an honorable solution to the slavery problem. In less than two decades, Francis Wayland—arguably the most influential northern Baptist leader of the antebellum era—had moved from a well-publicized willingness to welcome back repentant prodigal slaveholders and a position highly critical of abolitionism to the widespread conviction that a Christian nation simply cannot tolerate human bondage. To Southerners, he had turned into just another abolitionist. In a footnote to his 1860 publication of Thornton Stringfellow's "The Bible Argument: or, Slavery in the Light of Divine Revelation," E. N. Elliott identified Wayland and Unitarian leader William Ellery Channing as two abolitionist "writers on public law." By the time of the secession movement in the winter of 1860–61, Wayland was in full agreement with Northerners like Daniel D. Whedon, a Methodist professor at the University of Michigan, who looked forward to the day when the United States would be a nation free of slavery.[117] But it took him a long time to get there. Starting from opposite positions, Wayland and the Virginia Baptist leaders moved toward each other until, passing somewhere in the middle, each stood where the other had started. In their evolving attitudes toward race and slavery, many northern and most southern Baptists were mirror images of each other.

The Civil War eliminated the legal institution of chattel slavery, but it did not significantly change Baptist attitudes toward blacks, and the church remained in the forefront of the Christian campaign against racial equality. During the antebellum period, slave ownership had determined the rules by which people of "African descent"—as Lincoln called them—had been kept in their "place." After the war, social pressures performed that same function; and since the southern church was one of the most influential arbiters of social priorities, Baptist clergymen were among the leaders of what quickly became "the dogma of Negro inferiority." According to Jeremiah Bell Jeter, editor of the popular Baptist *Religious Herald*,[118] the only way to avoid that most horrible of all consequences, the amalgamation of the races, was to separate blacks completely from whites, beginning in the churches themselves.

As before the war, national agencies like the American Baptist Publication Society and the American Baptist Home Mission Society staunchly supported the separation of the races. After officials of the Home Mission Society made overtures to the Southern Baptist Convention for cooperation over a formal plan to "lift up the millions of freedmen to the exercise of all the rights and duties of citizenship and Christian brotherhood," they were rebuffed because such an effort, Southerners feared, would cultivate the dreaded social equality of the races. When some Southern Baptists threatened to discontinue using Publication Society materials because of the agency's invitations to black Baptists for publication contributions, the invitations were withdrawn. One upshot was the formation, in 1895, of the all-black National Baptist Convention. "White racism," religion historian H. Shelton Smith wrote, "was probably the greatest single factor in moving black people to establish churches of their own."[119]

To many Southern Baptists there was also the problem of reconciling the Christian ideal with the basic realities of everyday life. While black and white souls presumably had the same access to heaven, the "immutable laws of race" governed day-to-day activities in the physical world. Obviously the Baptist's hallowed tradition of "liberty of conscience" did not extend to liberty of person. It should have surprised no one, then, that some of the most aggressive supporters of separate *and* independent black congregations in the United States were white Baptist clergymen, who justified their position with the argument that, while all humans may indeed be equal in the eyes of God, the races had been created with "varied capacities" and that black people, accordingly, had been consigned to a subservient status from which they could seek the kingdom of God.[120] If racial differences were God's work, was not everyone obliged to accept them? It was, of course, nothing more than a continuation of the old proslavery argument that subjugating the African was God's will.

However, allegiance to God's will kept Southern Baptists from endorsing some of the more bizarre white-supremacist theories. In 1867, many church members were repelled by Buckner Payne's charge, set forth in *The Negro: What Is His Ethnological Status?*, that Africans were not humans and did not have souls; and their views were essentially the same when, thirty-three years later, Charles Carroll expanded on Payne's theme in his notorious *"The Negro a Beast"* (1900).[121] Of course, no one should mistake these reactions for manifestations of an equalitarian spirit. By the end of the nineteenth century, Southern Baptists, holding that "the religious destiny of the world is lodged in the hands of the English-speaking people," supported the American move toward Christian imperialism. "To the Anglo-Saxon race," one church spokesman said, "God seems to have committed the enterprise of the world's salvation."[122]

There was probably no more outrageous champion of white supremacy than Thomas Dixon, Jr., the son of a Baptist preacher who joined the ministry himself in 1886 after trying his hand at, variously, acting, politics, and the law. Born in Shelby, North Carolina, Dixon held pastorates in North Carolina, Boston, and New York City before he turned to full-time lecturing and writing in 1899. Because of the spectacular success of his fanatical white-supremacist novel *The Leopard's Spots: A Romance of the White Man's Burden, 1865–1900* (1902), Dixon decided to make a career out of condemning "the black ape," and he soon published two companion stories, *The Clansman: An Historical Romance of the Ku Klux Klan* (1905) and *The Traitor: A Story of the Fall of the Invisible Empire* (1907), both of which were similarly successful and the former subsequently adapted to film as D. W. Griffith's *The Birth of a Nation* (1915). While it would be incorrect and unfair to characterize Dixon as a typical Southern Baptist, it cannot be denied that the "massive sales" enjoyed by his white-supremacist trilogy were ominous testimony to the popularity of his ideas.[123] It stretches a person's credulity to accept the thought that Dixon was a product of the same denomination that had, a century earlier, produced John Leland and David Barrow. But then again the same thing could be said of individuals in each of the schismatic denominations.

If there was a countervailing Baptist polemic to Dixon's works, it was Benjamin F. Riley's *The White Man's Burden* (1910). Giving up his Texas pastorate to work full time for blacks, Riley insisted that most of the former slave's problems had been imposed on him by whites. But even someone as obviously concerned about justice for blacks as Riley could not avoid the missionary's inherent proclivity to be paternalistic and condescending.[124] Similarly, Baptists in Alabama, who for the previous three decades had taken little interest in the welfare of the former slaves, acknowledged after 1900 that they had a responsibility.[125] But Baptist dogmatism was unrelenting. In Alabama, as virtually everywhere else, the black person was seen as an object of respect only within the context of Christianity. "We are dealing with the Negroes as fellow Christians, as fellow Baptists, as Christ's freemen," a white preacher wrote in the *Alabama Baptist* in 1904. "As such they are entitled to courteous and considerate treatment, and must have all of their individual rights respected."[126] Why *as such*? Did this mean that unconverted black people were not "entitled" to such treatment and that whites could ignore their individual rights? Such an attitude was, in fact, little different from the seventeenth-century Puritan missionary's belief that the heathen deserved respect and justice only when he stopped being a heathen.

The Protestant Tradition of Separation

While it would be easy to attribute the southern Baptists' militant resistance to abolitionism to their congregational independence, the fact that the organizational structure of each of the divided denominations was different from the others suggests that congregationalism had little to do with the Baptist schism of 1845. Be its system of organization presbyterian, episcopalian, or congregational, each mainline church seemed helpless to cool the ardor of its antislavery factions or prevent the defection of its proslavery constituents. The schisms were probably more revealing as measures of the overwhelming political and economic power of the slaveholders than as manifestations of doctrinal or organizational differences. From the very beginning of the nation's constitutional existence, the slaveholders' influence in public affairs had been far out of proportion to their numbers—even in the South, where they were only a fraction of the white population. It should not be forgotten that before the election of Abraham Lincoln in 1860, thirteen of the fifteen presidents of the United States—from George Washington to James Buchanan—had been either southern slaveholders or Northerners who had usually sympathized with slaveholders; and prior to the Compromise of 1850 senators from the slave states had maintained a "balance of equality" that had enabled them to obstruct any congressional action that threatened the interests of the South, although the slave-state percentage of the population had become a declining minority long before. Such was the omnipresent power of the "peculiar institution." By the middle of the nineteenth century, that power could no longer be tolerated by Americans who could not reconcile human bondage with the ideals of Christian love and charity. Since the division in the churches was only a symptom of a larger malaise, the outcome was inevitable. As one historian put it, "The divided churches painfully exposed the deep moral chasm between North and South, furthering the alienation between sections and contributing to the eventual disruption of the Union."[127]

Anyone who wanted an object lesson on the influence of what abolitionists derisively called the "slave power" needed only to note that the southern Protestant obsession with preserving the slaveholding way of life united in a common brotherhood denominations that for decades, even centuries, had been driven apart by fundamental doctrinal and organizational differences. The colonies had been settled by dissenting religious forces, a condition that fed Christianity's amoebic inclination to divide and redivide. Founded by the Separatist followers of Robert Browne, some of whom had earlier relocated in the Netherlands, Plimouth Plantation was only the first such settlement; and the Puritans, who established the much larger Massachusetts Bay Colony to the north, had challenged the Anglican church only to find themselves challenged by the likes of Roger Williams, John Wheelwright, Anne Hutchinson, and Thomas Hooker. By the early eighteenth century, the "plethora of new sects" in English North

America had become "notoriously contemptuous of tradition and authority."[128] From the imperious Anglicans of Virginia and the Carolinas to the unobtrusive Schwenkfelders of Pennsylvania, there seemed to be no end to the proliferation of Christian denominations, each claiming to be the true church. And the disestablishmentarian principle—by which the law perceived churches as exclusively voluntary organizations and which evolved after 1787 into the doctrine of the separation of church and state—encouraged the impulse to splinter.

When the "hermeneutical awakening"—the early-nineteenth-century movement to unify Protestant denominations through independent interpretations of the Bible—led, not surprisingly, to still more fragmentation, it appeared that the United States was heading inexorably toward a society consisting almost entirely of independent splinter churches in every city and town. Such a consequence should really have surprised few people. Dissent and disunion, in the greatest tradition of the Protestant Reformation, had been around as long as Christianity itself—Gnostics, Montanists, Neo-Platonists, Monarchians, orthodoxy, heresy—and was as American as purple mountains, fruited plains, and amber waves of grain. Why should the Presbyterians, Methodists, and Baptists of the nineteenth-century United States have been immune to their lure, especially over an issue as patently contentious as slavery?

But slavery was also a countervailing force in the American tradition of religious dissent. As southern Presbyterians, Methodists, and Baptists left their northern brethren, they found a common ground. Perhaps more to the point, southern Christian unity was a tribute not so much to the power of slavery as to the fear of a society without slavery, a fear that brought the seceding denominations together around three general themes. Mainline Protestants in the slaveholding states agreed, first, that mistreating a bondsman was sinful but that the institution of slavery was not; second, that immediate emancipation would "turn loose upon the nation a horde of illiterate, uncouth, and undisciplined blacks"; and third, that the abolitionist goal of extending equality to former slaves would endanger the "purity of the white race" and expose the American people to the vile prospect of miscegenation.[129]

In 1863, an expression of this unity appeared in the Richmond *Central Presbyterian* under the title "An Address to the Christians of the World." It was drafted by five ministers and signed by ninety-six Christian leaders—including bishops, religious editors, college presidents, theology professors, and many "eminent parish ministers"—from eleven denominations (mostly Baptist, Methodist, and Presbyterian) and representing every Confederate state except Arkansas. The publication of the "Address," called by one historian the "most significant proslavery document" of the period, was apparently timed to look like a southern Protestant reply to the Emancipation Proclamation. In reality, the list of signatures was more impressive than the document's contents, which consisted of all the old proslavery clichés, including the sophism that enslavement was God's way of getting the gospel to the African.[130] Nonetheless, there is a painful irony in the fact that the cause of human bondage was able to do for Christian unity, at least in the southern states, what promises of an everlasting life could not. Moral priorities had been turned upside down. The power of fear, it seems, was more compelling than the power of faith.

The power of fear notwithstanding, many white southern Protestants, according to two researchers, did not spend all of their time trying to justify a white-supremacist society, and did, in fact, challenge popular assumptions about the moral and practical conditions of a slave society. Writing in the *Journal of Southern History* (1973), James Brewer Stewart asserted that "during the early and middle 1820s a number of deeply religious individuals living in the upper South [especially Tennessee] felt impelled to develop stringent criticisms of slavery and its influence upon churches, society, and politics." Similarly, Kenneth K. Bailey, conceding that "racial discrimination ought to be studied in southern Protestantism and elsewhere and that it ought to be deplored," argued two years later in the same journal that there were "happier aspects" of the situation and that "the southern churches were not so comfortably aligned with the racial mores of their region during the slavery era as now seems to be believed."[131] To these scholars, the common historical wisdom, though not incorrect, is incomplete.

Both writers are convincing, but their accounts, unfortunately, serve mainly as the exceptions that prove the rule. To begin with, Stewart restricted his study to a period before cotton cultivation had become extensively established in the South (and to a region in which cotton was to become only marginally significant) and before the popular philosophical defense of slavery had been fully articulated. More specifically, his heavy dependence on Benjamin Lundy's antislavery periodical *Genius of Universal Emancipation* (1821–25), and his admission that it was "the only continuing source to be found for the subject during this period," do little more than call attention to the fact that early southern evangelical abolitionists were conspicuously out of step with the common southern view on race. Bailey, likewise, drew a misleading portrait because he focused primarily on the white treatment of blacks who were members of Protestant churches and on the successes of certain black ministers, most notably Andrew Marshall, pastor of the Savannah First African Baptist Church. "Had the churches of the South in fact been captives of their regional culture," he wrote, "blacks would have no place in the clergy."[132] The problem with this conclusion is that it was based solely on a narrow examination of the receptions of a small number of blacks within the context of church activities. There were many black Baptists, Methodists, and Presbyterians whose lives were improved as a result of the kindness and understanding of white fellow worshipers; but how did the black population at large, the vast majority of whom did not affiliate with organized churches, benefit from all of this? More to the point, how were the destructive consequences of the South's fundamental "racial mores," as Bailey called them—white racism generally and the institution of slavery in particular—diminished by such "happier aspects"?

Until these questions can be answered, the premise that slaves generally were beneficiaries of southern Protestantism calls for a greater suspension of disbelief than most students of the history of race relations are willing to make. Moreover, the presence of black clergymen did not necessarily mean a more congenial Protestant South. There were, as noted earlier, more than a few black Baptist ministers prior to 1830, but that certainly did not stop the majority of white Baptists from hardening their view toward slavery.

The capitulation of the three mainline Protestant churches and their inevitable schisms also serve to illuminate the power of social privilege and vested interests. By the second quarter of the nineteenth century the plantation system had become so widely entrenched and the beneficiaries of that system so convinced of its virtues that no amount of moralizing could have the slightest effect on the status quo, and it is in this context that the acquiescence of churchmen like Francis Asbury and Charles Colcock Jones should be assessed. "Negro servitude was so intricately woven into the fabric of society that it compromised values, institutions, and perspectives by which it might otherwise have been weakened," Donald G. Mathews wrote. "Christianity, the Revolution, democracy, equality—all the abstractions of American national romanticism existed in varying degrees of subordination to the facts of slavery." Moreover, white Southerners had developed an "almost pathological fear of antislavery" and an unrelenting attachment "to a structure of race domination and social control" that easily deflected what they perceived to be sanctimonious and totally unjust attacks on their way of life. It could be argued that it was *race*—that is, "the determination to maintain white supremacy"—and not slavery, that was the critical element in their intransigence.[133]

And the slaveholder enjoyed more than a little support from unexpected quarters. For example, the popular rationalization of many northern clergymen that slavery was a political and not a moral issue and therefore a matter that should be of no concern to the churches was a total repudiation of the belief that Christianity's most fundamental qualities were things like love, charity, mercy, compassion, humility, and selflessness. In other words, to assert that human bondage was not a moral issue was to say that human suffering had nothing to do with morality. To a modern civil libertarian—not to mention a modern Christian—it defies belief that such a view could be sustained among men who considered themselves messengers of Jesus Christ.

The defection of the southern factions also needs to be viewed against the less-than-humanitarian posture of the northern churches. Largely ignoring the plight of the slave, many evangelicals in the late eighteenth and early nineteenth centuries had believed that slavery should be eliminated because it "undermined the spirituality of the master." Similarly, the subsequent Methodist perfectionism and New School Presbyterian revivalism maintained an "uncompromising stance against slavery *as a sin.*" Nor were religious institutions the only ones deluded by this concern. "The first great principle of the [American Anti-Slavery] Society, and indeed one from which all others are deduced," William Jay wrote in 1835, "is the *sinfulness of slavery.*" Thus even an ostensibly nonsectarian organization was seduced by an essentially religious theme. Of course, for the more zealous revivalists of the Jacksonian era, the abolition of slavery provided a convenient and timely moral platform. In his book *Slavery and the Church* (1853), William Hosmer said virtually nothing about the suffering endured by slaves; but on almost every one of its two hundred pages he called attention to the evil of slavery and what righteous people must do to escape punishment for tolerating it. Echoing a complaint first heard from the Quakers in the seventeenth century, northern Presbyterians, Methodists, and Baptists seemed to be more concerned with improving their chances of going to heaven than with relieving the burdens of bondage from the backs of millions of oppressed men and women. Some researchers have suggested that dissenting antislavery ministers and communicants established splinter churches not because they wanted to eliminate human bondage but because they had lost faith in the traditional church's ability to answer the question "What shall I do to be saved?" Even the Wesleyan Methodists, Freewill Baptists, Franckean Lutherans, and certain Presbyterians and Quakers, all of whom broke away from their respective parent churches over what they considered vacillating antislavery postures, fit this suggestion.[134] These Protestant factions deserved their reputations for humanitarian service, but that does not diminish the fact that their first purpose in establishing splinter congregations was one of spiritual self-cleansing. In the end, even the most radical Christian abolitionist judged his own actions, as he believed God would, in the light of the righteousness of his behavior.

Many Christians also probably took great comfort in the thought that their religious conviction was the one thing they would never compromise. After all, if a person's faith was based on a belief in eternal truths, there should have been no reason for that faith to waver. But in antebellum America such a sanguine attitude was simply not realistic. In a world of profit and power, moral concerns, from the earliest times, had been easily brushed aside by the forces of capital and politics. To appease the slaveholding class, Anglican clergymen in the seventeenth century repudiated the common-law connection of baptism and emancipation; two centuries later, for essentially the same reason, southern Protestants defined their faith to suit the interests of the slave power. Eternal truths notwithstanding, when it came to matters involving racial issues, Christianity's readiness to accommodate secular interests was second to none. The only truth that was eternal was the truth of self-interest.

When northern antislavery clergymen called for the expulsion of slaveholding members, southern ministers rationalized that the existence of slavery was a political issue to be dealt with by the government, not a moral issue to be settled by the church. Ironically, war—the government's ultimate political solution—resolved the moral controversy that proslavery Christians insisted was none of their business. Surprisingly, many officials in the postwar northern churches, despite three decades of abolitionist pressures, refused to acknowledge "the inherent sinfulness of slaveholding and the equality of all races." Not surprisingly, the abolition of slavery did not change very many southern minds and the churches remained bitterly divided. Beginning with the southern Presbyterian General Assembly just eight months after the end of the war and continuing into the twentieth century with the phenomenal growth of the Southern Baptist Church, virtually every effort at conciliation between the bodies that had divided before the Civil War failed.[135]

Even in those rare instances where reconciliation was achieved, David H. Reimers wrote in *White Protestantism and the Negro* (1965), such as "the northern Presbyterian Church's union with the Cumberland Presbyterians in the first decade of the twentieth century and in the active negotiations over Methodist unity that began in 1910," it was possible only because a "growing number of northern Protestants were willing to sacrifice Negro rights." If there has been a consistent theme in the American religious experience, another historian argued, "it has been that where a racial factor is present, the values of 'forgiveness, reconciliation, and love' have been largely impotent—even in church—to resolve conflict and stave off strife." It has been racism, more than anything else, C. C. Goen wrote in *Broken Churches, Broken Nation* (1985), "that has undermined the credibility of Christian charity throughout American history."[136]

NINE ✿ MELTING POT CHRISTIANS: THE IMMIGRANT CHURCHES

There will always be poor people in the land. Therefore I command you to be openhanded toward your brothers and toward the poor and needy in your land.

DEUTERONOMY 15:11

Then the King will say to those on his right, "Come, you who are blessed by my Father; take your inheritance, the kingdom prepared for you since the creation of the world. For I was hungry and you gave me something to eat, I was thirsty and you gave me something to drink, I was a stranger and you invited me in, I needed clothes and you clothed me, I was sick and you looked after me, I was in prison and you came to visit me."

Then the righteous will answer him, "Lord, when did we see you hungry and feed you, or thirsty and give you something to drink? When did we see you a stranger and invite you in, or needing clothes and clothe you? When did we see you sick or in prison and go to visit you?"

The King will reply, "I tell you the truth, whatever you did for one of the least of these brothers of mine, you did for me."

MATTHEW 25:34–40

Huddled Masses

The United States has long been known as a nation of immigrants. Dozens of books have been written about the subject, and one of them—Oscar Handlin's *The Uprooted* (1951)—is an American classic. The immigration theme stands alongside those other grand ideas by which Americans perceive their past—rugged individualism, the frontier movement, self-determination, free enterprise, and so on. While the theme may embody a few contradictions, most citizens manage to rationalize them away. Thus Americans cherish, on the one hand, the "melting pot" notion, with its emphasis on the singularity of their belief in democratic principles and economic opportunities and, on the other, the "tossed salad" idea of a society consisting of many unique components, each of which retains its distinctive—and, of course, commendable—characteristics.[1]

The American city at the turn of the century was a circus of sounds, sights, and smells. Ethnic foods, religions, festivals, newspapers, music, and languages reflected the pluralism of society. While hyphenated designations like Irish-American, German-American, or Chinese-American are cumbersome and not always in fashion, most Americans nonetheless proudly call attention to their racial and ethnic ancestries, be they Jewish, Italian, Japanese, Greek, Armenian, or whatever; and, not so surprisingly, some of them do so despite the fact that their immigrant forebears left the old countries two or three centuries ago. Ethnic identification seems to satisfy two fundamental human needs: the need to be different and the need to be the same.

The Statue of Liberty was dedicated in October 1886, as the country was moving into the fourth, and greatest, immigration wave in its history. In each of the first two years of the Civil War, the number of aliens taking up permanent residence in the United States dipped below 100,000 for the first time since 1844 (a low that would not be reached again until 1931). But it soon began creeping upward, reaching almost 800,000 in 1882, leveling off for two decades, then soaring again to new highs that diminished only with the beginning of the Great War. In fact, the number of arrivals in the fifteen years before the war was nothing less than mind-boggling. In the last forty years of the nineteenth century, almost 14 million people came to the United States, a figure that was matched in the following fifteen years. To put it another way, between 1880 and 1900 immigration into the United States averaged almost 450,000 annually, an increase of 59 percent over the annual rate of the previous decade; but in the first decade and a half of the twentieth century the annual average soared to 862,000, with six of those years counting over 1 million immigrants each and the peak year of 1907 claiming almost 1.3 million. Anyone who is still unimpressed need only note that the number of immigrants entering the United States in those fifteen years was over 15 percent of the total American population in 1900.[2]

As overwhelming as these numbers were, however, the most important differences between the old and new immigrants were qualitative rather than quantitative. In the First Census (1790), 83.5 percent of the white population had claimed an English cultural background, with most of the remainder divided among the Scotch-Irish, Germans, Dutch, Irish, and their descendants. While the percentages shifted dramatically in the ensuing years, the nationalities did not—until the last two decades of the nineteenth century, when immigrants from southern and eastern European countries, where the religions, languages, traditions, and political systems were radically different from the homelands of earlier immigrant nationalities, poured into eastern and midwestern cities. They even looked different: the swarthy Mediterranean and Slavic Europeans contrasted sharply with the fairer Anglo-Saxon (or Nordic, Teutonic, Aryan) types who had migrated in earlier times from northern and western Europe.

The most important of the new nationalities were the Italians. In 1880 immigrants from Italy had constituted less than 3 percent of all foreigners coming to the United States (12,354 out of 457,257); but by 1890 their percentage had climbed to 11.4, a figure that doubled by the end of the century and peaked in 1901 at almost 28 (135,996 out of 487,918), a larger percentage than all who came from northern and western Europe combined, including Germany. While the Italian percentage of total immigration declined slightly after 1903, the actual number continued to increase rapidly, averaging over 200,000 per year during the first decade and a half of the twentieth century. The number of Italians was exceptional, but the rate of increase was about the same as the rates for immigrants from Poland, the Slavic countries, Russia, and the Baltic States in the same years.[3]

Not only was the new immigration greater in numbers and different in composition from the earlier waves, but the range of its settlement and the concentrations of its neighborhoods altered the American landscape radically. Except for the Irish, many of those who had migrated in the years before the Civil War had moved on to the newer regions of the nation, especially the Midwest. The antebellum German immigrants had become prosperous members of the middle class, and some of their fellow countrymen who immigrated later in the century continued to settle, along with Scandinavians, in the upper Midwest and the Great Plains. As late as 1910 one-fifth of the people in Wisconsin and Illinois were foreign-born, mostly Germans and Scandinavians, a fraction that was matched or exceeded in parts of Nebraska and the Dakotas. But these were the exceptions. The late-nineteenth-century immigrant was most likely a peasant who lacked the resources and skills to continue on to the more distant corners of the nation, assuming he had ever wanted to go.

While political oppression had been a significant element in many decisions to leave Europe, the foreigners' incentive had been primarily economic and thus they gravitated to the factories of the eastern cities, where the jobs were. In some cases the attraction was virtually irresistible. With promises of free transportation and guaranteed employment, labor contractors rounded up thousands of young men and women in European cities specifically for work in American industry. "Though less than one fifth of the American people lived in the big cities" in 1900, Carl Degler noted, "almost two fifths of all immigrants did." The disparity became even greater with the second generation as over one third of that stock "lived in the thirty-eight cities over 100,000 population, though only one tenth of the old native population lived in those cities."[4] The result was ghettos and slums where these strange people, with their unfamiliar languages, peculiar habits, and suspicious political opinions, made up one level of a stratified society that was viewed with growing distrust and contempt by the other. When Frederick Jackson Turner introduced his famous frontier hypothesis at the annual meeting of the American Historical Association in Chicago in 1893, he was, in fact, warning Americans to beware of the dangers posed by the new immigration because the vast wilderness that had absorbed and regenerated earlier invasions of aliens was gone.

For many "native" Americans, the most detestable ingredient of the new immigration was religious. Some of the newcomers simply added to the established faiths, such as the Irish Catholics whom many Protestants had held in contempt since the 1850s; others were the less obtrusive Christian Reformed (Dutch) Church, German Mennonites from Russia, and various Lutheran sects from Germany and the Scandinavian countries. But the biggest numbers came as Catholics from Italy, Poland, Germany, Austria, Hungary, and the Baltic states, and as Eastern Orthodox and Jews from Russia and the Balkans. The result was a resurgence of the ugly nativism that had first been spawned in the decade before the Civil War with the rise of the American Party—the Know-Nothings.

In the earlier period the nation had gone through an orgy of religious fanaticism as pseudo-patriotic organizations like the Order of the Star-Spangled Banner had organized hate campaigns against Irish Catholics fleeing the great potato famine. The new nativism, on the other hand, fed by the growing popularity of an evolutionary theory that "brought a semblance of scientific support to old notions of 'Nordic' superiority," was much more inclusive, sweeping up almost all non–Western Europeans in its net.[5] In *Race or Mongrel* (1908), Alfred P. Schultz argued that the history of the rise and fall of the great empires of the past demonstrated conclusively that societies were brought down by mingling with inferior "alien stocks," and that the only way to save the United States from such a fate was to restrict severely the immigration of non–Western Europeans, a view echoed eight years later by Madison Grant, who, in *The Passing of the Great Race*, offered scientific "proof" that the "greatest danger which threatens the American republic to-day" is the dying out of Anglo-Saxon European hereditary traits.[6] There was no room for Emma Lazarus's "huddled masses" and "wretched refuse" in this America. As for people of color, they were so despicable that Schultz and Grant did not think it necessary even to mention them.

For the conservative Protestant, of course, the greatest threat was Catholicism, and his reaction to it was no less venomous than it had been four decades earlier. In 1887, seven men led by Henry F. Bowers of Clinton, Iowa, founded the American Protective Association, a secret anti-Catholic society committed to the belief that every economic problem faced by the nation was the iniquitous work of immigrants from Ireland and southern

Europe. Bowers, whom Sydney E. Ahlstrom identified as "a paranoid crony of the mayor of Clinton," was convinced that the mayor had been defeated for reelection by the local Irish labor vote. The APA, its leaders vowed, would save Protestant America from the long reach of the Vatican. Bowers and his successor, William J. Traynor, saw to it that members of the association swore "never to vote for a Catholic and if possible never to hire or strike with one." It was an organization of vengeance and retaliation. John Higham noted that surprisingly the APA "lacked a race consciousness that might have appealed to the [white] South" and, in fact, its leaders actually "welcomed Negro support."[7] The prospect was more than just paradoxical: black Americans, the greatest victims of racial bigotry, joining an organization of bigots dedicated to the suppression of people whose own bigotry toward blacks was well documented.

As it happened, of course, northern blacks were *objects* of discrimination and racial violence, not creators, and no small amount of that racism could be laid at the feet of the European immigrant, a situation that was more than obvious to James B. Clarke writing in the 1913 edition of *The Annals of the American Academy of Political and Social Science.*

> I do not pretend to say that the immigrant is not often to be found among those who keep alive the torch of liberty and justice of America, but I do believe that the continuance of racial hatred in the North is traceable to the Europeans whose lack of contact with the Negro has been exploited and played upon by native whites who have nothing to think and talk about but an exaggerated idea of the virtues and capacities of the Anglo-Saxon race.[8]

In the decade before the Civil War, emancipation was a radical idea and the immigrants' "cultural isolation" made them inherently conservative. When Irish and German Catholics realized that Protestant clergymen dominated the antislavery movement and were mostly Republicans, they quickly began filling the ranks of the Democratic party—the Germans predominantly and the Irish overwhelmingly—where they could spout their white-supremacy views without disagreement. The Democrats, for their part, jumped at the chance to exploit the perceived threat to jobs and wages that was sure to follow hordes of emancipated slaves spreading across the northern states. "It was among the foreign-born proletariat of the cities and small farmers of Southern origin that the specter was most disturbing," Wood Gray wrote in *The Hidden Civil War* (1942). "The Negroes were expected to compete with the whites for unskilled urban employment and thus force wages down to disastrous levels."[9]

It was a theme that could be found in political campaigns, both great and small, all across the nation. "A vote for Seymour is a vote to protect our white laborers against the association and competition of Southern negroes," the editor of the staunchly Democratic New York *World* wrote during the New York gubernatorial election in 1862, while "a vote for Wadsworth is a vote to elbow aside our white immigrant population and repel it from our shore." Running the following year to retain his seat in the Pennsylvania State Legislature, a Germantown Republican named William F. Smith woke up one morning to a four-page leaflet that, in a blatant attempt to foment discontent among Irish Catholics, accused his abolitionist supporters of "burning nunneries, mobbing Catholic priests, hanging Irishmen, and urging the passage of laws to disfranchise and degrade our adopted citizens." Considering their fanaticism on racial matters, advocates of this view certainly could not be expected to observe the niceties of good taste. Recounting a fictitious conversation between a northern banker and an abolitionist Protestant minister, one critic predicted that the Republicans planned to create a race of human "mules" by breeding immigrants with former slaves. "Ireland and Germany will supply us with fresh horses (poor white trash)," A. C. Harness wrote in 1873, "and the supply of asses (negroes) on hand is pretty large."[10]

There were probably more than a few unskilled immigrants who did not mind occupying the bottom rung of the ladder; they just did not want to share it with anybody—especially people whom they considered racially inferior. "You think this fall in wages is owing to the Chinaman?" English traveler William Hepworth Dixon asked an Irish laborer in San Francisco after the Civil War.

> What else, Captain? Why, before the brute came in, my ould woman got her bit of washing and ironing, enough anyhow to buy a drop of drink; but now the squinting villain robs the women as well as he robs the men. If it were not for soiling one's hands, I'd like to squash them head and heels into the bay—just there, by Hunter's Point.
>
> You don't say, Live and let live, eh, Pat?
>
> Live! Why, Captain, he's a heathen Chinee; a real heathen Chinee! What business has the loikes of him over here? Is not Chinay big enough for him?
>
> Come, Pat, haven't you come over from County Cork?
>
> That's thrue, Captain; but then the country's ours. We conquered it from the Injuns and the Mexicans. Let the Chinese try to conquer it from us![11]

In most other cities, such as Boston in the 1850s, competition between racial groups was not a problem, as Irish workers, who could not unfairly be described as northern equivalents of southern slaves, dominated the unskilled labor market and considered the frequent comparison to slaves as studied insults to their pride.[12] Even in places as remote as Iowa, over half of the state's almost 200,000 people in 1850 were foreign born, and over half of those were from Ireland and Germany. While many of them melted inconspicuously into the midwestern countryside, the Irish in Dubuque and the Germans in Davenport retained much of their ethnic culture, becoming productive components of their communities. These earlier immigrants, most of them in agriculture, unskilled services, or pre-factory manufacturing, did not face a great deal of economic resistance. The rise of the factory changed all of this. By 1900, thousands of Russian Jews, Irish, and Italians were clustered in ethnic enclaves within the largest northern cities, adding to those who had arrived before the Civil War.[13] The American ghetto was born.

Low pay, excessive hours, unsafe working conditions, few benefits, no job security, unhealthful living environment, exploitation by abusive managers, and manipulation by venal politicians—the foreign-born city dweller certainly could not be blamed for wondering if life in the United States was really any better than in his homeland. But the status of the urban white unskilled worker and the prejudices he faced, as bad as they were, in no way compared to the condition of the former slave. All the immigrant had done was relocate, presumably, and in many cases assuredly, for the purpose of improving his economic condition. And time was on his side. Although he started out at the bottom, he could eventually work his way into the general population, as Max Lerner described it, "yielding the role of strangeness in turn to the still later comers." For the most part, the hardships diminished with each generation. In fact, the eventual achievements of a few immigrant nationalities were remarkable. By the end of the nineteenth century, for example, many of the descendants of Irish immigrants who had arrived before the Civil War were electing mayors and controlling municipal governments in places like New York City, Pittsburgh, Boston, St. Louis, Omaha, New Orleans, and San Francisco. Similarly, German immigrants began to dominate politics in parts of Missouri and Wisconsin. In short, in just a few decades these newcomers and their children, originally viewed by the older residents as the dregs of humanity, had moved into the mainstream of American political and economic life.[14] Can anyone imagine very many former slaves doing anything even remotely similar?

The European immigrant had a distinctive national heritage, with all that entailed. "To many ethnic groups," Carl N. Degler wrote, "the silent terror of being in a new land, thousands of miles from native roots, strengthened rather than weakened the loyalty to and dependence upon the old religion." From this connection "sprang an attachment between the people and the Church" that held them together against all of the disruptive forces of their new environment. Changes there were many, of course. The tensions of adapting to an alien and threatening environment forced immigrants to accommodate their "tenacious ties to European culture and church traditions" to the institutions and ideals of their new country.[15]

But the black person's heritage was *slavery*; he had no cultural ties to accommodate. He did not even have an ancestral nationality, at least not one he could identify with any confidence. Africa was a continent of many nations and cultures, and most of the former slaves were centuries removed from all of them. No ancestral religion, no common language (except the master's), no ethnic traditions, no relatives in the old country, and no place called "home." In short, no cultural continuity.

German Piety and Lutheran Resolve

Although the Lutheran church had been around for over two hundred years before the Civil War, it could still be characterized as an "immigrant religion" because of its chronological separation into two distinct populations. The first Lutherans arrived in 1638 with the Swedish founding of Fort Christina on the Delaware, while the oldest continuous parishes date to New Netherland in 1649. These settlers were subsequently joined by those émigrés who, along with the various German sects, found colonial Pennsylvania and New York to be especially tolerant of their unorthodox religious views. There were four Lutheran congregations in English North America as early as 1660, but growth was slow and that number had increased only to seven by the end of the century. In the succeeding years, however, a new wave of immigration made the Lutherans more than an isolated continental sect. Between 1708 and 1710 the influx of Palatine Germans to New York and North Carolina accounted for the first surge of growth; and when the proprietors of Georgia received their charter in 1732, the distressed Lutherans of Salzburg led the greatest exodus of refugees from Europe in the eighteenth century. The new arrivals pushed the number of Lutheran churches to ninety-five by 1740, and forty years later the 240 Lutheran churches in the new nation, led by men like Henry Melchior Mühlenberg in Pennsylvania, were exceeded in number only by the Congregationalists, Presbyterians, Baptists, and Episcopalians.[16]

The second Lutheran population did not become significant until 1820 and, especially, after 1830, when the number of immigrants from Germany increased dramatically, peaking in 1854 with 215,009 arrivals. In 1830 there were 569 Lutheran congregations, claiming 42,876 communicants among a total constituency of over 200,000, and organized into ten regional synods in thirteen states. During the following decade, while the nation's population grew by one-third, the number of Lutherans went up at four times the national rate. And the pace continued. As political upheavals in Germany and crop failures in the Rhine Valley drove emigrants to American shores at a record pace—almost one million in the ten years before the Civil War—the number of Lutherans increased accordingly. By 1860 there were 2,128 Lutheran churches in the United States, still far behind the Methodists, Baptists, and Presbyterians but about even with the Catholics, Congregationalists, Episcopalians, and Disciples of Christ.

The greatest surge of all was still to come. In 1870 there were a half million Lutherans, a number that increased almost five times by 1910, easily surpassing the Presbyterians. Thus, although the church had come to America only thirty-one years after the founding of Jamestown, it was the sheer magnitude of the nineteenth-century influx that defined Lutheranism as an imported faith. Furthermore, unlike the colonial generations, which had adapted to the slave systems that had existed everywhere, most of the later Lutheran immigrants settled in the northern states long after slavery had been abolished there. Lutherans in older German communities were often uncomfortable, and even a little embarrassed, by the "eccentric" ideas and conduct of the newcomers, and that discomfiture was reflected in the diversity of Lutheran churches and synods. Language differences and other cultural obstacles, one church historian wrote, kept American Lutherans "largely isolated from Protestant churches until the twentieth century." With twenty independent Lutheran groups in the United States in 1900, many Lutherans were also isolated from each other.[17]

It was not, needless to say, a situation conducive to a unified position on race and slavery, a situation best seen in the emergence of two divergent—and extreme—factions at almost the same time. In 1837 four dissident ministers and a group of lay members from the Hartwick Synod west of Albany, New York, unhappy over their leaders' refusal to adopt a hardline position against slavery, formed the Franckean Synod (named after the great pietist August Herman Francke of Saxony), a body that was to become one of the most radical Protestant abolitionist factions in the United States. "The attitude and activity of the Franckean Synod with respect to slavery represents the greatest degree of opposition to that institution to be found among Lutheran bodies," Robert Fortenbaugh wrote in his old but still useful study; "and, indeed, it is doubtful if any group in any denomination exhibited a more extreme position."

To oppose the church's leading periodical, the Baltimore-based *Lutheran Observer*—which had criticized slavery but also denounced the abolitionists—the Franckeans established the *Lutheran Herald*, which, as expected, condemned both slavery and the American Colonization Society. The ACS had enlisted extensive support from many Christian clergymen, including Lutherans—not to mention the endorsement of prominent political figures like Andrew Jackson, Henry Clay, and William Crawford. But the Franckean ministers, recognizing the movement as an effort that, by getting rid of the allegedly troublesome free black population, would actually have made human bondage even more secure, repudiated its professed goal of colonizing former slaves in Africa. No one could accuse the Franckeans of being disingenuous. In 1841 the synod's leaders unanimously resolved that every Christian had a moral duty to denounce slavery. Six years later they voted to amend their constitution so as to deny seats in conventions to anyone who did not publicly oppose slavery. As far as the Franckeans were concerned, it was not enough for a Lutheran slaveholder quietly to set free his human property or for a southern Lutheran simply to say nothing about slavery. Each had to go the full measure and declare his opposition to bondage to all the world.[18]

The Franckean Synod, despite its high profile and controversial views, grew steadily but slowly and remained throughout its antebellum life a small and radical element on the fringe of the Lutheran church. By 1850 there were 50 Franckean congregations claiming 3,213 communicants and served by 25 pastors, impressive measures of growth in just thirteen years but still extremely small fractions of the corresponding figures for the total American Lutheran population. By 1860 there were over two thousand Lutheran congregations in the United States, and Isabella Bishop's calculations for 1859 reported one thousand ministers serving almost a quarter million members and running eight seminaries. And the overwhelming majority simply ignored the slavery issue. It should thus surprise no one that the Franckeans were little noticed by the General Synod, or anybody else, for that matter. "In 1842 the [Franckean] synod sent an appeal to every other synod in the United States, calling for them to express themselves on the abolition issue," Lutheran scholar H. George Anderson wrote, referring to the *Fraternal Appeal*. "The next year it published the results of its survey and revealed that no other synod had chosen to take a public stand."

Some churches did speak out on the issue and more than a few individual Lutherans privately condemned slavery. Fifteen years before the Franckean defection, the Tennessee Synod had agreed that slavery was indeed "a great evil" and "that government, if possible, would devise some means as an antidote to this evil." In 1845, the Pittsburgh Synod, with jurisdiction over parts of Pennsylvania and Ohio, issued a strong statement against bondage, and many of the German Lutherans who had immigrated to the United States during the two decades before the Civil War made no effort to conceal their opposition to slavery. Similarly, the less demonstrative Swedish and Norwegian Lutherans expressed their disapproval of slavery by settling as far from the institution as possible, mainly in Wisconsin, the Minnesota territory, and the Dakota region. Eventually, in 1860, representatives of both nationalities formed the Scandinavian Augustana Synod. But that was the extent of the Lutheran church's antislavery actions.[19]

If the Franckean Synod represented the extreme antislavery position of a largely indifferent Lutheran church, the Missouri Synod spoke for those clergy and members, at least outside the deep South, who saw nothing inherently wrong with human bondage. Many of the German Lutherans who had migrated to the United States in the nineteenth century opposed slavery, but in 1839 a small group of pietistic Saxon Lutherans in eastern Missouri established a dissident faction, which Carl F. W. Walther officially organized eight years later as the German Evangelical Lutheran Synod of Missouri, Ohio, and Other States.[20] Concentrated near St. Louis and in Perry County, the Missouri Lutherans insisted there was no biblical reason to criticize bondage. "The claim that all men were free and equal because Christ died to liberate them was to Walther and his associates a serious misunderstanding of Scripture," Ralph L. Moellering wrote. "Spiritual freedom was not to be identified with temporal freedom . . . [and] could be preserved within the framework of a servant-master relationship."[21]

Like Christians everywhere throughout the South, the Lutherans in Missouri saw nothing ambiguous about the Apostle Paul's admonitions to servants. It is important to note that there were also complex theological differences among various Lutheran groups that partially accounted for their views on slavery and race. The recent German influx included a strong conservative element that eschewed challenges to the status quo, emphasized the confessional aspects of worship, and above all stressed the belief that the church should confine itself to ecclesiastical issues. To one for whom devotional matters were primary, social reform simply was not a vital religious concern.[22] In time, this pietistic, nonsecular ideal, for which the Missouri Synod is best known, appeared in synods in Pennsylvania, New York, Ohio, Tennessee, and Iowa.

While the Lutherans of the Missouri Synod have usually been associated with the larger collection of immigrants that had settled mainly in the Midwest, it should not be forgotten that Missouri was a slave state, which, during the Kansas crisis of the 1850s, had been a hotbed of proslavery activity, and that the southern branches of virtually every Protestant denomination vigorously supported bondage, three of them to the point of seceding from their respective national organizations. When Walther criticized abolitionism and cited the Bible in defense of bondage, he was only doing what southern Baptists, Methodists, Presbyterians, and Episcopalians had been doing for years. The Missouri Synod, though consisting mainly of Lutherans who identified with northern members, had to accommodate all of the political and economic forces that defined life in a slave state, making it, in effect, a southern church. In short, while the Lutheran church was not a major southern denomination, many of its communicants consistently adhered to the southern view on slavery.

In 1835, the South Carolina Synod, with thirty-one congregations, fourteen ministers, and almost two thousand members, resolved that the abolitionists were "enemies of our beloved country; whose mistaken zeal is calculated to injure the cause of morals and religion." At their convention in the same year, delegates to the Virginia Synod called abolitionism "a combination of ignorance, fanaticism, and dishonesty," and four years later they described the Franckean Synod's efforts to entice other Lutherans into the antislavery camp as an "arrogant assumption of synodical censorship."[23] The most prominent southern Lutheran was probably John Bachman, a pastor in Charleston for over forty years, president of the General Synod in 1835, and the author of religious and scientific works that became centerpieces of the proslavery literary effort.[24] That someone as militantly racist as Bachman could be elected to lead the General Synod said a great deal about the attitude of the national leadership.[25] The number of southern Lutherans may have been small, but their enthusiasm in upholding human bondage, best exemplified by Bachman, was great.

In fact, southern Lutherans had embraced slavery from the very beginning. When Mühlenberg arrived in Charleston from Germany in 1742, he was shocked by what he saw and wondered what terrible consequences awaited "people who pretend to be Christians" but do not worry about the souls of those who serve them in bondage.[26] "This is a horrible state of affairs," he recorded in his journal, "and it will entail a severe judgment."[27] Mühlenberg was undoubtedly referring to God's wrath, but his speculation came to a temporal realization in the early-morning hours of April 12, 1861, when General P. G. T. Beauregard opened fire on Fort Sumter. Unfortunately, Mühlenberg had stayed in the South only long enough to visit the Salzburger Lutheran congregation at Ebenezer, Georgia, before he set out for Pennsylvania.

Had he remained, he would have found himself in the company of more than a few northern Lutheran farmers who had criticized slavery but later changed their minds after moving south and acquiring plantations, a not uncommon occurrence among other Americans who made the same move. In fact, slavery was so much a part of everyday life in the South that it did not even take something as compelling as plantation ownership to make a slaveholder out of a Lutheran, and even the church itself could not resist the opportunity to get into the slavery business. For example, as early as 1719 the Swedish congregation in Christina, Delaware, sold part of its property in order to purchase slaves for service in the parsonage. Five years later a church in Wilmington paid £40 for "a Negress named Peggy" who was considered "part of the inventory at the parsonage," but whose value declined with age until, after eighteen years, she was sold for only seven shillings. In 1734 the first Lutheran church in Virginia, located in Madison County, went so far as to dispatch two members to Germany and the Netherlands to raise funds, in Willis D. Weatherford's words, "to build a church, to purchase a farm and home for the pastor, and to purchase slaves to work the farm."[28] In none of these situations did church members see themselves as doing anything out of the ordinary. In the South the ownership of slaves was as much a part of life as the ownership of a cow or horse.

Many Lutheran slaveholders did appear to be conscientious about providing Christian instruction for their bondsmen, although apparently with no more success than slaveholders of other denominations. In the end, the church caved in to the economic and political realities of the agrarian South. In Georgia, for example, a rule adopted by the proprietors in 1733 banned the importation of slaves, but it was overturned in 1750. Like many clergymen who eventually defended slavery, John Martin Boltzius of Ebenezer was initially pleased that "no black slaves may be imported into our colony," but then rationalized that, as distasteful as the institution might be, it did facilitate the Africans' conversion to Christianity. Labor was in short supply in Georgia in 1740 and it was almost universally believed by whites everywhere that Africans "were better off as slaves in America than as freemen in Africa," even though it would be another ten years before the prohibition of slavery was repealed. Except for the size of its membership, southern Lutheranism, in the end, was no different from southern Methodism or any other southern Protestant denomination. Since the church was organized roughly along geographic lines, each congregation and synod adapted to the conditions of its region. Accordingly, southern Lutherans, like Southerners of every faith, supported secession and the Confederate war effort and withdrew from the General Synod to reorganize an independent General Synod, South. Somewhat surprisingly, not even this action or something as drastic as war itself could drive the northern church to an unequivocal position on slavery. A year after the Civil War began, the General Synod, convening in Lancaster, Pennsylvania, "disfellowshipped" the southern synods not for any slavery-related issue but for supporting the "cause of treason and insurrection." As far as the northern Lutheran church was concerned, slavery remained an invisible issue.[29]

Since its doctrinal roots were in the teachings of the greatest dissenter in Christendom, it should have surprised no one that the Lutheran church itself would be torn by dissent. This was made possible, in large measure, by the church's synodical structure, which allowed, even encouraged, doctrinal disagreement, administrative decentralization, geographic particularism, and a division of authority for which there were no more conspicuous examples than the Franckean and Missouri synods. In fact, so autonomous were the regional bodies that in 1835 two of them, the South Carolina Synod and the New York Ministerium, were able to ensure by threats of boycott that the General Synod would never be anything more than an advisory body. Depending on one's point of view, the system had the virtues of diversity or the weaknesses of fragmention.

Yet the Lutheran church in America was probably not as decentralized as it appeared. Despite the variety of synods, the differences among them were not so much differences of belief as they were differences of language, region, and "varying degrees of Americanization." In fact, the synods were unified by faith in a measure among large churches equaled only by the Catholics. However the situation was perceived, it could still be said that the church, as a widely dispersed national denomination consisting of many enclaves of non-English-speaking recent immigrants, held fast to the belief that social reform was "inappropriate for consideration by an ecclesiastical body" and did virtually nothing to challenge the institution of human bondage. It was a response—or, more to the point, a lack of response—that was inherent in the nature of the controversy. By doing nothing, the Lutherans, like every church that declared its neutrality, were, in effect, approving the status quo, that is, supporting slavery.[30]

The widespread Lutheran insistence that slavery was not an ecclesiastical issue may have had its roots in the early Protestant separation of church and state and in the teaching of Luther himself. Beginning with Constantine in Rome in the fourth century and culminating in the unification of Western Christendom in the eleventh and twelfth centuries, Christianity had been intimately entangled with government. Emperors, kings, and czars claimed to rule by divine right and were crowned by bishops and popes, who, in turn, shared in the monarchy's wealth, were protected by law, and were guaranteed a monopoly in all religious matters. In other words, church and state enjoyed a mutually self-perpetuating relationship. But there was at least one critic who believed that the Protestant Reformation was responsible for a breakdown in that relationship which changed dramatically the church's basic responsibility for racial attitudes. "Hans Kohn has attributed the seemingly more powerful appeal of racial exclusiveness to Protestant nations to their early separation of religion and politics," Thomas F. Gossett wrote in *Race: The History of an Idea in America* (1963). "Luther left the settlement of all specifically non-religious questions to the state, argues Kohn, and this decision led in turn to the creation of powerful nationalist and racist doctrines on the part of the state."[31] In other words, the Lutheran disengagement from the state made possible, or at least more likely, the state's cultivation of nationalism and racism.

The operative word in Gossett's assessment may be "seemingly." Kohn's argument assumed, first, that the governments of Protestant nations were "more" racist than those of Catholic nations; second, that slavery was a "nonreligious" question; and, third, that a church would have been able somehow to restrain the racist excesses of the state. There is no evidence to support the first assumption—Catholic countries were every bit as racist as Protestant countries; the second was simply an example of the church's defining a condition to suit itself—calling slavery a "nonreligious" issue did not make it so; and the third was betrayed by the fact that Catholic and Protestant churches alike were, from their earliest days, among the most influential supporters of "nationalist and racist doctrines."

If imperialism is nothing more than nationalism exported, then Christianity's role in the exploitation of the New World made the church a full partner in the "appeal of racial exclusiveness." One can only wonder with amazement how much more imperialistic the United States would have been if, say, Josiah Strong had been Secretary of State during and after the Spanish-American War. If Kohn's thesis is valid, one would have a right to expect an *increase* in legal racism as ecclesiastical influence in secular matters diminished in modern times, but exactly the opposite has actually happened. If there was any connection at all between the degree of racism and the extent of the relationship between church and state, modern developments have shown that the liberation of government from sectarian ties usually produced an enlargement of human rights, not a diminishment.

The Catholic Dilemma: Majority as Minority

Understanding the racial position of the Catholic church in America before the twentieth century poses some problems not faced when reviewing the status of the Protestant sects. The only other religious body with a hierarchy as tightly structured and authoritarian as the Catholic episcopacy was the Church of England. But the latter was the state church of the mother country as well as the Established Church of Virginia and several of the other colonies, not an alien denomination, whose priests and members remained largely non-English objects of derision and hostility long after it had become the largest religious group in the United States. As early as 1660 there were twelve Catholic congregations in the colonies, more than either the Baptists or Presbyterians and only one less than the Dutch Reformed. That number grew steadily but also very slowly—twenty-two in 1700 and twenty-seven in 1740. By the end of the War for Independence, there were fifty-six Catholic churches in the young republic; but since the Protestant churches had increased at a much faster rate, that was far fewer than all but the smallest sects. Of course, individual churches ranged considerably in size; thus the relative numbers of churches did not necessarily translate into an equivalent proportion of communicants. When Father John Carroll of Baltimore submitted his report to Cardinal Antonelli in 1785, he could account for only 25,000 Catholics in all of the Confederation—15,800 in Maryland (including 3,000 slaves), 7,000 in Pennsylvania (with a few slaves), 1,500 in New York, 200 in Virginia, and the remainder scattered around the other states. There were also French Catholics in the Louisiana territory, who would be coming under American jurisdiction in 1803. However the numbers were calculated and distributed, for all of the colonial period and well into the nineteenth century the American Catholic population remained small, the facilities meager, and priests few (between twenty and twenty-five ex-Jesuits in 1783).[32] In fact, the American church did not actually become part of the hierarchy until 1790, when Carroll traveled to England to be consecrated as the first American bishop.

But the decades just before the Civil War told an entirely different story. Between 1820 and 1860 the number of Catholic churches increased over twenty times, from 127 to 2,550—more churches than the Congregationalists, Episcopalians, Lutherans, or Disciples of Christ. Only the Methodists (19,883), Baptists (12,150), and Presbyterians (6,406) could count more congregations; but even these denominations, starting with much larger numbers, had increased only two to seven times in the same forty-year period.[33] The Catholic increase was so rapid that the number of priests available to serve them, insufficient to start with, fell even farther. As late as 1856 in heavily Catholic Louisiana, Mother Mary Hyacinth Le Conniat of the Daughters of the Cross and the Superior of Presentation Convent in Avoyelles Parish, confessed, in a letter to her brother, that "it is very difficult here to follow one's religion, because of the distances between the people and their pastor."[34]

The annexation of Texas in 1845, with its substantial Hispanic population, had partially accounted for the dramatic increase; but the greatest single reason was the immigration from Ireland (mostly from Eire as opposed to the earlier Scotch-Irish migration from Protestant Northern Ireland) before the Civil War. Between 1847 and 1854, Irish immigration, provoked by both agricultural failures and political oppression, averaged almost 150,000 annually, hitting a peak of 221,253 in 1851. To put these figures in perspective one need only note that the number of Irish immigrating to the United States during those eight years—almost 1.2 million—was over 44 percent of the total immigration from *all* countries!

And that increase was reflected in the church population. According to statistics compiled by Isabella Lucy Bishop, there were an estimated 3,250,000 Roman Catholics in the United States in 1859, over twice the number of the largest Protestant denomination, the Methodists.[35] It was a position they have never relinquished. Of course, the national distribution of that majority was very uneven. As late as 1900, with the great immigration wave from the Catholic countries of southern and eastern Europe already underway, the South was still overwhelmingly Protestant. Church membership for that year was 96.6 percent Protestant in the former slave states east of the Mississippi River, with percentages ranging from 99.4 in North Carolina to 90.3 in Florida. Only in Louisiana were Protestants in the minority, and Maryland was the only other southern state with a significant Catholic population.[36]

In point of time, the Catholic church's participation in the enslavement of Africans goes back at least to the middle of the fifteenth century, when Prince Henry of Portugal was so impressed with a gift of ten West Coast blacks that he offered them to the Pope. It must never be forgotten, a Ugandan critic noted, that "it was a Papal Bull which authorized the opening of the slave market in Lisbon in the first decade of the sixteenth century."[37] In the North American colonies, Catholics had owned slaves almost from the day that Maryland had received its charter in 1632. Beginning in 1711, Jesuits in the colony—conceived by George Calvert as a sanctuary for England's harried Catholics—acquired plantations worked by slaves, eventually controlling "six estates of almost twelve thousand acres and over one hundred slaves." By the early nineteenth century, more than a few priests were masters, including Archbishop Carroll, whose manservant, Charles, was not freed until after the archbishop's death.[38] One could argue that it was Carroll's humanity that led him to include a manumission proviso in his will. One could also argue that it was his lack of humanity that kept him from freeing Charles sooner.

It should be noted that, although priests, bishops, and religious orders, "as holders of diocesan property," were listed in local records as the legal owners, many slaves, in fact, were owned by the church as an institution. For example, a diocese often purchased slaves as both servants and field workers for convents, schools, and seminaries. An individual priest, especially a bishop, might be able to afford a slave from his own income, but an order of nuns committed to a lifetime of poverty certainly could not. "Father Tumoine is thinking of buying [a slave] at a sale which will take place on the twenty-sixth of this month," Mother Hyacinth wrote to Bishop Auguste M. Martin in January 1856. "If he is not too expensive, may we buy him?" Less than two months earlier, she had told her brother, Yves, of her repugnance at the bishop's suggestion that the nuns purchase a slave, but by March the convent had its bondsman. "Through the advice of our Bishop and our pastor we bought a slave," Mother Hyacinth wrote to Yves. "He is a mulatto named Simon, aged forty-five years, and the father of eight children." The church, not the nuns, paid $1,400 for Simon when his deceased master's heirs settled the accounts of the former owner's estate.[39] Similarly, the Capucine and Ursuline orders possessed slaves; and a convent in Nazareth, Kentucky, was so dependent on its bondsmen that it held on to them until January 1, 1865, over two years after emancipation had become the "second war aim" of the Union government.[40]

Without official divestment, most Catholic slaveholders, like slaveholders everywhere, kept their slaves until forced to manumit them. The Catholic's allegiance to his ecclesiastical leadership may have been stronger than that of any other slaveholder, but he was also a citizen of his region and state and subject to the same compelling political and social pressures as any other master. Archbishop Carroll was only the best-known Catholic slaveholder who refused to give up his bondsman as long as both of them were still alive. Another was Irish-born Michael H. Healy, president of Georgetown University and owner of a plantation in Georgia with sixteen hundred acres and seventeen slaves. The Jesuit masters in Maryland started selling off their slaves in 1823 when a contingent of bondsmen was sent to Missouri to work in Indian missions. Over the next fifteen years more slaves were sold or sent elsewhere until the final group left for Louisiana in 1838. But no one should look for a humanitarian motive from the Maryland Jesuits. They simply were losing money. In other words, they were acknowledging the unprofitability of their venture, not the inhumanity of it. Despite over a century of plantation experience, the Jesuits apparently had not learned a great deal about agricultural management. In 1819 one observer described all but one of the six estates as "in wretched condition" with the bondsmen living under circumstances "almost universally unfit for human beings." Ten years later another critic claimed he saw many slaves being underfed and mistreated, including pregnant women being whipped. In the end, Madeleine Hooke Rice wrote in her study on Catholicism and slavery, Catholic slaveholders "did not differ from owners of other creeds nor were they actuated by any loftier motives."[41] The preponderant factor was their status as masters, not their status as Christians.

There was also an incriminating dimension to this situation that did not obtain in the Protestant churches. The institutional ownership of a slave meant that a priest held his bondsmen, at least theoretically, at the pleasure of the hierarchy. Moreover, Catholic laymen could hold slaves only with the church's toleration. But forthrightness was never a Christian virtue.

On October 7, 1462, barely two decades after the first Portuguese venture along the African west coast, Pope Pius II condemned the slave trade. By 1888, when Leo XIII delivered to the Brazilian bishops "the most memorable statement" of all against slavery, at least nine popes had issued statements against slavery or the slave trade, including declarations of protection for Indians by Paul III and Urban VIII.[42] It should be noted that the Holy See did not specifically prohibit human bondage, even among its priests. If the church had established a doctrinal ban on slavery—as it had so readily banned many other things over the centuries—Catholic slave ownership would have been far more difficult. But, like their Protestant counterparts, Catholic slaveholders were true to their faith only so long as such profession did not jeopardize their economic well-being. Since their almost certain defiance would have ultimately weakened the church's authority, there were no papal decrees making bondage a basis for excommunication. By issuing occasional condemnations of slavery and the slave trade but failing to prohibit slavery outright, the Roman Catholic church, an institution that thrived on tradition and precedent, made clear its inability—or unwillingness—to make sudden changes, a situation that eventually placed the hierarchy in an awkward position in the United States.

In the late eighteenth and early nineteenth centuries, Methodist, Baptist, and Presbyterian leaders had publicly condemned bondage, but the slaveholding members of their denominations, including not a few clergymen, ignored them. Protestant officials who faced the defiance of slaveholding clergymen could always escape responsibility by claiming, as many did, that they lacked authority to enforce orders to slaveholders. In short, the Protestant churches could plead that they did not command the kind of allegiance that the Catholic hierarchy presumably enjoyed. But it was that very allegiance, resolute or not, that placed the full burden of responsibility for the tacit Catholic approval of human bondage squarely on the shoulders of the hierarchy—all the way to Rome. The Catholic slaveholder could always argue that he was only doing what his church allowed. An organization that claims ultimate power must also accept ultimate responsibility.

Unable to shed its ambivalence, the church institutionalized it. Islam and Judaism, sociologist Orlando Patterson wrote in *Slavery and Social Death*, were "too this-worldly and too strongly monistic" to sustain the Augustinian dualism that medieval Christianity had exalted. This left a Catholic church, he concluded, "stoutly declaring slavery a sin, yet condoning the institution to the point where it was itself among the largest slaveholders."[43] Unfortunately, Patterson did not examine the Catholic's distinction between an "evil" and a "sin," a distinction that was at the heart of the church's position. Over the years, numerous spokesmen tried to reconcile the obvious contradiction between slavery and Christianity by arguing, like many Protestant apologists, that slavery was not really a sin, a rationalization made necessary in 1838, according to one Catholic historian, by Pope Gregory XVI's reiteration of the church's condemnation of the slave trade.[44] To denounce the *process* by which slaves were acquired while remaining silent on—or approving—the *holding* of slaves forced the church's defenders to come up with a plausible explanation, an explanation that ultimately condemned specific practices but endorsed the general principle.

The result was a thicket of equivocation. Bondage, in the minds of the Catholic theologians, was an "evil disposition" produced by the Fall. "Accepting slavery, then, as a consequence of original sin and not of itself sinful," Rice wrote, "the Fathers were concerned rather for the moral or spiritual equality of the slave than for his worldly status when they struck at certain evils associated with that status." The church taught that "human bondage was not morally wrong *per se* provided the conditions laid down by theologians as necessary for a 'just servitude' were observed." Similarly, according to John Tracy Ellis, one of the nation's most eminent Catholic historians, the church taught that slavery, "thought of theoretically and apart from specific abuses to human dignity, was not opposed to the divine or natural law."[45]

Ellis could have been talking about Francis Patrick Kenrick, the Dublin-born author of the three-volume *Theologia Moralis* (1840–43) and, as Archbishop of Baltimore, successor to John Carroll and occupant of what Sydney E. Ahlstrom called "the most influential post in the American hierarchy."[46] According to Kenrick, Joseph D. Brokhage explained, the church recognized slavery as being lawful if the slave was held by one of four "valid" titles: "capture in war, punishment for crime, sale, and nativity." When Kenrick taught that "slavery was not contrary to natural law," Brokhage added, "he was not talking about slavery as it existed in practice in America, but slavery as defined by him and the theologians."[47] Unfortunately, such rationalizations failed for obvious reasons. Slavery in the abstract was not evil because nothing in the abstract is evil. The only slavery that mattered was slavery "as it existed in practice." How could something that was itself an abuse to human dignity be thought of apart from, as Ellis put it, its "specific abuses to human dignity"? After all, apologists like Kenrick were only addressing the issue because of its controversial existence in the United States. What other slavery was there for them to talk about? References to "just," "theoretical," or "theologically defined" slavery were nothing but pathetic expressions of sophistry. It made no difference how the hairs were split; the conclusion that the Catholic church officially endorsed human bondage was inescapable.

If there had been many Catholics who had misgivings about slavery, most said little or nothing, especially in the South, where social pressures made it virtually impossible to speak out against an institution that had long been a vital component of the region's economy and was rapidly becoming a benchmark of sectional loyalty. Even in predominantly Catholic French Louisiana—where M. Bienville's famous "Code Noir" of 1724, calling for the humane treatment of slaves, remained in force until 1803—the church hierarchy, one student of that region noted, "sought to ameliorate the lot of the bondsmen, but made no frontal attack on slavery as an institution." In an obvious reference to the fear of slave insurrections, Kenrick urged in 1841 that "nothing should be attempted against the laws nor anything be done or said that would make [the slaves] bear their yoke unwillingly." It had been just a decade since the Nat Turner uprising. Kenrick was only the best-known southern Catholic official to speak out.

Assuming the leadership of the Charleston diocese in 1821, John England, publishing his views in 1832 and 1840, argued that if slavery was evil the church would have condemned it long ago and that, accordingly, only "abuses accompanying the institution" should be denounced. By the beginning of the Civil War, some members of the southern hierarchy were almost as truculent as their Protestant counterparts. Augustin Verot, Bishop of Georgia and East Florida, arguing that slavery "accorded with both the law of nature and the law of the gospel," insisted that the tragedy of secession and war "lies in the misrepresentation of ignorant and fanatical zealots, who desecrate and pollute the Divine word, speaking in the name of God although they gainsay all the teachings of God." Other southern Catholic critics included Bishop Martin of Natchitoches, Louisiana, who defined slavery as "an arrangement eminently Christian by which millions pass from intellectual darkness to the sweet brilliance of the Gospel"; Bishop George F. Pierce of Georgia, who declared that slavery should be put "upon its scriptural basis," which would prove that it was "consistent with the highest development and the greatest happiness of the negro race"; and Courtney Jenkins, editor of the Baltimore *Catholic Mirror*, who predicted that emancipation would destroy the black race. In 1861, in an exchange of letters with New York's Archbishop John Hughes that were subsequently printed in several of the city's newspapers, Bishop Patrick N. Lynch, England's successor in Charleston, criticized Abraham Lincoln, the Union war effort, the influence of the abolitionists, and the general northern position on slavery.[48]

That position, as it happened, was not enthusiastically antislavery and, at times, was extremely vague. In 1854 Archbishop Hughes defined bondage as it existed in the United States as a "comparative"—rather than an "unmitigated"—evil, which was "to be preferred to the condition under which the Negroes would have lived, if they had not been brought from Africa." He meant, of course, "to be preferred" by *him*, not by the African victims of enslavement. Two weeks after the firing on Fort Sumter, bishops in Cincinnati reiterated what was by then one of the most popular religious evasions—Protestant as well as Catholic—when they said that they did not "think it their province to enter into the political arena." The northern Catholic public, on the other hand, reacted to secession much the same as everyone else; and northern Catholic newspapers, sometimes disagreeing with each other, frequently aroused "antagonism within Catholic ranks by their views." Seven years after Hughes set forth his "comparative" evil thesis, the New York *Metropolitan Record* reprinted the statement with similar arguments appearing in the *New York Freeman's Journal and Catholic Register* and the Boston *Pilot*. The following year, on the first anniversary of the firing on Fort Sumter, the editors of the *Metropolitan Record*, claiming that their newspaper was the archbishop's official organ, emphatically condemned calls for emancipation.[49] Against this chorus of proslavery rhetoric was Father Edward Purcell's liberal Cincinnati *Catholic Telegraph*, the oldest Catholic newspaper in the United States and one of the few to support the antislavery movement. In fact, so aggressive was Purcell that some church members insisted his editorial of April 8, 1863, put him squarely in the abolitionist camp.[50]

Despite these declarations and the southern sympathies of people like Hughes, the northern episcopacy, by and large, remained neutral. "Some might characterize this policy as an abdication of moral leadership," Ellis speculated, but, since there were Catholics "on both sides of the barricades," he believed the bishops acted "with wisdom." One could quarrel with the belief that the church should stand silent if there are strong feelings on opposing sides of a moral issue, especially, as in this situation, if silence is tantamount to approving human bondage. One could just as easily conclude that the hierarchy's primary concern was not to do the right thing but to do the pragmatic thing and avoid alienating southern Catholics.

Between 1837 and 1861 church leaders had watched the Presbyterian, Methodist, and Baptist systems wrench apart over the sectional crisis. But, while southern Catholics differed little from southern Protestants on the slavery issue, the hierarchy never publicly entertained the idea of schism. Accordingly, the pastoral letters of each assembly of bishops between 1840 and 1852 "remained silent on the nation's moral dilemma." Right up to the beginning of the war, Ellis pointed out, "Catholic bishops from above and below the Mason and Dixon line continued to meet in councils of the Church with no attendant rift in their ecclesiastical deliberatiions by reason of sectional differences."

The commitment to unity, perhaps the most vital element of the episcopal system, kept the American hierarchy intact, even while Catholic editors and individual parishioners disagreed vehemently over the question of human bondage. This was possible, in part, because the bishops, a careful student of the issue maintained, managed to separate slavery from the moral issues that the church was rightfully concerned with, an equivocation that must have embarrassed equalitarians among the faithful. After all, since Catholic "social philosophy" taught that it was sinful to violate basic human rights, Madeleine Hooke Rice queried, "were not Catholic leaders evading what was actually a moral issue, made so by the conflict between the inequities of the slave system and the rights of the slave as a human being?"[51]

Ambivalence also characterized the attitudes of the northern Catholic lay population in the years prior to the Civil War. For example, many church members agreed that the institution of slavery was evil but conceded that there seemed to be no practical way of abolishing it. To most of them, some kind of gradual emancipation was the only realistic course. Orestes Brownson, a former Unitarian and transcendentalist who had converted to Catholicism in 1844, was one of the few prominent lay Catholics who spoke out against slavery, an expression that was probably influenced more by the liberal habits of his Unitarian and transcendentalist past than by anything in his new faith. But even Brownson, despite his intellectual agreement with the antislavery movement, saw slavery as an evil only when the master abused his stewardship. Aligning himself with Kenrick, he concluded that slavery, in and of itself, was not necessarily evil. Like most critics who followed this line, Brownson did not specify just what constituted "abuse." Obviously, things like the denial of personal freedom, the separation of family members, the withholding of the most basic human rights, or the slave code that defined the bondsman as chattel personal were not on his list. Like many pious Christians, Brownson believed that ensuring the salvation of the slave's soul was the most important thing the church could do. It was not until the Civil War actually began that he finally came out strongly for emancipation, a declaration that, considering his intellectual moorings, was unavoidable, but which, not surprisingly, angered Archbishop Hughes.[52]

There was also the simple matter of numbers. During the colonial and early national period, the Catholic population was too small to influence critical social issues significantly. Priests and parishioners could never forget that they were a minority that had been persecuted by the Established Church in England and disfranchised by a Puritan majority in colonial Maryland. The malevolent attitude toward "Papists" and the "Romish" church that had crossed the Atlantic Ocean with the first English settlers lingered among many Protestants well into the twentieth century, erupting along the way into the emotional nativistic outbursts that produced the Know-Nothing movement in the early 1850s and the American Protective Association forty years later.

The Catholic with strong antislavery feelings learned early on that silence was usually the most prudent expression. If a Protestant spoke against slavery he could always find some agreement from other Protestants, most of whom perceived themselves collectively as the dominant religious interest in the nation. If a Catholic criticized slavery, however, many Protestant opponents of abolitionism would have used the occasion as an excuse to attack Catholicism. Even though this began to change with the mid-century immigration wave from Ireland, and the Roman Catholic Church by 1850, perhaps sooner, claimed more members than the largest Protestant denomination in the nation, many Catholics continued to suffer from a minority consciousness, which argued against taking strong positions on controversial political or social issues. Of course, any group that commands an impressive plurality in anything will eventually recognize its power, and it did not take long for the Catholic immigrant to identify his political bedfellows. Because the antislavery movement included so many Protestant clergymen and because most of them had become Republicans, the sons of Erin overwhelmingly joined the Democratic party.[53] Unfortunately, when Catholic reticence finally began to subside, it turned into ugly expressions of anger and racism.

It is doubtful that any immigrant nationality, except for the original English settlers who crossed the Atlantic Ocean in the seventeenth century, had as great an impact on the character of American life in a brief period as the Irish who emigrated to the United States during the decade following the great potato famine, an impact magnified by the fact that they tended to cluster together in a few eastern cities rather than, like the Germans and Scandinavians, spreading out across the interior. If anyone needs a reminder of how many people left Ireland for the United States in the century and a half after 1820, he need only note that the Irish were virtually tied with the British and exceeded only by the Germans and Italians, all people from much larger countries than Ireland. While the German Catholics came from a relatively liberal Catholic background, the overwhelming majority of the Irish immigrants were poor, uneducated peasants and, in the United States, were among those highly conservative and puritanical Catholics who "more and more explicitly rejected the liberal society that surrounded them."[54]

The American church's "social doctrine exalted harmony and stability," Rowland Berthoff wrote, which, to a black person, meant preserving the status quo. If, in an age of slavery, the subjugation of the oppressed is inherent in the conservative ethic, then the Roman Catholic Church, an institution whose very ethos rests on tradition and conservatism, must stand accused of advocating the oppression of black Americans. A few Irish-Americans, such as Daniel O'Connell, were outspoken supporters of the antislavery movement, but they were rare, and the nationality as a whole quickly earned the reputation of being "among the worst enemies of the colored race in the United States." During the notorious New York City draft riots of July 1863, in which the hatred and fear of blacks—not resistance to the draft—were the main issue, Irishmen were the primary antagonists. The conscription law of March 3 bore heavily on the poor because anyone with $300 could buy his way out. More to the point, however, unskilled white laborers were convinced they were being drafted to fight for the freedom of people who would eventually dominate unskilled employment. Since Irish immigrants were primarily low-income workers, they believed, like William Hepworth Dixon's Irish acquaintance in San Francisco, that they were more threatened than anyone by black job competition. It was no surprise, then, that when New York City officials posted a list of the whites who had been killed during the rioting, fifty-two of the eighty-two names were Irish and seven were German.[55] There were few Daniel O'Connells to be found here.

Catholics in America were also unable to claim great success in winning the souls of black folk to the church. One of southern Catholicism's most respected students reported that there may have been as many as one hundred thousand black Catholics throughout the South in 1860—an estimate that he admitted was "generous" and one that was still less than 2.5 percent of the free and slave black population—but they were located in isolated pockets or so widely scattered that it was virtually impossible to minister to them, a problem compounded by the dearth of priests everywhere in the southern states. Without pastoral care, the church could not even reach many of the slaves it claimed to have converted. Had there been black priests, at least part of the problem might have been resolved—after all, there were many black Protestant ministers in both North and South, especially in the Methodist and Baptist churches. But only two black Americans were ordained as Catholic priests in the nineteenth century, and as late as 1930 there were only three working in the American church. And opportunity did not necessarily mean achievement. The reluctance of the slave to convert to Catholicism was the result of several factors, not the least of which was his tendency to follow the faith of his master. As a minority religion, especially outside of Louisiana and Maryland, the church claimed few slaveholders, which meant that when a Catholic slave was sold he would probably be purchased by a Protestant master who would not allow him to continue practicing his faith.[56] Moreover, Catholicism was a formal, highly structured religion unlikely to appeal to people who, by nature and tradition, were drawn to the "more emotionalized evangelical faith" of most Protestant churches.[57]

Nor did the end of human bondage change many minds. In 1867 the American hierarchy decided to make a concerted effort to convert former slaves, but, despite this and other well-intentioned plans, Catholic missionary activity in behalf of the freedmen was virtually nonexistent before 1900. And one presumably neutral observer criticized the decision because of the church's ostensible rejection of racism. "The imposing ceremonials of the Romish Church, its system of Absolution, its worship of the Virgin, and its repudiation of distinctions of race and colour," Scottish traveler David Macrae sneered in 1868, "are likely to make it popular amongst the negroes." Macrae's strong commitment to his Protestant heritage accounted for his anti-Catholic sarcasm, but his prediction that a repudiation of racism would attract blacks to the faith revealed a fundamental ignorance about the pervasiveness of white supremacy. When, shortly after the war, the Bishop of New Orleans tried to integrate the parochial schools in his jurisdiction, he encountered strong resistance not only from lay Catholics but from members of the religious orders as well, a situation that repeated itself "in almost every diocese of the South."[58]

Even some of the black American's ostensible friends unwittingly exposed the insidiousness of white racism. In December 1885, John Boyle O'Reilly, an immensely popular radical priest whom the British had deported from Ireland to Australia because of his Fenian activities, was invited to address a colored men's convention in Boston. Expressing his belief that the law and the political system could do no more for the black man, O'Reilly said:

> The negro will never take his full stand beside the white man till he has given the world proof of the truth and beauty of heroism and power that are in his soul. And only by the organs of the soul are these delivered—by self-respect and self-reflection, by philosophy, religion, poetry, art, love, and sacrifice.[59]

Ten years later, Booker T. Washington, in his famous speech at the Atlanta Cotton States and International Exposition, would add sweat, labor, and thrift to essentially the same topic.

One extraneous development was soon to overwhelm well-intentioned efforts like those of the Josephites, an order of priests founded in 1893 to work with "colored missions." The tremendous surge in the immigration of unskilled and poorly educated Catholics from southern Europe that began in the last decade of the nineteenth century "so dwarfed all other problems with which the Church had to cope" that the 1866 declaration of the forty-five American bishops who met in Baltimore for the Second Plenary Council calling for religious instruction for blacks was never carried out.[60]

The Social Gospel and the Sin of Indifference

It was fitting, if unfortunate, that the most profound religious reform of the era did not originate among those who were suffering but "out of moral and intellectual dissatisfaction with the suffering of others." As with abolitionism, the Social Gospel movement was led by middle-class, educated men who were distressed by what they saw as injustice and exploitation. In short, it was élitist. Accordingly, when Sydney Ahlstrom wrote that "Protestantism derived its power and had its firm foundations far from the teeming multitudes,"[61] he was acknowledging that, although the American church may have appeared radical in its support of certain social issues, such as human bondage in another part of the country, when it came to economic matters close to home Christians suddenly became very conservative. Protestantism after the Civil War presented "a massive, almost unbroken front in its defense of the status quo," Henry F. May pointed out in *The Protestant Churches and Industrial America* (1949),[62] and if there was one thing that always worked against black people it was the status quo.

Nevertheless, in a democratic society, human suffering will ultimately generate some kind of response. And since governments can be notoriously slow to act against injustice, individuals and private organizations will almost always move in. Thus any reform was better than none because it at least called attention to the fact that injustice existed. To Ahlstrom, the Social Gospel was "the most distinctive contribution of the American churches to world Christianity," and Carl N. Degler agreed that it was "the distinguishing characteristic of American Christianity." It may have been all that, and more; but it also surely did nothing for the millions of black men and women, North and South, whose working and living conditions were far worse than anything even imagined by the oppressed foreign-born city dweller, and who could not have cared less about the white man's reforms. "While white men struggled to restrain the oppressions of the railroads, using the new instrument of the Interstate Commerce Commission, black men knew the humiliation of newly enacted Jim Crow laws," historian Paul A. Carter wrote; "while rural southern poor whites challenged the corporate control of their states, in the process they sacrificed the rights of rural southern Negroes."[63] Whether or not the Social Gospel brought about significant changes is arguable—many of the most effective Christian social service organizations, such as the Salvation Army and the Young Men's and Women's Christian Associations, preceded the movement. But there is no doubt that it would be a very long time after the movement ended before Protestant churches in the United States would again play a leading role in the cause of human rights.

The Social Gospel movement of the late nineteenth and early twentieth centuries was a largely liberal Protestant response to the obvious excesses and abuses of an unregulated industrial society, which to some critics seemed out of control. As factories became bigger and produced faster, their appetite for unskilled workers grew insatiable and their propensity to exploit them increased. The fact that there were millions of black men and women in the southern states who constituted an ideal and seemingly inexhaustible supply of cheap labor apparently was not even noticed by northern captains of industry. It is not unreasonable to assume that if it had occurred to any of them, the sheer logistics of relocation—not to mention the explosive political consequences of introducing large numbers of black people into northern white communities—easily discouraged further consideration. And few black Southerners had the resources to make it on their own. Frederick Douglass had predicted that emancipation would lead to a mass migration of former slaves into the cities of America, and many white Northerners feared just that; but, as urban historian Gunther Barth noted, "[r]elatively few black people were able to make the move in the nineteenth century."[64]

The entrepreneur's eventual solution to his need for labor was to encourage and subsidize the immigration of hordes of Europeans, many from the Mediterranean and Slavic regions of the continent, who, happy to have work, would man the machines of the new smoke-belching giants. No complaints, no racism, no problems, and no laws to restrain owners and managers who included among their closest friends members of Congress and the state legislatures. The upshot was urban congestion and its concomitant conditions: poverty, lawlessness, child labor, worker exploitation, and lack of public services.

The same reform spirit that had fueled the antislavery movement was now turned to the plight of the urban poor. The Roman Catholic Church, reacting to the fact that many of the worst conditions existed in the predominantly Catholic neighborhoods of the industrial centers of the East, was probably the first Christian church to establish programs that were humanitarian rather than evangelical. By the 1880s, several Protestant denominations had taken up the cause. "In 1887," Carl Degler wrote, "a number of Episcopalians in New York City organized the Church Association for the Advancement of the Interests of Labor, which gradually spread to other cities in the nation." Episcopalians later founded and led the reformist Christian Social Union. Social historian E. Digby Baltzell thought it important to note that "the Church of wealth, culture and aristocratic lineage" should be more "receptive to the new Social Gospel" than any other Protestant denomination. Five years after the New York City Episcopalians acted, "the Baptists, led by Walter Rauschenbusch, established the Brotherhood of the Kingdom."[65] These were only among the earliest efforts of Christian churches to establish contact with the urban masses. The Social Gospel was underway.

"Social Gospel" was only a new term; it was an idea that was as old as Christianity itself. And the resistance to it was just as old:

> Now a man came up to Jesus and asked, "Teacher, what good thing must I do to get eternal life?"
>
> "Why do you ask me about what is good?" Jesus replied. "There is only One who is good. If you want to enter life, obey the commandments."
>
> "Which ones?" the man inquired.
>
> Jesus replied, " 'Do not murder, do not commit adultery, do not steal, do not give false testimony, honor your father and mother, and love your neighbor as yourself.' "
>
> "All these I have kept," the young man said. "What do I still lack?"
>
> Jesus answered, "If you want to be perfect, go, sell your possessions and give to the poor, and you will have treasure in heaven. Then come, follow me."
>
> When the young man heard this, he went away sad, because he had great wealth.[66]

In early America the moral and religious antecedents of the Social Gospel could be found in Puritanism; by the nineteenth century, the Second Great Awakening and subsequent evangelical movement had intensified the reform tendency. In the 1840s, as immigration surged, several clergymen began to address the question of urban poverty. By 1851, the Young Men's Christian Association had moved from Great Britain. Within nine years there would be 205 local YMCA chapters in the United States, many of them addressing the needs of the poor and destitute in the northern cities with varying degrees of success (and a generous share of failures). Antebellum revivalism had shown a strong concern for social reform and evangelical Protestants had played a major role in the antislavery movement. "Abolitionism, with its hymns, slogans, and prophetic zeal, was a decisive prelude to the Social Gospel," religion historian Sydney E. Ahlstrom wrote. "The line from Theodore Dwight Weld and Elijah Lovejoy to Washington Gladden and Walter Rauschenbusch must never be ignored."[67]

But it should also not be overdrawn. Social reform did indeed rise and fall through several cycles in the American past, but there were many like Christ's questioner who walked away less than perfect. Most important of all, Gladden and Rauschenbusch, like virtually all of their contemporaries, never even asked what they might do for the poor black masses of the South.

For decades American Christianity had been mainly evangelical Christianity, committed to the belief that the primary—indeed, to some, exclusive—purpose of the church was to win souls to Jesus Christ. This belief had been the fountainhead of the southern preacher's argument that the best way for a servant to get to heaven was to be a good servant—which was also, not coincidentally, the best way to keep the black person in perpetual bondage. It was also part of the popular thesis, expressed by Christian ministers both North and South, who opposed the radicalism of the antislavery movement, that the best way to reform an institution was to reform the individuals who were in it.

Francis Wayland was only one of many evangelical Christians who were personally opposed to bondage but who also disapproved of any political action to abolish it and were convinced that "once the individual was converted, he would abstain from vice and thus social problems would be automatically solved." Revivalist Charles Grandison Finney, despite his abolitionist fervor, was similarly certain that social reform would inevitably follow individual conversion. Except for the Pittsburgh and Passavant and Stuckenberg synods, few Lutherans were involved in the Social Gospel movement because they believed that reform began with individuals, not groups. "The program to save men by changing their environment," Abdel Ross Wentz wrote in 1923, "was held to be nothing more than golden-rule ethics which forfeits the spiritual worth of the individual."[68]

This idea was based on the assumption that since a community consisted of many people it had a collective—though not an independent—conscience, and at least one Christian socialist seemed to agree. "The fact that individual Christians manumitted their slaves," Reinhold Niebuhr wrote in *Moral Man and Immoral Society* (1932), "proves that the principles of the gospel could inspire individuals more readily than they could prompt social and political policies." The abolitionists, who counted numerous men of the cloth among their ranks, had never devised a practical, systematic plan for bringing the former slave into the mainstream of American life because most of them had never expected him to be there. In a sense, the men and women who drove the antislavery movement were better compared to muckrakers than to reformers. Like many people who demanded change, they had no formula for dealing with the vacuum that would inevitably follow. Certainly to many of them—perhaps most—emancipation did not mean equality. For a long time the former slave would be just trying to catch up. In the years immediately after the Civil War, various freedmen's aid societies, the most active of which was probably the American Missionary Association, moved into the occupied states mainly to establish schools. The needs of the freedmen were fundamental. They had to be "civilized"—that is, Christianized and educated—first. Things like skills, jobs, property, and political activities could only come after the black person had been rescued from the lure of his heathen ancestry and liberated from the psychological shackles of a lifetime of dependency.[69]

It should thus come as no surprise that most southern Protestants in the late nineteenth century, like their antebellum forebears, continued to believe that the church's fundamental responsibility was to save souls, not meddle with the social order. A modern version of this belief appeared during the civil rights movement of the 1960s when northern clergymen, nuns, and seminarians who had marched through southern cities with Martin Luther King, Jr., and members of his Southern Christian Leadership Conference were often taunted by local white preachers, who asked, "How many souls have you saved today?" It should not be forgotten that reform before the Civil War—be it temperance, women's rights, public education, mental asylums, prisons, communitarianism, or antislavery—had been almost entirely a northern phenomenon. In stark contrast, the slaveholder had been the preeminent figure in a conservative, agrarian society committed to the perpetuation of the status quo.

The abolition of chattel slavery may have redefined the legal basis of the southern labor system, but it did not change the white Southerner's way of thinking. Well into the twentieth century, the South remained a bastion of resistance to change in many human activities, and in the area of race relations southern Christianity was a major force in that resistance. Isolated from the large-scale industry that was becoming the dominant fact of life in the northern states, the southern clergyman was, historian Frederick A. Bode wrote, convinced that he "must shun anything that smacked of social criticism" but, at the same time, saw nothing wrong with incorporating a "probusiness bias into the old framework of sin, grace, and salvation." The Civil War taught the South that it had to industrialize to progress. There was no reason why Christian leaders could not incorporate that lesson into their ministries. "Railroads, mines, and factories could become instruments of divine grace and means of regeneration if southern

Protestantism seized its opportunity and accepted the challenge of the New South."[70] There was no southern Social Gospel.

In the end, social Christianity turned the salvation priority on its head. Although Niebuhr called attention to the influence of the gospel on the consciences of individual slaveholders, he was really pointing out that it would take a lot more than private manumissions to change "social and political policies." No one would ever claim that those southern planters who had voluntarily freed their slaves had inspired mass manumissions. The Seventh Census (1850) counted 1,467 black people who had been manumitted during the previous year—one-half of one-thousandth of the total slave population! The fraction for the Eighth Census was three-fourths of one-thousandth. These insignificant numbers (or significant, depending on one's point of view) decline to virtually nonexistent when it is noted that some manumissions occurred under the terms of a deceased master's will and therefore could be questioned as acts of conscience. Whatever the circumstances of private manumissions, anyone looking for a trend would have had a long wait. Individual piety was commendable, but fundamental and sweeping changes would come only when institutions reformed—or, more to the point, were compelled to reform. Rauschenbusch, without actually denigrating the importance of personal conversions, was only one of many spokesmen for the cause who believed that the traditional Christian imperative of dealing with the souls of sinners must yield to the task of healing the ills of a corrupt economic system.[71] Thus the most distinctive characteristic of the Social Gospel was its denial of the "innate sinfulness of man" and its emphasis on changing an errant society. "All imperfection and brutalities of man were attributed to social maladjustments which would yield easily to correction when once exposed to the light of reason and Christian idealism," James Dombrowski wrote in 1936. "Human nature became evil or anti-social only when it was corrupted by society or ignorance." As a rejection of the "excessive individualism of Protestant theology," the emphasis here was on saving society, not individuals. If human nature was essentially good, all that was needed to overcome suffering was to "reorganize and reform the social setting."[72]

It is impossible to identify one person as the prime mover of the modern Social Gospel movement. Like the Great Awakening, the independence movement, the antislavery movement, the agrarian revolt, and other social upheavals, social Christianity was one of those impulses that emerged spontaneously in several places at the same time. Among those who contributed, in varying degrees, to its ideology and articulation were Francis Greenwood Peabody, Richard T. Ely, Albion W. Small, Henry George, Lester Ward, Shailer Mathews, Edward Bellamy, Jesse Henry Jones, William D. P. Bliss, Theodore Munger, Walter Rauschenbusch, Lyman

Abbott, Washington Gladden, George D. Herron, and Josiah Strong. Of these names, two seem to appear more in the histories of the subject than the others: Gladden and Rauschenbusch.

Religion historian Sydney E. Ahlstrom contended that Gladden, a Congregational minister with strong liberal leanings, "deserves first mention" in any discussion of the Social Gospel. Following ministries in Brooklyn and Morrisania, New York, and North Adams and Springfield, Massachusetts, Gladden, who did not go by his biblical first name of Solomon, spent most of his career at the First Congregational Church in Columbus, Ohio (1882–1918). Though he was never a socialist, his criticism of free enterprise grew stronger over the years and, progressing from "abstract moral protest to a specific critique of American economic institutions," he eventually came to advocate government ownership of public utilities. Gladden's "theology of social action" was simple: In works like *Tools and the Man* (1893) and *Social Salvation* (1902), "he demanded that the churches concern themselves with social injustice, and that they help bring the economic aspects of American life under the laws of God's kingdom by example and advocacy." Similarly, in *Social Facts and Forces* (1897), Gladden castigated those churches that sided with employers and against laborers and, though himself a staunch Protestant, ridiculed those who feared Catholics.[73]

Rauschenbusch, whose socialistic proclivities were more clearly defined than Gladden's, followed a different route to the same destination. He was the American-born son of a German Baptist preacher, who had descended from a long line of Lutheran ministers but had converted to the Baptist faith prior to emigrating to the United States in 1854. The young Rauschenbusch assumed his first pulpit at the Second German Baptist Church in New York City, where, like Gladden, he got a close look at impoverished immigrants and exploited laborers, among whom the process of disorganization and the loss of familiar ties of kinship and neighborhood were endemic.[74] But while his tenure at the Second Church put him close to the problems of the immigrants, Rauschenbusch, according to one writer, also feared that America's Anglo-German blood was being corrupted by the heavy infusion of Poles, Russians, and Jews, an attitude that certainly would not have made him an advocate of racial equality.[75]

At the same time that his level of consciousness over immigrant problems was rising, he began to show concern about the "deep conservatism" of his Baptist colleagues. In 1897, Rauschenbusch, partly because an illness nine years earlier had left him almost totally deaf, gave up parish work to become professor of New Testament interpretation at Rochester Theological Seminary, from which he had graduated eleven years earlier. In 1902 he was appointed professor of church history. Free to teach as he pleased and to concentrate on writing, he found himself in a much better position to influence the future of the church. With the publication of *Christianity and the Social Crisis* (1907), which was translated into several languages and was probably the most widely read of all Social Gospel works, Rauschenbusch became the conscience of social Christianity.[76]

The racist sin of the Social Gospel was the sin of indifference. Beginning with Henry Ward Beecher, who, even before the Civil War, became a prophet of the secularization of Christianity when he declared that ministers should address public issues, to the founding of the Federal Council of Churches of Christ in America in 1908, some of the most distinguished Protestant spokesmen in the United States championed the cause of the oppressed and exploited working people in northern industrial cities but said little about the most oppressed and exploited people of all.[77] Not surprisingly, one such spokesman even failed to recognize the sin in himself. In June 1891, Lyman Abbott, editor of the *Christian Union* and one of the nation's foremost Social Gospel advocates, told the delegates to a conference at Lake Mohonk, New York, that "[t]he selfish prejudice of indifference is not one whit more holy than the selfish prejudice of open aggression."[78]

There also may have been more than coincidence in the fact that the founding of the National Association for the Advancement of Colored People followed the establishment of the Federal Council by just one year. It would not be unreasonable to assume that the NAACP and its forerunner Niagara movement were, at least in part, reactions to the Social Gospel's inability, or unwillingness, to take a stand on the race issue. By this time, anyone with a genuine interest in the welfare of black Americans must have realized that he could expect little from the nation's white Christian churches. As it happened, the Council moved with glacierlike speed even on its own agenda. It was not until 1914 that the thirty-three Protestant denominations that constituted its membership, having adopted the Methodist "Social Creed," committed themselves to recognizing the problems of working people.[79] In a short time, war in Europe would command everyone's attention and domestic issues would be deferred or forgotten altogether. The race issue had never commanded anyone's attention and therefore could not even be forgotten.

In the meantime, one opportunity had already come and gone and hardly anybody noticed. The Afro-American National League of the United States—founded in 1890 and led by T. Thomas Fortune of New York, a black editor and journalist, who was concerned mainly with economic issues—would have been an ideal conduit for liberal Protestants interested in lifting the burden of discrimination from the backs of black working people, but no such effort was made and the league died in a few years from lack of interest and money.[80] The liberal ministers also could have responded to the dissident agrarian movement that began in 1867 with Oliver H. Kelley's Patrons of Husbandry (the Grange), continued with the Farmers' Alliances, and culminated with the entry of the People's party (the Populists) onto the national political scene. Tom Watson of Georgia and other leaders of the Southern Farmers' Alliance had initially invited black farmers and sharecroppers, who had organized a separate Colored Farmers' National Alliance, to join their crusade against big business.

But of the two basic responses of the common people to the predatory practices of businessmen and bankers—the trade union movement and the agrarian revolt—the Social Gospel gave only oblique attention to the first and none at all to the latter. It needs to be remembered that most of the advocates of social Christianity occupied pulpits in northern cities, where the conditions they addressed were highly visible. The majority of blacks, on the other hand, were scattered throughout the southern countryside, far from the eyes of big-city preachers. Moreover, as Sydney E. Ahlstrom pointed out, Populism, though it embodied a strong religious sensitivity through spokesmen like William Jennings Bryan, was influential only among people who were theologically conservative.[81]

It is not an exaggeration to suggest that black Protestants had always believed in social Christianity. From the time of the organization of independent black congregations in the North beginning in the late eighteenth century to the establishment in the South of separate churches for former slaves after the Civil War, the black church had been far more to black people than the white church had been to whites. Provider of education, dispenser of relief, or sanctuary for the runaway slave, the black church was the most vital institution in the black world and the black clergyman the most influential person in his community. In 1908 the "Colored Methodist Bishops' Appeal to White America," calling for an end to racial injustice, appeared in the March 19 issue of *The Christian Index*. But few white Christians appeared to be listening.

It must have been obvious to the fifty-three signers (including Rabbi Stephen S. Wise and the Reverend John Haynes Holmes) of Oswald Garrison Villard's call for the national conference that ultimately led to the creation of the National Association for the Advancement of Colored People that the Protestant proponents of the Social Gospel had no interest in becoming part of a racial dialogue. This had been more than obvious to Bishop Henry M. Turner of the African Methodist Episcopal Church, who wondered why black people should get excited over tariff revision when it was hard enough just finding something to eat. Ridiculing the white man's silly reforms and sounding ominously like Marcus Garvey, who would rise to prominence two decades later with his African Orthodox Church, Turner defiantly advocated black nationalism and emigration to Africa. There was no point, he was convinced, in continuing to struggle for equality in a land where the majority would *never* grant it.[82] It seems almost an ironic twist of fate that during and after the First World War, when black families finally began moving out of the South and into the industrial centers of the North in numbers rivaling those of the oppressed European immigrants, the Social Gospel was no longer there to care.

Indeed, some of social Christianity's adherents went out of their way to explain their indifference. Lyman Abbott insisted that racism was strictly a regional problem that southern blacks and whites needed to work out among themselves. When federal officials complained about the movement that had begun in Virginia and South Carolina to disfranchise black voters, Abbott espoused the conservative belief that the national government had no business interfering with the voting policies of the states. Acknowledging that little had been done in behalf of the former slave population, Rauschenbusch implied that there was probably nothing that could be done. "They are free now, under nobody's ownership, but also under nobody's care," he wrote in an 1896 issue of *The American Journal of Sociology*. "It is probably fair to say," he concluded in what could only be described as a monument to understatement, "that the benefits resulting from their emancipation have not been as great as had been hoped." In 1910 the Reverend Percy Stickney Grant, in *Socialism and Christianity*, and the Reverend John R. Rogers, in an undated pamphlet entitled "The Importance of Time in the Solution of the Negro Problem," argued that the black man, as a member of a child race, would require years of nurturing before he would be ready for the responsibilities of equality. Grant was one of the few contemporary Social Gospel writers who openly argued for black rights, but even he began from an assumption that black people were inferior because of evolutionary forces and that it would therefore take a very long time for them to adapt.[83]

Others intimated that the situation of the northern factory worker, not the plight of the former slaves, was the greatest injustice in the nation. Richard T. Ely, probably the most influential nonclerical Social Gospel spokesman, revealed his moral blind spot when he suggested that the burden of the slave had been no worse than the suffering endured by the exploited white city dweller. In *The Social Law of Service* (1896), he wrote about a man whose son had complained that emancipation left no evils to reform: "Alas! evils still exist, evils as bad as slavery," the father replied, "and those who fight the world, the flesh, and the devil will have opportunity to suffer."[84] To most of the proponents of the Social Gospel, the black person's great anguish had been slavery, an evil that had been exorcised only after over 600,000 men had died in the bloodiest war in the nation's history. After such a terrible price had been paid, it would have been very difficult to admit that the job was not finished.[85]

Despite the almost total indifference toward the welfare of black people on the part of the leading spokesmen for the Social Gospel, there were a few notable exceptions. One was Francis Greenwood Peabody, a "social ethics" professor at Harvard Divinity School and author of *Jesus Christ and the Social Question* (1900), a work that Rauschenbusch considered one of the definitive books on the Social Gospel. Peabody was genuinely interested in "Negro education and racial questions," Ahlstrom noted; "and he is among the very few Americans of that period whose words on these matters could be read without embarrassment a half-century later."[86] Another exception was Edgar Gardner Murphy, an Episcopal priest in Texas, who protested the harsh treatment suffered by blacks at the hands of whites. Similarly, Willis D. Weatherford, a leader in the southern YMCA movement and author of a work on blacks and churches in America, and Baptist preacher Benjamin F. Riley were vigorous advocates of "social Christianity" for black people. Even Rauschenbusch, perhaps aware of the fundamental flaw in the Social Gospel movement, finally addressed the race issue in 1914 when, in an article in *American Missionary*, he called upon whites to take "our belated black brother by the hand." It was not clear just how blacks were "belated." With the probable exception of Weatherford, no one should confuse these seemingly benevolent positions with anything even resembling equalitarianism. Murphy, holding that black people were biologically inferior and should not be allowed to vote, argued that racial segregation served the interests of both races, thus even the black person's "friends" continued to reflect the racist assumptions of their time.[87]

The ease with which Social Gospel advocates ignored the race issue is certainly more obvious to a modern observer than it was to most of the movement's contemporary critics. The Social Gospel was actually a submovement within the larger pattern of a liberal Protestant impulse that had been evolving since the Jacksonian era. For decades, the Protestant churches had been dominated by evangelical interests; thus liberal Protestantism had its roots in a conservative religious tradition, and people like Gladden, Rauschenbusch, Abbott, and even Bryan were the heirs and beneficiaries of that tradition. These men, James Dombrowski wrote in 1936, were "liberals advocating an ethic of charity consonant with a conservative and aristocratic society and based on an assumption of a permanently class-divided world." It was a class division that was even obvious to evangelicals like Arthur T. Pierson and Adoniram Judson Gordon, whose sympathy for the working poor was just as sincere as that of the better-known liberals. Pierson, the editor of the *Missionary Review of the World*, believed that the religious "estrangement of the masses" was a consequence of modern Christianity's "caste spirit." If the urban masses are unclean and prone to temptation, he wrote, it is because the miserable conditions under which they have been forced to live have driven them to it. In other words, as "victims" of capitalism, they have repudiated the churches that they believe have been partners in their oppression. "[I]t is not an orthodox creed which repels the masses," Gordon warned, "but an orthodox greed."[88]

Part of the public resistance to social reform in the nineteenth century was grounded in the long-held belief that poverty was the fault of the impoverished and the only people who were poor were those who were shiftless and lazy. Indeed, since no one, presumably, had to be impoverished, there were many who believed it was a sin to be poor and, accordingly, considered wealth and success to be the consequences of moral superiority.[89] "[N]o man in this land suffers from poverty unless it be more than his fault—unless it be his *sin*," Brooklyn Congregational minister Henry Ward Beecher proclaimed in the 1870s. "Because God called nobody into mendicancy and inactivity," as Ahlstrom put it, "those who begged and did not work either were being or ought to be punished for their sins." That meant that any effort to be charitable not only ran counter to the "Calvinist ethic of frugality and industry," but, if impoverishment and suffering were God's punishment for "vice and indolence," anyone who gave to the poor would be guilty of "an undue interference with divine justice."[90] Or even with the divine itself. When the disciples criticized a woman who poured expensive perfume over Christ instead of selling it and giving the money to the poor, Christ admonished them:

> Why are you bothering this woman? She has done a beautiful thing to me. The poor you will always have with you, but you will not always have me. When she poured this perfume on my body, she did it to prepare me for burial. I tell you the truth, wherever this gospel is preached throughout the world, what she has done will also be told, in memory of her.[91]

It would be easy to believe that Christ was predicting that there would always be poor people so there would be many opportunities to do something for them, but his own glorification came only once. But this is a belief that only a Christian would not consider uncharitable. It is far less easy to reconcile that interpretation with the admonition in Deuteronomy 15:11 that the poor will always be in the world and should be cared for by the able, or with Christ's parable in Matthew 25:40 calling for aid to the weak and sick. In fact, Christ's admonition of the disciples was in direct contradiction to Matthew 19:21, in which he instructed the rich man to sell all his possessions and give the money to the poor.

For the Christian American of the late nineteenth century, the idea that the poor were largely responsible for their condition may not have been specifically applied to the former slaves, but even a subconscious assumption that, somehow, poverty is self-induced and wealth is a reflection of God's will was bound to make a person reluctant to be generous. It was an idea that the affluent willingly embraced because not only was it a divine endorsement of their economic status but it also convinced them of their moral superiority. There was, of course, a certain familiarity in the assumption. Keeping people in poverty, then criticizing them for being poor was no different from withholding education from the slave, then criticizing him for being ignorant.

It should also be remembered that although many of the Social Gospel leaders maintained high profiles and their words were extensively recorded both in their own time and since, they were never more than a small minority of the American clergy, a status vividly underscored by the fact that some of the most vicious racist literature of the period was produced by conservative representatives of mainstream denominations. For example, William Montgomery Brown, author of *The Crucial Race Question, or, Where and How Shall the Color Line Be Drawn* (1907), was an Episcopal bishop in the Arkansas church when he called for the repeal of the Fifteenth Amendment and insisted that whites must dominate blacks. Although the Episcopal hierarchy denounced Brown and eventually defrocked him for alleged communist sympathies, more than a few southern Protestant leaders held views "not radically different from his." Even someone as ostensibly equalitarian as Baptist missionary Thomas J. Morgan was worried about the "menace" posed by black majorities in certain sections of the South.[92]

Despite the liberals' breakaway from "institutional Protestantism's social conservatism," Herbert G. Gutman wrote, "Gilded Age Protestantism" remained a "conformist, 'culture bound' Christianity that warmly embraced the rising industrialist, drained the aspiring rich of conscience, and confused or pacified the poor." Liberal Protestantism was the moral and ethical keystone of what was to become the progressive political movement that church historian Winthrop S. Hudson defined as "a manifestation of middle-class idealism." The progressive reform of the decades prior to World War I that is so often associated with the Populist revolt, the trade-union movement, federal antitrust campaigns against railroads and manufacturers, and efforts to clean up corruption in politics and government, was, like all reforms, an attempt to *return* to some presumed halcyon era when institutions were incorruptible, motives were pure, and leaders were noble.[93]

Of course, the "good old days," as every historian knows, were more old than good. One of liberal Protestantism's most perceptive critics was theologian H. Richard Niebuhr, younger brother to Reinhold and himself a social activist, who saw in the liberal movement an attempt by Social Gospel leaders to protect and enlarge American political and ecclesiastical institutions. "In the days of the slavery conflict [the reformers] had little interest in slaves," he wrote in *The Kingdom of God in America* (1937), "but a profound concern for the conservative institutions threatened by the political power of the slaveholder and a great desire to extend their own patterns of life over the whole country." Similarly, religious reformers, threatened by the political power of the entrepreneur, often seemed only interested in "using the social gospel as a means for the maintenance of [the church]." In a commentary on the "cultural aggressiveness" of the Social Gospel, Harvard University's William R. Hutchison argued that liberal Protestantism was a fundamental element in Christian imperialism. "Most liberals, even if they got put out of the business of personal evangelism," he wrote in *Errand to the World* (1987), "continued to express ultimate aims in the terminology not only of world evangelization but of Christian finality and 'right of conquest.' " Scratch a liberal Protestant, Hutchison seemed to be saying, and you will find an evangelical Christian. Whatever else he believed, the liberal could not escape the missionary impulse and its inherently arrogant baggage. It was impossible to be a Christian and not believe in a Christian solution to the world's problems.[94]

Beginning from the somewhat dubious premise that there are attitudes worse than indifference, if anything positive can be said about the racial views of the advocates of social Christianity it is that few were as driven by a commitment to Anglo-Saxon superiority as Josiah Strong. He was pastor of the Central Congregational Church in Cincinnati and, more important, general secretary of the Evangelical Alliance, a Protestant organization which, ironically but appropriately, had been founded by Horace Bushnell in 1846 to counteract the growing influence of the Roman Catholic Church. The "extinction of inferior races before the advancing Anglo-Saxon," Strong wrote, "certainly appears probable."[95] In his editorial comments in *The Social Gospel in America*, religion historian Robert T. Handy held that "proponents of the social gospel . . . tended to accept the views of race held by progressives generally," but that Strong "was closer to being obsessed with the idea of Anglo-Saxon superiority" than most of the others. But it would be misleading to imply that he was on the fringe of social Christianity. Sydney E. Ahlstrom considered him "the most irrepressible spirit of the Social Gospel movement." Similarly, Thomas F. Gossett wrote that Strong was "one of the most influential of the Social Gospel clergymen," who argued that racial inequality was not something to be condemned but was, in fact, "a triumphant demonstration of the workings of the Almighty." For example, since God had placed races and societies in various ascending and descending positions, the extermination of the American Indian was nothing more than his way of getting the land ready for occupation by the Anglo-Saxon race,[96] an argument virtually identical with the Puritan belief that the epidemic that had killed thousands of Indians in New England in the second decade of the seventeenth century had been part of God's design for English settlement.[97]

In his study of Thomas Jefferson and slavery, John Chester Miller identified an undercurrent of racism inherent in the "belief in the natural and inalienable rights of man." By verifying the former while exalting the latter, Miller argued, Jefferson "set the tone for much of subsequent American liberalism which, throughout a large part of its long struggle for a more just and economically equitable society, preserved its acknowledged but nevertheless pervasive racial prejudices intact." The Social Gospel was a willing handmaiden to Christian imperialism, and Strong was a leading spokesman for both. The proponents of the Social Gospel, like the advocates of Manifest Destiny, claimed to be carrying out God's will. The same divine power that drove one drove the other. Although Strong was undoubtedly the most conspicuous representative of Christianity's marriage to racism in the late nineteenth century, it was a commentary on his contemporaries that no one saw any contradiction in a leading advocate of social Christianity as an exponent of imperialism and Anglo-Saxon superiority. How strange it was that these champions of justice and defenders of the weak and oppressed never saw the "oppression, dispossession, and even extermination" of nonwhite races that accompanied the white Christians' relentless advance to the four corners of the world. To the missionary mind, winning souls to Christ justified conversion by conquest. While men like Munger, Gladden, Rauschenbusch, Abbott, and Herron might have been expected to take exception to Strong's virulent racism, in fact, Gossett pointed out, "the Social Gospel did not produce even one opponent of Strong's racist ethic," and some praised him. Rauschenbusch, for example, considered Strong, along with Gladden and Ely, one of the "pioneers of Christian social thought in America."[98]

As it happened, Rauschenbusch, nurturing "the dream of an American-German-English axis to dominate the world," had the same vision for the future of "Teutonic" peoples that Strong had for "Anglo-Saxons." Agreeing with Herron's proposition that Christianity had been a critical element in the evolution of the Anglo-Saxon's love of freedom, he was also critical of immigrants from Catholic countries, where clerical celibacy had allegedly "damaged" the racial stock.[99] Similarly, one of Strong's most ardent supporters contrived an even narrower ethnocentric application to certain Europeans. In 1915—the year before Strong's death—the Reverend John Brandt, a minister for the Disciples of Christ, published *Anglo-Saxon Su-*

premacy, in which he described German, Austrian, Italian, and Irish women as best suited for the "inferior stations" they occupied as domestic servants and as residents of slums, places one presumably would never find an Anglo-Saxon woman.[100] The best that can be said of most Social Gospel advocates is that they were guilty only of complicity. Strong was simply the most vocal supporter of racial differentiation. In determining his place in the pantheon of the movement's luminaries, the question that remains to be answered is: If his racial views were not at the center of the social Christian position, how far from it were they?

Fin de Siècle: *Protestantism's "Halcyon Years"*

If God had not answered the prayers of either side completely, as Lincoln said in his second inaugural address, he at least had obviously answered the prayers of the victorious Union to a far greater extent than those of the defeated Confederacy. The South had lost the Civil War, and four million black slaves, valued at between two and four billion dollars, had been emancipated. The ratification of the Fifteenth Amendment to the Constitution in 1870 seemingly culminated a human-rights movement that had begun somewhere back in the seventeenth century, when that unknown first person spoke out publicly against human bondage. It had been an agonizingly long and slow struggle. The earliest Quaker critics, like William Edmundson, George Keith, and the authors of the Germantown Protest, had been followed by the even more emphatic John Woolman and Anthony Benezet. But they had been a lonely number, ignored, criticized, or ridiculed by virtually everyone else—including fellow Quakers—and overwhelmed by the sheer weight of public indifference and the economic and political power of those who profited from slavery. When the mainline Christian churches joined the issue in the nineteenth century, they divided initially along pragmatic lines, with many, perhaps most, of the northern Protestant clergy decrying both slavery and abolitionism, and a few southern clergy, like George Bourne and David Barrow, condemning bondage. But ultimately they divided along sectional lines as the schisms gave the nation glimpses of secession. Finally, two centuries after the first voices had been raised, the descendants of those early African immigrants not only were free but were guaranteed their civil rights, including the right to participate in the selection of those who would create and administer the laws under which everyone would live. The political reformers had gone as far as they could—or so they said. Whatever remained to be done would have to begin in the minds and hearts of men and women who knew that laws were just words on paper until they came to life in human conduct.

The four million former slaves were now four million powerless and dependent people, largely unskilled, overwhelmingly illiterate, without land or other economic resources, and located in fifteen southern and border states. Perhaps most crippling was their lack of experience as free and independent people. Two hundred and fifty years of bondage had left them with no precedents on which to build and no tradition of self-determination. The habit of dependency would not fade quickly or easily. Slavery had given the bondsmen only one strength that, theoretically at least, they could exploit: They monopolized the southern unskilled labor market—hardly a significant power base for elevating the quality of life for so many. In short, the only category of life they dominated was the lowest one, which, of course, was where everyone else wanted to keep them.

Compounding their difficulty was the fact that they lived in a changing world that not only no longer wanted them but now no longer needed them. The former slave was whipsawed by a system that was rapidly moving away from the world of agriculture—the only world he knew—to a world of commerce and industry, leaving him on the fringes of an economy that could afford to ignore his needs.[101] The last three decades of the nineteenth century in the United States were characterized by a startling transition from a rural agricultural economy, with its agrarian values and traditions, to an urban industrialized society, which consisted primarily of northern whites, whose numbers had been dramatically enlarged by a mass of immigrants from southern and eastern Europe. And the churches were part of that world. As the surge of free enterprise and finance capitalism created new victims, the reform-minded ministers, convinced that they had done all they could for blacks, discovered the new oppressed. The old (and still) oppressed were forgotten.

On its face, the emergence of the Social Gospel was one of many reactions to the coming together of two irrepressible forces: (1) the rise of the city and (2) the displacement of the farm by the factory as the nexus of the American economy. For virtually all of the three centuries from the founding of Jamestown to the beginning of the twentieth century, America had been a largely agrarian society. Jefferson envisioned a nation of 200 million independent farmers, but even in his own lifetime conditions began to change. At the time of the First Census (1790), nine out of ten families lived on farms or in rural communities dependent on farming. By the beginning of the Civil War, more people were still engaged in agricultural pursuits than in all other occupations combined, and the value of farm products far exceeded the value of manufactured goods. But in the four decades following the war, there were radical and fundamental changes in the United States that revolutionized political and economic life in a way that Jefferson would never have recognized (or liked).

In fact, the number of workers engaged in manufacturing did not actually surpass the number in farming until the second decade of the twentieth century, but the *value* of nonagricultural goods exceeded the value of agricultural goods at least by 1890, if not sooner—which meant that the factory worker for some time had been more economically productive than the farmer. The problems created by this situation for the black worker were obvious—and overwhelming. At the end of the Civil War, three out of four of the former slaves had been field hands in cotton, sugar, rice, and tobacco production. As late as 1910, 72.6 percent of the almost ten million black Americans nationwide were still residents of rural areas.[102] During these same years the black Southerner, increasingly bound to a land-tenancy system that was slavery in all but name, moved even farther from the center of the new economy. Although southern cities like Atlanta and Birmingham had moved impressively ahead in industrial growth, the overwhelming preponderance of manufacturing was in the cities of the Northeast and the Great Lakes region—New York, Philadelphia, Pittsburgh, Cleveland, Detroit, Chicago. Thus the southern agricultural worker was rapidly becoming an economic anachronism. The black sharecropper and the northern factory worker were separated only by about a thousand miles geographically, but by light-years politically, economically, and socially.

The big city also presented problems for the traditional Protestant church, which, "suffused with the Calvinist ethic of individual achievement and responsibility," as Carl N. Degler put it, "could not easily understand an era characterized by class warfare, ruthless monopolies, and the squalor of tenement-filled cities."[103] American Christianity reflected the values of American culture at large—agrarian, conservative, provincial, geographically fragmented, locally controlled, and ideologically wrapped up in the dogma of Manifest Destiny. Despite the existence of influential clergymen in places like New York and Boston, evangelical Christianity in the United States was essentially a religion of the country and small town, a condition that persisted well into the third decade of the twentieth century, when urban residents finally outnumbered the rural population.

The problems of the city "were unfamiliar to a Protestantism that had flourished in small-town America," Ahlstrom wrote, "and the missionary movement was slow in regrouping its forces and reorienting its thinking." From George Whitefield and the Great Awakening to the Methodist camp meetings and the preaching of Charles Grandison Finney, revivalism had been the most distinctive American contribution to Christianity. But it was essentially a rural phenomenon, a style of preaching and a way of thinking that exalted conservative, small-town values and appealed to simple folk who preferred simple answers. As these people began moving into the cities, they organized congregations based on their country experiences "with little concern for other groups or for the needs of the cities."[104] The emergence of Dwight L. Moody was an urban manifestation of the old-time gospel revivalist. Like conservative Protestants of the antebellum era, who believed that changing the hearts of individual slaveholders was the best way to bring freedom to slaves, Moody insisted that institutional reform, like the Social Gospel movement, was not necessary because public morality could be achieved simply by saving individual souls. It has always been a feature of the evangelical ethic that if every soul embraced Christ there would be no evil in the world. The fact that such a simplistic belief was valid only in theory was not as important as the fact that those who believed it would not entertain any other remedies for the problems at hand. Such ossified single-mindedness left no room for alternatives.

In *A History of Christianity* (1953), Kenneth Scott Latourette called the nineteenth century—the century that began with the Second Great Awakening and closed with the triumphant emergence of liberal Protestant theology—the "Great Century" in American Christian history.[105] The achievements of the period were indeed impressive. By 1900 the United States was on the threshold of becoming the world's greatest power. Its factories were churning out goods in record amounts, and they were increasingly coming within reach of the masses; the military and missionary forces were establishing footholds in the far corners of the world; its largest cities were receiving immigrants in unprecedented numbers; and its government was entering a new era of progressive reform. The Christian churches of America responded to this exhibition of positive energy by, on the one hand, embarking on their own programs of bringing the gospel of Jesus Christ to millions of people worldwide who had never heard of the Bible and, on the other, of meeting the needs of the teeming newcomers who were swarming all across the northeastern and midwestern regions of the nation.

The problems were obvious and compelling, the outburst of business consolidations in the first four years of the century among companies that were already huge was ominous, but the mood was still one of optimism. Theodore Roosevelt sent the Navy's entire fleet of sixteen battleships around the world in a demonstration of power and commitment. The American government had prevented a decadent and vulnerable China from falling into the hands of the adventurous nations of Japan and Europe but wasted no time in overpowering the brown-skinned people of the Philippines who simply wanted to be left alone. The United States was embarking on a new era of political and economic achievement, and the only people who would not share in it were those with serious deficiencies and peculiarities. Encased in the myth of rugged individualism was the belief that the Anglo-American had the God-given right to export his religious beliefs everywhere on the globe, whether the foreigners welcomed them or not. And trapped at the bottom of all this were the black Americans, many of whom could still remember the years when the law did not recognize them as completely human.

With large churches being constructed, Sunday-morning services packed, and various humanitarian and missionary programs underway, the "decades bridging the turn of the century," church historian Winthrop S. Hudson wrote, "were the halcyon years of American Protestantism." It was also, he added, the "great age of the American pulpit," as preachers such as Phillips Brooks, Russell Conwell, George A. Gordon, Washington Gladden, Lyman Abbott, Newell Dwight Hillis, and Charles M. Sheldon, to name only a few, were acclaimed nationwide through their books, sermons, and syndicated columns.[106] But for black and brown people within the American orbit, the period was a "great age" of political and economic repression and "halcyon years" of public indifference. One can only speculate how much the one had to do with the other; but the delegates to the second convention of the Niagara Movement had no difficulty seeing a connection. Meeting in 1906 at Harpers Ferry, Virginia, they approved a resolution drafted by W. E. B. Du Bois angrily condemning the disfranchisement of southern black voters.

> Never before in the modern age has a great and civilized folk threatened to adopt so cowardly a creed in the treatment of its fellow-citizens, born and bred on its soil. Stripped of verbose subterfuge and in its naked nastiness, the new American creed says: fear to let black men even try to rise lest they become the equals of the white. And in this land that professes to follow Jesus Christ. The blasphemy of such a course is only matched by its cowardice.[107]

Notes

PREFACE

1. Thomas F. Pettigrew, *Racially Separate or Together?* (New York, 1971), p. xviii.

2. Bertram Wyatt-Brown, *Yankee Saints and Southern Sinners* (Baton Rouge, La., 1985), pp. ix, 28–29.

3. Joseph B. Earnest, Jr., *The Religious Development of the Negro in Virginia* (Charlottesville, Va., 1914), p. 10.

4. Georges Fisch, *Nine Months in the United States during the Crisis* (London, 1863), p. 114.

5. Harriet A. Jacobs, *Incidents in the Life of a Slave Girl, Written by Herself* (Cambridge, Mass., 1987 [1861]), p. 49.

6. Stephen F. Teiser, *The Ghost Festival in Medieval China* (Princeton, N.J., 1988), p. 15. See also C. K. Yang, *Religion in Chinese Society: A Study of Contemporary Social Functions of Religion and Some of Their Historical Factors* (Berkeley, Calif., 1961), pp. 28–57, 294–96, and passim.

7. Max Lerner, *America as a Civilization: Life and Thought in the United States Today* (New York, 1957), pp. 505–507, 510, 512, 513.

8. Harry S. Stout, "Word and Order in Colonial New England," *The Bible in America: Essays in Cultural History* (ed. Nathan O. Hatch and Mark A. Noll, New York, 1982), pp. 19–38; Margaret T. Hillis, *The English Bible in America: A Bibliography of Editions of the Bible & the New Testament Published in America, 1777–1957* (New York, 1961), passim.

9. For an extreme example of this process, see the description of John Eliot's Algonquin Bible in chapter 7.

CHAPTER ONE

1. Horace Bushnell, *Christian Nurture* (rev. ed., New York, 1861), pp. 93, 106, 112–13, 123–61, 173–93.

2. Daniel Walker Howe, "The Social Science of Horace Bushnell," *Journal of American History*, vol. 70, no. 2 (September 1983), p. 310. Bushnell may have had in mind the emphasis on religious indoctrination endured by children in his native New England during the colonial period. See Philip Greven, *The Protestant Temperament: Patterns of Child-Rearing, Religious Experience, and the Self in Early America* (New York, 1977), and Gusti Wiesenfeld Frankel, "Between Parent and Child in Colonial New England: An Analysis of the Religious Child-Oriented Literature and Selected Children's Works" (Ph.D. dissertation, University of Minnestoa, 1976).

3. William R. Hutchison, "Cultural Strain and Protestant Liberalism," *American Historical Review*, vol. 76, no. 2 (April 1971), pp. 402–403; George M. Fredrickson, *The Black Image in the White Mind: The Debate on Afro-American Character and Destiny, 1817–1914* (New York, 1971), p. 156.

4. Quoted in Charles C. Cole, Jr., "Horace Bushnell and the Slavery Question," *New England Quarterly*, vol. 23, no. 1 (March 1950), p. 29.

5. See *infra*, chapter 4.

6. Gary B. Nash, *Red, White, and Black: The Peoples of Early America* (2nd ed., Englewood Cliffs, N.J., 1982), p. 31.

7. Alexis de Tocqueville, *Democracy in America* (ed. J. P. Mayer and Max Lerner, translated by George Lawrence, New York, 1966 [1835]), pp. 235–37.

8. Arnold Toynbee, *An Historian's Approach to Religion* (2nd ed., Oxford, U.K., 1979), pp. 256–57, citing John Locke's *A Letter Concerning Toleration* (1689).

9. Melville J. Herskovits, *The Myth of the Negro Past* (New York, 1958 [1941]). See also Leonard E. Barrett, *Soul-Force: African Heritage in Afro-American Religion* (Garden City, N.Y., 1974); Henry H. Mitchell, *Black Belief: Folk Beliefs of Blacks in America and West Africa* (New York, 1975); and Patricia Jones-Jackson, *When Roots Die: Endangered Traditions on the Sea Islands* (Athens, Ga., 1987).

10. Eugene D. Genovese, *Roll, Jordan, Roll: The World the Slaves Made* (New York, 1972), pp. 197–202.

11. Nash, *Red, White, and Black*, p. 187.

12. The strongest argument against Herskovits's thesis has come from E. Franklin Frazier: *The Negro Church in America* (New York, 1964), pp. 1–9; *The Negro Family in the United States* (Chicago, 1966), pp. 3–16; and *The Negro in the United States* (rev. ed., New York, 1957), pp. 3–13. Other critics include: Martin E. Marty, *Righteous Empire: The Protestant Experience in America* (New York, 1970), p. 25; Kenneth M. Stampp, *The Peculiar Institution: Slavery in the Ante-Bellum South* (New York, 1956), pp. 371, 375; Genovese, *Roll, Jordan, Roll*, p. 172; Olli Alho, *The Religion of the Slaves: A Study of the Religious Tradition and Behaviour of the Plantation Slaves in the United States, 1830–1865* (Helsinki, 1976), pp. 43, 48; and Lawrence W. Levine, *Black Culture and Black Consciousness: Afro-American Folk Thought from Slavery to Freedom* (New York, 1977), pp. 3–5.

13. For an extended discussion of the debate, especially between Herskovits and Frazier, over "persistent Africanisms" in American slave religion, see Albert J. Raboteau, *Slave Religion: The "Invisible Institution" in the Antebellum South* (New York, 1978), pp. 48–60. Raboteau believes that Herskovits was right to the extent that the existence of African habits and customs in the New World ranged from pervasive in Dutch Guiana to occasional in the United States. In Haiti and Brazil it was possible to identify Africanisms that could be traced to specific countries such as Nigeria or Dahomey. It was Frazier's contention, on the other hand, that the Africanisms in the United States were only the exceptions that proved the rule that the slave's traditional culture had been destroyed, and that "the vacuum thus created was filled by Christianity, which became the new bond of social cohesion."

14. Orlando Patterson, *Sociology of Slavery: An Analysis of the Origins, Development, and Structure of Negro Slave Society in Jamaica* (Rutherford, N.J., 1969 [1967]), pp. 183–95; Raboteau, *Slave Religion*, p. 49.

15. For a fuller discussion of African gods, see *infra*, chapter 5.

16. Herskovits, *The Myth of the Negro Past*, p. 249.

17. Genovese, *Roll, Jordan, Roll*, pp. 209–11; Raboteau, *Slave Religion*, pp. 22–25, 87–92. The blending of traditional African religious practices and Catholic rituals has continued to the present day. At the 41st International Eucharistic Congress in Philadelphia in 1976, church leaders from both Africa and Latin America complained of the influence of "pagan practices" among converts. For example, Cardinal Maurice Otunga, archbishop of Nairobi, Kenya, claimed that blacks often confuse the Catholic habit of wearing religious medals with the African's proclivity for charms and amulets. Similarly, the Most Reverend Helder Camara, archbishop of Recife, Brazil, found that in celebrations of the feast of the Immaculate Conception many black Catholics "mix Our Lady with Iomonja, the 'Goddess of the Seas.' " Even the Eucharist itself, which Catholics perceive as the body and blood of Christ, has been equated with African animal sacrifices. See Providence *Journal*, August 5, 1976.

18. William R. Hutchison, *Errand to the World: American Protestant Thought and Foreign Missions* (Chicago, 1987), pp. 15–16.

19. Peter Kolchin, "Reevaluating the Antebellum Slave Community: A Comparative Perspective," *Journal of American History*, vol. 70, no. 3 (December 1983), p. 587.

20. Ralph Barton Perry, *Puritanism and Democracy* (New York, 1944), pp. 551–82.

21. Samuel Worcester, *Paul on Mars Hill: Or a Christian Survey of the Pagan World* (Andover, Mass., 1815), pp. 19–20.

22. Lois W. Banner, "Religious Benevolence as Social Control: A Critique of an Interpretation," *Journal of American History*, vol. 50, no. 1 (June 1973), pp. 38–39; Walter Rauschenbusch, *Christianity and the Social Crisis* (New York, 1907), p. 421–22.

23. See Andrew Sharp, *Ancient Voyages in Polynesia* (Berkeley, Calif., 1964), pp. 33–53; and two works by Douglas L. Oliver: *The Pacific Islands* (rev. ed., Garden City, N.Y., 1961 [1951]), pp. 14–25; and *Oceania: The Native Cultures of Australia and the Pacific Islands* (2 vols., Honolulu, 1989), vol. I, pp. 406–22.

24. This expression (or variations of it) has been attributed to many people, including gangster Al Capone.

25. Tocqueville, *Democracy in America*, p. 313.

26. Harriet Martineau, *Society in America* (Gloucester, Mass., 1968 [New York, 1837]), pp. 220, 332–33.

27. Carl N. Degler, *Out of Our Past: The Forces That Shaped Modern America* (New York, 1959), pp. 53–54; Sydney E. Ahlstrom, *A Religious History of the American People* (New Haven, Conn., 1972), p. 761; Rowland Berthoff, *An Unsettled People: Social Order and Disorder in American History* (New York, 1971), p. 252.

28. David T. Bailey, *Shadow of the Church: Southwestern Evangelical Religion and the Issue of Slavery, 1783–1860* (Ithaca, N.Y., 1985), pp. 65 ff; Paul Jacobs, Saul Landau, and Eve Pell, eds., *To Serve the Devil* (2 vols., New York, 1971), vol. I, *Natives and Slaves*, pp. 51–52; T. C. McLuhan, ed., *Touch the Earth: A Self-Portrait of Indian Existence* (New York, 1971), p. 63. For a discussion of Quaker fragmentation in the nineteenth century, see Thomas D. Hamm, *The Transformation of American Quakerism: Orthodox Friends, 1800–1907* (Bloomington, Ind., 1988).

29. Tocqueville, *Democracy in America*, p. 267; Martineau, *Society in America*, p. 334; Francis J. Grund, *The Americans in Their Moral, Social, and Political Relations* (New York, 1968 [1837]), pp. 164–65. Grund was a German who had been born and educated in Vienna; but, after living in the United States for ten years, he considered himself a "committed democrat." His work was a conscious effort to counteract some of the unfavorable commentaries on life in the United States written by other recent European travelers, e.g., Frances Trollope's *Views of Society and Manners in America* (London, 1821), and, especially, *Domestic Manners of the Americans* (London, 1832).

30. Milton Bryan Powell, "The Abolitionist Controversy in the Methodist Episcopal Church, 1840–1864" (Ph.D. dissertation, State University of Iowa, 1963), p. 11, quoting *Methodist Quarterly Review* (October 1845), p. 491; Robert Baird, *Religion in the United States of America* (Glasgow and Edinburgh, 1844).

31. Martineau, *Society in America*, p. 334; Norman A. Graebner, "Christianity and Democracy: Tocqueville's Views of Religion in America," *Journal of Religion*, vol. 56, no. 3 (July 1976), pp. 263–64; Grund, *The Americans in Their Moral, Social, and Political Relations*, p. 158; Tocqueville, *Democracy in America*, pp. 267, 268–69.

32. Perry Miller argued that it is easy to make too much of the Puritan commitment to individualism. "There was, it is true, a strong element of individualism in the Puritan creed; every man had to work out his own salvation, each soul had to face his maker alone. But at the same time, the Puritan philosophy demanded that in society all men, at least all regenerate men, be marshaled into one united array. . . . The theorists of New England thought of society as a unit, bound together by inviolable ties; they thought of it not as an aggregation of individuals but as an organism, functioning for a definite purpose, with all parts subor-

dinate to the whole, all members contributing a definite share, every person occupying a particular status. . . . The state . . . was an active instrument of leadership, discipline, and, wherever necessary, of coercion; it legislated over any or all aspects of human behavior, it not merely regulated misconduct but undertook to inspire and direct all conduct." See *Errand into the Wilderness* (Cambridge, Mass., 1956), pp. 143–44.

33. Degler, *Out of Our Past*, p. 16.

34. Edward H. Madden, *Civil Disobedience and Moral Law in Nineteenth-Century American Philosophy* (Seattle, 1968), pp. 6–7.

35. These numerical and geographical limitations did not apply to the Universalists. This group, which did not formally unite with the Unitarians until 1961, was virtually identical to the Unitarians except in social status. Introduced into English North America in 1770 by John Murray, Universalism appealed to the rural, lower-middle-class folk and by the middle of the nineteenth century easily exceeded the Unitarians in numbers, especially in the Midwest. See Winthrop S. Hudson, *Religion in America* (New York, 1981), pp. 162–63, 392.

36. William R. Hutchison, ed., *American Protestant Thought: The Liberal Era* (New York: 1968), p. 3; Grund, *The Americans*, p. 160.

37. Robert T. Handy, *A Christian America: Protestant Hopes and Historical Realities* (New York, 1971), p. viii; Jacobs, Landau, and Pell, eds., *To Serve the Devil*, vol. I, pp. 47–48; Francis Jennings, *The Invasion of America: Indians, Colonialism, and the Cant of Conquest* (Chapel Hill, N.C., 1975), p. 48. For an example of missionary attitudes of superiority toward converts, see Myra Dinnerstein, "The American Zulu Mission in the Nineteenth Century: Clash over Customs," *Church History*, vol. 45, no. 2 (June 1976), pp. 235–46. The Franklin story is related in full in Nancy B. Black and Bette S. Weidman, eds., *White on Red: Images of the American Indian* (Port Washington, N.Y., 1976), p. 104.

38. James Axtell, *The Invasion Within: The Contest of Cultures in Colonial North America* (New York, 1985), p. 13; A. R. Radcliffe-Brown, *Structure and Function in Primitive Society: Essays and Addresses* (New York, 1965 [1952]), p. 153. In *A Key into the Language of America* (1743), Roger Williams explained the Indians' reaction to the idea of monotheism. "They will generally confess that God made all: but then in special, although they deny not that *English-Mans* God made *English* Men, and the Heavens and the Earth there! yet their Gods made them and the Heaven and Earth where they dwell." See *The Complete Writings of Roger Williams* (7 vols., New York, 1963), vol. I, pp. 207–208.

39. Quoted in Pauline Moffitt Watts, "Prophecy and Discovery: On the Spiritual Origins of Christopher Columbus's 'Enterprise of the Indies,' " *American Historical Review*, vol. 90, no. 1 (February 1985), pp. 73, 99. Columbus was obviously referring to Revelation 21:1: "Then I saw a new heaven and a new earth, for the first heaven and the first earth had passed away, and there was no longer any sea."

40. Stephen Neill contended that many European missionaries did not hold the extreme view that the white man had an *obligation* "to bring the whole world under his dominion" or that the "propagation of Christianity is a natural and inevitable accompaniment of the expansion of the West." See *Colonization and Christian Mission* (London, 1966), pp. 412–13. But that may have been beside the point. If there were political forces that did believe they had such an obligation, and Christian missionaries availed themselves of the opportunities afforded by conquest, then these men of God were really culpable.

41. R. Pierce Beaver, *Church, State, and the American Indians: Two and a Half Centuries of Partnership in Missions between Protestant Churches and Government* (St. Louis, 1966), pp. 8–9; Norman Lewis, "English Missionary Interest in the Indians of North America, 1578–1700" (Ph.D. dissertation, University of Washington, 1968), pp. 75–103.

42. Hutchison, *Errand to the World*, p. 24; Sir Charles Lucas, *Religion, Colonising & Trade: The Driving Forces of the Old Empire* (London, 1930), pp. 6–9.

43. Miller, *Errand into the Wilderness*, p. 101; Roy Harvey Pearce, *The Savages of America: A Study of the Indian and the Idea of Civilization* (rev. ed., Baltimore, 1965), p. 6; George M. Fredrickson, *White Supremacy: A Comparative Study in American and South African History* (New York, 1981), p. 12; George Maclaren Brydon, *Virginia's Mother Church and the Political Conditions under Which It Grew* (2 cols., Richmond, Va., 1947), vol. I, p. 52; Herbert S. Klein, *Slavery in the Americas: A Comparative Study of Virginia and Cuba* (Chicago, 1967), p. 105; Beaver, *Church, State, and the American Indians*, pp. 10–11; and Hutchison, *Errand to the World*, p. 24.

44. Quoted in Marty, *Righteous Empire*, p. 9. Italics added.

45. Miller, *Errand into the Wilderness*, p. 101.

46. Matthew 28:19. See also Mark 16:15, 1 Corinthians 9:16, Romans 15:14–21, and Revelation 5:9.

47. Alden T. Vaughan, *New England Frontier: Puritans and Indians, 1620–1675* (rev. ed., New York, 1979), p. 236; Kenneth Scott Latourette, *Missions and the American Mind* (Indianapolis, 1949), pp. 3–4. See also Hutchison, *Errand to the World*, p. 24.

48. Cotton Mather, *India Christiana: A Discourse Delivered unto the Commissioners for the Propagation of the Gospel among American Indians. . .* (Boston, 1721), p. 27. See also Jesse Page, *David Brainerd: The Apostle to the North American Indians* (New York, [1900?]), p. 125, and Neal Salisbury, "Red Puritans: The 'Praying Indians' of Massachusetts Bay and John Eliot," *William and Mary Quarterly*, vol. 31 (January 1974), pp. 29–30.

49. Lewis, "English Missionary Interest in Indians," pp. 80–99; Beaver, *Church, State, and the American Indians*, pp. 4, 13–14, 24, 85; Miller, *Errand into the Wilderness*, p. 101. See also R. Pierce Beaver, "American Missionary Motivation before the Revolution," *Church History*, vol. 31, no. 2 (June 1962), pp. 216–26.

50. Lucas, *Religion, Colonising & Trade*, pp. 6–9; Brydon, *Virginia's Mother Church*, vol. I, pp. 56, 84; Beaver, *Church, State, and the American Indians*, pp. 12–13; Maxwell Ford Taylor, Jr., "The Influence of Religion on White Attitudes toward Indians in the Early Settlement of Virginia" (Ph.D. dissertation, Emory University, 1961), pp. 204ff. Taylor also disagreed with Winthrop D. Jordan's later conclusion that it was not until after 1660 that "the tradition associating slavery and heathenism was manifested." Because of the aftermath of the massacre, Virginians had already formed such an association, Taylor argued; when Africans began arriving the attitude was already in place. "The colonists' earlier experience with the Indians within the context of an avowed missionary concern left them convinced of the entrenched heathenism of the Indians, so much so that only by means of forceful subjugation was it believed possible to achieve the conversion of any Indians at all." See p. 259 and Jordan, *White over Black: American Attitudes toward the Negro, 1550–1812* (Chapel Hill, N.C., 1968), p. 92.

51. Brydon, *Virginia's Mother Church*, vol. I, pp. 299, 342–43. For fuller discussions of English-Indian relations in early Virginia, see Bernard Sheehan, *Savagism and Civility: Indians and Englishmen in Colonial Virginia* (Cambridge, U.K., 1980); Taylor, "The Influence of Religion on White Attitudes toward Indians"; and A. Mark Conrad, "The Christianization of Indians in Colonial Virginia" (Th.D. dissertation, Union Theological Seminary, Richmond, 1979).

52. Nash, *Red, White, and Black*, p. 78; Vaughan, *New England Frontier*, pp. 236, 388; Salisbury, "Red Puritans," pp. 29–30. For a fuller discussion of Puritan efforts to "civilize" Indians, see *infra*, chapter 7.

53. Clayton J. Drees, "Augustine of Hippo and Bernard of Clairvaux: A Medieval Justification for War," *Perspectives: A Journal of Historical Inquiry*, vol. 14 (1987), p. 7. The Puritan idea of a just war has been thoroughly explored in Timothy George, "War and Peace in the Puritan Tradition," *Church History*, vol. 53, no. 4 (December 1974), pp. 492–503; and Peter Lloyd, "The Emergence of Racial Prejudice towards the Indians in Seventeenth

Century New England: Some Notes on an Explanation" (Ph.D. dissertation, Ohio State University, 1975), pp. 51–53.

54. Quoted in Keith W. F. Stavely, *Puritan Legacies:* Paradise Lost *and the New England Tradition, 1630–1890* (Ithaca, N.Y., 1987), p. 86.

55. Edmund S. Morgan, *The Puritan Family: Religion & Domestic Relations in Seventeenth-Century New England* (rev. ed., New York, 1966), p. 110. According to a study by Ann Kibbey, the Puritan's war against the Indians was far more than a response to perceived dangers. Rather, it was inherent in his faith. "Both the [Pequot] war and the [Antinomian] controversy [occurring within months of each other] demonstrate that prejudice was rationalized by religion in Puritan society," Kibbey wrote. "[This rationalization] was in many respects only the outcome of a more profound synthesis of religion and prejudice in the perception of material shapes. . . . [T]he Puritan belief in the necessity and righteousness of deliberate physical harm was deeply indebted to the ideology of Protestant iconoclasm in Reformation Europe. The violent destruction of artistic images of people developed into a mandate for sacrosanct violence against human beings, especially against people whose material 'image,' whose physical characteristics, differed from the Puritan's own." See *The Interpretation of Material Shapes in Puritanism: A Study in Rhetoric, Prejudice, and Violence* (Cambridge, U.K., 1986), p. 2.

56. Quoted in George S. Brookes, *Friend Anthony Benezet* (Philadelphia, 1937), p. 366.

57. H. Shelton Smith, Robert T. Handy, and Lefferts A. Loetscher, eds., *American Christianity: An Historical Interpretation with Representative Documents* (2 vols., New York, 1960), vol. I, p. 547; Samuel Worcester, *Paul on Mars Hill: Or a Christian Survey of the Pagan World* (Andover, Mass., 1815), pp. 26–27. See also Hutchison, *Errand to the World,* pp. 47–48.

58. Okot p'Bitek, *African Religions in Western Scholarship* (Kampala, [1970]), p. 59.

59. Dorothea R. Muller, "Josiah Strong and American Nationalism: A Reevaluation," *Journal of American History,* vol. 53, no. 3 (December 1966), p. 491. See especially Josiah Strong, *Our Country: Its Possible Future and Its Present Crisis* (New York, 1885).

60. Robert E. Speer, *Christianity and the Nations* (New York, 1910), from the chapter "Christianity and the Non-Christian Religions." The six chapters of this book were originally presented in Scotland as the Duff Missionary Lectures.

61. Quoted in Hutchison, *Errand to the World,* p. 91.

62. Alden T. Vaughan, ed., *The Puritan Tradition in America, 1620–1730* (Columbia, S.C., 1972), pp. 265–66; Ola Elizabeth Winslow, *John Eliot, Apostle to the Indians* (Boston, 1968), p. 102; Hutchison, *Errand to the World,* pp. 31–32.

63. Jacobs, Landau, and Pell, eds., *To Serve the Devil,* vol. I, pp. 51–52; W. C. Vanderwerth, *Indian Oratory: Famous Speeches by Noted Indian Chiefs* (Norman, Okla., 1971), pp. 45–46; McLuhan, ed., *Touch the Earth,* pp. 60–61; Robert F. Berkhofer, *Salvation and the Savage: An Analysis of Protestant Missions and American Indian Response, 1787–1862* (Westport, Conn., 1977 [1965]), p. 107; Lewis, "English Missionary Interest in Indians," p. 456; Grund, *The Americans,* p. 226n., quoting *Red Jacket's Reply to the Missionaries, by Thomas Jefferson;* Louis Thomas Jones, *Aboriginal American Oratory: The Tradition of Eloquence among the Indians of the United States* (Los Angeles, 1965), p. 55. Red Jacket was described by one historian as "the most outstanding Indian orator of the 18th century," a description reflected in his tribal name, Sa-Go-Ye-Wat-Ha, which translated as "He who keeps his tribe awake."

64. Berkhofer, *Salvation and the Savage,* p. 108.

65. Williams, *Complete Writings,* vol. I, pp. 219–20. Among New England Indians Southwest was a common name for the afterlife. For a fuller discussion of Indian beliefs on life after death, see Åke Hultkrantz, *The Religions of the American Indians* (Translated by Monica Setterwall, Berkeley, Calif., 1967), chapter 9.

66. Charles A. Litzinger, "Conflict between Christians and Non-Christians in Rural

Chihli, 1860–1895," *Essays in Memory of Professor Chao T'ieh-han* (Taipei, 1978). In 1987 a Nepalese Christian was arrested and jailed for trying to persuade some of his countrymen to convert. American church officials protested, but their reaction was, in fact, a reflection of their inability—or unwillingness—to recognize and respect the fundamental nature of a non-Christian society. In Nepal, where religion is an imperative aspect of culture, it is against the law for anyone to try to change someone else's religion. To a Christian, that is not a good enough reason to leave others alone. Like evangelical Protestants everywhere, he believes that where a peron's immortal soul is at stake he is not obliged to observe the laws of man.

67. John S. Mbiti, *African Religions & Philosophy* (New York, 1969), p. 4.

68. Eric Hoffer, *The True Believer: Thoughts on the Nature of Mass Movements* (New York, 1951), p. 112. See also Kenneth Scott Latourette, *A History of the Expansion of Christianity* (7 vols., New York, 1937–1945), vol. I, p. 164.

69. Fyodor Dostoyevsky, *The Brothers Karamazov* (trans. by Constance Garnett, New York, n.d. [1879–1880]), p. 260.

70. A modern—and nonfictional—example of this situation may be found in the Catholic Church's attempt to exonerate Galileo Galilei, who, in 1616, had been convicted of heresy by the Italian Inquisition for arguing that the earth revolved around the sun. In 1980—364 years later—Pope John Paul II ordered the Pontifical Academy of Science to review the case. But the wheels of ecclesiastical justice move slowly. In this case, they stopped completely. Eight years after the Pope's order, nothing had been done and a Vatican representative told a reporter for the Los Angeles *Times* (May 31, 1988) that "The case is closed." The hierarchy was embarrassed in being caught between the truth and the doctrine of papal infallibility. Like Dostoyevsky's Grand Inquisitor, the Holy See considered it more important to ignore reality and retain the confidence of the faithful than to admit a mistake and possibly undermine that confidence.

71. Bertrand Russell, *Why I Am Not a Christian, and Other Essays on Religion and Related Subjects* (New York, 1957), p. 202.

72. Thomas Jefferson, *Notes on the State of Virginia* (Chapel Hill, N.C., 1955 [London, 1787]), p. 160.

73. Hudson, *Religion in America*, p. 64.

74. For a fuller discussion on the Puritan "Morphology of Conversion," see Edmund S. Morgan, *Visible Saints: The History of a Puritan Idea* (New York, 1963), pp. 69–70, 90–92. In modern times this attitude is found among some conservative Protestant denominations where the practices of *confession* and giving *testimony* are common and even required.

75. Samuel Stanhope Smith, *An Essay on the Causes of the Variety of Complexion and Figure in the Human Species* (Cambridge, Mass., 1965, reprint of the 2nd ed., New York, 1810 [1787]), pp. x–xi, from the introduction by Winthrop D. Jordan.

76. Leland J. Bellot, "Evangelicals and the Defense of Slavery in Britain's Old Colonial Empire," *Journal of Southern History*, vol. 37, no. 1 (February 1971), p. 22.

77. There are even some who believe that Christianity can be seen as the handmaiden of free enterprise. In a book co-published by the Hoover Institution, Senior Fellows Peter Duignan and L. H. Gann, discussing commerce, Christianity, and colonization to 1865, argued that "supporters of the missionary movement both before and after [Olaudah Equiano] believed there was a close link among the spreading of the Gospel; the destruction of the slave trade; the development of a new economic system founded on free labor and free trade, with resultant prosperity for the new manufacturing industries; and material progress for all." See *The United States and Africa: A History* (Cambridge, U.K., and New York, 1984), p. 91. The authors did not say if anyone believed there was a "close link" between the spreading of the gospel and the creation and expansion of the slave trade; nor did they bother to explain why some of the most ardent advocates of free trade were also militant Christian

defenders of slave labor. It should be noted that Equiano was a Nigerian Christian convert who, contrary to the implication of Duignan and Gann, condemned the role of Christianity in the enslavement of Africans. See Philip D. Curtin, ed., *Africa Remembered: Narratives by West Africans from the Era of the Slave Trade* (Madison, Wis., 1967), pp. 97–98; and Olaudah Equiano, *The Interesting Narrative of the Life of Olaudah Equiano, or Gustavus Yassa, the African, Written by Himself* (2 vols., New York, 1969 [1789]), vol. I, pp. 218–19; vol. II, pp. 249–50.

78. Galatians 3:26–29.

79. William R. Brock, *The Evolution of American Democracy* (New York, 1970), p. 131.

80. Michael C. Coleman, "Not Race, but Grace: Presbyterian Missionaries and American Indians, 1837–1893," *Journal of American History*, vol. 67, no. 1 (June 1980), p. 55. Italics added.

81. Franklin H. Littell, *The Free Church* (Boston, 1957), p. 61.

82. See Alho, *The Religion of the Slaves*, pp. 46–47. See also J. Spencer Trimingham, *A History of Islam in West Africa* (London, 1982 [1970]), and *The Influence of Islam upon Africa* (2nd ed., London, 1980 [1968]).

83. Orlando Patterson, *Slavery and Social Death: A Comparative Study* (Cambridge, Mass., 1982), pp. 114–15, 117–18, 128, 204, 276; [Benjamin Rush], *A Vindication of the Address to the Inhabitants of the British Settlements* (Philadelphia, 1773), p. 7n.

84. Patterson, *Slavery and Social Death*, pp. 121–22.

85. Arye Oded, *Islam in Uganda: Islamization through a Centralized State in Pre-Colonial Africa* (New York, 1974), p. 47.

86. See Patterson, *Slavery and Social Death*, p. 145.

87. Trimingham, *The Influence of Islam upon Africa*, pp. 92–93.

88. Louis Brenner, *The Shehus of Kukawa: A History of the Al-Kanemi Dynasty of Bornu* (London, 1973), pp. 89–103; Patterson, *Slavery and Social Death*, pp. 308–309; J. D. Fage, *A History of Africa* (New York, 1978), pp. 163, 183. The word *mamluk* specifically identified a Caucasian male purchased in the slave market or captured, while *abid*, the plural of *abd*, almost always referred to Negro slaves.

89. Patterson, *Slavery and Social Death*, pp. 41, 58, 93, 176.

90. Ibid., p. 97. See especially pages 97–101, "Hegel and the Dialectics of Slavery."

91. Oded, *Islam in Uganda*, pp. 269–70.

92. Marty, *Righteous Empire*, pp. 9, 50–52; Stephen Neill, *Colonization and Christian Mission* (London, 1966), pp. 413, 415–16; Robert F. Berkhofer, *The White Man's Indian: Images of the American Indian from Columbus to the Present* (New York, 1978), p. 121; Charles M. Segal and David C. Stineback, *Puritans, Indians, and Manifest Destiny* (New York, 1977), p. 35. See also John R. Bodo, *The Protestant Clergy and Public Issues, 1812–1848* (Princeton, N.J., 1954), pp. 90–93, 108.

93. Yasuhide Kawashima, *Puritan Justice and the Indian* (Middletown, Conn., 1966), pp. 110–13.

94. Donald G. Mathews, "The Methodist Mission to the Slaves, 1829–1844," *Journal of American History*, vol. 51, no. 4 (March 1965), p. 617. The arrogance of faith has been as enduring as it has been pervasive, and it has not been confined to missionaries. In 1949, while serving as president of the American Historical Association, Yale University's Kenneth Scott Latourette praised Christian missions for "helping the Indians adjust themselves *wholesomely* to the changed conditions brought by the dominance of the white man and his culture," and for assisting the Negro "in making a *wholesome* adjustment to the culture into which he had been involuntarily thrust" (italics added). For Americans of an earlier time to compel Indians and Africans to adjust to an alien culture was one thing. For a modern scholar to perceive those adjustments as "wholesome" is quite another. See Latourette, *Missions and the American Mind*, pp. 21, 23.

95. "The White Man's Burden: The United States and the Philippine Islands" (1899), in Rudyard Kipling, *Complete Verse: Definitive Edition* (New York, 1989 [1940]), p. 321.

96. John C. Van Horne, ed., *Religious Philanthropy and Colonial Slavery: The American Correspondence of the Associates of Dr. Bray, 1717–1777* (Champaign, Ill., 1985), passim.

97. Ronald T. Takaki, *Iron Cages: Race and Culture in the Nineteenth Century* (New York, 1979), pp. 95–96; Coleman, "Not Race, but Grace," p. 41–42. Unfortunately, much of Coleman's article reads like an apology for Presbyterian missions. His main thesis, that "these supremely ethnocentric missionaries were not racist in their attitudes toward Indian people," is a contradiction in terms. Indians who converted to Christianity, he wrote, found "a far higher privilege." *Higher* is a qualitative term that implies *better*. Coleman also quoted missionary statements on the "transformation of character"—which meant that the Indian's native "character" needed transforming—the "utter worthlessness of Indian ways," and the denunciation of Indian religion. He made no objections to pejorative expressions like "a real wild Indian" who can learn if "she only becomes tame" (p. 49). In a later version of this article, chapter 7 of *Presbyterian Missionary Attitudes toward American Indians* (Jackson, Miss., 1985), Coleman insisted there is a difference between ethnocentricism and racism. The first is an attitude of cultural superiority that does not deny "inferior" cultures the ability to be elevated; the second is based on inherited and immutable racial characteristics which forever condemn a people to an inferior condition. Presbyterian missionaries, he argued, were guilty only of an "extreme" (which replaced "supreme" in the earlier essay) form of ethnocentricism (pp. 139–40). But, in the end, did that really matter? If the consequences of each were equally destructive, the distinction is irrelevant. As Coleman himself wrote (p. 161) when describing William C. McLoughlin's views on missionary relationships with the Cherokees, "To those on the receiving end, . . . there was little perceptible difference between judgments of cultural inferiority and racial inferiority."

98. John Fiske, *History of the United States* (Boston, 1894), pp. 3, 8, 103, 110.

99. Berkhofer, *The White Man's Indian*, pp. 15–16. For a perceptive analysis of the moral bias inherent in the historian's use of code words, see James Axtell, "Forked Tongues: Moral Judgments in Indian History," *Perspectives: American Historical Association Newsletter*, vol. 25, no. 2 (February 1987), pp. 10–13.

100. Williams, *Complete Writings*, vol. VII, pp. 31–32, from the work entitled *Christenings Make Not Christians, or A Briefe Discourse Concerning that Name* Heathen, *Commonly Given to the Indians. As also Concerning that Great Point of Their Conversion* (London, 1645), pp. 1–2.

101. p'Bitek, *African Religions in Western Scholarship*, pp. ii–iii.

102. Pearce, *Savages of America*, pp. 8–9, 15.

103. Ibid., p. 22; Fredrickson, *White Supremacy*, 25–26; Segal and Stineback, *Puritans, Indians, and Manifest Destiny*, pp. 35, 106–107, 132–33, 182.

104. The most prolific writer on the Devil has been Jeffrey Burton Russell, whose four books cover the years from antiquity to modern times. Russell agrees that the Devil is "a Judeo-Christian-Muslim idea," (*Lucifer*, p. 12), but, unfortunately, much of his work is marred by his perception of mythology and abstraction as reality. For example, in *The Devil* (p. 12), he admits his belief in the existence of Satan, which means he must also believe in the existence of God. But a belief in the existence of Satan carries with it a belief that the source of evil behavior is extraneous to the individual, i.e., that the thief can claim "the Devil made me do it!" Similarly, Russell does not acknowledge that people are guilty of theft, rape, murder, and every other offense against persons and property because they are greedy, sick, lazy, hungry, jealous, or in some way driven by a desire or emotion that is entirely *within themselves*. He also makes frequent allusions to nonscholarly and nonscientific phantasmata, e.g., that humanity moves with a purpose because there is some force *outside* of humanity that gives it that impulse. That may be a comforting idea in a theological treatise,

but it does not belong in a scholarly work. Moreover, his religious bias aside, Russell is also guilty of ethnocentrism. Although he identifies evil as a *universal* phenomenon, he discusses it only within the context of Western culture, offering no insights as to how his thesis applies to Asia, Africa, or any non-Western society in which the Judeo-Christian-Islamic notion of Satan has no equivalent. See *The Devil: Perceptions of Evil from Antiquity to Primitive Christianity* (Ithaca, N.Y., 1977); *Satan: The Early Christian Tradition* (Ithaca, N.Y., 1981); *Lucifer: The Devil in the Middle Ages* (Ithaca, N.Y., 1984); and *Mephistopheles: The Devil in the Modern World* (Ithaca, N.Y., 1986).

105. Cited in Ralph C. Moellering, *Christian Conscience and Negro Emancipation* (Philadelphia, 1965), p. 25.

106. John Hope Franklin, *From Slavery to Freedom: A History of Negro Americans* (5th ed., New York, 1980), p. 32; Joseph Houldsworth Oldham, *Christianity and the Race Problem* (New York, 1969 [1924]), passim; Jacob Stroyer, *My Life in the South* (Salem, Mass., 1898 [1879]), p. 99; Conrad James Engelder, "The Churches and Slavery: A Study of the Attitudes toward Slavery of the Major Protestant Denominations" (Ph.D. dissertation, University of Michigan, 1964), pp. 32–34.

107. Ahlstrom, *A Religious History of the American People*, p. 635.

108. Christianity has also discriminated against Africans and Indians by excluding them from its history. James G. Moseley's *A Cultural History of Religion in America* (Westport, Conn., 1981) refers briefly to "Black religion," including a comment on the role of people like Martin Luther King, Jr., but otherwise manages to discuss the *cultural* role of religion without ever mentioning racial issues. Likewise, Sidney E. Mead, whom Moseley called the "dean of American church history" (p. 84), published a collection of essays under the title *The Lively Experiment: The Shaping of Christianity in America* (New York, 1963), which, like Moseley's work, listed no entries in the index under "slavery," "Negro," "race," or "black." Even a work focusing on race and Christianity can miss the mark. In his *Presbyterians and the Negro—A History* (Philadelphia, 1966), p. ix, Andrew E. Murray contended that "Negro and white Christians share a common Christianity, and that it is only the existence of racial segregation that prevents each group from recognizing this basic oneness," a contention that ignores both the importance of the slave's traditional religion and the conditions under which he embraced Christianity. Similarly, Kenneth Scott Latourette, a professor at Yale University and, in 1949, outgoing president of the American Historical Association, claimed that the federal government tried to improve its services to the Indians by delegating "the nomination of its Indian agents to the various religious bodies engaged in missions." Left unsaid was the question of whether or not a mission official would select an agent who was not religiously motivated. See *Missions and the American Mind*, pp. 21–22.

CHAPTER TWO

1. Grant Wacker of the University of North Carolina has pointed out that it is important to "distinguish an articulated doctrine of biblical inerrancy from an unarticulated assumption that the Bible is without error." The former view was probably imported into the United States in the middle of the nineteenth century from Swiss scholasticism and refined by theologians at Princeton Seminary, but the latter was most common among evangelical Protestants. On the eve of the twenty-first century, the belief in biblical inerrancy among American Protestants remains strong, ranging from 33 percent for Methodists to 53 percent for Southern Baptists, and probably even more among independent fundamentalist congregations. See Wacker, "The Demise of Biblical Civilization," *The Bible in America: Essays in Cultural History*, ed. Nathan O. Hatch and Mark A. Noll (New York, 1982), pp. 121–38,

and Richard J. Mouw, "The Bible in Twentieth-Century Protestantism: A Preliminary Taxonomy," *The Bible in America: Essays in Cultural History*, ed. Nathan O. Hatch and Mark A. Noll (New York, 1982), pp. 139–62.

2. Ralph L. Moellering, *Christian Conscience and Negro Emancipation* (Philadelphia, 1965), p. 50.

3. William R. Hutchison, ed., *American Protestant Thought: The Liberal Era* (New York, 1968), pp. 28–36; William Newton Clarke, *Sixty Years with the Bible: A Record of Experience* (New York, 1909), passim; Norman K. Gottwald, *The Hebrew Bible—A Socio-Literary Introduction* (Philadelphia, 1985), pp. 16–22; Robert T. Handy, ed., "Conflict over Biblical Criticism," *Religion in the American Experience: The Pluralistic Style* (Columbia, S.C., 1972), pp. 122–29; and Sydney E. Ahlstrom, *A Religious History of the American People* (New Haven, Conn., 1972), p. 812n.

4. Nathan O. Hatch, "*Sola Scriptura* and *Novus Ordo Seclorum*," *The Bible in America: Essays in Cultural History*, ed. Nathan O. Hatch and Mark A. Noll (New York, 1982), pp. 73–75. See also in the same volume George M. Marsden, "Every One's Own Interpreter?: The Bible, Science, and Authority in Mid-Nineteenth Century America," pp. 79–100.

5. C. C. Goen, *Broken Churches, Broken Nation: Denominational Schisms and the Coming of the Civil War* (Macon, Ga., 1985), p. 117.

6. For a brief but trenchant account of the biblical justification of slavery, see H. Shelton Smith, *In His Image, but . . .: Racism in Southern Religion, 1780–1910* (Durham, N.C., 1972), pp. 129–36. There is no way of determining who "won" the biblical argument, nor would there be any point in doing so, but that does not mean there have not been those who have tried. John R. Bodo, in *The Protestant Clergy and Public Issues, 1812–1848* (Princeton, N.J., 1954), pp. 143–45, wrote: "On Biblical grounds the Southern defenders of slavery undoubtedly carried the day," and "by suggesting that abolitionism was not of Christian but infidel origin the Southern clergy could rest secure in their pro-slavery views which few of the theocrats could or dared attack." But in a footnote to the latter sentence, he stated that "clerical abolitionists constantly used Biblical arguments, often outdoing in literalism and fanciful interpretation the Southern pro-slavery position." To assert that the defenders of slavery "carried the day" is a subjective opinion that cannot be statistically verified. As for abolitionist clergymen who, Bodo argued, could not or dared not attack the proslavery position, their list of antislavery pamphlets and sermons is as long as, if not longer than, any collection of proslavery works by southern clerics.

7. David Brion Davis, *The Problem of Slavery in Western Culture* (Ithaca, N.Y., 1966), p. vii.

8. Josiah Quincy, *Figures of the Past from the Leaves of Old Journals* (Boston, 1883), p. 355.

9. This calculates to reading the entire Bible almost thirty times.

10. John William Ward, *Andrew Jackson: Symbol for an Age* (New York, 1962 [1953]), pp. 101–32.

11. Ronald T. Takaki, *Iron Cages: Race and Culture in the Nineteenth Century* (New York, 1979), p. 103; John Spencer Bassett, *The Life of Andrew Jackson* (2 vols., New York, 1916), vol. I, pp. 91, 117. In a chapter entitled "Jackson: Metaphysician of Indian-Hating," Takaki described Jackson as a person who helped Americans rationalize their cruelty toward Indians by hating them. As Cherokee John Ross put it, "the perpetrator of a wrong never forgives his victims." See *Iron Cages*, pp. 92–107.

12. Probably the most sympathetic account of Jackson's attitude toward Indians is Francis Paul Prucha's "Andrew Jackson's Indian Policy: A Reassessment," *Journal of American History*, vol. 56, no. 3 (December 1969), pp. 527–39. In challenging what he called a "devil theory" of Indian policy, Prucha argued that the traditional portrait of Jackson as an "Indian-hater" is "simplistic" and "unacceptable." He conceded that Indians "who committed outrages against whites were to be summarily punished," but, at the same time, asserted that

Jackson insisted that "the rights of friendly Indians were to be protected." Unfortunately, the article is a classic example of setting out to prove a point only to make a case for the contrary. For instance, to illustrate Jackson's determination to punish "bad" Indians, Prucha described the general's reaction to the capture of a white woman by the Creeks. In order to rescue the woman and punish the offenders, Jackson said he would not stop short of "laying waste their villages, burning their houses, killing their warriors and leading into Captivity their wives and children" (p. 529). All of this for snatching one white woman! Since Prucha simply left the matter there, one can easily doubt that Jackson would have been driven to such drastic actions against whites who had captured an Indian woman. Prucha also appeared to endorse Jackson's policy of "rescuing the Indians from the evil effects of too-close contact with white civilization, so that in the end they too might become civilized" (p. 539). That sounds painfully similar to Ronald Reagan's comment at the 1988 summit meeting in Moscow that the federal government devised the reservation program to ensure the survival of the Indian's traditional culture. In one of his Walter Lynwood Fleming Lectures at Louisiana State University in 1984, Robert V. Remini, in a line of reasoning almost identical with Prucha's, chastised historians who have been critical of Jackson's racism. In fact, Remini argued, Jackson considered himself something of a benevolent father figure toward the Indians, and his behavior toward them "varied hardly at all from his behavior toward anyone else." As long as the Indians "obeyed him and followed his instructions and commands," he would be "kind and loving 'Great Father,' " Remini added. "But if they challenged him in any way, if they dared to disobey, contradict, or argue with him, he could be savage and vindictive." Was Remini saying that Jackson was savage and vindictive toward anyone—black, white, or red—who disobeyed him? Did it matter that the Indians might have had good reason for challenging, disobeying, contradicting, or arguing with Jackson? See *The Legacy of Andrew Jackson: Essays on Democracy, Indian Removal, and Slavery* (Baton Rouge, La., 1988), p. 46. A contrary view is Michael Paul Rogin, *Fathers and Children: Andrew Jackson and the Subjugation of the American Indian* (New York, 1975).

13. One of the best accounts of this subject is Arda Walker, "The Religious Views of Andrew Jackson," *East Tennessee Historical Society's Publications*, no. 17 (1945). Despite all of the hoopla that accompanied Jackson's invocation of divine retribution, he did not actually become a member of a church until the last years of his life. In 1838, one year after leaving the presidency and seven years before his death, he joined the Presbyterian church in Nashville. If, as H. S. Turner wrote in 1892, Jackson "was a believer in predestination, and trusted and believed in special Providence," then his choice of denominations is understandable. See Turner, "Andrew Jackson and Davy Crockett," *Magazine of American History*, vol. 27 (May 1892), pp. 386–87; and Ward, *Andrew Jackson*, pp. 202–203, 246n.

14. William Sumner Jenkins, in his *Pro-Slavery Thought in the Old South* (Chapel Hill, N.C., 1935), pp. 39, 201–202, 206–207, called the biblical justification the "cornerstone" of both the moral *and* political defenses of slavery, a justification that began as early as 1701 with John Saffin's *A Brief and Candid Answer to a Late Printed Sheet, Entitled, the Selling of Joseph* ([Boston]). Interestingly, Saffin's reply to Samuel Sewall's antislavery tract was also the *only* published defense of slavery for a long time. The first edition of Samuel Stanhope Smith's *Essay on the Causes of the Variety of Complexion and Figure in the Human Species* appeared in 1787 (2nd ed., New York, 1810), but, since it made no reference to slavery and was not written as a response to abolitionist criticism, it differed in both form and substance from most biblical arguments.

15. Harriet Martineau, *Society in America*, ed. Seymour Martin Lipset (Gloucester, Mass., 1968 [New York, 1837]), p. 335; B. M. Palmer, "Slavery a Divine Trust: Duty of the South to Preserve and Perpetuate It," *Fast Day Sermons: The Pulpit on the State of the Country* (New York, 1861), in Gilbert Osofsky, ed., *The Burden of Race: A Documentary History of Negro-White Relations in America* (New York, 1967), pp. 90–93.

16. Thomas Virgil Peterson, *Ham and Japheth: The Mythic World of Whites in the Antebellum South* (Metuchen, N.J., 1978), pp. 14–15. See also Jenkins, *Pro-Slavery Thought in the Old South*, pp. 201–202, 206–207; Moellering, *Christian Conscience*, p. 50; and James Oscar Farmer, Jr., *The Metaphysical Confederacy: James Henley Thornwell and the Synthesis of Southern Values* (Macon, Ga., 1986), p. 231.

17. The eminent English jurist Sir Edward Coke interpreted the Roman *servus* to mean no more than a "villein," a term that described a class of serfs in feudal England who, by the thirteenth century, had become freemen in their legal relations to everyone except their liege lords, to whom they remained subject as slaves. It was this "villenage" that existed in England until 1661, but which never transferred to the colonies. See John Codman Hurd, *The Law of Freedom and Bondage in the United States* (2 vols., New York, 1968 [1858–62]), vol. I, pp. 136–37.

18. William F. Arndt and F. Wilbur Gingrich, *A Greek-English Lexicon of the New Testament and Other Early Christian Literature* (trans. and adapted from Walter Bauer, *Griechisch-Deutsches Wörterbuch zu den Schriften des Neuen Testaments und der übrigen urchristlichen Literatur* [Chicago, 1979]), p. 205.

19. Oscar Handlin, *Race and Nationality in American Life* (New York, 1957 [1948]), p. 10; Lorenzo Johnston Greene, *The Negro in Colonial New England, 1620–1776* (New York, 1966 [1942]), p. 168; Edmund S. Morgan, *The Puritan Family: Religion & Domestic Relations in Seventeenth-Century New England* (rev. ed., New York, 1966), p. 109.

20. Ephesians 6:5–8. Paul repeated the same admonition, verbatim, in Colossians 3:22–25.

21. Thornton Stringfellow, *Scriptural and Statistical Views in Favor of Slavery* (4th ed., Richmond, Va., 1856), pp. 72–74; Albert Taylor Bledsoe, *Liberty and Slavery: or, Slavery in the Light of Moral and Political Philosophy*, in E. N. Elliott, ed., *Cotton Is King, and Pro-Slavery Arguments: Comprising the Writings of Hammond, Harper, Christy, Stringfellow, Hodge, Bledsoe, and Cartwright, on This Important Subject* (Augusta, Ga., 1860), pp. 360–63.

22. George Junkin, *The Integrity of Our National Union vs. Abolitionism: Being Part of a Speech Delivered before the Synod of Cincinnati, on the Subject of Slavery, September 19th and 20th, 1843* (Cincinnati, 1843), pp. 25–29, 35–38; John Robinson, *The Testimony and Practice of the Presbyterian Church in Reference to American Slavery . . .* (Cincinnati, 1852), pp. 92, 95–96; W[illiam] P[ope] Harrison, *The Gospel among the Slaves: A Short Account of Missionary Operations among the African Slaves of the Southern States* (Nashville, 1893), p. 18.

23. Leviticus 25:44–46. Conservative Protestants usually accept without question Moses's authorship of the Pentateuch, but the debate over how much he actually wrote has gone on since the days of the early church. See Richard Elliott Friedman, *Who Wrote the Bible?* (New York, 1987), pp. 17–29. Also useful is Friedman's *The Creation of Sacred Literature: Composition and Redaction of Biblical Texts* (Berkeley, Calif., 1981).

24. Moses Finley: "Slavery," *Encyclopedia of Social Sciences*, 2nd ed., vol. XIV, pp. 307–13; and "The Idea of Slavery," in Laura Foner and Eugene D. Genovese, eds., *Slavery in the New World: A Reader in Comparative History* (Englewood Cliffs, N.J., 1969), p. 260; Orlando Patterson, *Slavery and Social Death: A Comparative Study* (Cambridge, Mass., 1982), p. 7, and passim.

25. Leviticus 25:8–16.

26. George B. Cheever, *God against Slavery: And the Freedom and Duty of the Pulpit to Rebuke It, as a Sin against God* (Miami, 1969 [New York, 1857]), pp. 148–49; Charles Elliott, *The Bible and Slavery* (Cincinnati, 1857), pp. 186–88.

27. William W[ells] Brown, *Narrative of William Wells Brown, a Fugitive Slave, Written by Himself* (Boston, 1847), p. 52.

28. Most Christian antislavery publications, like most proslavery documents, were very short, some of them nothing more than pamphlet versions of sermons. One remarkable exception was Charles Elliott's *Sinfulness of American Slavery*, printed in two volumes in Cincinnati in 1850. Totaling over 700 pages, with an extensive index and a bibliography of

216 titles that included virtually every extant antislavery work published up to that time, it may very well be the longest antislavery document ever produced.

29. Davis, *The Problem of Slavery in the Age of Revolution, 1770–1823* (Ithaca, N.Y., 1975), pp. 523–24; Albert Barnes, *An Inquiry into the Scriptural Views of Slavery* (Philadelphia, 1855 [1846]), p. 64; and Cheever, *God Against Slavery*, passim, and *The Guilt of Slavery and the Crime of Slaveholding, Demonstrated from the Hebrew and Greek Scriptures* (Boston, 1860), passim, especially pp. iii–x; Sarah M. Grimké, *An Epistle to the Clergy of the Southern States* (New York, 1836), pp. 6–7; Executive Committee, *Journal of the American Baptist Anti-Slavery Convention*, vol. I, no. 3 (Worcester, Mass., July, 1841), p. 78. While describing a case of enslavement for debt, Louis Wallis, to signify the lowest social class, i.e., slaves, twice used the word *abadim*, which sounded seductively similar to *èbed*. See *God and the Social Process: A Study in Hebrew History* (Chicago, 1935), p. 168.

30. Moellering, *Christian Conscience*, pp. 67–68.

31. Morgan, *The Puritan Family*, p. 109.

32. Gerhard Kittel, ed., *Theological Dictionary of the New Testament* (10 vols., Grand Rapids, Mich., 1964), trans. by Geoffrey W. Bromiley from *Theologisches Wörterbuch zum Neuen Testament* (1933), vol. II, "Secular Usage of Slave Words," pp. 270–71; Moellering, *Christian Conscience*, pp. 68–69; Cheever, *God Against Slavery*, p. 149; Jenkins, *Pro-Slavery Thought in the Old South*, pp. 219–20, 220n.; Barnes, *Scriptural Views of Slavery*.

33. Barnes, *Scriptural Views of Slavery*, passim.

34. Robinson, *Testimony and Practice*, p. 92; Junkin, *Integrity of Our National Union*, pp. 25–29.

35. Barnes, *Scriptural Views of Slavery*, pp. 64–68. *Latris* did not occur in the early biblical manuscripts but derivatives like *latreia* (service) and *latreuo* (to serve)—always referring to religious service—were common.

36. Jude 13.

37. Song of Solomon, 1:5–6.

38. Jeremiah 13:23.

39. Anthony Gerard Barthelemy, *Black Face, Maligned Race: The Representation of Blacks in English Drama from Shakespeare to Southerne* (Baton Rouge, La., 1987), pp. 2–3; Frank M. Snowden, Jr., *Before Color Prejudice: The Ancient View of Blacks* (Cambridge, Mass., 1983), pp. 100–101, 103–104, 107–108.

40. See *infra*, chapter 3.

41. Patterson, *Slavery and Social Death*, p. 176. A more recent example of the Chinese antipathy toward dark skin could be seen in the attacks on visiting African students in the winter of 1988–89.

42. Roger Bastide, "Color, Racism, and Christianity," *Daedalus: Journal of the American Academy of Arts and Sciences* (Spring 1967), pp. 314–15; Josiah Priest, *Slavery, As It Relates to the Negro, or African Race* (Albany, N.Y., 1843), pp. 136–39.

43. Arnold A. Sio, "Interpretations of Slavery: The Slave Status in the Americas," *Comparative Studies in Society and History*, vol. 7., no. 3 (April 1965), pp. 7–8; Carl N. Degler, *Neither Black Nor White: Slavery and Race Relations in Brazil and in the United States* (New York, 1971), p. 105. See also Donald J. Horowitz, "Color Differentiation in the American Systems of Slavery," *Journal of Interdisciplinary History*, vol. 3, no. 3 (Winter 1973), pp. 509–41.

44. Kenneth M. Stampp, *The Peculiar Institution: Slavery in the Ante-Bellum South* (New York, 1956), p. 196. Stampp also noted, however, that light-skinned slaves, partly because it was easier for them to run away, were often considered more trouble than they were worth.

45. What was probably the most absurd example of color differentiation was a state law in North Carolina, finally repealed in 1966, that prohibited racial intermarriage. The law did permit marriages between blacks and Indians provided the Indian was not a descendant of the

"Croatoan" tribe that had presumably absorbed the "Lost Colony" of English settlers of Roanoke in the late sixteenth century. North Carolina's lawmakers assumed that such an Indian *might* have a trace of white blood and therefore should not be allowed to marry a black person.

46. David Macrae, *Americans at Home* (New York, 1952 [Edinburgh, 1870]), p. 311; Bastide, "Color, Racism, and Christianity," p. 325; Hinton Rowan Helper, *Nojoque: A Question for a Continent* (New York, 1867), pp. 99–100; B. A. Botkin, ed., *Lay My Burden Down: A Folk History of Slavery* (Chicago, 1945), facing p. 139.

47. Red was actually a color more specifically denoting sin than black. "Come now, and let us reason together, saith the Lord: Though your sins be as scarlet, they shall be as white as snow; though they be red like crimson, they shall be as wool" (Isaiah 1:18).

48. *Records of Salem Witchcraft, Copied from the Original Documents* (New York, 1969 [Roxbury, Mass., 1864]), pp. 46, 55.

49. Theologian Reinhold Niebuhr was not averse to using biblical symbolism when he titled his book *The Children of Light and the Children of Darkness* (New York, 1944).

50. See, for example, 2 Kings 7:3, 8. The Hebrew word for leprosy was used for a variety of skin diseases.

51. Louis Filler, ed., *Abolition and Social Justice in the Era of Reform* (New York, 1972), p. 53. For an excellent summary of the origins of black as the color of evil in Western thought, see chapter 1, "Satan's Livery: Blackness and the Western Tradition," in Barthelemy's *Black Face, Maligned Race*, pp. 1–17.

52. It is paradoxical that modern translators have articulated a more clearly defined biblical slavery than did those scholars who four centuries ago produced the Authorized, or King James, Version. In *The Living Bible* (1971), the words "slave-girl," "slave," "slave-owner," and "slave-wife," have replaced, respectively, "maid," "servant," "master," and "bondwoman." The *New International Version of the Holy Bible* (1978) shows most of the same changes and also extends "under the yoke" to "under the yoke of slavery." For a discussion of these differences, see Wallis, *God and the Social Process*, pp. 307–308.

53. Paul Jacobs, Saul Landau, and Eve Pell, eds., *To Serve the Devil* (2 vols., New York, 1971), vol. I, *Natives and Slaves*, p. 133. While Hagar, the maidservant of Abram's wife, Sarah, was referred to as an Egyptian slave in the Old Testament, she was never identified as black, and Pinckney's claim that "millions sprang" from her—probably based on biblical references to children "too numerous to count" who will "make a great nation"—was pure fantasy, not to mention irrelevant.

54. Jenkins, *Pro-Slavery Thought in the Old South*, p. 202. *Leviticus* means, literally, "about the Levites," who were God's priests, and the book of Leviticus contains many rules that God gave the people of Israel to help them lead holy lives. For a brief but excellent review of Leviticus 25, see Dale Patrick, *Old Testament Law* (Atlanta, Ga., 1985), p. 184.

55. Isaiah 24:2.

56. "Sister Sallie," *The Color Line. Devoted to the Restoration of Good Government, Putting an End to Negro Authority and Misrule, and Establishing a White Man's Government in the White Man's Country, by Organizing the White People of the South* (n.p., 1868?), p. 25; Conrad James Engelder, "The Churches and Slavery: A Study of the Attitudes toward Slavery of the Major Protestant Denominations" (Ph.D., dissertation, University of Michigan, 1964), p. 16–17.

57. Deuteronomy 28:15–68. See also Jeremiah 17:4.

58. Many American clergymen in the nineteenth century viewed the Bible in terms of its three great ages: the *Patriarchal Age*, from Noah to the receiving of the law by Moses; the *Mosaic*, or *Legal Dispensation*, from Moses on Mount Sinai to the birth of Christ; and the *Gospel Dispensation*, from Christ to Revelation.

59. [Iveson L. Brookes], *A Defence of Southern Slavery, against the Attacks of Henry Clay and Alex'r Campbell* . . . ([Hamburg, S.C., 1851]), pp. 2–3. Robert L. Dabney's *A Defence of Virginia, and through Her, of the South, in Recent and Pending Contests against the Sectional Party* (New York, 1867), written in 1862 but actually published after the Civil War, devoted a long chapter (pp. 94–145) to Old Testament arguments justifying slavery.

60. Harry M. Orlinsky, *Ancient Israel* (Ithaca, N.Y., 1954), pp. 12–13, 17–18; John Bright, *A History of Israel* (3rd ed., Philadelphia, 1981), pp. 93–95; H[enk] Jagersma, *A History of Israel in the Old Testament Period* (trans. by John Bowden, Philadelphia, 1983), pp. 10–11. Biblical scholars have disagreed over the significance of the tantalizing similarity between "'Apiru" and "Hebrew." Bright conceded that there was some relationship, but he also contended that the word "Hebrew," or "*ibri*," apparently popularly derived from the name of the ancestor Eber (Genesis 11:14–17) "who, in turn, descended directly from Shem through Arphaxad and Shelah." See also Genesis 10:21. Gottwald, *The Hebrew Bible*, pp. 270, 273, identified the 'Apiru as "social outsiders" but made no close connection between them and the ancient Israelites. Jagersma, on the other hand, contended that it "seems virtually certain" that the Egyptian 'Apiru, the Babylonian and Hittite Hapiru and Habiru, and the Ugaritic *'aprm* all referred to the same people.

61. Judges 1:28, 30, 35.

62. Wallis, *God and the Social Process*, pp. 307–308; Patterson, *Slavery and Social Death*, pp. 125, 404n.32. The "strict religious law" Patterson referred to was set forth in Leviticus 25:39–40: "If one of your countrymen becomes poor among you and sells himself to you, do not make him work as a slave. He is to be treated as a hired worker or temporary resident among you; he is to work for you until the Year of the Jubilee."

63. Orlinsky, *Ancient Israel*, pp. 95, 138; Nehemiah 5:5.

64. A detailed and comprehensive account of the slave code of ancient Israel can be found in *The Code of Maimonides: Book Twelve, The Book of Acquisition* (trans. by Isaac Klein, New Haven, Conn., 1951), pp. 245–82.

65. Many of the same terms listed in Exodus 21:1–11 are repeated in Deuteronomy 15:12–18. Needless to say, there is no equivalent set of rules for a male slave and his relationship to his mistress.

66. Dorothy Mills, *The People of Ancient Israel* (New York, 1932), pp. 57–58, 94–95; Patterson, *Slavery and Social Death*, p. 192; Patrick, *Old Testament Law*, pp. 7, 75–76, 199. For the biblical bases of these conditions, see Exodus 21:26–27 and Deuteronomy 5:14.

67. Genesis 17:12.

68. Abram Leon Sachar, *A History of the Jews* (New York, 1968), pp. 95–96. For the story of Sarah and Hagar and the subsequent banishment of Hagar and Ishmael, see Genesis 16:1–15, 21:9–21, and 25:12; and Galatians 4:21–31. For the story of Rachel and Bilhah, see Genesis 30:1–7.

69. Exodus 22:21, 23:9; Deuteronomy 15:15, 24:22. See also Orlinsky, *Ancient Israel*, p. 153, and Victor Tcherikover, *Hellenistic Civilization and the Jews* (trans. by S. Applebaum, Philadelphia, 1966), p. 342.

70. For a succinct explanation of those rules that had been set forth in the slave's interests, not the master's, see Patrick, *Old Testament Law*, pp. 69–72.

71. Sachar, *A History of the Jews*, p. 95; Salo Wittmayer Baron, *The Social and Reli-gious History of the Jews* (20 vols., 2nd ed., New York, 1952 [1937]), vol. I, *To the Begin-ning of the Christian Era*, pp. 267–68. According to Orlando Patterson, most slaves in Israel were Israelites, not outsiders, and recent papyric evidence supports the suspicion that many Jewish masters ignored the six-year limitation. See *Slavery and Social Death*, p. 275.

72. Tcherikover, *Hellenistic Civilization and the Jews*, pp. 342, 442n.36.

73. Patrick, *Old Testament Law*, pp. 55–56; Exodus 21:16; Deuteronomy 24:7.

74. Deuteronomy 23:15–16; Isaiah 16:3; Patrick, *Old Testament Law*, p. 133.

75. Cheever, *God Against Slavery*, pp. 140–42, referring to Exodus 22:9–11 and 23:4.

76. Jeremiah 34:8–22.

77. Obadiah 14–15.

78. Lawrence W. Levine, *Black Culture and Black Consciousness: Afro-American Folk Thought from Slavery to Freedom* (New York, 1977), pp. 23, 33, 37.

79. Joseph B. Earnest, Jr., *The Religious Development of the Negro in Virginia* (Charlottesville, Va., 1914), pp. 153–54.

80. Ola Elizabeth Winslow, *John Eliot, Apostle to the Indians* (Boston, 1968), p. 143.

81. Richard Fuller and Francis Wayland, *Domestic Slavery Considered as a Scriptural Institution* (New York, 1856), passim.

82. James Henley Thornwell, *Report on the Subject of Slavery: Presented to the Synod of South Carolina* . . . (Columbia, S.C., 1852), pp. 5–7, 9–10. See also John B. Adger and John L. Girardeau, eds., *The Collected Writings of James Henley Thornwell, D.D., LL.D.* (4 vols., Richmond, Va., 1871–73), vol. 4, pp. 382–88. For an extended discussion of Thornwell's efforts to defend slavery see Farmer, *The Metaphysical Confederacy*, pp. 216–33.

83. Richard Nisbet, *Slavery Not Forbidden by Scripture. Or a Defence of the West-Indian Planters from the Aspersions Thrown Out against Them, by the Author of a Pamphlet, entitled "An Address . . . upon Slave-Keeping"* (Philadelphia, 1773), p. 83; Fuller and Wayland, *Domestic Slavery*, passim. See also Jenkins, *Pro-Slavery Thought in the Old South*, p. 203; Smith, *In His Image*, p. 133.

84. Robinson, *Testimony and Practice*, p. 37.

85. Quoted in Olli Alho, *The Religion of the Slaves: A Study of the Religious Tradition and Behavior of Plantation Slaves in the United States, 1830–1865* (Helsinki, 1976), pp. 62–63.

86. Dabney, *A Defence of Virginia*, pp. 198–205.

87. A group of mainly liberal Protestant and Catholic scholars, who began meeting in 1986 as the "Jesus Seminar," concluded in 1989 that "way less than 25 per cent" of the New Testament words attributed to Christ were actually uttered by him but, rather, had been composed by later writers. Needless to say, conservative Christians considered this conclusion to be heresy. See Los Angeles *Times*, March 5, 1989.

88. Albert Barnes, *The Church and Slavery* (Philadelphia, 1857), pp. 41–48, quoted in Handy, ed., *Religion in the American Experience*, pp. 110–15; George Bourne, *The Book and Slavery Irreconcilable, with Animadversions upon Dr. Smith's Philosophy* (Philadelphia, 1816), pp. 4–5; Jenkins, *Pro-Slavery Thought in the Old South*, pp. 218–19, 222; Goldwin Smith, *Does the Bible Sanction American Slavery?* (Cambridge, Mass., 1864), pp. 86–87; Davis, *The Problem of Slavery in the Age of Revolution, 1770–1823*, p. 553, citing James Dana, *The African Slave Trade: A Discourse Delivered in the City of New-Haven, September 9, 1790, Before the Connecticut Society for the Promotion of Freedom* (New Haven, 1791), pp. 6–11, 26–28; Jonathan Edwards, Jr., *The Injustice and Impolity of the Slave-Trade, and of Slavery of the Africans* (Providence, R.I., 1792), pp. 14–17; David Barrow, *Involuntary, Unmerited, Perpetual, Absolute, Hereditary Slavery, Examined: on the Principles of Nature, Reason, Justice, Policy and Scripture* (Lexington, Ky., 1808), pp. 14–16, 27, 31; Carl N. Degler, *The Other South: Southern Dissenters in the Nineteenth Century* (New York, 1974), pp. 31–32.

89. Jenkins, *Pro-Slavery Thought in the Old South*, p. 222; Smith, *Does the Bible Sanction American Slavery?* pp. 86–87; Alexander McCaine, *Slavery Defended from Scripture* (Baltimore, 1842), pp. 14, 18.

90. Jenkins, *Pro-Slavery Thought in the Old South*, pp. 8–10, 223–24, and citing Sandiford, *A Brief Examination of the Practice of the Times* (1729); Coleman, *Testimony Against Making Slaves of Men* (1733); and Lay, *All Slave-Keepers that Keep the Innocent in Bondage, Apostates* (1738). See also Louis Ruchames, ed., *Racial Thought in America* (Amherst, Mass., 1969), vol. I, pp. 79–110.

91. Anthony Benezet and John Wesley, *Views of American Slavery, Taken a Century Ago* (Philadelphia, 1858), pp. 47–48.

92. Robinson, *Testimony and Practice*, p. 24.

93. Olaudah Equiano, *The Interesting Narrative of the Life of Olaudah Equiano, or Gustavus Vassa, the African. Written by Himself* (2 vols., New York, 1969 [1789]), vol. I, p. 87. See also Philip D. Curtin, ed., *Africa Remembered: Narratives by West Africans from the Era of the Slave Trade* (Madison, Wis., 1967), pp. 97–98.

94. Lester B. Scherer, *Slavery and the Churches in Early America, 1619–1819* (Grand Rapids, Mich., 1975), pp. 34–35.

95. Perry Miller, *Errand Into the Wilderness* (Cambridge, Mass., 1956), p. 148.

96. Ephesians 5:22–23.

97. Jenkins, *Pro-Slavery Thought in the Old South*, pp. 225–26.

98. Colossians 4:1; Fuller and Wayland, *Domestic Slavery Considered as a Scriptural Institution*, p. 202.

99. H. Shelton Smith, Robert T. Handy, and Lefferts A. Loetscher, eds., *American Christianity: An Historical Interpretation with Representative Documents* (2 vols., New York, 1960), vol. 2, p. 185; James H. Thornwell, "Slavery and the Religious Instruction of the Coloured Population," *Southern Presbyterian Review* (July 1850), p. 135. See also Farmer, *The Metaphysical Confederacy*, p. 25; Moellering, *Christian Conscience*, p. 62; and Smith, *In His Image*, p. 134, 134n. Others who advanced similar arguments included William T. Hamilton, *The Duties of Masters and Slaves Respectively: or, Domestic Servitude as Sanctioned by the Bible: A Discourse, Delivered in the Government-Street Church, Mobile, Ala., on Sunday Night, December 15, 1844* (Mobile, Ala., 1845), p. 16; Albert T. Bledsoe, *An Essay on Liberty and Slavery* (Philadelphia, 1856), pp. 77–79; and William A. Smith, *Lectures on the Philosophy and Practice of Slavery* (Nashville, 1856), pp. 136–38.

100. Smith, Handy, and Loetscher, eds., *American Christianity*, vol. II, p. 208; Dabney, *A Defence of Virginia*, p. 197; Martineau, *Society in America*, pp. 122–23.

101. Smith, *In His Image*, p. 98; Junkin, *Integrity of Our National Union*, pp. 77–78.

102. *Christian Advocate and Journal*, October 20, 1837, in Smith, *In His Image*, p. 103.

103. *Minutes of Several Conversations Between the Rev. Thomas Coke, L.L.D., the Rev. Francis Asbury, and Others, at a Conference, Begun in Baltimore, in the State of Maryland, on Monday, the 27th of December, in the Year 1784* (Philadelphia, 1785), p. 15, in Smith, *In His Image*, p. 103.

104. Ephesians 6:5–9.

105. Ruchames, ed., *Racial Thought in America*, vol. I, p. 404; Clifton Herman Johnson, "The American Missionary Association, 1846–1861: A Study in Christian Abolitionism" (Ph.D. dissertation, University of North Carolina, 1958), pp. 11–12; Jeremiah Bell Jeter, *The Recollections of a Long Life* (Richmond, Va., 1891), pp. 229–30; Gerald Francis De Jong, "The Dutch Reformed Church and Negro Slavery in Colonial America," *Church History*, vol. 40, no. 4 (December 1971), pp. 424–25; Samuel Blanchard How, *Slaveholding Not Sinful: Slavery, the Punishment of Man's Sin; Its Remedy the Gospel of Christ. An Argument before the General Synod of the Reformed Protestant Dutch Church, October 1855* (n.p., 1855); Robinson, *Testimony and Practice*, p. 98; Abdel Ross Wentz, *A Basic History of Lutheranism in America* (rev. ed., Philadelphia, 1955), pp. 170–71.

106. Edward H. Madden, *Civil Disobedience and Moral Law in Nineteenth-Century American Philosophy* (Seattle, 1968), pp. 27–28, 176–77. For a brief but excellent discussion of Francis Wayland's works in moral philosophy, see chapter 2 (pp. 16–29). See also Wayland's *The Elements of Moral Science* (New York, 1855 [1835]) and *The Limitations of Human Responsibility* (Boston, 1838), the latter being, essentially, a Baptist argument against abolitionism.

107. Matthew 25:21, 23.

108. Stiles Bailey Lines, "Slaves and Churchmen: The Work of the Episcopal Church

among Southern Negroes" (Ph.D. dissertation, Columbia University, 1960), p. 181. The passages in question were: Matthew 18:23–35, 24:45–51, and 25:14–30; Luke 12:42–48; 1 Corinthians 7:20–22; Ephesians 6:5–8; Colossians 3:22–25; 1 Timothy 6:1–2; Titus 2:9–10; and 1 Peter 2:18–25.

109. 1 Peter 2:18–20.

110. Smith, *In His Image*, p. 98.

111. William Grimes, *Life of William Grimes, the Runaway Slave, Brought Down to the Present Time. Written by Himself* (New Haven, Conn., 1855), p. 78.

112. Charles H. Nichols, *Many Thousand Gone: The Ex-Slaves' Account of Their Bondage and Freedom* (Leiden, Netherlands, 1963), p. 82.

113. Berry was obviously referring to Matthew 22:15–22. Verse 21 is the familiar: "Render therefore unto Caesar the things which are Caesar's; and render unto God the things that are God's."

114. Lewis McCarroll Purifoy, Jr., "The Methodist Episcopal Church, South, and Slavery, 1844–1865" (Ph.D. dissertation, University of North Carolina, 1965), pp. 329–33.

115. Romans 13:1; Hebrews 13:17; 1 Peter 2:13–14.

116. David E. Harrell, Jr., *Quest for a Christian America: The Disciples of Christ and American Society to 1866* (Nashville, 1966), pp. 131–32. See also A. B. Longstreet, *Letters on the Epistle of Paul to Philemon* (Charleston, 1845).

117. Philemon 8–20; Harrison Berry, *Slavery and Abolitionism, as Viewed by a Georgia Slave* (Atlanta, 1861), p. 13.

118. [John England], *Letters of the Late Bishop England to the Hon. John Forsyth, on the Subject of Domestic Slavery* (Baltimore, 1844), pp. 31–39. Letter dated October 21, 1840. A total of eighteen letters were written from England to Forsyth and were originally published in *United States Catholic Miscellany*.

119. John Tracy Ellis, ed., *Documents of American Catholic History* (3 vols., Wilmington, Del., 1987), vol. 2 (1866–1966), pp. 378–83. See also A[ngelina] E[mily] Grimké, *Appeal to the Christian Women of the South* (n.p., n.d.), p. 14.

120. Moellering, *Christian Conscience*, p. 52n.; Junkin, *Integrity of Our National Union*, pp. 58–62; Ephesians 6:5.

121. Modern biblical scholars have revised "in the flesh" in Philemon 16 to mean "as a man," and "according to the flesh" in Ephesians 6:5 as "earthly." Cf. the Authorized Version and the New International Version.

122. For example, see Barnes, *Scriptural Views of Slavery*, pp. 318–30; Elliott, *The Bible and Slavery*, pp. 326–54; and Dabney, *A Defence of Virginia*, pp. 176–85.

123. 1 Timothy 1:10; 1 Corinthians 7:21.

124. J. F. Feeks, pub., *Copperhead Minstrel: A Choice Collection of Democratic Poems and Songs, for the Use of Political Clubs and the Social Circle* (New York, 1863), pp. 21–24.

125. French theologian Maurice Goguel has argued that, while Christ was the *cause* of the Christian church, it was Paul who was responsible for the church's establishment "in the form in which we find it." See *The Primitive Church* (London, 1963 [1947]), p. 10.

126. William M. Manross, *A History of the American Episcopal Church* (3rd ed., New York, 1959), pp. 148–50.

127. Quoted in Scherer, *Slavery and the Churches*, pp. 83, 96–97.

128. Since many slave catechisms were produced only for local use and there are few extant copies, it can never be known exactly how many existed. Among the antebellum clerical and lay authors were Benjamin Palmer, William Capers, James Smylie, Charles Colcock Jones, Robert Ryland, Nathaniel Hyatt, John A. Hoff, William Meade, James C. Furman, John Mines, Samuel J. Bryan, A. W. Chambliss, John Girardeau, Christopher Gadsden, Paul Trapier, and William H. Barnwell. For fuller discussions of the catechisms, see Alho, *Religion*

of the Slaves, pp. 66–67, 135–39, 170–71, and Blake Touchstone, "Planters and Slave Religion in the Deep South," *Masters & Slaves in the House of the Lord: Race and Religion in the American South, 1740–1870* (John B. Boles, ed., Lexington, Ky., 1988), pp. 114–15.

129. Alho, *Religion of the Slaves*, p. 54.

130. These lines appeared, in one form or another, in virtually every slave catechism. See Gilbert Osofsky, ed., *Puttin' on Ole Massa: The Slave Narratives of Henry Bibb, William Wells Brown, and Solomon Northup* (New York, 1969), pp. 32–33; Alho, *Religion of the Slaves*, pp. 64–66; and Ernest Trice Thompson, *Presbyterians in the South* (2 vols., Richmond, Va., 1963), vol. I, p. 439.

131. W. David Stacey, *The Pauline View of Man: In Relation to Its Judaic and Hellenistic Background* (London, 1956), pp. 7–8. But Stacey also saw Paul as master of adaptation. "Paul did what every teacher must. He explained the unknown by means of the known. He used whatever terms were available, asking only that they should fairly describe the subject and be intelligible to the readers. Wherever he found a word that would forward his appeal, he used it, whether it was taken from Judaism, Alexandrian literature, the Mystery cults, the Hermetica, or the philosophical schools, and he used it, not precisely in its original sense, but adjusted to the particular purpose for which he required it" (page 237). By applying Pauline principles to bondage, the Christian slaveholder was only carrying on that tradition of adaptation.

132. Titus 2:9.

133. John W. Blassingame, ed., *Slave Testimony: Two Centuries of Letters, Speeches, Interviews, and Autobiographies* (Baton Rouge, La., 1977), pp. 642–43.

134. Ibid., pp. 410–11.

135. Ibid., p. 538.

136. C. Eric Lincoln, *Race, Religion, and the Continuing American Dilemma* (New York, 1984), p. 56.

137. Osofsky, ed., *Puttin' on Ole Massa*, p. 33.

138. Solomon Northup, *Twelve Years a Slave: Narrative of Solomon Northup, a Citizen of New York, Kidnapped in Washington City in 1841, and Rescued in 1853, from a Cotton Plantation* (Auburn, N.Y., 1853), pp. 93–96.

139. Historian George M. Fredrickson has argued that most southern clergy "did not contribute significantly to the case for inherent black inferiority because they concentrated their efforts on converting slaves to Christianity and the masters to Christian paternalism." The ideology of black inferiority "was promulgated primarily by secular defenders of the institution; and it was this secular or naturalistic argument that made the greater contribution to the public ideology of white supremacy." See *White Supremacy: A Comparative Study in American and South African History* (New York, 1981), pp. 172–73. There is no doubt that "secular defenders" of slavery played a prominent role in shaping opinions, but what kind of statistical data can be cited to justify the use of the term *primarily*? Fredrickson also seemed to be suggesting that there was a recognizable separation between religious and secular thinking when, in fact, racist religious tracts were filled with appeals to natural history and secular spokesmen made frequent references to biblical and other Christian themes. Northern and southern clergymen often alluded, both in and out of the pulpit, to their belief in white supremacy; and the various slave catechisms were stark reminders that these men of the cloth believed slaves should forever remain in a state of subjugation. Considering the importance of Christianity in the lives of so many Americans, can it be assumed that the racist declarations of Protestant clergymen only secondarily influenced public opinion, especially when those clergymen were saying what many people wanted to hear?

140. Frederick Law Olmsted, *Journey in the Seaboard Slave States* (New York, 1856), p. 119; Alho, *Religion of the Slaves*, p. 63.

141. The idea, which, John W. Storey wrote, "required something of an intellectual somersault," remained widespread after the Civil War. Southern Baptists reconciled their belief in the "theoretical equality of all men before God, Nature, and Law" with their belief in the racial inferiority of blacks by arguing that "God and Nature had given man varied capacities." See "The Negro in Southern Baptist Thought, 1865–1900" (Ph.D. dissertation, University of Kentucky, 1968), pp. 208, 211–20.

142. Stacey, *The Pauline View of Man*, p. 178. For an extended discussion of Paul and dualism, see pages 174–205.

143. Patterson, *Slavery and Social Death*, p. 72.

144. Edmund A. Moore, *Robert J. Breckinridge and the Slavery Aspect of the Presbyterian Schism of 1837* (Chicago, 1932), p. 7. Also reprinted in *Church History*, vol. 4, no. 4 (December 1935).

145. It is also an idea that has not easily gone away. Discussing the views of theologian Ernst Troeltsch, Reinhold Niebuhr maintained that the notion of human equality may be politically useful, but, by suggesting that "equality before God need not imply equality in historic social relations," the influence of religion can undermine that usefulness. In other words, rational thought is essential to the religious principle that all humans are equal; but the religious belief that spiritual equality is not tantamount to civil equality contradicts the essence of that principle. In short, religion stands in the way of equality. See *Moral Man and Immoral Society: A Study in Ethics and Politics* (New York, 1960 [1932]), p. 59.

146. De Jong, "The Dutch Reformed Church and Negro Slavery," pp. 424–25. Capitein was also the first known black person ordained into any Protestant ministry.

147. Galatians 3:28; Benjamin Fawcett, *A Compassionate Address to Christian Negroes in Virginia* (New York, 1975 [London, 1756]), pp. 11–12; John 8:32, 36.

148. Farmer, *The Metaphysical Confederacy*, p. 223; Junkin, *Integrity of Our National Union*, p. 48; Moellering, *Christian Conscience*, pp. 89–90.

149. Joseph W. Phillips, *Jedidiah Morse and the New England Congregationalists* (New Brunswick, N.J., 1983), p. 222.

150. Davis, *The Problem of Slavery in Western Culture*, p. 201; Donald G. Mathews, *Religion in the Old South* (Chicago, 1977), p. 144.

151. Nehemiah Adams, *South-Side View of Slavery; or, Three Months at the South, in 1854* (Boston, 1854), p. 204. Adams was a Boston clergyman who returned from a trip through the South convinced that emancipation was not the answer to the slavery crisis. His anti-slavery colleagues then began referring to him sarcastically as "South-Side Adams." Two years later, another Bostonian, Benjamin Drew, published what appeared to be a counter-argument, although he made no specific reference to Adams. See *A North-Side View of Slavery; The Refugee; or, The Narratives of Fugitive Slaves in Canada. Related by Themselves, with an Account of the History and Condition of the Colored Population of Upper Canada* (New York, 1928 [1856]).

152. See "Christians as *doloui* of God and Christ," in Kittel, ed., *Theological Dictionary*, vol. II, pp. 273–77. For a discussion of the "Servant of Yahweh," see Bright, *A History of Israel*, pp. 358–60. Examples of the "servant poems" can be found in Isaiah 42:1–9, 43:10, 49:1–6, 50:10, and 52:13.

153. Davis, *The Problem of Slavery in Western Culture*, pp. 304, 307; Gerald Sorin, *Abolitionism: A New Perspective* (New York, 1972), p. 36. The Great Awakening as a countervailing force to the ideal of dualism can be reviewed in Lincoln, *Race, Religion, and the Continuing American Dilemma*, pp. 48–49; Alho, *Religion of the Slaves*, p. 52; and Luther P. Jackson, "Religious Development of the Negro in Virginia from 1760 to 1860," *Journal of Negro History*, vol. 16, no. 2 (April 1931), p. 172.

154. Stampp, *Peculiar Institution*, p. 158; Smith, *In His Image*, p. 98; Timothy L. Smith,

"Slavery and Theology: The Emergence of Black Christian Consciousness in Nineteenth-Century America," *Church History*, vol. 41, no. 4 (December 1972), pp. 497–98.

155. 1 Corinthians 7:20–24; Colossians 3:24–25; Ephesians 6:5–8; and 1 Peter 2:18–20.

156. Jupiter Hammon, *America's First Negro Poet: The Complete Works of Jupiter Hammon of Long Island* (Port Washington, N.Y., 1970), pp. 59–65. See also Benjamin Brawley, *Early Negro American Writers: Selections with Biographical and Critical Introductions* (Chapel Hill, N.C., 1935), p. 26.

157. Smith, *In His Image*, p. 54; Charles Cotesworth Pinckney, *An Address Delivered in Charleston, before the Agricultural Society of South Carolina at Its Anniversary Meeting, on Tuesday, the 18th of August, 1829* (Charleston, S.C., 1829). See also Kyle Haselden, *The Racial Problem in Christian Perspective* (New York, 1964 [1959]), pp. 35–36; and Donald G. Mathews, "The Methodist Mission to the Slaves, 1829–1844," *Journal of American History*, vol. 51, no. 4 (March 1965), p. 618.

158. Quoted in Herbert G. Gutman, "Protestantism and the American Labor Movement: The Christian Spirit in the Gilded Age," *American Historical Review*, vol. 72, no. 1 (October 1966), p. 91.

159. George P. Rawick, ed., *The American Slave: A Composite Autobiography* (31 vols., Wesport, Conn., 1972–78), vol. II, part I, p. 43.

160. For a comprehensive review of the Bible as inspiration for slave spirituals, see John Lovell, Jr., *Black Song: The Forge and the Flame. The Story of How the Afro-American Spiritual Was Hammered Out* (New York, 1972), pp. 245–63, 475–77. The serious collection of black American folk music began in the first year of the Civil War and has continued to recent times. Nevertheless, the total number of slave songs, spiritual and otherwise, will probably never be known, in part because many of them passed from usage before anyone had a chance to write them down; but, since there were numerous regional variations of the same songs and their forms and lyrics often changed over the years, they unquestionably numbered in the thousands. The songs cited here and elsewhere in this work can be found in many collections, including: William Francis Allen, Charles Pickard Ware, and Lucy McKim Garrison, eds., *Slave Songs of the United States* (New York, 1951 [1867]); John Nelson Clark Coggin, ed., *Plantation Melodies and Spiritual Songs for Evangelistic Meetings, Schools and Colleges* (Philadelphia, n.d.); R. Nathaniel Dett, ed., *Religious Folk-Songs of the Negro as Sung at Hampton Institute* (Hampton, Va., 1927 [1874, 1891, 1909]); Thomas P. Fenner, Frederic G. Rathburn, and Bessie Cleaveland, arrs., *Cabin and Plantation Songs as Sung by the Hampton Students* (New York, 1977 [1874, 1901]); William Arms Fisher, ed., *Seventy Negro Spirituals* (New York, 1926); Emily Hallowell, ed., *Calhoun Plantation Songs* (Boston, 1907 [1901]); Lydia Parrish, *Slave Songs of the Georgia Sea Islands* (Hatboro, Pa., 1965 [1942]); and Harold Courlander, *Negro Folk Music, U.S.A.* (New York, 1963). Together these eight volumes list over 800 different titles. Lovell based his research for *Black Song* on 500 spirituals out of more than 6,000 that he had consulted. See especially p. 637.

161. Allen, Ware, and Garrison, eds., *Slave Songs of the United States;* pp. 23–24, from the song, "Michael, Row the Boat Ashore." Reversing "wide" and "deep" would have produced a rhyme, but none of the twenty-two lines rhymed. This was not unusual in slave-song lyrics. Although rhyme making was common in many areas of Africa, it apparently was not in some of the regions from which slaves were brought, and its only occasional appearance in the spirituals may have been partly the result of the influence of its familiar usage in English writing. Some slave songs had several verses, but as a general rule the songs were very short and there were numerous repeats. For an extended discussion of rhyme in plantation songs and poems, see Thomas W. Talley, *Negro Folk Rhymes: Wise and Otherwise* (New York, 1922), pp. 228–326.

162. Dett, ed., *Religious Folk-Songs of the Negro as Sung at Hampton Institute*, p. 102, from "Swing Low."

163. Ibid., pp. 98–99, from "Oh, Wasn't Dat a Wide Riber."

164. Fisher, ed., *Seventy Negro Spirituals*, p. 20, from "Deep River."

165. Courlander, *Negro Folk Music, U.S.A.*, pp. 258–59, from "I'm Crossing Jordan River."

166. Ibid., p. 50, from "Rock, Chariot, I Told You to Rock."

167. The "going home" theme was also vividly preserved by Anton Dvořák in the haunting strains of the "Largo" movement from his Symphony No. 9 in E Minor, Op. 95, "The New World."

168. For a concise review of the meaning of death in the early Christian world through the sixteenth century, see David E. Stannard, *The Puritan Way of Death: A Study in Religion, Culture, and Social Change* (New York, 1977), chapter 1, "Death in the Western Tradition."

169. John C. Van Horne, ed., *Religious Philanthropy and Colonial Slavery: The American Correspondence of the Associates of Dr. Bray, 1717–1777* (Champaign, Ill., 1985), p. 100.

170. Allen, Ware, and Garrison, eds., *Slave Songs of the United States*, p. 31, from "Travel On."

171. Coggin, ed., *Plantation Melodies and Spiritual Songs*, no. 43, from "On the Other Shore."

172. Courlander, *Negro Folk Music, U.S.A.*, p. 253, from "Way Bye and Bye."

173. Coggin, ed., *Plantation Melodies and Spiritual Songs*, no. 140. Also in Joseph B. Earnest, Jr., *The Religious Development of the Negro in Virginia* (Charlottesville, Va., 1914), p. 155.

174. Jacob Stroyer, *My Life in the South* (Salem, Mass., 1898 [1879]), p. 41.

175. Nichols, *Many Thousand Gone*, p. 101.

176. John B. Cade, "Out of the Mouths of Ex-Slaves," *Journal of Negro History*, vol. 20, no. 3 (July 1935), p. 329; B. A. Botkin, ed., *Lay My Burden Down: A Folk History of Slavery* (Chicago, 1945), pp. 25, 273; [Charles Ball], *Fifty Years in Chains; or, The Life of an American Slave* (New York, 1858), pp. 188–90. See also Julius Lester, ed., *To Be a Slave* (New York, 1968), pp. 81–82, 86–87.

177. Donald J. D'Elia, "Dr. Benjamin Rush and the Negro," *Journal of the History of Ideas*, vol. 30, no. 3 (July–September 1969), p. 422; Scherer, *Slavery and the Churches*, pp. 86, 89.

178. Philippians 3:10.

179. Proverbs 28:6.

180. William Wells Brown, *My Southern Home: or, The South and Its People* (Boston, 1880), pp. 16–17.

181. Matthew 5:10.

CHAPTER THREE

1. The "Curse of Canaan" story theme of many proslavery documents. For example, see Samuel A. Cartwright, *Essays, Being Inductions from the Baconian Philosophy Proving the Truth of the Bible and the Justice and Benevolence of the Decree Dooming Canaan to Be a Servant of Servants; and Answering the Question of Voltaire:* "On demande quel droit des étrangers tels que les Juifs avaient sur pays de Canaan?" *In a Series of Letters to the Rev. William Winans, by Samuel A. Cartwright, M.D., of Natchez, Miss.* (Vidalia, [La.], 1843); Frederick A. Ross, *Slavery Ordained of God* (Philadelphia, 1859); New York *Daily News*, April 16, 1864; Robert L. Dabney, *A Defence of Virginia, and Through Her, of the South, in Recent and Pending Contests Against the Sectional Party* (New York, 1867); Robert A. Young, *The Negro: A Reply to Ariel . . .* (Nashville, Tenn., 1867); *The Mystery Finished: The Negro Has a Soul . . .* (Memphis, Tenn., 1868);

P[hilip] C. Friese, *Letter to the President and the People of the United States* . . . (Baltimore, 1869); and "A Citizen of Georgia," *Remarks upon Slavery, Occasioned by Attempts Made to Circulate Improper Publications in the Southern States* (n.p., n.d.).

2. Genesis 9:24 of the New International Version of the Bible identifies Ham as the "youngest" of Noah's sons, but the King James Version uses the word "younger" and the continuous placement of Ham's name second in the order of brothers, especially in Genesis 6:10, suggests that he was the middle son, an assertion supported by most dictionaries. On the other hand, biblical scholar Umberto Cassuto has made a persuasive argument for the youngest-son theory. See *A Commentary on the Book of Genesis* (2 vols., Jerusalem, 1961 [1944]), vol. II, *From Noah to Abraham*, pp. 164–65.

3. B. A. Botkin, ed., *Lay My Burden Down: A Folk History of Slavery* (Chicago, 1945), pp. 15, 272.

4. Dabney, *A Defence of Virginia*, pp. 101–108.

5. Thomas Virgil Peterson, *Ham and Japheth: The Mythic World of Whites in the Antebellum South* (Metuchen, N.J., 1978), p. xiii.

6. Goldwin Smith, *Does the Bible Sanction American Slavery?* (Cambridge, Mass., 1864), p. 29.

7. Cotton Mather, *The Negro Christianized; An Essay to Excite and Assist the Good Work, the Instruction of Negro Servants in Christianity* (Boston, 1706), quoted in Louis Ruchames, ed., *Racial Thought in America* (2 vols., Amherst, Mass., 1969), vol. I, p. 60; Increase N. Tarbox, *The Curse; or, The Position in the World's History Occupied by the Race of Ham* (Boston, 1864), pp. 14–21.

8. Quoted in H. Shelton Smith, *In His Image, but . . . : Racism in Southern Religion, 1780–1910* (Durham, N.C., 1972), p. 28.

9. Recent scholarship continues to make the connection. Michael Grant, in *The History of Ancient Israel* (New York, 1984), cited Genesis 9:25 as the basis of the enslavement of Canaan's descendants. This is not simply a case of drawing a conclusion based on unverifiable evidence—as many biblical scholars often do—but a case of drawing a conclusion based on evidence that is not in the Bible at all. For an older example of the same error, see Louis Wallis, *God and the Social Process: A Study in Hebrew History* (Chicago, 1935), pp. 91–92.

10. [Iveson L. Brookes], *A Defence of Southern Slavery, against the Attacks of Henry Clay and Alex'r Campbell* . . . ([Hamburg, S.C., 1851]), p. 5.

11. Conor Cruise O'Brien, *God Land: Reflections on Religion and Nationalism* (Cambridge, Mass., 1988), pp. 9–10. The principle of *Limpieza de Sangre*, purity of blood, simply stated that a guiltless person inherited the sins of his forebears. "The blood of a converted Jew was impure; even if he personally was not a blasphemer, his ancestors had been. So he could, indeed had to be, excluded from the Christian community. By the exact same reasoning, American slaveowners justified holding black Christians as slaves. They might be Christians *now*, but their ancestors had been heathens, and rightfully enslaved, and therefore so should they be."

12. David Barrow, *Involuntary, Unmerited, Perpetual, Absolute, Hereditary Slavery, Examined: on the Principles of Nature, Reason, Justice, Policy and Scripture* (Lexington, Ky., 1808), p. 29. By interpolating certain meanings into Hebrew and Akkadian sentence structures and speech patterns and comparing them to selected Old Testament passages, it is possible to conclude that Canaan's descendants were also cursed; but such an explanation is still stretching it. See Cassuto, *A Commentary on the Book of Genesis*, vol. II, pp. 166–70.

13. Smith, *Does the Bible Sanction American Slavery?*, pp. 29–30.

14. George M. Fredrickson, *White Supremacy: A Comparative Study in American and South African History* (New York, 1981), p. 10.

15. Cartwright, *Essays*, p. 33.

16. John H. Hopkins, *Bible View of Slavery* (New York, 1863), p. 2, also printed in the

Philadelphia *Age*, December 8, 1863. Hopkins was the first Protestant Episcopal Bishop of Vermont; in 1851, he delivered a sermon in Buffalo, New York, entitled "Slavery: Its Religious Sanction." The sermon was published the same year and received extensive circulation, undoubtedly, in part, because he was a prominent northern Christian leader. But Hopkins also generated strong opposition. Shortly after his sermon appeared in print, 116 Episcopal clergymen signed a statement criticizing his use of the pulpit to support his racist views. See "The Voice of the Clergy" ([Philadelphia, 1863]), a leaflet.

17. Ross, *Slavery Ordained of God*, p. 50. For a discussion of the idea that Japheth was given authority over *both* Shem and Ham, see Peterson, *Ham and Japheth*.

18. Genesis 9:19, 10:32.

19. Thomas Smyth, *The Unity of the Human Races, Proved To Be the Doctrine of Scripture, Reason, and Science* (New York, 1850), pp. 31–45; Cartwright, *Essays*, p. 5.

20. Olaudah Equiano, *The Interesting Narrative of Olaudah Equiano, or Gustavus Vassa, the African. Written by Himself* (2 vols., New York, 1969 [1789]), vol. I, pp. 37–39; Philip D. Curtin, ed., *Africa Remembered: Narratives of West Africans from the Era of the Slave Trade* (Madison, Wis., 1967), p. 82; John Josselyn, *An Account of Two Voyages to New-England, Made during the Years 1638, 1663* (Boston, 1865), pp. 143–44; W. S. Armistead, *The Negro Is a Man: A Reply to Professor Charles Carroll's Book "The Negro Is a Beast; or, In the Image of God"* (Tifton, Ga., 1903), pp. 316–17; Donald J. D'Elia, "Dr. Benjamin Rush and the Negro," *Journal of the History of Ideas*, vol. 30, no. 3 (July–September 1969), pp. 421–22.

21. [Josiah Priest], *Slavery, as It Relates to the Negro, or African Race, Examined in the Light of Circumstances, History and the Holy Scripture; . . .* (Albany, N.Y., 1843), pp. 27–28. The reference to the color of Ham's parents was based on Priest's belief that up to this time the universal skin color was not white but *red*, since the Hebrew word *adam* translated as "one that is red." See also Peterson, *Ham and Japheth*, p. 42.

22. [Priest], *Slavery, as It Relates to the Negro, or African Race*, p. 135. One can only wonder if Priest had read George Best's *A True Discourse of the Late Voyages of discoverie, for the finding of a Passage to Cathaya . . .* (London, 1758), in which Canaan and his descendants were made "so blacke & lothsome." See Alden T. Vaughan, "The Origins Debate: Slavery and Racism in Seventeenth-Century Virginia," *Virginia Magazine of History and Biography*, vol. 97, no. 3 (July 1989), p. 350.

23. David E. Harrell, Jr., *Quest for a Christian America: The Disciples of Christ and American Society to 1866* (Nashville, 1966), 127; Gerald Sorin, *Abolitionism: A New Perspective* (New York, 1972), pp. 24–25.

24. Howell Cobb, *A Scriptural Examination of the Institution of Slavery in the United States* (Georgia, 1856), passim; E. Brooks Holifield, *The Gentleman Theologians: American Theology in Southern Culture, 1795–1860* (Durham, N.C., 1978), p. 153; Dabney, *A Defence of Virginia*, p. 103.

25. Quoted in Franklin H. Littell, *The Free Church* (Boston, 1957), pp. 83–84. The modern revival of the idea of original sin, especially as expounded by Paul Tillich and Reinhold Niebuhr, is well summarized in H. Shelton Smith, *Changing Conceptions of Original Sin: A Study in American Theology Since 1750* (New York, 1955), pp. 206–29.

26. John Codman Hurd, *The Law of Freedom and Bondage in the United States* (2 vols., New York, 1968 [1858–1862]), vol. I, p. 161n.; William L. Westermann, *The Slave Systems of Greek and Roman Antiquity* (Philadelphia, 1955), pp. 97, 135.

27. Frank M. Snowden, Jr., *Before Color Prejudice: The Ancient View of Blacks* (Cambridge, Mass., 1983), pp. 107–108; William McKee Evans, "From the Land of Canaan to the Land of Guinea," *American Historical Review*, vol. 85, no. 1 (February 1980), pp. 24–28.

28. Anthony Gerard Barthelemy, *Black Face, Maligned Race: The Representation of Blacks in English Drama from Shakespeare to Southerne* (Baton Rouge, La., 1987), p. 7.

29. Evans, "From the Land of Canaan to the Land of Guinea," p. 34.

30. Hollis Read, *The Negro Problem Solved; or, Africa as She Is, and as She Shall Be. Her Curse and Her Cure* (New York, 1864), pp. 39–41.

31. Olli Alho, *Religion of the Slaves: A Study of the Religious Tradition and Behaviour of Plantation Slaves in the United States, 1830–1865* (Helsinki, 1976), p. 62.

32. [Buckner H. Payne], *The Negro: What Is His Ethnological Status; Is He a Progeny of Ham? Is He a Descendant of Adam and Eve? Has He a Soul? Or Is He a Beast in God's Nomenclature? What Is His Status as Fixed by God in Creation? What Is His Relation to the White Race?* (2nd ed., Cincinnati, 1867), pp. 4–5. An "enlarged version" that included comments from Payne's critics was published in 1872. See Cartwright, *Essays*, p. 5.

33. "Sister Sallie," *The Color Line. Devoted to the Restoration of Good Government, Putting an End to Negro Authority and Misrule, and Establishing a White Man's Government in the White Man's Country, by Organizing the White People of the South* (n.p., [1868?]), pp. 16–23.

34. Ross, *Slavery Ordained of God*, p. 50.

35. William Sumner Jenkins, *Proslavery Thought in the Old South* (Chapel Hill, N.C., 1935), pp. 269–70. See also Josiah C. Nott and George R. Gliddon, *Types of Mankind: or, Ethnological Researches, Based upon the Ancient Monuments, Paintings, Sculptures, and Crania of Races, and upon Their Natural, Geographical, Philological and Biblical History* (Philadelphia, 1855). In the twentieth century, ethno-archaeologists working in the Tassili-n-Ajjer region of southeast Algeria have discovered rock and cave paintings dating back as far as 5,000 B.C. that feature people with distinctive Negroid facial features. See Henri Lohte, "Oasis of Art in the Sahara," *National Geographic*, vol. 172, no. 2 (August 1987), pp. 180–91.

36. Josiah Clark Nott, *Two Lectures on the Connection Between the Biblical and Physical History of Man, Delivered by Invitation, from the Chair of Political Economy, etc., of the Louisiana University, in December, 1848* (New York, 1969 [1849]), p. 29. See also Nott, *Two Lectures on the Natural History of the Caucasian and Negro Races* (Mobile, Ala., 1844).

37. The sons of Japheth were Gomer, Magog, Madai, Javan, Tubal, Meshech, and Tiras. The sons of Ham were Cush, Mizraim, Phut, and Canaan. The sons of Shem were Elam, Asshur, Arphaxad, Lud, and Aram. See Genesis 10:2, 6, 22. These verses say nothing about daughters.

38. Smyth, *The Unity of the Human Races*, p. 74; Jenkins, *Proslavery Thought in the Old South*, p. 269.

39. In fact, Bachman proclaimed an exact number: 2,362,749,914,214,046.

40. John Bachman, *The Doctrine of the Unity of the Human Race Examined on the Principles of Science* (Charleston, S.C., pp. 282–85.

41. George B. Cheever, *God against Slavery: And the Freedom and Duty of the Pulpit to Rebuke It, as a Sin against God* (New York, 1857), pp. 100–101; Read, *The Negro Problem Solved*, pp. 36–50.

42. David Brion Davis, *The Problem of Slavery in Western Culture* (Ithaca, N.Y., 1966), p. 307.

43. James Axtell, *The Invasion Within: The Contest of Cultures in Colonial North America* (New York, 1985), pp. 219–20.

44. Josselyn, *An Account of Two Voyages to New-England*, pp. 96–97; Cotton Mather, *Magnalia Christi Americana; or, The Ecclesiastical History of New-England; from Its First Planting, in the Year 1620, unto the Year of Our Lord 1698* (2 vols., New York, 1967, reproduced from the 1852 edition [1st ed., 1702]), vol. I, p. 51.

45. Quoted in Ola Elizabeth Winslow, *John Eliot, Apostle to the Indians* (Boston, 1968), p. 86.

46. Gary B. Nash, *Red, White, and Black: The Peoples of Early America* (2nd ed., Englewood Cliffs, N.J., 1982), pp. 76–77, 79; Mather, *Magnalia Christi Americana*, vol. I, p. 51;

R. Pierce Beaver, *Church, State, and the American Indians: Two and a Half Centuries of Partnership in Missions between Protestant Churches and Government* (St. Louis, 1966), pp. 25–26, quoting Nathaniel Appleton's *A Sermon Preached October 9, Being a Day of Public Thanksgiving Occasioned by the Surrender of Montreal, and all Canada* (Boston, 1760), p. 17.

47. *The Book of Mormon: An Account Written by the Hand of Mormon upon Plates Taken from the Plates of Nephi*, translated by Joseph Smith, Jun. (Salt Lake City, 1981), 2 Nephi 5:21–24. See also 1 Nephi 12:23; Alma 3:6; and Mormon 5:15.

48. The best study of the Mormon church's racial policies is Newell G. Bringhurst's *Saints, Slaves, and Blacks: The Changing Place of Black People Within Mormonism* (Westport, Conn., 1981), which superseded the sketchy, superficial, and totally inadequate article-length "book" by Stephen G. Taggart, *Mormonism's Negro Policy: Social and Historical Origins* (Salt Lake City, 1970). Both authors were Mormons. Of the general histories, Leonard J. Arrington and Davis Bitton's *The Mormon Experience: A History of the Latter-Day Saints* (New York, 1979) is the best work by Mormon historians; while Klaus J. Hansen's brief but incisive *Mormonism and the American Experience* (Chicago, 1981) and Robert Gottlieb and Deter Wiley's *America's Saints: The Rise of Mormon Power* (New York, 1984) lead the short list by non-Mormon scholars. In a class by itself is Fawn M. Brodie's *No Man Knows My History: The Life of Joseph Smith, the Mormon Prophet* (2nd ed., New York, 1971). Because of her Mormon background and her challenge to the authenticity of the *Book of Mormon*, Brodie drew sharp rebukes from the LDS leadership, which was clearly stung by the doubt she cast over Mormon doctrines. And being a woman did not make her any dearer to the hierarchy. Mormon leaders classify all publications about the church as either "faith-promoting" or "faith-destroying." Books by "gentiles" or, worse, by excommunicated saints, are often relegated to the latter group. Since historians of sectarian works usually fall into two categories—church members, who tend to be defensive (if not hostile), and nonmembers, who have an axe to grind—Brodie's unique situation generated a measure of credibility rarely seen in denominational studies.

49. John Chester Miller, *Wolf by the Ears: Thomas Jefferson and Slavery* (New York, 1977), pp. 52–55.

50. Thomas Jefferson, *Notes on the State of Virginia* (Chapel Hill, N.C., 1955 [London, 1787]), p. 102. See also pages 43–65 for his speculations on animals and Indians.

51. Fredrickson, *White Supremacy*, pp. 10–11.

52. Thomas F. Gossett, *Race: The History of an Idea in America* (New York, 1965), pp. 58–59.

53. For example, see William Aikman, *The Future of the Colored Race in America: Being an Article in the Presbyterian Quarterly Review, of July, 1862* (Philadelphia, 1862), p. 28.

54. New York *Daily News*, April 16, 1864. For a discussion of the political controversy over miscegenation, see Forrest G. Wood, *Black Scare: The Racist Response to Emancipation and Reconstruction* (Berkeley, Calif., 1968), chapter 4.

55. Samuel G. Morton, *Crania Americana* (Philadelphia, 1839), p. 3. See also Ruchames, ed., *Racial Thought in America*, vol. I, pp. 441–48; William Stanton, *The Leopard's Spots: Scientific Attitudes toward Race in America, 1815–1859* (Chicago, 1960), pp. 25–35 and passim; and Herbert Hovenkamp, *Science and Religion in America, 1800–1860* (Philadelphia, 1978), pp. 166–68.

56. Smith, *In His Image*, pp. 157–58; Nott, *Two Lectures, on the Natural History of the Caucasian and Negro Races*, pp. 30–34.

57. Smith, *In His Image*, pp. 156–57; Edward J. Larson, *Trial and Error: The American Controversy over Creation and Evolution* (New York, 1985), p. 8; Ruchames, ed., *Racial Thought in America*, vol. I, pp. 457–61. For the fullest account of Agassiz's position, see his article "The Diversity of the Origin of the Human Race," *Christian Examiner and Religious Miscellany*, vol. 49 (Boston, July 1850).

58. Jenkins, *Proslavery Thought in the Old South*, pp. 268–84; Peterson, *Ham and Japheth*, p. 24; Josiah Clark Nott, *An Essay on the Natural History of Mankind, Viewed in Connection with Negro Slavery: Delivered before the Southern Rights Association, 14th December, 1850* (Mobile, Ala., 1851), pp. 19–21. See also Smith, *In His Image*, p. 159.

59. Nott, *Two Lectures, on the Natural History of the Caucasian and Negro Races*, p. 5.

60. Franz Boas, *The Mind of Primitive Man* (rev. ed., New York, 1963 [1938]), p. 5. From the foreword by Melville J. Herskovits.

61. One of the most outspoken critics was Samuel Stanhope Smith, an American Presbyterian minister. See *Essay on the Causes of the Variety of Complexion and Figure in the Human Species* (Cambridge, Mass., 1965 issue of the 2nd ed., New York, 1810 [1787]), pp. 187–212. See also John C. Greene, "The American Debate on the Negro's Place in Nature, 1780–1815," *Journal of the History of Ideas*, vol. 15, no. 3 (June 1954), pp. 384–96.

62. Oscar Handlin, *Race and Nationality in American Life* (New York, 1957 [1948]), p. 42. For an extended discussion of the "ancient idea of the Great Chain of Being which had become so popular in the eighteenth century," see Winthrop D. Jordan's introduction to Samuel Stanhope Smith's *Essay*, p. xxvi.

63. Robert F. Berkhofer, *The White Man's Indian: Images of the American Indian from Columbus to the Present* (New York, 1978), pp. 36–37; Jenkins, *Proslavery Thought in the Old South*, p. 273; Reginald Horsman, *Race and Manifest Destiny: The Origins of American Racial Anglo-Saxonism* (Cambridge, Mass., 1981), p. 135. For an extended discussion of the unity versus polygenesis debate see Horsman, pp. 48–52, 129–30, 132–33, 145–51.

64. Hovenkamp, *Science and Religion in America*, p. 163. Examples of Christian arguments on the unity of the races can be found in Moses Ashley Curtis, "Unity of the Races," *Southern Quarterly Review*, vol. 7 (1849); M. B. Hope, "On the Unity of the Human Race," *Biblical Repertory and Princeton Review*, vol. 22 (1850); Samuel Davies Baldwin, *Dominion, or the Unity and Eternity of the Human Race* (Nashville, Tenn., 1857); and Thomas A. Davies, *Cosmogony, or the Mysteries of Creation* (New York, 1857).

65. Peterson, *Ham and Japheth*, pp. 25–26.

66. Quoted in John W. Storey, "The Negro in Southern Baptist Thought, 1865–1900" (Ph.D. dissertation, University of Kentucky, 1968), pp. 17–18.

67. *Notes on the State of Virginia*, p. 47; Miller, *Wolf by the Ears*, p. 53.

68. In his comparison of American and European animal life, Jefferson conceded that mammoths could not be found in any of the places where civilized people dwell. But this did not mean they did not exist somewhere. "Such is the economy of nature, that no instance can be produced of her having permitted any one race of her animals to become extinct; of her having formed any link in her great work so weak as to be broken. To add to this, the traditionary testimony of the Indians, that this animal still exists in the northern and western parts of America, would be adding the light of a taper to that of the meridian sun." (*Notes*, pp. 53–54.) See also Berkhofer, *The White Man's Indian*, p. 56.

69. For a discussion of the Christian critics of polygenesis, see Hovenkamp, *Science and Religion in America*, "The Unity of Man," pp. 165–86.

70. Acts 17:26.

71. Genesis 3:20 and 11:1. See also Dabney, *A Defence of Virginia*, p. 23.

72. S. S. Smith, *Essay*, pp. xlviii–xlix; Nott, *Two Lectures on the Connection between the Biblical and Physical History of Man*, passim; George Howe, *Southern Presbyterian Review* (January 1850), pp. 427–90; Peterson, *Ham and Japheth*, pp. 25–26; Smith, *In His Image*, pp. 160–61; Holifield, *The Gentleman Theologians*, pp. 152–53; Smyth, *The Unity of the Human Races*, pp. 348–81.

73. W[illiam] T. Hamilton, *The "Friend of Moses"; or, a Defence of the Pentateuch as the Production of Moses and an Inspired Document, against the Objections of Modern Skepticism* (New

York, 1852), pp. 408–97; Smyth, *The Unity of the Human Races*, p. xix. See also J. William Flinn, ed., *Complete Works of Rev. Thomas Smyth, D.D.* (Columbia, S.C., 1910), vol. VIII.

74. Ruchames, ed., *Racial Thought in America*, vol. I, pp. 449–56; Smith, *In His Image*, pp. 161–63; Bachman, *Unity of the Human Race*, pp. 7–8; Bachman, *An Examination of Professor Agassiz's Sketch of the Natural Provinces of the Animal World* (Charleston, S.C., 1855), passim.

75. There is more than a little irony in the fact that Charles Darwin's findings on evolution eventually discredited the theory of polygenesis, only to provide an even greater challenge for Protestant fundamentalists.

76. For a detailed discussion of this subject, see Winthrop D. Jordan, *White Over Black: American Attitudes Toward the Negro, 1550–1812* (Chapel Hill, N.C., 1968), pp. 17–20.

77. Peterson, *Ham and Japheth*, pp. 25–26.

78. [Payne], *The Negro*, pp. 4–5. See also Prospero (pseud.), *Caliban: A Sequel to "Ariel"* (New York, 1868); Sister Sallie (pseud.), *The Color Line;* David Macrae, *The Americans at Home* (New York, 1952 [Edinburgh, 1870]), pp. 299–392.

79. Other negative reviews included [W. J. Scott], "Our Tripod: The Ethnological Status of the Negro," *Scott's Monthly Magazine*, vol. V, no. 3 (March 1868), pp. 149–51; *The Adamic Race: Reply to "Ariel," Drs. Young and Blackie, on the Negro*, by "M.S." (New York, 1868); and Harrison Berry, *A Reply to Ariel* (Macon, Ga., 1869)—the same Harrison Berry who, as a "slave," eight years earlier purportedly wrote a biblical justification of his own enslavement. See *supra*, chapter 2. See also *The Six Species of Men, with Cuts Representing the Types of the Caucasian, Mongul, Malay, Indian, Esquimaux and Negro, with Their General Physical and Mental Qualities, Laws of Organization, Relations to Civilization, etc.* (New York, 1866).

80. William G. Schell, *Is the Negro a Beast?: A Reply to Chas. Carroll's Book Entitled "The Negro a Beast," Proving that the Negro is Human from Biblical, Scientific, and Historical Standpoints* (Moundsville, W. Va., 1901), pp. 180–81. For a discussion of the Christian reaction to Darwinism see John H. Roberts, *Darwinism and the Divine in America: Protestant Intellectuals and Organic Evolution, 1859–1900* (Madison, Wis., 1988).

81. Fredrika Teute Schmidt and Barbara Ripel Wilhelm, "Early Proslavery Petitions in Virginia," *William and Mary Quarterly*, 3rd series, vol. 30, no. 1 (January 1973), pp. 143–44. The petition was dated November 10, 1785.

82. Ralph L. Moellering, *Christian Conscience and Negro Emancipation* (Philadelphia, 1965), p. 50; Harrell, *Quest for a Christian America*, p. 52.

83. It is interesting that people who accept the allegories of the Bible as factually accurate often condemn serious literature as the work of the Devil. Jonathan Blanchard, appointed in 1860 as the founding president of fundamentalist Wheaton College, once declared that "a novel is at best a well-told lie." For a discussion of modern Christian fiction writers, see David S. Reynolds, *Faith in Fiction: The Emergence of Religious Literature in America* (Cambridge, Mass., 1981).

84. Quoted in Jenkins, *Pro-Slavery Thought in the Old South*, pp. 205–206.

85. See Alan O. Grimes, *Equality in America: Religion, Race, and the Urban Majority* (New York, 1964), pp. 50–51, 86. For a brief review of the continued use of the Bible to justify racial segregation in the twentieth century, see James O. Buswell III, *Slavery, Segregation, and Scripture* (Grand Rapids, Mich., 1964), pp. 55–92.

86. Quoted in *Life* magazine (March 18, 1966), p. 91.

87. C. E. McLain, *The Place of Race* (New York, 1965).

88. David Brion Davis, *The Problem of Slavery in the Age of Revolution, 1770–1823* (Ithaca, N.Y., 1975), p. 555; Moellering, *Christian Conscience and Negro Emancipation*, p. 67; Smith, *Revivalism and Social Reform*, pp. 220–21.

89. Davis, *The Problem of Slavery in the Age of Revolution*, pp. 540–41, 553–54; Smith, *Does the Bible Sanction American Slavery?*, pp. 29–30; Read, *The Negro Problem Solved*, pp. 39–41.

90. Norman K. Gottwald, *The Hebrew Bible—A Socio-Literary Introduction* (Philadelphia, 1985), pp. 16–22.

91. Davis, *The Problem of Slavery in the Age of Revolution*, p. 523; [Isabella Lucy Bishop], *Aspects of Religion in the United States* (London, 1859), p. 85.

92. The passage of time and the presence of a more enlightened generation apparently has not made a great deal of difference. At a conference at the University of Michigan in the spring of 1985 on the subject "Jesus in History and Myth" sponsored by the humanist-oriented magazine *Free Inquiry*, Van Harvey of Stanford University's religious studies department pointed to the difficulty New Testament scholars confront when their findings do not agree with the commonly held views of the lay population. Much of what conservative Protestants believe is based on faith in the *literal* truth of the Bible, Harvey asserted, but most of the miracles and other stories about Jesus cannot be verified when they are subjected to the canons of historical research. Harvey dismissed the work of conservative biblical scholars because, he argued, most of them only look for evidence that reinforces what they already believe rather than, as the unbiased scholar would, allow the evidence to determine their conclusions. See Los Angeles *Times*, April 27, 1985.

93. Jenkins, *Pro-Slavery Thought in the Old South*, pp. 218–19; H. Shelton Smith, Robert T. Handy, and Lefferts A. Loetscher, eds., *American Christianity: An Historical Interpretation with Representative Documents* (2 vols., New York, 1960), vol. II, pp. 177–78.

94. By carefully selecting isolated bits of biological, geological, and historical data that do not conflict with their religious beliefs and marshaling them under the inherently contradictory term "scientific creationism," modern Christian fundamentalists, in the face of overwhelming empirical evidence to the contrary, continue to deny the reality of biological evolution.

CHAPTER FOUR

1. Olli Alho, *Religion of the Slaves: A Study of the Religious Tradition and Behaviour of Plantation Slaves in the United States, 1830–1865* (Helsinki, 1976), p. 49; George M. Fredrickson, *White Supremacy: A Comparative Study in American and South African History* (New York, 1981), p. 72; William Sumner Jenkins, *Pro-Slavery Thought in the Old South* (Chapel Hill, N.C., 1935), pp. 18–19; William M. Manross, *A History of the American Episcopal Church* (New York, 1959 [1935]), p. 147.

2. It was also possible to construe the common law as applicable only to enslaved whites. See John Codman Hurd, *The Law of Freedom and Bondage in the United States* (2 vols., New York, 1968 [1858–1862]), vol. I, pp. 124–32. Slaves in the Muslim world had it both better and worse. Under Islamic law, the conversion of an infidel slave did not necessarily mean freedom, but no one *born* a Muslim could be enslaved. See Moses I. Finley, "Slavery," *Encyclopedia of Social Sciences*, XIV (2nd ed., New York, 1968), pp. 307–13. In one respect, at least, Islamic slavery was little different from the slavery of the Christian world. While the law prohibited the enslavement of Muslims, Orlando Patterson wrote, "the history of Islam shows that political and economic factors triumphed over religious sentiment whenever the two were in conflict." As with Christianity, piety usually yielded to profits. See *Slavery and Social Death: A Comparative Study* (Cambridge, Mass., 1982), p. 276.

3. David S. Lovejoy, *Religious Enthusiasm in the New World: Heresy to Revolution* (Cambridge, Mass., 1985), pp. 197–98.

4. George Maclaren Brydon, *Virginia's Mother Church and the Political Conditions under which It Grew* (2 vols., Richmond, Va., 1947), vol. I, pp. 186–87, 470; Helen Tunnicliff Catterall, ed., *Judicial Cases Concerning American Slavery and the Negro* (5 vols., Washington, D.C., 1929–1937), vol. I, pp. 55n., 57; Hurd, *The Law of Freedom and Bondage in the United States*,

vol. I, pp. 232, 249. For a discussion of the various cases in Virginia that addressed the manumission issue, see Catterall, pp. 55–61. For a review of two cases in early Virginia that reflected the hardening attitude toward baptizing slaves, see Warren M. Billings, "The Case of Fernando and Elizabeth Key: A Note on the Status of Blacks in Seventeenth Century Virginia," *William and Mary Quarterly*, 3rd series, vol. 30, no. 3 (July 1973), p. 470; and Alden T. Vaughan, "The Origins Debate: Slavery and Racism in Seventeenth-Century Virginia," *Virginia Magazine of History and Biography*, vol. 97, no. 3 (July 1989), pp. 329–30.

5. John C. Van Horne, ed., *Religious Philanthropy and Colonial Slavery: The American Correspondence of the Associates of Dr. Bray, 1717–1777* (Champaign, Ill., 1985), pp. 27–28; Hurd, *The Law of Freedom and Bondage in the United States*, vol. I, pp. 234–35, 240, 243, 250n., 252, 297, 300–301.

6. Fredrickson, *White Supremacy*, pp. 72–73; Patricia U. Bonomi, *Under the Cope of Heaven: Religion, Society, and Politics in Colonial America* (New York, 1986), pp. 120–21; Lorenzo Johnston Greene, *The Negro in Colonial New England* (New York, 1966 [1942]), pp. 261, 263–64, 267; Van Horne, ed., *Religious Philanthropy*, pp. 27–28.

7. Quoted in Louis Ruchames, ed., *Racial Thought in America* (vol. I, *From the Puritans to Abraham Lincoln*, Amherst, Mass., 1969), pp. 66–67.

8. Hurd, *The Law of Freedom and Bondage in the United States*, vol. I, p. 173; Marcus W. Jernagan, "Slavery and Conversion in the American Colonies," *American Historical Review*, vol. 21, no. 3 (April 1916), pp. 506–507; Van Horne, ed., *Religious Philanthropy*, pp. 27–28; Stanley Feldstein, ed., *The Poisoned Tongue: A Documentary History of American Racism and Prejudice* (New York, 1972), p. 30.

9. Fredrickson, *White Supremacy*, pp. 76–80; S. Charles Bolton, *Southern Anglicanism: The Church of England in Colonial South Carolina* (Westport, Conn., 1982), p. 109; W. D. Weatherford, *American Churches and the Negro: An Historical Study from Early Slave Days to the Present* (Boston, 1957), pp. 31–32; Frank J. Klingberg, *An Appraisal of the Negro in Colonial South Carolina: A Study in Americanization* (Washington, D.C., 1941), pp. 13, 21n.; Hurd, *The Law of Freedom and Bondage in the United States*, vol. I, pp. 300–301. Historians have also spelled Le Jau as "Le Jeau," "Le Jan," and "Le Jeon."

10. Quoted in Jenkins, *Pro-Slavery Thought in the Old South*, p. 19. See also Oscar Handlin, *Race and Nationality in American Life* (New York, 1957 [1948]), pp. 16–17; Martin E. Marty, *Righteous Empire: The Protestant Experience in America* (New York, 1970), p. 26; and Weatherford, *American Churches and the Negro*, p. 34. For the full texts of Gibson's letters, see Frederick Dalcho, *Historical Account of the Protestant Episcopal Church in South Carolina* (Charleston, 1820), pp. 104–12. A brief but excellent discussion of the legal aspects of the issue of conversion and emancipation in the colonial period can be found in Hurd, *The Law of Freedom and Bondage in the United States*, vol. I, pp. 165–70, 188, 189, 210, and 358.

11. Gerald Francis De Jong, "The Dutch Reformed Church and Negro Slavery in Colonial America," *Church History*, vol. 40, no. 4 (December 1971), p. 423.

12. Ibid., p. 426, quoting J. A. Grothe, ed., *Archief voor de Geschiedenis der Oude Hollandoche Zending* (6 vols., Utrecht, 1884–1891), vol. II, p. 240.

13. De Jong, "The Dutch Reformed Church and Negro Slavery in Colonial America," p. 430; Catterall, ed., *Judicial Cases Concerning American Slavery and the Negro*, pp. 55n., 57; E. Clifford Nelson, *The Lutherans in North America* (Philadelphia, 1975), vol. I, p. 74.

14. Frank J. Klingberg, *Anglican Humanitarianism in Colonial New York* (Philadelphia, 1940), p. 188; Emma Willard, *History of the United States or Republic of America* (New York, 1845), pp. 119–20.

15. Carl N. Degler, *Out of Our Past: The Forces That Shaped Modern America* (New York, 1959), p. 38n.; Weatherford, *American Churches and the Negro*, p. 35; Lester B. Scherer, *Slavery and the Churches in Early America, 1619–1819* (Grand Rapids, Mich., 1975), pp. 90–91.

See especially "*Opinion of Sir Philip York[e], then Attorney-General, and Mr. Talbot, Solicitor-General*," 33 Dict. of Dec. 14547, 1729, in Catterall, ed., *Judicial Cases*, vol. I, pp. 3, 12.

16. Historian George M. Fredrickson has suggested that, since slavery had existed in the Christian world long before the founding of Jamestown, the controversy over whether or not a baptized slave should be emancipated has been exaggerated. See *White Supremacy*, pp. 71–74, 77. But a problem that, after a century of legal and ecclesiastical debate, remained unresolved in the minds of so many people obviously had a life that went beyond conventional solutions. The baptism issue did not come up in American courts—although the suits for freedom in Massachusetts in 1773 raised the question of whether or not an enslaved person could perform his Christian duties—but there were more than a few English court cases that addressed the matter, e.g., *Butts v. Penney*, 3 *Keble* 785, 84 *Eng. Rep.* 1011 (1677); *Sir Thomas Grantham's Case*, 3 *Mod.* 120–21, 87 *Eng. Rep.* 77 (1686–1687); *Chamberlaine v. Harvey* 5 *Mod.* 186, 187, 87 *Eng. Rep.* 586 (1696); *Pearne v. Lisle, Ambler* 75 (1749); *Sheddan v. a Negro*, 33 Dict. of Dec. 14545 (Scottish Case), (1757); and *Somerset v. Stewart*, Lofft I [20 How. St. Tr. I], (1772). See Jenkins, *Pro-Slavery Thought in the Old South*, pp. 20n.–21n.; and Catterall, ed., *Judicial Cases*, vol. I, pp. 9, 10, 12, 13, 15, 17. For a concise discussion of these and other English court cases dealing with the "increasing conflict between slavery and the ideal of Christian service," see David Brion Davis, *The Problem of Slavery in Western Culture* (Ithaca, N.Y., 1966), pp. 207–11.

17. Scherer, *Slavery and the Churches*, pp. 90–91; William R. Riddell, "The Baptism of Slaves in Prince Edward Island," *Journal of Negro History*, vol. 6, no. 1 (July 1921), p. 308.

18. Robert T. Lewit, "Indian Missions and Antislavery Sentiment: A Conflict of Evangelical and Humanitarian Ideals," *Mississippi Valley Historical Review*, vol. 50, no. 2 (June 1963), pp. 41, 43.

19. Ibid., pp. 50, 53–54.

20. Jesse T. Peck, *The History of the Great Republic, Considered from a Christian Standpoint* (New York, 1868), p. 46; Fredrickson, *White Supremacy*, p. 76; William W. Sweet, *The Story of Religion in America* (New York, 1950 [1930]), p. 170; Willard, *History of the United States*, p. 46.

21. The other two were the three-fifths compromise for determining the representation of the slave population and a call for a fugitive slave law.

22. Quoted in the Waterloo (Iowa) *Black Hawk Courier*, January 18, 1859.

23. Peter Duignan and L. H. Gann, *The United States and Africa: A History* (New York, 1984), p. 100; John R. McKivigan, *The War Against Proslavery Religion: Abolitionism and the Northern Churches, 1830–1865* (Ithaca, N.Y., 1984), p. 107.

24. Jernagan, "Slavery and Conversion in the American Colonies," p. 505; Colin A. Palmer, "Religion and Magic in Mexican Slave Society, 1570–1650," *Race and Slavery in the Western Hemisphere: Quantitative Studies* (Stanley L. Engerman and Eugene D. Genovese, eds., Princeton, N.J., 1975), pp. 312–13.

25. Herbert S. Klein, "Anglicanism, Catholicism, and the Negro Slave," *Slavery in the New World: A Reader in Comparative History* (Laura Foner and Eugene D. Genovese, eds., Englewood Cliffs, N.J., 1969), p. 140. Reprinted from *Comparative Studies in Society and History*, vol. VIII, no. 3 (April 1966), pp. 295–327.

26. Peck, *The History of the Great Republic*, p. 45. For a detailed discussion of Las Casas and his early support of black slavery, see Ronald Sanders, *Lost Tribes and Promised Lands: The Origins of American Racism* (Boston, 1978), chapter XIV, especially pp. 158–60. Also useful is Stephen Neill, *Colonization and Christian Mission* (London, 1966), pp. 51ff. In "The Church and Racism: Toward a More Fraternal Society" (February 23, 1989), p. 616, the Vatican's Pontifical Justice and Peace Commission described Las Casas's "resolute commitment on the side of the Indians" and praised his work as "one of the first contributions to the doctrine of universal human rights, based on the dignity of the person, regardless of his or her ethnic or religious affiliation." The

document said nothing about his initial proposal calling for the enslavement of thousands of Africans. Except for a brief footnote acknowledging that the report's historical review (pp. 615–17) "by no means implies an effort to gloss over the weaknesses and even, at times, the complicity of certain church leaders, as well as other members of the church," the Commission in fact had only praise for the Catholic church's "constant concern for the deeper respect of indigenous peoples."

27. Gary B. Nash, *Red, White, and Black: The Peoples of Early America* (Englewood Cliffs, N.J., 1982 [1974]), pp. 155–56, 274; Mary Veronica Miceli, "The Influence of the Roman Catholic Church on Slavery in Colonial Louisiana under French Domination, 1718–1763" (Ph.D. dissertation, Tulane University, 1979), p. 58.

28. For a discussion of this point, see Frederick Perry Noble, *The Redemption of Africa: A Story of Civilization, with Maps, Statistical Tables and Select Bibliography of the Literature of African Missions* (Chicago, 1899), vol. I, p. 7; and C. Eric Lincoln, *Race, Religion, and the Continuing American Dilemma* (New York, 1984), pp. 28–29. See also C. Vann Woodward, *American Counterpoint: Slavery and Racism in the North-South Dialogue* (New York, 1983 [1964]), pp. 47–77.

29. *Five Slave Narratives: A Compendium* (New York, 1968), p. vi, quoting Cartwright, "Slavery in the Light of Ethnology," pp. 713–26; William Wells Brown, *My Southern Home: or, The South and Its People* (Boston, 1880), p. 12; Alice Felt Tyler, *Freedom's Ferment: Phases of American Social History from the Colonial Period to the Civil War* (New York, 1962 [1944]), p. 519.

30. Patterson, *Slavery and Social Death*, pp. 273–75. In his introduction to the 1962 edition of Harriet Martineau's *Society in America* (New York, 1837), p. 10, Seymour Martin Lipset argued that Martineau assumed "that the country's basic moral values were a major factor in determining its institutional character." When those moral values conflicted with "institutional reality," they "engendered a strong force towards bringing the practices into line—though she recognized that changes in other institutions, particularly the economic and political, could greatly affect the value system." It is not clear just what "other institutions," besides the economic and political, Lipset had in mind. Moreover, economic and political forces did not just "greatly affect" the value system; in the South they redefined it. Virtually every Protestant church in early-nineteenth-century America had criticized slavery. By 1830 the southern constituencies of these same denominations had become bastions of proslavery sentiment. See *infra*, chapter 8.

31. Jernagan, "Slavery and Conversion in the American Colonies," pp. 509–10; Herbert S. Klein, *Slavery in the Americas: A Comparative Study of Virginia and Cuba* (Chicago, 1967), p. 113; Nash, *Red, White, and Black*, p. 187.

32. Greene, *The Negro in Colonial New England*, p. 269.

33. Ruchames, ed., *Racial Thought in America*, p. 64. The full title of Mather's work is *The Negro Christianized: An Essay to Excite and Assist that Good Work, the Instruction of Negro Servants in Christianity* (Boston, 1706). See also Gilbert Osofsky, ed., *The Burden of Race: A Documentary History of Negro-White Relations in America* (New York, 1967), pp. 35–39.

34. Lovejoy, *Religious Enthusiasm in the New World*, p. 198; James D. Essig, *The Bonds of Wickedness: American Evangelicals against Slavery, 1770–1808* (Philadelphia, 1983), pp. 11–13.

35. John Lee Eighmy, *Churches in Cultural Captivity; A History of the Social Attitudes of Southern Baptists* (rev. ed., Knoxville, Tenn., 1987), pp. 5–6, citing Richard Furman, *Exposition of the Baptists in Relation to the Colored Populations of the United States in a Communication to the Governor of South Carolina* (Charleston, 1823).

36. Pinckney, *An Address Delivered in Charleston, before the Agricultural Society of South Carolina at Its Anniversary Meeting, on Tuesday, the 18th of August, 1829* (Charleston, S.C., 1829). The published version of the speech "ran through two editions," Susan Markey Fickling wrote, "and was reviewed at length by Dr. James O. Andrews of Augusta, Georgia, in the *Methodist Magazine and Quarterly Review* for July 1831, when nearly the whole

address was quoted." See Fickling, *Slave-Conversion in South Carolina, 1830–1860* (Columbia, S.C., 1924), p. 15. See also Kyle Haselden, *The Racial Problem in Christian Perspective* (New York, 1964 [1959]), pp. 35–36; and Donald G. Mathews: "The Methodist Mission to the Slaves, 1829–1844," *Journal of American History*, vol. LI, no. 4 (March 1965), p. 618, and *Religion in the Old South* (Chicago, 1977), p. 140.

37. William W. Brown, *Narrative of William Wells Brown, a Fugitive Slave, Written by Himself* (Boston, 1847), pp. 83–84. See also Julius Lester, ed., *To Be a Slave* (New York, 1968), p. 78; and Gilbert Osofsky, ed., *Puttin' On Ole Massa: The Slave Narratives of Henry Bibb, William Wells Brown, and Solomon Northup* (New York, 1969), p. 211.

38. Lester, ed., *To Be a Slave*, p. 78.

39. De Jong, "The Dutch Reformed Church and Negro Slavery in Colonial America," p. 431; Lawrence W. Levine, *Black Culture and Black Consciousness: Afro-American Folk Thought from Slavery to Freedom* (New York, 1977), p. 60. See also Alho, *The Religion of the Slaves*, pp. 54, 58–59.

40. Quoted in John Frederick Woolverton, *Colonial Anglicanism in North America* (Detroit, 1984), p. 72. See also George H. Moore, *Notes on the History of Slavery in Massachusetts* (New York, 1968 [1866]), p. 79.

41. Quoted in Klingberg, *An Appraisal of the Negro in Colonial South Carolina*, pp. 6–7.

42. Brydon, *Virginia's Mother Church*, vol. I, pp. 186–87, 368, 399–400, 470.

43. Klingberg, *Anglican Humanitarianism in Colonial New York*, passim; Jernagan, "Slavery and Conversion in the American Colonies," pp. 518, 521–22; Herbert S. Klein, *Slavery in the Americas: A Comparative Study of Virginia and Cuba* (Chicago, 1967), p. 114; Thomas F. Gossett, *Race: The History of an Idea in America* (New York, 1965 [1963]), p. 31; Van Horne, ed., *Religious Philanthropy and Colonial Slavery*, passim; Robert Baird, *The Progress and Prospects of Christianity in the United States of America; with Remarks on the Subject of Slavery in America; and on the Intercourse between British and American Churches* (London, [1851]), p. 2.

44. Lincoln, *Race, Religion, and the Continuing American Dilemma*, p. 38. The resistance to slave conversion was strong throughout the Protestant New World. Methodist and Baptist missionaries in Jamaica not only faced opposition from planters but—when the churches launched attacks on the transplanted African's heathen "superstitions" and preached the "virtues of thrift, industry, and social peace"—from the slaves themselves. Similarly, the Calvinist churches in the Dutch West Indies supported many missionaries, but ended up with little to show for it. Between the opposition of the planters and the lingering influence of the slave's traditional religion, the Protestant missionary influence in the Caribbean remained negligable at least to the end of the eighteenth century. See Eugene D. Genovese, *Roll, Jordan, Roll: The World the Slaves Made* (New York, 1972), pp. 168–69, 173–74; and Orlando Patterson, *Sociology of Slavery: An Analysis of the Origins, Development, and Structure of Negro Slave Society in Jamaica* (Rutherford, N.J., 1969 [1967]), pp. 72–73, 207.

45. Albert J. Raboteau, *Slave Religion: The "Invisible Institution" in the Antebellum South* (New York, 1978), p. 66.

46. Allan Gallay, "The Origins of Slaveholders' Paternalism: George Whitefield, the Bryan Family, and the Great Awakening in the South," *Journal of Southern History*, vol. 53, no. 3 (August 1987), p. 373; H. Shelton Smith, *In His Image . . . : Racism in Southern Religion, 1780–1910* (Durham, N.C., 1972), p. 8; Jernagan, "Slavery and Conversion in the American Colonies," pp. 521–22; Woolverton, *Colonial Anglicanism*, p. 161; Stephen J. Stein, "George Whitefield on Slavery: Some New Evidence," *Church History*, vol. 42, no. 2 (June 1973), p. 244; Lovejoy, *Religious Enthusiasm in the New World*, p. 199; Alho, *The Religion of the Slaves*, p. 50; Curtis P. Nettels, *The Roots of American Civilization: A History of American Colonial Life* (New York, 1963), p. 479; Bonomi, *Under the Cope of Heaven*, p. 119; Luther P. Jackson, "Religious

Development of the Negro in Virginia from 1760 to 1860," *Journal of Negro History*, vol. 16, no. 2 (April 1931), p. 168; Greene, *The Negro in Colonial New England*, p. 257.

47. Van Horne, ed., *Religious Philanthropy*, p. 68.

48. Olmsted, *The Cotton Kingdom*, p. 461. Stiles Bailey Lines argued that the masters' resistance to slave conversion eroded significantly after 1840. See "Slaves and Churchmen: The Work of the Episcopal Church among Southern Negroes" (Ph.D. dissertation, Columbia University, 1960), pp. 118–23. Confining himself exclusively to the Episcopal church in South Carolina—which, in itself, limited the significance of his conclusion—Lines quoted numerous statements by clergymen exhorting planters to permit their bondsmen to be converted, but he did not indicate if there were any positive results. An analysis of church membership figures suggests that the ministers failed miserably. In 1840, approximately 2,500 of South Carolina's slave and free black people—less than 1 percent—were considered members of the Episcopal church. By the Eighth Census (1860), the percentage was almost exactly the same. For the nation as a whole, the numbers were even less impressive. In February 1861, the *Christian Observer* counted 7,000 black Episcopalians, or one out of every 635 black Americans. See Fickling, *Slave-Conversion in South Carolina*, pp. 49–50; Joel Williamson, *The Crucible of Race: Black-White Relations in the American South since Emancipation* (New York, 1984), p. 21; and Alho, *The Religion of the Slaves*, p. 58. For estimates of the black membership of some of South Carolina's Episcopal congregations before 1840, see Weatherford, *American Churches and the Negro*, pp. 38–40.

49. John B. Cade, "Out of the Mouths of Ex-Slaves," *Journal of Negro History*, vol. 20, no. 3 (July 1935), p. 331.

50. Harriet A. Jacobs, *Incidents in the Life of a Slave Girl, Written by Herself* (Cambridge, Mass., 1987 [1861]), p. 72.

51. Brown, *My Southern Home*, p. 3. In 1840, the year that Brown was referring to, blacks in Missouri constituted less than 16 percent of the state's population. At the other extreme were South Carolina, Louisiana, and Mississippi with 56, 55, and 52 percent, respectively.

52. B. A. Botkin, ed., *Lay My Burden Down: A Folk History of Slavery* (Chicago, 1945), pp. 25, 273.

53. Quoted in Klein, *Slavery in the Americas*, p. 121.

54. Henry Bibb, *Narrative of the Life and Adventures of Henry Bibb, an American Slave, Written by Himself* (New York, 1849), chapter 11, passim. See also Osofsky, ed., *Puttin' on Ole Massa*, pp. 123–29.

55. Cade, "Out of the Mouths of Ex-Slaves," pp. 329–31; Federal Writers' Project, *Slave Narratives: A Folk History of Slavery in the United States from Interviews with Former Slaves* (17 vols., Washington, D.C., 1941), vol. 17 (typescript), pp. 11–12. The term "paddy rollers," a slave colloquialism for slave "patrollers," has been reproduced in written form with several spellings, e.g., patterollers, patarollers, and patarolls. The title of a short poem recited by slaves was "Run Nigger Run—De Patarolls Ketch Yuh Jes 'fo Day." See the testimony of 83-year-old Henry Baker of Alabama in John W. Blassingame, ed., *Slave Testimony: Two Centuries of Letters, Speeches, Interviews, and Autobiographies* (Baton Rouge, La., 1977), pp. 656–59.

56. Van Horne, ed., *Religious Philanthropy*, p. 112.

57. Klein, *Slavery in the Americas*, p. 121; Alho, *The Religion of the Slaves*, p. 59; Winthrop D. Jordan, *White Over Black: American Attitudes toward the Negro, 1550–1812* (Chapel Hill, N.C., 1968), p. 363; Bolton, *Southern Anglicanism*, pp. 109–11.

58. Lester, ed., *To Be a Slave*, p. 82.

59. Osofsky, ed., *Puttin' on Ole Massa*, p. 68; Jacobs, *Incidents in the Life of a Slave Girl*, p. 73; Blassingame, ed., *Slave Testimony*, p. 712; Olmstead, *The Cotton Kingdom*, p. 473; Solomon Northup, *Twelve Years as a Slave: Narrative of Solomon Northup, a Citizen of New York*,

Kidnapped in Washington City in 1841, and Rescued in 1853, from a Cotton Plantation Near the Red River of Louisiana (Baton Rouge, La., 1968 [1853]), p. 69.

60. Joshua Coffin, *An Account of Some of the Principal Slave Insurrections and Others, Which Have Occurred, or Been Attempted, in the United States and Elsewhere, during the Last Two Centuries* (New York, 1860), pp. 10–11; Van Horne, ed., *Religious Philanthropy*, pp. 31–32; Lawrence W. Levine, "Slave Songs and Slave Consciousness," *Anonymous Americans: Explorations in Nineteenth-Century Social History* (Tamara K. Hareven, ed., Englewood Cliffs, N.J., 1971), pp. 120–21.

61. John Lovell, Jr., *Black Song: The Forge and the Flame: The Story of How the Afro-American Spiritual Was Hammered Out* (New York, 1972), pp. 228–29.

62. Lester, *To Be a Slave*, p. 82.

63. Lovell, *Black Song*, p. 191.

64. Vincent Harding, *There Is a River: The Black Struggle for Freedom in America* (New York, 1981), pp. 111, 117–19, and passim.

65. Lovell, *Black Song*, pp. 113–17. Lovell posited an unusual theory when he contradicted the common opinion that the slave sang of his next life because he knew he would never improve his status in this one. On the contrary, he argued, the *white* spirituals of the camp meetings were primarily about the hereafter since life in this world was about as good as it would get but the "perfections of heaven" promised improvement in the next life. On the other hand, the slave's earthly life could get no worse, so the anticipation of improving it was real. Thus he sang of "the most banal incidents of everyday life," telling of "life in the fields, . . . in the shops, at home, in religious meeting." For black people, Lovell concluded, the spirituals covered "the whole range of group experience, except sex."

66. On the order of his master, Edwin Epps, Northup had whipped Patsey mercilessly. His later description clearly reflected his agony over being forced to treat a fellow slave with such cruelty: "She had a dim perception of God and of eternity, and a still more dim perception of a Saviour who had died even for such as her. She entertained but confused notions of a future life—not comprehending the distinction between the corporeal and spiritual existence. Happiness, in her mind, was exemption from stripes—from labor—from the cruelty of masters and overseers." See *Twelve Years as a Slave*, pp. 199–200.

67. Gerald W. Mullin, *Flight and Rebellion: Slave Resistance in Eighteenth-Century Virginia* (New York, 1972), p. 149; Harding, *There Is a River*, pp. 55, 67–69, 85–88, 94–95; Marty, *Righteous Empire*, pp. 28–31; Kenneth M. Stampp, *The Peculiar Institution: Slavery in the Ante-Bellum South* (New York, 1956), pp. 156–57; Genovese, *Roll, Jordan, Roll*, p. 185; John B. Duff and Peter M. Mitchell, eds., "Confessions of Nat Turner," John B. Duff and Peter M. Mitchell, eds., *The Nat Turner Rebellion: The Historical Event and the Modern Controversy* (New York, 1971), pp. 17–18.

68. Herbert Aptheker, *American Negro Slave Revolts* (New York, 1943); Joseph C. Carroll, *Slave Insurrections in the United States, 1800–1860* (Boston, 1938); and Nicholas Halasz, *Rattling Chains: Slave Unrest and Revolt in the Antebellum South* (New York, 1966); Degler, *Out of Our Past*, pp. 168–69.

69. Gallay, "The Origins of Slaveholders' Paternalism," p. 380; Lovejoy, *Religious Enthusiasm in the New World*, p. 199; Alho, *Religion of the Slaves*, p. 50; Van Horne, ed., *Religious Philanthropy*, p. 34; Woolverton, *Colonial Anglicanism*, p. 161; Lovell, *Black Song*, pp. 149–50; Olmsted, *The Cotton Kingdom*, pp. 349, 461–62.

70. Fredrika Bremer, *The Homes of the New World: Impressions of America* (trans. by Mary Howitt, 2 vols., New York, 1853), vol. II, p. 190; Olmsted, *The Cotton Kingdom*, pp. 462–66.

71. Thomas W. Talley, *Negro Folk Rhymes: Wise and Otherwise* (New York, 1922), pp. 300–301; Olmsted, *The Cotton Kingdom*, pp. 461, 466.

72. Davis, *The Problem of Slavery in Western Culture*, pp. 26–27; Greene, *The Negro in*

Colonial New England, pp. 276–77; William Dillon Piersen, "Afro-American Culture in Eighteenth Century New England: A Comparative Examination" (Ph.D. dissertation, Indiana University, 1975), p. 132; Nash, *Red, White, and Black*, p. 187; Lincoln, *Race, Religion, and the Continuing American Dilemma*, p. 41; Nettels, *The Roots of American Civilization*, p. 480.

73. Peter H. Wood, *Black Majority: Negroes in Colonial South Carolina, from 1670 through the Stono Rebellion* (New York, 1974), pp. 141–42; Andrew E. Murray, *Presbyterians and the Negro—A History* (Philadelphia, 1966), p. 10; Bonomi, *Under the Cope of Heaven*, pp. 252–53n.; Alho, *Religion of the Slaves*, p. 51.

74. Nettels, *The Roots of American Civilization*, p. 479; Levine, *Black Culture and Black Consciousness*, p. 61. See also Jernagan, "Slavery and Conversion in the American Colonies," pp. 504, 517, 517n., and passim; Klingberg, *Anglican Humanitarianism*, p. 131; Lovell, *Black Song*, p. 181; [Isabella Lucy (Bird) Bishop], *The Aspects of Religion in the United States* (London, 1859), p. 96; and Manross, *A History of the American Episcopal Church*, p. 137.

75. Alho, *Religion of the Slaves*, p. 51; Melville J. Herskovits, *The Myth of the Negro Past* (New York, 1958 [1941]), pp. 232–35. Donald G. Mathews, the chief chronicler of the early Methodists, has pointed out that the Baptist conversions were not part of an *organized* missionary effort, as was the case with the Methodists, but were largely the result of the Baptists' congregational independence. See "The Methodist Mission to the Slaves, 1829–1844," p. 628.

76. Levine, *Black Culture and Black Consciousness*, p. 42; Leon F. Litwack, *Been in the Storm So Long: The Aftermath of Slavery* (New York, 1979), pp. 458–60.

77. C. C. Goen, *Broken Churches, Broken Nation: Denominational Schisms and the Coming of the Civil War* (Macon, Ga., 1985), p. 118; Alho, *Religion of the Slaves*, pp. 53–54.

78. The Presbyterians were not the only ones who ridiculed the Methodists for their lack of restraint, and the criticism reached beyond the southern camp meetings. The Methodists, for their part, did not believe there was reason to be embarrassed. "They saw emotion as a legitimate part of religious worship," Richard Carwardine has written. "Revivals they agreed could sometimes be noisy, but they made no apologies for this, arguing that it was sheer presumption to question the way in which the Holy Spirit operated." See "The Second Great Awakening in the Urban Centers: An Examination of Methodism and the 'New Measures,' " *Journal of American History*, vol. 59, no. 2 (September 1972), pp. 351–52.

79. Robert L. Hall, "Black and White Christians in Florida, 1822–1861," *Masters & Slaves in the House of the Lord: Race and Religion in the American South, 1740–1870* (John B. Boles, ed., Lexington, Ky., 1988), p. 94; Sarah M. Grimké, *An Epistle to the Clergy of the Southern States* (New York, 1836), p. 13; Murray, *Presbyterians and the Negro*, p. 65; Stampp, *Peculiar Institution*, pp. 371–73; Raboteau, *Slave Religion*, pp. 55–57; Lines, "Slaves and Churchmen," p. 135; Lincoln, *Race, Religion, and the Continuing American Dilemma*, p. 47; Williamson, *The Crucible of Race*, p. 21.

80. Sweet, *The Story of Religion in America*, p. 58. See also Katherine L. Dvorak, "After Apocalypse, Moses," *Masters & Slaves in the House of the Lord*, p. 189.

81. Cf. Alho, *Religion of the Slaves*, pp. 55–56, 58; Hall, "Black and White Christians in Florida, 1822–1861," p. 88; and Ben J. Wattenberg, ed., *The Statistical History of the United States: From Colonial Times to the Present* (New York, 1976), p. 392. The increase for all Methodists was from 65,000 in 1800 to 1,661,000 in 1860. Since these figures include black members, the rate of increase for whites only was even higher than two to one.

82. Fickling, *Slave-Conversion in South Carolina*, pp. 49–50; Williamson, *The Crucible of Race*, p. 21.

83. James W. C. Pennington, *The Fugitive Blacksmith; or, Events in the History of James W. C. Pennington* (London, 1849), p. 51; Mathews, *Religion in the Old South*, p. 137; Alho, *Religion of the Slaves*, p. 58.

84. Smith, *In His Image*, p. 229. But the conversion success of southern Methodists

apparently did not last. Between 1860 and 1866, according to one researcher's calculations, the number of black Methodists in the South declined by over 62 percent; and "[t]hose who remained were set apart by the General Conference" into the "Colored Methodist Episcopal Church." See Lewis McCarroll Purifoy, Jr., "The Methodist Episcopal Church, South, and Slavery, 1844–1865" (Ph.D. dissertation, University of North Carolina, 1965), p. 228.

85. Henry Warner Bowden, *American Indians and Christian Missions: Studies in Cultural Conflict* (Chicago, 1981), p. xv; Yasuhide Kawashima, *Puritan Justice and the Indian* (Middletown, Conn.), pp. 106–107, 110–13; Robert F. Berkhofer, *Salvation and the Savage: An Analysis of Protestant Missions and American Indian Response* (Westport, Conn., 1977 [1965]), p. 153; Linda K. Kerber, "The Abolitionist Perception of the Indian," *Journal of American History*, vol. 62, no. 2 (September 1975), pp. 283–85; Roy Harvey Pearce, *The Savages of America: A Study of the Indian and the Idea of Civilization* (rev. ed., Baltimore, 1965 [1953]), p. 61; Philip Borden, "Found Cumbering the Soil: Manifest Destiny and the Indian in the Nineteenth Century," *The Great Fear: Race and the Mind of America* (Gary B. Nash and Richard Weiss, eds., New York, 1970), pp. 76–77.

86. Genovese, *Roll, Jordan, Roll*, pp. 184–85; Levine, "Slave Songs and Slave Consciousness," p. 114; Patterson, *Slavery and Social Death*, p. 73; E. Franklin Frazier, *The Negro Church in America* (New York, 1964), pp. 6–19; Timothy L. Smith, "Slavery and Theology: The Emergence of Black Christian Consciousness in Nineteenth-Century America," *Church History*, vol. 41, no. 4 (December 1972), p. 497; John B. Boles, ed., *Masters & Slaves in the House of the Lord*, p. 5; Williamson, *The Crucible of Race*, p. 21.

87. Winthrop S. Hudson, "The American Context as an Area for Research in Black Church Studies," *Church History*, vol. 52, no. 2 (June 1983), p. 159.

88. John W. Blassingame, *The Slave Community: Plantation Life in the Antebellum South* (rev. ed., New York, 1979), p. 93.

89. The "vast" and "overwhelming" majorities described by Hudson and Blassingame simply have no basis in fact. Neither writer cited any empirical, circumstantial, or even impressionistic data to support such astonishing conclusions. The only evidence that was overwhelming was the testimony of both slaves and clergymen on the opposition of the slaveholders and the paucity of converted slaves, testimony that was virtually unchanged from Morgan Godwyn (1680) to Frederick Law Olmsted (1856). Blassingame identified as one source (p. 93, n. 86) the *Journals* of the annual conventions of the Episcopal church in eight southern states from 1839 to 1860, an unlikely source of overwhelming numbers since, according to the *Christian Observer* (February 1861), there were only 7,000 black Episcopalians in all fifteen slave states—less than .002 percent of the total slave population. He also listed articles in the *Southern Presbyterian Review*, *Religious Herald* (Baptist), and *Southern Episcopalian*; and WPA interviews of eleven former slaves collected in George P. Rawick, ed., *The American Slave: A Composite Autobiography* (31 vols., Westport, Conn., 1972–78). Three of the former slaves said nothing about religion. Of the remaining eight, two mentioned masters who read the Bible to their bondsmen, one described a mistress who read Bible stories to the slaves, one identified a master who called his slaves in for evening prayers, and one described a plantation where slaves "occasionally" attended their master's church. Only three of those interviewed said that everyone went to church on Sunday. Equally unsubstantiated was Boles's declaration that a "majority of slaves" became Christians in the century after 1750. Using Blassingame as his authority, he criticized Sterling Stuckey for citing the same figures as Albert Raboteau but coming to the opposite conclusion. Stuckey and Raboteau had quoted the calculation that had originally appeared in *Christian Observer* (February 1861), showing 468,000 black church members in the South in 1859, but only Stuckey was surprised that the number was so small—perhaps because it was barely 11 percent of the southern black (slave and free) popula-tion. Moreover, the fact that so many observers, like

Olmsted, considered it a rare master who allowed his slaves to hear the gospel is completely contrary to Boles's contention that far more blacks attended church than were members. See Boles, ed., *Masters & Slaves in the House of the Lord,* p. 193; Raboteau, *Slave Religion,* pp. 209–10; and Sterling Stuckey, *Slave Culture: Nationalist Theory and the Foundations of Black America* (New York, 1987), p. 367.

90. Agreement on when and how many slaves converted has not been unanimous. Olli Alho argued that the effort to convert slaves actually *declined* in the latter part of the eighteenth century and that the year 1830 marked an upward turning point in the effort to convert slaves into Christians mainly because of "a growing activism in Georgia and South Carolina." See Alho, *The Religion of the Slaves,* pp. 53–54, 55.

91. [Bishop], *Aspects of Religion in the United States,* p. 108; William Aikman, *The Future of the Colored Race in America: Being an Article in the Presbyterian Quarterly Review, of July, 1862* (Philadelphia, 1862), pp. 29–30; Milton Bryan Powell, "The Abolitionist Controversy in the Methodist Episcopal Church, 1840–1864" (Ph.D. dissertation, State University of Iowa, 1963), p. 10; Baird, *Progress and Prospects of Christianity in the United States,* pp. 33–34.

92. Marty, *Righteous Empire,* p. 27.

93. Peter G. Mode, *The Frontier Spirit in American Christianity* (New York, 1923), p. 17, citing Gookin, "Historical Collections of Indians in New England," *Collections Massachusetts Historical Society,* series I, vol. I, p. 195.

94. Clifton H. Johnson, *God Struck Me Dead: Religious Conversion Experiences and Autobiographies of Ex-Slaves* (Philadelphia, 1965), p. ix, also available in Rawick, ed., *The American Slave,* vol. XIX, p. vi; Lovell, *Black Song,* pp. 147–54, 182–83, 193; Levine, "Slave Songs and Slave Consciousness," p. 115; Stuckey, *Slave Culture,* p. 27.

95. In the late 1940s, psychologist B. F. Skinner generated a heated controversy by dismissing things like mind, feelings, religion, and freedom as essential elements in developmental psychology in favor of *operant conditioning,* a reward-and-punishment view of human behavior that he had formulated as a result of experiments with pigeons. According to Skinner's thesis, freedom is an illusion and human behavior is shaped exclusively by external forces; feelings and mental processes are the by-products of a continuous cycle of stimulus and response, in which one repeats actions that are rewarded and eschews those that result in punishment or those for which there is no response at all. According to operant conditioning, the transplanted African, responding to favorable stimuli, was simply adapting to his environment. Accordingly, his adoption of the master's religion was nothing more than the repetition of an action that was rewarded.

96. Harding, *There Is a River,* p. 43. This was also a fundamental theme of the chapter on "The Poor" in Eric Hoffer's *The True Believer: Thoughts on the Nature of Mass Movements* (New York, 1951): "It is obvious that a proselytizing mass movement must break down all existing group ties if it is to win a considerable following. The ideal potential convert is the individual who stands alone, who has no collective body he can blend with and lose himself in and so mask the pettiness, meaninglessness and shabbiness of his individual existence" (p. 36).

97. Alexis de Tocqueville, *Democracy in America* (ed. J. P. Mayer and Max Lerner, trans. by George Lawrence, New York, 1966 [1835]), p. 292; Stampp, *Peculiar Institution,* p. 371; Genovese, *Roll, Jordan, Roll,* pp. 161–68, 183–93.

98. *Poems on Various Subjects, Religious and Moral* (Boston, 1773), from the poem "To the University of Cambridge in New England," in Julian D. Mason, Jr., ed., *The Poems of Phillis Wheatley* (Chapel Hill, N.C., 1966), p. 5. See also M. A. Richmond, *Bid the Vassal Soar: Interpretive Essays on the Life and Poetry of Phillis Wheatley (ca. 1753–1784) and George Moses Horton (ca. 1797–1883)* (Washington, D.C., 1974); and John C. Shields, ed., *The Collected Works of Phillis Wheatley* (New York, 1988).

99. Benjamin Brawley, *The Negro in Literature and Art in the United States* (New York, 1934), p. 31; Mason, ed., *Poems of Phillis Wheatley*, p. xiii.

100. Wheatley was only the best-known black poet to extol the virtues of Christianity. In 1760, Jupiter Hammon published the first of several poetic and prose works, heavily supported by biblical references, that were passionate tributes to his faith, including, in 1778, "An Address to Mis Phillis Wheatley." See Stanley A. Ransom, ed., *America's First Negro Poet: The Complete Works of Jupiter Hammon of Long Island* (Port Washington, N.Y., 1970).

101. Mason, ed., *The Poems of Phillis Wheatley*, p. 7. Some scholars have suggested that Wheatley was originally from the Senegal region of West Africa, but this has never been confirmed. Nor was she the last black poet to praise white Christians for rescuing the damned of Africa. On New Year's Day, 1808, a service at Absalom Jones's St. Thomas African Episcopal Church in Philadelphia included a hymn with these lines by Michael Fortune:

Lift up your souls to God on high,
The fountain of eternal grace,
Who, with a tender father's eye,
Look'd down on Afric's helpless race!
The nations hear His stern commands!
Britannia kindly sets us free;
Columbia tears the galling bands,
And gives the sweets of liberty.

See Ruth Miller, ed., Blackamerican Literature: 1760 to Present (Beverly Hills, Calif., 1971), pp. 41–42.

102. Mason, ed., *The Poems of Phillis Wheatley*, p. 7; William L. Van Deburg, *Slavery and Race in American Popular Culture* (Madison, Wis., 1984), p. 57.

103. Mason, ed., *The Poems of Phillis Wheatley*, pp. xi–xvi.

104. Roger Bastide, "Color, Racism, and Christianity," *Daedalus: Journal of the American Academy of Arts and Sciences* (Spring 1967), p. 324.

105. Max Lerner, *America as a Civilization: Life and Thought in the United States Today* (New York, 1957), p. 18.

106. Patterson, *Slavery and Social Death*, pp. 74–76.

107. A conspicuous exception was the Ewe people of Abomey.

108. Patterson, *Sociology of Slavery*, p. 183; John S. Mbiti, *African Religions & Philosophy* (New York, 1969), p. 103; Geoffrey Parrinder, *Religion in Africa* (New York, 1969), p. 26.

109. Genovese, *Roll, Jordan, Roll*, p. 211. Genovese also argued that the early Jews accommodated this idea by shifting the blame for their historical oppression from God to themselves. If persecution was punishment for misbehavior, God, since he could not do anything wrong, was exonerated from all responsibility for whatever suffering one endures. The ultimate consequence of this posture, of course, has been the celebrated self-flagellation that has become so much a part of the collective Jewish psyche.

110. Paul Jacobs, Saul Landau, and Eve Pell, eds., *To Serve the Devil* (2 vols., New York, 1971), vol. I, *Natives and Slaves*, p. 46.

111. Ibid., vol. I, pp. 65–66.

112. Louis Thomas Jones, *Aboriginal American Oratory: The Tradition of Eloquence among the Indians of the United States* (Los Angeles, 1965), pp. 64–65.

113. Stampp, *Peculiar Institution*, p. 374; Van Horne, ed., *Religious Philanthropy and Colonial Slavery*, p. 34. For specific biblical references, see Deuteronomy 18:9–12 and Isaiah 47:9–13.

114. Levine, *Black Culture and Black Consciousness*, p. 59.

115. According to Richard Weisman, *Witchcraft, Magic, and Religion in Seventeenth-Century Massachusetts* (Amherst, Mass., 1983), pp. 8–12, the "seminal work" of the witch-devil association "is generally acknowledged by historians to be the *Malleus Maleficarum* composed in 1486 by the German inquisitors Heinrich Institoris and Jakob Sprenger under the authority of a papal bull issued by Innocent VIII in 1484." This was an enormously popular work and, between 1487 and 1669, was reprinted in twenty-nine editions in Italy, France, and Germany. The first English translation did not appear until 1584, which was also the publication date of Reginald Scot's *Discoverie of Witchcraft*. In his introduction to Marin L. Starkey's *The Devil in Massachusetts: A Modern Inquiry into the Salem Witch Trials* (New York, 1949), p. xviii, Aldous Huxley wrote that the "lore of witchcraft was given its definitive forms" in *Malleus Maleficarum* (literally, *The Hammer of Witches*) and identified the authors as Sprenger and a Father Kramer, both Dominican priests. For a review of the European background to American witchcraft, see Alan C. Kors and Edward Peters, eds., *Witchcraft in Europe, 1100–1700: A Documentary History* (Philadelphia, 1972); Peters, *The Magician, the Witch, and the Law* (Philadelphia, 1982); Donald Nugent, "The Renaissance and/of Witchcraft," *Church History*, vol. 40, no. 1 (March 1971), pp. 69–78; Julio Caro Baroja, *The World of the Witches* (trans. by O.N.Y. Glendinning, Chicago, 1961); and Michael Kunze, *Highroad to the Stake: A Tale of Witchcraft* (trans. by William E. Yuill, Chicago, 1987).

116. Joseph Klaits, *Servants of Satan: The Age of the Witch Hunts* (Bloomington, Ind., 1985), p. 1; David E. Stannard, *The Puritan Way of Death: A Study in Religion, Culture, and Social Change* (New York, 1977), p. 36.

117. Weisman, *Witchcraft, Magic, and Religion*, p. 5. For another perspective of this point, see Jon Butler, "Magic, Astrology, and the Early American Religious Heritage, 1600–1760," *American Historical Review*, vol. 84, no. 2 (April 1979), pp. 317–46.

118. Lovell, *Black Song*, p. 30.

119. Palmer, "Religion and Magic in Mexican Slave Society, 1570–1650," p. 319.

120. Stampp, *Peculiar Institution*, pp. 374–75; Geoffrey Parrinder, *Witchcraft: European and African* (London, 1963 [1958]), pp. 117–18.

121. Arthur Miller, *The Crucible: A Play in Four Acts* (Bantam ed., New York, 1959 [1952]), pp. 30–31. "When it is recalled that until the Christian era the underworld was never regarded as a hostile area," Miller added, "that all gods were useful and essentially friendly to man despite occasional lapses; when we see the steady and methodical inculcation into humanity of the idea of man's worthlessness—until redeemed—the necessity of the Devil may become evident as a weapon, a weapon designed and used time and time again in every age to whip men into surrender to a particular church or church-state."

122. Cotton Mather, *On Witchcraft: Being the Wonders of the Invisible World* (New York, 1974 [Boston, 1692]), pp. 3, 6. See also Increase Mather, *Essay for the Recording of Illustrious Providences* (Boston, 1684), and Cotton Mather, *Memorable Providences, Relating to Witchcrafts and Possessions* (Boston, 1689).

123. Cotton Mather, *Magnalia Christi Americana; or, The Ecclesiastical History of New-England; from Its First Planting, in the Year 1620, unto the Year of Our Lord 1698* (2 vols., New York, 1967 [1702]), vol. II, p. 473. Mather's "learn'd writers" were "Keeble on the Common Law, Chapt. *Conjuration*, (an author approv'd by the twelve judges of our nation:) also, Sir Matthew Hale's Trial of Witches, printed An. 1682; Glanvil's Collection of Sundry Trials in England and Ireland in the year 1658, 61, 63, 64, and 81; Bernard's Guide to Jury-men; Baxter's and R. B., their Histories about Witches, and their Discoveries; C. Mather's '*Memorable Providences*,' relating to witchcrafts, printed 1685."

124. Frederick C. Drake, "Witchcraft in the American Colonies, 1647–62," *American Quarterly*, vol. 20, no. 4 (Winter 1968), pp. 694–725. For an in-depth account of superstition in Puritan America, see John P. Demos, *Entertaining Satan: Witchcraft and the Culture of Early New*

England (New York, 1982). An older but still useful work is George L. Kittredge, *Witchcraft in Old and New England* (Cambridge, Mass., 1929). A description of the social conditions that led to the outbreak in Salem village in 1692 can be found in Paul Boyer and Stephen Nissenbaum, *Salem Possessed: The Social Origins of Witchcraft* (Cambridge, Mass., 1978).

125. George Lincoln Burr, ed., *Narratives of the Witchcraft Cases, 1648–1706* (New York, 1946 [1914]), pp. 309–10, 420.

126. Some historians have described Tituba as black and others as a West Indian immigrant of mixed African-Indian extraction. Her tormentors apparently considered her only an Indian. In the ten letters, affidavits, and other documents pertaining to her testimony, dated February 29 to May 23, 1692, she was always identified as "Tituba Indian," as though that was her full name. This was also how Mather saw her. See *Records of Salem Witchcraft, Copied from the Original Documents* (New York, 1969 [1864]), pp. 41–50; and Mather, *Magnalia Christi Americana*, vol. II, p. 471. For a provocative account of the role played by Tituba, see Starkey, *The Devil in Massachusetts*, pp. 41–46.

127. Larry M. James, "Biracial Fellowship in Antebellum Baptist Churches," *Masters & Slaves in the House of the Lord*, pp. 37–57. For another example of this predicament, see Mechal Sobel, *The World They Made Together: Black and White Values in Eighteenth-Century Virginia* (Princeton, N.J., 1987), chapter 4. Describing the interracial adaptation of the races, Sobel meticulously analyzed the contacts between whites and slaves in colonial Virginia but said virtually nothing about the many slaves who had few contacts with whites.

128. Gallay, "The Origins of Slaveholders' Paternalism," p. 35; Olmsted, *The Cotton Kingdom*, pp. 462, 468.

129. Hall, "Black and White Christians in Florida, 1822–1861," pp. 37–57; Gallay, "The Origins of Slaveholders' Paternalism," p. 393; Olmsted, *The Cotton Kingdom*, p. 378; Lines, "Slaves and Churchmen," pp. 134–35; Alho, *Religion of the Slaves*, pp. 58, 189–91; Levine, "Slave Songs and Slave Consciousness," p. 125.

130. Lines, "Slaves and Churchmen," pp. 137–41.

131. Blassingame, ed., *Slave Testimony*, pp. 410–11.

132. Jacobs, *Incidents in the Life of a Slave Girl*, p. 73.

133. Olmsted, *The Cotton Kingdom*, p. 473; Bibb, *Narrative*, p. 73.

134. Alden T. Vaughan, ed., *The Puritan Tradition in America, 1620–1730* (Columbia, S.C., 1972), p. 271; Greene, *The Negro in Colonial New England*, p. 288; Brown, *Narrative*, in Osofsky, ed., *Puttin' on Ole Massa*, p. 206; [Charles Ball], *Fifty Years in Chains; or The Life of an American Slave* (New York, 1858), p. 150. See also Piersen, "Afro-American Culture in Eighteenth Century New England," pp. 133–36.

135. Robert F. Berkhofer, Jr., *The White Man's Indian: Images of the American Indian from Columbus to the Present* (New York, 1978), pp. 19–20.

136. Norman Lewis, "English Missionary Interest in the Indians of North America, 1578–1700" (Ph.D. dissertation, University of Washington, 1968), p. 456; Berkhofer, *Salvation and the Savage*, p. 107; T. C. McCluhan, ed., *Touch the Earth: A Self-Portrait of Indian Existence* (New York, 1971), pp. 60–61, 63.

137. This sentence was part of a hypothetical response from a "noble savage" in a series of London debates in which SPG missionaries looked for ways to overcome the Indian's resistance to conversion: "I grant what you say, that the Christian religion doth propose many excellent advantages to those that believe and embrace it; but I have been otherwise educated, and cannot easily part with all my progenitors have lived and died in, and must have very convincing reasons to oblige me to forsake it: . . . [G]ive me a plain and positive answer, whether a heathen, continuing to be, may not be saved, if he take nature and reason to be his guide, and live soberly and virtuously? And why must all the world submit to you?" *Soberly and virtuously?* Even playing the Devil's Advocate, the Christian could not help

applying his moral standards to the Indian's perception of proper behavior. See Klingberg, *An Appraisal of the Negro in Colonial South Carolina*, p. 36.

138. Berkhofer, *Salvation and the Savage*, pp. 125, 127–28. One apologist for the Cayuse Indians who had attacked the mission at Wailatpu described the massacre as "humane" (by Indian standards) because—except for Marcus Whitman's wife—all the victims were men. This humaneness, Thomas E. Jessett claimed, resulted from the fact that the Indians were Christians. Such a conclusion calls for a complete suspension of disbelief. In the first place, if the Indians had converted, why did they believe they needed to kill anyone? Moreover, killing only men and adopting women and children was not an unusual Indian practice. Most absurd was the implication that if one is a Christian it is humane to murder only men. See Thomas E. Jessett, "Christian Missions to the Indians of Oregon," *Church History*, vol. 28, no. 2 (June 1969), p. 155. For a general discussion of the missionary problems with Indians in the Northwest, see Frederick A. Norwood, "Two Contrasting Views of the Indians: Methodist Involvement in the Indian Troubles in Oregon and Washington," *Church History*, vol. 49, no. 2 (June 1980), pp. 178–87.

139. Chirouse to Father Pascal Richard (January 12, 1849), in John Tracy Ellis, ed., *Documents of American Catholic History* (3 vols., Wilmington, Del., 1987), vol. II, pp. 296–300.

140. Blassingame, *The Slave Community*, p. 75; Genovese, *Roll, Jordan, Roll*, pp. 183–84; John K. Thornton, *The Kingdom of Kongo: Civil War and Transition, 1641–1718* (Madison, Wis., 1983), pp. 63–64. The adaptation of Christianity to a native's traditional religion was also common among Indians of Central and South America, where Catholic missionaries sometimes complained that it was Christianity that was doing *all* the adapting.

141. Quoted in Alho, *Religion of the Slaves*, p. 50.

142. Handlin, *Race and Nationality in American Life*, p. 30.

143. Kawashima, *Puritan Justice and the Indian*, pp. 110–13. Bad ideas take a long time to go away. In 1949, Yale University's Kenneth Scott Latourette, outgoing president of the American Historical Association and a recognized authority on American church history, praised the Christian missions for helping the Indians "adjust themselves wholesomely" to white culture. A few minutes later he complimented missionaries who had helped "the Negro in making a wholesome adjustment" to his new environment. Beginning from the assumption that Christianity was a necessary and beneficial force in the lives of Indians and slaves, Latourette could not ascribe to their native cultures anything worth preserving. See *Missions and the American Mind* (Indianapolis, 1949), pp. 21, 23. On the other hand, Robert F. Berkhofer maintained that the Americans' belief in their cultural superiority "forced the Indian to remain savage and guaranteed the failure of the missionary program." See *Salvation and the Savage*, p. 159.

144. Ola Elizabeth Winslow, *John Eliot, Apostle to the Indians* (Boston, 1968), p. 148; Lewis, "English Missionary Interest in Indians," p. 388; Marty, *Righteous Empire*, p. 8; Charles Lloyd Cohen, *God's Caress: The Psychology of Puritan Religious Experience* (New York, 1986), pp. 5–6.

145. Klingberg, *Anglican Humanitarianism in Colonial New York*, p. 131; Handlin, *Race and Nationality in American Life*, pp. 30–31; Berkhofer, *Salvation and the Savage*, p. 159; Francis J. Grund, *The Americans in Their Moral, Social, and Political Relations* (New York, 1968 [1837]), p. 226.

CHAPTER FIVE

1. For a brief but excellent review of the Lake Nyos disaster, see Curt Stager, *National Geographic*, vol. 172, no. 3 (September 1987), pp. 404–20.

2. See, for example, Eugene D. Genovese, *Roll, Jordan, Roll: The World the Slaves Made* (New York, 1972), pp. 183–93; and Orlando Patterson, *Slavery and Social Death: A Comparative Study* (Cambridge, Mass., 1982), p. 73.

3. John S. Mbiti, *African Religions & Philosophy* (New York, 1969), pp. 233–34; Robin Horton, "Stateless Societies in the History of West Africa," in J. F. A. Ajayi and Michael Crowder, eds., *History of West Africa* (2 vols., New York, 1972–73), vol. II, p. 106; Galbraith Welch, *Africa, Before They Came* (New York, 1965), p. 6; Mary H. Kingsley, *West African Studies* (London, 1901), p. 108.

4. For a discussion of the varieties and definitions of African traditional religion, see E. Bolagi Idowu, *African Traditional Religion: A Definition* (Maryknoll, N.Y., 1973).

5. Margo Jefferson and Elliott P. Skinner, *Roots of Time: A Portrait of African Life and Culture* (Garden City, N.Y., 1974), pp. 70–71.

6. P. C. Lloyd, "Osifekunde of Ijebu," in Philip D. Curtin, ed., *Africa Remembered: Narratives by West Africans from the Era of the Slave Trade* (Madison, Wis., 1967), pp. 274, 274n.; Welch, *Africa, Before They Came*, pp. 177–80.

7. *The Interesting Narrative of the Life of Olaudah Equiano, or Gustavus Vassa, the African, Written by Himself* (2 vols., London, 1789), vol. I, p. 27. The African perception of the High God was virtually identical to the Great Spirit that American Indians referred to, even when discussing nonreligious matters. See Louis Thomas Jones, *Aboriginal American Oratory: The Tradition of Eloquence among the Indians of the United States* (Los Angeles, 1965).

8. The names of the African High God ranged from Wele and Mulungu in East Africa to Nyambe and Oloroun in parts of West Africa. Although without physical form, the High God was almost always perceived as a male. The female Mawu of Dahomey, whose male counterpart was Lisa, was an exception. One of the reasons for the great variety of names, according to Nigerian scholar E. Bolagi Idowu, was the combination of suffixes and prefixes that were "descriptive of his character and emphatic of the fact that he is a reality and that he is not an abstract concept." For example, the Ibo's Chukwu combined Chi, meaning "Source-Being," and -ukwu, which means "great, immense, or undimensional." See Idowu, *African Traditional Religion*, pp. 149–50; Welch, *Africa, Before They Came*, pp. 177–80; Geoffrey Parrinder, ed., *World Religions: From Ancient History to the Present* (New York, 1983 [1971]), p. 62; Jefferson and Skinner, *Roots of Time*, pp. 70–71; and I. A. Akinjogbin, "The Expansion of Oyo and the Rise of Dahomey, 1600–1800," in Ajayi and Crowder, eds., *History of West Africa*, vol. II, p. 306. The New World Indians' High God had almost as many names as the Africans'. See Åke Hultkrantz, *The Religions of the American Indians* (Berkeley, Calif., 1967), pp. 15–26.

9. Okot p'Bitek, *African Religions in Western Scholarship* (Kampala, Uganda, [1970]), p. 125. See also Oli Alho, *The Religion of the Slaves: A Study of the Religious Tradition and Behaviour of Plantation Slaves in the United States, 1830–1865* (Helsinki, 1976), p. 45. One exception might be the "native high god" of the Ewe- and Tshi-speaking Ashanti peoples called Tando, who, appearing "to his priesthood as a giant, tawny-skinned, lank-haired, and wearing the Ashantee robe," inflicted disease upon those who had fallen behind in their sacrifices to him. See Kingsley, *West African Studies*, p. 98.

10. For a concise but complete discussion of the belief in a High God in that part of Africa from which most of the slaves were brought to the New World, see Geoffrey Parrinder, *West African Religions: A Study of the Beliefs and Practices of Akan, Ewe, Yoruba, Ibo, and Kindred Peoples* (London, 1969 [1949]), chapter 3. See also Parrinder, *Religion in Africa* (New York, 1969), chapter 3; Edwin W. Smith, ed., *African Ideas of God: A Symposium* (London, 1950), passim; and Newell S. Booth, Jr., "God and the Gods in West Africa," *African Religions: A Symposium* (ed. Newell S. Booth, Jr., New York, 1977), pp. 159–81.

11. Quoted in Parrinder, *West African Religions*, p. 14.

12. Harold Courlander, *Negro Folk Music, U.S.A.* (New York, 1963), p. 38.

13. "Theistic Beliefs of the Yoruba and Ewe Peoples of West Africa," in Smith, ed., *African Ideas of God*, p. 229; Parrinder, *West African Religions*, p. 24.

14. In this respect the African High God was not all that different from the Christian God perceived by John Calvin. "Indeed, his essence is incomprehensible," Calvin wrote in *Institutes*, "hence, his divineness far escapes all human perception." The Puritans believed that God was "not to be understood but to be adored," Perry Miller wrote. "He is simply the sum of all perfections, that being who is at one and the same the embodiment of perfect goodness and justice, perfect power and mercy, absolute righteousness and knowledge." The Calvinist may have believed in an inscrutable God, but understanding that status of the African supreme being nonetheless demanded a leap in open-mindedness that was restrained by the Christian's own ambivalence about the nature of God. In the West, Gordon D. Kaufman wrote, the word "God" signified, on the one hand, a being who is "faithful to man, trustworthy, loving, forgiving, merciful, and kind," and, on the other, a stern God who "demands 'perfection' of men (Matt. 5:48): before him one feels deeply his own lowliness, guilt, and sinfulness." See Hugh T. Kerr, ed., *Readings in Christian Thought* (Nashville, Tenn., 1966), p. 165; Perry Miller, *Errand into the Wilderness* (Cambridge, Mass., 1956), p. 51; and Gordon D. Kaufman, *God the Problem* (Cambridge, Mass., 1972), p. 91. It is not surprising that Kaufman does not even try to escape his own cultural blinders. Confining himself to Western conceptions of God, he virtually ignores Asian, African, or pre-Columbian New World notions of a supreme being. When he discusses systematic theology, he means *Christian* theology; and a chapter on "cultural history" describes only Western culture. See especially pp. 88–89, 99.

15. Kingsley, *West African Studies*, pp. 95–152; Welch, *Africa, Before They Came*, pp. 184, 186; Smith, ed., *African Ideas of God*, pp. 224–25; Benjamin C. Ray, *African Religions: Symbol, Ritual, and Community* (Englewood Cliffs, N.J., 1976), pp. 50–52, 64–65; Gary B. Nash, *Red, White, and Black: The Peoples of Early America* (2nd ed., Englewood Cliffs, N.J., 1982), p. 186; Curtin, ed., *Africa Remembered*, p. 274.

16. Akin Mabogunje, "The Land and People of West Africa," in Ajayi and Crowder, eds., *History of West Africa*, p. 23; Welch, *Africa, Before They Came*, p. 182. For a discussion of the cult of Shango and Christianity, see Lamin Sanneh, *West African Christianity: The Religious Impact* (London, 1983), pp. 84ff. Like the Africans, the American Indians counted spirits for virtually everything. In New England alone, according to a report by Roger Williams in 1643, the Nanhiggonsicks listed over three dozen gods, including a main god, Manit-manittó-wock, and gods for each direction on the compass, members of a family, heavenly bodies, and important forces like fire and sea. The familiar thunderbird that decorates Indian art throughout the New World was believed to create thunder by flapping its huge wings. See Hultkrantz, *The Religions of American Indians*, pp. 50–52. Many of the Indian god names, like those of the West African Ibo gods, were multisyllabic combinations of suffixes and prefixes which, when spelled phonetically in English, were real tongue twisters, e.g., Wompanànd, Chekesuwànd, Muckquachuckquànd, Keesuckquànd, Squàuanit, and Wunnanaméanit. See *The Complete Writings of Roger Williams* (7 vols., New York, 1963), vol. I, pp. 207–10, from *A Key into the Languages of America*, pp. 147–50.

17. For example, the Mandingo and Bambara recognized demon dwarfs called *Wokolo*; while the natives of the Lake Chad region tried to enhance their sex lives by invoking *Megboula*. The Mossi people recognized tree dwellers called *Tise*—demons larger than humans with feet on the tops of their bodies and heads at the bottom—who caused skin afflictions like pimples and boils; and protectors of children and pregnant women called *Kikirisi*, "some black, some red, who were about an inch tall, who loved sweets," but who became angry if offered something bitter or sour. The Zulus believed in a "furry dwarf"

called *Thikololoshi;* the Niger claimed that water spirits led by a chief named *Faro* lived in a fine house on the bottom of the river; and Ethiopians acknowledged demons called *Boudas*. In Dahomey and Yoruba, victims of smallpox were believed to have been infected by *Sapatan;* and people in the Ivory Coast feared *Asom*, the god of syphilis.

18. Welch, *Africa, Before They Came*, pp. 187–90.

19. Deuteronomy 18:9–12.

20. B[enjamin] A. Botkin, ed., *Lay My Burden Down: A Folk History of Slavery* (Chicago, 1945), pp. 36–38, 274.

21. Gilbert Osofsky, ed., *Puttin' on Ole Massa: The Slave Narratives of Henry Bibb, William Wells Brown, and Solomon Northup* (New York, 1969), pp. 36–37.

22. William Wells Brown, *The Negro in the American Rebellion: His Heroism and His Fidelity* (Boston, 1867), p. 113.

23. Ray, *African Religions*, p. 150.

24. Harriet A. Jacobs, *Incidents in the Life of a Slave Girl, Written by Herself* (Cambridge, Mass., 1987 [1861]), p. 70.

25. Botkin, ed., *Lay My Burden Down*, pp. 39, 274. WPA testimony of eighty-nine-year-old Ank Bishop of Livingstone, Alabama.

26. William Wells Brown, *My Southern Home: or, The South and Its People* (Boston, 1880), pp. 68, 124; Alho, *Religion of the Slaves*, pp. 110–12; John W. Blassingame, *The Slave Community: Plantation Life in the Antebellum South* (rev. ed., New York, 1979), p. 146.

27. Thomas W. Talley, *Negro Folk Rhymes: Wise and Otherwise* (New York, 1922), pp. 103, 228.

28. Parrinder, *West African Religion*, p. 113; Albert J. Raboteau, *Slave Religion: The "Invisible Institution" in the Antebellum South* (New York, 1978), p. 32.

29. Smith, ed., *African Ideas of God*, p. 227.

30. Ray, *African Religions*, p. 134; Henry Warner Bowden, *American Indians and Christian Missions: Studies in Cultural Conflict* (Chicago, 1981), p. 69.

31. George Bird Grinnell, *Pawnee Hero Stories and Folk Tales, with Notes on the Origin, Customs and Character of the Pawnee People* (New York, 1889), pp. 350–59, cited in Robert T. Handy, ed., "Religion among American Indians—Two Accounts," *Religion in the American Experience: The Pluralistic Style* (Columbia, S.C., 1972), p. 136.

32. Hilrie Shelton Smith, *Changing Conceptions of Original Sin: A Study in American Theology since 1750* (New York, 1955), p. 88.

33. Romans 7:18.

34. Genovese, *Roll, Jordan, Roll*, pp. 211–12; Parrinder, *West African Religions*, p. 56.

35. Alden T. Vaughan, ed., *The Puritan Tradition in America, 1620–1730* (Columbia, S.C., 1972), pp. 265–66; Bowden, *American Indians and Christian Missions*, pp. 82–83.

36. Charles Lloyd Cohen, *God's Caress: The Psychology of Puritan Religious Experience* (New York, 1986), p. 15; Mbiti, *African Religions & Philosophy*, pp. 4–5.

37. Quoted in Lindley Spring, *The Negro at Home* . . . (New York, 1868), p. 147.

38. Parrinder, *Religion in Africa*, pp. 84–85.

39. See *supra*, chapter 2.

40. To Rev. Samuel Smith (October 10, 1748), from the American Correspondence of the Associates of Dr. Bray, in John C. Van Horne, ed., *Religious Philanthropy and Colonial Slavery: The American Correspondence of the Associates of Dr. Bray, 1717–1777* (Champaign, Ill., 1985), p. 100.

41. Ray, *African Religions*, pp. 140–41.

42. Christians talked about a variety of chronologies which Africans and other non-Christians probably could never comprehend. The second coming of Christ was based on a projection of a period of 1,000 years—millennialism—during which Christ would reign on

earth. Premillennialism meant that Christ would return before the millennial era began; postmillennialism was the belief that Christ would return after the millennial era and take with him back to heaven all of the saved—the Rapture. See James West Davidson, *The Logic of Millennial Thought: Eighteenth-Century New England* (New Haven, Conn., 1977).

43. Equiano, *Narrative*, vol. I, p. 27; Curtin, ed., *Africa Remembered*, p. 78; Ray, *African Religions*, p. 41. For most black Africans, John S. Mbiti pointed out, time was two-dimensional "with a long *past*, a *present*, and virtually *no future*." Conversely, the Western conception of *time*, with an "indefinite past, present and finite future, is practically foreign to African thinking." For such people, reality was defined as experience in a corporeal world, therefore the future did not exist because its events had not yet occurred. To them, *actual time* was simply the past and the present—the *Zamani* and the *Sasa*, to the Akamba and Gikuyu of Kenya. While Africans understood that future events would occur—especially those in the process of unfolding and therefore constituting the immediate future—there were no specific words in many of the continent's languages that carried the idea of a *distant* future. The difficulty of reconciling African perceptions of time to Western thought can be seen in the Kikamba and Gikuyu verb tenses, in which the three basic English tenses of past, present, and future assumed as many as nine forms, each with its own pronunciation and with the most distant future tense projecting only two to six months. See Mbiti, *African Religions & Philosophy*, p. 18. For a discussion of verb forms among some Bantu languages, especially Swahili, see Pierre Alexandre, *Languages and Language in Black Africa* (trans. by F. A. Leary, Evanston, Ill., 1972), p. 41. Also useful are Edgar A. Gregerson, *Language in Africa: An Introductory Survey* (New York, 1977); and Maurice Houis, *Anthropologie linguistique de l'Afrique noire* (Paris, 1971).

44. Lawrence W. Levine, "Slave Songs and Slave Consciousness," in Tamara K. Hareven, ed., *Anonymous Americans: Explorations in Nineteenth-Century Social History* (Englewood Cliffs, N.J., 1971), p. 117; Mbiti, *African Religions & Philosophy*, pp. 15–23. See also Mechal Sobel, *The World They Made Together: Black and White Values in Eighteenth-Century Virginia* (Princeton, N.J., 1987), pp. 18–19, 21–30.

45. For a brief but illuminating discussion of how Westerners perceive the African conception of time, and a comparison of the *cyclic* time of pre-European Africans to the *linear* time of modern industrialized societies, see Bonnie J. Barthold, *Black Time: Fiction of Africa, the Caribbean, and the United States* (New Haven, Conn., 1981), pp. 5–7, 9–18.

46. Lawrence W. Levine, *Black Culture and Black Consciousness: Afro-American Folk Thought from Slavery to Freedom* (New York, 1977), p. 37; John Lovell, Jr., *Black Song: The Forge and the Flame: The Story of How the Afro-American Spiritual Was Hammered Out* (New York, 1972), pp. 301–302.

47. Courlander, *Negro Folk Music, U.S.A.*, p. 252.

48. Frederick Law Olmsted, *The Cotton Kingdom: A Traveller's Observations on Cotton and Slavery in the American Slave States* (New York, 1970 [1861]), p. 467; David Macrae, *The Americans at Home* (New York, 1952 [Edinburgh, 1870]), pp. 354–55, 366–69.

49. Clifton H. Johnson, ed., *God Struck Me Dead: Religious Conversion Experiences and Autobiographies of Ex-Slaves* (Philadelphia, 1969), p. 122.

50. Ibid., pp. 145–46.

51. Ibid., p. 141.

52. Blassingame, *The Slave Community*, p. 146; Levine, "Slave Songs and Slave Consciousness," pp. 115, 116.

53. Osofsky, *Puttin' on Ole Massa*, p. 23; Courlander, *Negro Folk Music, U.S.A.*, p. 39; Roger D. Abrahams, ed., *Afro-American Folktales* (New York, 1985), pp. 62–63.

54. Parrinder, ed., *World Religions*, p. 62.

55. Parrinder, *West African Religions*, p. 60.

56. *The Analects of Confucius* (trans. by Arthur Waley, New York, 1938), Book 11:11.

57. Alho, *Religion of the Slaves*, p. 44; Parrinder, *Religion in Africa*, p. 27.

58. The written records of Taoists and Buddhists reveal a belief in an afterlife, as do other philosophical writings, but otherwise most of what has been learned about such a belief has been found in archaeological evidence. The subject of Chinese philosophy and religion is too vast and complex to be discussed in a footnote. For an introduction to the sense of the matter and how it can enlarge an understanding of American religion and racism, see: Alfred Forke, *The World-Conception of the Chinese* (New York, 1975 [1925]); John B. Henderson, *The Development and Decline of Chinese Cosmology* (New York, 1984); Hok-lam Chan and William Theodore de Bary, eds., *Yüan Thought: Chinese Thought and Religion under the Mongols* (New York, 1982); Charles Moore, ed., *The Chinese Mind: Essentials of Chinese Philosophy and Culture* (Honolulu, Hawaii, 1967); Benjamin I. Schwartz, *The World of Thought in Ancient China* (Cambridge, Mass., 1985); and, especially, C. K. Yang, *Religion in Chinese Society: A Study of Contemporary Social Functions of Religion and Some of Their Historical Factors* (Berkeley, Calif., 1967).

59. "Chinese Beliefs in the Afterworld," in Los Angeles County Museum of Art, Overseas Archaeological Exhibition Corporation, and the People's Republic of China, *The Quest for Eternity: Chinese Ceramic Structures from the People's Republic of China* (Los Angeles and San Francisco, 1987), pp. 1, 3–5. For a discussion of the importance of continuity in Chinese life, see Frank Ching, *Ancestors: 900 Years in the Life of a Chinese Family* (New York, 1988).

60. Ray, *African Religions*, p. 140; Parrinder, *Religion in Africa*, pp. 69–70; Nash, *Red, White, and Black*, p. 186; Equiano, *Narrative*, vol. I, p. 28; Curtin, ed., *Africa Remembered*, p. 78; Orlando Patterson, *Sociology of Slavery: An Analysis of the Origins, Development, and Structure of Negro Slave Society in Jamaica* (Rutherford, N.J., 1969 [1967]), p. 198; Alho, *Religion of the Slaves*, p. 45; Welch, *Africa, Before They Came*, pp. 191–92; Smith, ed., *African Ideas of God*, p. 243. For a discussion of the cult of ancestors, see Meyer Fortes, "Some Reflections on Ancestor Worship in Africa," *African Systems of Thought: Studies Presented and Discussed at the Third International Africa Seminar in Salisbury, December 1960* (London, 1965), pp. 122–42.

61. Deuteronomy 18:11.

62. Ecclesiastes 9:5.

63. A. R. Radcliffe-Brown, *Structure and Function in Primitive Society: Essays and Addresses* (New York, 1965 [1952]), pp. 163–64, 173–75.

64. Meyer Fortes, *Œdipus and Job in West African Religion* (Cambridge, U.K., 1959), pp. 29–31, 66.

65. T. C. McLuhan, ed., *Touch the Earth: A Self-Portrait of Indian Existence* (New York, 1971), p. 39.

66. For a discussion of the slave's alienation from his past, see Patterson, *Slavery and Social Death*, pp. 7–11.

67. Although individual commitment was the cornerstone of Christian belief, not everyone believed that Christianity was best served by appeals to individuals. Horace Bushnell, a prominent antebellum Congregational minister, advocated a social order in which individual interests were subordinated to the common Christian good. "Instead of seeing society as the creation of individuals, the way the dominant social contract theory did," Daniel Walker Howe wrote, "Bushnell saw the individual as the creation of society." Convinced that the revival "overemphasized individualism and conscious choice as factors in religion," Bushnell focused on the importance of family influence and argued that a proper religious attitude was "more effectively transmitted as part of a total cultural heritage and personality structure," an idea that was almost identical to the traditional African and American Indian postures toward religion. See "The Social Science of Horace Bushnell," *Journal of American History*, vol. 70, no. 2 (September 1983), p. 310.

68. Carl N. Degler, *Out of Our Past: The Forces That Shaped Modern America* (New York, 1959), p. 16; Robert N. Bellah, Richard Madsen, William M. Sullivan, Ann Swidler, and Steven M. Tipton, *Habits of the Heart: Individualism and Commitment in American Life* (Berkeley, Calif., 1985), p. 222.

69. *Christian Examiner*, vol. XIV (July 1833), quoted in Lois W. Banner, "Religious Benevolence as Social Control: A Critique of an Interpretation," *Journal of American History*, vol. 60, no. 1 (June 1973), p. 39.

70. Bellah et al., *Habits of the Heart*, pp. 56–57, 222. For a detailed discussion of the significance of individualism in American life, see especially chapters 2 and 6.

71. Frederick E. Hoxie, "The Indians Versus the Textbooks: Is There a Way Out?" *Perspectives: American Historical Association Newsletter*, vol. 23, no. 4 (April 1985), p. 21; Bowden, *American Indians and Christian Missions*, p. 72.

72. For an account of the importance of *guanxi* in modern China, see Jay Mathews and Linda Mathews, *One Billion: A China Chronicle* (New York, 1985).

73. Schwartz, *The World of Thought in Ancient China*, pp. 62, 67. While the *Analects* represent the thoughts of Confucius, the *tao* of Taoism is, ironically, based on the teaching of Confucius's philosophical opposite, Lao Zi (Lao-tse), who advocated simplicity and selflessness.

74. Ibid., p. 105. In this regard, Confucianist thought and Christianity may have more in common than Schwartz has allowed. When popes, bishops, and preachers interpreted the Bible to suit their purposes and invoked the law to force compliance, were they not behaving like a "ruling élite"? If events like inquisitions and witch trials are taken into account, the moral and ecclesiastical rigidity of the Christian churches in earlier times suggests that their adherents were similarly "dependent."

75. Ray, *African Religions*, pp. 132–33. For the fullest account of Dinka religious practices, see Godfrey Lienhardt, *Divinity and Experience: The Religion of the Dinka* (London, 1961).

76. John K. Thornton, *The Kingdom of Kongo: Civil War and Transition, 1641–1718* (Madison, Wis., 1983), pp. 62–63. There were, however, distinct inequalities among people of different ranks.

77. Radcliffe-Brown, *Structure and Function in Primitive Society*, pp. 218–19.

78. Mill, *On Liberty*, pp. 1, 72.

79. Mbiti, *African Religions & Philosophy*, pp. 104–109; Alho, *Religion of the Slaves*, p. 45.

80. Mbiti, *African Religions & Philosophy*, p. 2. It does not appear that much has changed. In a study on Christianity in modern Cameroon, one writer observed that "a Christian was defined as 'one who has abandoned his customs.' " See R. Bureau, "Influence de la Christianisation sur les institutions traditionnelles des ethnies cotières du Cameroun," *Christianity in Tropical Africa* (London/Oxford, 1968), quoted in Mbiti, *African Religions & Philosophy*, p. 238.

81. Patterson, *Slavery and Social Death*, passim; Alho, *Religion of the Slaves*, p. 48.

82. Ray, *African Religions*, p. 78; Evan M. Zeusse, *Ritual Cosmos: The Sanctification of Life in African Religions* (Athens, Ohio, 1979), p. 238; Radcliffe-Brown, *Structure and Function in Primitive Society*, pp. 154–55, 157, 158–59, 160; Schwartz, *The World of Thought in Ancient China*, p. 67. See also "A Discussion of Rites," *Basic Writings of Mo Tzu, Hsün Tzu, and Han Fei Tzu* (trans. by Burton Watson, New York, 1967), and *Li Chi, Book of Rites: An Encyclopedia of Ancient Ceremonial Usages, Religious Creeds, and Social Institutions* (trans. by James Legge, 2 vols., New Hyde Park, N.Y., 1967), vol. II, pp. 92–131.

83. Lovell, *Black Song*, p. 193; Mbiti, *African Religions & Philosophy*, p. 123; Parrinder, *Religion in Africa*, p. 77; Raboteau, *Slave Religion*, pp. 55–75, 339–40.

84. Moncure Daniel Conway, *Testimonies Concerning Slavery* (London, 1864), pp. 3–4.

85. Courlander, *Negro Folk Music, U.S.A.*, p. 195.

86. Levine, *Black Culture and Black Consciousness*, pp. 38, 42; Raboteau, *Slave Religion*, pp. 63–64.

87. Levine, *Black Culture and Black Consciousness*, p. 19.

88. Quoted in Kenneth M. Stampp, *The Peculiar Institution: Slavery in the Ante-Bellum South* (New York, 1956), p. 157.

89. Blassingame, *The Slave Community*, p. 137.

90. Cohen, *God's Caress*, pp. 5–6; Marty, *Righteous Empire*, p. 9; Roy Harvey Pearce, *The Savages of America: A Study of the Indian and the Idea of Civilization* (rev. ed., Baltimore, 1965 [1953]), p. 66.

91. To Rev. Samuel Smith (October 10, 1748), from the American Correspondence of the Associates of Dr. Bray, in Van Horne, ed., *Religious Philanthropy*, p. 100.

92. John Frederick Woolverton, *Colonial Anglicanism in North America* (Detroit, 1984), p. 152; Kingsley, *West African Studies*, p. 107.

93. For a perceptive account of the African's adaptation to his New World environment, see Ira Berlin, "Time, Space, and the Evolution of Afro-American Society on British Mainland North America," *American Historical Review*, vol. 85, no. 1 (February 1980), pp. 44–78. See also C. Eric Lincoln, *Race, Religion, and the Continuing American Dilemma* (New York, 1984), especially pp. 60–86.

94. Omitted entirely from this discussion is the matter of physiological adaptation. The effect of *cultural* evolution on *biological* development—specifically, how environment influences the way information is organized and processed in the brain—is a research field that is in its infancy, but it poses some provocative questions. What, for example, is the significance of the different ways in which aboriginal and white Australians solve the same problems. Aboriginal children, who do poorly in language skills, excel in solving spatial problems. While these children silently rearrange rocks in a particular order by studying them with their eyes, white children taking the same test verbalize the solution by talking to themselves. It is fairly obvious that the two groups are *thinking* in fundamentally different ways. Similarly, the Japanese hear natural sounds—rainfall, birds, crickets—as language, and those sounds are, accordingly, processed in the left hemisphere of the brain. On the other hand, people in the West tend to hear such sounds as *noises* and process them in the right hemisphere. If the enslaved African came from a cultural environment that was fundamentally alien to the Christian world, it is not unreasonable to wonder if he was capable of responding to the forces imposed on him in a way that his white oppressors could understand.

95. Nigel Davies, *The Rampant God: Eros Throughout the World* (New York, 1984), p. 169.

96. For example, see Proverbs 6:25, Colossians 3:5, 1 John 2:16, and 1 Peter 2:11.

97. Matthew 15:19.

98. Davies, *The Rampant God*, pp. 176–81.

99. 1 Corinthians 6:18. See also 1 Corinthians 7:1.

100. 1 Thessalonians 4:3 and Hebrews 13:4. See also 1 Corinthians 5:9, 6:13, and 10:8; and Ephesians 5:3.

101. Joseph Klaits, *Servants of Satan: The Age of Witch Hunts* (Bloomington, Ind., 1985), p. 66. For a summary of Tertullian's equation of "the depreciation of sex and the idea of universality of sinfulness," see Paul Tillich, *A History of Christian Thought: From Its Judaic Origins to Existentialism* (ed. Carl E. Braaten, New York, 1967), pp. 98–99.

102. Davies, *The Rampant God*, p. 181.

103. Stephen Sapp, *Sexuality, the Bible, and Science* (Philadelphia, 1977), pp. 63, 68, 126; Joseph Blenkinsopp, *Sexuality and the Christian Tradition* (Dayton, Ohio, 1969), p. 102. For a modern discussion of the fundamentalist Christian view that people who have sex outside of marriage have "lost control" of their feelings, see Tim Stafford, "Great Sex: Reclaiming a Christian Sexual Ethic," *Christianity Today*, vol. 31, no. 14 (October 2, 1988), pp. 23–46.

104. Sapp, *Sexuality, the Bible, and Science*, p. 126; Reinhold Niebuhr, *The Children of Light and the Children of Darkness* (New York, 1944), p. 61.

105. Tillich, *History of Christian Thought*, pp. 109–10.

106. *Confessions of St. Augustine*, book 2.

107. Quoted in William Sumner Jenkins, *Pro-Slavery Thought in the Old South* (Chapel Hill, N.C., 1935), p. 19.

108. Ralph Barton Perry, *Puritanism and Democracy* (New York, 1944), p. 87; Klaits, *Servants of Satan*, p. 66; Davies, *The Rampant God*, p. 169; Peter Gardella, *Innocent Ecstasy: How Christianity Gave America an Ethic of Sexual Pleasure* (New York, 1985), pp. 10–11. For a discussion of the evolution of the Christian church's doctrines on sexuality, see James A. Brundage, *Law, Sex, and Christian Society in Medieval Europe* (Chicago, 1987).

109. Ruth Miller, ed., *Blackamerican Literature: 1760–Present* (Beverly Hills, Calif., 1971), pp. 41–42, from a hymn entitled "New Year's Anthem," by Michael Fortune, sung at St. Thomas African Episcopal Church in Philadelphia, January 1, 1808.

110. Tillich, *History of Christian Thought*, p. 127. For a fuller discussion of the history of sexuality, see Philippe Ariès and André Bejin, eds., *Western Sexuality: Practice and Precept in Past and Present Times* (trans. by Anthony Forster, New York, 1986).

111. Davies, *The Rampant God*, pp. 85–115, 145–67, 204, 237–61.

112. Ibid., pp. 92–97; Bronislaw Malinowski, *The Sexual Life of Savages: An Ethnographic Study of Courtship, Marriage, and Family Life among the Natives of the Trobriand Islands, British New Guinea* (New York, 1929). For a comprehensive analysis of this work, see Davies, *The Rampant God*, pp. 53–63.

113. Islam, with wide swings from wanton eroticism to fanatical puritanism, was in a class by itself. See Davies, *The Rampant God*, pp. 185–201.

114. Gardella, *Innocent Ecstasy*, p. 3.

115. Samuel Richardson, *Pamela, or Virtue Rewarded* (London, 1740); Thomas Hardy, *Tess of the d'Urbervilles: A Pure Woman* (London, 1891). The titles of both books call attention to the Victorian code.

116. Carl Degler argued that it is incorrect to assert that Puritans were against matters of pleasure. "It was against excess of enjoyment that the Puritan cautioned and legislated," he wrote in *Out of Our Past* (p. 9). But this raised a question, which Degler never answered, of what constituted "excess" and who was responsible for defining it. If "excess of enjoyment" was against God's will, and a clerical oligarchy intent on controlling the populace interpreted that will, then the rules became entirely arbitrary. Like the writers referred to above who applied Christian standards to their definition of "improper" sexual activity, it all depended on whose ox was being gored.

117. James Michener, *Hawaii* (New York, 1959), pp. 194–95.

118. Edmund S. Morgan, *The Puritan Family: Religion & Domestic Relations in Seventeenth-Century New England* (rev. ed., New York, 1966), p. 48, quoting John Cotton, *A Practical Commentary, or An Exposition with Observation, Reasons and Uses upon the First Epistle Generall of John* (London, 1656), pp. 126, 200. Morgan also quoted Cotton on page 131 and repeated the point in citing Thomas Hooker, *A comment upon Christ's Last Prayer* (London, 1650), p. 178; John Norton, *The Orthodox Evangelist* (London, 1654), p. 194; and Increase Mather, *Practical Truths Plainly Delivered* (Boston, 1718), pp. 56, 59. See *The Puritan Family*, pp. 20, 165–66, 166n.

119. Quoted in Morgan, *The Puritan Family*, p. 166.

120. For an excellent summary of the New England Puritan's attitude toward sex, see ibid., pp. 48–64. Max Weber also considered sexuality an important aspect of the Puritan psyche. "Combined with the harsh doctrines of the absolute transcendentality of God and the corruption of everything pertaining to the flesh, this inner isolation of the individual

contains, on the one hand, the reason for the entirely negative attitude of Puritanism to all the sensuous and emotional elements in culture and religion, because they are of no use toward salvation and promote sentimental illusions and idolatrous superstitions. Thus it provides a basis for a fundamental antagonism to sensuous culture of all kinds." See *The Protestant Ethic and the Spirit of Capitalism* (trans. by Talcott Parsons, New York, 1958 [1930]), pp. 105–106.

121. David Leverenz, *The Language of Puritan Feeling* (New Brunswick, N.J., 1980), pp. 150–58; Philip Greven, *The Protestant Temperament: Patterns of Child-Rearing, Religious Experience, and the Self in Early America* (New York, 1977), p. 132.

122. Gardella, *Innocent Ecstasy*, pp. 10–11; Greven, *The Protestant Temperament*, pp. 129–32. See also 1 Corinthians 6:18.

123. Gardella, *Innocent Ecstasy*, pp. 44–67, 80–81, 102–103.

124. Degler, *Out of Our Past*, pp. 12–13.

125. *New England Quarterly*, vol. XV (1942), pp. 591–607. Reprinted in Leonard Dinnerstein and Kenneth T. Jackson, eds., *American Vistas, 1607–1877* (4th ed., New York, 1983), pp. 18–31.

126. Roger Thompson, *Sex in Middlesex: Popular Mores in a Massachusetts County, 1649–1699* (Amherst, Mass., 1986), p. 195; Robert C. Twombly and Robert H. Moore, "Black Puritan: The Negro in Seventeenth-Century Massachusetts," *William and Mary Quarterly*, 3rd series, vol. 24, no. 2 (April 1967), pp. 229–31; Vaughan, ed., *The Puritan Tradition in America*, p. 266. The code also set a fine of five shillings for a woman whose hair hangs loose or a man who wears "long locks," or any person who kills lice between his teeth.

127. Morgan agreed that "Americans, by comparison with Europeans or Asiatics, are squeamish when confronted with the facts of life," but that the Puritans, "those bogeymen of the modern intellectual, are not responsible for it." See Dinnerstein and Jackson, eds., *American Vistas, 1507–1877*, p. 19.

128. David Rice, *Slavery Inconsistent with Justice and Good Policy* (Philadelphia, 1792), pp. 7–10; Degler, *Out of Our Past*, p. 173.

129. 1 Thessalonians 4:3–5; Leviticus 25:44–45.

130. William M. Manross, *A History of the American Episcopal Church* (3rd ed., New York, 1959 [1935]), p. 147. There are very few direct plantation—or other—records indicating the extent of slave breeding. It appears that many masters practiced it, but few would admit to it, a tacit recognition of its inhumanity, not to mention its gross violation of Christian morality. There is, however, substantial indirect evidence that the breeding and selling of slaves in the upper South, especially during the decade of the 1850s, was extensive. See Richard Sutch, "The Breeding of Slaves for Sale and the Westward Expansion of Slavery, 1850–1860," *Race and Slavery in the Western Hemisphere: Quantitative Studies* (ed. Eugene D. Genovese and Stanley L. Engerman, Princeton, N.J., 1975), pp. 173–210.

131. George H. Moore, *Notes on the History of Slavery in Massachusetts* (New York, 1968 [1866]), p. 256. See also Ruchames, ed., *Racial Thought in America*, vol. I, p. 158.

132. Act II, Scene 3. All of the Shakespearean references were taken from the Charles Symmons edition of *The Complete Works of William Shakespeare* (London, 1980).

133. Act V, Scene 1.

134. Act I, Scene 2. For an analysis of the racial themes of *The Merchant of Venice*, *Titus Andronicus*, and *Othello*, see Lemuel A. Johnson, *The Devil, the Gargoyle, and the Buffoon: The Negro as Metaphor in Western Literature* (Port Washington, N.Y., 1969), pp. 38–49. See also Anthony Gerard Barthelemy, *Black Face, Maligned Race: The Representation of Blacks in English Drama from Shakespeare to Southerne* (Baton Rouge, La., 1987); and Errol Hill, *Shakespeare in Sable: A History of Black Shakespearean Actors* (Amherst, Mass., 1984).

135. Mary Frances Berry and John W. Blassingame, *Long Memory: The Black Experience in America* (New York, 1982), p. 120.

136. Thomas Jefferson, *Notes on the State of Virginia* (Chapel Hill, N.C., [London, 1787]), p. 139. See also William Cohen, "Thomas Jefferson and the Problem of Slavery," *Journal of American History*, vol. 56, no. 3 (December 1969), p. 513.

137. Jefferson, *Notes*, p. 138. Jefferson apparently made the same mistake in identifying primates that many Europeans and Americans did. The word *orangutan* was derived from the Malayan term "man of the forest" and the animals were found only in Sumatra and Borneo. Although the first English description of the African gorilla had been published in 1613, it was known only by its skeletal remains prior to 1855, twenty-nine years after Jefferson had died. The "orangutans" referred to in the various African travel studies that he and others cited were probably chimpanzees.

138. John Chester Miller, *The Wolf by the Ears: Thomas Jefferson and Slavery* (New York, 1977), pp. 62–63.

139. See especially Genesis 18:16–33, 19:1–29. After Lot and his family had been spared from the destruction of Sodom and Gomorrah and his wife turned to "a pillar of salt" for looking back at the scene, Lot's two daughters, "to preserve our family line through our father," conspired to have sexual intercourse with him by getting him so drunk he would not realize he was with his own daughters. The women subsequently gave birth to Moab and Ben-Ammi.

140. John Tracy Ellis, ed., *Documents of American Catholic History* (3 vols., Wilmington, Del., 1987), vol. II, pp. 325–29.

141. The American Book and Bible House and the Adamic Publishing Company, respectively.

142. For a brief but excellent discussion of white fantasies of blacks as sex beasts during the years 1889–1915, see Joel Williamson, *The Crucible of Race: Black-White Relations in the American South since Emancipation* (New York, 1984), pp. 306–10.

143. Woolverton, *Colonial Anglicanism*, p. 68.

144. Francis Jennings, *The Invasion of America: Indians, Colonialism, and the Cant of Conquest* (Chapel Hill, N.C., 1975), pp. 49, 147.

145. Philip Borden, "Found Cumbering the Soil: Manifest Destiny and the Indian in the Nineteenth Century," *The Great Fear: Race in the Mind of America* (Gary B. Nash and Richard Weiss, eds., New York, 1970), p. 74.

146. Michael Rogin, *Ronald Reagan, the Movie, and Other Episodes in Political Demonology* (Berkeley, Calif., 1987), pp. 191, 206–207. A brief but excellent discussion of Dixon's two works is George M. Fredrickson's *The Black Image in the White Mind: The Debate on Afro-American Character and Destiny, 1817–1914* (New York, 1971), pp. 276–81. For a summary of Dixon's life and an analysis of the psychosexual demons that tormented him, see Williamson, *The Crucible of Race*, chapter 5, "Tom Dixon and *The Leopard's Spots*." Another perspective can be found in Trudier Harris, *Exorcising Blackness: Historical and Literary Lynching and Burning Rituals* (Bloomington, Ind., 1985), p. 20: "James Baldwin has long argued that the prevailing metaphor for understanding the white man's need to suppress the black man is that attached to sexual prowess. White men have originated and passed along to their women the myth of the black man's unusual ability in sexual intercourse. So long has the myth been a part of his culture and his psyche that the white man can no longer separate reality from the larger-than-life beliefs that his ancestors created."

147. Helen V. McLean, "Psychodynamic Factors in Racial Relations," *The Annals of the American Academy of Political and Social Science* (March 1966), p. 164. For a discussion of this subject in the twentieth century, see Sander L. Gilman, *Difference and Pathology: Stereotypes*

of Sexuality, Race, and Madness (Ithaca, N.Y., 1985), especially chapter 4, "Black Sexuality and Modern Consciousness." For an amusing but serious reflection on the modern white man's preoccupation with the black male's alleged virility, see Wayland Young's *Eros Denied* (London, 1965), pp. 271–73. A candid but entirely impressionistic account is Calvin C. Hernton's *Sex and Racism in America* (New York, 1965).

148. Among modern black males, the matter of sexual equality apparently has the lowest priority. According to Gunnar Myrdal's "Rank Order of Discriminations," black men want economic equality first, with sexual equality falling last on a list of six priorities. But, according to another survey, this is exactly the reverse of what white men *believe* the black man wants, a glaring reflection of their obsession with his sexuality. See *An American Dilemma: The Negro Problem and Modern Democracy* (New York, 1962 [1944]), pp. 60–61. For analyses of the Myrdal report, see Brewton Berry, *Race and Ethnic Relations* (Boston, 1958), pp. 262–63; and Bernard Bereleson and Gary A. Steiner, *Human Behavior: An Inventory of Scientific Findings* (New York, 1964), p. 511.

149. Frank M. Snowden, Jr., *Before Color Prejudice: The Ancient View of Blacks* (Cambridge, Mass., 1983), p. 96; Kyle Haselden, *The Racial Problem in Christian Perspective* (New York, 1964 [1959]), p. 51; John H. Russell, *The Free Negro in Virginia, 1619–1865* (New York, 1969 [Baltimore, 1913]), pp. 123–24. See also James C. Ballagh, *A History of Slavery in Virginia*, (Baltimore, 1902).

150. For the strongest case supporting the Jefferson-Hemings love affair, see Fawn Brodie, *Thomas Jefferson: An Intimate Biography* (New York, 1974), pp. 14–17, 293–302; and "The Great Jefferson Taboo," in Dinnerstein and Jackson, eds., *American Vistas*, pp. 118–40.

151. Quoted in C. Vann Woodward, *American Counterpoint: Slavery and Racism in the North-South Dialogue* (New York, 1983 [1964]), p. 74. There are various editions of Chesnut's *A Diary from Dixie*, not all of which include this entry. Written from Augusta, Georgia, on March 18, 1861, the statement also can be found in *Mary Chesnut's Civil War* (ed. C. Vann Woodward, New Haven, Conn., 1981), p. 29; and *The Private Mary Chesnut: The Unpublished Civil War Diaries* (ed. C. Vann Woodward and Elizabeth Muhlenfeld, New York, 1984), p. 42.

152. For an analysis of these groups, see Lawrence Foster, *Religion and Sexuality: Three American Communal Experiments of the Nineteenth Century* (New York, 1981), chapters 2 and 3. A more general account is Sidney Ditzion, *Marriage, Morals, and Sex in America: A History of Ideas* (New York, 1953).

153. Lillian Smith, *Killers of the Dream* (rev. ed., New York, 1961), pp. 120–21; Vernon Lane Wharton, *The Negro in Mississippi, 1865–1900* (Chapel Hill, N.C., 1947), p. 150; *Proceedings of the State Convention of Colored Men of Texas, Held at the City of Austin, July 10–12, 1883*, in Herbert Aptheker, ed., *A Documentary History of the Negro People in the United States* (New York, 1951), pp. 687–88; Jeffrey Brackett, *Notes on the Progress of Colored People of Maryland since the War* (Baltimore, 1890), pp. 412–13. In all fairness it should be noted that laws against interracial marriage were not uncommon in the North, especially in the western states, where the Indian and Chinese minorities were substantial. Although they were only sporadically enforced, most such statutes were not overturned by the courts or repealed until well into the twentieth century. Oregon rescinded its law in 1951, followed by Montana in 1953, North Dakota in 1955, Colorado and South Dakota in 1957, California, Idaho, and Nevada in 1959; Arizona in 1962, Nebraska and Utah in 1963, and Wyoming and Indiana in 1965. By the centennial anniversary of the Thirteenth Amendment, only the eighteen southern and border states still had laws prohibiting the marriage of people of different races. One bizarre variation obtained in North Carolina, where Indians and blacks were permitted to intermarry except for the Indian descendants of the "Croatoan" people, who, because their ancestors had presumably absorbed Virginia Dare's "lost colony" of Roanoke

Island sometime between 1587 and 1591, *might* be part white. Such was the fanaticism of racial purity. On June 12, 1967, the United States Supreme Court in the case of *Loving* v. *Virginia* invalidated all remaining state laws denying freedom of choice in marriage. But old habits die hard. As recently as 1987, voters in Mississippi repealed a state law against intermarriage by a narrow 52 to 48 percent margin. Since the law had been unenforceable, the decision to put it on the ballot was only symbolic. The ominous margin of victory was not.

154. The white man's alleged fascination for black women has been a subject of continuing interest. "Biological integration presupposes an attraction and desire in both white men and Negroes, since without such mutual attraction no problem would exist," Helen V. McLean wrote in 1946. "The attraction is a condensation of many pregenital and genital feelings of the individual. In calling the Negro a child of nature, simple, lovable, without ambition, a person who gives way to every impulse, white men have made a symbol which gives secret gratification to those who are inhibited and crippled in their instinctual satisfactions." See "Psychodynamic Factors in Racial Relations," p. 165. For more recent accounts, see Romanzo Adams, "Interracial Marriage and Social Change," *Race: Individual and Collective Behavior* (Edgar T. Thompson and Everett C. Hughes, eds., Glencoe, Ill., 1958), pp. 428–30; James H. Chaplin, "A Report on Sexual Behavior: Six Case Histories from Northern Rhodesia," *Advances in Sex Research: A Publication of the Society for the Scientific Study of Sex* (Hugh G. Beigel, ed., New York, 1963), pp. 13–26; John Dollard, "Hostility and Fear in Social Life," *Race, Class, and Power* (Raymond W. Mack, ed., New York, 1963), pp. 103–17; and Robert Seidenberg, "The Sexual Basis of Social Prejudice," *Psychoanalytic Review*, vol. 39 (1952), pp. 90–95.

155. Smith, *Killers of the Dream*, pp. 121, 141; Rice, *Slavery Inconsistent with Justice and Good Policy*, pp. 7–10; Klaits, *Servants of Satan*, p. 67; Oscar Handlin, *Race and Nationality in American Life* (New York, 1957 [1948]), pp. 154–55.

156. Mary Boykin Chesnut would have none of that. "Thank God for my countrywomen, but alas for the men!" she wrote in her diary. "They are probably no worse than men everywhere, but the lower their mistresses, the more degraded they must be." See *Mary Chesnut's Civil War*, p. 29.

157. Smith, *Killers of the Dream*, p. 141; Williamson, *The Crucible of Race*, p. 307; Jacobs, *Incidents in the Life of a Slave Girl*, pp. 31–36; Myrta Lockett Avary, *Dixie after the War: An Exposition of Social Conditions Existing in the South, during the Twelve Years Succeeding the Fall of Richmond* (New York, 1906), p. 395; Leon F. Litwack, *Been in the Storm So Long: The Aftermath of Slavery* (New York, 1979), p. 458.

158. United States Department of Commerce, Bureau of the Census, *Negro Population, 1790–1915* (Washington, D.C., 1918), pp. 208, 218. The exact number was 588,363 out of a total black population of 4,441,830.

159. John Hope Franklin, "The Great Confrontation: The South and the Problem of Change," *Journal of Southern History*, vol. 38, no. 1 (February 1972), p. 7.

160. Handlin, *Race and Nationality in American Life*, pp. 155–56; Smith, *Killers of the Dream*, pp. 116–18.

161. See *infra*, chapter 6.

162. Equiano, *Narrative*, vol. I, p. 67; Curtin, ed., *Africa Remembered*, pp. 79–80, 79n., 80n., 91; Mbiti, *African Religions & Philosophy*, pp. 141–47.

163. Thornton, *The Kingdom of Kongo*, p. 58; Miller, ed., *Blackamerican Literature*, p. 14; Curtin, ed., *Africa Remembered*, p. 71; Joshua Coffin, *An Account of Some of the Principal Slave Insurrections*. . . (New York, 1860), pp. 7–8; John Josselyn, *An Account of Two Voyages to New England, Made during the Years 1638, 1663* (Boston, 1865), p. 26.

164. Mbiti, *African Religions & Philosophy*, p. 147.

CHAPTER SIX

1. Genesis 12:1–3.

2. Exodus 19:5–6.

3. The seven dispossessed nations were the Hittites, Girgashites, Amorites, Canaanites, Perizzites, Hivites, and Jebusites.

4. Deuteronomy 7:1–8. The New International Version repeats "treasured possession" in 26:18. The Authorized Version uses "special people" and "peculiar people" in the same places. See also Ralph L. Moellering, *Christian Conscience and Negro Emancipation* (Philadelphia, 1965), p. 67.

5. Goldwin Smith, *Does the Bible Sanction American Slavery?* (Cambridge, Mass., 1864), p. 23.

6. Genesis 15:13.

7. Conor Cruise O'Brien, *God Land: Reflections on Religion and Nationalism* (Cambridge, Mass., 1988), p. 41.

8. *Life*, December 8, 1967. According to Toynbee, the Jew is exceeded in "race-consciousness" only by the high-caste Hindu. The Ango-Saxon is third.

9. Ironically, this reasoning was the abiding principle of the United States Supreme Court's desegregation ruling in *Brown* v. *Board of Education* (1954), in which the justices ruled unanimously that, because the separation of races was *inherently* unequal, the separated person was denied the equal protection of the laws guaranteed by the Fourteenth Amendment to the Constitution.

10. Genesis 12:6–7; 15:18–21. Six of the ten were included among the seven—along with the Hivites—later designated by Moses to be destroyed. See note 3 above. The four others were the Kenites, Kenizzites, Kadmonites, and Raphaites.

11. See also O'Brien, *God Land*, p. 3, and Dale Patrick, *Old Testament Law* (Atlanta, 1985), pp. 160–61.

12. Heman Humphrey, *The Promised Land: A Sermon, Delivered at Goshen, (Conn.) at the Ordination of the Rev. Messrs. Hiram Bingham & Asa Thornton, as Missionaries to the Sandwich Islands, Sept. 29, 1819* (Boston, 1819), p. 5.

13. 1 Peter 2:9. For a review of Christianity's inheritance of antiquity's "linking the idea of a given to the idea of the divine," see O'Brien, *God Land*, pp. 11–19. "This was the cult of heroes who had died for . . . *patria*," which subsequently became "a part of the heritage of medieval Christendom."

14. Darrett B. Rutman, *American Puritanism: Faith and Practice* (Philadelphia, 1970), p. 23; Ola Elizabeth Winslow, *John Eliot, Apostle to the Indians* (Boston, 1968), p. 86; Cotton Mather, *Magnalia Christi Americana: or, The Ecclesiastical History of New-England; from Its First Planting, in the Year 1620, unto the Year of Our Lord 1698* (2 vols., New York, 1967 [1702]), vol. I, p. 51, vol. II, pp. 390–91, 580–644; William R. Brock, *The Evolution of American Democracy* (New York, 1970), p. 29.

15. Merrill D. Peterson, ed., *Thomas Jefferson: Writings* (New York, 1985), p. 523.

16. Robert T. Handy, *A Christian America: Protestant Hopes and Historical Realities* (New York, 1971), pp. 105–106.

17. *Congressional Record*, 56th Cong., 1st Sess. (January 9, 1900), pp. 704–12. See also Beveridge's "March of the Flag" speech in Daniel M. Smith, ed., *Major Problems in American Diplomatic History: Documents and Readings* (2 vols., Boston, 1964), vol. II, pp. 287–90.

18. Timothy L. Smith, "Religion and Ethnicity in America," *American Historical Review*, vol. 83, no. 5 (December 1978), pp. 1177, 1182. The titles of two of Miller's most important works, *Errand into the Wilderness* and *Nature's Nation*, suggest a quality of exclusiveness that is realized in overcoming the challenges of the natural landscape.

19. Lawrence W. Levine, "Slave Songs and Slave Consciousness," *Anonymous Americans: Explorations in Nineteenth-Century Social History* (Tamara K. Hareven, ed., Englewood Cliffs, N.J., 1971), p. 111.

20. Thomas F. Gossett, *Race: The History of an Idea in America* (New York, 1965 [1963]), pp. 190–92.

21. *Time*, November 10, 1986.

22. Thomas Virgil Peterson, *Ham and Japheth: The Mythic World of Whites in the Antebellum South* (Metuchen, N.J., 1978), p. xii; John William Ward, *Andrew Jackson: Symbol for an Age* (New York, 1962 [1953]), pp. 113–14; William R. Hutchison, *Errand to the World: American Protestant Thought and Foreign Missions* (Chicago, 1967), p. 7.

23. Josiah Strong, *The New Era; or, the Coming Kingdom* (New York, 1893), pp. 79–80.

24. Albert Katz Weinberg, *Manifest Destiny: A Study of Nationalist Expansionism in American History* (New York, 1979 [1935]), p. 160.

25. William Stanton, *The Leopard's Spots: Scientific Attitudes toward Race in America, 1815–1859* (Chicago, 1960), p. 174; Josiah Clark Nott and George R. Gliddon, *Types of Mankind: or, Ethnological Researches, Based upon the Ancient Monuments, Paintings, Sculptures, and Crania of Races, and upon Their Natural, Geographical, Philological and Biblical History* (Philadelphia, 1855); Nott, *Indigenous Races of the Earth: or, New Chapters of Ethnological Inquiry* (Philadelphia, 1857). For a detailed discussion of Nott's racial theories, see Reginald Horsman, *Josiah Nott of Mobile: Southerner, Physician, and Racial Theorist* (Baton Rouge, La., 1987). The English translation of the Gobineau work was published in one volume as *The Moral and Intellectual Diversity of Races, with Particular Reference to Their Respective Influence in the Civil and Political History of Mankind* (Philadelphia, 1856), and is also available, with the same title, in a later translation by Adrian Collins (New York, 1967 [1915]). A comprehensive analysis of Gobineau's theories is Michael D. Biddiss's *Father of Racist Ideology: The Social and Political Thought of Count Gobineau* (New York, 1970). Biddiss pointed out that Gobineau rejected the "egalitarian implications" of religions like Buddhism and Christianity and believed, like many conservative Protestants in the United States, that the latter's "chief concern is not with earthly existence." Moreover, he went on, "Christianity is seen as uplifting the spirit of man, but it can only do this to the degree that the racial make-up of the individual allows" (pp. 152–53).

26. Edward Lurie, *Louis Agassiz: A Life in Science* (Chicago, 1960), pp. 257–58, 260–62, 305–306.

27. The best work available on this subject is Reginald Horsman's *Race and Manifest Destiny: The Origins of American Racial Anglo-Saxonism* (Cambridge, Mass., 1981). Unfortunately, Horsman limited himself to antebellum sources of racism. One can only hope for a second volume dealing with the years since the Civil War and focusing on the eruption of Manifest Destiny at the turn of the century.

28. Van Evrie was a New York physician who wrote and edited numerous racist publications. His best-known work was *Negroes and Negro "Slavery": The First an Inferior Race: The Latter Its Normal Condition* (New York, 1861). The title of the 1870 edition was *White Supremacy and Negro Subordination.* Van Evrie also wrote several pamphlets condemning emancipation; edited a white-supremacist newspaper, the New York *Weekly Day Book* (known officially for two years as *The Caucasian*); and in June 1862 founded a monthly journal, *The Old Guard*, which remained in publication for nine years.

29. *Congressional Globe*, 56th Congress, 1st Sess. (January 9, 1900), pp. 704–12; Robert H. Ferrell, *American Diplomacy: A History* (New York, 1969), pp. 475–76; Walter L. Williams, "United States Indian Policy and the Debate over Philippine Annexation: Implications for the Origins of American Imperialism," *Journal of American History*, vol. 66, no. 4 (March 1980), pp. 830–31; Alexander De Conde, *A History of American Foreign Policy* (New York, 1963), p. 355.

30. *Congressional Record*, 55th Congress, 3rd Sess., pp. 1430–31.

31. Stephen Neill, *Colonization and Christian Mission* (London, 1966), pp. 412–13; O'Brien, *God Land*, pp. 11–12; Henry F. May, *The Protestant Churches and Industrial America* (New York, 1963 [1949]), p. 5; Winthrop S. Hudson, ed., *Nationalism and Religion in America: Concepts of American Identity and Mission* (New York, 1970), p. 153; Gary B. Nash, *Red, White, and Black: The Peoples of Early America* (2nd ed., Englewood Cliffs, N.J., 1982), p. 79; George M. Fredrickson, *White Supremacy: A Comparative Study in American and South African History* (New York, 1981), p. 8; Robert F. Berkhofer, *The White Man's Indian: Images of the American Indian from Columbus to the Present* (New York, 1978), p. 121.

32. See especially Charles M. Segal and David C. Stineback, *Puritans, Indians, and Manifest Destiny* (New York, 1977).

33. R. Pierce Beaver, *Church, State, and the American Indians: Two and a Half Centuries of Partnership in Missions between Protestant Churches and Government* (St. Louis, 1966), pp. 25–26; Nash, *Red, White, and Black*, pp. 81–82.

34. Winthrop S. Hudson, *Religion in America* (New York, 1981), p. 76. The term "Manifest Destiny" first appeared in an article written by journalist John L. O'Sullivan in *The Democratic Review* in 1845 and pertained to the idea that Americans had a "manifest" right to occupy the western portion of the continent.

35. Donald J. D'Elia, "Dr. Benjamin Rush and the Negro," *Journal of the History of Ideas*, vol. 30, no. 3 (July–September 1969), p. 416.

36. David E. Harrell, Jr., *Quest for a Christian America: The Disciples of Christ and American Society to 1866* (Nashville, Tenn., 1966), p. 53. Apparently many of Rice's fellow Presbyterians were not persuaded. Six years after his death in 1831, the church formally divided into Old School and New School divisions, and by 1861 each of these groups had northern and southern branches. See *infra*, chapter 8.

37. Joshua 13:1; Humphrey, *The Promised Land*, pp. 5–6, 9–10. See also Hudson, ed., *Nationalism and Religion in America*, p. 97.

38. Samuel A. Cartwright, *Essays, Being Inductions from the Baconian Philosophy Proving the Truth of the Bible and the Justice and Benevolence of the Decree Dooming Canaan To Be a Servant of Servants; and Answering the Question of Voltaire:* "On demande quel droit des étrangers tels que Juifs avaient sur pays de Canaan?" *In a Series of Letters to the Rev. William Winans, by Samuel A. Cartwright, M.D., of Natchez, Miss.* (Vidalia, [La.], 1843). The first letter to Winans was dated November 17, 1841, but none of the others was dated. See also William Sumner Jenkins, *Pro-Slavery Thought in the Old South* (Chapel Hill, N.C., 1935), p. 205; Moellering, *Christian Conscience and Negro Emancipation*, pp. 52–53.

39. Timothy L. Smith, *Revivalism and Social Reform: American Protestantism on the Eve of the Civil War* (Baltimore, 1980 [1957]), p. 188; Hollis Read, *The Hand of God in History* (Hartford, Conn., 1849), passim; J. Earl Thompson, Jr., "Lyman Beecher's Long Road to Conservative Abolitionism," *Church History*, vol. 42, no. 1 (March 1973), p. 90; William Bernard Gravely, "Gilbert Haven, Radical Equalitarian" (Ph.D. dissertation, Duke University, 1960), p. 3.

40. John Ireland, *The Church and Modern Society* (Chicago, 1896), p. 174. This is a collection of "lectures and addresses" given by Ireland in the late nineteenth century. The "Church" in the title refers specifically to the Roman Catholic Church. Ireland was a leader of the modernist movement that called for "religious liberty, separation of church and state, interfaith cooperation, and greater lay initiative," but after the Vatican announced its opposition to modernism Ireland became one of the movement's harshest critics. See Neil T. Storch, "John Ireland and the Modernist Controversy," *Church History*, vol. 54, no. 3 (September 1985), pp. 353–65.

41. Smith, ed., *Major Problems in American Diplomatic History*, vol. II, pp. 287–90; De Conde, *A History of American Foreign Policy*, p. 352; Julius W. Pratt, *A History of United States Foreign Policy* (2nd ed., Englewood Cliffs, N.J., 1965), p. 215. The Quakers and Unitarians,

seeing no benefit to be derived for anyone from the acquisition of the Philippines, remained skeptical throughout the imperialism controversy. Similarly, many Roman Catholics, distressed by the Protestant argument that the Filipinos needed to be "Christianized," opposed annexation, although some Catholics supported the idea of "civilizing" Asians. For a review of American Catholic concerns over the acquisition of the Philippines, see Frank T. Reuter, *Catholic Influence on American Colonial Policy, 1898–1904* (Austin, Tex., 1967). Despite the fact that it is more descriptive than analytical, Kenton J. Clymer's *Protestant Missionaries in the Philippines, 1898–1916: An Inquiry into the American Colonial Mentality* (Urbana and Chicago, 1986), pp. 65–92, is an informative account of the American missionary's attitude toward the Filipinos. For a discussion of American missions as "a moral equivalent for imperialism," see Hutchison, *Errand to the World*, pp. 91–124.

42. Josiah Strong, *Our Country: Its Possible Future and Its Present Crisis* (Cambridge, Mass., 1963 [1885, revised 1891]), p. 201.

43. See the "Editor's Introduction" by Jurgen Herbst in the Belknap Press edition (Cambridge, 1963), p. ix. Henry F. May called *Our Country* "the *Uncle Tom's Cabin* of city reform." See *The Protestant Churches and Industrial Reform*, pp. 115–16.

44. At least two historians have argued that the view of Strong as a racist and imperialist is inaccurate. Dorothea R. Muller, "Josiah Strong and American Nationalism: A Revaluation," *Journal of American History*, vol. 53, no. 3 (December 1966), pp. 489–90, 494, argued that Strong "envisioned evangelizing the world through the persuasive power of example and practice of Christian civilization carried by its people to all parts of the world as they traveled or migrated—but not by the extension of American political power or force." Such an assessment ignored the obvious. A call to evangelize the world may not have included a political mandate, but it served as a stalking horse for those who did advocate political aggression. Politicians, businessmen, and missionaries calling for the acquisition of the Philippines formed an imperialistic partnership. And Muller's contention that "Anglo-Saxon supremacy did not necessarily mean racial hostility" is a contradiction in terms. Similarly, James A. Field, Jr., "American Imperialism: The Worst Chapter in Almost Any Book," *American Historical Review*, vol. 83, no. 3 (June 1978), pp. 647, 649, contended that people like Strong believed that Anglo-Saxons had simply demonstrated their cultural superiority, but were not racists in an anthropological sense. Field neglected to point out that the victims of imperialism suffered just the same. Also, calling attention to the absence of policy makers who were influenced by Strong is irrelevant. A racist who is a product of public opinion rather than a creator of it is still a racist. See also Muller, "The Social Philosophy of Josiah Strong: Social Christianity and American Progressivism," *Church History*, vol. 28, no. 2 (June 1959), pp. 183–201.

45. W[illiam] P[ope] Harrison, *Gospel among the Slaves: A Short Account of Missionary Operations among the African Slaves of the Southern States* (Nashville, Tenn., 1893), p. 35.

46. Quoted in Martin E. Marty, *Righteous Empire: The Protestant Experience in America* (New York, 1970), p. 7. See also Francis Paul Prucha, *The Churches and the Indian Schools, 1888–1912* (Lincoln, Neb., 1979), pp. 240–41; Philip Borden, "Found Cumbering the Soil: Manifest Destiny and the Indian in the Nineteenth Century," *The Great Fear: Race in the Mind of America* (Gary B. Nash and Richard Weiss, eds., New York, 1970), pp. 71–97; and, especially, Weinberg, *Manifest Destiny*, chapter 3, "The Destined Use of the Soil."

47. Henry Steele Commager, ed., *Documents of American History* (2 vols., 8th ed., New York, 1963), vol. I, pp. 407, 410, 445.

48. Clayton J. Drees, "Augustine of Hippo and Bernard of Clairvaux: A Medieval Justification for War," *Perspectives: A Journal of Historical Inquiry*, vol. 14 (1987), pp. 1–22.

49. Commager, ed., *Documents*, vol. II, p. 209.

50. Los Angeles *Times*, February 13, 1987.

51. Timothy L. Smith, "Protestant Schooling and American Nationality," *Journal of American History*, vol. 53, no. 4 (March 1967), p. 680.

52. Marty, *Religious Empire*, pp. 15–16. For a comprehensive analysis of this theme, see Ray Allen Billington, *The Protestant Crusade, 1800–1860: A Study of the Origins of American Nativism* (New York, 1938).

53. Sydney E. Ahlstrom, *A Religious History of the American People* (New Haven, Conn., 1972), p. 798.

54. Ironically, some Roman Catholics almost seemed to agree. The editor of *The Pittsburgh Catholic* defended the invasion of Cuba as "bed-rock Christianity" and predicted that the United States would carry out "the designs of Providence on this continent for the betterment of the race and the upholding and conserving the rights of the individual MAN." See Hudson, ed., *Nationalism and Religion in America*, p. 120.

55. McKinley's comments to the visiting Methodists were first printed in the *Christian Advocate*, January 22, 1903. Since this was over a year after he had been assassinated, there was no way the White House could confirm or deny their accuracy. But, inasmuch as McKinley's exact words have been so universally accepted and extensively quoted, a check of their authenticity is long overdue. The source of the *Christian Advocate* account was Brigadier General James F. Rusling, a member of the visiting delegation of Methodists, who, in a book he had published a few years earlier, *Men and Things I Saw in Civil War Days* (New York, 1899), pp. 14–15, recounted a similar story of presidential piety involving Abraham Lincoln. In July 1863, Rusling claimed to have witnessed a conversation between Lincoln and Major General Daniel E. Sickles, who had been wounded in the Battle of Gettysburg. After Sickles questioned Lincoln's sublime confidence about winning a battle that could have been easily lost, the President told how he had dropped to his knees and prayed to God for victory at Gettysburg. "I told Him that this was His country, and the war was His war, but that we really couldn't stand another Fredericksburg or Chancellorsville," Rusling quoted Lincoln as saying, "And then and there I made a solemn vow with my Maker, that if He would stand by you boys at Gettysburg, I would stand by Him. After thus wrestling with the Almighty in prayer, I don't know how it was, and it is not for me to explain, but, somehow or other, a sweet comfort crept into my soul, that God Almighty had taken the whole business there into His own hands, and we were bound to win at Gettysburg!" There was a disturbing similarity between the two anecdotes. Since there was no verification of the conversation from Sickles and the whole story was uncharacteristic of Lincoln, the question of Rusling's credibility in *both* situations is worth considering. See also Ferrell, *American Diplomacy*, pp. 402–405.

56. Ferrell, *American Diplomacy*, p. 400.

57. For a fuller discussion of the American Protective Association, see *infra*, chapter 9.

58. Marty, *Righteous Empire*, pp. 17, 23. See also Philip Schaff, *America: A Sketch of the Political, Social, and Religious Character of the United States of America, in Two Lectures, Delivered at Berlin with a Report Read Before the German Diet at Frankfort-am-Maine, September 1854* (New York, 1855). Schaff's most important work was probably his 8-volume *History of the Christian Church* (Grand Rapids, Mich., 1964–1967 [1907–1910]) which stretched a head-spinning 6,946 pages.

59. Marty, *Righteous Empire*, p. 15; Hutchison, *Errand to the World*, p. 8.

60. Quoted in Hutchison, *Errand to the World*, p. 24.

61. Nash, *Red, White, and Black*, pp. 3–4; Stephen Neill, *A History of Christian Missions* (Middlesex, U.K., 1964), p. 243; Franklin H. Littell, "The Churches and the Body Politic," *Daedalus: Journal of the American Academy of Arts and Sciences* (Winter 1967), pp. 23–24; Mather, *Magnalia Christi Americana*, vol. I, p. 51.

62. James Oscar Farmer, Jr., *The Metaphysical Confederacy: James Henley Thornwell and the Synthesis of Southern Values* (Macon, Ga., 1986), p. 107; Robert Baird, *The Progress and Prospects of Christianity in the United States of America; with Remarks on the Subject of Slavery in America; and on the Intercourse between British and American Churches* (London, [1851]), p. 5. See also Gossett, *Race*, pp. 184–85.

63. Ahlstrom, *Religious History of the American People*, p. 845.

64. For example, see Octavius Brooks Frothingham, *Recollections and Impressions, 1822–1890* (New York, 1891), p. 50.

65. Ebenezer Davies, *American Scenes and Christian Slavery; A Recent Tour of Four Thousand Miles in the United States* (London, 1849), p. 30; Alan Heimert, *Religion and the American Mind: From the Great Awakening to the Revolution* (Cambridge, Mass., 1966), p. 429; Roy Harvey Pearce, *The Savages of America: A Study of the Indian and the Idea of Civilization* (rev. ed., Baltimore, 1965), p. 63, quoting James Knowles, *Memoir of Roger Williams* (Boston, 1834), pp. 95, 98.

66. Frederick M. Binder, *The Color Problem in Early National America as Viewed by John Adams, Jefferson and Jackson* (The Hague and Paris, 1968), p. 150.

67. Weinberg, *Manifest Destiny*, pp. 84–85; Ahlstrom, *Religious History of the American People*, pp. 789–90; Harrison, *The Gospel among Slaves*, p. 30.

68. Arnold Toynbee, *An Historian's Approach to Religion* (2nd ed., Oxford, U.K., 1979), pp. 228–32; Pearce, *Savages of America*, pp. 7–8; David E. Stannard, *The Puritan Way of Death: A Study in Religion, Culture, and Social Change* (New York, 1977), p. 26, quoting Sibbes, *The Saints Cordial* (London, 1637), p. 188.

69. Cotton Mather, *On Witchcraft: Being the Wonders of the Invisible World* (New York, [1974] [1692]), p. 14.

70. Psalms 8:5–8. Of course, the same people who cited these verses ignored Genesis 2:15, in which God told Adam to take care of the Garden of Eden.

71. Matthew 6:26; Luke 12:7.

72. James 3:7.

73. J[acob] J. Finkelstein, *The Ox That Gored* (Transactions of the American Philosophical Society, vol. 71, part 2, Philadelphia, 1981), pp. 12–13. See also Patrick, *Old Testament Law*, pp. 250–51.

74. Reynolds, *A Treatise of the Passions and Faculties of the Soule of Man* (London, 1658), quoted in Perry Miller, *The New England Mind* (2 vols., Boston, 1961 [1939]), vol. I, *The Seventeenth Century*, pp. 270–71. For a full discussion of the Puritan's notions about nature, see pp. 181–82, and especially 208–35.

75. Jonathan Edwards, *Images or Shadows of Divine Things* (New Haven, Conn., 1948), p. 98; Heimert, *Religion and the American Mind*, pp. 103–105, 307.

76. Sarah M. Grimké, *An Epistle to the Clergy of the Southern States* (New York, 1836), pp. 3–5.

77. A[ngelina] E[mily] Grimké, *Appeal to the Christian Women of the South* (n.p., [1836]), p. 13.

78. Ibid., p. 3.

79. William Graham Sumner, *The Challenge of Facts and Other Essays* (New Haven, Conn., 1913), p. 25. See also E. Digby Baltzell, *The Protestant Establishment: Aristocracy and Caste in America* (New York, 1964), pp. 13–14.

80. It is possible that Secretary of the Interior James Watt, when he testified before the House Interior Committee, was thinking of the first verse of Revelation, where John predicted that "things will shortly come to pass," or the next-to-last verse, where Christ promised to return soon. "My responsibility is to follow the Scriptures which call upon us to occupy the land until Jesus returns," Watt replied when asked about protecting the wilder-

ness. "I do not know how many future generations we can count on before the Lord returns." See Coleman McCarthy, "The Perils of Having a Pipeline to God," Los Angeles *Times*, May 26, 1981; Michael Rogin, *Ronald Reagan, the Movie, and Other Episodes in Political Demonology* (Berkeley, Calif., 1987), p. 36. In March 1989, the thirty Catholic and Protestant biblical scholars of the Jesus Seminar, meeting in Sonoma, California, at Robert Funk's Westar Institute, voted overwhelmingly that nowhere in the New Testament did Christ indicate he would return to the earth. See Los Angeles *Times*, March 5, 1989.

81. Hermann Hesse, *Siddartha* (New York, 1951), p. 11–12; Benjamin J. Schwartz, *The World of Thought in Ancient China* (Cambridge, Mass., 1985), pp. 201, 206.

82. But Gagudju culture is dying a slow death. As more and more of the aborigines migrate to the cities, they leave behind only the elderly, whose task it is to pass on the arts, skills, legends, traditions, and history of the past; and the very young, few of whom will stay long enough to learn them. See Stanley Breeden, "The First Australians," *National Geographic*, vol. 173, no. 2 (February 1988), pp. 266–94.

83. T. C. McLuhan, ed., *Touch the Earth: A Self-Portrait of Indian Existence* (New York, 1971), pp. 5, 6, 8, 16–19, 22, 23.

84. Ibid., p. 23.

85. Miller, *The New England Mind*, vol. I, p. 218.

86. McLuhan, ed., *Touch the Earth*, pp. 15, 169–71; Carl N. Degler, *Out of Our Past: The Forces That Shaped Modern America* (New York, 1959), p. 4; Max Lerner, *America as a Civilization: Life and Thought in the United States Today* (New York, 1957), p. 297; Henry Adams, *History of the United States during the Administrations of Jefferson and Madison* (9 vols., New York, 1889–1891), vol. VI, pp. 74–75. See also Jefferson's letter to Governor William Henry Harrison of the Indiana Territory (February 27, 1803), in Peterson, ed., *Thomas Jefferson: Writings*, pp. 1117–19. For a fuller discussion of Jefferson's views on Indian removal, see Bernard W. Sheehan, *Seeds of Extinction: Jeffersonian Philanthropy and the American Indian* (New York, 1973), pp. 243–75.

87. James D. Foreman, *People of the Dream* (New York, 1972), p. 22; Hugh A. Dempsey, *Crowfoot: Chief of the Blackfeet* (Edmonton, Alb., n.d.), p. 103.

88. Dempsey, *Crowfoot*, p. 105. See also Hana Samek, *The Blackfoot Confederacy, 1880–1920: A Comparative Study of Canadian and U.S. Indian Policy* (Albuquerque, N.M., 1987).

89. Paul Jacobs, Saul Landau, and Eve Pell, eds., *To Serve the Devil* (2 vols., New York, 1971), vol. I, *Natives and Slaves*, pp. 3–4.

90. John Lovell, Jr., *Black Song: The Forge and the Flame: The Story of How the Afro-American Spiritual Was Hammered Out* (New York, 1972), pp. 263–72, excerpted from various poems and songs.

91. Ibid., pp. 263–72.

92. The first Uncle Remus publication was *Uncle Remus: His Songs and Sayings* (1880), followed by *Nights with Uncle Remus* (1883). Harris published *Uncle Remus and Br'er Rabbit* in 1906. See Richard M. Dorson, *Negro Tales from Pine Bluff, Arkansas, and Calvin, Michigan* (Bloomington, Ind., 1958 [1939]), pp. 11–42, 158–71.

93. Thomas W. Talley, *Negro Folk Rhymes: Wise and Otherwise* (New York, 1922), p. 160.

94. Ibid., p. 170.

95. B. A. Botkin, ed., *Lay My Burden Down: A Folk History of Slavery* (Chicago, 1945), pp. 24, 273.

96. Talley, *Negro Folk Rhymes*, p. 205.

97. George M. Marsden, "Everyone One's Own Interpreter?: The Bible, Science, and Authority in Mid-Nineteenth Century America," *The Bible in America* (Nathan O. Hatch and Mark A. Noll, eds., New York, 1982), pp. 79–100.

98. That humankind is not merely of this world is a Christian, not just a fundamentalist

Protestant, notion. In his Gifford Lectures, published as *The Nature and Destiny of Man: A Christian Interpretation* (2 vols., New York, 1941), theologian Reinhold Niebuhr argued persuasively that man, possessing a body and a soul, is *both* a child of nature and a spiritual being who stands outside of nature. For a brief discussion of this thesis, see James G. Moseley, *A Cultural History of Religion in America* (Westport, Conn., 1981), pp. 109–15.

99. John Henderson Russell, *The Free Negro in Virginia, 1619–1865* (Baltimore, 1913), pp. 123–24; C. Eric Lincoln, *Race, Religion, and the Continuing American Dilemma* (New York, 1984), pp. 39–40. See also Kyle Haselden, *The Racial Problem in Christian Perspective* (New York, 1964 [1959]), p. 51.

100. Nash, *Red, White, and Black*, pp. 81–82; Segal and Stineback, *Puritans, Indians, and Manifest Destiny*, p. 35; Pearce, *The Savages of America*, p. 22.

101. Quoted in Fredrickson, *White Supremacy*, pp. 8–9.

102. Genesis 3:1.

103. 2 Peter 2:12.

104. Roger Williams, *The Complete Writings of Roger Williams* (7 vols., New York, 1963), vol. 7, p. 31.

105. Mather, *Magnalia Christi Americana*, vol. I, p. 44; George H. Moore, *Notes on the History of Slavery in Massachusetts* (New York, 1968 [1866]), pp. 63–65; John Frederick Woolverton, *Colonial Anglicanism in North America* (Detroit, 1984), p. 163; S. Charles Bolton, *Southern Anglicanism: The Church of England in Colonial South Carolina* (Westport, Conn., 1982), p. 107; Ronald T. Takaki, *Iron Cages: Race & Culture in the Nineteenth Century* (New York, 1979), pp. 95–96; Richard F. Burton, *Mission to Gelele, King of Dahome: With Notices of the So-Called "Amazons," the Grand Customs, the Yearly Customs, the Human Sacrifices, the Present State of the Slave Trade, and the Negro's Place in Nature* (2nd ed., 2 vols., London, 1864); [Albert Taylor Bledsoe], "Baker's African Explorations," *Southern Review*, vol. 2 (October 1867), pp. 330–58; "Ape-Like Tribes of Men," *Old Guard*, vol. 4, no. 9 (September 1866), pp. 557–62; W. Winwood Reade, *Savage Africa: Being a Narrative on a Tour in Equatorial, Southwestern, and Northwestern Africa; with Notes on the Habits of the Gorilla; on the Existence of Unicorns and Tailed Men; on the Slave Trade; on the Origin, Character and Capabilities of the Negro, and on the Future Civilization of Western Africa* (New York, 1864). Classifying slaves as farm animals was also common in colonial Virginia where, Philip Alexander Bruce wrote, the enslavement of Africans was due partly to "sincere doubts in the minds of many Englishmen as to whether the place of the negro in the general system of life was higher than that of the horse or the ox." See *Economic History of Virginia in the Seventeenth Century: An Inquiry Into the Material Condition of the People Based Upon Original and Contemporaneous Records* (2 vols., New York, 1865), vol. II, p. 65.

106. *The American Annual Cyclopedia and Register of Important Events* (84 vols., New York, 1870–1903), (1868), p. 86.

107. Quoted in Marty, *Righteous Empire*, p. 12.

108. Weinberg, *Manifest Destiny*, p. 83; Frederick Law Olmsted, *The Cotton Kingdom: A Traveller's Observations on Cotton and Slavery in the American Slave States* (New York, 1970 [1861]), p. 512; Sidney Andrews, *The South since the War: As Shown by Fourteen Weeks of Travel and Observation in Georgia and the Carolinas* (Boston, 1866), p. 28.

109. [Buckner H. Payne], *The Negro: What Is His Ethnological Status; Is He Progeny of Ham? Is He a Descendant of Adam and Eve? Has He a Soul? Or Is He a Beast in God's Nomenclature? What Is His Status as Fixed by God in Creation? What Is His Relation to the White Race?* (Cincinnati, 1867), passim; David Macrae, *The Americans at Home* (New York, 1952 [Edinburgh, 1870]), pp. 299–301.

110. For example, see Prospero (pseud.), *Caliban: A Sequel to "Ariel"* (New York, 1868); and Sister Sallie (pseud.), *The Color Line. Devoted to the Restoration of Good Government, Putting*

an End to Negro Authority and Misrule, and Establishing a White Man's Government in the White Man's Country, by Organizing the White People of the South (n.p., [1868?]).

111. The 1872 booklength edition had the same 50-word title as the original followed by: *Enlarged, and with a Review of His Reviewers, Exhibiting the Learning of the "Learned"* (Cincinnati, 1872). The title of the 1876 pamphlet was *Ariel's Reply to the Rev. John [Joseph] A. Seiss, D.D., of Philadelphia; also, His Reply to the Scientific Geologist and Other Learned Men, in Their Attacks on the Credibility of the Mosaic Account of Creation and the Flood* (Cincinnati, 1876).

112. Charles Carroll, *The Tempter of Eve*, 289–314, 337. Like Payne's book, the full titles of both of Carroll's books indicated clearly his basic theme: *"The Negro a Beast"; or, "In the Image of God"; the Reasoner of the Age, the Revelator of the Century! The Bible as It Is! The Negro and His Relation to the Human Family! The Negro a Beast, but Created with Articulate Speech, and Hands, that He May Be of Service to His Master—the White Man. The Negro Not the Son of Ham, Neither Can It Be Proven by the Bible and the Argument of the Theologian Who Would Claim Such, Melts to Mist before the Thunderous and Convincing Arguments of this Masterful Book* (St. Louis, 1900); and *The Tempter of Eve; or, the Criminality of Man's Social, Political, and Religious Equality with the Negro, and the Amalgamation to which These Crimes Inevitably Lead. Discussed in the Light of the Scriptures, the Sciences, Profane History, Tradition, and the Testimony of the Monuments* (St. Louis, 1902).

113. Gilbert Osofsky, *The Burden of Race: A Documentary History of Negro-White Relations in America* (New York, 1967), p. 90.

114. All five incorrectly identified the title of *"The Negro a Beast,"* and four were published in small southern towns. See C[alvin] H[erlock] Brooks, *The Race Problem Solved, or, A Reply to a Book Entitled, "The Negro Is a Beast," by Charles Carroll* (Elgin, Tex., 1901); William G. Schell, *Is the Negro a Beast?: A Reply to Chas. Carroll's Book Entitled "The Negro Is a Beast," Proving that the Negro Is Human from Biblical, Scientific, and Historical Standpoints* (Moundsville, West, Va., 1901); W. S. Armistead, *The Negro Is a Man: A Reply to Professor Charles Carroll's Book "The Negro Is a Beast; or, In the Image of God"* (Tifton, Ga., 1903); H. P. Eastman, *The Negro, His Origin, History, and Destiny; Containing a Reply to "The Negro Is a Beast"* (Boston, 1905); and M. B. Thompson, *The Negro, Not a Beast, but a Descendant of Adam: A Reply to Prof. Chas. Carroll's Work, " 'The Negro Is a Beast' or 'In the Image of God' "* (Mt. Juliet, Tenn., 1906). Brooks was a member of the Texas Universal Conference, Methodist Episcopal Church, South. Thompson was the former slave.

115. Armistead, *The Negro Is a Man*, pp. iv–v; Eastman, *The Negro*, p. 5; David M. Reimers, *White Protestantism and the Negro* (New York, 1965), p. 27.

116. Quoted in Charles Grier Sellers, Jr., "The Travail of Slavery," *The Southerner as American* (Charles Grier Sellers, Jr., ed., Chapel Hill, N.C., 1960), pp. 58–59.

117. Arnold A. Sio, "Interpretations of Slavery: The Slave Status in the Americas," *Comparative Studies in Society and History*, vol. VII, no. 3 (April 1965), pp. 300–302. See also Kenneth M. Stampp, *The Peculiar Institution: Slavery in the Ante-Bellum South* (New York, 1956), pp. 192–93.

CHAPTER SEVEN

1. The "church," as defined here, is not the spiritual "church" of the individual who has partaken of the "Body of Christ," but the temporal organization that ranges from the vast and hierarchical Roman Catholic Church to the independent neighborhood congregation established and supported entirely by local worshipers.

2. Francis J. Grund, *The Americans in Their Moral, Social, and Political Relations* (New York,

1968 [1837]), p. 46; Harriet Martineau, *Society in America* (Gloucester, Mass., 1962 [New York, 1837]), p. 344.

3. Martineau, *Society in America*, p. 30, from Seymour Martin Lipset's introductory essay to the 1962 abridged edition, quoting Max Berger, *The British Traveler in America* (2 vols., New York, 1943), vol. I, p. 314.

4. Wilbur S. Shepperson, *Emigration & Disenchantment: Portraits of Englishmen Repatriated from the United States* (Norman, Okla., 1965), p. 142.

5. C. C. Goen, *Broken Churches, Broken Nation: Denominational Schisms and the Coming of the Civil War* (Macon, Ga., 1985), p. 31. See also David O. Moberg, *The Church as a Social Institution: The Sociology of American Religion* (Englewood Cliffs, N.J., 1962), p. 2.

6. Ralph Barton Perry, *Puritanism and Democracy* (New York, 1944), p. 557.

7. Shepperson, *Emigration and Disenchantment*, p. 96; John Tracy Ellis, ed., *Documents of American Catholic History* (3 vols., Wilmington, Del., 1987), vol. II, pp. 325–29; Rowland Berthoff, *An Unsettled People: Social Order and Disorder in American History* (New York, 1971), p. 235; Franklin Hamlin Littell, *From State Church to Pluralism: A Protestant Interpretation of Religion in American History* (Chicago, 1962), p. 32, and "The Churches and the Body Politic," *Daedalus: Journal of the American Academy of Arts and Sciences* (Winter 1967), p. 33.

8. Jon Butler, "Magic, Astrology, and the Early American Religious Heritage, 1600–1760," *American Historical Review*, vol. 84, no. 2 (April 1979), p. 317.

9. Patricia U. Bonomi, *Under the Cope of Heaven: Religion, Society, and Politics in Colonial America* (New York, 1986), p. 220. For a more detailed discussion of this view, see Bonomi and Peter R. Eisenstadt, "Church Adherence in the Eighteenth-Century British Colonies," *William and Mary Quarterly*, 3rd series, vol. 39, no. 2 (April 1982), pp. 245–86. Bonomi based her calculations on a comparison of church membership with population, but such an explanation has its pitfalls. She agreed that the "evangelical" nineteenth century was, in the traditional view, a more church-oriented century. Unfortunately for her thesis, this may not have been a helpful argument since church membership was not very high in that century either. The Eighth Census (1860) counted 31,443,321 Americans. The previous year, English traveler Isabella Lucy Bishop, using the reports of all but the very smallest sects—ranging from the Roman Catholics at 3,250,000 to the Moravians at 12,000—calculated the official membership of the Christian churches of the United States at 7,149,331, or 22.7 percent of the population—very close to Littell's Civil War estimate. See *The Aspects of Religion in the United States* (London, 1859), pp. 33–47. If, as other accounts indicate, church membership increased steadily throughout the antebellum era, these admittedly imperfect statistics suggest that the actual number of churchgoers in antebellum America probably lay somewhere between the two extremes, albeit closer to Littell's smaller figures.

10. Needless to say, even the most inflated of these figures would not set well with present-day conservative politicians and evangelical Protestants, who, lamenting what they see as a disastrous decline in American moral values, frequently allude to the nation's presumed Christian origins. If church membership is any indication, modern Americans are far more religious than their forebears. "During the century and a half [from the early nineteenth to the mid-twentieth centuries] of mass evangelism," Littell wrote, "church membership was brought from about 7 per cent to about 70 per cent of the population." See "The Churches and the Body Politic," p. 36.

11. Winthrop S. Hudson, *American Protestantism* (Chicago, 1961), pp. 109–10; Frances Trollope, *Domestic Manners of the Americans* (London, 1974 [1832]), p. 93.

12. In reality, the small independent congregation, more than likely led by a charismatic individual who has attracted a personal following, has not been very democratic. Disillusioned members usually just leave. But this does not change the validity of the assumption that, for the believer, the church's authority can be far-reaching.

13. Nathan O. Hatch, "*Sola Scriptura* and *Novus Ordo Seclorum*," *The Bible in America: Essays in Cultural History* (ed. Nathan O. Hatch and Mark A. Noll, New York, 1982), pp. 59–78; Hudson, *American Protestantism*, p. 2; James G. Moseley, *A Cultural History of Religion in America* (Westport, Conn., 1981), pp. 58–59.

14. The most notable exception was probably the Dutch Reformed Church, which had won its full independence from the mother church in The Netherlands in 1772. The American church's leadership took no position on slavery, although more than a few Dutch Reformed ministers were concerned about salvation for slaves, winning only a handful of converts in English North America, the West Indies, and South America. See Gerald Francis De Jong, "The Dutch Reformed Church and Negro Slavery in Colonial America," *Church History*, vol. 40, no. 4 (December 1971), pp. 426, 430.

15. William W. Sweet, *The Story of Religion in America* (New York, 1950 [1930]), pp. 5, 293.

16. Richard Bauman, *For the Reputation of Truth: Politics, Religion, and Conflict among Pennsylvania Quakers, 1750–1800* (Baltimore, [1971]), pp. 191–99; James David Essig, "A Very Wintry Season: Virginia Baptists and Slavery, 1785–1797," *Virginia Magazine of History and Biography*, vol. 88, no. 2 (April 1980), p. 181.

17. Perry, *Puritanism and Democracy*, p. 80. Perry included as Calvinist the Congregationalists (mainly New England Puritans), 575,000; Presbyterians (mainly Scotch-Irish), 410,000; Dutch Reformed, 75,000; German Reformed, 50,000; and Baptists (excluding "Free Will Baptists" of Rhode Island), 25,000.

18. Alden T. Vaughan, ed., *The Puritan Tradition in America, 1620–1730* (Columbia, S.C., 1972), pp. xi–xiv; Max Lerner, *America as a Civilization: Life and Thought in the United States Today* (New York, 1957), p. 187.

19. Curtis P. Nettels, *The Roots of American Civilization: A History of American Colonial Life* (2nd ed., New York, 1963), p. 326; Robert C. Twombly and Robert H. Moore, "Black Puritan: The Negro in Seventeenth-Century Massachusetts," *William and Mary Quarterly*, 3rd series, vol. 24, no. 2 (April 1967), p. 224; George H. Moore, *Notes on the History of Slavery in Massachusetts* (New York, 1968 [1866]), p. 51; Edmund S. Morgan, *The Puritan Family. Religion & Domestic Relations in Seventeenth-Century New England* (rev. ed., New York, 1966), p. 111n.

20. United States Department of Commerce, Bureau of the Census, *Negro Population in the United States, 1790–1915* (Washington, D.C., 1918), pp. 45, 51, 57. Connecticut, Rhode Island, and New Hampshire also still reported slaves. Moore, *Notes on the History of Slavery in Massachusetts*, p. 51, cited a census count for Massachusetts of 6,001 for 1790 but did not identify the source for that figure. The Massachusetts State Constitution of 1780 officially abolished slavery, but there were court challenges that were not resolved for several years. See also pp. 200–23.

21. Twombly and Moore, "Black Puritan," pp. 238–39; Morgan, *The Puritan Family*, p. 109.

22. There are only three brief page references under "slavery" in the index and, amazingly, no listing at all for Indians.

23. Perry Miller, *Nature's Nation* (Cambridge, Mass., 1967), p. 5. Considering Perry's and Miller's stature among New England scholars, their failure to say anything about slavery and race tells us a great deal about them, and perhaps about historians generally. In his introduction to the 1967 edition of *Nature's Nation*, Kenneth B. Murdock praised Miller as the consummate historian and literature scholar, who "found the classics of Greece and Rome, the writings of the Middle Ages, and the whole range of literature, American and foreign, past and present, necessary for any approach to comprehension of the past and present history of his country" (p. xii). Yet in all of his "comprehension," Miller said virtually nothing about slavery, race, Africans, or black people, as though such people were indeed invisible in the history of colonial

New England. Such was the tunnel vision of the Western historian, who assumed that anything that was non-Western was simply not worth considering.

24. Twombly and Moore, "Black Puritan," p. 225; Yasuhide Kawashima, *Puritan Justice and the Indian* (Middletown, Conn., 1986), pp. 121–22; Vaughan, ed., *The Puritan Tradition in America*, pp. 267–68.

25. Moore, *Notes on the History of Slavery in Massachusetts*, p. 12. See also Morgan, *The Puritan Family*, pp. 110–11, and Carl N. Degler, *Out of Our Past: The Forces That Shaped Modern America* (New York, 1959), p. 36.

26. William Sumner Jenkins, *Pro-Slavery Thought in the Old South* (Chapel Hill, N.C., 1935), p. 4; Moore, *Notes on the History of Slavery in Massachusetts*, pp. 73–74.

27. Quoted in Degler, *Out of Our Past*, pp. 36–37.

28. George M. Fredrickson, *White Supremacy: A Comparative Study in American and South African History* (New York, 1981), pp. 72–73; Lorenzo Johnston Greene, *The Negro in Colonial New England, 1620–1776* (New York, 1966 [1942]), p. 262.

29. Quoted in Morgan, *The Puritan Family*, pp. 117–18.

30. Greene, *The Negro in Colonial New England*, pp. 257, 282; Lester B. Scherer, *Slavery and the Churches in Early America, 1619–1819* (Grand Rapids, Mich., 1975), p. 83; Vaughan, ed., *The Puritan Tradition in America*, p. 271.

31. Jenkins, *Pro-Slavery Thought in the Old South*, p. 7; Greene, *The Negro in Colonial New England*, pp. 265–66, 285.

32. Scherer, *Slavery and the Churches in Early America*, pp. 96–97; Louis R. Ruchames, ed., *Racial Thought in America* (Vol. I, *From the Puritans to Abraham Lincoln*, Amherst, Mass., 1969), pp. 63–64. See also Gilbert Osofsky, ed., *The Burden of Race: A Documentary History of Negro-White Relations in America* (New York, 1967), pp. 35–39. The full title of Mather's work is *The Negro Christianized; An Essay to Excite and Assist that Good Work, the Instruction of Negro Servants in Christianity* (Boston, 1706).

33. Morgan, *The Puritan Family*, pp. 109, 112–13.

34. Matthew 20:26–28.

35. Historians who have cited Sewall's antislavery thesis include a traditional colonialist (Nettels, *The Roots of American Civilization*, 2nd ed., p. 465), the most respected black historian in the United States (John Hope Franklin, *From Slavery to Freedom*, [5th ed., New York, 1980], p. 195), and a leading scholar in the history of race relations (Winthrop D. Jordan, *White over Black: American Attitudes toward the Negro, 1550–1812* [Chapel Hill, S.C., 1968], pp. 195–96). The *first* antislavery document printed in North America was probably George Keith's *An Exhortation & Caution to Friends Concerning Buying and Keeping Negroes* ([Philadelphia], 1793).

36. There is more than a little irony in the fact that the two matters for which Judge Sewall is best remembered are this antislavery pamphlet and his earlier role as the "hanging judge" in the trials and executions of accused witches in Salem.

37. Samuel Sewall, *The Selling of Joseph, A Memorial* (ed. with notes and commentary by Sidney Kaplan [Boston], 1969 [1701]), p. 10; Ruchames, ed., *Racial Thought in America*, vol. I, p. 46. See also Scherer, *Slavery and the Churches of Early America*, pp. 68–69.

38. Alice Felt Tyler, *Freedom's Ferment: Phases of American Social History from the Colonial Period to the Civil War* (New York, 1962 [1944]), p. 464; Jordan, *White over Black*, pp. 199–200.

39. The full text is reprinted in Stanley Feldstein, ed., *The Poisoned Tongue: A Documentary History of American Racism and Prejudice* (New York, 1972), pp. 36–37. For an analysis of Saffin's argument, see Kaplan's extensive comments in the 1969 reprint of *The Selling of Joseph*, pp. 35–45.

40. Degler, *Out of Our Past*, p. 31.

41. R. H. Tawney, *Religion and the Rise of Capitalism: A Historical Study* (New York, 1954 [1926]), p. 99.

42. Max Weber, *The Protestant Ethic and the Spirit of Capitalism* (trans. by Talcott Parsons, New York, 1958 [1930]). See also Ernst Troeltsch, *Die Soziallehren der Christlichen Kirchen* (1912), pp. 70–74; and G. von Schulze-Gaevernitz, *Britischer Imperialismus und Englischer Freihandel* (1906). For a critical view of Weber, see Tawney, *Religion and the Rise of Capitalism*, pp. 176–77, 261–63n.; and Lujo Brentano, *Die Anfänge des modernen Kapitalismus* (1916), pp. 117–57.

43. Degler, *Out of Our Past*, pp. 6–7.

44. William R. Brock, *The Evolution of American Democracy* (New York, 1970), p. 9. The confluence of work and religious devotion did not end with the Puritans. Two sects that have virtually made a sacrament of hard labor—the Mormons of Joseph Smith and the Black Muslims of Elijah Muhammad—have, ironically, often been objects of public obloquy.

45. Roger Bastide, "Color, Racism, and Christianity," *Daedalus: Journal of the American Academy of Arts and Sciences* (Spring 1967), pp. 322–23.

46. Roy Harvey Pearce, *The Savages of America: A Study of the Indian and the Idea of Civilization* (rev. ed., Baltimore, 1965 [1953]), pp. 25–26; Bastide, "Color, Racism, and Christianity," pp. 320–21; Neal Salisbury, "Red Puritans: The 'Praying Indians' of Massachusetts Bay and John Eliot," *William and Mary Quarterly*, vol. 31, no. 1 (January 1974), pp. 33–35, 41; Miller, *Nature's Nation*, pp. 81–82; Norman Lewis, "English Missionary Interest in the Indians of North America, 1578–1700" (Ph.D. dissertation, University of Washington, Seattle, 1968), pp. 189–292; Vaughan, ed., *The Puritan Tradition in America*, pp. 233–59, 261–62.

47. Ola Elizabeth Winslow, *John Eliot, Apostle to the Indians* (Boston, 1968), pp. 1–3, 90–95, 137–47; Lewis, "English Missionary Interest in the Indians of North America," pp. 269–71; John Josselyn, *An Account of Two Voyages to New-England, Made During the Years 1638, 1663* (Boston, 1865), p. 206. Eliot was not the only—or even the first—to write religious material in an Indian tongue. John Campanius, a Swedish Lutheran who lived in the Delaware Valley from 1643 to 1648, "reduced to writing the sounds of the Indian speech which he heard, and then he laboriously translated Luther's Small Catechism into the dialect of the Lenapes." Returning to Sweden, he revised the work into what eventually became the 1696 edition, 500 copies of which were sent back to the Delaware region. Unlike Eliot, Campanius apparently intended the translation only for the missionaries' use. Like Eliot's, his labor was relatively unproductive. "Some missionary efforts were made with the use of the translation but virtually nothing was accomplished." See E. Clifford Nelson, ed., *The Lutherans in North America* (Philadelphia, 1975), pp. 72–73.

48. Salisbury, "Red Puritans," pp. 28, 32–34; Vaughan, ed., *The Puritan Tradition in America, 1620–1730*, p. 266; Wiliam R. Hutchison, *Errand to the World: American Protestant Thought and Foreign Missions* (Chicago, 1987), pp. 27–28. See also James Axtell, *The Invasion Within: The Contest of Cultures in Colonial North America* (New York, 1985), pp. 173–78.

49. Josselyn, *Two Voyages*, p. 105; Miller, *Nature's Nation*, pp. 81–82.

50. Alden T. Vaughan, *New England Frontier: Puritans and Indians, 1620–1675* (rev. ed., New York, 1979), pp. xii–xiii, 237. Vaughan has pointed out that he uses "transculturation" to indicate the "complete acculturation" of the individual rather than the more common anthropological designation of group adaptation.

51. Pearce, *The Savages of America*, pp. 29–31; Hutchison, *Errand to the World*, pp. 38–39.

52. Cotton Mather, *Magnalia Christi Americana: or, The Ecclesiastical History of New-England; from Its First Planting, in the Year 1620, unto the Year of Our Lord 1698* (2 vols., New York, 1967 [1702]), vol. II, pp. 390–91, and appendix, "*Decennium Luctuosum:* An History of Remarkable Occurences in the Long War, which New-England Hath Had with the Indian Salvages,

from the Year 1688 to the Year 1698, Faithfully Composed and Improved," vol. II, pp. 580–644.

53. Ibid., vol. I, pp. 42, 215; vol. II, p. 552; Cotton Mather, *India Christiana: A Discourse Delivered unto the Commissioners for the Propagation of the Gospel among the American Indians* (Boston, 1721), p. 29.

54. Peter G. Mode, *The Frontier Spirit in American Christianity* (New York, 1923), p. 17; and Francis Jennings, *The Invasion of America: Indians, Colonialism, and the Cant of Conquest* (Chapel Hill, N.C., 1975), pp. 250–51; both quoting Gookin, "Historical Collections of Indians in New England," *Collections Massachusetts Historical Society*, series I, vol. I, p. 195. Jennings listed all fourteen villages—the first group of Natick, Hassenmeist, Magunkaquogt, Punkapoag, Okammakamesit, Wamessit, and Nashobah; and the "new" towns of Manchage, Chabanalongkomun, Maanexit, Quantisset, Wabqyisset, Pakachoog, and Waeuntag—but no Nonantum or Noonatomen!

55. Salisbury, "Red Puritans," pp. 33–35, 54; Kawashima, *Puritan Justice and the Indian*, pp. 106–107, 110–13; Fredrickson, *White Supremacy*, pp. 25–26. For a sympathetic view of Eliot, see Winslow, *John Eliot, Apostle to the Indians*. Obviously favorably disposed toward her subject, Winslow has contended that Eliot did not perceive the Indians as savage "dregs of humanity," which was the common view among most whites. "To him the Indian was a human being, created in God's image, but 'lost.' He must be found and it must be the Christian white man who gave him this chance" (p. 72). For a highly critical view, see Axtell, *The Invasion Within*, pp. 131–78, 218–41. Throughout a chapter entitled "Early Missionary Activity, 1620–1650," Alden T. Vaughan contended that Eliot and Mayhew had "many" followers among the Indians, but, except for Mayhew's meager 22, he gave no numbers and did not explain how many "many" was. See *New England Frontier*, pp. 233–59.

56. Pearce, *The Savages of America*, pp. 29–31.

57. Vaughan, *New England Frontier*, pp. xlii–xliii.

58. Mather, *Magnalia Christi Americana*, vol. I, p. 51; Winslow, *John Eliot*, p. 86.

59. Vaughan, *New England Frontier*, p. 313.

60. Bastide, "Color, Racism, and Christianity," pp. 320–21; Paul Tillich, *A History of Christian Thought: From Its Judaic and Hellenistic Origins to Existentialism* (ed. Carl E. Braaten, New York, 1967), p. 268.

61. Quoted in David E. Stannard, *The Puritan Way of Death: A Study in Religion, Culture, and Social Change* (New York, 1977), pp. 72–73.

62. Translated by J. T. McNeill and excerpted in Hugh T. Kerr, ed., *Readings in Christian Thought* (Nashville, Tenn., 1966), p. 170; Stannard, *The Puritan Way of Death*, p. 27.

63. Michael Wigglesworth, "Day of Doom" (1662), in Roy Harvey Pearce, ed., *Colonial American Writing* (New York, 1950), p. 243.

64. Tillich, *A History of Christian Thought*, p. 269.

65. Ibid., pp. 267, 269; Fredrickson, *White Supremacy*, pp. 25–26; Jenkins, *Pro-Slavery Thought in the Old South*, p. 6.

66. Quoted in Thomas F. Gossett, *Race: The History of an Idea in America* (New York, 1965 [1963]), p. 26.

67. Robert F. Berkhofer, *The White Man's Indian: Images of the American Indian from Columbus to the Present* (New York, 1978), p. 81.

68. The belief that God had set aside a *place* for everyone extended far beyond and long after the Puritan's world and time and, in fact, became a cornerstone of the religious defense of slavery and, later, racial segregation. For example, after the Civil War Southern Baptists continued to argue that God had predetermined society's order and that no person should interfere with it. Racial segregation was a reasonable consequence of divine will; since the black person's inferiority was innate, his "menial role in society was predetermined." See

John W. Storey, "The Negro in Southern Baptist Thought, 1865–1900" (Ph.D. dissertation, University of Kentucky, 1968), p. xi.

69. Kerr, ed., *Readings in Christian Thought*, p. 170; Tillich, *A History of Christian Thought*, p. 268.

70. Pearce, ed., *Colonial American Writing*, pp. 277–78.

71. Tillich, *A History of Christian Thought*, p. 267.

72. Pearce, ed., *Colonial American Writing*, pp. 242–43.

73. Tillich, *A History of Christian Thought*, p. 269.

74. Quoted in Marcus W. Jernagan, "Slavery and Conversion in the American Colonies," *American Historical Review*, vol. 21, no. 3 (April 1916), p. 513.

75. Jordan, *White Over Black*, p. 298; Sweet, *The Story of Religion in America*, pp. 171, 286; W[illis] D. Weatherford, *American Churches and the Negro: An Historical Study from Early Slave Days to the Present* (Boston, 1957), p. 217.

76. Gerald Sorin, *Abolitionism: A New Perspective* (New York, 1972), p. 52; Ruchames, ed., *Racial Thought in America*, vol. I, pp. 438–40; Sydney E. Ahlstrom, *A Religious History of the American People* (New Haven, Conn., 1972), pp. 666–67; Degler, *Out of Our Past*, p. 180. See also Timothy L. Smith, *Revivalism and Social Reform: American Protestantism on the Eve of the Civil War* (New York, 1965 [1957]), p. 190.

77. Jernagan, "Slavery and Conversion in the American Colonies," p. 510; Nettels, *The Roots of American Civilization*, p. 480; Greene, *The Negro in Colonial New England*, p. 269; Ahlstrom, *A Religious History of the American People*, pp. 219–21.

78. Jenkins, *Pro-Slavery Thought in the Old South*, p. 13; Scherer, *Slavery and the Churches in Early America*, pp. 31–33; Gary B. Nash, *Red, White, and Black: The Peoples of Early America* (2nd ed., Englewood Cliffs, N.J., 1982), p. 187; Sweet, *Religion in America*, p. 287; Moore, *Notes on the History of Slavery in Massachusetts*, p. 79; Frank J. Klingberg, *An Appraisal of the Negro in Colonial South Carolina: A Study in Americanization* (Washington, D.C., 1941), p. 123; Olli Alho, *The Religion of the Slaves: A Study of the Religious Tradition and Behaviour of Plantation Slaves in the United States, 1830–1865* (Helsinki, 1976), p. 50; Tyler, *Freedom's Ferment*, p. 519; H. Shelton Smith, *In His Image but . . . : Racism in Southern Religion, 1780–1910* (Durham, N.C., 1972), p. 8; and Herbert S. Klein, *Slavery in the Americas: A Comparative Study of Virginia and Cuba* (Chicago, 1967), pp. 113, 124–25.

79. John C. Van Horne, ed., *Religious Philanthropy and Colonial Slavery: The American Correspondence of the Associates of Dr. Bray, 1717–1777* (Urbana, Ill., 1985), p. 5.

80. Ahlstrom, *A Religious History of the American People*, pp. 219–21. Herbert S. Klein has called Bray's enterprise a "short-lived experiment," but, according to Klein's own evidence, the last school did not close until 1774. See *Slavery in the Americas*, p. 123.

81. Quoted in Frank J. Klingberg, *Anglican Humanitarianism in Colonial New York* (Philadelphia, 1940), p. 131.

82. Van Horne, ed., *Religious Philanthropy and Colonial Slavery*, p. 6.

83. J. D. Fage, *A History of Africa* (New York, 1978), p. 55; Robert W. July, *A History of the African People* (New York, 1970), pp. 45–46; C. Eric Lincoln, *Race, Religion, and the Continuing American Dilemma* (New York, 1984), p. 45.

84. Sir Charles Lucas, *Religion, Colonising & Trade: The Driving Forces of the Old Empire* (London, 1930), pp. 56–57.

85. John Frederick Woolverton, *Colonial Anglicanism in North America* (Detroit, 1984), p. 162. For an extended summary of Le Jau's efforts, with abundant quotations, see Klingberg, *An Appraisal of the Negro in Colonial South Carolina*, pp. 10–26.

86. Klein, *Slavery in the Americas*, p. 111; Lincoln, *Race, Religion, and the Continuing American Dilemma*, p. 38.

87. Sorin, *Abolitionism*, p. 29. See also Klingberg, *Anglican Humanitarianism in Colonial*

New York, passim, and *An Appraisal of the Negro in Colonial South Carolina*, pp. 6–7; Klein, *Slavery in the Americas*, p. 114; and William M. Manross, *A History of the American Episcopal Church* (3rd ed., New York, 1959 [1935]), p. 137.

88. An example of the kind of distortion by omission that can occur when the history of a denomination is written by one of its members is Nelson Waite Rightmyer's *Maryland's Established Church* (Baltimore, 1956). Writing for the Church Historical Society for the Diocese of Maryland, Rightmyer, who was identified as the "Historiographer" of the diocese, covered virtually every topic in Maryland's early history from its founding in the seventeenth century to the Revolution—except slavery. The index lists only one page number under "slavery," but that page does not mention slavery at all. There are eight references listed for the SPG, but none of them mentions slaves or Indians. On the other hand, there is plenty of discussion of *comparative salaries*. Although Rightmyer had a great deal to say about tobacco, he said nothing whatever about the people whose labor made it the most profitable commodity in Maryland's economy. That anyone could write the history of a major denomination in a plantation colony without mentioning slavery—which itself calls attention to the disjunction of the denomination and the slaves—is indicative of the institutional blinders that can afflict the writer who attempts to describe the history of his own church.

89. C. P. Groves, *The Planting of Christianity in Africa* (4 vols., London, 1948), vol. I, pp. 173–74; Klingberg, *An Appraisal of the Negro in Colonial South Carolina*, pp. 4–5. The latter work also includes extensive excerpts from the society's reports.

90. Greene, *The Negro in Colonial New England*, p. 270; Lincoln, *Race, Religion, and the Continuing American Dilemma*, p. 41.

91. Sweet, *Religion in America*, p. 170; S. Charles Bolton, *Southern Anglicanism: The Church of England in Colonial South Carolina* (Westport, Conn., 1982), chapter 6; Leland J. Bellot, "Evangelicals and the Defense of Slavery in Britain's Old Colonial Empire," *Journal of Southern History*, vol. 37, no. 1 (February 1971), pp. 30, 38–39.

92. Jon Butler, "Enlarging the Body of Christ: Slavery, Evangelism, and the Christianization of the White South, 1690–1790," *The Evangelical Tradition in America* (ed. Leonard I. Sweet, Atlanta, Ga., 1984), pp. 102–103, 111. In view of the Established Church's role in cultivating white supremacy in the American South, Butler has criticized Frank Klingberg's use of the word "humanitarianism" in the title *Anglican Humanitarianism in Colonial New York*. Butler may also have had in mind Klingberg's description of the SPG missionaries in South Carolina who saw "the Negro not alone as a producer, but, more fundamentally, as a human being." They not only guided him "into his new environmental adaptation but also intervened for him with the white masters," Klingberg added. "Under the Society's observation, and with its assistance, the Negro in the United States began the slow process of winning his civil and religious rights." The import of this last sentence is diminished by the fact that the SPG ceased to exist before there was a "United States." See *An Appraisal of the Negro in Colonial South Carolina*, p. 139.

93. Jernagan, "Slavery and Conversion in the American Colonies," pp. 517, 517n.; Hutchison, *Errand to the World*, p. 29; Jennings, *The Invasion of America*, pp. 53–56; George Maclaren Brydon, *Virginia's Mother Church and the Political Conditions Under Which It Grew* (2 vols., Richmond, Va., 1947), vol. I, p. 101. While Brydon gave the Indians a close look in Volume I of this work, it is revealing that in two volumes totaling over twelve hundred pages, there is, except for a few references to baptism and the feeble efforts to convert slaves, virtually nothing about slavery. A reader who did not know otherwise could easily conclude that bondage had never existed in Virginia before 1814.

94. Ahlstrom, *A Religious History of the American People*, p. 844; Lincoln, *Race, Réligion, and the Continuing American Dilemma*, p. 46; Bonomi, *Under the Cope of Heaven*, pp. 124–25.

95. Stephen J. Stein, "George Whitefield on Slavery: Some New Evidence," *Church History*,

vol. 42, no. 2 (June 1973), p. 244; Alho, *The Religion of the Slaves*, p. 52; Alan Gallay, "The Origins of Slaveholders' Paternalism: George Whitefield, the Bryan Family, and the Great Awakening in the South," *Journal of Southern History*, vol. 53, no. 3 (August 1987), p. 380.

96. For example, see David S. Lovejoy, *Religious Enthusiasm in the New World: Heresy to Revolution* (Cambridge, Mass., 1985), p. 201.

97. Bellot, "Evangelicals and the Defense of Slavery in Britain's Old Colonial Empire," pp. 20–22, quoting Sir Reginald Coupland, *The British Anti-Slavery Movement* (New York, 1964), p. 57. In 1784, Wesley led dissident Anglicans in both Great Britain and the United States into the new Methodist Episcopal Church; but Whitefield, whose appeal was ecumenical, remained in the English church.

98. Lovejoy, *Religious Enthusiasm in the New World*, p. 199. Lovejoy also argued that "[t]he moral issue of slavery aside, Whitefield did preach a God who was no respecter of color." This may have been hypothetically true, but it was also irrelevant; slavery was a "moral issue," which, in the final analysis, was impossible to put "aside." Whatever "good intentions" Whitefield may have had, as long as he believed slavery was morally acceptable he was no better than any other slaveholder.

99. Bellot, "Evangelicals and the Defense of Slavery in Britain's Old Colonial Empire," pp. 20–22, quoting Sir Reginald Coupland, *The British Anti-Slavery Movement* (New York, 1964), p. 57.

100. Stein, "George Whitefield on Slavery," pp. 243, 245, 246, 248; Gallay, "The Origins of Slaveholders' Paternalism," p. 391; David Brion Davis, *The Problem of Slavery in Western Culture* (Ithaca, N.Y., 1966), p. 388. Davis noted that Jonathan Edwards, without the pressures of a plantation economy, also owned slaves. With Gilbert Tennent joining the group, the slaveholding triumvirate of the Great Awakening was complete. See James D. Essig, *The Bonds of Wickedness: American Evangelicals against Slavery, 1770–1808* (Philadelphia, 1983), p. 14.

101. Ahlstrom, *A Religious History of the American People*, p. 667; Winthrop S. Hudson, *Religion in America* (New York, 1981), p. 204; Tyler, *Freedom's Ferment*, p. 519.

102. Quoted in Carl N. Degler, *The Other South: Southern Dissenters in the Nineteenth Century* (New York, 1974), p. 20. One of the popular abolitionist versions of this theme was: The slaveholder refuses to allow his bondsmen to learn to read, then he criticizes them for being illiterate.

103. Manross, *A History of the American Episcopal Church*, p. 290; John R. McKivigan, *The War against Proslavery Religion: Abolitionism and the Northern Churches, 1830–1865* (Ithaca, N.Y., 1984), p. 165; John H. Hopkins: *Bible View of Slavery* (No. 8 of *Papers from the Society for the Diffusion of Political Knowledge*, New York, 1863), and *Scriptural, Ecclesiastical, and Historical View of Slavery, from the Days of the Patriarch Abraham, to the Nineteenth Century* (New York, 1969 [1864]).

104. Smith, *In His Image*, pp. 196–97, quoting the *Journals* of the Protestant Episcopal Church in the Confederate States of America; *Negroes and Religion: The Episcopal Church of the South, Memorial to the General Convention of the Protestant Episcopal Church in the United States of America* (Charleston, S.C., [1863?]).

105. For an antebellum account of Bishop Polk's operation of his plantation and his devotion to converting his bondsmen to "the Church," see Frederick Law Olmsted, *The Cotton Kingdom: A Traveller's Observations on Cotton and Slavery in the American Slave States* (New York, 1970 [1861]), pp. 460n.–462n., quoting Henry Caswall's "America and the American Church," *The Western World Revisited* (1854).

106. Smith, *In His Image*, pp. 223, 246–48, 301–303.

107. David M. Reimers, *White Protestantism and the Negro* (New York, 1965), pp. 4–5; Sorin, *Abolitionism*, p. 29; Thomas E. Drake, *Quakers and Slavery in America* (Gloucester,

Mass., 1965 [New Haven, Conn., 1950]), p. 5; Anthony Benezet and John Wesley, *Views of American Slavery, Taken a Century Ago* (Philadelphia, 1858), pp. 47–48.

108. Scherer, *Slavery and the Churches in Early America*, pp. 41–42; Stephen B. Weeks, *Southern Quakers and Slavery: A Study in Institutional History* (New York, 1969 [1896]), p. 198. Arriving in the colonies in 1672, Edmundson settled in Albemarle and became the founder of the first Quaker meeting house in what later became North Carolina. His location there may have been one reason why North Carolina became the only southern colony with a substantial Quaker population. See Sorin, *Abolitionism*, p. 35.

109. Drake, *Quakers and Slavery in America* pp. 9–10; Davis, *The Problem of Slavery in Western Culture*, p. 308. "It seems probable," Davis wrote, "that men who had suffered from religious persecution were more likely to see a connection between bodily and spiritual liberty." Davis may have been reaching a little. The Puritans, among others, migrated to avoid the persecution of the Established Church, but they were not particularly concerned about a connection between "bodily and spiritual liberty." Nevertheless, for a comprehensive look at Quakers and slavery, one could do worse than the designated sections of Davis's three major works on slavery: *The Problem of Slavery in Western Culture*, chapter 10, "Religious Sources of Antislavery Thought: Quakers and the Sectarian Tradition"; *The Problem of Slavery in the Age of Revolution, 1770–1823* (Ithaca, N.Y., 1975), chapter 5, "The Quaker Ethic and the Antislavery International"; and *Slavery and Human Progress* (New York, 1984), pp. 136–40. The best single volume on the subject is still Thomas E. Drake's *Quakers and Slavery in America*. The title of Jean R. Soderlund's *Quakers & Slavery: A Divided Spirit* (Princeton, N.J., 1985) suggests a revision of Drake's study but, in fact, it is disappointing in its narrow focus on selected meetings in the Delaware Valley during the last 100 years of the colonial period; and Stephen B. Weeks's old but still valuable volume *Southern Quakers and Slavery: A Study in Institutional History* (New York, 1968 [1896]) examines Quaker activities in the slave states.

110. Ruchames, ed., *Racial Thought in America*, vol. I, pp. 41–45, 77–110; Jenkins, *Pro-Slavery Thought in the Old South*, pp. 8–9. Jenkins has given 1713 as the publication date for Hepburn's piece and 1738 for Lay's.

111. Quoted in George S. Brookes, *Friend Anthony Benezet* (Philadelphia, 1937), p. 77.

112. Ruchames, ed., *Racial Thought in America*, vol. I, pp 111–23; Drake, *Quakers and Slavery in America*, p. 56.

113. Smith, *In His Image*, p. 29. But another historian attributed this statement to Benezet. See Brookes, *Friend Anthony Benezet*, p. 76.

114. Ruchames, ed., *Racial Thought in America*, vol. I, pp. 124–32; Tyler, *Freedom's Ferment*, p. 465; Brookes, *Friend Anthony Benezet*, pp. 84–85. Titles and publication dates varied. Tyler listed the publication year of *Some Historical Account of Guinea* as 1772; and Brookes, *Friend Anthony Benezet*, pp. 82, 89, gave both 1762 and 1784 (the year of his death) for *A Caution and Warning to Great Britain and Her Colonies*. The unknown Quaker editor of *Views of American Slavery, Taken a Century Ago*, pp. 22–23, listed 1767 for both and gave a slightly different title for the former.

115. Brookes, *Friend Anthony Benezet*, p. 77.

116. Ibid., pp. 45–48 and 228–53, from the "Benezet Letters"; Ruchames, ed., *Racial Thought in America*, vol. I, p. 124.

117. Lovejoy, *Religious Enthusiasm in the New World*, pp. 151–52; Jenkins, *Pro-Slavery Thought in the Old South*, p. 10. See especially Benezet's *A Short Account of that Part of Africa Inhabited by Negroes*, and Woolman's *Some Considerations on the Keeping of Negroes*.

118. Ruchames, ed., *Racial Thought in America*, vol. I, p. 41.

119. For a discussion of Keith's differences with the Quaker leadership, see two works by Jon Butler: " 'Gospel Order Improved': The Keithian Schism and the Exercise of Quaker

Ministerial Authority in Pennsylvania," *William and Mary Quarterly*, 3rd series, vol. 31, no. 3 (July 1974), pp. 431–52; and "Power, Authority, and the Origins of American Denominational Order: The English Churches in the Delaware Valley, 1680–1730," *Transactions of the American Philosophical Society*, vol. 68, part 2 (1978), pp. 32–40.

120. Sweet, *The Story of Religion in America*, pp. 288–89; Bauman, *For the Reputation of Truth*, pp. 105, 193; Ahlstrom, *A Religious History of the American People*, p. 650; Sorin, *Abolitionism*, p. 33.

121. Davis, *The Problem of Slavery in Western Culture*, p. 304; Drake, *Quakers and Slavery in America*, p. 6; Weatherford, *American Churches and the Negro*, p. 52; Jenkins, *Pro-Slavery Thought in the Old South*, p. 7; Scherer, *Slavery and the Churches*, pp. 40–41.

122. Scherer, *Slavery and the Churches*, pp. 40–41; Ruchames, ed., *Racial Thought in America*, p. 42; Franklin H. Littell, *The Free Church* (Boston, 1957), pp. 62–63; Drake, *Quakers and Slavery in America*, pp. 4, 5, 11; Tyler, *Freedom's Ferment*, p. 465; Phillips Moulton, "John Woolman's Approach to Social Action—as Exemplified in Relation to Slavery," *Church History*, vol. 30, no. 4 (December 1966); John Woolman, *A Journal of the Life, Gospel Labours, and Christian Experiences of that Faithful Minister of Jesus Christ, John Woolman, Late of Mount-Holly, in the Province of New-Jersey* (Secaucus, N.J., 1961 reprint of 1871 edition [Philadelphia, 1774]), p. 118.

123. Weeks, *Southern Quakers and Slavery*, pp. vii–viii, 1–2, 201–206; Sweet, *The Story of Religion in America*, p. 289. According to Weeks, the southern Quaker migration, "especially into Ohio and Indiana," made the Midwest "the greatest stronghold of Quakerism in the world." Today, Indiana and Ohio claim two of the largest and most active Quaker populations in the United States.

124. Weatherford, *American Churches and the Negro*, p. 67; Weeks, *Southern Quakers and Slavery*, pp. 206–207, 224–29.

125. Drake, *Quakers and Slavery in America*, pp. 11–12. The full text of the Germantown Protest can be found in several anthologies dealing with religion or race, e.g., Ruchames, ed., *Racial Thought in America*, vol. I, pp. 38–40; and H. Shelton Smith, Robert T. Handy, and Lefferts A. Loetscher, eds., *American Christianity: An Historical Interpretation with Representative Documents* (2 vols., New York, 1960), vol. I, pp. 181–82.

126. Quoted in Weatherford, *American Churches and the Negro*, p. 62.

127. Nettels, *The Roots of American Civilization*, p. 545.

128. Davis, *The Problem of Slavery in Western Culture*, p. 30; Smith, *In His Image*, pp. 34–35; Sorin, *Abolitionism*, pp. 63–64; Pearce, *The Savages of America*, pp. 35–40. For an example of Quaker communication with Indians, see Woolman, *Journal*, pp. 145–56.

129. Auguste Jorns, *The Quakers as Pioneers in Social Work* (trans. by Thomas Kite Brown, Jr., from *Studien über die Sozialpolitik der Quäker* [1931], Montclair, N.J., 1969), pp. 197–98. Barbados, the first West Indian island to become English, was, along with Jamaica, a popular New World relocation site for banished Quakers.

130. Drake, *Quakers and Slavery in America*, p. 197.

131. Ibid., pp. 9–10.

132. Weatherford, *American Churches and the Negro*, pp. 43–48; Davis, *The Problem of Slavery in Western Culture*, p. 291.

133. Bauman, *For the Reputation of Truth*, p. 193.

134. Quoted in Weatherford, *American Churches and the Negro*, p. 63.

135. Brookes, *Friend Anthony Benezet*, pp. 280–81, from "Benezet Letters"; Drake, *Quakers and Slavery in America*, pp. 51, 53; Bauman, *For the Reputation of Truth*, p. 105; Woolman, *Journal*, p. 93. See also Moulton, "John Woolman's Approach to Social Action," especially pp. 400–401.

136. Brookes, *Friend Anthony Benezet*, pp. 285, 291, 294–95, from "Benezet Letters."

137. Quoted in Degler, *The Other South*, pp. 28–29.

138. John Parrish, *Remarks on the Slavery of the Black People; Addressed to the Citizens of the United States, Particularly to Those Who Are in Legislative or Executive Stations in the General or State Governments; and also to Such Individuals as Hold Them in Bondage* (Philadelphia, 1806).

139. [Society of Friends], *The Appeal of the Religious Society of Friends of Pennsylvania, New York, New Jersey, Delaware, etc., to Their Fellow-Citizens of the United States on Behalf of the Coloured Races* (Philadelphia, 1858), pp. 3–5; McKivigan, *The War against Proslavery Religion*, pp. 105–106, 163.

140. Drake, *Quakers and Slavery in America*, p. 4; Bauman, *For the Reputation of Truth*, pp. 191–99; Weeks, *Southern Quakers and Slavery*, pp. 232–33.

CHAPTER EIGHT

1. H. Shelton Smith, *In His Image but . . . : Racism in Southern Religion, 1780–1910* (Durham, N.C., 1972), p. 127.

2. Sydney E. Ahlstrom, *A Religious History of the American People* (New Haven, Conn., 1972), pp. 666–67.

3. C. C. Goen, *Broken Churches, Broken Nation: Denominational Schisms and the Coming of the Civil War* (Macon, Ga., 1985), p. 113.

4. For an excellent discussion of the deep divisions in the churches, see chapter 12, "Christian Liberty and Human Bondage: The Paradox of Slavery," in Timothy L. Smith, *Revivalism and Social Reform: American Protestantism on the Eve of the Civil War* (New York, 1965 [1957]), pp. 178–203.

5. This is the central theme of Franklin H. Littell's "The Churches and the Body Politic," *Daedalus: Journal of the American Academy of Arts and Sciences* (Winter 1967), pp. 22–42. American churches passed through three stages, Littell wrote. During the first, "Congregationalism and Anglicanism were dominant." In the second, "Baptists, Methodists, and Disciples or Christians achieved major statistical growth and influence." In the most recent period, " 'late-bloomers,' like the Lutherans—once confined to linguistic ghettos—are exercising a major liturgical and theological influence" (see pages 33–34).

6. George M. Marsden, *The Evangelical Mind and the New School Presbyterian Experience: A Case Study of Thought and Theology in Nineteenth-Century America* (New Haven, Conn., 1970), p. 89; Clifford E. Clark, Jr., "The Changing Nature of Protestantism in Mid-Nineteenth Century: Henry Ward Beecher's *Seven Lectures to Young Men*," *Journal of American History*, vol. 57, no. 4 (March 1971), pp. 839–40; James D. Essig, *The Bonds of Wickedness: American Evangelicals against Slavery, 1770–1808* (Philadelphia, 1983), p. 69.

7. William R. Brock, *The Evolution of American Democracy* (New York, 1970), p. 130; Alexis de Tocqueville, *Democracy in America* (ed. J. P. Mayer and Max Lerner, translated by George Lawrence, New York, 1966 [1835]), p. 267; Reinhold Niebuhr, *Moral Man and Immoral Society: A Study in Ethics and Politics* (New York, 1960 [1932]), passim; Kyle Haselden, *The Racial Problem in Christian Perspective* (New York, 1964 [1959]), p. 62; James G. Moseley, *A Cultural History of Religion in America* (Westport, Conn., 1981), pp. 107–108.

8. Frances Trollope, *Domestic Matters of the Americans* (London, 1974 [1832]), p. 93; Harriet Martineau, *Society in America* (ed. Seymour Martin Lipset, Gloucester, Mass., 1968 [1837]), pp. 347–50; David Macrae, *The Americans at Home* (New York, 1952 [Edinburgh, 1870]), p. 588.

9. Marsden, *The Evangelical Mind and the New School Presbyterian Experience*, p. 89. See also Goen, *Broken Churches, Broken Nation*, p. 188.

10. Tocqueville, *Democracy in America*, p. 265; John R. McKivigan, *The War against Pro-*

slavery Religion: Abolitionism and the Northern Democracy, 1830–1865 (Ithaca, N.Y., 1984), p. 172; Richard Bryant Drake, "The American Missionary Association and the Southern Negro, 1861–1888" (Ph.D. dissertation, Emory University, 1957), p. 4; Clifton Herman Johnson, "The American Missionary Association, 1846–1861: A Study of Christian Abolitionism" (Ph.D. dissertation, University of North Carolina, Chapel Hill, 1958), pp. 1–2; David M. Reimers, *White Protestantism and the Negro* (New York, 1965), p. 9.

11. Martineau, *Society in America*, p. 335; Carl N. Degler, *Out of Our Past: The Forces That Shaped Modern America* (New York, 1959), p. 180; Ebenezer Davies, *American Scenes and Christian Slavery: A Recent Tour of Four Thousand Miles in the United States* (London, 1849), p. 25; Reimers, *White Protestantism and the Negro*, pp. 4, 19, 25, 27, 39–40; Joel Williamson, *The Crucible of Race: Black-White Relations in the American South since Emancipation* (New York, 1984), pp. 276–83.

12. Smith, *Revivalism and Social Reform*, pp. 179–80. See Gilbert H. Barnes, *The Antislavery Impulse, 1830–1844* (New York, 1933), and Barnes and Dwight L. Dumond, eds., *Letters of Theodore Dwight Weld, Angelina Grimké Weld and Sarah Grimké, 1822–1844* (New York, 1934).

13. Many northern Protestant ministers spoke against slavery without joining an abolitionist organization. According to David M. Reimers, Methodists and Congregationalists were the most vociferous. See *White Protestantism and the Negro*, p. 23.

14. McKivigan, *The War against Proslavery Religion*, pp. 90–91, 200; William Warren Sweet, *Methodism in American History* (rev. ed., Nashville, Tenn., 1953), p. 233, and *The Story of Religion in America* (New York, 1950 [1930]), p. 5; Goen, *Broken Churches, Broken Nation*, pp. 11, 188. For an especially critical denunciation of the racial insensitivity of the modern church, see Haselden, *The Racial Problem in Christian Perspective*, pp. 13–14.

15. [Carlyle McKinley], *An Appeal to Pharaoh: The Negro Problem and Its Radical Solution* (New York, 1889), pp. 120–30.

16. Sweet, *The Story of Religion in America*, p. 293; Joseph W. Phillips, *Jedidiah Morse and the New England Congregationalists* (New Brunswick, N.J., 1983), pp. 187, 189.

17. Henry Clay, *An Address, Delivered to the Colonization Society of Kentucky, at Frankfort, December 17, 1829* (Lexington, Ky., 1829), pp. 3–4. For similar arguments, see: [Edward Carbery], *Inducements to the Colored People of the United States to Emigrate to British Guiana* (Boston, 1840); David Christy, *A Lecture on African Colonization, Delivered in the Hall of the House of Representatives of Ohio* (Cincinnati, 1849), and *A Lecture on the Present Relations of Free Labor to Slave Labor, in Tropical and Semi-Tropical Countries* (Cincinnati, 1850); Robert J. Breckinridge, *The Black Race: Some Reflections on Its Position and Destiny as Connected with Our American Dispensation. A Discourse Delivered before the Kentucky Colonization Society, at Frankfort, on the 6th of February, 1851* (Frankfort, Ky., 1851); *The Annual Report of the Colonization Society of the State of Iowa, with the Proceedings of the Second Anniversary, in the Capitol, January 23, 1851* (Iowa City, Ia., [1857]); and James Mitchell, *Letter on the Relation of the White and African Races in the United States, Showing the Necessity of the Colonization of the Latter. Addressed to the President of the United States* (Washington, D.C., 1862).

18. J[ohn] K[endrick] Converse, *A Discourse on the Moral, Legal and Domestic Condition of Our Colored Population, Preached before the Vermont Colonization Society, at Montpelier, October 17, 1832* (Burlington, Vt., 1832), pp. 3–6; Fredrika Bremer, *The Homes of the New World: Impressions of America* (trans. by Mary Howitt, 2 vols., New York, 1853), vol. II, pp. 445–48. See also Donald G. Mathews, "The Methodist Mission to the Slaves, 1829–1844," *Journal of American History*, vol. 51, no. 4 (March 1965), p. 617; and John R. Bodo, *The Protestant Clergy and Public Issues, 1812–1848* (Princeton, N.J., 1954), pp. 113–32, 139–42, 147–51.

19. William R. Hutchison, *Errand to the World: American Protestant Thought and Foreign Missions* (Chicago, 1987), pp. 31–32; H. Shelton Smith, Robert T. Handy, and Lefferts A. Loetscher, eds., *American Christianity: An Historical Interpretation with Representative Docu-*

ments (2 vols., New York, 1960), vol. I, p. 335; Joseph Conforti, "Jonathan Edwards' Most Popular Work, 'The Life of David Brainerd' and Nineteenth-Century Evangelical Culture," *Church History*, vol. 54, no. 2 (June 1985), pp. 188–89; Lefferts A. Loetscher, *A Brief History of the Presbyterians* (3rd ed., Philadelphia, 1978), p. 69. Jesse Page's *David Brainerd: The Apostle to the Indians* (New York, [1901?]) glorifies the subject too much to be very useful.

20. Conforti, "Jonathan Edwards' Most Popular Work," passim.

21. Andrew E. Murray, *Presbyterians and the Negro—A History* (Philadelphia, 1966), p. 10; Lester B. Scherer, *Slavery and the Churches in Early America, 1619–1819* (Grand Rapids, Mich., 1975), p. 92; Samuel Stanhope Smith, *An Essay on the Causes of the Variety of Complexion and Figure in the Human Species* (ed. Winthrop D. Jordan, Cambridge, Mass., 1965, reprint of the 2nd edition, 1810 [1787]).

22. Marsden, *The Evangelical Mind and the New School Presbyterian Experience*, pp. 89–90.

23. John Robinson, *The Testimony and Practice of the Presbyterian Church in Reference to American Slavery* (Cincinnati, 1852), p. 24. The proclamation is reproduced in full in Smith, Handy, and Loetscher, eds., *American Christianity*, vol. II, pp. 179–82.

24. Sweet, *The Story of Religion in America*, p. 292; [James Gillespie Birney], *The American Churches—The Bulwarks of American Slavery* (New York, 1969 [1842]), p. 29; Loetscher, *A Brief History of the Presbyterians*, p. 94; Smith, *In His Image*, p. 77.

25. George Bourne, *The Book and Slavery Irreconcilable, with Animadversions upon Dr. Smith's Philosophy* (Philadelphia, 1816), pp. 4–5; Murray, *Presbyterians and the Negro*, pp. 20–28; Louis Ruchames, ed., *Racial Thought in America* (Amherst, Mass., 1969), vol. I, p. 261; Ernest Trice Thompson, *Presbyterians in the South* (vol. I, 1607–1861, Richmond, Va., 1963), pp. 328–31; Smith, *In His Image*, pp. 61–66. In 1845 Bourne published a 91-page book that was virtually a passage-by-passage refutation of the most popular proslavery biblical arguments, including the Curse of Canaan, the Jubilee, the Onesimus story, Pauline obedience, and etymological analysis. See *A Condensed Anti-Slavery Bible Argument; By a Citizen of Virginia* (New York).

26. Gerald Sorin, *Abolitionism: A New Perspective* (New York, 1972), p. 52; Loetscher, *A Brief History of the Presbyterians*, p. 69; Alice Felt Tyler, *Freedom's Ferment: Phases of American Social History from the Colonial Period to the Civil War* (New York, 1962 [1944]), p. 520; McKivigan, *The War Against Proslavery Religion*, p. 102; Smectymnuus (pseud.), *Slavery and the Church* (Boston, 1856).

27. Victor B. Howard, "The Southern Aid Society and the Slavery Controversy," *Church History*, vol. 41, no. 2 (June 1972), pp. 208–24; Smith, *Revivalism and Social Reform*, pp. 186, 196–97; Sorin, *Abolitionism*, p. 52.

28. Donald G. Mathews, *Religion in the Old South* (Chicago, 1977), p. 139; and "Charles Colcock Jones and the Southern Evangelical Crusade to Form a Biracial Community," *Journal of Southern History*, vol. 41, no. 3 (August 1975), pp. 301, 305.

29. Mathews, *Religion in the Old South*, p. 141; South Carolina and Georgia Synod, *Report of the Committee to Whom Was Referred the Subject of the Religious Instruction of the Colored Population . . .* (Charleston, S.C., 1834), quoted in Murray, *Presbyterians and the Negro*, p. 56.

30. Thompson, *Presbyterians in the South*, vol. I, pp. 338–441; Loetscher, *A Brief History of the Presbyterians*, pp. 94–95; Mathews, "Charles Colcock Jones," pp. 310–12.

31. Olli Alho, *The Religion of the Slaves: A Study of the Religious Tradition and Behaviour of Plantation Slaves in the United States, 1830–1865* (Helsinki, 1976), p. 56; Smith, *In His Image*, p. 79.

32. Smith, *In His Image*, pp. 82–93.

33. See the resolutions of the various synods in [Birney], *The American Churches*, pp. 35–36. It should be noted that since there were far fewer southern New School churches than Old School, there were many more proslavery Presbyterians in the latter. See Goen,

Broken Churches, Broken Nation, pp. 68–78; and McKivigan, *The War against Proslavery Religion*, pp. 82–84, 165–66.

34. Elwyn A. Smith, "The Role of the South in the Presbyterian Schism of 1837–38," *Church History*, vol. 29, no. 1 (March 1960), p. 45; S. B. Treadwell, *American Liberties and American Slavery: Morally and Politically Illustrated* (New York, 1969 [1838]), p. 255.

35. Smith, *Revivalism and Social Reform*, p. 185; Winthrop S. Hudson, *Religion in America* (New York, 1981), pp. 202–205; C. Bruce Staiger, "Abolitionism and the Presbyterian Schism of 1837–1838," *Mississippi Valley Historical Review*, vol. 36, no. 3 (December 1949), p. 391 and passim. See also Marsden, *The Evangelical Mind and the New School Presbyterian Experience*, pp. 93–103.

36. John Hope Franklin, *From Slavery to Freedom: A History of Negro Americans* (New York, 1980), p. 145 in the fifth edition; [Isabella Lucy (Bird) Bishop], *Aspects of Religion in the United States* (London, 1859), pp. 33–40.

37. Murray, *Presbyterians and the Negro*, p. 65.

38. James Oscar Farmer, Jr., *The Metaphysical Confederacy: James Henley Thornwell and the Synthesis of Southern Values* (Macon, Ga., 1986), p. 201. See also E. Brooks Holifield, *The Gentleman Theologians: American Theology in Southern Culture, 1795–1860* (Durham, N.C., 1978), p. 221n.; and Randy J. Sparks, "Religion in Amite County. 1800–1861," *Masters & Slaves in the House of the Lord: Race and Religion in the American South, 1740–1870* (John B. Boles, ed., Lexington, Ky., 1988), p. 68.

39. Edmund A. Moore, *Robert J. Breckinridge and the Slavery Aspect of the Presbyterian Schism of 1837* (Chicago, 1932), passim, reprinted from *Church History*, vol. 4, no. 4 (December 1935).

40. Ahlstrom, *A Religious History of the American People*, p. 660; Moore, *Robert J. Breckinridge and the Slavery Aspect of the Presbyterian Schism of 1837*, p. 7; Robinson, *The Testimony and Practice of the Presbyterian Church*.

41. McKivigan, *The War Against Proslavery Religion*, pp. 167–70; Carl N. Degler, *The Other South: Southern Dissenters in the Nineteenth Century* (New York, 1974), pp. 29–31.

42. Ahlstrom, *A Religious History of the American People*, p. 660; Smith, *In His Image*, p. 196; Robert Manson Myers, ed., *The Children of Pride: Selected Letters to the Family of Rev. Dr. Charles Colcock Jones from the Years 1860–1868, with the Addition of Several Previously Unpublished Letters* (abridged ed., New Haven, Conn., 1984), D. H. Porter to C. C. Jones, Sr. (April 27, 1861), and C. C. Jones, Sr., to D. H. Porter (April 30, 1861), pp. 54–55; Smith, Handy, and Loetscher, eds., *American Christianity*, vol. II, pp. 205–10.

43. Thompson, *Presbyterians in the South*, vol. I, p. 550; Smith, *In His Image*, pp. 205–206.

44. Myers, ed., *The Children of Pride:* C. C. Jones, Sr., to C. C. Jones, Jr. (April 20, 1861), p. 53; C. C. Jones, Jr., to C. C. Jones, Sr. (September 10, 1862), p. 291; C. C. Jones, Sr., to C. C. Jones, Jr. (September 30, 1862), pp. 297–98.

45. Quoted in Smith, *In His Image*, p. 205.

46. *The American Annual Cyclopedia and Register of Important Events* (84 vols., New York, 1870–1903), (1865), p. 706.

47. The market value of the slave population in 1860 is impossible to calculate with any accuracy. According to the Eighth Census there were 3,953,760 slaves in fifteen southern and border states. An average price of $500 per slave would have meant a value of $2 billion. Most historical estimates have been higher.

48. Smith, *In His Image*, pp. 237–44, 266–67; William A. Clebsch, "Christian Interpretations of the Civil War," *Church History*, vol. 30, no. 2 (June 1961), pp. 214–15.

49. "Race Problem in the South" (July 1900), quoted in Smith, *In His Image*, pp. 271–73; Loetscher, *A Brief History of the Presbyterians*, p. 125; David M. Reimers, "The Race Problem and Presbyterian Union," *Church History*, vol. 31, no. 2 (June 1962), pp. 203–15.

50. Ahlstrom, *A Religious History of the American People*, p. 661. See also Ben J. Wattenberg, ed., *The Statistical History of the United States: From Colonial Times to the Present* (New York, 1976), p. 390.

51. Donald G. Mathews, *Slavery and Methodism: A Chapter in American Morality, 1780–1845* (Princeton, N.J., 1965), p. 283.

52. Ahlstrom, *A Religious History of the American People*, p. 371, says 80 percent. Goen, *Broken Churches*, pp. 111–12, says 90 percent.

53. C. Eric Lincoln, *Race, Religion, and the Continuing American Dilemma* (New York, 1984), p. 47; Peter Gardella, *Innocent Ecstasy: How Christianity Gave America an Ethic of Sexual Pleasure* (New York, 1985), p. 86.

54. Moseley, *Cultural History of Religion in America*, p. 57. A comparison with other reports suggests that these figures are on the high side.

55. Goen, *Broken Churches, Broken Nation*, pp. 111–12.

56. Ibid., p. 187, quoting Edwin S. Gausted, *Historical Atlas of Religion in America* (New York, 1962), pp. 52, 96. Note that the 1800 figure of 70,000 is *less* than the 1791 count of 76,150 cited above (and attributed to Moseley, *Cultural History of Religion in America*, p. 57), which is, if nothing else, a reminder that church-membership numbers varied widely depending on who was doing the counting.

57. McKivigan, *The War against Proslavery Religion*, p. 92, quoting the Methodist Episcopal Church, *The Methodist Almanac for the Year of Our Lord, 1849* (New York, 1849), p. 21; Gausted, ed., *The Statistical History of the United States*, p. 392. The 1849 count divided into 629,660 members of the (northern) Methodist Episcopal Church and 465,553 members of the Methodist Episcopal Church, South. The same report cited a figure of 1,190,700 Roman Catholics, a number that, of course, included many recent immigrants from Ireland. Thus, at a time when most Americans (and many since then) thought of their nation as predominantly Protestant, the Catholic Church was already the largest *single* Christian church in the United States, reaching 3.25 million by 1860—double the combined Methodist membership for that year.

58. Smith, *In His Image*, p. 113; Lewis McCaroll Purifoy, Jr., "The Methodist Episcopal Church, South, and Slavery, 1844–1865" (Ph.D. dissertation, University of North Carolina, Chapel Hill, 1965), p. 341; Ahlstrom, *Religious History of the American People*, p. 661.

59. Mathews, "The Methodist Mission to the Slaves, 1829–1844," pp. 615, 628.

60. There is more than a little disparity in the various reports. The Statistical Office of the Methodist Church, 1790–1948, in *Methodist History as Revealed in Statistical Form* (Chicago, 1949), counted 856,000 members in 1840. See Ben J. Wattenberg, ed., *The Statistical History of the United States: From Colonial Times to the Present* (New York, 1976), pp. 390, 392. See also Katherine L. Dvorak, "After Apocalypse, Moses," *Masters & Slaves in the House of the Lord*, p. 189. For numbers of black Methodists in Florida, see Robert L. Hall, "Black and White Christians in Florida," *Masters & Slaves in the House of the Lord*, p. 88.

61. Smith, *In His Image*, p. 94.

62. Alho, *Religion of the Slaves*, pp. 55–56; W. D. Weatherford, *American Churches and the Negro: An Historical Study from Early Slave Days to the Present* (Boston, 1957), p. 95. See also *supra*, chapter 4.

63. John Nelson Norwood, *The Schism in the Methodist Episcopal Church, 1844: A Study of Slavery and Ecclesiastical Politics* (Philadelphia, 1976 [New York, 1923]), pp. 12–13.

64. For the story on Benezet's inspiration of Wesley, see Tyler, *Freedom's Ferment*, p. 465; Thomas E. Drake, *Quakers and Slavery in America* (New Haven, Conn., 1950), p. 91; and George S. Brookes, *Friend Anthony Benezet* (Philadelphia, 1937), pp. 84–85. Applying a modern definition of *plagiarism* may be unfair to Wesley. In what Brookes called "a century of free plagiarism," the practice of repeating someone else's words was not considered especially opprobrious. In fact, Benezet apparently had been flattered. Writing to Wesley on May 23,

1774, he acknowledged *Thoughts on Slavery* and said it gave him "much satisfaction." Indeed, Benezet even "plagiarized"—if that is the correct word—from himself. In three letters written six months apart in 1772, he described the brutalizing effect of slavery on whites using almost exactly the same words and sentences. See *Friend Anthony Benezet*, "Benezet Letters" to Wesley, p. 318; and to John and Henry Gurney, Granville Sharp, and Richard Shackleton, pp. 285, 291, 294–95. In 1858, a Quaker group called the Association of Friends for the Diffusion of Religious and Useful Knowledge published Wesley's essay and two of Benezet's other works under the title *Views of American Slavery, Taken a Century Ago.*

65. Ahlstrom, *Religious History of the American People*, p. 650; Sweet, *Story of Religion in America*, p. 291; Milton Bryan Powell, "Abolitionist Controversy in the Methodist Episcopal Church" (Ph.D. dissertation, State University of Iowa, 1963), pp. 121–28; Norwood, *The Schism in the Methodist Episcopal Church, 1844*, p. 13.

66. Mathews, *Slavery and Methodism*, pp. 8–13, 26, 47; Paul Otis Evans, "The Ideology of Inequality: Asbury, Methodism, and Slavery" (Ph.D. dissertation, Rutgers University, 1981), passim; Mathews, "The Methodist Mission to Slaves," *Journal of American History*, vol. 51, no. 4 (March 1965), p. 615.

67. Quoted in William Sumner Jenkins, *Pro-Slavery Thought in the Old South* (Chapel Hill, N.C., 1935), p. 54.

68. M[oncure] D[aniel] Conway, *Testimonies Concerning Slavery* (London, 1864), pp. 1–2, 36.

69. Smith, *In His Image*, p. 98; Sorin, *Abolitionism*, p. 52; Tyler, *Freedom's Ferment*, p. 520.

70. Purifoy, "The Methodist Episcopal Church, South," p. 325, quoting *Journal of the General Conference of the Methodist Episcopal Church, 1796–1836*. See also [Birney], *The American Churches*, pp. 10–26.

71. Smith, *In His Image*, pp. 100–102; Mathews, "The Methodist Mission to the Slaves," pp. 621–23, 629–30.

72. This principle has continued to serve conservative Protestantism. During the civil rights demonstrations of the 1960s, clergymen and nuns who marched through southern communities with Martin Luther King, Jr., were often confronted by local preachers who asked, "How many souls have you saved today?"

73. Smith, *In His Image*, pp. 106–107; Smith, *Revivalism and Social Reform*, pp. 184–85; Charles Baumer Swaney, *Episcopal Methodism and Slavery: With Sidelights on Ecclesiastical Politics* (Boston, 1926), pp. 59–100; Norwood, *The Schism in the Methodist Episcopal Church*, pp. 25–26, 48. The Wesleyan Methodist Connection of America was formally created on May 31, 1843. See Smith, Handy, and Loetscher, eds., *American Christianity*, vol. II, pp. 198–200.

74. Blake Touchstone, "Planters and Slave Religion in the Deep South," *Masters & Slaves in the House of the Lord*, p. 100; Purifoy, "The Methodist Episcopal Church, South," p. 325n.; Swaney, *Episcopal Methodism and Slavery*, pp. 120–28; Norwood, *The Schism in the Methodist Episcopal Church*, pp. 66–80, 82–101; McKivigan, *The War against Proslavery Religion*, p. 86; Ahlstrom, *Religious History of the American People*, pp. 661–62.

75. Purifoy, "The Methodist Episcopal Church, South," pp. 326–29.

76. Ibid., p. 338; Wesley L. Norton, "The Religious Press and the Compromise of 1850" (Ph.D. dissertation, University of Illinois, 1959), passim. The Methodist church had not been the first denomination to benefit from McTyeire's proslavery writings. In 1849, while serving in New Orleans, he was one of three ministers whose essays were chosen for $200 cash awards by the Baptist State Convention of Alabama as the best statements on the proper biblical relationship between masters and servants. See H[olland] N[immons] McTyeire, C. F. Sturgis, and A. Holmes, *Duties of Masters to Servants: Three Premium Essays* (Charleston, S.C., 1851).

77. Smith, *In His Image*, pp. 113–14; McKivigan, *The War against Proslavery Religion*, p. 171. See also Goen, *Broken Churches, Broken Nation*, p. 138.

78. For a brief but excellent historical analysis of the "three forms of Christian polity" in America—congregational, presbyterian, and episcopal—see Ralph Barton Perry, *Puritanism and Democracy* (New York, 1944), pp. 105–106.

79. Norwood, *The Schism in the Methodist Episcopal Church*, from the preface; Ahlstrom, *A Religious History of the American People*, p. 661.

80. Reimers, *White Protestantism and the Negro*, p. 23; Smith, *Revivalism and Social Reform*, pp. 220–21. For examples of Haven's views, see his *Sermons, Speeches, and Letters on Slavery and Its War. From the Passage of the Fugitive Slave Bill to the Election of President Grant* (New York, 1969 [Boston, 1869]).

81. Quoted in Robert T. Handy, *A Christian America: Protestant Hopes and Historical Realities* (New York, 1971), pp. 107–108.

82. Smith, *In His Image*, pp. 229–37; William Bernard Gravely, "Gilbert Haven, Racial Equalitarian" (Ph.D. dissertation, Duke University, 1969), passim.

83. Ralph E. Morrow, *Northern Methodism and Reconstruction* (East Lansing, Mich., 1956), pp. 187–88, 199–200; *Methodist Advocate*, February 23, 1875.

84. Kenneth K. Bailey, "The Post-Civil War Racial Separation in Southern Protestantism: Another Look," *Church History*, vol. 46, no. 4 (December 1977), pp. 453–73; Reimers, *White Protestantism and the Negro*, pp. 56–57, 62–64; George M. Fredrickson, *The Black Image in the White Mind: The Debate on Afro-American Character and Destiny, 1817–1914* (New York, 1971), p. 241. Hamilton was a poor prognosticator. The Eighteenth Census (1960) counted 22.6 million black Americans. See Wattenberg, ed., *The Statistical History of the United States*, p. 12.

85. Williamson, *The Crucible of Race*, pp. 88–93; Smith, Handy, and Loetscher, eds., *American Christianity*, vol. II, pp. 373–77.

86. Kenneth M. Stampp, *The Peculiar Institution: Slavery in the Ante-Bellum South* (New York, 1956), p. vii.

87. Fredrickson, *The Black Image in the White Mind*, p. 241; McKivigan, *The War against Proslavery Religion*, p. 107.

88. In 1660 there were only 4 Baptist churches in all of English North America, compared to 41 Anglican and 75 Congregational (Puritan). By 1740 their respective numbers had increased to 96, 246, and 423, plus 160 Presbyterian. Forty years later the count was 457, 406, 749, and 495. Of course, these figures do not take into account the different sizes of congregations. See Gausted, *Historical Atlas of Religion in America*, pp. 3–4.

89. Smith, *In His Image*, p. 47; W. Harrison Daniel, "Virginia Baptists and the Negro in the Early Republic," *The Virginia Magazine of History and Biography*, vol. 80, no. 1 (January 1972), p. 65; James D. Essig, "A Very Wintry Season: Virginia Baptists and Slavery," *Virginia Magazine of History and Biography*, vol. 88, no. 2 (April 1980), pp. 181–82, and *Bonds of Wickedness*, pp. 67–69, 145–48; Goen, *Broken Churches, Broken Nation*, p. 166.

90. Smith, *In His Image*, p. 49. The full title of Barrow's work was *Involuntary, Unmerited, Perpetual, Absolute, Hereditary Slavery, Examined: on the Principles of Nature, Reason, Justice, Policy, and Scripture* (Lexington, Ky., 1808).

91. Smith, *In His Image*, p. 49; David E. Harrell, Jr., *Quest for a Christian America: The Disciples of Christ and American Society to 1866* (Nashville, 1966), p. 100; John Lee Eighmy, *Churches in Cultural Captivity: A History of the Social Attitudes of Southern Baptists* (Knoxville, Tenn., 1987), p. 5.

92. Ahlstrom, *A Religious History of the American People*, p. 650; Sweet, *Story of Religion*, pp. 290–91; Smith, *In His Image*, pp. 114–15.

93. Smith, *In His Image*, p. 118.

94. Lincoln, *Race, Religion, and the Continuing American Dilemma*, p. 47.

95. Daniel, "Virginia Baptists and the Negro in the Early Republic," p. 60. See also Larry M. James, "Biracial Fellowship in Antebellum Baptist Churches," *Masters & Slaves in the House of the Lord*, pp. 37–57.

96. Daniel, "Virginia Baptists and the Negro in the Early Republic," p. 62; Alho, *Religion of the Slaves*, pp. 51, 56–57; Eighmy, *Churches in Cultural Captivity*, pp. 27–28.

97. Mathews, "The Methodist Mission to the Slaves, 1829–1844," p. 628; Eighmy, *Churches in Cultural Captivity*, pp. 25–26; Frederick Law Olmsted, *The Cotton Kingdom: A Traveller's Observations on Cotton and Slavery in the American Slave States* (New York, 1970 [1861]), p. 349.

98. Melville J. Herskovits, *The Myth of the Negro Past* (New York, 1958 [1941]), pp. 232–33. For a discussion of African spirit beliefs, see *infra*, chapter 5.

99. Eighmy, *Churches in Cultural Captivity*, p. 26; Daniel, "Virginia Baptists and the Negro in the Early Republic," p. 65; Goen, *Broken Churches, Broken Nation*, p. 166.

100. Jeremiah Bell Jeter, *Recollections of a Long Life* (Richmond, Va., 1891), pp. 67–71; Touchstone, "Planters and Slave Religion," p. 107; Daniel, "Virginia Baptists and the Negro in the Early Republic," pp. 67–68. See also Iveson L. Brookes: *A Defence of the South against the Reproaches and Incroachments of the North . . .* (Hamburg, S.C., 1850); and *A Defence of Southern Slavery, against the Attacks of Henry Clay and Alex'r Campbell . . .* ([Hamburg, S.C., 1851]).

101. Daniel, "Virginia Baptists and the Negro in the Early Republic," p. 69.

102. The Baptist Declaration of 1822 was published as *Rev. Dr. Richard Furman's Exposition of the Views of the Baptists, Relative to the Coloured Population of the United States, in a Communication to the Governor of South-Carolina* (Charleston, S.C., 1823). See also Smith, Handy, and Loetscher, eds., *American Christianity*, vol. II, pp. 183–86; and Eighmy, *Churches in Cultural Captivity*, pp. 5–6.

103. Goen, *Broken Churches, Broken Nation*, pp. 150–51. Fitzhugh's two major works are *Sociology for the South* (Richmond, Va., 1854), and *Cannibals All! or, Slaves without Masters* (Richmond, Va., 1857). Both works, with commentary, are available in one volume in Harvey Wish, ed., *Antebellum: Writings of George Fitzhugh and Hinton Rowan Helper on Slavery* (New York, 1960).

104. [Birney], *The American Churches*, pp. 26–27; Goen, *Broken Churches, Broken Nation*, pp. 91, 93.

105. Goen, *Broken Churches, Broken Nation*, pp. 94–98; Tyler, *Freedom's Ferment*, p. 520. Of the three mainline Protestant churches that divided into northern and southern divisions before the Civil War, only the Southern Baptists have retained their distinctive sectional identity. In fact, the Baptist tradition of decentralization has resulted in a number of independent systems and congregations; but the Southern Baptist Church has become a *national* organization and is the largest Protestant denomination in the United States.

106. Sweet, *Story of Religion*, p. 287; O. K. and Margorie M. Armstrong, *The Indomitable Baptists: A Narrative of Their Role in Shaping American History* (Garden City, N.Y., 1967), pp. 164–67. The work by the Armstrongs is one of two recent books about the Southern Baptists that reveal the racial blinders still common among the faithful. The subtitle of their volume is certainly sweeping enough to justify high expectations, but the work suffers from the predictable lack of objectivity when members of a church write about themselves. In a chapter on the schism of 1845 the authors said nothing about the moral issues involved in the debate over slavery and race relations; and in another chapter on the emergence of the black Baptist movement, there is no explanation of the reasons for the separatist impulse and no discussion of the racist conditions under which black Baptists organized. In his more scholarly study, *Tried as by Fire: Southern Baptists and the Religious Controversies of the 1920s* (Macon, Ga., 1982), James J. Thompson described the familiar conflicts over the fundamentalist issues of evolution, urbanism, and conservatism in the decade after World War I, but he ignored the race question

altogether. The index lists eleven different page references under "prohibition," but there are no entries at all for "race," "Negro," "segregation," or any related topic. In the Epilogue the author did note that after World War II Southern Baptists *started* "facing the South's number one social problem"—which only makes one wonder why he made no effort to explain their earlier lack of interest in it. In fairness to Thompson, it needs to be pointed out that the Southern Baptists of the twenties probably did not believe they had a racial problem and, in any event, believed it was not a religious matter. Such a posture, of course, was only one more manifestation of the insidiousness of institutional racism.

107. Eighmy, *Churches in Cultural Captivity*, pp. 14–16; Jeter, *Recollections of a Long Life*, pp. 232, 234–37.

108. Essig, "A Very Wintry Season," p. 185; Eighmy, *Churches in Cultural Captivity*, pp. 11–12; E. N. Elliott, ed., *Cotton Is King, and Pro-Slavery Arguments: Comprising the Writings of Hammond, Harper, Christy, Stringfellow, Hodge, Bledsoe, and Cartwright, on this Important Subject* (Augusta, Ga., 1860), pp. 492–508; Smith, *In His Image*, pp. 116, 118, 120–21.

109. McKivigan, *The War against Proslavery Religion*, pp. 87–90; Eighmy, *Churches in Cultural Captivity*, p. 8; Essig, *Bonds of Wickedness*, pp. 68, 145; Ahlstrom, *A Religious History of the American People*, pp. 663, 665–66.

110. Essig, "A Very Wintry Season," pp. 181–82. See also [Birney], *American Churches*, pp. 26–28.

111. Sorin, *Abolitionism*, pp. 52, 63–64.

112. Smith, *In His Image*, pp. 116–18.

113. Essig, *The Bonds of Wickedness*, p. 5. Italics added.

114. McKivigan, *The War against Proslavery Religion*, pp. 162–63, 177; Drake, *Quakers and Slavery in America*, pp. 165–66; Goen, *Broken Churches, Broken Nation*, pp. 94, 114–15.

115. Edward H. Madden, *Civil Disobedience and Moral Law in Nineteenth-Century American Philosophy* (Seattle, 1968), pp. 30–33; Francis Wayland, *The Limitations of Human Responsibility* (Boston, 1838), pp. 161–88; Smith, *In His Image*, pp. 116–18.

116. The letters were published as *Domestic Slavery Considered as a Scriptural Institution* (New York, 1856).

117. Madden, *Civil Disobedience and Moral Law*, pp. 41–43; Elliott, ed., *Cotton Is King, and Pro-Slavery Arguments*, p. 521; Goen, *Broken Churches, Broken Nation*, pp. 114–15.

118. The *Religious Herald* of Richmond, Virginia, was one of the most popular of the Southern Baptist periodicals that supported the call for a divinely ordained separation of the races. Others included the *Baptist Record* (Jackson, Mississippi), *Baptist Standard* (Dallas), *Christian Index* (Atlanta), *Biblical Recorder* (Raleigh, North Carolina), *Baptist and Reflector* (Nashville), *Working Christian* (Columbia, South Carolina), *Baptist Courier* (Greenville, South Carolina), *The Baptist* (Tennessee), *Alabama Baptist*, *Florida Baptist Witness*, *Texas Baptist*, *Texas Baptist Herald*, and *Tennessee Baptist*. For a review of some of the articles in these journals, see John W. Storey, "The Negro in Southern Baptist Thought, 1865–1900" (Ph.D. dissertation, University of Kentucky, 1968).

119. Eighmy, *Churches in Cultural Captivity*, pp. 30–31, 33–34, 38–40; Reimers, *White Protestantism and the Negro*, pp. 27, 57–58; Smith, *In His Image*, pp. 226–29, 264–65.

120. Storey, "The Negro in Southern Baptist Thought," pp. xi, 32, 208.

121. Ibid., pp. 42–47. For a discussion of Payne's and Carroll's works, see *supra*, chapters 3 and 6.

122. Handy, *A Christian America*, pp. 106–107.

123. The well eventually ran dry. Dixon's last book, *The Flaming Sword* (1939), went unnoticed, and he died seven years after its publication, as committed a white supremacist as ever. See Smith, *In His Image*, pp. 274–77.

124. B[enjamin] F. Riley, *The White Man's Burden: A Discussion of the Interracial Question*

with Special Reference to the Responsibility of the White Race to the Negro Problem (Birmingham, Ala., 1910), passim; Wayne Flynt, "Dissent in Zion: Alabama Baptists and Social Issues, 1900–1914," *Journal of Southern History*, vol. 35, no. 4 (November 1969), p. 537.

125. Flynt, "Dissent in Zion," pp. 524, 537–38. This 20-page article purports to deal with social issues in Alabama between 1900 and 1914, but the author did not even address Alabama's, and the South's, primary social problem until the fifteenth page and then for only four paragraphs.

126. Quoted in Flynt, "Dissent in Zion," pp. 538–39.

127. Goen, *Broken Churches, Broken Nation*, p. 4.

128. Ibid., pp. 117–18.

129. Smith, *In His Image*, pp. 127–28. The word "miscegenation" was not coined until 1863, when certain Democrats brought it into use to discredit Lincoln and the Republicans during the presidential campaign of 1864. Prior to that time, the world "amalgamation" was usually used to designate racial mixture, and "mongrelization" was a favorite term among white supremacists. See Forrest G. Wood, *Black Scare: The Racist Response to Emancipation and Reconstruction* (Berkeley, Calif., 1968), chapter 4.

130. Smith, *In His Image*, pp. 197–98.

131. James Brewer Stewart, "Evangelicalism and the Radical Strain in Southern Antislavery Thought During the 1820s," *Journal of Southern History*, vol. 39, no. 3 (August 1973), p. 379; Kenneth K. Bailey, "Protestantism and Afro-Americans in the Old South: Another Look," *Journal of Southern History*, vol. 41, no. 4 (November 1975), p. 452.

132. Stewart, "Evangelicalism and the Radical Strain," p. 381n.; Bailey, "Protestantism and Afro-Americans," p. 471.

133. Donald G. Mathews, "The Abolitionists on Slavery: The Critique Behind the Social Movement," *Journal of Southern History*, vol. 33, no. 2 (May 1967), p. 174; Goen, *Broken Churches, Broken Nation*, p. 5; Robert E. Shalhope, "Race, Class, Slavery, and the Antebellum Southern Mind," *Journal of Southern History*, vol. 37, no. 4 (November 1971), p. 561.

134. Essig, *Bonds of Wickedness*, p. 70; William Jay, *An Inquiry into the Character and Tendency of the American Colonization and American Anti-Slavery Societies* (New York, 1835), p. 128; Smith, *Revivalism and Social Reform*, p. 70; William Hosmer, *Slavery and the Church* (New York, 1969 [1853]), p. 98; McKivigan, *The War against Proslavery Religion*, p. 109.

135. McKivigan, *The War against Proslavery Religion*, pp. 90–91, 200.

136. Reimers, *White Protestantism and the Negro*, pp. 51–52; Goen, *Broken Churches, Broken Nation*, pp. 11, 188.

CHAPTER NINE

1. The term "melting pot" apparently was popularized by writer Israel Zangwill, *The Melting Pot* (New York, 1923).

2. Ben J. Wattenberg, ed., *The Statistical History of the United States: From Colonial Times to the Present* (New York, 1976), pp. 105–106.

3. Martin E. Marty, *Righteous Empire: The Protestant Experience in America* (New York, 1970), p. 16; Wattenberg, ed., *The Statistical History of the United States*, pp. 105–106.

4. Carl E. Degler, *Out of Our Past: The Forces That Shaped Modern America* (New York, 1959), pp. 281–82, 290.

5. Sydney E. Ahlstrom, *A Religious History of the American People* (New Haven, Conn., 1972), pp. 45, 848.

6. Alfred P. Schultz, *Race or Mongrel: A Brief History of the Rise and Fall of the Ancient Races of the Earth: A Theory that the Fall of Nations Is Due to Intermarriage with Alien Stocks. A*

Demonstration that a Nation's Strength Is Due to Racial Purity. A Prophecy that America Will Sink to Early Decay unless Immigration Is Rigorously Restricted (Boston, 1908); Madison Grant, *The Passing of the Great Race* (4th ed., New York, 1921 [1916]).

7. Ahlstrom, *A Religious History of the American People*, p. 853; John Higham, *Strangers in the Land: Patterns of American Nativism, 1860–1925* (New York, 1965), pp. 62–63, 80–87. For a good summary of the APA's activities, see Gustavus Myers, *History of Bigotry in the United States* (ed. and rev. by Henry M. Christman, New York, 1960 [1943]), pp. 163–91. It is revealing that in a work on the history of bigotry in America, Myers mentioned the race issue—a discussion of the Ku Klux Klan in the 1920s—in only *one* out of thirty-one chapters. For the most comprehensive analysis of the APA, see Donald L. Kinzer, *An Episode in Anti-Catholicism: The American Protective Association* (Seattle, 1964). For a copy of "The Secret Oath of the American Protective Association, October 31, 1893," see John Tracy Ellis, ed., *Documents of American Catholic History* (3 vols., Wilmington, Del., 1987), vol. II, pp. 483–85.

8. James B. Clarke, "The Negro and the Immigrant in the Two Americas: An International Aspect of the Color Problem," *The Negro's Progress in Fifty Years. The Annals of the American Academy of Political and Social Science*, vol. 49, no. 138 (September 1913), p. 35.

9. Degler, *Out of Our Past*, p. 295; Wood Gray, *The Hidden Civil War: The Story of the Copperheads* (New York, 1942), p. 99.

10. New York *World*, November 4, 1862; *Abolition Philanthropy! The Fugitive Slave Law. Too Bad for Southern Negroes, but Good Enough for Free Citizens of Foreign Birth! Handcuffs for White Men! Shoulder Straps for Negroes! Voters Read!* ([Philadelphia, 1863]); A. C. Harness, *The Great Trial; or, The Genius of Civilization Brought to Judgement* (Philadelphia, 1873), p. 54.

11. William Hepworth Dixon, *White Conquest* (2 vols., London, 1876), vol. II, pp. 237–38.

12. Degler, *Out of Our Past*, p. 280. See also Leon F. Litwack, *North of Slavery: The Negro in the Free States* (Chicago, 1961), p. 163.

13. Degler, *Out of Our Past*, pp. 291–92.

14. Max Lerner, *America as a Civilization: Life and Thought in the United States Today* (New York, 1957), p. 503; Degler, *Out of Our Past*, pp. 286–87.

15. Degler, *Out of Our Past*, pp. 294–95; Ahlstrom, *A Religious History of the American People*, p. 751.

16. E. Clifford Nelson, ed., *The Lutherans in North America* (Philadelphia, 1975), pp. 33–34; Edwin S. Gausted, ed., *A Historical Atlas of Religion in America* (New York, 1962), pp. 3–4.

17. Wattenberg, ed., *The Statistical History of the United States*, p. 106; Robert Fortenbaugh, "American Lutheran Synods and Slavery, 1830–1860," *Journal of Religion*, vol. 13, no. 1 (January 1933), p. 72; Gausted, ed., *A Historical Atlas of Religion in America*, pp. 43–44, 54–55; Ahlstrom, *A Religious History of the American People*, p. 756; John T. Handy, ed., "The Manifold Transplantations of Lutheranism," *Religion in the American Experience: The Pluralistic Style* (Columbia, S.C., 1972), p. 24. Actually, it was possible to divide these 20 Lutheran groups into as many as 66 semi-independent bodies.

18. W. D. Weatherford, *American Churches and the Negro: An Historical Study from Early Slave Days to the Present* (Boston, 1957), p. 154; Nelson, ed., *The Lutherans in North America*, pp. 142–43; Fortenbaugh, "American Lutheran Synods and Slavery," p. 75; Abdel Ross Wentz, *A Basic History of Lutheranism in America* (rev. ed., Philadelphia 1955 [1923]), pp. 162, 163–64; John R. McKivigan, *The War against Proslavery Religion: Abolitionism and the Northern Churches, 1830–1865* (Ithaca, N.Y., 1984), p. 165; Fortenbaugh, "American Lutheran Synods and Slavery," pp. 75, 81, 83.

19. Wentz, *Lutheranism in America*, pp. 163–64, 168, 171; Ralph L. Moellering, *Christian Conscience and Negro Emancipation* (Philadelphia, 1965), p. 85; Gausted, *A Historical Atlas of Religion in America*, pp. 43–44, 54–55; [Isabella Lucy (Bird) Bishop], *The Aspects of Religion in*

the United States (London, 1859), pp. 41–47; Douglas C. Stange, *Radicalism for Humanity: A Study of Lutheran Abolitionism* (St. Louis, 1970), pp. 14–19; Nelson, ed., *The Lutherans in North America*, pp. 142–43; Fortenbaugh, "American Lutheran Synods and Slavery," pp. 81, 89–90.

20. Ahlstrom, *A Religious History of the American People*, p. 757; Moellering, *Christian Conscience and Negro Emancipation*, pp. 89–90; Fortenbaugh, "American Lutheran Synods and Slavery," pp. 88–90.

21. Moellering, *Christian Conscience and Negro Emancipation*, pp. 89–90. See also Wentz, *Lutheranism in America*, pp. 168–69.

22. Fortenbaugh, "American Lutheran Synods and Slavery," pp. 72–73.

23. Wentz, *Lutheranism in America*, pp. 164–66; Weatherford, *American Churches and the Negro*, pp. 143–44; Fortenbaugh, "American Lutheran Synods and Slavery," pp. 79–80.

24. See especially *The Doctrine of the Unity of the Human Race Examined on the Principles of Science* (Charleston, 1850) and *Examination of Prof. Agassiz's Sketch of the Natural Provinces* (Charleston, 1855). Abdel Ross Wentz, in *A Basic History of Lutheranism in America*, p. 166, asserted that Bachman's "vindication of slaveholders" was "one of the best ever written." But Wentz, who was ordained in the United Lutheran Church in America, did not clarify "best," and his use of the term "vindication"—which means to prove right and absolve of guilt—raises some serious questions about his objectivity, questions underscored by his frequently hyperbolic conclusions and unwillingness to include any documentation. A modern history of the Lutherans was long overdue and, fortunately, it came in the much more scholarly collaborative effort edited by E. Clifford Nelson, *The Lutherans in North America*.

25. Nelson, ed., *The Lutherans in North America*, p. 127.

26. Ibid., p. 74.

27. Quoted in Ahlstrom, *A Religious History of the American People*, p. 255.

28. Wentz, *Lutheranism in America*, p. 57; Nelson, ed., *The Lutherans in North America*, p. 74; Weatherford, *American Churches and the Negro*, pp. 142–43.

29. Weatherford, *American Churches and the Negro*, p. 140; Nelson, ed., *The Lutherans in North America*, p. 74; Ahlstrom, *A Religious History of the American People*, p. 667; Moellering, *Christian Conscience and Negro Emancipation*, p. 85; Wentz, *Lutheranism in America*, p. 167.

30. Nelson, ed., *The Lutherans in North America*, p. 127; Ahlstrom, *A Religious History of the American People*, p. 761; Fortenbaugh, "American Lutheran Synods and Slavery," pp. 73, 86; McKivigan, *The War Against Proslavery Religion*, pp. 105, 165; Gerald Sorin, *Abolitionism: A New Perspective* (New York, 1972), pp. 52–53.

31. Thomas F. Gossett, *Race: The History of an Idea in America* (New York, 1965 [1963]), p. 26, citing Kohn, *Nationalism in the Soviet Union* (London, 1933), p. 123.

32. Gausted, *Historical Atlas of Religion in America*, pp. 3–4; H. Shelton Smith, Robert T. Handy, and Lefferts A. Loetscher, eds., *American Christianity: An Historical Interpretation with Representative Documents* (2 vols., New York, 1960), vol. I, p. 360; Ahlstrom, *A Religious History of the American People*, pp. 529, 531; Madeleine Hooke Rice, *American Catholic Opinion in the Slavery Controversy* (New York, 1948), p. 43.

33. Gausted, *Historical Atlas of Religion in America*, pp. 43–44, 54–55.

34. Mother Hyacinth to Yves-Marie Le Conniat (August 25, 1856), in (Sister) Dorothea Olga McCants, ed., *They Came to Louisiana: Letters of a Catholic Mission, 1854–1882* (Baton Rouge, La., 1970), p. 44.

35. Wattenberg, ed., *The Statistical History of the United States*, p. 106; [Bishop], *Aspects of Religion*, pp. 41–47. Wattenberg's figures for the Catholic church do not go back beyond 1891, but his numbers for the Methodists in 1859 match Bishop's count almost exactly. It should be noted that the Catholic church customarily counted all of the people in a Catholic community as Catholic even though many of them did not actually profess the faith, while

Protestant churches usually counted only those who had formally joined. The most extreme example of Catholic inflation of numbers could be found in the baptism of Indians in Latin America, where a missionary, simply with a wave of his hand, would "baptize" masses of Indians standing before him. Of course, most of the Indians had no idea what had happened, but the missionary could nonetheless file a report with his superiors in which he claimed to have baptized "thousands."

36. John W. Storey, "The Negro in Southern Baptist Thought, 1865–1900" (Ph.D. dissertation, University of Kentucky, 1968), p. vi.

37. Okot p'Bitek, *African Religions in Western Scholarship* (Kampala, Uganda, [1970]), p. 3. Protestant England was not far behind. Parliament legalized the purchase of slaves in 1565.

38. Randall M. Miller, "Slaves and Southern Catholicism," *Masters & Slaves in the House of the Lord: Race and Religion in the American South, 1740–1870* (ed. John B. Boles, Lexington, Ky., 1988), pp. 128–29; John Tracey Ellis, *American Catholicism* (2nd ed., Chicago, 1969), pp. 90–91; Joseph D. Brokhage, *Francis Patrick Kenrick's Opinion of Slavery* (Washington, D.C., 1955), p. 37.

39. Mother Hyacinth to Yves-Marie Le Conniat (November 17, 1855), to Bishop Martin (January 12, 1856), and to Yves-Marie Le Conniat (March 24, 1856), in McCants, ed., *They Came to Louisiana*, pp. 28, 36, 39.

40. Brokhage, *Kenrick's Opinion of Slavery*, p. 37; James Hennesey, *American Catholics: A History of the Roman Catholic Community in the United States* (New York, 1981), p. 144.

41. Ellis, *American Catholicism*, pp. 90–91; R. Emmett Curran, S. J., " 'Splendid Poverty': Jesuit Slaveholding in Maryland, 1805–1838," *Catholics in the Old South: Essays on Church and Culture* (ed. Randall M. Miller and Jon L. Wakelyn, Macon, Ga., 1983), pp. 125–26; Hennesey, *American Catholics*, p. 144; Miller, "Slaves and Southern Catholicism," pp. 128–29; Rice, *American Catholic Opinion in the Slavery Controversy*, pp. 41–43.

42. Joseph Butsch, "Catholics and the Negro," *Journal of Negro History*, vol. 2, no. 4 (October 1917), p. 397.

43. Orlando Patterson, *Slavery and Social Death: A Comparative Study* (Cambridge, Mass., 1982), p. 72.

44. Hennesey, *American Catholics*, p. 145.

45. Rice, *American Catholic Opinion*, pp. 12, 152; Ellis, *American Catholicism*, p. 89.

46. Ahlstrom, *A Religious History of the American People*, pp. 667–68.

47. Brokhage, *Kenrick's Opinion of Slavery*, pp. 115, 242. Like many authors who are devout members of the church they are writing about—e.g., Mary Veronica Miceli, "The Influence of the Roman Catholic Church on Slavery in Colonial Louisiana under French Domination, 1718–1763" (Ph.D. dissertation, Tulane University, 1979)—Brokhage, trying to put Kenrick in the most favorable light, was unable to be altogether objective in his criticisms.

48. Miceli, "The Influence of the Roman Catholic Church on Slavery in Colonial Louisiana under French Domination, 1718–1763," p. 58; Ellis, *American Catholicism*, p. 90; John C. Murphy, "An Analysis of the Attitudes of American Catholics toward the Immigrant and the Negro, 1825–1925" (Ph.D. dissertation, Catholic University of America, 1940), pp. 40–43; Thomas Virgil Peterson, *Ham and Japheth: The Mythic World of Whites in the Antebellum South* (Metuchen, N.J., 1978), p. 21; H. Shelton Smith, *In His Image but . . . : Racism in Southern Religion, 1780–1910* (Durham, N.C., 1972), pp. 198–201; Ellis, ed., *Documents of American Catholic History*, vol. II, pp. 347–56.

49. Murphy, "Attitudes of American Catholics," pp. 46–51, 53–56, 137; Ellis, *American Catholicism*, pp. 92–94.

50. Murphy, "Attitudes of American Catholics," pp. 46–51; Ellis, ed., *Documents of American Catholic History*, vol. II, pp. 378–83. Father Purcell would not be the last urban Catholic cleric to incur the wrath of his parishioners over the race issue. In November 1969, syndi-

cated columnist D. J. R. Bruckner wrote: "Bishop Fulton Sheen tried innovations in his Rochester, N.Y., diocese which so isolated him from his conservative people that he had to resign. In 1966, Catholics in Chicago insulted and threatened John Cardinal Cody because he supported Dr. Martin Luther King. In 1967 Archbishop William Cousins of Milwaukee refused to censure the Rev. James Groppi, the civil rights leader, and the people of the diocese cut their charity contributions drastically." See Los Angeles *Times*, November 1, 1969.

51. Ellis, *American Catholicism*, pp. 92–94; Jon L. Wakelyn, "Catholic Elites in the Slave-holding South," *Catholics in the Old South*, p. 216; Ahlstrom, *A Religious History of the American People*, pp. 667–68; Winthrop S. Hudson, *Religion in America* (New York, 1981), p. 204; Rice, *American Catholic Opinion in the Slavery Controversy*, pp. 158–59.

52. Murphy, "Attitudes of American Catholics," pp. 60–79, 137; Ahlstrom, *A Religious History of the American People*, p. 550.

53. Weatherford, *American Churches and the Negro*, p. 244; Miller, "Slaves and Southern Catholicism," p. 130; C. Eric Lincoln, *Race, Religion, and the Continuing American Dilemma* (New York, 1984), p. 38; John La Farge, S.J., *The Catholic Viewpoint on Race Relations* (rev. ed., Garden City, N.Y., 1960), pp. 52–53; Brokhage, *Kenrick's Opinion of Slavery*, p. 39.

54. Ahlstrom, *A Religious History of the American People*, p. 750, citing the Department of Justice, Immigration and Naturalization Service, *Annual Reports* (the exact numbers were: Germany 6,906,465; Italy, 5,149,119; Great Britain, 4,777,727; and Ireland, 4,712,680); Degler, *Out of Our Past*, p. 293.

55. Rowland Berthoff, *An Unsettled People: Social Order and Disorder in American History* (New York, 1971), pp. 251–52; Rice, *American Catholic Opinion in the Slavery Controversy*, pp. 80–82, 124, 161; Jay P. Dolan, *The Immigrant Church: New York's Irish and German Catholics, 1815–1865* (Baltimore, 1975), pp. 24–25; Williston H. Lofton, "Northern Labor and the Negro during the Civil War," *Journal of Negro History*, vol. 34, no. 3 (July 1949), pp. 256–71.

56. Rice, *American Catholic Opinion in the Slavery Controversy*, p. 159; Brokhage, *Kenrick's Opinion of Slavery*, p. 37; Randall M. Miller, "The Failed Mission: The Catholic Church and Black Catholics in the Old South," *Catholics in the Old South*, pp. 149–70; Jay P. Dolan, *The American Catholic Experience: A History from Colonial Times to the Present* (Garden City, N.Y., 1985), p. 360; Miller, "Slaves and Southern Catholicism," p. 127, 131ff.

57. Rice, *American Catholic Opinion in the Slavery Controversy*, p. 59. A counterargument holds that the Catholic system of saints to whom believers prayed for intercession made it highly compatible with the Africans' traditional belief in a pantheon of gods and therefore a religion that blacks were *more* likely to be attracted to. In places like Cuba and Brazil, where close ties to Africa were maintained for many years and where the Catholic Church dominated religious life, this argument seems to hold up. On the other hand, the early abolition of the foreign slave trade in the predominantly Protestant United States precluded any such development. For a fuller discussion of this topic see Albert J. Raboteau, *Slave Religion: The "Invisible Institution" in the Antebellum South* (New York, 1978), pp. 22–25, 87–92. See also *supra*, chapter 1.

58. Murphy, "Attitudes of American Catholics," pp. 56–57, 114–35; La Farge, *The Catholic Viewpoint on Race Relations*, pp. 54–55; David Macrae, *The Americans at Home* (New York, 1952 [Edinburgh, 1870]), p. 375; Miller, "Slaves and Southern Catholicism," pp. 150ff.; Ellis, *American Catholicism*, pp. 101–102.

59. Ellis, ed., *Documents of American Catholic History*, vol. II, pp. 432–36.

60. Dolan, *The American Catholic Experience*, p. 360; Ellis, *American Catholicism*, p. 103. The "St. Joseph's Society of the Sacred Heart" was founded in 1866 in Mill Hill, London, by Herbert Vaughan, later the Cardinal Archbishop of Westminster. In response to a plea from the Baltimore Plenary Council for priests to serve former slaves and a concomitant request

for a mission assignment from Vaughan, Pope Pius IX suggested that the order take on the American field. Eventually, it became obvious that an American community of priests could better serve the mission, and in 1893, as a result of an agreement between Vaughan and Cardinal James Gibbons of Baltimore, a new group, the Society of St. Joseph, assumed responsibility for meeting the special needs of black Catholics. By 1917 there were Josephite branches in most of the southern and border states. In 1964 the largest contingent was in Louisiana, where 66 priests served 71,265 parishioners. See *New Catholic Encyclopedia* (17 vols., New York, 1967), vol. 7, pp. 1119–20.

61. Henry F. May, *The Protestant Churches and Industrial America* (New York, 1963 [1949]), p. 235; Ahlstrom, *A Religious History of the American People*, p. 842.

62. May, *The Protestant Churches and Industrial America*, p. 91. May's book, Aaron Ignatius Abell's *The Urban Impact on American Protestantism, 1865–1900* (Cambridge, Mass., 1943), and Charles Howard Hopkins's *The Rise of the Social Gospel in American Protestantism, 1865–1913* (New Haven, Conn., 1940) are the three works most often listed as "indispensable" in any study of the Social Gospel, but all three, ironically, say virtually nothing about the Social Gospel in relation to the most oppressed Americans of all.

63. Ahlstrom, *A Religious History of the American People*, p. 786; Degler, *Out of Our Past*, p. 348; Paul A. Carter, *The Spiritual Crisis of the Gilded Age* (DeKalb, Ill., 1971), pp. 151–53.

64. Gunther Barth, *City People: The Rise of Modern City Culture in Nineteenth-Century America* (New York, 1980), p. 16. For a discussion of the whites' fear of former slaves' migrating north, see Forrest G. Wood, *Black Scare: The Racist Response to Emancipation and Reconstruction* (Berkeley, Calif., 1968), chapter 2.

65. Degler, *Out of Our Past*, p. 343; E. Digby Baltzell, *The Protestant Establishment: Aristocracy and Caste in America* (New York, 1964), p. 161.

66. Matthew 19:16–22.

67. Timothy L. Smith, *Revivalism and Social Reform: American Protestantism on the Eve of the Civil War* (New York, 1965 [1957]), p. 163; Winthrop S. Hudson, *American Protestantism* (Chicago, 1961), pp. 112–15; Ahlstrom, *A Religious History of the American People*, p. 787.

68. Edward H. Madden, *Civil Disobedience and Moral Law in Nineteenth-Century American Philosophy* (Seattle, 1968), pp. 30–33; Clifford E. Clark, Jr., "The Changing Nature of Protestantism in Mid-Nineteenth Century: Henry Ward Beecher's *Seven Lectures to Young Men*," *Journal of American History*, vol. 57, no. 4 (March 1971), pp. 839–40; James H. Moorehead, "Social Reform and the Divided Conscience of Antebellum Protestantism," *Church History*, vol. 48, no. 4 (December 1979), p. 424; Wentz, *Lutheranism in America*, pp. 327–32.

69. Reinhold Niebuhr, *Moral Man and Immoral Society: A Study in Ethics and Politics* (New York, 1960 [1932]), p. 77; Leon F. Litwack, *Been in the Storm so Long: The Aftermath of Slavery* (New York, 1979), pp. 477ff.

70. Frederick A. Bode, "Religion and Class Hegemony: A Populist Critique in North Carolina," *Journal of Southern History*, vol. 37, no. 3 (August 1971), pp. 417–18, 425–26.

71. United States Department of Commerce, Bureau of the Census, *Negro Population, 1790–1915* (Washington, D.C., 1918), pp. 54–55; James G. Moseley, *A Cultural History of Religion in America* (Westport, Conn., 1981), p. 94; Degler, *Out of Our Past*, pp. 346–47.

72. James Dombrowski, *The Early Days of Christian Socialism in America* (New York, 1936), pp. 17, 19–20. See also Baltzell, *The Protestant Establishment*, p. 161.

73. Ahlstrom, *A Religious History of the American People*, pp. 792–95; Washington Gladden, *Social Facts and Forces: The Factory—the Labor Union—the Corporation—the Railway—the City—the Church* (Port Washington, N.Y., 1971 [1897]), p. 212.

74. Rauschenbusch, "The Ideals of Social Reformers," *American Journal of Sociology*, vol. 2 (July 1896–May 1897), pp. 202–219, in Robert T. Handy, ed., *The Social Gospel in America, 1870–1920: Gladden, Ely, and Rauschenbusch* (New York, 1966), p. 280.

75. John R. Aiken, "Walter Rauschenbusch and Education for Reform," *Church History*, vol. 36, no. 4 (December 1967), pp. 460–61.

76. For an excellent critique of Rauschenbusch's influence, see Robert D. Cross's introduction to the Harper Torchbook edition of *Christianity and the Social Crisis* (New York, 1964), pp. viii–xx.

77. Clark, "The Changing Nature of Protestantism in Mid-Nineteenth Century," pp. 839–40; David M. Reimers, *White Protestantism and the Negro* (New York, 1965), pp. 53–54. Spokesmen for the Social Gospel were not the only ones who ignored the racial issues. Paul Boyer covered an entire century of urban development in *Urban Masses and Moral Order in America, 1820–1920* (Cambridge, Mass., 1978), but, except for a reference in a footnote to black migration to northern cities in the early twentieth century, he said nothing at all about black Americans. In *The Rise of the Social Gospel in American Protestantism, 1865–1913*, Charles Howard Hopkins frequently mentions the "race problem," but there is no discussion of any attempt to deal with it. See especially pp. 92, 112, 261–62, 266, 271, 277, and 319. On pages 141–44, Hopkins described the career of Charles M. Sheldon, the pastor of the Central Congregational Church in Topeka, Kansas, and author of *In His Steps: What Would Jesus Do?* (1898), who tried to get the feel of the city by living with various groups—"railroad men, college students, professional people, Negroes, and newspaper workers"—but who subsequently said nothing about "Negroes." See also Degler, *Out of Our Past*, pp. 371–72.

78. Ralph E. Luker, "The Social Gospel and the Failure of Racial Reform," *Church History*, vol. 46, no. 1 (March 1977), p. 81.

79. Degler, *Out of Our Past*, pp. 346–47.

80. Fortune was editor of the New York *Globe* and author of *Black and White: Land, Labor, and Politics in the South* (New York, 1884).

81. Ahlstrom, *A Religious History of the American People*, p. 788. For a discussion of Bryan's conservative position on the Social Gospel, see Willard H. Smith, "William Jennings Bryan and the Social Gospel," *Journal of American History*, vol. 53, no. 1 (June 1966), pp. 41–60.

82. Carter, *The Spiritual Crisis of the Gilded Age*, pp. 150–53. For the only full account of Turner's African emigration efforts, see Edwin S. Redkey, "Bishop Turner's African Dream," *Journal of American History*, vol. 54, no. 2 (September 1967), pp. 271–90.

83. Gossett, *Race*, p. 196; Rauschenbusch, "The Ideals of Social Reformers," *The Social Gospel in America*, p. 280; George M. Fredrickson, *The Black Image in the White Mind: The Debate on Afro-American Character and Destiny, 1817–1914* (New York, 1971), pp. 302–303; Percy Stickney Grant, *Socialism and Christianity* (New York, 1910), pp. 123–50.

84. Richard T. Ely, *The Social Law of Service* (New York, 1896), in Handy, ed., *The Social Gospel in America*, p. 234. See also Benjamin G. Rader, "Richard T. Ely: Spokesman for the Social Gospel," *Journal of American History*, vol. 53, no. 1 (June 1966), pp. 61–74.

85. Moellering, *Christian Conscience and Negro Emancipation*, p. 72; Gossett, *Race*, p. 177; Ahlstrom, *A Religious History of the American People*, p. 923; Hopkins, *The Rise of the Social Gospel in American Protestantism*, pp. 12–13, 319; Reimers, *White Protestantism and the Negro*, pp. 53–54; Handy, ed., *The Social Gospel in America, 1870–1920*, p. 29.

86. Ahlstrom, *A Religious History of the American People*, p. 795. Unfortunately, the one work of Peabody's that Ahlstrom did cite, *Jesus Christ and the Social Question*, discusses Christ's teachings and how they apply to the poor but does not, in 374 pages, mention blacks at all.

87. Fredrickson, *The Black Image in the White Mind*, pp. 288–89, 303–304; Smith, *In His Image*, pp. 285–89. In his study of Southern Baptists, John Lee Eighmy, in a chapter entitled "The Social Gospel Moves South," discussed issues like child labor and slum improvement, but mentioned the race issue only twice in passing. In the following chapter, "The Social Gospel Compromised," the race issue does not appear at all except in relation to the diatribe

of a Josiah Strong type named Victor I. Masters of the Southern Baptist Home Mission Board. See *Churches in Cultural Captivity: A History of the Social Attitudes of Southern Baptists* (Knoxville, Tenn., 1987), pp. 57–71. Attempts by Baptists in Alabama to improve race relations, Wayne Flynt wrote, looked good only when compared to earlier Baptist actions. "Yet any attempt to bridge the gap between the races—even if only to evangelize or pass prohibition legislation or guarantee against lynching and the more overt forms of racism—moved Baptists beyond their nineteenth-century attitude of ignoring the Negro's very existence." See "Dissent in Zion: Alabama Baptists and Social Issues, 1900–1914," *Journal of Southern History*, vol. 35, no. 4 (November 1969), pp. 538–39.

88. Smith, "William Jennings Bryan and the Social Gospel," pp. 44–45; Ahlstrom, *A Religious History of the American People*, p. 733; Dombrowski, *The Early Days of Christian Socialism in America*, p. 21; Grant Wacker, "The Holy Spirit and the Spirit of the Age in American Protestantism, 1880–1910," *Journal of American History*, vol. 72, no. 1 (June 1985), p. 46.

89. Baltzell, *The Protestant Establishment*, pp. 158–59. Baltzell also argued that this idea began to change until what had been blamed on heredity in rural Republican America before 1880 was, in the urban Democratic America of the 1930s, blamed on the environment. This was simply another way of saying what God had done to man before, man was now doing to himself.

90. Sidney E. Mead, *The Lively Experiment: The Shaping of Christianity in America* (New York, 1963), p. 160; Ahlstrom, *A Religious History of the American People*, p. 786; Smith, *Revivalism and Social Reform*, p. 163.

91. Matthew 26:10–13.

92. William Montgomery Brown, *The Crucial Race Question, or, Where and How Shall the Color Line Be Drawn* (Little Rock, Ark., 1907), pp. 111–18; Reimers, *White Protestantism and the Negro*, pp. 27–28; T[homas] J[efferson] Morgan, *The Negro in America and the Ideal American Republic* (Philadelphia, 1898), pp. 155–56. Other conservative Protestants and their works included Carlyle McKinley, *An Appeal to Pharaoh: The Negro Problem and Its Radical Solution* (New York, 1889), John L. Brandt, *Anglo-Saxon Supremacy, or, Race Contributions to Civilization* (Boston, 1915), and the various works of Charles Carroll and Thomas Dixon, Jr.

93. Gutman, "Protestantism and the American Labor Movement," pp. 76–77; Ahlstrom, *A Religious History of the American People*, p. 786; Degler, *Out of Our Past*, pp. 376–77; Hudson, *Religion in America*, p. 317. For examples of the writings of liberal Protestant thinkers, including Beecher, Mathews, and Rauschenbusch, see William R. Hutchison, ed., *American Protestant Thought: The Liberal Era* (New York, 1968).

94. H. Richard Niebuhr, *The Kingdom of God in America* (New York, 1937), pp. 183–84; Hutchison, *Errand to the World*, p. 111.

95. Quoted in Gossett, *Race*, p. 189. Gossett has been one of Strong's severest critics. See, especially, pages 185–90.

96. Handy, ed., *The Social Gospel in America, 1870–1920*, p. 29; Ahlstrom, *A Religious History of the American People*, p. 798; Gossett, *Race*, p. 178.

97. See *supra*, chapter 3.

98. John Chester Miller, *The Wolf by the Ears: Thomas Jefferson and Slavery* (New York, 1977), p. 59; Ahlstrom, *A Religious History of the American People*, pp. 852–53; Gossett, *Race*, pp. 193, 196–97, 476n.

99. David Alan McClintock, "Walter Rauschenbusch: The Kingdom of God and the American Experience" (Ph.D. dissertation, Case Western Reserve University, 1975), pp. 350–52, 355, 358; Gossett, *Race*, pp. 194–95. See also George D. Herron, *The Christian Society* (New York, 1894), p. 22.

100. Brandt, *Anglo-Saxon Supremacy*, pp. 176–77. See also Gossett, *Race*, pp. 192–93.

101. For the fullest account of this situation, see Litwack, *Been in the Storm So Long*.

102. Department of Commerce, Bureau of the Census, *Negro Population, 1790–1915*, p. 88.

103. Degler, *Out of Our Past*, p. 340.

104. Ahlstrom, *A Religious History of the American People*, pp. 741, 743–48, 846. See also Hudson, *American Protestantism*, p. 11.

105. Kenneth Scott Latourette, *A History of Christianity* (New York, 1953), chapter 45.

106. Hudson, *American Protestantism*, p. 124.

107. Quoted in John Hope Franklin, *From Slavery to Freedom: A History of Negro Americans* (5th ed., New York, 1980), p. 318.

Bibliography

CONTEMPORARY WORKS ORIGINATING BEFORE 1800

The Analects of Confucius. Translated by Arthur Waley. New York, 1938.

Basic Writings of Mo Tzu, Hsün Tzu, and Han Fei Tzu. Translated by Burton Watson. New York, 1967.

Benezet, Anthony, and Wesley, John. *Views of American Slavery, Taken a Century Ago*. Philadelphia, 1858.

Black, Nancy B., and Weidman, Bette S., eds. *White On Red: Images of the American Indian*. Port Washington, N.Y., 1976.

Burr, George Lincoln, ed., *Narratives of the Witchcraft Cases 1648–1706*. New York, 1946 (1914).

The Code of Maimonides: Book Twelve, The Book of Acquisition. Translated by Isaac Klein. New Haven, Conn., 1951.

Curtin, Philip D., ed. *Africa Remembered: Narratives by West Africans from the Era of the Slave Trade*. Madison, Wis., 1967.

Edwards, Jonathan. *Images or Shadows of Divine Things*. Edited by Perry Miller. New Haven, Conn., 1948.

Edwards, Jonathan, Jr. *The Injustice and Impolity of the Slave-Trade, and of Slavery of the Africans*. Providence, R. I., 1792.

Equiano, Olaudah. *The Interesting Narrative of the Life of Olaudah Equiano, or Gustavus Vassa, the African. Written by Himself*. 2 vols. London, 1969 (1789).

Fawcett, Benjamin. *A Compassionate Address to the Christian Negroes in Virginia*. New York, 1975 (London, 1756).

Hammon, Jupiter. *America's First Negro Poet: The Complete Works of Jupiter Hammon of Long Island*. Port Washington, N.Y., 1970.

Jefferson, Thomas. *Notes on the State of Virginia*. Chapel Hill, N.C., 1955 (London, 1787).

Josselyn, John. *An Account of Two Voyages to New-England, Made during the Years 1638, 1663*. Boston, 1865 (1674).

Keith, George. *An Exhortation & Caution to Friends Concerning Buying or Keeping of Negroes*. [Philadelphia], 1693.

Knox, William. *Three Tracts, Respecting the Conversion and Instruction of the Free Indians, and Negro Slaves in the Colonies*. London, 1789.

Lay, Benjamin. *All Slaveholders that Keep the Innocent in Bondage, Apostates Pretending to Lay Claim to the Pure Holy Christian Religion*. Philadelphia, 1737.

Li Chi: Book of Rites. An Encyclopedia of Ancient Ceremonial Usages, Religious Creeds, and Social Institutions. 2 vols. Translated by James Legge, edited by Ch'u Chai and Winberg Chai. New Hyde Park, N.Y., 1967.

Mason, Julian D., ed. *The Poems of Phillis Wheatley*. Chapel Hill, N.C., 1966.

Mather, Cotton. *India Christiana: A Discourse, Delivered unto the Commissioners, for the Propagation of the Gospel among the American Indians which Is Accompanied with Several Instruments Relating to the Glorious Design of Propagating Our Holy Religion, in the Eastern, as Well as the Western Indies. An Entertainment which They that Are Waiting for the Kingdom of God Will Receive as Good News from a Far Country*. Boston, 1721.

———. *Magnalia Christi Americana: or, The Ecclesiastical History of New-England; from Its First Planting, in the Year 1620, unto the Year of Our Lord 1698*. 2 vols. New York, 1967, reproduced from the 1852 edition (1702).

———. *Memorable Providence, relating to Witchcrafts and Possessions*. Boston, 1689.

———. *The Negro Christianized; An Essay to Excite and Assist that Good Work, the Instruction of Negro Servants in Christianity*. Boston, 1706.

———. *On Witchcraft: Being the Wonders of the Invisible World*. New York, 1974 (Boston, 1692).

Mather, Increase. *Essay for the Recording of Illustrious Provinces*. Boston, 1684.

Nisbet, Richard. *Slavery Not Forbiden by Scripture. Or a Defence of the West-Indian Planters from the Aspersions Thrown Out against Them, by the Author of a Pamphlet, entitled "An Address . . . Upon Slave-Keeping*." Philadelphia, 1773.

Pearce, Roy Harvey, ed. *Colonial American Writing*. New York, 1950.

Peterson, Merrill, D., ed. *Thomas Jefferson: Writings*. New York, 1985.

Records of Salem Witchcraft, Copied from the Original Documents. 2 vols. in one. New York, 1969 (Roxbury, Mass., 1864).

Rice, David. *Slavery: Inconsistent with Justice and Good Policy, Proved by a Speech Delivered in the Convention, Held at Danville, Kentucky*. Philadelphia, 1792.

Richardson, Samuel. *Pamela, or, Virtue Rewarded*. London, 1740.

Ruchames, Louis, ed. *Racial Thought in America: A Documentary History*. Vol. I: *From the Puritans to Abraham Lincoln*. Amherst, Mass., 1969.

[Rush, Benjamin]. *An Address to the Inhabitants of the British Settlements, on the Slavery of the Negroes in America*. 2nd ed., Philadelphia, 1773.

———. *A Vindication of the Address to the Inhabitants of the British Settlements, on the Slavery of the Negroes in America, in Answer to a Pamphlet Entitled, "Slavery Not Forbidden by Scripture; Or a Defence of the West-India Planters from the Aspersions Thrown Out against Them by the Author of the Address*." Philadelphia, 1773.

Saffin, John. *A Brief and Candid Answer to a Late Printed Sheet, Entitled, the Selling of Joseph*. [Boston], 1701.

Sewall, Samuel. *The Selling of Joseph, a Memorial*. Edited, with Notes and Commentary, by Sidney Kaplan. Northampton, Mass., 1969 (Boston, 1700).

Shields, John C., ed. *The Collected Works of Phillis Wheatley*. New York, 1988.

Van Horne, John C., ed. *Religious Philanthropy and Colonial Slavery: The American Correspondence of the Associates of Dr. Bray, 1717–1777*. Urbana, Ill., 1985.

Williams, Roger. *The Complete Writings of Roger Williams*. 7 vols. New York, 1963.

Woolman, John. *A Journal of the Life, Gospel Labours, and Christian Experiences of that Faithful Minister of Jesus Christ, John Woolman, Late of Mount-Holly, in the Province of New-Jersey*. Philadelphia, 1774 (John Greenleaf Whittier edition, 1871).

CONTEMPORARY WORKS ORIGINATING SINCE 1800

Abolition Philanthropy! The Fugitive Slave Law: Too Bad for Southern Negroes, but Good Enough for Free Citizens of Foreign Birth! Handcuffs for White Men! Shoulder Straps for Negroes! Voters Read! [Philadelphia, 1863].

The Adamic Race: Reply to "Ariel," Drs. Young and Blackie, on the Negro. By "M. S." New York, 1868.

Adams, Nehemiah. *South-Side View of Slavery; or, Three Months at the South, in 1854*. New York, 1969 (Boston, 1854).

Adger, John B., and Girardeau, John L., eds. *The Collected Writings of James Henley Thornwell, D.D., LL.D.* Vol. IV. Richmond, Va., 1871–73.

Agassiz, Louis. "The Diversity and Origin of the Human Race." *The Christian Examiner and Religious Miscellany*. Vol. 49. Boston, July, 1850.

Aikman, William. *The Future of the Colored Race in America: Being an Article in the Presbyterian Quarterly Review, of July, 1862.* Philadelphia, 1862.

Allen, William Francis; Ware, Charles Pickford; and Garrison, Lucy McKim, eds. *Slave Songs of the United States.* New York, 1951 (1867).

The American Annual Cyclopedia and Register of Important Events. 84 vols. New York, 1870–1903.

Andrews, Sidney. *The South since the War: As Shown by Fourteen Weeks of Travel and Observation in Georgia and the Carolinas.* Boston, 1866.

The Annual Report of the Colonization Society of the State of Iowa, with the Proceedings of the Second Anniversary, in the Capitol, January 23, 1857. Iowa City, Ia., [1857].

"Ape-Like Tribes of Men." *The Old Guard.* Vol. IV, no. 9 (September 1866), pp. 557–62.

Armistead, W. S. *The Negro Is a Man: A Reply to Professor Charles Carroll's Book "The Negro Is a Beast; or, In the Image of God."* Tifton, Ga., 1903.

Avary, Myrta Lockett. *Dixie after the War: An Exposition of Social Conditions Existing in the South, during the Twelve Years Succeeding the Fall of Richmond.* New York, 1906.

Bachman, John. *The Doctrine of the Unity of the Human Race, Examined on the Principles of Science.* Charleston, S.C., 1850.

———. *An Examination of Professor Agassiz's Sketch of the Natural Provinces of the Animal World and Their Relation to the Different Types of Man, with a Tableau Accompanying the Sketch.* Charleston, S.C., 1855.

Bacon, Leonard. *Slavery Discussed in Occasional Essays, from 1833 to 1846.* New York, 1846.

Baird, Robert. *The Progress and Prospects of Christianity in the United States of America; with Remarks on the Subject of Slavery in America; and on the Intercourse between British and American Churches.* London, [1851].

———. *Religion in America.* New York, 1844.

Baldwin, Samuel Davis. *Dominion, or the Unity and Eternity of the Human Race.* Nashville, Tenn., 1857.

[Ball, Charles]. *Fifty Years in Chains; or, The Life of an American Slave.* New York, 1858.

Baptist Church. Executive Committee. *Journal of the American Baptist Anti-Slavery Convention.* Vol. I, no. 3 (Worcester, Mass., July 1841).

Barnes, Albert. *The Church and Slavery.* Philadelphia, 1857.

———. *An Inquiry into the Scriptural Views of Slavery.* Philadelphia, 1855 (1846).

Barnes, Gilbert H., and Dumond, Dwight L., eds. *Letters of Theodore Dwight Weld, Angelina Grimké Weld, and Sarah Grimké, 1822–1844.* New York, 1934.

Barrow, David. *Involuntary, Unmerited, Perpetual, Absolute, Hereditary Slavery, Examined: on the Principles of Nature, Reason, Justice, Policy and Scripture.* Lexington, Ky., 1808.

Berry, Harrison. *Slavery and Abolitionism, as Viewed by a Georgia Slave.* Atlanta, 1861.

Bibb, Henry. *Narrative of the Life and Adventures of Henry Bibb, an American Slave, Written by Himself.* New York, 1849.

[Birney, James Gillespie]. *The American Churches, the Bulwarks of American Slavery. By an American.* 2nd American ed., rev., Newburyport, Mass., 1842.

[Bishop, Isabella Lucy (Bird)]. *The Aspects of Religion in the United States of America.* London, 1859.

Blassingame, John W., ed. *Slave Testimony: Two Centuries of Letters, Speeches, Interviews, and Autobiographies.* Baton Rouge, La., 1977.

[Bledsoe, Albert Taylor]. "Baker's African Explorations." *The Southern Review.* Vol. 2, no. 4 (October 1867), pp. 330–58.

———. *An Essay on Liberty and Slavery.* Philadelphia, 1856.

The Book of Mormon: An Account Written by the Hand of Mormon upon Plates Taken from the Plates of Nephi. Translated by Joseph Smith, Jun. Salt Lake City, Utah, 1981.

Bourne, George. *The Book and Slavery Irreconcilable, with Animadversions Upon Dr. Smith's Philosophy*. Philadelphia, 1816.
———. *A Condensed Anti-Slavery Bible Argument; By a Citizen of Virginia*. New York, 1845.
Brackett, Jeffrey R. *Notes on the Progress of the Colored People of Maryland since the War*. Baltimore, 1890.
Brandt, John L. *Anglo-Saxon Supremacy, or, Race Contributions to Civilization*. Boston, 1915.
Brawley, Benjamin. *Early Negro American Writers: Selections with Biographical and Critical Introductions*. Freeport, N.Y., 1968 (1935).
Breckinridge, Robert J. *The Black Race: Some Reflections on Its Position and Destiny, as Connected with Our American Dispensation. A Discourse Delivered before the Kentucky Colonization Society, at Frankfort, on the 6th of February, 1851*. Frankfort, Ky., 1851.
Bremer, Fredrika. *The Homes of the New World: Impressions of America*. Translated by Mary Howitt. 2 vols. New York, 1853.
[Brookes, Iveson L.] *A Defence of Southern Slavery, against the Attacks of Henry Clay and Alex'r Campbell. In which Much of the False Philanthropy and Mawkish Sentime[n]talism of the Abolitionists Is Met and Refuted. In Which It Is Moreover Shown that the Association of the White and Black Races in the Relation of Master and Slave Is the Appointed Order of God, as Set Forth in the Bible, and Constitutes the Best Social Condition of Both Races and the Only True Principle of Republicanism. By a Southern Gentleman*. [Hamburg, S.C., 1851.]
———. *A Defence of the South against the Reproaches and Encroachments of the North: In Which Slavery Is Shown To Be an Institution of God Intended to Form the Basis of the Best Social State and the Only Safeguard to the Permanence of a Republican Government*. Hamburg, S.C., 1850.
Brooks, C[alvin] H[erlock]. *The Race Problem Solved, or, A Reply to a Book Entitled, "The Negro a Beast," by Chas. Carroll*. Elgin, Tex., 1901.
Brown, William Montgomery. *The Crucial Race Question, or, Where and How Shall the Color Line Be Drawn*. Little Rock, Ark., 1907.
Brown, William Wells. *My Southern Home: or, the South and Its People*. Boston, 1880.
———. *Narrative of William Wells Brown, a Fugitive Slave, Written by Himself*. Boston, 1847.
———. *The Negro in the American Rebellion: His Heroism and His Fidelity*. Miami, Fla., 1969 (Boston, 1880 [1867]).
Burton, Richard F. *Mission to Gelele, King of Dahome: With Notices of the So-Called "Amazons," the Grand Customs, the Yearly Customs, the Human Sacrifices, the Present State of the Slave Trade, and the Negro's Place in Nature*. 2 vols. 2nd ed., London, 1864.
Bushnell, Horace. *Christian Nurture*. New York, 1861 (1847).
[Carbery, Edward]. *Inducements to the Colored People of the United States to Emigrate to British Guiana*. Boston, 1840.
Carroll, Charles. *"The Negro a Beast"; or, "In the Image of God"; the Reasoner of the Age, the Revelator of the Century! The Bible as It Is! The Negro and His Relation to the Human Family! . . . The Negro Not the Son of Ham. . . .* St. Louis, 1900.
———. *The Tempter of Eve; or, the Criminality of Man's Social, Political, and Religious Equality with the Negro, and the Amalgamation to Which These Crimes Inevitably Lead. Discussed in the Light of the Scriptures, the Sciences, Profane History, Tradition, and the Testimony of the Monuments*. St. Louis, 1902.
Cartwright, Samuel A. *Essays, Being Inductions from the Baconian Philosophy Proving the Truth of the Bible and the Justice and Benevolence of the Decree Dooming Canaan To Be a Servant of Servants; and Answering the Question of Voltaire:* "On demande quel droit des étrangers tels que les Juifs avaient sur pays de Canaan?" *In a series of Letters to the Rev. William Winans, by Samuel A. Cartwright, M.D., of Natchez, Miss.* Vidalia, [La.], 1843.
Cheever, George B. *God Against Slavery: And the Freedom and Duty of the Pulpit to Rebuke It, as a Sin Against God*. Miami, Fla., 1969 (New York, 1857).

———. *The Guilt of Slavery and the Crime of Slaveholding, Demonstrated from the Hebrew and Greek Scriptures*. Boston, 1860.

Chesnut, Mary Boykin. *A Diary from Dixie: As Written by Mary Chesnut, Wife of James Chesnut, Jr., United States Senator from South Carolina, 1859–1861, and Afterward an Aide to Jefferson Davis and a Brigadier-General in the Confederate Army*. Edited by Isabella D. Martin and Myrta Lockett Avary, Gloucester, Mass., 1961 (1905).

———. *Mary Chesnut's Civil War*. Edited by C. Vann Woodward, New Haven, Conn., 1981.

———. *The Private Mary Chesnut: The Unpublished Civil War Diaries*. Edited by C. Vann Woodward and Elizabeth Muhlenfeld, New York, 1984.

Christy, David. *A Lecture on African Colonization, Delivered in the Hall of the House of Representatives of Ohio*. Cincinnati, 1849.

———. *A Lecture on the Present Relations of Free Labor to Slave Labor, in Tropical and Semi-Tropical Countries: Presenting an Outline of the Commercial Failure of West Indian Emancipation, and Its Effects upon Slavery and the Slave Trade, Together with Its Final Effect upon Colonization to Africa. Addressed to the Constitutional Convention of the State of Ohio, 1850*. Cincinnati, 1850.

"A Citizen of Georgia." *Remarks upon Slavery, Occasioned by Attempts Made to Circulate Improper Publications in the Southern States*. N.p., n.d.

Clarke, James B. "The Negro and the Immigrant in the Two Americas: An International Aspect of the Color Problem." *The Negro's Progress in Fifty Years. The Annals of the American Academy of Political and Social Science*. Vol. 49, no. 138 (September 1913), pp. 32–37.

Clay, Henry. *An Address, Delivered to the Colonization Society of Kentucky, at Frankfort, December 17, 1829*. Lexington, Ky., 1829.

Cobb, Howell. *A Scriptural Examination of the Institution of Slavery in the United States; with Its Objects and Purposes*. Georgia (Printed for the Author), 1856.

Coffin, Joshua. *An Account of Some of the Principal Slave Insurrections, and Others, Which Have Occurred, or Been Attempted, in the United States and Elsewhere, during the Last Two Centuries*. New York, 1860.

Coggin, John Nelson Clark, ed. *Plantation Melodies and Spiritual Songs for Evangelistic Meetings, Schools and Colleges*. Philadelphia, n.d.

Converse, J[ohn] K[endrick]. *A Discourse on the Moral, Legal, and Domestic Condition of Our Colored Population, Preached before the Vermont Colonization Society, at Montpelier, October 17, 1832*. Burlington, Vt., 1832.

Conway, M[oncure] D[aniel]. *Testimonies Concerning Slavery*. London, 1864.

Curtis, Moses Ashley. "Unity of the Races." *Southern Quarterly Review*. Vol. 7 (1849).

Dabney, Robert L. *A Defence of Virginia, and Through Her, of the South, in Recent and Pending Contests Against the Sectional Party*. New York, 1867.

Dalcho, Frederick. *Historical Account of the Protestant Episcopal Church in South Carolina*. Charleston, 1820.

———. *Practical Considerations Founded on the Scriptures Relative to the Slave Population of South Carolina*. Charleston, S.C., 1823.

Davies, Ebenezer. *American Scenes, and Christian Slavery: A Recent Tour of Four Thousand Miles in the United States*. London, 1849.

Davies, Thomas A. *Cosmogony, or the Mysteries of Creation*. New York, 1857.

Dennis, James S. *Christian Missions and Social Progress*. 3 vols. New York, 1897–1906.

Dett, R[obert] Nathaniel, ed. *Religious Folk-Songs of the Negro as Sung at Hampton Institute*. Hampton, Va., 1927 (1874, 1891, 1909).

Dixon, Thomas. *The Clansman: An Historical Romance of the Ku Klux Klan*. Ridgewood, N.J., 1967 (1905).

———. *The Flaming Sword*. Atlanta, 1939.

———. *The Leopard's Spots: A Romance of the White Man's Burden, 1865–1900*. New York, 1902.

———. *The Traitor: A Story of the Fall of the Invisible Empire*. New York, 1907.

Dixon, William Hepworth. *White Conquest*. 2 vols. London, 1876.

Drew, Benjamin. *A North-Side View of Slavery; The Refugee; or, The Narratives of Fugitive Slaves in Canada. Related by Themselves, with an Account of the History and Condition of the Colored Population of Upper Canada*. New York, 1928 (1856).

Eastman, H. P. *The Negro: His Origin, History, and Destiny: Containing a Reply to "The Negro Is a Beast."* Boston, 1905.

Elliott, Charles. *The Bible and Slavery: In Which the Abrahamic and Mosaic Discipline Is Considered with the Most Ancient Forms of Slavery; and the Pauline Code on Slavery as Related to Roman Slavery and the Discipline of the Apostolic Churches*. Cincinnati, 1857.

———. *Sinfulness of American Slavery: Proved from Its Evil Sources; Its Injustice; Its Wrongs; Its Contrariety to Many Scriptural Commands, Prohibitions and Principles, and to the Christian Spirit, and from Its Evil Effects; Together with Observations on Emancipation, and the Duties of American Citizens in Regard to Slavery*. 2 vols. Cincinnati, 1850.

Elliott, E. N., ed. *Cotton Is King, and Pro-Slavery Arguments: Comprising the Writings of Hammond, Harper, Christy, Stringfellow, Hodge, Bledsoe, and Cartwright, on This Important Subject*. Augusta, Ga., 1860.

[England, John]. *Letters of the Late Bishop England to the Hon. John Forsyth, on the Subject of Domestic Slavery*. Baltimore, 1844.

Feeks, J. F., pub. *Copperhead Minstrel: A Choice Collection of Democratic Poems and Songs, for the Use of Political Clubs and the Social Circle*. New York, 1863.

Fenner, Thomas P.; Rathburn, Frederic G.; and Cleaveland, Bessie; arrs. *Cabin and Plantation Songs as Sung by the Hampton Students*. New York, 1977 (1874, 1901).

Fisch, Georges. *Nine Months in the United States during the Crisis*. London, 1863.

Fisher, William Arms, ed. *Seventy Negro Spirituals*. New York, 1926.

Five Slave Narratives: A Compendium. New York, 1968.

Flinn, J. William, ed. *The Complete Works of Rev. Thomas Smyth, D.D.* Columbia, S.C., 1910.

Fortune, T. Thomas. *Black and White: Land, Labor, and Politics in the South*. New York, 1884.

Friese, P[hilip] C. *Letter to the President and the People of the United States, Showing that the President Cannot Lawfully Execute an Unconstitutional Law, and that the So-Called Reconstruction Acts Are Both Unconstitutional and Repugnant to the Republican Party's Original Higher Law Policy; with a Postscript, Proving that All Positive Law is Subject to a Sovereign Equity in the Courts, and Suggesting the Formation of a White Man's Party of Law and Order, Combining All of the Conservative Elements of the Country Under the Democratic Name, to Support the Dignity and the Freedom of the Courts, and to Oppose the Destructive and Unconstitutional Action of the White Negro Party*. Baltimore, 1869.

Frothingham, Octavius Brooks. *Recollections and Impressions, 1822–1890*. New York, 1891.

Fuller, Richard, and Wayland, Francis. *Domestic Slavery Considered as a Scriptural Institution: In a Correspondence Between the Rev. Richard Fuller, of Beaufort, S.C., and the Rev. Francis Wayland, of Providence, R.I.* Rev. ed., New York, 1856 (1845).

Furman, Richard. *Rev. Dr. Richard Furman's Exposition on the Views of the Baptists, Relative to the Coloured Population of the United States, in a Communication to the Governor of South-Carolina*. Charleston, 1823.

Gladden, Washington. *Social Facts and Forces. The Factory—the Labor Union—the Corporation—the Railway—the City—the Church*. Port Washington, N.Y., 1971 (1897).

Gobineau, Joseph Arthur de. *The Moral and Intellectual Diversity of Races, with Particular Reference to Their Respective Influence in the Civil and Political History of Mankind*. Translated from *Essai sur l'inégalité des races humaines*. Philadelphia, 1856.

Grant, Madison. *The Passing of the Great Race*. 4th ed., New York, 1921 (1916).

Grant, Percy Stickney. *Socialism and Christianity*. New York, 1910.

Grimes, William. *Life of William Grimes, the Runaway Slave, Brought Down to the Present Time. Written by Himself.* New Haven, Conn., 1855. Reprinted in *Five Black Lives* (Middletown, Conn., 1971).

Grimké, A[ngelina] E. *Appeal to the Christian Women of the South.* N.p., [1836].

Grimké, Sarah M. *An Epistle to the Clergy of the Southern States.* New York, 1836.

Grund, Francis J. *The Americans in Their Moral, Social, and Political Relations.* With a new introduction by Robert F. Berkhofer, Jr., New York and London, 1968 (1837).

Hallowell, Emily, ed. *Calhoun Plantation Songs.* 2nd ed., Boston, 1907.

Hamilton, W[illiam] T. *The Duties of Masters and Slaves Respectively: or, Domestic Servitude as Sanctioned by the Bible: A Discourse, Delivered in the Government-Street Church, Mobile Ala., on Sunday Night, December 15, 1844.* Mobile, 1845.

———. *The "Friend of Moses"; or, A Defence of the Pentateuch as the Production of Moses and an Inspired Document, against the Objections of Modern Skepticism.* New York, 1852.

Hammond, J. W. *Two Letters on Slavery in the United States, Addressed to Thomas Clarkson, Esq.* Columbia, S.C., 1845.

Handy, Robert T., ed. *The Social Gospel in America, 1870–1920: Gladden, Ely, Rauschenbusch.* New York, 1966.

Hardy, Thomas. *Tess of the d'Urbervilles: A Pure Woman.* London, 1891.

Harness, A. C. *The Genius of Democracy; or, The Fall of Babylon.* Philadelphia, 1873.

———. *The Great Trial; or, The Genius of Civilization Brought to Judgement.* Philadelphia, 1873.

Harrison, W[illiam] P[ope], ed. *The Gospel among the Slaves: A Short Account of Missionary Operations among the African Slaves of the Southern States.* Nashville, Tenn., 1893.

Haven, Gilbert. *Sermons, Speeches, and Letters on Slavery and Its War: From the Passage of the Fugitive Slave Bill to the Election of President Grant.* New York, 1969 (Boston, 1869).

Helper, Hinton R. *Nojoque: A Question for a Continent.* New York, 1867.

Herron, George D. *The Christian Society.* New York, 1984.

Hope, M. B. "On the Unity of the Human Race." *Biblical Repertory and Princeton Review.* Vol. 22 (1850).

Hopkins, John H. *Bible Views of Slavery.* No. 8 of *Papers from the Society for the Diffusion of Political Knowledge.* New York, 1863.

———. *Scriptural, Ecclesiastical, and Historical View of Slavery, from the Days of the Patriarch Abraham, to the Nineteenth Century.* New York, 1969 (1864).

Horlacher, Jacob. *Is Slavery Condemned by the Bible or Prohibited by the Constitution of the United States[?].* N.p., 1862.

Hosmer, William. *Slavery and the Church.* New York, 1969 (1853).

How, Samuel Blanchard. *Slaveholding Not Sinful: Slavery, the Punishment of Man's Sin; Its Remedy, the Gospel of Christ. An Argument before the General Synod of the Reformed Protestant Dutch Church, October, 1855.* N.p., 1855.

Humphrey, Heman. *The Promised Land: A Sermon, Delivered at Goshen, (Conn.) at the Ordination of the Rev. Messrs. Hiram Bingham & Asa Thurston, as Missionaries to the Sandwich Islands, Sept. 29, 1819.* Boston, 1819.

Hurd, John Codman. *The Law of Freedom and Bondage in the United States.* 2 vols. New York, 1968 (1858–62).

Ireland, John (Most Rev.). *The Church and Modern Society: Lectures and Addresses.* Chicago, 1896.

Jacobs, Harriet A. *Incidents in the Life of a Slave Girl, Written by Herself.* Edited by L. Maria Child (1861); edited and with an Introduction by Jean Fagan Yellin. Cambridge, Mass., 1987 (1861).

Jacobs, Paul; Landau, Saul; and Pell, Eve, eds. *To Serve the Devil.* 2 vols. Vol. I, *Natives and Slaves.* New York, 1971.

Jay, William. *An Inquiry into the Character and Tendency of the American Colonization, and the American Anti-Slavery Societies.* New York, 1835.

Jeter, Jeremiah Bell. *The Recollections of a Long Life.* Richmond, Va., 1891.

Jones, Charles Colcock. *Suggestions on the Religious Instruction of Negroes in the Southern States.* Philadelphia, 1847.

Junkin, George. *The Integrity of Our National Union vs. Abolitionism: An Argument from the Bible, in Proof of the Position that Masters Ought to Be Honored and Obeyed by Their Servants, and Tolerated in, Not Excommunicated from, the Church of God: Being Part of a Speech Delivered before the Synod of Cincinnati, on the Subject of Slavery, September 19th and 20th, 1843.* Cincinnati, 1843.

Kipling, Rudyard. *Complete Verse: Definitive Edition.* New York, 1989 (1940).

Lester, Julius, ed. *To Be a Slave.* New York, 1968.

Longstreet, A. B. *Letters on the Epistle of Paul to Philemon.* Charleston, S.C., 1845.

Macrae, David. *The Americans at Home.* New York, 1952 (Edinburgh, 1870).

Martineau, Harriet. *Society in America.* Edited, abridged and with an introductory essay by Seymour Martin Lipset. Gloucester, Mass., 1968 (1962 [New York, 1837]).

McCaine, Alexander. *Slavery Defended from Scripture, against the Attacks of the Abolitionists, in a Speech Delivered before the General Conference of the Methodist Episcopal Church, in Baltimore, 1842.* Baltimore, 1842.

McTyeire, H[olland] N[immons]; Sturgis, C. F.; and Holmes, A. *Duties of Masters to Servants: Three Premium Essays.* Charleston, S.C., 1851.

Mill, John Stuart. *On Liberty.* New York, 1947 (London, 1859).

Mitchell, James. *Letter on the Relation of the White and African Races in the United States, Showing the Necessity of the Colonization of the Latter. Addressed to the President of the U.S.* Washington, D.C., 1862.

Moore, George H. *Notes on the History of Slavery in Massachusetts.* New York, 1968 (1866).

Morgan, T[homas] J[efferson]. *The Negro in America and the Ideal American Republic.* Philadelphia, 1898.

Morton, Samuel George. *Crania Americana, or, A Comparative View of the Skulls of Various Aboriginal Nations of North and South America: To which Is Prefixed an Essay on the Varieties of the Human Species.* Philadelphia, 1839.

Myers, Robert Manson, ed. *The Children of Pride: Selected Letters of the Family of Rev. Dr. Charles Colcock Jones from the Years 1860–1868, with the Addition of Several Previously Unpublished Letters.* Abridged ed., New Haven, Conn., 1984.

The Mystery Finished: The Negro Has a Soul; His Normal Relation is that of a Servant of Tribute to Shem and Japheth; the Negro is not a Citizen of the State, but a Member of the Church by Divine Appointment; the Negro Is Only Made a Citizen While the "Two Witnesses Are Dead"—These are Moses and Christ, Civil Law and Ecclesiastical or Social; this Death is for Forty-Two Months, or for Three and a Half Years. Nashville, Tenn., 1868.

Negroes and Religion: The Episcopal Church of the South, Memorial to the General Convention of the Protestant Episcopal Church in the United States of America. Charleston, S.C., [1863?].

Noble, Frederick Perry. *The Redemption of Africa.* Chicago, 1899.

Northup, Solomon. *Twelve Years a Slave: Narrative of Solomon Northup, a Citizen of New-York, Kidnapped in Washington City in 1841, and Rescued in 1853, from a Cotton Plantation Near the Red River, in Louisiana.* Auburn, N.Y., 1853.

Nott, Josiah C. *An Essay on the Natural History of Mankind, Viewed in Connection with Negro Slavery: Delivered before the Southern Rights Association, 14th December, 1850.* Mobile, Ala., 1851.

———. *Indigenous Races of the Earth: or, New Chapters of Ethnological Inquiry.* Philadelphia, 1857.

———. *Two Lectures on the Connection Between the Biblical and Physical History of Man, Delivered by Invitation, from the Chair of Political Economy, etc., of the Louisiana University, in December, 1848.* New York, 1969 (1849).

———. *Two Lectures on the Natural History of the Caucasian and Negro Races.* Mobile, Ala., 1844.

———, and Gliddon, George R. *Types of Mankind: or, Ethnological Researches, Based upon the Ancient Monuments, Paintings, Sculptures, and Crania of Races, and upon Their Natural, Geographical, and Philological and Biblical History.* Philadelphia, 1855.

Olmsted, Frederick Law. *The Cotton Kingdom: A Traveller's Observations on Cotton and Slavery in the American Slave States.* Based upon Three Former Volumes of Journeys and Investigations by the Same Author. Edited, with an Introduction, by Arthur M. Schlesinger, New York, 1970 (1856, 1860, and London, 1861).

———. *Journey in the Seaboard Slave States.* New York, 1856.

Osofsky, Gilbert, ed. *Puttin' On Ole Massa: The Slave Narratives of Henry Bibb, William Wells Brown, and Solomon Northup.* New York, 1969.

Parrish, John. *Remarks on the Slavery of the Black People; Addressed to the Citizens of the United States, Particularly to Those Who Are in Legislative or Executive Stations in the General or State Governments; and also to Such Individuals as Hold Them in Bondage.* Philadelphia, 1806.

Parrish, Lydia. *Slave Songs of the Georgia Sea Islands.* Hatboro, Pa., 1965 (1942).

[Payne, Buckner H.] *The Negro: What Is His Ethnological Status; Is He a Progeny of Ham? Is He a Descendant of Adam and Eve? Has He a Soul? Or Is He a Beast in God's Nomenclature? What Is His status as Fixed by God in Creation? What Is His Relation to the White Race?* Cincinnati, 2nd ed. 1867, 3rd ed. 1872, with a review of his reviewers.

Peabody, Francis Greenwood. *Jesus Christ and the Social Question: An Examination of the Teaching of Jesus in Its Relation to Some of the Problems of Modern Social Life.* New York, 1920 (1900).

Peck, Jesse T. *The History of the Great Republic, Considered from a Christian Stand-Point.* New York, 1868.

Pennington, James W. C. *The Fugitive Blacksmith; or, Events in the History of James W. C. Pennington.* London, 1849.

Pinckney, Charles Cotesworth. *An Address Delivered in Charleston, before the Agricultural Society of South Carolina at Its Anniversary Meeting, on Tuesday, the 18th of August, 1829.* Charleston, S.C., 1829.

[Priest, Josiah]. *Slavery, As It Relates to the Negro, or African Race, Examined in the Light of Circumstances, History and the Holy Scriptures; with an Account of the Origin of the Black Man's Color, Causes of His State of Servitude and Traces of His Character as Well in Ancient as in Modern Times: with Strictures on Abolitionism.* Albany, N.Y., 1843.

Prospero (pseud.). "Caliban: A Sequel to 'Ariel.' " New York, 1868.

Quincy, Josiah. *Figures of the Past from Leaves of the Old Journals.* Boston, 1883.

Ransom, Stanley A., ed. *America's First Negro Poet: The Complete Works of Jupiter Hammon of Long Island.* Port Washington, N.Y., 1970.

Read, Hollis. *The Hand of God in History.* Hartford, Conn., 1849.

———. *The Negro Problem Solved; or, Africa as She Is, and as She Shall Be. Her Curse and Her Cure.* New York, 1864.

Reade, W. Winwood. *Savage Africa: Being a Narrative of a Tour in Equatorial, Southwestern, and Northwestern Africa; with Notes on the Habits of the Gorilla; on the Existence of Unicorns and Tailed Men; on the Slave Trade; on the Origin, Character and Capabilities of the Negro, and on the Future Civilization of Western Africa.* New York, 1864.

Riley, B[enjamin] F. *The White Man's Burden: A Discussion of the Interracial Question with Special Reference to the Responsibility of the White Race to the Negro Problem.* Birmingham, Ala., 1910.

Robinson, John. *The Testimony and Practice of the Presbyterian Church in Reference to American Slavery*. Cincinnati, 1852.

Robinson, John Bell. *Pictures of Slavery and Anti-Slavery: Advantages of Negro Slavery and the Benefits of Negro Freedom; Morally, Socially, and Politically Considered.* Philadelphia, 1863.

———. *A Reply to the Resolutions Passed by the Late Philadelphia Annual Conference of the Methodist Episcopal Church in March, 1864, with a Slight Notice of the Acts of the Late General Conference of Said Church in the Following May*. Philadelphia, 1864.

Ross, Frederick A. *Slavery Ordained of God*. Philadelphia, 1859.

Sawyer, Leicester A. *A Dissertation on Servitude: Embracing an Examination of the Scripture Doctrines on the Subject, and an Inquiry into the Character and Relations of Slavery*, N.p., 1837.

Schaff, Philip. *America: A Sketch of the Political, Social, and Religious Character of the United States of America, in Two Lectures, Delivered at Berlin with a Report Read before the German Diet at Frankfort-am-Maine, September 1854*. New York, 1855.

———. *History of the Christian Church*. 8 vols., Grand Rapids, Mich., 1964–67 (1907–10).

Schell, William G. *Is the Negro a Beast?: A Reply to Chas. Carroll's Book Entitled "The Negro Is a Beast." Proving that the Negro Is Human from Biblical, Scientific, and Historical Standpoints.* Moundsville, West Va., 1901.

Schultz, Alfred P. *Race or Mongrel: A Brief History of the Rise and Fall of the Ancient Races of the Earth. A Theory that the Fall of Nations Is Due to Intermarriage with Alien Stocks. A Demonstration that a Nation's Strength Is Due to Racial Purity. A Prophecy that America Will Sink to Early Decay unless Immigration Is Rigorously Restricted.* Boston, 1908.

[Scott, W. J.] "Our Tripod: The Ethnological Status of the Negro." *Scott's Monthly Magazine*. Vol. 5, no. 3 (March 1868), pp. 149–51.

Sister Sallie (pseud.). *The Color Line. Devoted to the Restoration of Good Government, Putting an End to Negro Authority and Misrule, and Establishing a White Man's Government in the White Man's Country, by Organizing the White People of the South*. [N.p., 1868?]

The Six Species of Men, with Cuts Representing the Types of the Caucasian, Mongul, Malay, Indian, Esquimaux and Negro, with Their General Physical and Mental Qualities, Laws of Organization, Relations to Civilization, etc. New York, 1866.

Smectymnuus (pseud.). *Slavery and the Church: Two Letters Addressed to Rev. N. L. Rice, D.D., in Reply to His Letters to the Congregational Deputation, on the Subject of Slavery. Also a Letter to Rev. Nehemiah Adams, D.D., in Answer to the "South Side View of Slavery."* Boston, 1856.

Smith, Goldwin. *Does the Bible Sanction Slavery?* Cambridge, Mass., 1864.

Smith, Samuel Stanhope. *An Essay on the Causes of the Variety of Complexion and Figure in the Human Species*. Edited by Winthrop D. Jordan. Cambridge, Mass., 1965 (2nd ed., New York, 1810 [1787]).

Smith, William A. *Lectures on the Philosophy and Practice of Slavery*. Nashville, 1856.

Smyth, Thomas. *The Unity of the Human Races, Proved To Be the Doctrine of Scripture, Reason, and Science: With a Review of the Present Position and Theory of Professor Agassiz*. New York, 1850.

[Society of Friends]. *The Appeal of the Religious Society of Friends in Pennsylvania, New Jersey, Delaware, etc., to Their Fellow-Citizens of the United States on Behalf of the Coloured Races*. Philadelphia, 1858.

Speer, Robert E. *Christianity and the Nations*. New York, 1910.

Spring, Lindley. *The Negro at Home: An Inquiry after His Capacity for Self-Government and the Government of Whites for Controlling, Leading, Directing, or Co-operating in; the Civilization of the Age; Its Material, Intellectual, Moral, Religious, Social and Political Interests; the Objects of Society and Government; the Business and Duties of Our Race; the Offenses of Legislation*. New York, 1868.

Stringfellow, Thornton. *Scriptural and Statistical Views in Favor of Slavery*. 4th ed., Richmond, Va., 1856.

Strong, Josiah. *The New Era; or, the Coming Kingdom.* New York, 1893.
———. *Our Country. Its Possible Future and Its Present Crisis.* Edited by Herbst Jurgen. Cambridge, Mass., 1963 (New York, 1885, rev., 1891).
Stroyer, Jacob. *My Life in the South.* Salem, Mass., 1898 (1879).
Sumner, William Graham. *The Challenges of Facts and Other Essays.* New Haven, Conn., 1913.
Tarbox, Increase N. *The Curse: or, The Position in the World's History Occupied by the Race of Ham.* Boston, 1864.
Thompson, M. B. *The Negro, Not a Beast, but a Descendant of Adam: A Reply to Prof. Chas. Carroll's Work, " 'The Negro Is a Beast' or 'In the Image of God.' "* Mt. Juliet, Tenn., 1906.
Thornwell, J[ames] H[enley]. *Report on the Subject of Slavery, Presented to the Synod of South Carolina, at Their Sessions in Winnsborough, November 6, 1851.* Columbia, S.C., 1852.
———. "Slavery and Religious Instruction of the Coloured Population." *Southern Presbyterian Review.* July 1850.
Tocqueville, Alexis de. *Democracy in America.* Edited by J. P. Mayer and Max Lerner. Translated by George Lawrence. New York, 1966 (1835).
Treadwell, S[eymour] B[oughton]. *American Liberties and American Slavery: Morally and Politically Illustrated.* New York, 1838.
Trollope, Frances. *Domestic Manners of the Americans.* London, 1974 (1832).
Tyson, Bryan. *The Institution of Slavery in the Southern States, Religiously and Morally Considered in Connection with Our Sectional Troubles.* N.p., [1863].
Van Evrie, John H. *Negroes and Negro "Slavery": The First an Inferior Race: The Latter Its Normal Condition.* New York, 1861.
"Voice of the Clergy." [Philadelphia, 1863].
Wayland, Francis. *The Elements of Moral Science.* New York, 1855 (1835).
———. *The Limitations of Human Responsibility.* Boston, 1838.
Wheat, Marvin T. *The Progress and Intelligence of Americans; Collateral Proof of Slavery, from the First to the Eleventh Chapter of Genesis, as Founded on Organic Law; and from the Fact of Christ Being a Caucasian, Owing to His Peculiar Parentage; Progress of Slavery South and South-West, with Free Labor Advancing Through the Acquisition of Territory, Advantages Enumerated and Explained.* Louisville, Ky., 1862.
Willard, Emma. *History of the United States or Republic of America.* New York, 1845.
Worcester, Samuel. *Paul on Mars Hill: or, A Christian Survey of the Pagan World. A Sermon, Preached at Newburyport, June 21, 1815, at the Ordination of the Reverend Messrs. Samuel J. Mills, James Richards, Edward Warren, Horatio Bardwell, Benjamin C. Meigs, and Daniel Poor, to the Office of Christian Missionaries.* Andover, Mass., 1815.
Young, Robert A. *The Negro: A Reply to Ariel. The Negro Belongs to the Genus Homo—He Is a Descendant of Adam and Eve—He Is the Offspring of Ham—He Is Not a Beast, but a Human Being—He Has an Immortal Soul—He May Be Civilized, Enlightened, and Converted to Christianity.* Nashville, Tenn., 1867.

MODERN SECONDARY WORKS

Abell, Aaron Ignatius. *The Urban Impact on American Protestantism, 1865–1900.* Cambridge, Mass., 1943.
Abrahams, Roger D., ed. *Afro-American Folktales: Stories from Black Traditions in the New World.* New York, 1985.
Adams, Henry. *History of the United States during the Administrations of Jefferson and Madison.* 9 vols. New York, 1889–91.
Adams, Romanzo. "Interracial Marriage and Social Change." *Race: Individual and Collective*

Behavior. Edited by Edgar T. Thompson and Everett C. Hughes. Glencoe, Ill., 1958, pp. 428–30.

Ahlstrom, Sydney E. *A Religious History of the American People*. New Haven, Conn., 1972.

Aiken, John R. "Walter Rauschenbusch and Education for Reform." *Church History*. Vol. 36, no. 4 (December 1967), pp. 456–69.

Ajayi, J. F. A., and Crowder, Michael, eds. *History of West Africa*. 2 vols. New York, 1972–73.

Alexandre, Pierre. *Languages and Language in Black Africa*. Translated by F. A. Leary. Evanston, Ill., 1972.

Alho, Olli. *The Religion of the Slaves: A Study of the Religious Tradition and Behaviour of Plantation Slaves in the United States, 1830–1865*. Helsinki, 1976.

Aptheker, Herbert. *American Negro Revolts*. New York, 1943.

———, ed. *A Documentary History of the Negro People in the United States*. New York, 1951.

Aries, Philippe, and Bejin, André, eds. *Western Sexuality: Practice and Precept in Past and Present Times*. Translated by Anthony Forster. New York, 1986.

Armstrong, O. K., and Marjorie M. *The Indomitable Baptists: A Narrative of Their Role in Shaping American History*. Garden City, N.Y., 1967.

Arndt, William F., and Gingrich, F. Wilbur. *A Greek-English Lexicon of the New Testament and Other Early Christian Literature*. Translated and adapted from Walter Bauer, *Griechisch-Deutsches Wörterbuch zu den Schriften des Neuen Testaments und der übrigen urchristlichen Literatur*. Chicago, 1979.

Arrington, Leonard J., and Britton, Davis. *The Mormon Experience: A History of the Latter-Day Saints*. New York, 1979.

Axtell, James. "Forked Tongues: Moral Judgments in Indian History." *Perspectives: American Historical Association Newsletter*. Vol. 25, no. 2 (February 1987), pp. 10–13.

———. *The Invasion Within: The Contest of Cultures in Colonial North America*. New York, 1985.

Bailey, Kenneth K. "The Post-Civil War Racial Separations in Southern Protestantism: Another Look." *Church History*. Vol. 46, no. 4 (December 1977), pp. 453–73.

———. "Protestantism and Afro-Americans in the Old South: Another Look." *Journal of Southern History*. Vol. 41, no. 4 (November 1975), pp. 451–72.

Bailey, Thomas D. *Shadow on the Church: Southwestern Evangelical Religion and the Issue of Slavery, 1783–1860*. Ithaca, N.Y., 1985.

Ballagh, James C. *A History of Slavery in Virginia*. Baltimore, 1901.

Balmer, Randall. *A Perfect Babel of Confusion: Dutch Religion and English Culture in the Middle Colonies*. New York, 1989.

Baltzell, E. Digby. *The Protestant Establishment: Aristocracy and Caste in America*. New York, 1964.

Banner, Lois W. "Religious Benevolence as Social Control: A Critique of an Interpretation." *Journal of American History*. Vol. 40, no. 1 (June 1973), pp. 23–41.

Barnes, Gilbert H. *The Antislavery Impulse, 1830–1844*. New York, 1933.

Baroja, Julio Caro. *The World of the Witches*. Translated by O. N. V. Glendinning. Chicago, 1961.

Baron, Salo Wittmayer. *The Social and Religious History of the Jews*. 20 vols. 2nd ed., New York, 1952 (1937).

Barrett, Leonard E. *Soul-Force: African Heritage in Afro-American Religion*. 1st ed., Garden City, N.Y., 1974.

Barth, Gunther. *City People: The Rise of Modern City Culture in Nineteenth-Century America*. New York, 1980.

Barthelemy, Anthony Gerard. *Black Face, Maligned Race: The Representation of Blacks in English Drama from Shakespeare to Southerne*. Baton Rouge, La., 1987.

Barthold, Bonnie J. *Black Time: Fiction of Africa, the Caribbean, and the United States*. New Haven, Conn., 1981.

Bassett, John Spencer. *The Life of Andrew Jackson*. 2 vols. New York, 1967 [1916].

Bastide, Roger. "Color, Racism, and Christianity." *Daedalus: Journal of the American Academy of Arts and Sciences*. Spring 1967, pp. 312–27.

Bauman, Richard. *For the Reputation of Truth: Politics, Religion, and Conflict Among the Pennsylvania Quakers, 1750–1800*. Baltimore, Md., 1971.

Beaver, R. Pierce. "American Missionary Motivation before the Revolution." *Church History*. Vol. 31, no. 2 (June 1962), pp. 216–26.

———. *Church, State, and the American Indians: Two and a Half Centuries of Partnership in Missions Between Protestant Churches and Government*. St. Louis, Mo., 1966.

Bellah, Robert N.; Madsen, Richard; Sullivan, William M.; Swidler, Ann; and Tipton, Steven M. *Habits of the Heart: Individualism and Commitment in American Life*. Berkeley, Calif., 1985.

Bellot, Leland J. "Evangelicals and the Defense of Slavery in Britain's Old Colonial Empire." *Journal of Southern History*. Vol. 37, no. 1 (February 1971), pp. 19–40.

Berelson, Bernard, and Steiner, Gary A. *Human Behavior: An Inventory of Scientific Findings*. New York, 1964.

Berkhofer, Robert F., Jr. *Salvation and the Savage: An Analysis of Protestant Missions and American Indian Response, 1787–1862*. New York, 1972 (Lexington, Ky., 1965).

———. *The White Man's Indian: Images of the American Indian from Columbus to the Present*. New York, 1978.

Berlin, Ira. "Time, Space, and the Evolution of Afro-American Society on British Mainland North America." *American Historical Review*. Vol. 85, no. 1 (February 1980), pp. 44–78.

Berry, Brewton. *Race and Ethnic Relations*. Boston, 1958.

Berry, Mary Frances, and Blassingame, John W. *Long Memory: The Black Experience in America*. New York, 1982.

Berthoff, Rowland. *An Unsettled People: Social Order and Disorder in American History*. New York, 1971.

Biddiss, Michael D. *Father of Racist Ideology: The Social and Political Thought of Count Gobineau*. New York, 1970.

Billington, Ray Allen. *The Protestant Crusade, 1800–1860: A Study of the Origins of American Nativism*. New York, 1938.

Binder, Frederick M. *The Color Problem in Early National America as Viewed by John Adams, Jefferson and Jackson*. The Hague and Paris, 1968.

Black, Nancy B., and Weidman, Bette S., eds. *White on Red: Images of the American Indian*. Port Washington, N.Y., 1976.

Blassingame, John W. *The Slave Community: Plantation Life in the Antebellum South*. Rev. and enlarged ed., New York, 1979.

Blenkinsopp, Joseph. *Sexuality and the Christian Tradition*. Dayton, Ohio, 1969.

Boas, Franz. *The Mind of Primitive Man*. Rev. ed., New York, 1963 (1938).

Bode, Frederick A. "Religion and Class Hegemony: A Populist Critique in North Carolina." *Journal of Southern History*. Vol. 37, no. 3 (August 1971), pp. 415–38.

Bodo, John R. *The Protestant Clergy and Public Issues, 1812–1848*. Princeton, N.J., 1954.

Boles, John B., ed. *Masters & Slaves in the House of the Lord: Race and Religion in the American South, 1740–1870*. Lexington, Ky., 1988.

Bolton, S. Charles. *Southern Anglicanism: The Church of England in Colonial South Carolina*. Westport, Conn., 1982.

Bonomi, Patricia U. *Under the Cope of Heaven: Religion, Society, and Politics in Colonial America*. New York, 1986.

———, and Eisenstadt, Peter R. "Church Adherence in the Eighteenth-Century British Colonies." *William and Mary Quarterly*. 3rd series, vol. 39, no. 2 (April 1982), pp. 245–86.

Booth, Newell S., Jr. "God and the Gods in West Africa." *African Religions: A Symposium*. Edited by Newell S. Booth, Jr. New York, 1977, pp. 159–81.

Borden, Philip. "Found Cumbering the Soil: Manifest Destiny and the Indian in the Nineteenth Century." *The Great Fear: Race in the Mind of America*. Edited by Gary B. Nash and Richard Weiss. New York, 1970, pp. 71–97.

Botkin, B. A., ed. *Lay My Burden Down: A Folk History of Slavery*. Chicago, 1945.

Bowden, Henry Warner. *American Indians and Christian Missions: Studies in Cultural Conflict*. Chicago, 1981.

Boyer, Paul. *Urban Masses and Moral Order in America, 1820–1920*. Cambridge, Mass., 1978.

———, and Nissenbaum, Stephen. *Salem Possessed: The Social Origins of Witchcraft*. Cambridge, Mass., 1978.

Brenner, Louis. *The Shehus of Kukawa: A History of the Al-Kanemi Dynasty of Bornu*. London, 1973.

Bright, John. *A History of Israel*. 3rd ed., Philadelphia, 1981.

Bringhurst, Newell G. *Saints, Slaves, and Blacks: The Changing Place of Black People Within Mormonism*. Westport, Conn., 1981.

Brock, William R. *The Evolution of American Democracy*. New York, 1970.

Brodie, Fawn M. "The Great Jefferson Taboo." *American Vistas*. Edited by Leonard Dinnerstein and Kenneth T. Jackson. 4th ed., New York, 1983, pp. 118–40.

———. *No Man Knows My History: The Life of Joseph Smith the Mormon Prophet*. 2nd ed., New York, 1971 (1945).

———. *Thomas Jefferson: An Intimate Biography*. New York, 1974.

Brokhage, Joseph D. *Francis Patrick Kenrick's Opinion on Slavery*. Washington, D.C., 1955.

Brookes, George S. *Friend Anthony Benezet*. Philadelphia, 1937.

Bruce, Philip Alexander. *Economic History of Virginia in the Seventeenth Century: An Inquiry Into the Material Condition of the People Based Upon Original and Contemporaneous Records*. 2 vols. New York, 1895.

Brundage, James A. *Law, Sex, and Christian Society in Medieval Europe*. Chicago, 1987.

Brydon, George Maclaren. *Virginia's Mother Church and the Political Conditions Under Which It Grew*. 2 vols. Vol. I, *An Interpretation of the Records of the Colony of Virginia and the Anglican Church of That Colony, 1607–1727*. Vol. II, *The Story of the Anglican Church and the Development of Religion in Virginia, 1727–1814*. Philadelphia, 1947.

Buswell, James O., III. *Slavery, Segregation, and Scripture*. Grand Rapids, Mich., 1964.

Butler, Jon. "Enlarging the Body of Christ: Slavery, Evangelism, and the Christianization of the White South, 1690–1790." *The Evangelical Tradition in America*. Edited by Leonard I. Sweet. Atlanta, 1984, pp. 87–112.

———. " 'Gospel Order Improved': The Keithian Schism and the Exercise of Quaker Ministerial Authority in Pennsylvania." *William and Mary Quarterly*. 3rd series, vol. 31, no. 3 (July 1974), pp. 431–52.

———. "Magic, Astrology, and the Early American Religious Heritage, 1600–1760." *American Historical Review*. Vol. 84, no. 2 (April 1979), pp. 317–46.

———. "Power, Authority, and the Origins of American Denominational Order: The English Churches in the Delaware Valley, 1680–1730." *Transactions of the American Philosophical Society*. Vol. 68, part 2 (1978).

Butsch, Joseph. "Catholics and the Negro." *Journal of Negro History*. Vol. 2, no. 4 (October 1917), pp. 393–410.

Cade, John B. "Out of the Mouths of Ex-Slaves." *Journal of Negro History*. Vol. 20, no. 3 (July 1935), pp. 294–337.

Carroll, Joseph. *Slave Insurrections in the United States, 1800–1860*. Boston, 1938.

Carter, Paul A. *The Spiritual Crisis of the Gilded Age*. DeKalb, Ill., 1971.

Carwardine, Richard. "The Second Great Awakening in the Urban Centers: An Examination of Methodism and the 'New Measures.' " *Journal of American History*. Vol. 61, no. 2 (September 1972), pp. 327–40.

Cassuto, U[mberto]. *A Commentary on the Book of Genesis*. 2 vols., Jerusalem, 1961 (1944).

Catterall, Helen Tunnicliff, ed. *Judicial Class concerning American Slavery and the Negro*. 5 vols. New York, 1968 (1926).

Chan, Hok-lam, and William Theodore de Bary, eds. *Yüan Thought: Chinese Thought and Religion under the Mongols*. New York, 1982.

Chaplin, James H. "A Report on Sexual Behavior: Six Case Histories from Northern Rhodesia." *Advances in Sex Research: A Publication of the Society for the Scientific Study of Sex*. Edited by Hugo G. Beigel. New York, 1963, pp. 13–26.

Cheatham, Thomas Richard. "The Rhetorical Structure of the Abolitionist Movement within the Baptist Church, 1833–1845." Ph.D. dissertation, Purdue University, 1969.

Ching, Frank. *Ancestors: 900 Years in the Life of a Chinese Family*. New York, 1988.

Clark, Clifford E., Jr. "The Changing Nature of Protestantism in Mid-nineteenth Century: Henry Ward Beecher's *Seven Lectures to Young Men*." *Journal of American History*. Vol. 57, no. 4 (March 1971), pp. 832–46.

Clarke, William Newton. *Sixty Years with the Bible: A Record of Experience*. New York, 1909.

Clebsch, William A. "Christian Interpretation of the Civil War." *Church History*. Vol. 30, no. 2 (June 1961), pp. 212–22.

Clymer, Kenton J. *Protestant Missionaries in the Philippines, 1898–1916: An Inquiry into the American Colonial Mentality*. Urbana and Chicago, 1986.

Cohen, Charles Lloyd. *God's Caress: The Psychology of Puritan Religious Experience*. New York, 1986.

Cohen, William. "Thomas Jefferson and the Problem of Slavery." *Journal of American History*. Vol. 56, no. 3 (December 1969), pp. 503–26.

Cole, Charles C., Jr. "Horace Bushnell and the Slavery Question." *New England Quarterly*. Vol. 13, no. 1 (March 1950), pp. 19–30.

Coleman, Michael C. "Not Race, but Grace: Presbyterian Missionaries and American Indians, 1837–1893." *Journal of American History*. Vol. 67, no. 1 (June 1980), pp. 41–60.

———. *Presbyterian Missionary Attitudes Toward American Indians, 1837–1893*. Jackson, Miss., 1985.

Commager, Henry Steele, ed. *Documents of American History*. 2 vols. 8th ed., New York, 1963.

Conforti, Joseph. "Jonathan Edwards's Most Popular Work: 'The Life of David Brainerd' and Nineteenth-Century Evangelical Culture." *Church History*. Vol. 54, no. 2 (June 1985), pp. 188–201.

Conrad, A. Mark. "The Christianization of Indians in Colonial Virginia." Th.D. dissertation, Union Theological Seminary, Richmond, 1979.

Courlander, Harold. *Negro Folk Music, U.S.A.* New York, 1963.

Curran, R. Emmett, S.J. " 'Splendid Poverty': Jesuit Slaveholding in Maryland, 1805–1838." *Catholics in the Old South: Essays on Church and Culture*. Edited by Randall M. Miller and Jon L. Wakelyn. Macon, Ga., 1983, pp. 125–46.

Daniel, W. Harrison. "Virginia Baptists and the Negro in the Early Republic." *The Virginia Magazine of History and Biography*. Vol. 80, no. 1 (January 1972), pp. 60–69.

Davidson, James West. *The Logic of Millennial Thought: Eighteenth-Century New England*. New Haven, Conn., 1977.

Davies, Nigel. *The Rampant God: Eros Throughout the World*. New York, 1984.

Davis, David Brion. *The Problem of Slavery in the Age of Revolution, 1770–1823*. Ithaca, N.Y., 1975.

———. *The Problem of Slavery in Western Culture*. Ithaca, N.Y., 1966.

———. *Slavery and Human Progress*. New York, 1984.

Degler, Carl N. *Neither Black Nor White: Slavery and Race Relations in Brazil and the United States*. New York, 1971.

———. *The Other South: Southern Dissenters in the Nineteenth Century*. New York, 1974.

———. *Out of Our Past: The Forces That Shaped Modern America*. New York, 1959.

De Jong, Gerald Francis. "The Dutch Reformed Church and Negro Slavery in Colonial America." *Church History*. Vol. 40, no. 4 (December 1971), pp. 423–36.

D'Elia, Donald J. "Dr. Benjamin Rush and the Negro." *Journal of the History of Ideas*. Vol. 30, no. 3 (July–September 1969), pp. 413–22.

Demos, John P. *Entertaining Satan: Witchcraft and the Culture of Early New England*. New York, 1982.

Denton, Charles Richard. "American Unitarians, 1840–1865: A Study of Religious Opinion on War, Slavery, and the Union." Ph.D. dissertation, Michigan State University, 1969.

Dinnerstein, Leonard, and Jackson, Kenneth T., eds. *American Vistas, 1607–1877*. 4th ed., New York, 1983.

Dinnerstein, Myra. "The American Zulu Mission in the Nineteenth Century: Clash over Cultures." *Church History*. Vol. 45, no. 2 (June 1976), pp. 235–46.

Ditzion, Sidney. *Marriage, Morals, and Sex in America: A History of Ideas*. New York, 1953.

Dolan, Jay P. *The American Catholic Experience: A History from Colonial Times to the Present*. Garden City, N.Y., 1985.

———. *The Immigrant Church: New York's Irish and German Catholics, 1815–1865*. Baltimore, 1975.

Dollard, John. "Hostility and Fear in Social Life." *Race, Class, and Power*. Edited by Raymond W. Mack. New York, 1963, pp. 103–117.

Dombrowski, James. *The Early Days of Christian Socialism in America*. New York, 1966 (1936).

Dorson, Richard M. *Negro Tales from Pine Bluff, Arkansas, and Calvin, Michigan*. Bloomington, Ind., 1958.

Dostoyevsky, Fyodor. *The Brothers Karamazov*. Translated by Constance Garnett. New York [Moscow, 1879–80].

Drake, Frederick C. "Witchcraft in the American Colonies, 1647–62." *American Quarterly*. Vol. 20, no. 4 (Winter 1968), pp. 694–725.

Drake, Richard Bryant. "The American Missionary Association and the Southern Negro, 1861–1888." Ph.D. dissertation, Emory University, 1957.

Drake, Thomas E. *Quakers and Slavery in America*. Gloucester, Mass., 1965 (1950).

Drees, Clayton J. "Augustine of Hippo and Bernard of Clairvaux: A Medieval Justification for War." *Perspectives: A Journal of Historical Inquiry*. Vol. 14 (1987), pp. 1–22.

Duff, John B., and Mitchell, Peter M., eds. *The Nat Turner Rebellion: The Historical Event and the Modern Controversy*. New York, 1971.

Duignan, Peter, and Gann, L. H. *The United States and Africa: A History*. Cambridge, U.K., and New York, 1984.

Dvorak, Katherine L. "After Apocalypse, Moses." *Masters & Slaves in the House of the Lord: Race and Religion in the American South, 1740–1870*. Edited by John B. Boles. Lexington, Ky., 1988, pp. 173–91.

Earnest, Joseph B., Jr. *The Religious Development of the Negro in Virginia*. Charlottesville, Va., 1914.

Eighmy, John Lee. *Churches in Cultural Captivity: A History of the Social Attitudes of Southern Baptists*. Rev. ed., Knoxville, Tenn., 1987.

Ellis, John Tracy. *American Catholicism.* 2nd rev. ed., Chicago, 1969.
———, ed. *Documents of American Catholic History.* 3 vols. Wilmington, Del., 1987.
Elsbree, Oliver Wendell. *The Rise of the Missionary Spirit in America, 1790–1815.* Williamsport, Pa., 1928.
Engelder, Conrad James. "The Churches and Slavery: A Study of the Attitudes toward Slavery of the Major Protestant Denominations." Ph.D. dissertation, University of Michigan, 1964.
Erdoes, Richard, and Oritz, Alfonso, eds. *American Indian Myths and Legends.* New York, 1984.
Essig, James D. *The Bonds of Wickedness: American Evangelicals Against Slavery, 1770–1808.* Philadelphia, 1982.
———. "A Very Wintry Season: Virginia Baptists and Slavery, 1785–1797." *Virginia Magazine of History and Biography.* Vol. 88, no. 2 (April 1980), pp. 170–85.
Evans, Paul Otis. "The Ideology of Inequality: Asbury, Methodism, and Slavery." Ph.D. dissertation, Rutgers University, 1981.
Evans, William McKee. "From the Land of Canaan to the Land of Guinea: The Strange Odyssey of the 'Sons of Ham.'" *American Historical Review.* Vol. 85, no. 1 (February 1980), pp. 15–43.
Fage, J. D. *A History of Africa.* New York, 1978.
Farmer, James Oscar, Jr. *The Metaphysical Confederacy: James Henley Thornwell and the Synthesis of Southern Values.* Macon, Ga., 1986.
Farrison, William E. *William Wells Brown: Author and Reformer.* Chicago, 1969.
Federal Writers' Project. *Slave Narratives: A Folk History of Slavery in the United States from Interviews with Former Slaves.* 17 vols. Washington, D.C., 1941.
Feldstein, Stanley, ed. *The Poisoned Tongue: A Documentary History of American Racism and Prejudice.* New York, 1972.
Fickling, Susan Markey. *Slave-Conversion in South Carolina, 1830–1860.* Columbia, S.C., 1924.
Field, James A., Jr. "American Imperialism: The Worst Chapter in Almost Any Book." *American Historical Review.* Vol. 83, no. 3 (June 1978), pp. 645–68.
Filler, Louis, ed. *Abolition and Social Justice in the Era of Reform.* New York, 1972.
Finkelstein, J[acob] J. *The Ox That Gored.* Transactions of the American Philosophical Society. Vol. 71, part 2. Philadelphia, 1981.
Finley, Moses I. "The Idea of Slavery: Critique of David Brion Davis's *The Problem of Slavery in Western Culture.*" *Slavery in the New World: A Reader in Comparative History.* Edited by Laura Foner and Eugene D. Genovese. Englewood Cliffs, N.J., 1969, pp. 256–61.
———. "Slavery." *Encyclopedia of Social Sciences.* 2nd ed., vol. 14, pp. 307–13.
Flynt, Wayne. "Dissent in Zion: Alabama Baptists and Social Issues, 1900–1914." *Journal of Southern History.* Vol. 35, no. 4 (November 1969), pp. 523–42.
Foner, Laura, and Genovese, Eugene D., eds. *Slavery in the New World: A Reader in Comparative History.* Englewood Cliffs, N.J., 1969.
Forke, Alfred. *The World-Conception of the Chinese.* New York, 1975.
Forman, James D. *People of the Dream.* New York, 1972.
Fortenbaugh, Robert. "American Lutheran Synods and Slavery, 1830–1860." *Journal of Religion.* Vol. 13 (January 1933), pp. 72–92.
Fortes, Meyer. *Œdipus and Job in West African Religion.* Cambridge, U.K., 1959.
———. "Some Reflections on Ancestor Worship in Africa." *African Systems of Thought: Studies Presented and Discussed at the Third International Africa Seminar in Salisbury, December 1960.* London, 1965, pp. 122–42.
Foster, Lawrence. *Religion and Sexuality: Three American Communal Experiments of the Nineteenth Century.* New York, 1981.

Frankel, Gusti Wiesenfeld. "Between Parent and Child in Colonial New England: An Analysis of the Religious Child-Oriented Literature and Selected Children's Works." Ph.D. dissertation, University of Minnesota, 1976.

Franklin, John Hope. *From Slavery to Freedom: A History of Negro Americans.* 5th ed., New York, 1980.

———. "The Great Confrontation: The South and the Problem of Change." *Journal of Southern History.* Vol. 38, no. 1 (February 1972), pp. 3–20.

Frazier, E. Franklin. *The Negro Church in America.* New York, 1964.

Fredrickson, George M. *The Black Image in the White Mind: The Debate on Afro-American Character and Destiny, 1817–1914.* New York, 1971.

———. *White Supremacy: A Comparative Study in American and South African History.* New York, 1981.

Friedman, Richard Elliott, ed. *The Creation of Sacred Literature: Composition and Redaction of the Biblical Text.* Berkeley, Calif., 1981.

———. *Who Wrote the Bible?* New York, 1987.

Gallay, Alan. "The Origins of Slaveholders' Paternalism: George Whitefield, the Bryan Family, and the Great Awakening in the South." *Journal of Southern History.* Vol. 53, no. 3 (August 1987), pp. 369–94.

———. "Planters and Slaves in the Great Awakening." *Masters & Slaves in the House of the Lord: Race and Religion in the American South, 1740–1870.* Edited by John B. Boles. Lexington, Ky., 1988, pp. 19–36.

Gardella, Peter. *Innocent Ecstasy: How Christianity Gave America the Ethic of Sexual Pleasure.* New York, 1985.

Gausted, Edwin S., ed. *Historical Atlas of Religion in America.* New York, 1962.

Genovese, Eugene D. *Roll, Jordan, Roll: The World the Slaves Made.* New York, 1974.

Gilman, Sander L. *Difference and Pathology: Stereotypes of Sexuality, Race, and Madness.* Ithaca, N.Y., 1985.

Goen, C. C. *Broken Churches, Broken Nation: Denominational Schisms and the Coming of the Civil War.* Macon, Ga., 1985.

Gossett, Thomas F. *Race: The History of an Idea in America.* New York, 1965 (Dallas, 1963).

Gottlieb, Robert, and Wiley, Peter. *America's Saints: The Rise of Mormon Power.* New York, 1984.

Gottwald, Norman K. *The Hebrew Bible—A Socio-Literary Introduction.* Philadelphia, 1985.

Graebner, Norman A. "Christianity and Democracy: Tocqueville's Views of Religion in America." *Journal of Religion.* Vol. 56, no. 3 (July 1976), pp. 263–73.

———, ed. *Ideas and Diplomacy: Readings in the Intellectual Tradition of American Foreign Policy.* New York, 1964.

Grant, Michael. *The History of Ancient Israel.* New York, 1984.

Gravely, William Bernard. "Gilbert Haven, Racial Equalitarian: A Study of His Career in Racial Reform, 1850–1880." Ph.D. dissertation, Duke University, 1969.

Gray, Virginia. "Anti-Evolution Sentiment and Behavior: The Case of Arkansas." *Journal of American History.* Vol. 57, no. 2 (September 1970), pp. 352–66.

Gray, Wood. *The Hidden Civil War: The Story of the Copperheads.* New York, 1942.

Greenberg, Joseph. *The Languages of Africa.* Bloomington, Ind., 1963.

———. *Studies in African Languages.* 1955.

Greene, John C. "The American Debate on the Negro's Place in Nature, 1780–1815." *Journal of the History of Ideas.* Vol. 15, no. 3 (June 1954), pp. 384–96.

Greene, Lorenzo Johnston. *The Negro in Colonial New England, 1620–1776.* New York, 1966 (1942).

Gregerson, Edgar A. *Language in Africa: An Introductory Survey.* New York, 1977.

Greven, Philip. *The Protestant Temperament: Patterns of Child-Rearing, Religious Experience, and the Self in Early America.* New York, 1977.

Grimes, Alan P. *Equality in America: Religion, Race, and the Urban Majority.* New York, 1964.

Groves, C. P. *The Planting of Christianity in Africa.* 4 vols. London, 1948.

Halasz, Nicholas. *Rattling Chains: Slave Unrest and Revolt in the Antebellum South.* New York, 1966.

Hall, Robert L. "Black and White Christians in Florida, 1822–1861." *Masters & Slaves in the House of the Lord: Race and Religion in the American South, 1740–1870.* Edited by John B. Boles. Lexington, Ky., 1988, pp. 81–98.

Hamm, Thomas D. *The Transformation of American Quakerism: Orthodox Friends, 1800–1907.* Bloomington, Ind., 1988.

Handlin, Oscar. *Race and Nationality in American Life.* New York, 1957 (1948).

Handy, Robert T. *A Christian America: Protestant Hopes and Historical Realities.* New York, 1971.

———, ed. *Religion in the American Experience: The Pluralistic Style.* Columbia, S.C., 1972.

Hansen, Klaus J. *Mormonism and the American Experience.* Chicago, 1981.

Harding, Vincent. *There Is a River: The Black Struggle for Freedom in America.* New York, 1981.

Harrell, David Edwin, Jr. *Quest for a Christian America: The Disciples of Christ and American Society to 1866.* Volume I of *A Social History of the Disciples of Christ.* Nashville, Tenn., 1966.

Harris, Trudier. *Exorcising Blackness: Historical and Literary Lynching and Burning Rituals.* Bloomington, Ind., 1984.

Haselden, Kyle. *The Racial Problem in Christian Perspective.* New York, 1964 (1959).

Hatch, Nathan O. "*Sola Scriptura* and *Novus Ordo Seclorum.*" *The Bible in America: Essays in Cultural History.* Edited by Nathan O. Hatch and Mark A. Noll. New York, 1982, pp. 59–78.

Heimert, Alan. *Religion and the American Mind: From the Great Awakening to the Revolution.* Cambridge, Mass., 1966.

Henderson, John B. *The Development and Decline of Chinese Cosmology.* New York, 1984.

Hennesey, James, S.J. *American Catholics: A History of the Roman Catholic Community in the United States.* New York, 1981.

Herskovits, Melville J. *The Myth of the Negro Past.* New York, 1958 (1941).

Hesse, Hermann. *Siddartha.* Translated by Hilda Rosner. New York, 1951.

Higham, John. *Strangers in the Land: Patterns of American Nativism, 1860–1925.* New York, 1965.

Hillis, Margaret T. *The English Bible in America: A Bibliography of Editions of the Bible & the New Testament Published in America, 1777–1957.* New York, 1961.

Hoffer, Eric. *The True Believer: Thoughts on the Nature of Mass Movements.* New York, 1963 (1951).

Holifield, E. Brooks. *The Gentleman Theologians: American Theology in Southern Culture, 1795–1860.* Durham, N.C., 1978.

Hopkins, Charles Howard. *The Rise of the Social Gospel in American Protestantism, 1865–1915.* New Haven, Conn., 1940.

Horowitz, Donald L. "Color Differentiation in the American Systems of Slavery." *Journal of Interdisciplinary History.* Vol. 3, no. 3 (Winter 1973), pp. 509–41.

Horsman, Reginald. *Josiah Nott of Mobile: Southerner, Physician, and Racial Theorist.* Baton Rouge, La., 1987.

———. *Race and Manifest Destiny: The Origins of American Racial Anglo-Saxonism.* Cambridge, Mass., 1981.

Houis, Maurice. *Anthropologie linguistique de l'Afrique noire.* Paris, 1971.

Hovenkamp, Herbert. *Science and Religion in America, 1800–1860*. Philadelphia, 1978.

Howard, Victor B. "The Southern Aid Society and the Slavery Controversy." *Church History*. Vol. 41, no. 2 (June 1972), pp. 208–24.

Howe, Daniel Walker. "The Social Science of Horace Bushnell." *Journal of American History*. Vol. 70, no. 2 (September 1983), pp. 305–22.

Howe, George. *Southern Presbyterian Review*. January 1950, pp. 427–90.

Hoxie, Frederick E. "The Indians Versus the Textbooks: Is There a Way Out?" *Perspectives: American Historical Association Newsletter*. Vol. 23, no. 4 (April 1985), pp. 18–22.

Hudson, Winthrop S. "The American Context as an Area for Research in Black Church Studies." *Church History*. Vol. 52, no. 2 (June 1983), pp. 157–71.

———. *American Protestantism*. Chicago, 1961.

———, ed. *Nationalism and Religion in America: Concepts of Identity and Mission*. New York, 1970.

———. *Religion in America*. New York, 1981.

Hultkrantz, Åke. *The Religions of the American Indians*. Translated by Monica Setterwall. Berkeley, Calif., 1967.

Hutchison, William R., ed. *American Protestant Thought: The Liberal Era*. New York, 1968.

———. "Cultural Strain and Protestant Liberalism." *American Historical Review*. Vol. 76, no. 2 (April 1971), pp. 386–411.

———. *Errand to the World: American Protestant Thought and Foreign Missions*. Chicago, 1987.

Idowu, E. Bolaji. *African Traditional Religion: A Definition*. Maryknoll, N.Y., 1973.

Jackson, Luther P. "Religious Development of the Negro in Virginia from 1760 to 1860." *Journal of Negro History*. Vol. 16, no. 2 (April 1931), pp. 168–239.

Jagersma, H[enk]. *A History of Israel in the Old Testament Period*. Translated by John Bowden. Philadelphia, 1983.

James, Larry M. "Biracial Fellowship in Antebellum Baptist Churches." *Masters & Slaves in the House of the Lord: Race and Religion in the American South, 1740–1870*. Edited by John B. Boles. Lexington, Ky., 1988, pp. 37–57.

Jefferson, Margo, and Skinner, Elliott P. *Roots of Time: A Portrait of African Life and Culture*. Garden City, N.Y., 1974.

Jenkins, William Sumner. *Pro-Slavery Thought in the Old South*. Chapel Hill, N.C., 1935.

Jennings, Francis. *The Invasion of America: Indians, Colonialism, and the Cant of Conquest*. Chapel Hill, N.C., 1975.

Jernagan, Marcus W. "Slavery and Conversion in the American Colonies." *American Historical Review*. Vol. 21, no. 3 (April 1916), pp. 504–27.

Jessett, Thomas E. "Christian Missions to the Indians of Oregon." *Church History*. Vol. 28, no. 2 (June 1959), pp. 147–56.

Johnson, Clifton Herman. "The American Missionary Association, 1846–1861: A Study of Christian Abolitionism." Ph.D. dissertation, University of North Carolina, 1958.

———, ed. *God Struck Me Dead: Religious Conversion Experiences and Autobiographies of Ex-slaves*. Philadelphia, 1969.

Johnson, Lemuel A. *The Devil, the Gargoyle, and the Buffoon: The Negro as Metaphor in Western Literature*. Port Washington, N.Y., 1969.

Jones, Louis Thomas. *Aboriginal American Oratory: The Tradition of Eloquence Among the Indians of the United States*. Los Angeles, 1965.

Jones-Jackson, Patricia. *When Roots Die: Endangered Traditions on the Sea Islands*. Athens, Ga., 1987.

Jordan, Winthrop D. *White Over Black: American Attitudes Toward the Negro, 1550–1812*. Chapel Hill, N.C., 1968.

Jorns, Auguste. *The Quakers as Pioneers in Social Work*. Translated by Thomas Kite Brown, Jr., from *Studien über die Sozialpolitik der Quäker* (1931). Montclair, N.J., 1969.

July, Robert W. *A History of the African People.* New York, 1970.

Kaufman, Gordon D. *God the Problem.* Cambridge, Mass., 1972.

Kawashima, Yasuhide. *Puritan Justice and the Indian: White Man's Law in Massachusetts, 1630–1763.* Middletown, Conn., 1986.

Keller, Robert H., Jr. *American Protestantism and United States Indian Policy, 1869–82.* Lincoln, Neb., 1983.

Kerber, Linda K. "The Abolitionist Perception of the Indian." *Journal of American History.* Vol. 62, no. 2 (September 1975), pp. 271–95.

Kerr, Hugh T., ed. *Readings in Christian Thought.* Nashville, Tenn., 1966.

Kibbey, Ann. *The Interpretation of Material Shapes in Puritanism: A Study of Rhetoric, Prejudice, and Violence.* Cambridge, U.K., 1986.

Kingsley, Mary H. *West African Studies.* London, 1901.

Kinzer, Donald L. *An Episode in Anti-Catholicism: The American Protective Association.* Seattle, 1964.

Kittel, Gerhard, ed. *Theological Dictionary of the New Testament.* Translated by Geoffrey W. Bromiley from *Theologisches Wörterbuch zum Neuen Testament* (1933). 10 vols. Grand Rapids, Mich., 1964.

Kittredge, George L. *Witchcraft in Old and New England.* Cambridge, Mass., 1929.

Klaits, Joseph. *Servants of Satan: The Age of the Witch Hunts.* Bloomington, Ind., 1985.

Klein, Herbert S. "Anglicanism, Catholicism, and the Negro Slave," *Slavery in the New World: A Reader in Comparative History.* Edited by Laura Foner and Eugene D. Genovese. Englewood Cliffs, N.J., 1969, pp. 138–66. Reprinted from *Comparative Studies in Society and History.* Vol. 3, no. 3 (April 1966), pp. 295–327.

———. *Slavery in the Americas: A Comparative Study of Virginia and Cuba.* Chicago, 1967.

Klingberg, Frank J. *Anglican Humanitarianism in Colonial New York.* Philadelphia, 1940.

———. *An Appraisal of the Negro in Colonial South Carolina: A Study in Americanization.* Washington, D.C., 1941.

Kohn, Hans. *Nationalism in the Soviet Union.* New York, 1966 (London, 1933).

Kolchin, Peter. "Reevaluating the Antebellum Slave Community: A Comparative Perspective." *Journal of American History.* Vol. 70, no. 3 (December 1983), pp. 579–601.

Kors, Alan C., and Edward Peters, eds. *Witchcraft in Europe, 1100–1700. A Documentary History.* Philadelphia, 1972.

Kunze, Michael. *Highroad to the Stake: A Tale of Witchcraft.* Translated by William E. Yuill. Chicago, 1987.

La Farge, John. *The Catholic Viewpoint on Race Relations.* Rev. ed., Garden City, N.Y., 1960.

Larson, Edward J. *Trial and Error: The American Controversy Over Creation and Evolution.* New York, 1985.

Latourette, Kenneth Scott. *A History of Christianity.* New York, 1953.

———. *Missions and the American Mind.* Indianapolis, Ind., 1949.

Lerner, Max. *America as a Civilization: Life and Thought in the United States Today.* New York, 1957.

Leverenz, David. *The Language of Puritan Feeling: An Exploration in Literature, Psychology, and Social History.* New Brunswick, N.J., 1980.

Levine, Lawrence W. *Black Culture and Black Consciousness: Afro-American Folk Thought from Slavery to Freedom.* New York, 1977.

———. "Slave Songs and Slave Consciousness: An Exploration in Neglected Sources." *Anonymous Americans: Explorations in Nineteenth-Century Social History.* Edited by Tamara K. Hareven. Englewood Cliffs, N.J., 1971.

Lewis, Norman. "English Missionary Interest in the Indians of North America, 1578–1700." Ph.D. dissertation, University of Washington, 1968.

Lewit, Robert T. "Indian Missions and Antislavery Sentiment: A Conflict of Evangelical and Humanitarian Ideals." *Mississippi Valley Historical Review*. Vol. 50, no. 1 (June 1963), pp. 39–55.

Lincoln, C. Eric. *Race, Religion, and the Continuing American Dilemma*. New York, 1984.

Lines, Stiles Bailey. "Slaves and Churchmen: The Work of the Episcopal Church among Southern Negroes." Ph.D. dissertation, Columbia University, 1960.

Linkh, Richard. *American Catholicism and European Immigrants (1900–1924)*. Staten Island, N.Y., 1975.

Littell, Franklin Hamlin. "The Churches and the Body Politic." *Daedalus: Journal of the American Academy of Arts and Sciences* (Winter 1967), pp. 22–42.

———. *The Free Church*. Boston, 1957.

———. *From State Church to Pluralism: A Protestant Interpretation of Religion in American History*. Chicago, 1962.

Litwack, Leon F. *Been in the Storm So Long: The Aftermath of Slavery*. New York, 1979.

———. *North of Slavery: The Negro in the Free States*. Chicago, 1961.

Litzinger, Charles A., "Conflict between Christians and Non-Christians in Rural Chilhi, 1860–1895." *Essays in Memory of Professor Chao T'ieh-han*. Taipei, 1978.

Lloyd, Peter. "The Emergence of a Racial Prejudice towards the Indians in Seventeenth Century New England: Some Notes on Explanation." Ph.D. dissertation, Ohio State University, 1975.

Loetscher, Lefferts A. *A Brief History of the Presbyterians*. 3rd ed., Philadelphia, 1978.

Lohte, Henri. "Oasis of Art in the Sahara." *National Geographic*. Vol. 172, no. 2 (August 1987), pp. 180–91.

Los Angeles County Museum of Art, Overseas Archaeological Exhibition Corporation, and the People's Republic of China. *The Quest for Equality: Chinese Ceramic Structures from the People's Republic of China*. Los Angeles and San Francisco, 1987.

Lovejoy, David S. *Religious Enthusiasm in the New World: Heresy to Revolution*. Cambridge, Mass., 1985.

Lovell, John, Jr. *Black Song: The Forge and the Flame: The Story of How the Afro-American Spiritual Was Hammered Out*. New York, 1972.

Lucas, Sir Charles. *Religion, Colonising & Trade: The Driving Forces of the Old Empire*. London, 1930.

Luker, Ralph E. "Bushnell in Black and White: Evidence of the 'Racism' of Horace Bushnell." *New England Quarterly*. Vol. 45, no. 3 (September 1972), pp. 408–16.

———. "The Social Gospel and the Failure of Racial Reform." *Church History*. Vol. 46, no. 1 (March 1977), pp. 80–99.

Lurie, Edward. *Louis Agassiz: A Life in Science*. Chicago, 1960.

Madden, Edward H. *Civil Disobedience and Moral Law in Nineteenth-Century American Philosophy*. Seattle, Wash., 1968.

Malinowski, Bronislaw. *The Sexual Life of Savages: An Ethnographic Account of Courtship, Marriage, and Family Life Among the Natives of the Trobriand Islands, British New Guinea*. New York, 1929.

Manross, William Wilson. *A History of the American Episcopal Church*. 3rd ed., New York, 1959 (1935).

Marsden, George M. *The Evangelical Mind and the New School Presbyterian Experience: A Case Study of Thought and Theology in Nineteenth-Century America*. New Haven, Conn., 1970.

———. "Everyone One's Own Interpreter?: The Bible, Science, and Authority in Mid-Nineteenth Century America." *The Bible in America: Essays in Cultural History*. Edited by Nathan O. Hatch and Mark A. Noll. New York, 1982, pp. 79–100.

Marty, Martin E. *Righteous Empire: The Protestant Experience in America*. New York, 1970.

Mathews, Donald G. "The Abolitionists on Slavery: The Critique Behind the Social Movement." *Journal of Southern History.* Vol. 33, no. 2 (May 1967), pp. 163–82.

———. "Charles Colcock Jones and the Southern Evangelical Crusade to Form a Biracial Community." *Journal of Southern History.* Vol. 41, no. 3 (August 1975), pp. 299–320.

———. "The Methodist Mission to the Slaves, 1829–1844." *Journal of American History.* Vol. 51, no. 4 (March 1965), pp. 615–31.

———. *Religion in the Old South.* Chicago, 1977.

———. *Slavery and Methodism: A Chapter in American Morality, 1780–1845.* Westport, Conn., 1978 (1965).

Mathews, Jay, and Mathews, Linda. *One Billion: A China Chronicle.* New York, 1985.

May, Henry F. *The Protestant Churches and Industrial America.* New York, 1963 (1949).

Mbiti, John S. *African Religions & Philosophy.* New York, 1969.

McCants, Dorothea Olga, ed. *They Came to Louisiana: Letters of a Catholic Mission, 1854–1882.* Baton Rouge, La., 1970.

McCarthy, Michael James. "Africa and America: A Study of American Attitudes toward Africa and the African during the Late Nineteenth and Early Twentieth Centuries." Ph.D. dissertation, University of Minnesota, 1975.

McClintock, David Alan. "Walter Rauschenbusch: The Kingdom of God and the American Experience." Ph.D. dissertation, Case Western Reserve University, 1975.

McKivigan, John R. *The War against Proslavery Religion: Abolitionism and the Northern Churches, 1830–1865.* Ithaca, N.Y., 1984.

McLain, C. E. *Place of Race.* New York, 1965.

McLean, Helen V. "Psychodynamic Factors in Race Relations." *Annals of the American Academy of Political and Social Science.* March 1946.

McLoughlin, William G. "Indian Slaveholders and Presbyterian Missions, 1837–1861." *Church History.* Vol. 42, no. 4 (December 1973), pp. 535–51.

McLuhan, T. C., comp. *Touch the Earth: A Self-Portrait of Indian Existence.* New York, 1971.

Mead, Sidney E. *The Lively Experiment: The Shaping of Christianity in America.* New York, 1963.

Miceli, Mary Veronica. "The Influence of the Roman Catholic Church on Slavery in Colonial Louisiana under French Domination, 1718–1763." Ph.D. dissertation, Tulane University, 1979.

Michener, James A. *Hawaii.* New York, 1959.

Miller, Arthur. *The Crucible: A Play in Four Acts.* Bantam ed., New York, 1959 (1952).

Miller, John Chester. *The Wolf by the Ears: Thomas Jefferson and Slavery.* New York, 1977.

Miller, Perry. *Errand into the Wilderness.* New York, 1964 (1956).

———. *Nature's Nation.* Cambridge, Mass., 1967.

———. *The New England Mind.* 2 vols. Vol. I: *The Seventeenth Century.* Vol. II: *From Colony to Province.* Boston, 1961 (1939).

Miller, Randall M. "The Failed Mission: The Catholic Church and Black Catholics in the Old South." *Catholics in the Old South: Essays on Church and Culture.* Edited by Randall M. Miller and Jon L. Wakelyn. Macon, Ga., 1983, pp. 149–70.

———. "Slaves and Southern Catholicism." *Masters & Slaves in the House of the Lord: Race and Religion in the American South, 1740–1870.* Edited by John B. Boles. Lexington, Ky., 1988, pp. 127–52.

———, and Wakelyn, Jon L., eds. *Catholics in the Old South: Essays on Church and Culture.* Macon, Ga., 1983.

Miller, Ruth, ed. *Blackamerican Literature, 1760–Present.* Beverly Hills, Calif., 1971.

Mills, Dorothy. *The People of Ancient Israel.* New York, 1932.

Mitchell, Henry H. *Black Belief: Folk Beliefs of Blacks in America and West Africa.* New York, 1975.

Moberg, David O. *The Church as a Social Institution: The Sociology of American Religion.* 2nd ed., Grand Rapids, Mich., 1984.
Mode, Peter G. *The Frontier Spirit to American Christianity.* New York, 1923.
Moellering, Ralph L. *Christian Conscience and Negro Emancipation.* Philadelphia, 1965.
Moore, Charles, ed. *The Chinese Mind: Essentials of Chinese Philosophy and Culture.* Honolulu, Hawaii, 1967.
Moore, Edmund A. *Robert J. Breckinridge and the Slavery Aspect of the Presbyterian Schism of 1837.* Chicago, 1932.
Moorehead, James H. "Social Reform and the Divided Conscience of Antebellum Protestantism." *Church History.* Vol. 48, no. 4 (December 1979), pp. 416–30.
Morgan, Edmund S. *The Puritan Family: Religion & Domestic Relations in Seventeenth-Century New England.* Rev. and enlarged ed., New York, 1966.
———. "The Puritans and Sex." *American Vistas, 1607–1877.* Edited by Leonard Dinnerstein and Kenneth T. Jackson. New York, 1987. Originally published in *New England Quarterly,* Vol. 15 (1942), pp. 591–607.
———. *Visible Saints: The History of a Puritan Idea.* New York, 1963.
Morrow, Ralph E. *Northern Methodism and Reconstruction.* East Lansing, Mich., 1956.
Moseley, James G. *A Cultural History of Religion in America.* Westport, Conn., 1981.
Moulton, Phillips. "John Woolman's Approach to Social Action—as Exemplified in Relation to Slavery." *Church History.* Vol. 30, no. 4 (December 1966), pp. 399–410.
Mouw, Richard J. "The Bible in Twentieth-Century Protestantism: A Preliminary Taxonomy." *The Bible in America: Essays in Cultural History.* Edited by Nathan O. Hatch and Mark A. Noll. New York, 1982, pp. 139–62.
Muller, Dorothea R. "Josiah Strong and American Nationalism: A Reevaluation." *Journal of American History.* Vol. 53, no. 3 (December 1966), pp. 487–503.
———. "The Social Philosophy of Josiah Strong: Social Christianity and American Progressivism." *Church History.* Vol. 28, no. 2 (June 1959), pp. 183–201.
Mullin, Gerald W. *Flight and Rebellion: Slave Resistance in Eighteenth-Century Virginia.* New York, 1972.
Murphy, John C. "An Analysis of the Attitudes of American Catholics toward the Immigrant and the Negro, 1825–1925." Ph.D. dissertation, Catholic University of America, 1940.
Murray, Andrew E. *The Presbyterians and the Negro—A History.* Philadelphia, 1966.
Myers, Gustavus. *History of Bigotry in the United States.* New York, 1960 (1943).
Myrdal, Gunnar. *An American Dilemma: The Negro Problem and Modern Democracy.* New York, 1962 (1944).
Nash, Gary B. *Red, White, and Black: The Peoples of Early America.* 2nd ed., Englewood Cliffs, N.J., 1982.
———, and Weiss, Richard, eds. *The Great Fear: Race in the Mind of America.* New York, 1970.
Neill, Stephen. *Colonialism and Christian Missions.* London, 1966.
———. *A History of Christian Missions.* Harmondsworth, Middlesex, England, 1964.
Nelson, E. Clifford, ed. *The Lutherans in North America.* Philadelphia, 1975.
Nettels, Curtis. *The Roots of American Civilization: A History of American Colonial Life.* 2nd ed., New York, 1963.
New Catholic Encyclopedia. 17 vols. New York, 1967.
Nichols, Charles H. *Many Thousand Gone: The Ex-Slaves' Account of Their Bondage and Freedom.* Leiden, Netherlands, 1963.
Niebuhr, H. Richard. *The Kingdom of God in America.* New York, 1937.
Niebuhr, Reinhold. *The Children of Light and the Children of Darkness: A Vindication of Democracy and a Critique of Its Traditional Defense.* New York, 1944.

———. *Moral Man and Immoral Society: A Study in Ethics and Politics*. New York, 1960 (1932).
———. *The Nature and Destiny of Man: A Christian Interpretation*. 2 vols. New York, 1941.
Norton, L. Wesley. "The Religious Press and the Compromise of 1850: A Study of the Relationship of the Methodist, Baptist, and Presbyterian Press to the Slavery Controversy, 1846–1851." Ph.D. dissertation, University of Illinois, 1959.
Norwood, Frederick A. "Two Contrasting Views of the Indians: Methodist Involvement in the Indian Troubles in Oregon and Washington." *Church History*. Vol. 49, no. 2 (June 1980), pp. 178–87.
Norwood, John Nelson. *The Schism in the Methodist Episcopal Church, 1844: A Study of Slavery and Ecclesiastical Politics*. New York, 1923.
Nugent, Donald. "The Renaissance and/of Witchcraft." *Church History*. Vol. 40, no. 1 (March 1971), pp. 69–78.
O'Brien, Conor Cruise. *God Land: Reflections on Religion and Nationalism*. Cambridge, Mass., 1988.
Oded, Arye. *Islam in Uganda: Islamization through a Centralized State in Pre-colonial Africa*. New York, 1974.
Oldham, J. H. *Christianity and the Race Problem*. New York, 1969 (1924).
Oliver, Douglas L. *Oceania: The Native Cultures of Australia and the Pacific Islands*. Honolulu, Hawaii, 1989.
———. *The Pacific Islands*. Rev. ed., Garden City, N.Y., 1961 (1951).
Orlinsky, Harry N. *Ancient Israel*. Ithaca, N.Y., 1954.
Osofsky, Gilbert. *The Burden of Race: A Documentary History of Negro-White Relations in America*. New York, 1967.
Page, Jesse. *David Brainerd: The Apostle to the North American Indians*. New York, [1901?].
Palmer, Colin A. "Religion and Magic in Mexican Slave Society, 1570–1650." *Race and Slavery in the Western Hemisphere: Quantitative Studies*. Edited by Stanley L. Engerman and Eugene D. Genovese. Princeton, N.J., 1975, pp. 311–28.
Parrinder, Geoffrey. *Religion in Africa*. New York, 1969.
———. *West African Religions: A Study of the Beliefs and Practices of Akan, Ewe, Yoruba, Ibo, and Kindred Peoples*. London, 1969 (1949).
———. *Witchcraft: European and African*. London, 1963 (1958).
———, ed. *World Religions: From Ancient History to the Present*. New York, 1983 (1971).
Patrick, Dale. *Old Testament Law*. Atlanta, 1985.
Patterson, Orlando. *Slavery and Social Death: A Comparative Study*. Cambridge, Mass., 1982.
———. *Sociology of Slavery: An Analysis of the Origins, Development, and Structure of Negro Slave Society in Jamaica*. Rutherford, N.J., 1969 (1967).
p'Bitek, Okot. *African Religions in Western Scholarship*. Kampala, Uganda, [1970].
Pearce, Roy Harvey. *The Savages of America: A Study of the Indian and the Idea of Civilization*. Rev. ed., Baltimore, 1965 (1953).
Perry, Ralph Barton. *Puritanism and Democracy*. New York, 1944.
Peters, Edward. *The Magician, the Witch, and the Law*. Philadelphia, 1982.
Peterson, Thomas Virgil. *Ham and Japheth: The Mythic World of Whites in the Antebellum South*. Metuchen, N.J., 1978.
Pettigrew, Thomas F. *Racially Separate or Together?* New York, 1971.
Phillips, Joseph W. *Jedidiah Morse and New England Congregationalism*. New Brunswick, N.J., 1983.
Piersen, William Dillon. "Afro-American Culture in Eighteenth-Century New England: A Comparative Examination." Ph.D. dissertation, Indiana University, 1975.
Powell, Milton Bryan. "The Abolitionist Controversy in the Methodist Episcopal Church, 1840–1864." Ph.D. dissertation, State University of Iowa, 1963.

Prucha, F[rancis] P[aul]. "Andrew Jackson's Indian Policy: A Reassessment." *Journal of American History*. Vol. 56, no. 3 (December 1969), pp. 527–39.

———. *The Churches and the Indian Schools, 1888–1912*. Lincoln, Neb., 1979[?].

Purifoy, Lewis McCarroll, Jr. "The Methodist Episcopal Church, South, and Slavery, 1844–1865." Ph.D. dissertation, University of North Carolina, 1965.

———. "The Southern Methodist Church and the Proslavery Argument." *Journal of Southern History*. Vol. 32, no. 3 (August 1966), pp. 325–41.

Raboteau, Albert J. *Slave Religion: "The Invisible Institution" in the Antebellum South*. New York, 1978.

Radcliffe-Brown, A. R. *Structure and Function in Primitive Society: Essays and Addresses*. New York, 1965 (1952).

Rader, Benjamin G. "Richard T. Ely: Lay Spokesman for the Social Gospel." *Journal of American History*. Vol. 53, no. 1 (June 1966), pp. 61–74.

Rauschenbusch, Walter. *Christianity and the Social Crisis*. New York, 1907.

Rawick, George P., ed. *The American Slave: a Composite Autobiography*. 31 vols., Westport, Conn., 1972–78.

Ray, Benjamin C. *African Religions: Symbol, Ritual, and Community*. Englewood Cliffs, N.J., 1976.

Redkey, Edwin S. "Bishop Turner's African Dream," *Journal of American History*. Vol. 54, no. 2 (September 1967), pp. 271–90.

Reimers, David M. "The Race Problem and Presbyterian Union." *Church History*. Vol. 31, no. 2 (June 1962), pp. 203–15.

———. *White Protestantism and the Negro*. New York, 1965.

Remini, Robert V. *The Legacy of Andrew Jackson: Essays on Democracy, Indian Removal, and Slavery*. Baton Rouge, La., 1988.

Reuter, Frank T. *Catholic Influence on American Colonial Policy, 1898–1904*. Austin, Tex., 1967.

Reynolds, David S. *Faith in Fiction: The Emergence of Religious Literature in America*. Cambridge, Mass., 1981.

Rice, Madeleine Hooke. *American Catholic Opinion in the Slavery Controversy*. New York, 1944.

Richmond, M. A. *Bid the Vassal Soar: Interpretive Essays on the Life and Poetry of Phillis Wheatley (ca. 1753–1784) and George Moses Horton (ca. 1797–1883)*. Washington, D.C., 1974.

Riddell, William R. "The Baptism of Slaves in Prince Edward Island," *Journal of Negro History*. Vol. 6, no. 1 (July 1921), pp. 307–309.

Rightmyer, Nelson Waite. *Maryland's Established Church*. Baltimore, 1956.

Roberts, Jon H. *Darwinism and the Divine in America: Protestant Intellectuals and Organic Evolution, 1859–1900*. Madison, Wis., 1988.

Robinson, Forrest G. *In Bad Faith: The Dynamics of Deception in Mark Twain's America*. Cambridge, Mass., 1986.

Robinson, William H. *Phillis Wheatley and Her Writings*. New York, 1984.

Rogin, Michael Paul. *Fathers and Children: Andrew Jackson and the Subjugation of American Indians*. New York, 1975.

———. *Ronald Reagan, the Movie, and Other Episodes in Political Demonology*. Berkeley, Calif., 1987.

Rousselle, Aline. *Porneia: On Desire and the Body in Antiquity*. Translated by Felicia Pheasant. New York, 1988.

Russell, Bertrand. *Why I Am Not a Christian, and Other Essays on Religion and Related Subjects*. New York, 1957.

Russell, Jeffrey Burton. *The Devil: Perceptions of Evil from Antiquity to Primitive Christianity*. Ithaca, N.Y., 1977.

———. *Lucifer: The Devil in the Middle Ages*. Ithaca, N.Y., 1984.

———. *Mephistopheles: The Devil in the Modern World*. Ithaca, N.Y., 1986.
———. *Satan: The Early Christian Tradition*. Ithaca, N.Y., 1981.
Russell, John H. *The Free Negro in Virginia, 1619–1865*. New York, 1969 (Baltimore, 1913).
Rutman, Darrett B. *American Puritanism: Faith and Practice*. Philadelphia, 1970.
Sachar, Abram Leon. *A History of the Jews*. New York, 1968.
Salisbury, Neal. "Red Puritans: The 'Praying Indians' of Massachusetts Bay and John Eliot." *William and Mary Quarterly*. 3rd series, vol. 31, no. 1 (January 1974), pp. 27–54.
Samek, Hana. *The Blackfoot Confederacy, 1880–1920: A Comparative Study of Canadian and U.S. Indian Policy*. Albuquerque, N.M., 1987.
Sanders, Ronald. *Lost Tribes and Promised Lands: The Origins of American Racism*. Boston, 1978.
Sanneh, Lamin. *West African Christianity: The Religious Impact*. London, 1983.
Sapp, Stephen. *Sexuality, the Bible, and Science*. Philadelphia, 1977.
Scherer, Lester B. *Slavery and the Churches in Early America, 1619–1819*. Grand Rapids, Mich., 1975.
Schmidt, Fredrika Teute, and Wilhelm, Barbara Ripel. "Early Proslavery Petitions in Virginia." *William and Mary Quarterly*. 3rd series, vol. 30, no. 1 (January 1973), pp. 133–46.
Schwartz, Benjamin I. *The World of Thought in Ancient China*. Cambridge, Mass., 1985.
Segal, Charles M., and Stineback, David C. *Puritans, Indians, and Manifest Destiny*. New York, 1977.
Seidenberg, Robert. "The Sexual Basis of Social Prejudice." *Psychoanalytic Review*. Vol. 39 (1952), pp. 90–95.
Sellers, Charles Grier, Jr. "The Travail of Slavery." *The Southerner as American*. Edited by Charles Grier Sellers, Jr. Chapel Hill, N.C., 1960, pp. 40–71.
Senior, Robert C. "New England Congregationalists and the Anti-Slavery Movement, 1830–1860." Ph.D. dissertation, Yale University, 1954.
Shalhope, Robert E. "Race, Class, Slavery, and the Antebellum Southern Mind." *Journal of Southern History*. Vol. 37, no. 4 (November 1971), pp. 557–74.
Sharp, Andrew. *Ancient Voyagers in Polynesia*. Berkeley, Calif., 1964.
Sheehan, Bernard W. *Savagism and Civility: Indians and Englishmen in Colonial Virginia*. Cambridge, U.K., 1980.
———. *Seeds of Extinction: Jeffersonian Philanthropy and the American Indian*. New York, 1973.
Shepperson, Wilbur S. *Emigration & Disenchantment: Portraits of Englishmen Repatriated from the United States*. Norman, Okla., 1965.
Sio, Arnold A. "Interpretations of Slavery: The Slave Status in the Americas." *Comparative Studies in Society and History*. Vol. 7, no. 3 (April 1965), pp. 289–308.
Smith, Edwin W., ed. *African Ideas of God: A Symposium*. London, 1950.
Smith, Elwyn A. "The Role of the South in the Presbyterian Schism of 1837–38." *Church History*. Vol. 29, no. 1 (March 1960), pp. 44–63.
Smith, H. Shelton. *Changing Conceptions of Original Sin: A Study in American Theology since 1750*. New York, 1955.
———. *In His Image, but . . . : Racism in Southern Religion, 1780–1910*. Durham, N.C., 1972.
———, Handy, Robert T., and Loetscher, Lefferts A., eds. *American Christianity: An Historical Interpretation with Representative Documents*. 2 vols. New York, 1960.
Smith, Lillian. *Killers of the Dream*. Rev. ed., New York, 1961.
Smith, Timothy L. "Protestant Schooling and American Nationality, 1800–1850." *Journal of American History*. Vol. 53, no. 4 (March 1967), pp. 679–95.
———. "Religion and Ethnicity in America." *American Historical Review*. Vol. 83, no. 5 (December 1978), pp. 1155–85.
———. *Revivalism and Social Reform: American Protestantism on the Eve of the Civil War*. New York, 1965 (1957).

———. "Slavery and Theology: The Emergence of Black Christian Consciousness in Nineteenth-Century America." *Church History*. Vol. 41, no. 4 (December 1972), pp. 497–512.

Smith, Willard H. "William Jennings Bryan and the Social Gospel." *Journal of American History*. Vol. 53, no. 1 (June 1966), pp. 41–60.

Snowden, Frank M., Jr. *Before Color Prejudice: The Ancient View of Blacks*. Cambridge, Mass., 1983.

Sobel, Mechal. *The World They Made Together: Black and White Values in Eighteenth-Century Virginia*. Princeton, N.J., 1987.

Soderlund, Jean R. *Quakers and Slavery: A Divided Spirit*. Princeton, N.J., 1985.

Sorin, Gerald. *Abolitionism: A New Perspective*. Foreword by James P. Shenton. New York, 1972.

Sparks, Randy J. "Religion in Amite County, 1800–1861." *Masters & Slaves in the House of the Lord: Race and Religion in the American South, 1740–1870*. Edited by John B. Boles. Lexington, Ky., 1988, pp. 58–80.

Stacey, W. David. *The Pauline View of Man: In Relation to Its Judaic and Hellenistic Background*. London, 1956.

Stafford, Tim. "Great Sex: Reclaiming a Christian Sexual Ethic." *Christianity Today*. Vol. 31, no. 14 (October 2, 1988), pp. 23–46.

Stager, Curt. "Killer Lake." *National Geographic*. Vol. 172, no. 3 (September 1987), pp. 404–20.

Staiger, C. Bruce. "Abolitionism and the Presbyterian Schism of 1837–1838." *Mississippi Valley Historical Review*. Vol. 36, no. 3 (December 1949), pp. 391–414.

Stampp, Kenneth M. *The Peculiar Institution: Slavery in the Ante-Bellum South*. New York, 1956.

Stange, Douglas C. *Radicalism for Humanity: A Study of Lutheran Abolitionism*. St. Louis, 1970.

Stannard, David E. *The Puritan Way of Death: A Study in Religion, Culture, and Social Change*. New York, 1977.

Stanton, William. *The Leopard's Spots: Scientific Attitudes toward Race in America, 1815–59*. Chicago, 1960.

Starkey, Marion L. *The Devil in Massachusetts: A Modern Inquiry into the Salem Witch Trials*. New York, 1963 (1949).

Stavely, Keith W. F. *Puritan Legacies:* Paradise Lost *and the New England Tradition, 1630–1890*. Ithaca, N.Y., 1987.

Stein, Stephen J. "George Whitefield on Slavery: Some New Evidence." *Church History*. Vol. 42, no. 2 (June 1973), pp. 243–56.

Stewart, James Brewer. "Evangelicalism and the Radical Strain in Southern Antislavery Thought during the 1820s." *Journal of Southern History*. Vol. 39, no. 3 (August 1973), pp. 379–96.

Storch, Neil T. "John Ireland and the Modernist Controversy." *Church History*. Vol. 54, no. 3 (September 1985), pp. 353–65.

Storey, John W. "The Negro in Southern Baptist Thought, 1865–1900." Ph.D. dissertation, University of Kentucky, 1968.

Stout, Harry S. "Word and Order in Colonial New England," *The Bible in America: Essays in Cultural History*. Edited by Nathan O. Hatch and Mark A. Noll, New York, 1982, pp. 19–38.

Stuckey, Sterling. *Slave Culture: Nationalist Theory and the Foundations of Black America*. New York, 1987.

Sutch, Richard. "The Breeding of Slaves for Sale and the Westward Expansion of Slavery, 1850–1860." *Race and Slavery in the Western Hemisphere: Quantitative Studies*. Edited by Stanley L. Engerman and Eugene D. Genovese. Princeton, N.J., 1975, pp. 173–210.

Swaney, Charles Baumer. *Episcopal Methodism and Slavery: With Sidelights on Ecclesiastical Politics.* Boston, 1926.

Sweet, Leonard I., ed. *The Evangelical Tradition in America.* Atlanta, 1984.

Sweet, William Warren. *Methodism in American History.* Rev. ed., Nashville, Tenn., 1953.

———. *The Story of Religion in America.* New York, 1950 (1930).

Taggart, Stephen G. *Mormonism's Negro Policy: Social and Historical Origins.* Salt Lake City, Utah, 1970.

Takaki, Ronald T. *Iron Cages: Race and Culture in Nineteenth-Century America.* New York, 1979.

Talley, Thomas W. *Negro Folk Rhymes: Wise and Otherwise.* New York, 1922.

Tawney, R. H. *Religion and the Rise of Capitalism: A Historical Study.* New York, 1954 (1926).

Taylor, Maxwell Ford, Jr. "The Influence of Religion on White Attitudes toward Indians in the Early Settlement of Virginia." Ph.D. dissertation, Emory University, 1970.

Tcherikover, Victor. *Hellenistic Civilization and the Jews.* Translated by S. Applebaum. Philadelphia, 1966.

Teiser, Stephen F. *The Ghost Festival in Medieval China.* Princeton, N.J., 1988.

Thompson, Ernest Trice. *Presbyterians in the South.* Vol. I: 1607–1861. Richmond, Va., 1963.

Thompson, J. Earl, Jr. "Lyman Beecher's Long Road to Conservative Abolitionism." *Church History.* Vol. 42, no. 1 (March 1973), pp. 89–109.

Thompson, James J., Jr. *Tried as by Fire: Southern Baptists and the Religious Controversies of the 1920s.* Macon, Ga., 1982.

Thompson, Roger. *Sex in Middlesex: Popular Mores in a Massachusetts County, 1649–1699.* Amherst, Mass., 1986.

Thornton, John K. *The Kingdom of Kongo: Civil War and Transition, 1641–1718.* Madison, Wis., 1983.

Tillich, Paul. *A History of Christian Thought: From Its Judaic and Hellenistic Origins to Existentialism.* Edited by Carl E. Braaten. New York, 1967.

Touchstone, Blake. "Planters and Slave Religion in the Deep South." *Masters & Slaves in the House of the Lord: Race and Religion in the American South, 1740–1870.* Edited by John B. Boles. Lexington, Ky., 1988, pp. 99–126.

Toynbee, Arnold. *An Historian's Approach to Religion.* 2nd ed., Oxford, U.K., 1979 (1956).

Tracy, Arthur Linwood. "The Social Gospel, 'New' Immigration, and American Culture: An Analysis of the Attitudes of Charles Ellwood, Shailer Mathews, and Graham Taylor toward the 'New' Immigration." Ph.D. dissertation, American University, 1975.

Trimingham, J. Spencer. *A History of Islam in West Africa.* London, 1982 (1970).

———. *Influence of Islam upon Africa.* 2nd ed., London, 1980.

Twombly, Robert C., and Moore, Robert H. "Black Puritan: The Negro in Seventeenth-Century Massachusetts." *William and Mary Quarterly.* Vol. 24, no. 2 (April 1967), pp. 224–42.

Tyler, Alice Felt. *Freedom's Ferment: Phases of American Social History from the Colonial Period to the Civil War.* New York, 1962 (1944).

United States Department of Commerce. Bureau of the Census. *Negro Population in the United States 1790–1915.* Washington, D.C., 1918.

Van Deburg, William L. *Slavery and Race in American Popular Culture.* Madison, Wis., 1984.

Vanderwerth, W. C. *Indian Oratory: Famous Speeches by Noted Indian Chiefs.* Norman, Okla., 1971.

Vaughan, Alden T. *New England Frontier: Puritans and Indians, 1620–1675.* Rev. ed., New York, 1979.

———. "The Origins Debate: Slavery and Racism in Seventeenth-Century Virginia." *Virginia Magazine of History and Biography.* Vol. 97, no. 3 (July 1989), pp. 311–54.

———, ed. *The Puritan Tradition in America, 1620–1730.* Columbia, S.C., 1972.

Wacker, Grant. "The Demise of Biblical Civilization." *The Bible in America: Essays in Cultural History*. Edited by Nathan O. Hatch and Mark A. Noll. New York, 1982, pp. 121–38.

———. "The Holy Spirit and the Spirit of the Age in American Protestantism, 1880–1910." *Journal of American History*. Vol. 72, no. 1 (June 1985), pp. 45–62.

Wakelyn, Jon L. "Catholic Elites in the Slaveholding South." *Catholics in the Old South: Essays on Church and Culture*. Edited by Randall M. Miller and Jon L. Wakelyn. Macon, Ga., 1983, pp. 211–39.

Walker, Arda. "The Religious Views of Andrew Jackson." *East Tennessee Historical Society's Publications*. No. 17 (1945).

Wallis, Louis. *God and the Social Process: A Study in Hebrew History*. Chicago, 1935.

Ward, John William. *Andrew Jackson: Symbol for an Age*. New York, 1962 (1953).

Wattenberg, Ben J., ed. *The Statistical History of the United States: From Colonial Times to the Present*. New York, 1976.

Watts, Pauline Moffitt. "Prophecy and Discovery: On the Spiritual Origins of Christopher Columbus's 'Enterprise of the Indies.' " *American Historical Review*. Vol. 90, no. 1 (February 1985), pp. 73–102.

Weatherford, W. D. *American Churches and the Negro: An Historical Study from Early Slave Days to the Present*. Boston, 1957.

Weber, Max. *The Protestant Ethic and the Spirit of Capitalism*. New York, 1958 (1904–1905, 1920).

Weeks, Stephen B. *Southern Quakers and Slavery: A Study in Institutional History*. New York, 1968 (1896).

Weinberg, Albert K. *Manifest Destiny: A Study of Nationalist Expansion in American History*. Chicago, 1963 (1935).

Weisman, Richard. *Witchcraft, Magic, and Religion in 17th Century Massachusetts*. Amherst, Mass., 1984.

Welch, Galbraith. *Africa Before They Came: The Continent, North, South, East and West, Preceding the Colonial Powers*. New York, 1965.

Wentz, Abdel Ross. *A Basic History of Lutheranism in America*. Rev. ed., Philadelphia, 1955 (1923).

Westermann, William L. *The Slave Systems of Greek and Roman Antiquity*. Philadelphia, 1955.

Wharton, Vernon Lane. *The Negro in Mississippi, 1865–1890*. Chapel Hill, N.C., 1947.

Williams, Walter L. "United States Indian Policy and the Debate over Philippine Annexation: Implications for the Origins of American Imperialism." *Journal of American History*. Vol. 66, no. 4 (March 1980), pp. 810–31.

Williamson, Joel. *The Crucible of Race: Black-White Relations in the American South since Emancipation*. New York, 1984.

Winslow, Ola Elizabeth. *John Eliot, Apostle to the Indians*. Boston, 1968.

Wood, Forrest G. *Black Scare: The Racist Response to Emancipation and Reconstruction*. Berkeley, Calif., 1968.

Wood, Peter H. *Black Majority: Negroes in Colonial South Carolina, from 1670 through the Stono Rebellion*. New York, 1974.

Woodward, C. Vann. *American Counterpoint: Slavery and Racism in the North-South Dialogue*. New York, 1983 (1964).

Woolverton, John Frederick. *Colonial Anglicanism in North America*. Detroit, 1984.

Wyatt-Brown, Bertram. *Lewis Tappan and the Evangelical War against Slavery*. Cleveland, 1969.

———. *Yankee Saints and Southern Sinners*. Baton Rouge, La., 1985.

Yang, C. K. *Religion in Chinese Society: A Study of Contemporary Social Functions of Religion and Some of Their Historical Factors*. Berkeley, Calif., 1967.

Zeusse, Evan M. *Ritual Cosmos: The Sanctification of Life in African Religions*. Athens, Ohio, 1979.

Index

A NOTE ABOUT THE AUTHOR

Forrest G. Wood was born in Oak Park, Illinois, in 1931. He took his A.B. and M.A. at California State University, Sacramento, and his Ph.D. at the University of California, Berkeley. From 1963 to 1970 he was Assistant and then Associate Professor of History at Fresno State University. Since 1970 he has been Professor of History at California State University, Bakersfield. He has also been a visiting professor at the University of Iowa and the University of California, Santa Cruz. He is the author of Black Scare: The Racist Response to Emancipation and Reconstruction *(1968) and* The Era of Reconstruction, 1863–1877 *(1975).*

A NOTE ON THE TYPE

This book was set in a digitized version of Janson. The hot-metal version of Janson was a recutting made direct from type cast from matrices long thought to have been made by the Dutchman Anton Janson, who was a practicing type founder in Leipzig during the years 1668–1687. However, it has been conclusively demonstrated that these types are actually the work of Nicholas Kis (1650–1702), a Hungarian, who most probably learned his trade from the master Dutch type founder Dirk Voskens. The type is an excellent example of the influential and sturdy Dutch types that prevailed in England up to the time William Caslon (1692–1766) developed his own incomparable designs from them.

Composed by American–Stratford Graphic Services, Inc.
Brattleboro, Vermont

Printed and bound by R.R. Donnelley & Sons,
Harrisonburg, Virginia

Designed by Valarie J. Astor